Teaching International Law

Teaching International Law

Edited by

Peter Hilpold and Giuseppe Nesi

BRILL | NIJHOFF

LEIDEN | BOSTON

Library of Congress Cataloging-in-Publication Data

Names: Hilpold, Peter, 1965- editor. | Nesi, Giuseppe, editor.
Title: Teaching international law / edited by Peter Hilpold and Giuseppe Nesi.
Description: Leiden ; Boston : Brill/Nijhoff, 2024. | Includes index. | Summary: "Teaching International Law is a topic of great importance in international law academia. In the past renowned international lawyers and research institutions have dealt with this matter. This book brings together a larger number of established international lawyers who not only present the state of the art of this discipline but also their own vision and perspective. Traditionally, teachers of international law had considerable influence on the development and the understanding of this subject. The international legal system has profoundly changed but in time of enormous challenges for the survivel of mankind the voice of the teachers should again be heard"– Provided by publisher.
Identifiers: LCCN 2023042426 (print) | LCCN 2023042427 (ebook) | ISBN 9789004678873 (hardback) | ISBN 9789004678880 (ebook)
Subjects: LCSH: International law–Study and teaching.
Classification: LCC KZ1237 .T43 2024 (print) | LCC KZ1237 (ebook) | DDC 341.071/1–dc23/eng/20231002
LC record available at https://lccn.loc.gov/2023042426
LC ebook record available at https://lccn.loc.gov/2023042427

Typeface for the Latin, Greek, and Cyrillic scripts: "Brill". See and download: brill.com/brill-typeface.

ISBN 978-90-04-67887-3 (hardback)
ISBN 978-90-04-67888-0 (e-book)
DOI 10.1163/9789004678880

This book is printed on acid-free paper and produced in a sustainable manner.

Contents

PART III
National and Regional Perspectives, New Methodological Approaches

PART IV
Teaching Different Sub-disciplines of International Law

Prologue

This book is the result of a teaching and research project within the "Euregio" (Austria/Italy) involving the University of Innsbruck and Trento. It started in 2015 and continued over five years. Within this period a series of conferences were organized at the University of Innsbruck. Beginning with the year 2020 the papers published in this book were prepared, reviewed, discussed and finalized.

The editors of this book are planning to continue research activities in this field as they are convinced that "Teaching International Law" is still an under-researched topic which holds great promise for the discipline of International Law.

We are grateful for all the contributions and comments by many colleagues from several countries all over the globe. Only part of these contributions could be integrated in this book but we are looking forward to extended future editions.

The editors would like to acknowledge the generous financial support provided by the Vice Rectorate for Research of the Universität Innsbruck, the Stiftung Fürstlicher Kommerzienrat Guido Feger, the University of Trento, the Land Vorarlberg and the Helmut M. Merlin-Stiftung.

Peter Hilpold
Universität Innsbruck
Giuseppe Nesi
Università di Trento

Figures and Tables

Figures

Tables

Abbreviations

AAIL	Asian Academy of International Law
AAVV	Autori Vari
ABA	American Bar Association
AB	Appellate Body
AG HWIR	Harmonisierung des deutschen und des französischen Wirtschafts-und Insolvenzrechts
AI	Artificial Intelligence
AISDUE	Associazione Italiana Studiosi del Diritto Europeo
AJIL	American Journal of International Law
ALTA	Australian Law Teachers Association
Am.Pol.	Sci-Rev American Political Science Review
ANVUR	Agenzia Nazionale di Valutazione del sistema Universitario e della Ricerca
AnwBl	Anwaltsblatt
ASIL	American Society of International Law
ARD	Arbeitsgemeinschaft der öffentlich-rechtlichen Rundfunkanstalten der Bundesrepublik
AUS	Australia
AVR	Archiv des Völkerrechts
BA	Bachelor of Arts
BC	Before Christ
BDA	Brussels Diplomatic Academy
BDGIR	Berichte der Deutschen Gesellschaft für Internationales Recht
BGBl	Bundesgesetzblatt
BIT	Bilateral Investment Treaty
BL	Basic Law
BverfG	Bundesverfassungsgericht
BYIL	British Yearbook of International Law
CAC	Codex Alimentarius Commission
CBAMS	Carbon Border Adjustment Measures
CDC	Centre for Disease Control and Prevention
CDU	Christlich Demokratische Union (Christian Democratic Union)
CEDAM	Casa Editrice Dottor Antonio Milani
CETA	Comprehensive Economic Agreement with Canada
C.F.	*Confer*/Compare
CFSP	Common Foreign and Security Policy
Chic.JIntL	Chicago Journal of International Law
Cit.	Citation

CITES	Convention on International Trade in Endangered Species of Wild Fauna and Flora
CJEU	Court of Justice of the European Union
CLE	Continuing Legal Education
CLS	Critical Legal Studies
CMLRev	Common Market Law Review
CNN	Cable News Network
COE	Council of Europe
COJUR	Council Working Party on Public International Law
COM	Committee of Ministers
COVAX	Covid-19 Vaccines Global Access
CPTPP	Comprehensive and Progressive Transpacific Partnership
CSCE	Conference on Security and Cooperation in Europe
CSR	Corporate Social Responsibility
CSU	Christlich Soziale Union (Christian Social Union)
CTIR	Centre for Teaching International Relations
CTLS	Centre for Transnational Legal Studies
CUP	Cambridge University Press
Dem	Groupe démocrate
DFPV	Deutsch-Französische Parlamentarische Versammlung
DILA	Development of International Law in Asia
DPRK	Democratic People's Republic of Korea
DriG	Deutsches Richtergesetz
DSK	Dominique Strauss-Kahn
EC	European Council
ECHR	European Convention on Human Rights
ECT	Energy Charter Treaty
ECtHR	European Court of Human Rights
ECJ	European Court of Justice
Ed(s)	Edition(s)
EEA	European Economic Area
EFA	Education For All
EFILA	European Federation for Investment Law and Arbitration
e.g.	*exempli gratia*
EHRR	European Human Rights Reports
EJIL	European Journal of International Law
EJLE	European Journal of Legal Education
EJLS	European Journal of Legal Studies
ELFA	European Law Faculties Association
ELJ	European Law Journal

ELSA European Law Students' Association
ESA European Space Agency
ESIL European Society of International Law
Et al *et alii*
Etc. *Et cetera*
EU European Union
EuZW Europäische Zeitschrift für Wirtschaftsrecht
FAO Food and Agriculture Organization
FDI Foreign Direct Investment
FDP Freie Demokratische Partei
ff. following pages
FRG Federal Republic of Germany
FTAS Free Trade Agreements
GAL Global Administrative Law
GATS General Agreement on Trade in Services
GATT General Agreement on Tariffs and Trade
GB Great Britain
GEV Gruppi di Esperti della Valutazione
GHG Greenhouse Gas
HCCH Hague Conference on Private International Law
HRL Human Right Law
i.a. *inter alia*
IACtHR Inter-American Court of Human Rights
IAJ International Association of Judges
Ibid *ibidem*
IBM International Business Machines Corporation
ICANN Internet Corporation for Assigned Names and Numbers
ICC International Criminal Court
ICCPR International Covenant on Civil and Political Rights
ICESCR International Covenant on Economic, Social and Cultural Rights
ICH International Conference on Harmonization
ICJ International Court of Justice
ICLQ International and Comparative Law Quarterly
ICON International Journal of Constitutional Law
ICT Information and Communication Technology
ICTY International Criminal Tribunal for the former Yugoslavia
i.e. *id est*
IEL International Economic Law
IHL International Humanitarian Law
IIL International Investment Law

IL	International Law
ILA	International Law Association
ILC	International Law Commission
ILO	International Labour Organization
ILSA	International Law Students' Association
IMDb	Internet Movie Database
IMF	International Monetary Fund
IOE	Institute of Education
IOM	International Organization for Migration
IOS	International Organizations
IPA	International Public Authority
IRPA	Istituto di Ricerche sulla Pubblica Amministrazione
ISDS	InvestorStaat-Schiedsverfahren
ISIS	Islamic State of Iraq and Sham
ISO	International Organization for Standardization
IT	Information Technology
JAPrO	Juristenausbildungs- und Prüfungsordnung
JD	Juris Doctor
JEL	Journal of Economic Literature
J.Int.	Law Journal of International Law
JuS	Juristische Schulung
JZ	Juristenzeitung
LaREM	La République En Marche
LEUR	League of European Research Universities
LL.M.	*Legum Magister*
LJIL	Leiden Journal of International Law
L.R.	Law Review
LT	Libertés et territoires
MIC	Multilateral Investment Court
MichJIntL	Michigan Journal of International Law
MIT	Massachusetts Institute of Technology
MIUR	Ministero dell'educazione, dell'Università e della ricerca
MOOCS	Massive Online Courses
MOU	Memorandum of Understanding
MPEPIL	Max Planck Encyclopedia of Public International Law
N@HZ	Neue@Hochschulzeitung
NATO	Nort-Atlantic Treaty Organization
N.B.	Nota Bene
NDCS	Nationally Determined Contributions
NGO	Non-governmental Organization

NJIL	Nordic Journal of International Law
NJW	Neue Juristische Woschenschrift
NPM	New Public Management
NULR	Northwestern University School of Law Review
NUS	National University of Singapore
NWICO	New World Information and Communication Order
NYU	New York University
OECD	Organization for Economic Co-operation and Development
OHCHR	Office of the United Nations High Commissioner for Human Rights
OJLS	Oxford Journal of Legal Studies
OSCE	Organization for Security and Cooperation in Europe
OUP	Oxford University Press
Para	Paragraph
PBL	Problem Based Learning
PCIJ	Permanent Court of International Justice
PGA	President of the General Assembly
PGS	Public Goods
PhD	*Philosophiae Doctor*
PIL	Public International Law
PSPP	Public Sector Purchase Program
PWN	Państwowe Wydawnictwo Naukowe
R2P	Responsibility to Protect
RablesZ	Rabels Zeitschrift für ausländisches und internationales Privatrecht
RCEP	Regional Comprehensive Economic Partnership
RdC	Recueil de Cours
REDIAL	Repensando la Educación en Derecho Internacional en América Latina
REF	Research Excellence Framework
REIO	Regional Economic Integration Organization
RIO	Regional Integration Organization
SDGS	Sustainable Development Goals
SIDI	Società Italiana di Diritto Internazionale e del Diritto dell'Unione Europea
SILS	Society of International Law, Singapore
SOC	Groupe socialiste
SPD	Sozialdemokratische Partei Deutschlands
SSDI	Société suisse de droit international
SVIR	Schweizerische Vereinigung für Internationales Recht
SZIER	Schweizerische Zeitschrift für internationales und europäisches Recht
TBT	Technical Barriers to Trade
TCM	Text, Cases and Materials
TFEU	Treaty on the Functioning of the European Union

TIL	Teaching International Law
TINA	There Is No Alternative
TRILA	Teaching and Researching International Law in Asia
TRIPS	Trade-Related Aspects of International Property Rights
TTIP	Transatlantic Trade and Investment Partnership
TWAIL	Third-World Approaches to International Law
TWAILR	Third-World Approaches to International Law Review
UDHR	Universal Declaration of Human Rights
UG	Universitätsgesetz
UN	United Nations
UNCESCR	United Nations Committee on Economic Social and Cultural Rights
UNCITRAL	United Nations Commission on International Trade Law
UNCLOS	United Nations Convention on the Law of the Sea
UNCTAD	United Nations Conference on Trade and Development
UN Doc.	United Nations Documents
UNECE	United Nations Economic Commission for Europe
UNESCO	United Nations Educational, Scientific and Cultural Organization
UNFCCC	United Nations Framework Convention on Climate Change
UNGA	United Nations General Assembly
UNHCR	United Nations High Commissioner for Refugees
UNHRC	United Nations Human Rights Committee
UNITAR	United Nations Institute for Training and Research
UNSC	United Nations Security Council
UNTS	United Nations Treaty Series
UK	United Kingdom
URL	Uniform Resource Locator
U.S.	United States
USP	Unique Selling Point
USSR	Union of Soviet Socialist Republics
VCLT	Vienna Convention on the Law of Treaties
Vol.	Volume
VQR	Valutazione della Qualità della Ricerca
VUCA	Volatility, Uncertainty, Complexity and Ambiguity
WADA	World Anti-Doping Agency
WHO	World Health Organization
WPIA	UW Wydział Prawa i Administracji Uniwersytetu Warszawskiego
Wis. Int'L.L.J.	Wisconsin International Law Journal
WTO	World Trade Organization
WW I	World War I
WW II	World War II

ZaöRV	Zeitschrift für ausländisches öffentliches Recht und Völkerrecht
ZinsO	Zeitschrift für das gesamte Insolvenz- und Sanierungsrecht
ZSR	Zeitschrift für schweizerisches Recht

PART I

Introduction

Introduction

Peter Hilpold

In no other legal discipline does the teacher enjoy such a prominent role as in International Law (IL). This outstanding role was obvious even from the very beginning of this discipline's development – and it is no coincidence that IL's creation is closely associated with the names of theoreticians such as Francisco Suárez, Hugo Grotius, Thomas Hobbes, Samuel Pufendorf, and Emer de Vattel. It is still strongly perceptible today, albeit in a modified form adapted to the needs of modern times.

As will be shown in this volume, this role is interpreted very differently from region to region, from country to country and even from person to person. The teacher may be seen as a saint, a priest, a norm-creator, but also as a "tin soldier" and as a miserable apologist for and agent of the dominant powers. Any such judgement is, however, context-dependent, not only with regard to the teacher but also in relation to the observer.

Expectations as to the contributions the teacher of IL could and should make are often exaggerated and unrealistic. The teacher is not a norm-setter, even in IL, despite the fact that he or she may often have considerable interpretative leeway and may be able to influence the norm-creation process to some extent. But the opposite perspective is also wrong: Teachers, even if they are integrated in hierarchical systems need not be the politicians' yes-men, and handmaidens. Self-respect should inhibit the most extreme deference even for government advisors and even more so for University teachers.

In the end, however, teachers often find themselves between a rock and a hard place, and everyone has to find his or her role in the particular environment in which these teachers are operating. Each situation is, to a very large degree, particular and no obvious solution is available to each and every teacher.

Nonetheless, it is assumed here that an investigation into the present-day role of the IL teacher can provide useful insights into the reality of this profession which is currently facing extraordinary challenges, and these challenges are to some extent also representative of the situation of IL as a whole. It is contended that teachers of IL are important actors in its development, at least in the sense that they provide basic insights into a highly complex subject, and they can also operate as mediators between different positions, claims, and pretensions. Teachers can also be important discussants in the controversy about the values undergirding the international legal order, a fact that has

 | DOI:10.1163/9789004678880_002

gained enormous importance regionally (in particular in the European area, mediated through EU law) but also on a universal level. Finally, in the worldwide quest to tackle essential challenges for humankind such as environmental protection, the fight against climate change, the need to address migration and the struggle against poverty and terrorism teachers of IL assume a decisive role in the difficult communication and negotiation process between the relevant stakeholders, but also towards the broader public that in any democratic setting should be the repository of the final responsibility in the decision-making process.

Teachers are themselves part of the democratic decision-making process (to the extent that they are able to operate within a democratic setting). They do not stand above it, but neither are they prohibited from contributing their specific knowledge and their values. In this sense, it becomes extremely important that in their education, their professional formation, and their academic advancement teachers themselves are part of a democratic, value-based environment. If modern legal orders are based on a series of non-negotiable values that find their best expression in basic human rights and a UN order in which the preservation of peace is at center stage, it is an important mission for teachers of IL to convey the relevant information, to act as a focal point for all such information and to try to develop the values underlying IL further – always, of course, within a genuine democratic process. IL teachers can be important, decisive actors in any attempt to mediate between interests, to reconcile interests, to align positions in the international legal order. In this, if they want to count, to be taken seriously now, they have essentially to adopt a positivist approach. If they want to be remembered also in the future, to have a significant part in solving the challenges of tomorrow, they have to see the norms in their broader context, to at least take notice of demands for change, of a shifting consensus on values that might demand a re-definition of traditional interpretative outcomes. How far the international lawyer is willing and prepared to depart from the agreed core meaning of a norm and to espouse aspirational ideas will vary, and often it may not even be clear whether the interpretative outcome is to be located – "territorially speaking" – at the interpretative core, within its "penumbra"[1] or already slightly detached from it – with the lifeline to the core still intact.[2] The claim to argue "on the basis of the existing law" is a

1 See HLA Hart, Essay in Jurisprudence and Philosophy (Oxford, Clarendon Press, 1983), at 64–65, 71–72, cited according to A. Cassese, Five Masters of International Law (Oxford and Portland, Hart Publishing, 2011), at 258.

2 Antonio Cassese attributed the term "critical positivism" to such approaches. Ibid. A year later, in his last book he called for a "realistic utopia". See A. Cassese, Realizing Utopia (OUP: Oxford 2012) at xxi. One can only speculate whether this outspoken belief in and call

basic condition of entry into the club of "recognized international lawyers", but even if that lawyer sides with a prevailingly formalistic position he or she can make important contributions to IL's further development, for "civilizational progress", if thereby the confidence is acquired to make the interpretation of the international norm to some extent predictable, transparent, and unbiased and that "secrecy, dishonesty, fraud, or manipulation" are excluded as far as possible.[3]

To make this happen important societal pre-conditions have to be guaranteed. Regularly (with very few exceptions)[4] teachers are firm parts of a national educational system, and this system has to be conceived in such a way as to enable the teacher to rise to this mission.

Any analysis of the role of the teacher of IL as regards the consolidation and enhancement of basic societal values, any inquiry into the potential this role has for the promotion of aspirational goals that should advance human civilization in a peace-and consensus-oriented, human-rights-centered international order has therefore to focus not only on the person of the teacher but also on the institutional and societal environment he or she operates in.

For this reason, the following studies are undertaken from two vantage points.

- A specific focus, is, of course, directed at the teacher as an individual. This is to infer that there are elements of an IL teacher that can be generalized up to a certain point, and that can be noted independently of specific legal orders and cultural circumstances. The assumption is that, notwithstanding all national and regional differences, the image of what a truly international teacher really is, appears on the horizon. Even in the backyard any IL teacher is aware of being part of a universal community. The formula of

---

for utopia gave this book a far more satisfied and optimistic outlook than the book on "five masters" published a year before. There, recapitulating his interviews with René-Jean Dupuy, Eduardo Jiménez de Aréchaga, Sir Robert Jennings, Louis Henkin and Oscar Schachter, Cassese remarked that these great international lawyers displayed "relative serenity" in their attitude towards existential issues. He attributed the fact that they were not beset by greater anxieties i.a. to the fact that they took comfort in religion while he, as a "radical secular", felt himself to be among those who had "a more troublesome life". Ibid. at 268.

3 See Martti Koskenniemi, What is International Law For?, in: Malcom D. Evans (ed.), International Law, 5th ed. (Oxford, OUP 2018),28–50, at 32.

4 Of course, there are also international institutions IL teachers operate in, and some of these institutions are very famous. Such a setting is, however, still the exception and this specific environment does not contradict the findings: first of all, these teachers usually maintain strong relations with the national educational institutions they come from. Furthermore, these international institutions are regularly themselves in the forefront of the development and defense of national, regional, and international values.

the "invisible college of international lawyers" coined by the late Professor Oscar Schachter gets to the heart of the matter when it presents an essential trait of this profession: the fact of belonging to a world-wide community for which no formal membership card is necessary, no membership fee has to be paid, and no regular personal meetings are envisioned. To belong to this community it is sufficient to engage in some form of intellectual exchange that can be very informal and indirect, and can take place, for example, through the study of books and journals and the publication of articles and monographs. These very traditional activities may reveal considerable harmonizing forces, and the modern communication tools enhance these processes enormously.

- But, as already hinted at, there are also extreme national and regional differences that any study of the IL teacher has to be aware of. Most IL teachers have been educated against the backdrop of a specific national legal order whose specific cultural and philosophical essence will to a greater or lesser extent also influence his or her understanding of IL.[5] This specific national environment will usually continue to influence IL teachers throughout their careers if they remain in their country of origin or choose to migrate to countries with similar, related legal orders. As will be shown, the mobility of IL teachers continues to be low, even in Europe, for various reasons such as linguistic barriers, university systems that are reciprocally incompatible, and not least because of outright protectionism. And there is even more to this: to a considerable extent, IL teachers are the product of a specific university system and these systems are part of the broader educational system of a country and of a specific political environment. The introduction of a so-called "university autonomy" does not create a real exception to this. Hence, "university autonomy" is nothing more than a term than can have a myriad of meanings. To declare universities as "autonomous" does not exempt them from political influence. On the contrary, such autonomy can even augment this influence by local political forces, by rendering it less transparent and by excluding political control by opposition forces in parliamentarian bodies. What is decisive is rather the question whether the rule of law applies also to universities, whether decision-making is open, transparent, and inclusive, and whether basic democratic rules are respected also within these bodies. It is important to consider these working conditions in order to know whether IL teachers

5 We have tried to analyze these different viewpoints on IL in Europe in P. Hilpold, European International Law Traditions (Heidelberg: Springer 2021).

operate in an environment where they can develop their personalities, freely express their opinions, and teach a subject very close to politics and ideologies according to their true knowledge and conscience. Academic freedom can therefore be endangered in many ways: crude and brutal political interference by central or local governments, directly or through political representatives in university councils, but also through the opposite: if no guarantees are given that basic democratic rules and rule of law provisions are respected. In the latter case, universities are left to themselves and the power of the stronger (in scheming and abusing) becomes paramount. Lately, an additional threat seems to have materialized: that universities are becoming focal points of political correctness where tolerance of diverging opinions becomes ever more restricted for the sake of higher ideals, again defined and imposed by dominant groups.[6] This is, of course a debate going well beyond the specific situation of IL teachers, and this debate is surely not exclusive to them, but they are certainly also exposed to this struggle, and often even in a qualified manner due to the nature of the subject they study and teach.

If we have here referred to the IL teacher, a further caveat has to be added. IL teachers not only present different characteristics as to their formation and enjoy a different degree of academic freedom according to the legal and institutional order where they are actually working. IL teachers also display different professional characteristics according to the activities they are exercising. In fact, they may exclusively be teachers at law schools or universities or they may wear different "hats". They may have in the past been advisors to the government, public servants, working at international organizations or in law firms, and they may continue one or more of these activities. There can be no doubt that these activities will influence one another in the way IL is interpreted and understood. Some national orders will be more open to such additional activities than others. Also, this may explain national differences in the way IL is approached. Furthermore, some university curricula will attribute more or less importance to IL, they may foresee IL as an independent subject or combine it with other subjects. The working contracts of IL teachers will provide for greater or lesser teaching loads. Assessment of teaching activities will be more or less severe or demanding.

A comparative study that takes into account all these differences (and there are, of course, many more that could be considered) is probably impossible

6 See on this discussion Michael Ignatieff & Stephan Roch, Academic Freedom – A global challenge (Budapest: Central European University 2018.).

to undertake. Nonetheless, it is assumed that there is value as such in the attempts to develop different approaches to analyzing the role, the function, the potentials, and limits IL teachers are faced with. It is hoped that the picture of the IL teacher will thereby become somewhat sharper, that some foundations for further studies will be laid, and a better understanding of the world-wide dialogue between international lawyers will be created. Eventually this should also provide a further clue for a better understanding of IL itself and for international dialogue between experts and the broader public.

This book is divided into seven sections. It starts with an introduction by this author. The second section concerns the "global perspective", the third national and regional perspectives and new methodological approaches towards the issue of TIL, the fourth examines teaching issues specific to single sub-disciplines of IL, the fifth deals with tools, instruments, and resources, the sixth directs the focus towards scholarship on teaching IL. Final remarks by the two editors conclude this book.

In the introductory chapter, Peter Hilpold examines the role of the IL teacher from various vantage points. In particular, he tries to ascertain whether and how this teacher can come up to the high expectations that are often associated with this role. Hilpold argues that the teacher's role has surely changed profoundly over the centuries but IL teachers can still be game changers, in particular in view of the new challenges humankind is confronted with. These challenges require – more than ever – thinking in the IL dimension, a position fully confirmed by Charlotte Ku's contribution which follows. At the same time, Hilpold warns that the role of the IL teacher should not be seen as isolated from the broader context he or she operates in. First of all, in a democratic setting it is not up to IL teachers to claim an autocratic right to impose their own will purportedly based on better insights into complex international realities. Nonetheless, IL teachers can offer their knowledge to society and act as mediators, consultants, and promotors of new initiatives that should, however, always be based on a parliamentary, democratic process.

At the same time, it must be ensured that IL teachers can freely and independently fill this role. "Academic freedom" must be more than a slogan. It presupposes a high school structure that leaves sufficient space for the independent formation and expression of thought. As will be shown, "university autonomy" is not necessarily an instrument conducive to achieving this end. It may be another slogan and it may even be an instrument to increase pressure and to reduce transparency. Furthermore, it is important to permit and to foster free, keen competition among ideas and to avoid protectionism and parochialism.

To make this happen a series of institutional measures have to be adopted.

Charlotte Ku, when writing about "U.S. approaches to teaching international law in a global environment" profits from her long teaching experience both inside and outside the U.S. She both starts and ends her piece with a reference to the COVID pandemic that has again evidenced the importance of IL solutions to counter problems of a world-wide dimension. She also underscores that we should start from a broad notion of teaching which should encompass not only classroom teaching but also any form of disseminating knowledge about IL to a broader public. Instruction in IL should not stop with graduation from law school, but rather take the form of continuing education. She explains that the role of TIL at American law schools is a rather limited one, as these schools focus on preparing for employment and the bar examination. However, she also convincingly argues that not only does IL acquire an ever greater role for the actual practice of law, but at the same time the characteristics of IL thinking are becoming more and more relevant also for the proper understanding and application of national law. As regards the actual content of teaching she adopts a liberal approach, affirming that "there are a variety of approaches that are equally valid". It is for the individual teacher to find the balance between breadth and depth within the constraints of the rather limited number of hours at their disposal. When she writes that teachers of IL in the U.S. have rather limited foreign experience, she addresses a problem we encounter in many countries. She also refers to the heydays of IL teaching in the U.S. when academics from Europe having to flee repression and persecution brought invaluable intellectual capacity to the U.S. She emphasizes the need to avoid excessive fragmentation in IL and to teach it as a system and a process rather than as a set of rules. An important insight to be gleaned from Professor Ku's contribution could be the following: it is essential to instill interest in IL in the individual student. Once this fire is ignited the student will look for further information and instruction on his/her own and will proceed on the path of life-long learning. For teachers, to come up to their mission the number of available teaching hours should not be the decisive factor: enthusiasm for the subject and the ability to convey it should be of at least equal importance.

Carlo Focarelli delivers a broad panoply of ideas and concepts of teaching, drawing from literature and academic writings in pedagogics, law, and political sciences. He demonstrates that teaching can mean many things: providing information, technical training, an exercise of critique, communication (as an endeavor by the teacher to engage and attune with the learner), an act of reinforcement (of existing power structures) or of interaction. He demonstrates that usually the act and process are a combination of all of these elements which, however, can be given different weights. Focarelli's contribution clearly evidences his skepticism of the emphasis on technical training, now much *en vogue*, pleading instead for greater relevance of the element of interaction that valorizes both the teacher and the learner as human persons. He strongly criticizes the modern trend of creating "supermarketized universities", the trend to commodify education which attributes excessive importance to technical skills of immediate professional relevance while neglecting the long-term positive effects of a sound general education and, most of all, to provide space for students to grow into persons with empathy and capable of reasoning critically. He criticizes a widespread but incorrect understanding of what "academic freedom" means. Contrary to what is commonly held, at least in Western countries, academic freedom is less imperiled by (direct) state intervention and coercion and more by the fact that, to the contrary, the State is withdrawing from education in general and from high school instruction in particular. Universities are left to their own devices and they have to cope with the harsh reality of economic survival in the market. Here, Focarelli wades in and criticizes the commodification of university instruction, a tendency that also directly influences the position of the teacher.

This situation could also be qualified as a market failure or, from another perspective, a situation where the market should provide for public goods (in particular a broad education, associated with incentives to critical thinking) while there is no such market that would honor abilities for which there is no immediate, individual demand in monetary terms. A solid preparation in humanities, the ability to think critically, in context, and in system, the understanding that the learning process does not end with the awarding of a degree but has rather to be a life-long process not only are potential elements of personal fulfilment for the teacher but may also be decisive requisites for a society system to be able to adapt swiftly to new challenges, also of an economic nature. There is, however, no market for such qualifications. If a society works with a selection system according to which advancement is made dependent on having attended universities with overprized tuition systems, the social divide becomes ever larger while the signals emitted by this system are misleading for society as a whole: Students are thereby motivated to study subjects of short-term economic relevance and critical thinking becomes generally obsolete and distrusted.

The detrimental effects of such developments for an education system as a whole are evident, but they may even be qualified for the field of TIL, as this subject is particularly dependent on a broad education with interdisciplinary knowledge not only in law but also in the humanities or in fields such as economics. In a globalized society intercultural knowledge and the ability to think in context and to avoid strictly partisan positions are essential for a functioning cross-border dialogue. Strictly commercialized university instruction provides little incentive to opt for such an education, also in view of the fact that professional perspectives in the field of IL are still rather limited. In other words, society as a whole would surely need such capacities, especially in a long-term perspective, but there is no market that would offer sufficient and reliable price signals to opt for such instruction.

Of course, a purely market-based university instruction system is still the exception and an extreme model. In many countries, governments continue to finance universities but withdraw widely from controlling and steering them in the name of a misunderstood notion of "university autonomy". Such a development can lead to results that are even worse, if dominant groups at universities are thereby enabled to pursue their egoistic interests in a non-transparent situation, with public means and with full powers overs teachers and with the possibility to use this power at will by simple reference to the needs of a market that in reality does not exist, at least in the assumed form.

While it is worth being wary of perilous developments in the university system in general and in the field of IL teaching in particular, there remains, of course, space to remediate against such detrimental processes, and already the creation of transparency can be an important instrument to this end. Focarelli emphasizes the importance for the teacher of engaging in critical thinking, evidencing empathy, "liv[ing] by example", understanding that "teaching is ultimately tantamount to learning". In this sense, Focarelli's idea of IL as a social construct[7] where the human person has to be center stage reconnects very well with the approach of "critical positivism" as elaborated by Antonio Cassese and addressed above.[8]

In a concise but dense article, Natalino Ronzitti presents his view of what makes a good IL teacher. He seems to set the bar high when he demands i.a. a deep knowledge of all fields of IL, including foreign literature, experience acquired in practicing as counsel and/or as a legal advisor, the mastering of modern teaching tools, the ability to teach at all levels of IL instruction, as well as "independence". He explains what he means by these requirements and provides hints on how to achieve this form of excellence. On the whole, it becomes clear that Ronzitti sees this form of excellence as an "*optimum optimorum*" to be achieved through a life-long learning process which, however, requires full commitment and dedication to the classroom as a paramount virtue.

The points made by Natalino Ronzitti on good, effective teaching of IL are in several ways confirmed by Pierre-Marie Dupuy's piece on whether there is

7 See Carlo Focarelli, International Law as a Scoail Construct: The Struggle for Global Justice (Oxford: OUP 2012).

8 See note 1.

an art of teaching. At the same time, Dupuy adds important perspectives of a lawyer very much present both in academia and before international courts and arbitral tribunals.

On the one hand, he illustrates the importance of a solid teaching of the theory of law. On the other hand, he warns against dogmaticism and reports that before international courts and tribunals IL scholarship has only a reduced importance. He also warns against modern trends to "mix political philosophy, sociology and ideology more or less distilled by a certain 'political correctness' to the analysis of legal problems that are not always very rigorously defined". In this, he may take what is to a certain extent a minority position in modern academia where careers often seem to be made exactly by the doctrinal approaches criticized here.

When the author states that "[t]he confrontation of the different doctrines of international law with their practical effectiveness [...] remains a test to which the theories developed by the authors are subjected", he takes a strong, courageous, and important stance that may be taken as an invitation to counter or at least ignore certain aberrations in dogmatic IL discussions that lead to debates that are complacent, self-congratulatory, and materially void.

Giuseppe Nesi, the co-editor of this book, provides very personal insights into a career characterized by experiences as a researcher, practitioner, and teacher. He evidences that sometimes these different functions can enter into conflict with each other, but most of the time synergies prevail. Hence, Giuseppe Nesi's short autobiographical report can be interpreted also as an encouragement for teachers to gather practical experience beyond the "ivory tower" and as a conduit to overcome cynicism, to acquire greater credibility as a teacher, and to better convey to students enthusiasm for international law. At the same time, practice can profit from academic experience by providing a greater depth of knowledge as well as the structural thinking this activity is associated with.

Jan Wouters deals with the question whether in Europe teachers of IL should choose a specific "European" perspective. He is thoroughly convinced of such a need, having recently also published a manual with exactly that focus. For Wouters such a specific perspective becomes necessary also because in Europe we are confronted with a multilayered legal order which comprises not only national legal systems but also the legal order of the European Union and the system of the European Convention on Human Rights, which again find their origins in IL. Any attempt to ignore this complexity would lead to a misrepresentation of the existing legal system on the Old Continent.

In recent years the discipline of "Global Administrative Law" has been gaining ground in law teaching at various universities. Barbara Marchetti in her chapter provides, first of all, an introduction to this subject whose contours are still not yet fully clear. There can be no doubt that there are many areas of overlap between GAL and IL, even though this overlap is surely not complete, at least for the time being. Then she moves on to analyze how GAL should be taught. Due to the fact that this discipline deviates considerably from traditional law disciplines, no easy answer can be given to this question. She explains that "[t]eaching global administrative law therefore means, first of all, to analyze and distinguish between the different global regulators, to know how to trace their origins and constitutive powers, to examine their public or private traits, to discover their tools and instruments of action, to understand their relationships with States or national regulators, and to know their sources of law and procedural rules."

This author, too, believes that GAL provides important insights into the modern international law reality which is otherwise difficult to explain using traditional IL concepts and tools. In the meantime, however, GAL has achieved a very high degree of sophistication and autonomy, so that it will become difficult to merge with IL. On the other hand, it is doubtful whether GAL could one day replace IL. According to this author, it is rather probable that both disciplines will maintain their autonomy, and at the same time they can provide important reciprocal insights if studied concomitantly. For the foreseeable future, such an approach will probably be pursued only by a minority of teachers, but nonetheless they can make valuable contributions to a better understanding of IL.

Sergio Dellavalle deals with the "curious contradiction" that, on the one hand, legal disciplines become increasingly specialistic and therefore also exclusive areas for experts in this field and, at same time, interdisciplinarity has surged to the status of a mantra. Also for IL teachers it is more and more becoming a must to profess openness to interdisciplinarity, if not to swear an oath to this academic standpoint.

Dellavalle sets out to explain the intricacies of interdisciplinarity, which should, however, not discourage IL teachers from engaging in this approach as it may provide insights and perspectives that are essential to this discipline. Taking up this task, Dellavalle provides an overview of several methodological positions now of pivotal importance in IL doctrine.

Confronted with a standpoint, nowadays much in vogue in IL, according to which law is not the expression of an inherent material truth and according to which law schools could limit themselves to training students in the application of legal technicalities, he pleads for a more encompassing teaching mission. According to Dellavalle, "the expertise on legal technicalities should be integrated with the knowledge of the social processes that these technicalities are going to regulate and with an encompassing idea of the well-ordered society, which the legal system is assumed to stabilize and its operators are presumed to serve."

Andreas Ziegler deals with the paradox that many universities offer a rich panoply of courses on IL, but at the same time students seem not to get a necessary minimum of instruction in this field. As the author explains, the reasons for this are manifold: IL instruction is provided at too late a stage in the curriculum, it may not be compulsory, students' language skills are insufficient, teaching resources are concentrated on small groups, IL is not sufficiently closely related to national subjects, and there is not enough transparency regarding quality standards in relation to IL teaching at specific universities. These points of criticism already harbor an answer to where action should primarily be taken. As to the last point, the author proposes an international accreditation system of law schools and programs – a measure that surely would enhance academic competition. On the whole, Ziegler's contribution also makes it clear that many operators in the law area are not yet fully aware of the relevance of IL to every-day life – a problem that the whole IL community should try to counter more effectively.

Three shorter contributions on Germany by Rüdiger Wolfrum, Heribert Hirte, and Gerd Morgenthaler deal with the situation of TIL there. In order to examine the German academic situation, these essays were commissioned to provide insights into a reality which is both complex and influential on an international level. Wolfrum and Hirte, on the one hand, underscore IL's importance for the instruction of future lawyers that have to operate in an ever more globalized and interconnected world from which almost no area of national law can be separated. Nowadays, typical "national" law disciplines are also strongly influenced by norms set at the international law level and by norm interpretations stemming from subjects beyond national borders. On the other hand, the demands of many experts in Germany, forming a group that goes well beyond IL teachers who could be accused of arguing for egoistic interests, to strengthen the role of IL in the teaching curricula at German universities are as loud as they have been for decades. So far, however, these demands have gone unheard. As a consequence, in many areas of German society where IL knowledge would be important and is continuously gaining in relevance relevant expertise is lacking. At German universities there are very few chairs exclusively in IL. In most cases this subject is only an appendix to the description of a Public Law chair. Many German academics active (also) in the field of IL have become renowned experts in this area, but they have to exercise this activity alongside other duties in German public law and with a comparatively high teaching load of eight to nine weekly teaching hours for 15 weeks per semester.

The combination of IL with Public Law has also influenced to a certain extent the way IL is approached, studied, and taught in Germany. The more, however, the "invisible college of international lawyers" becomes a reality and the more international lawyers are interconnected, this specific "German approach to IL" loses weight in a global perspective.

Gerd Morgenthaler addresses a challenge of a more systematic nature, having effects on the teaching not only of law but also of other subjects: The threat to freedom of research and teaching resulting from ideas derived from the "New Public Management" philosophy is revealing itself slowly but with increasing force. This managerialism is often justified with output arguments, but in reality motivated by interests aspiring at more control over academic reality and eventually academic creativity and material output. Tendencies of such a kind, of an even more pronounced nature, have been identified by this author with respect to Austria.

While such a development has generally to be counteracted due to its detrimental effects on a university in a Humboldtian sense, in the area of TIL it becomes especially perilous due to the closeness of this subject to politics. Stricter control by politicians or specific group interests over universities might have particularly devasting effects on TIL by undermining the very essence of this discipline and transforming it into a servant without autonomy and character.

Ernst-Ulrich Petersmann examines the specific challenges teachers of International Economic Law (IEL) are faced with. First of all, IEL is not a subject with clear contours. There are many approaches to this discipline, many different views on what issues should be given priority within this area. Petersmann, on the one hand, admits that this "perspectivism" has to be recognized but, on the other hand, he advocates strongly for a value-oriented approach that takes into account the most urgent challenges human society is facing today, first of all more efficient and encompassing human rights protection and then environmental protection. For Petersmann, teaching IEL should focus on regulatory challenges common to all countries in order to realize their universally agreed "sustainable development goals" (SDGs); the regulatory diversity among national and regional IEL traditions; and on policy lessons from the historical evolution of IEL and from the close interrelationship between economic, political, legal, and social orders.

Such an approach must, of course, enter into conflict with methodological positions that are currently rather strong and which opine that law is substantially indeterminate and focus on the process of legal argumentation, not on values that always have to remain subjective and to be located outside the law. Petersmann instead also requires lawyers to take human rights as well as the 2030 UN Agenda for Sustainable Development seriously and to attribute objective binding relevance to these commitments. For Petersmann the teaching of IEL should also be characterized by these basic values and students should be confronted with them: "If law depends on the legal opinions of people and 'justice is the first virtue of social institutions' [Rawls], legal education should be based on theories of justice – also in IEL."

Repeatedly in this book we will address the question of how much specialization makes sense in IL, for example in the field of IEL. Here, the often-cited problem of "fragmentation" comes up. As to International Investment Law (IIL), a branch of IEL which is developing very dynamically, Nikos Lavranos stands for a "true holistic approach" in teaching and studying the subject. This standpoint coincides with that of other authors who have deplored excessive specialization of TIL leading to lesser knowledge of the broader framework. This knowledge, however, is often indispensable for understanding and applying specific international norms (see, for instance, the importance of the Vienna Convention on the Law of Treaties also in the area of IEL). Equally, Lavranos underscores the importance for universities of opening up to practice. Universities should also develop a network with relevant law firms so that students can early on obtain the opportunity to get acquainted with issues of International Investment and Arbitration Law.

If textbooks stand for tradition in TIL, Massive Open Online Courses ("MOOCs") and new tools for visualizing IL stand for modernity, for the future, either as an alternative to present instruments or as a means to their integration. Pierre d'Argent's MOOCs in IL are widely known and he is surely the ideal proponent of this new approach which he presents as an instrument for reaching new audiences on a potentially global level. He may make this instrument attractive to many more teachers when he writes that "MOOCs offer a true existential satisfaction" to scholars with a certain taste for teaching and outreach.

Movies and image references, presented by Markus Beham, Melanie Fink, and Ralph, constitute a tool that can be used both with traditional teaching and as part of online teaching. The authors discuss a broad spectrum of such tools and dedicate particular attention to film. A series of films is analyzed as to their relevance for TIL as they address specific questions of IL (for example, diplomatic immunity, genocide, UN law, human rights, prohibition of torture, law of the sea, space law etc.). Also these instruments can be used to inspire new audiences for IL issues. The authors, however, also add an important warning: "[a]n inevitable fact of academic life is the increasing age gap between student and teacher as the latter progresses along his or her career.

The issue lies less in the age gap itself than the fact that it is only the teacher that gets older. The use of a particular cultural reference may simply no longer be appreciated by a new generation of students or, in the worst case, appear as an inappropriate attempt at youthfulness". This is a problem that past generations of teachers who used to stick to traditional teaching material did not have or in any case had in a less pronounced way. In other words, in a fast-moving era to try to adapt teaching methods so that they are always absolutely "in fashion" may involve overwhelming efforts or become unfeasible.

The teaching and studying of IL usually have one pivotal element as common ground: the use of a textbook. Many international lawyers will tell one that their thinking was formed by the use of a specific textbook, and in many cases one may notice a life-long adherence to basic premises set out in their student textbooks. James Summers sheds light on the issue of what a "good textbook" may be, but also on the intricacies and travails of writing one. In doing so he provides insight into the particularities of the process of TIL, torn as it is between the aspiration to convey a good overview of an immensely broad and considerably complicated subject to a vast audience and the fact that it is often possible only to reach out to an epistemic community or even just parts of it.

Towards the end of this book Lucas Lixinski presents a broad overview of the literature on TIL. He shows that a shift has taken place in the focus of this literature, which he sees now as less concentrated on universalist projects which themselves have mostly fallen into disregard. The region-specific and country-specific focuses now prevail. Many experts in TIL write self-reflective pieces pretending to deal with pedagogics. For Lixinski most of these authors pay only lip service to interdisciplinary engagement in pedagogics. For the author the time has come to become serious about this promise.

The very last chapter is, however, dedicated to Manfred Lachs and his "Teacher in International Law". Throughout this collective volume we will meet Manfred Lachs and his abovementioned monograph. Although much criticism has been voiced about the present relevance of this book for TIL it cannot be denied that Manfred Lachs has decisively pre-shaped the research interest in this subject. Barthlomiej Krzan explains how many pivotal lessons can still today be drawn from this exceptional book. Krzan concludes his detailed analysis of Lachs' work by citing this eminent scholar's final remarks in the "Teacher" where he emphasizes the contribution the teacher of IL can make to creating a more human world. As is well known, not all scholars are confident about the feasibility of such an attempt.[9] As already mentioned, it will also be shown in this book that the teacher never stands above the democratic

9 Perhaps this need is felt more in some regions than in others. As one author (Lucas Lixinski) points out, the belief in the universalist idea may be stronger in Europe than, say, in Australia,

institutions so as to claim to have better knowledge than they do and to dictate political solutions. Teachers of IL, however, are surely, as a rule, qualified repositories of (technical) knowledge about IL. They are in the privileged position of having the time and means to study this extremely broad and complex discipline in detail and to present this knowledge to the institutions tasked with deciding on IL issues and implementing the relevant norms. In this, they can give special emphasis to the principles of humanity, to "true social humanism" in the words of Manfred Lachs. Even though often neglected on the practical level, this "true social humanism" has surely been a pivotal overall guide in the development of IL, in particular since WWII. In democratic orders, teachers of IL are part of a complex system of "check and balances" in which they can play an important role. It is the aim of this book to evidence the prerequisites necessary for this role to come to bear, as well as the potential, limits, and responsibilities of this position.

where Critical Legal Studies have a more prominent role and where universalist approaches are more easily "deconstructed". Nonetheless, it is argued here that idealism, the belief in progress and in the universalist idea, is a vision held by international lawyers on a universal level.

PART II

The "Global" Perspective

CHAPTER 1

Teaching International Law in the 21st Century

Opening the Hidden Room in the Palace of International Law

Peter Hilpold

1 Introduction[1]

Interest in Teaching International Law (TIL) goes far back in history but appears in an astonishingly discontinuous way.[2] Furthermore, it has a widely diverging meaning and focus. From time to time remarkable studies are published and study groups on this subject are even established, but there is no permanent engagement with this issue. Angles of perspective change continuously; study groups are abandoned notwithstanding promising results they have delivered;[3] the immediate motivation for academics to deal with TIL seems to vary constantly.

The list of publications in this field may be long,[4] but these studies exhibit hardly any common thread, concentrated as they mostly are on specific regional vantage points, on curricular issues of a transient nature, or on moral or ethical pleas which display highly subjective characteristics and are widely divergent in tone and formulation over the years. Some erudite studies when dealing with the "Teacher of International Law" deliver more of a philosophy and a history of international law rather than sort out what the timeless traits

1 Many thanks to Charlotte Ku and to Lucas Lixinski for their comments on an earlier version of this manuscript.

2 As John Gamble wrote in 2007, "the teaching of international law does not seem to be a major interest of professional associations devoted to international law or, for that matter, to most professors who teach the subject". See John Gamble, 'Teaching or Get Off the Lectern: Impediments to Improving International Law Teaching' (2007) 13 ILSA Journal of International & Comparative Law 379.

3 Reference can be made here to the activities of the International Law Association ILA in the period between 1998 and 2010, characterized by the adoption of a series of reports and resolutions. See 'Committees' (International Law Association ILA) <www.ila-hq.org/index.php/committees> accessed 25 October 2021.

4 This is remarked on by Gerry Simpson, 'On the Magic Mountain: Teaching Public International Law' (1999) 10 EJIL 70, citing in note 2 a series of publications, many from Anglo-Saxon countries.

 | DOI:10.1163/9789004678880_003

of the figure of the IL teacher, of his function, could be.[5] This situation may be puzzling at first sight, as the role of the teacher in developing the discipline of International Law, both as a system and as an academic discipline, has been a very prominent one in the past and continues to be so, though in a considerably modified form in the present. More recently, however, things appear to have changed. In the continuous quest to find new or previously neglected fields of research the area of teaching seems to be something like a hidden room in the palace of International Law studies. Everyone believes they have already been there, but nobody knows how to find its front door, nor how fully to describe its content. In this context, the subject of "outer space" might be easier to deal with than the adjacent field of the theory of teaching.

So we can say that showing interest in TIL may have become fashionable, but it is still hard to structure the tools to address this interest and to see a solid and sustainable foundation behind the relevant utterances and initiatives.

The reasons for this situation are manifold. In what follows, while not pretending to be complete, a first attempt will be made to sort out some of the most conspicuous aspects of this discussion.

It will be shown that one reason for TIL remaining an unwieldy subject is to be found in the fact that at universities pedagogics of law has long been a widely neglected field, and this has even more so been the case for International Law. Academic recognition and institutionalization are surely an important pre-requisite for a discipline to develop and to continue to find followers, be it out of true enthusiasm for the subject or for pragmatic or opportunistic professional reasons.

In a next step, the "Humboldtian dilemma", affecting all university teaching but International Law teaching in particular, will be examined. The unity or symbiosis of research and teaching, the concept of research-based teaching, so deeply entrenched in our understanding of university reality, often meets with

5 See, most prominently, Manfred Lachs, *The Teacher in International Law* (2nd edition, Martinus Nijhoff: Dordrecht/Boston/Lancaster 1987). As regards this book, John Gamble remarked rather caustically: "With all due respect to my friend, the late Judge Manfred Lachs, an expansive approach to teaching such as that advocated in Judge Lachs′ book is not the way to generate sustained interest." See Gamble (n 2) 385. The review by Otto Kimminich in the German journal, "Archiv des Völkerrechts", is more generous: "This book is complex [...] First of all it is a history of international law thinking. But theory and practice cannot be separated. The problem lies rather in combining them and to present their parallel historic development in a meaningful way" (translation by this author). Otto Kimminich attests to the fact that Manfred Lachs succeeded in this task. See Otto Kimminich, 'The Teacher in International Law by Manfred Lachs' (1986) 24 AVR 238.

hard challenges when put to the test in practice.[6] With ever higher demands associated with the position of a university/high school teacher individual teachers might find themselves at first sight between a rock and a hard place if they want to fully satisfy all the ambitions of the Humboldtian model. How can one be a good teacher and an extraordinary researcher at the same time? As will be shown in this contribution, in recent years in the social sciences different approaches have been developed that should make enterprises, service providers, but also the public sector and even higher education more effective. A series of concepts and buzzwords, such as "New Public Management", "Lean Management", or "VUCA", originally developed in other areas of society, may be referred to in this context. And in fact some attempts have already been made also to apply theories of this kind to the teaching of law. Taking advantage of first insights resulting from these studies, we will try to go a step further and to see what could be the consequences for TIL, from the perspective of both the teacher and the university. University teaching operating in a volatile, uncertain, complex,and ambiguous (VUCA) environment has to adapt to these new challenges if it wants to remain relevant and pertinent.

It is true that universities have to adapt to mounting international competitive pressure and they will often pass this pressure on to the teachers. On the other hand, teachers will have to adapt to these pressures and to compromise in order to satisfy in the best possible way the ever-growing demands with which they are confronted. It will be shown that this situation must not necessarily end in conflict: modern high school management is directed at reconciling the interests of the education institutions and those of the teachers in an open and participative process. This presupposes, however, an adequate legislative framework in which such a process can unfold.[7]

6 In a comment on an earlier version of this text Charlotte Ku formulated this problem as follows: "There seems some implicit assumption that if you are a good researcher, you would be a good teacher. We know, this is not the case. On the other hand, we do want teaching that is evidence and research based, right? In science, the basic courses teach scientific and research methods. We do not have the same kinds of basics in law. It in those basic courses that more consideration is given to teaching. In the U.S. we have the legal writing, analysis, and reasoning courses. Not surprisingly, some of our best and most thoughtful teachers come from that cohort, but they are not generally the law professors we recognize."
Perhaps part of this dilemma can be solved if we adopt a broad notion of "teaching" that also comprises written texts. Many of us might state that they have been strongly influenced by teachers they have never met personally. However, the problem that traditional teaching as such does not get enough academic recognition remains real.

7 As Charlotte Ku pointed out, in the U.S. parents are also very much involved in school governance so that there it is a political and governance framework as much as a legislative one.

In what follows we will try to provide a broad panoply of the resulting questions. First of all, we will show what the situation of teaching IL is in various regions and countries. No comprehensive picture of the situation world-wide can be delivered here, and as far as can be seen no such global studies exist. Nonetheless, the situations portrayed here should be able to show that the teaching of IL takes widely different forms depending on a variety of factors, such as traditions, the relevance of IL as such, or the overall university structure. Different teaching systems have again influenced the meaning and the relevance attributed to IL in various countries, so that the whole perspective has to be a dynamic one.

In law teaching, IL is regularly a discipline apart. In some countries (or at some universities) IL has a rather marginal role. On the other hand, in other situations the relevance of IL is given a very prominent role, at least formally. This stems from the fact that IL has an enormous outreach; it touches upon almost every national legal rule system and it harbors enormous potential for change. As IL teachers contribute to interpreting and also forming IL (in particular also through additional functions, such as those of judges, advisors, and counsels, that they often exercise contemporaneously) they may enjoy considerable power when it comes to conceiving or even creating a better future – bringing national and international legal frameworks more in conformity with broadly cherished values.

As a consequence, the IL teacher has to decide which role to take. Figuratively speaking these roles are placed on a broad spectrum, which, at its vanishing points, has a marginalized faculty member[8] teaching IL as an optional course, and at the other end of the spectrum a teacher having a role akin to that of a prophet, a priest, an "international norm engineer". It will be shown that exaggerations have to be avoided and compromises have to be found. Globalization and intense international interaction between societies, economies, and regulative systems have tremendously boosted the relevance of IL norms. National law and IL are more strongly intertwined than ever. International lawyers have an important mission and can make essential contributions to steering the future of the planet. At the same time, however, they are part of an extremely large community. Meaningful contributions to societal progress can be given only as a result of close interaction within this community and in an interdisciplinary dialogue. To make this possible, universities also have to change

8 See Martti Koskenniemi, 'Commitment and Cynicism' in Jean d'Aspremont and others (eds), *International Law as a Profession* (CUP: Cambridge 2017).

and to foster, in a decisive way, free dialogue, transparency, and international exchange.

This is the main focus of this contribution, which aims to speak not (only) to international lawyers but to universities in general and even society more broadly. In this sense, this contribution is not only "facing inward" but also, and to a considerable extent "facing outward".[9]

2 Pedagogics and IL at Universities

International Law teaching is mostly university teaching, or in any case teaching that takes place in institutions located at the upper end of the educational system (for example, in some countries in "law schools"). In this, International Law teaching is more or less in the same situation as law teaching in general. Therefore, we encounter here a situation that is very similar to top-level teaching in general. While pedagogics is surely an important field of research in humanities, finding its most prominent location at universities, university pedagogics, i.e. the study of university teaching, is a rather latecomer and underdeveloped. The explanation for this may be given by the essence of a principle developed in International Law: "*par in parem non habet imperium*": To give pedagogics the function of structuring the content, to assess the quality of university teaching in other disciplines would be tantamount to introducing a vertical structure in university teaching, with pedagogics placed at the top.[10] True, much has changed in recent years and the growing awareness and search for quality in university teaching has in the meantime opened the door for a pedagogical discussion in all areas of academic activity and for all disciplines. But this discussion is a very prudent, diplomatic one. Pedagogical concepts are not simply accepted and imported from the faculties of pedagogics, but have rather developed in a consensual dialogue, with the academics in the relevant scholarly fields having a strong say in this process. Furthermore, while pressure for rigorous quality management for all academic disciplines is surely strong, we are most probably only at the beginning of a long process. Tradition, the situation of the discipline within the academic system, and the standing of the discipline within the faculty contribute further to determining the importance of pedagogics within that discipline. By all measures, these elements are counter-intuitive for the greater relevance of pedagogics in International Law

9 Many thanks to Lucas Lixinski for inviting me to point out this aspect explicitly.

10 As John Gamble (n 2) 385 wrote, International Law teachers are often suspicious of those offering to help them to teach better.

university teaching. They indicate rather that this importance is much reduced in respect to law teaching in general. In fact, as will be shown in more detail below, International Law in many university and law school systems has a rather reduced importance. It has been integrated into the relevant curricula, if at all, at a rather late stage and it is academically, in this together with law in general, situated rather far distant from pedagogics (differently from, for example, linguistics or history).

Thus, if university disciplines were structured according to their traditional closeness to pedagogics, International Law would most probably be located near the bottom of such a list, with other law disciplines being ranked, if not at the top, somewhat higher. This fact is reflected in the relevant publications in this field. If it is true that the foundation of a journal on the subject is a significant sign of the academic recognition of a discipline (or a sub-discipline),[11] then "Teaching International Law" has not yet obtained full recognition. It could be seen as forming part of a more general subject of "legal education", but even this discipline, judging from the number and influence of the relevant journals on the market, is still in its infancy, with some promising developments in recent years.[12] A series of academic journals of law teaching have

11 In International Law this can be demonstrated very well with reference to the "turn to history" towards the end of the last millennium when, in 1999, the Journal of the History of International Law was founded. In 2001 Martti Koskenniemi's influential "Gentle Civilizer of Nations" was published, and in 2016 the first issue of "Ius Gentium – Journal of International Legal History" followed. The growing interest in "Corporate Social Responsibility" found expression in 2016 in the foundation of the "Business & Human Rights Journal" (which is interdisciplinary but with a legal, and in particular International Law, focus).

12 In 2013, the „Zeitschrift für Didaktik der Rechtswissenschaft" was founded in Germany. Before this journal began publication, the editors engaged in a market survey, looking for journals that would be competitors on the Anglo American market and they found the following titles:

- "The Law Teacher" (GB) edited by the Association of Law Teachers and published by Taylor and Francis (URL: https://www.tandfonline.com/action/journalInformation?journalCode=ralt20). This journal sets out its aim as follows: "*The Law Teacher* is a fully-refereed journal concerned with the teaching of law and issues affecting legal education at all academic levels. Whilst it is the journal of the UK-based Association of Law Teachers, both the Association and the journal are international in outlook and contributions from any jurisdiction are welcome in any section of the journal."
- In the past, also in the US, a journal entitled "The Law Teacher" was published (by the Institute for Law Teaching and Learning). In 2017 its publication ceased, but its previous activities continue in part via the "Law Teaching Blog" (URL: http://lawteaching.org/the-law-teacher/). On the homepage of the Institute for Law Teaching and Learning the aim of this journal (whose archives can still be used) is described as follows: "The Law Teacher encouraged readers to submit brief articles explaining

been founded in recent decades but the relevant market appears still to be a limited one with some journals having already ceased publication after a promising start.[13] As it seems, the market for journals on law teaching issues is a rather difficult one and hardly self-sustaining without strong support from professional institutions (in particular associations of law teachers). While many law journals are also subscribed to by practitioners, no relevant market of such a kind exists for journals on law teaching. If international lawyers are touted as an "epistemic community"[14] this characterization applies to experts on law teaching in an even more pronounced manner.

As for the discipline of international law in particular, as far as can be seen there is no law teaching journal devoted exclusively or predominantly to this subject. Only sporadically do law teaching journals deal with international law issues (in the broader sense). As of yet there are also no chairs of TIL. There can be no doubt that to institutionalize academic research in TIL in such a way would greatly advance this subject.

3 "Research-Informed Teaching" – the "Humboldtian Dilemma"

3.1 *Setting the Stage*

At first sight, one might be inclined to suppose that, of all lawyers, I nternational lawyers should be predestined to deal with didactic matters, as their professional reality is more characterized by teaching activities than is the case for most other lawyers. While this situation has changed somewhat in recent

---

interesting and practical ideas to help law professors become more effective teachers. The archive of past issues is a resource of teaching ideas and Institute activities."

- The "Journal of Legal Education" (US) is a publication of the Association of American Law Schools (URL: https://jle.aals.org/home/). According to this journal's mission statement, "[t]he primary purpose of the Journal is to foster a rich interchange of ideas and information about legal education and related matters, including but not limited to the legal profession, legal theory, and legal scholarship."
- The "International Journal of Clinical Legal Education" (GB) "addresses the role of clinic as an instrument for civic engagement, access to justice and societal change." (See the homepage of this journal at https://www.northumbriajournals.co.uk/index.php/ijcle/about). Many thanks to Jan-Hendrik Dietrich for making available to me his market study which has been updated here.

13 See the previous note. Alongside "The Law Teacher" (US) the "Journal of Professional Legal Education" (AUS) has also ceased publication.

14 On this concept see Andrea Bianchi, 'Epistemic Community' in Jean d'Aspremont and Sahib Singh (eds), *Concepts for International Law – Contributions to Disciplinary Thought* (Edward Elgar 2018), 251.

decades with international lawyers finding more opportunities for professional engagements outside academia, the reality is still that international lawyers in the stricter sense are mainly active in academia with "temptations" to work outside still being the exception.[15] Of course, as we will see throughout this contribution, the picture of the international lawyer is a varied one, in particular if we adopt a global, encompassing perspective that should provide a portrait of "the" international lawyer. In fact, professional curricula may vary very much regionally and even between countries in the same region.[16] In Europe, the situation is made even more complicated by the fact that some international lawyers are also European lawyers or even specialize exclusively in this field. Due to the far higher integration of national law and EU law and the fact that considerable parts of EU law enjoy direct effect within the Member States,[17] academics acting (part-time or exclusively) in the field of EU law enjoy professional opportunities somewhat more similar to those of "traditional" national lawyers. Nonetheless, as far as an attempt to generalize is possible and leaving aside, at first, the international lawyers within counseling enterprises acting before International Courts and Tribunals, for example in the area of corporate social responsibility,[18] or private persons or NGOs, for example in human rights issues, the typical international lawyer is still the academic who works mainly at a university or a high school/law school. There, he or she is confronted with the "Humboldtian challenge" which will often translate into a "Humboldtian dilemma", i.e. in the need to reconcile teaching and research

15 In her otherwise well written and engaging contribution in the Australian Yearbook of International Law of 2005, Gillian Triggs presents a situation according to which international lawyers now enjoy vast job opportunities. As will be shown below, as a description of a trend by which the national and international spheres overlap more and more and lawyers have thereby to deal more often with international issues, this analysis is surely correct. On the other hand, over-enthusiasm is not warranted in this regard. This is still a painstaking process and the development towards more openness for the international perspective has begun from a very low starting point. And it can hardly be said that in the over one-and-a-half decades that have passed since the publication of the article by Gillian Triggs much has changed in this regard. See Gillian Triggs, 'The Public International Lawyer and the Practice of International Law' (2005) 24 Australian Yearbook of International Law 201.

16 This is, for example, already the case within the European Union, where the status of lawyers, their education, and their professional functions diverge profoundly.

17 See Paul Craig/Gráinne De Búrca, *EU Law, Text, Cases and Materials* (6th edition, 2020).

18 See Peter Hilpold, 'Maßnahmen zur effektiven Durchsetzung von Menschen-und Arbeitsrechten – Völkerrechtliche Anforderungen' in Nico Krisch and others (eds), *50 Berichte der Deutschen Gesellschaft für Internationales Recht, Unternehmensverantwortung und Internationales Recht* (C.F. Müller 2020).

and to be productive or even excel in both.[19] This may explain why many international law academics show considerable unease when writing about teaching or avoid this subject altogether. In fact, the dual role of teaching and doing research (publishing) in international law, that many (but not all) of these academics have to fit into, hides many difficult compromises.

3.2 *What Does "Research-Informed Teaching" Mean?*

The term "research-informed teaching" has a strong positive connotation, and therefore most academics will not dare to challenge this approach openly. In reality, however, this concept has widely different meanings and, depending on which meaning one chooses, the consequences for the teacher in general and for the IL teacher in particular will vary considerably. Further questions arise as to the way this concept is to be implemented in practice. To this end, continuous assessment (of teachers, of university administrations, of curricula)[20] is necessary and this creates further challenges.

As has been set out in literature,[21] the concept of "research-informed teaching" may refer to an updated curriculum, the presence of world-leading experts in the team of teachers, and/or a strong relationship between a department's research and its study program.

At the same time, universities have to attribute primary importance to the employability of their students,[22] and many universities pride themselves on

---

19 Of course, there are different understandings of what the characteristic traits of the "Humboldtian University" are. According to a wider, general understanding the "Humboldtian University" consists exactly of binary holistic access to knowledge based on teaching and research. According to a more restrictive view, this term should be more appropriately reserved for the university model of German-speaking countries. See, for example, Alan Scott/Pier Paolo Pasqualoni, 'Invoking Humboldt: The German model' in James Côté and Andy Furlong (eds), *Routledge handbook of the sociology of higher education* (Routledge: London/New York 2016), 211. Here, the more general meaning is attributed to the term. In fact, although there can be no doubt that the Humboldtian University model finds its origin in the German-speaking area, at the same time it has, however, also to be recognized that this model later achieved world-wide acceptance (although with considerable regional nuances).

20 See Justyna Maciag, 'Six Sigma as a Method for Improving University Processes: The Case of the Academic Assessment Process' in Stephen Yorkstone (ed), *Global Lean for higher education: a themed anthology of case studies, approaches, and tools* (Routledge/Taylor & Francis: New York 2020).

21 See Alex Nicolson, 'Research-informed teaching: a clinical approach' (2017) 51 The Law Teacher 40, 41.

22 Ibid., 41.

their high positions in the relevant rankings.[23] Do these aims go together and, if not, how can one reconcile them?

3.3 *The Meaning of "Employability" – with Special regard to* TIL

In fact, as has been said,[24] most law students do not want to become academic researchers, but rather to practice law. Therefore, the added value of research-based teaching is rather to be found in the forming of openness for flexible thinking, continuous learning, continuous updating of legal knowledge becoming rapidly obsolete, for questioning the truth handed down by others, for thinking autonomously. Such a mindset is useful in practice in at least the same way as it is in academic research.

If we apply these criteria to TIL the perspective has again to be refocused. What the "employability" of IL students means has to be considered separately. As shown above, notwithstanding some euphoric analyses and predictions, it appears to be more realistic to be rather cautious as to the job opportunities of academics in IL in a narrower sense. In other words, only a very small number of students can expect to be employed later in the IL area in the proper sense. As to employment in academia, the prospects depend on the status of this subject in the different national law curricula, but also in this context traditional national disciplines such as civil, labor, or criminal law usually offer more promising opportunities. By adopting such a perspective one might at first sight be inclined to guess that universities would be well advised to invest as little as possible in TIL. The fact that very market-and profit-oriented universities also act otherwise gives us a first clue that something essential in these considerations may be missing. In fact, as has become clear from the considerations above, IL is in the meantime influencing and permeating all other disciplines of law. But there is more to this. IL also has a "bridging function" between various disciplines, as underlying IL norms often fulfil a more comprehensive function transcending specific disciplines.[25] Foundations and interrelations that might otherwise be lost thus become transparent. No law discipline is as vast and comprehensive as IL. Notwithstanding the problem of fragmentation,[26] which to a certain extent is real, IL offers a common

23 Like in university rankings in general, differences in the statistical methods, focus, and time horizon of the relevant rankings clear the way for many high or top positions in this field.

24 See Nicolson (n 21) 42.

25 See, for example, WTO law which spans broad areas of economic law, from tariffs to agricultural law, from intellectual property law to the law of services, to name just a few.

26 As to the need to fight against fragmentation and the "thinking in boxes" see also below at para 4.

language and a common understanding for overarching access to various law disciplines. And as to language, the centrality of English as a communication tool[27] is key to the introduction of that language into national law academia in general. If the internationalization of all national law disciplines becomes more and more necessary, the experience gained, the paths followed, and the instruments developed by international lawyers from various countries in their reciprocal communications and exchanges offer invaluable help. IL is regularly best suited for exchange programs like Erasmus, where students attend courses and have exams at universities in EU countries other than their own.[28] Subsequently or in parallel, students and teachers may engage in further academic endeavors in other law disciplines and prepare the basis for a more encompassing transborder professional activity.

Finally, a strong IL focus may considerably enhance the international visibility of a law faculty and strengthen its overall reputation. "Employability", often seen as one of the most important qualifications a university can give its students, is therefore a highly complex issue. With regard to the relevance of IL this issue reveals a pronounced relevance If employability in law professions is measured less on the basis of acquired knowledge (i.e. on a static, quickly outdated element) but on the basis of intellectual flexibility, inter-cultural knowledge, and thinking beyond strict national borders (i.e. a dynamic, process-based element), IL may be a subject that considerably improves the future position of a law student in the labor market.

4 "Lean University Management" and Its Applicability to Higher Education and to TIL in Particular

4.1 *The Growing Competition in TIL*

It goes without saying that these (possible) positive effects do not come about automatically. Their realization depends on the quality of TIL. In other words, it

27 See Christian Tomuschat, 'The (Hegemonic?) Role of the English Language' (2017) 86 NJIL 196.

28 And exchange initiatives like the Erasmus program again increase employability, as several studies suggest. Alongside increasing foreign language skills, the mobility programs improve awareness of other cultures as well as the ability to adapt to new situations. Reference is made in this context to socio-communicative skills such as intercultural awareness, adaptability, flexibility, innovativeness, productivity, motivation, endurance, problem solving abilities, and being able to work productively in a team. See European Commission, *The Erasmus Impact Study, Effects of mobility on the skills and employability of students and the internationalization of higher education institutions* (2014).

will not suffice to offer IL courses. If IL teaching is to have the effects described above, it has also to fulfil the necessary requisites and to evidence the ambition to reach highest standards. As a consequence, TIL may become extremely demanding. TIL at the Humboldtian law faculty requires teachers with a strong research and publication record, and at the same time they have to engage actively in teaching. Teachers have to understand that they are exposed to international competition not only with regard to research but also on the level of pedagogics, and perhaps there is no law discipline in which competition could be keener. In fact, IL curricula may evidence considerable differences in various countries, but these differences are still considerably smaller than in other "national" law disciplines. "Entrance barriers" into this subject are, even if national specifics are considered, far lower than in other fields. As is known from competition theory, differentiation and segmentation of markets lower competition pressure. In this sense, competition in the market for IL teaching and research should be keener than in all other law areas as, at least in principle, such differentiation and segmentation are harder to achieve.[29]

If the law teacher in student-focused pedagogies is now required to convey both knowledge and skills,[30] the exact mix of these competencies may vary from discipline to discipline and, with regard to national disciplines, from country to country. In IL the optimal mix will acquire a considerable degree of homogeneity in a highly competitive process. Unlike their colleagues in national law disciplines, the IL teacher therefore stands in direct competition with other IL teachers potentially on a world-wide level.

On this basis, in a research-informed law faculty with some openness to the international market the pressure on the individual will be considerable. The more the respective faculty is truly open and internationally oriented the less the individual teacher will be able to define what the standards of high-quality teaching in IL are. The teacher is in a similar position to the entrepreneur in a system of perfect competition: the standards and quality elements are widely pre-determined. In order to obtain a competitive edge excellence is required.[31]

29 However, reality is often different. As will be shown below with regard to the European IL "teaching and research market", high segmentation and strong protectionist barriers can be noticed.

30 See Nicholson (n 21) 45.

31 Of course, these considerations operate also in the opposite direction: Within a national university reality somewhat separated from the "global" academic reality (for example for linguistic, political, or geographical reasons) a rather small number of IL teachers might also be able to set their own (low) standards for IL teaching (and research) and influence the career of other IL teachers on the basis of criteria that have less to do with

There are two pivotal players in this game, which have partially divergent perspectives and often conflicting interests: the teacher and the university.

Two questions have immediately to be addressed in this regard:

- How can the IL teacher react or adapt to the challenges described in a somewhat competitive environment?[32]
- How can universities make sure that they fare well in this competition or how may they even be able to excel in this process?

4.2 *The Teacher's Perspective*

As described, the workload of the IL teacher in an internationally oriented Humboldtian law faculty can be enormous. He or she can either fully subscribe to this challenge and show total dedication and commitment or try to compromise and to invest time and energy strategically. While teachers may subscribe wholeheartedly to the ideal of research-informed teaching, eventually they will nonetheless experience the weight of time and resource constraints. Thus, many will be induced to compromise on teaching, to renounce the pleasure of a well-prepared lecture for the sake of long-lasting recognition and appreciation by the epistemic community, or at least for the abstract prospect of such adulation. On this basis, public commitments to the importance of teaching may be a kind of act of redemption soothing a bad conscience. The more emotional such a plea gets, the greater the awareness of past sins and the fear of future ones in this area may be. Emotional pleas as to the value of teaching may, however, also be openly insincere and thereby put to the test the abilities of the teacher as an actor. Teachers may see themselves as compelled openly to commit to a role they cannot or do not want to come up in full.

This situation is exacerbated by two tendencies that stand in mutual conflict but nonetheless appear in parallel. On the one hand, in many countries the teaching load, also as a consequence of economic constraints on education institutions, is continuously rising. On the other hand, publication achievements become measurable also in the field of IL. As contested as the respective algorithms may have been in the past, impact factor measurement becomes ever more sophisticated and reliable and, in the meantime, even very strong academic power structures can no longer provide effective protection against

internationally defined standards of academic merit and more with personal or political affinity, common club membership, or outright nepotism and corruption. They may even be able to steer the careers of their students – most effectively, however, only as far as these IL careers take place nationally.

32 The qualification of "somewhat competitive" appears to be necessary as it cannot be assumed that such a situation will necessarily come about. This will often be the case, but it cannot be claimed that in number they will be in the majority.

these developments. It becomes more and more difficult to auto-certify one's own academic standing in the field of IL or to let it be certified by a group of connected or dependent colleagues independently of real achievements. Thereby, old academic habits very much present also in the field of IL have to be put in question. While in the past, assessment committees in practice had almost unrestricted freedom in their judgment of academic achievements, in the meantime the jurors risk their own reputation in case of blatant abuses. If, for example jurors attest to the high academic impact to the friend or the friend's pupil with next to no publications while dismissing the other candidate with a far higher impact this malpractice might now become more easily public than in the past. Persistent feudalistic academic structures may still prevent these tendencies towards more transparency from becoming fully effective and it is often obvious which camps opposition to more objective assessment methods come from. The meaning, function, and scope of university assessment procedures are often misunderstood; they are neither a legitimate tool to enforce university hierarchy nor do they focus only or even prevailingly on teachers. Assessment procedures have rather to be comprehensive, all-encompassing, and the expression of an open, transparent, and cooperative approach involving all relevant stakeholders.

In an international community that is ever more connected, transparent, and dismissive of national academic hierarchies it becomes ever more difficult to conceal deficient achievements by political networking, scheming, and power plays.[33] Increasing the openness and transparency made possible also by modern communication instruments creates more objectivity, thereby intensifying competition and eventually also increasing the pressure on the individual teacher to catch up with rising standards. When academic publication achievements become easier to measure (at least on the basis of some criteria with general recognition) than the value of teaching activities, there is a strong incentive to concentrate on the former. Therefore, also in this perspective, a closer interest in teaching becomes imperative. The Humboldtian university as a holistic knowledge acquisition and instruction institution model is based, as already hinted at, on the idea that teaching and research are of more or less equal importance. Overemphasizing the relevance of only one of these pillars could jeopardize the whole system. If the Humboldtian university is to be preserved it is essential to re-determine the academic standing of teaching,

33 It goes without saying that „academic achievement" is again only partially accessible to objective assessment. And ranking and impact factors have, as already stated, their limits. But they set some barrier to blatant and strident abuse.

and also to this end it is necessary to acquire more knowledge and to develop a common understanding about this activity.

4.3 *The University Perspective – "Lean University Management" and "New Public Management"* (NPM)

Universities as institutions evidently have the opposite interest in making sure that the goals and ambitions of the Humboldtian university are adhered to to the utmost extent. At first sight, this can be achieved by control or by incentive. In recent years a new management approach, originally developed for the production sector but subsequently also extended to services, public administration, and eventually also high school teaching, has gained more and more appreciation and could now be considered also for providing more efficacy to IL.

Originally, the concept of "lean production" was developed by Toyota in the mid-twentieth century in Japan.[34] The evident success of this production method led to the creation of an entire "lean management method" which was, step by step, extended to ever broader areas and eventually also to services, public government, and higher education,[35] although in the last field this experiment is at only an "embryonic stage".[36]

At the center of this approach is the attempt to create customer value and to eliminate "waste". While such goals may lead to straightforward consequences in the field of car production, to apply such thinking to the services sector or even to higher education requires a series of adaptations and qualifications.

In their original field of application, Toyota production, lean production and lean management were directed at eliminating three types of inefficiencies: *"muda"* ("wastefulness, uselessness and futility"), *"mura"* (unevenness, non-uniformity, and irregularity"), and *"muri"* ("overburden and excessiveness").[37] These inefficiencies are closely interrelated as, for example, irregularity in the production process may soon lead to an overburden and subsequently to wastefulness.[38] Applied to higher education and TIL in particular, this philosophy

34 Alexander Nicholson/Alireza Pakgohar, 'Lean Thinking in a UK University Law Clinic: A Reflective Case Study' (2020) 27 International Journal of Clinical Legal Education 171, 177 who point out that the term "lean production" was coined by John Krafcik, 'Triumph of the Lean Production System' (1988) 30 Sloan Management Review 41.

35 See Stephan Höfer/Jörg Naeve, 'The Application of Lean Management in Higher Education' (2017) 16 International Journal of Contemporary Management 63.

36 Ibid., 63s, referring to Jiju Antony, 'Lean Six Sigma for Higher Education' (2015) 32 International Journal of Quality & Reliability Management.

37 See Doanh Do, 'What is Muda, Mura, and Muri?' (The Lean Way, 5 August 2017) <https://theleanway.net/muda-mura-muri> accessed 25 October 2021.

38 Ibid.

immediately reveals its limits but nonetheless there is value in it also for this area. The limits are already to be found in the identification of the "customer" for whom value has to be created. One might think in this context first of students, but in reality the benefits of research-informed TIL extend far beyond this group and will eventually concern society as a whole. If and to the extent that research outcomes are to be seen as international public goods, humankind as such can be seen as the customer.

Even more problematic is the concept of "waste". Here, a distinction is made between "obvious waste" and "hidden waste". While such a distinction may work fine, to a certain extent, for the industrial production process ("obvious waste" could be seen in a production process that failed, in the destruction of resources, in the sheer inactivity of collaborators; "hidden waste" relates to internal costs, for example transportation costs from one manufacturing facility to the other, for which the customer is not willing to pay),[39] it is difficult to transpose it to the services sector and even more so to higher education.

For example, it could be said that a failed experiment or an article rejected by a journal creates "hidden waste". On the other hand, a failed experiment may also provide new information and a rejected article may be accepted by another journal or induce the writer to improve it. It is, in any case, important that an internal learning process takes place. Over a certain period, this process must result in tangible output. A researcher who fails all experiments and an academic writer who never gets his papers accepted by a quality journal will have, sooner or later, to bear the consequences in a quality management system. It is even more difficult to identify "hidden waste" in higher education, as this would imply relating research (or, even more so, teaching) output to a specific customer demand defined in exact quantitative terms.

And there are even more hurdles to overcome for applying "lean management" methods to higher education. Any attempt to introduce a lean management approach at a university (and even more so at a law faculty) has to expect resistance using arguments that range from the political ("neoliberal approach") to the cultural ("Americanization of University instruction", "abandonment of the traditional, classical education model which constitutes the basis of our civilization"), and the sociological ("commercialization of instruction").

Endeavors to experiment with such strategies will therefore have to be introduced cautiously, perhaps not even having recourse to the official designation of this strategy. And it should be clear that this is a strategy and not a detailed

---

39 Ibid.

implementation plan. This way, the lean management strategy, as it has been concretized in recent years, contains a series of elements that are highly valuable for further improving TIL, for making it more effective and successful in an international competitive process. In this context it has been said that lean management as an expression of Top Quality Management in higher education has i.a. to provide for participative management, the development of a clear mission determined by objectives/goals, open communication, the allocation of resources for implementation and top-management support, employment involvement, commitment of leadership, and the mobilization of and efficient communication with the members of higher education institutions.[40]

Such goals can be implemented only if hierarchies are flat, communication is open and transparent, and career paths are based on objective criteria. Unfortunately, in Europe, developments in university legislation in recent years have moved partially in the opposite direction by strengthening hierarchy and making career decisions arbitrary.[41]

Efficiency problems in higher education have been noticed on a world-wide basis. The immediate response has often led to half-hearted reforms, worsening the situation even further. One of these reforms was the introduction of "university autonomy". If such autonomy is introduced while universities still continue to be financed almost exclusively by public contributions and in the absence of a somewhat competitive national university market, the question must arise what the real purpose of such a reform was. The situation worsens further if such reform goes together with the state's withdrawal from quality control and this control is delegated wholly to universities, which may or may not take them seriously.

In such a situation, the concept of "university autonomy", sold to the public as an approach to introducing more efficiency and market orientation, in

40 See Piotr Grudowski/Malgorzata Wisniewska, 'Lean Management Higher Education Institutions. How to Begin?' (2019) 137 Scientific Papers of Silesian University of Technology, Organization and Management 51 (with further references).

41 A hot debate has taken place in Austria as a consequence of the latest amendment of the University law (Universitätsgesetz 2002) according to which academic collaborators can remain at a university for only 8 years. Universities can offer a stable job, but they usually do not. For most academic collaborators no career paths in the academia are foreseen.

See Carina Altreiter, 'Befristete Uni-Stellen: Drei Fehlschlüsse mit gravierenden Folgen' *Der Standard* (23 July).

At the same time, some Universities hire professors "ad personam" with life-time appointments on the basis of token competitions where the "winner" of the procedure is known in advance with his name being registered in the university protocols even before the competition starts.

reality concentrates almost absolute power in the hands of local university leaders who can operate with public funds without assuming any substantive responsibility. University legislation may provide for mandatory assessment.[42] If such assessments have, however, no substantive consequences or if they are again to be decided at the local level, the whole proceeding risks becoming a farce, producing nothing other than additional costs ("obvious waste" according to the lean management terminology).

Even if such a development takes place, it can hardly be alleged that there was abusive intent by the legislator who created these norms. Such developments rather provide evidence of the fact that the particularities of higher education management are often poorly understood, and it is surely not enough to have recourse to business terminology to improve the situation. As shown, such attempts can even worsen the situation. In Germany and in Austria the decisive buzzword has been "New Public Management" (NPM), a well-sounding word that could mean everything and nothing. In Austria it was used to re-introduce hierarchy which had been very much reduced in 1975. In Germany, in the 1970s, university reform did not go as far as in Austria, and this may explain why there was not as much room for a backlash.[43]

A specific "NPM speech" was developed that created a series of euphemisms that cannot withstand closer scrutiny as to their having real substance or their corresponding to real facts.[44] In particular, it is not possible to see how the

---

42 See, for example, in Austria § 14 Universitätsgesetz 2002.

43 See on these processes Alain Scott/Pier Paolo Pasqualoni, 'Invoking Humboldt – The German model' in James Côté/Andy Furlong (eds), *Routledge Handbook of the Sociology of Higher Education* (Routledge: London/New York 2016), 211.

44 Thus, in Austria, the terms *„Leistungsvereinbarungen"* (performance agreements between the rectors and the government) und *"Zielvereinbarungen"* (target agreements between rectors and faculties) are used, conveying the image of an agreement on performance respecting internal university autonomy. In reality, however, these agreements are very generic, leaving extremely broad areas to the rectors. In Germany, in 2005, an "excellence initiative" (*"Exzellenzinitiative"*) was started which was to provide for extra funding for elite universities in order to catch up with top universities at a world-wide level. Some 15 years later the results are mixed, as the concept of "elite" is not only difficult to define but also culturally contrasted. See Fabian Mader, 'Wie viel Elite verträgt Deutschland?' (ARD alpha, 17 July 2019) <https://www.br.de/fernsehen/ard-alpha/sendungen/campus/exzellenz-initiative-foerderung-zeit-100.html> accessed 25 October 2021.

Scott/Pasqualoni (2016) further refer to the problem of federalism in Germany where federal states vie for such subsidies in a logic of "equal distribution of means" and not primarily on the basis of academic strengths. What is more, by far not all disciplines would be suitable for such an "excellence initiative". For example, the subject here at the center of interest, TIL, would hardly profit from such a concentration of financing in favor of a few selected universities.

"NPM logic" (as far as it exists beyond buzzwords) has in real life improved quality, for example with regard to the selection process of professors in university competitions.[45]

4.4 *A First Stock-Take*

On the whole, these developments evidence that new management methods, proposed for application in higher education, have to be examined in detail as to their real impact on the ground before one has recourse to them to introduce a major paradigm shift in higher education.

While NPM, widely devoid of substantive content and prone to be abused by restorative interests as it is, has hardly been able to make universities more efficient and more competitive, the "lean management strategy" may be a valuable concept that merits closer examination. Again, however, prudence is required. As shown, this new approach is no more than a general strategy and it is applicable to higher education only with many qualifications and caveats.[46] That said, it has to be acknowledged that this approach is based on several ideas and considerations that could enhance the efficiency of any institution including those dedicated to higher education. In particular, if the "lean management approach" advocates flat hierarchies, open communication, and cooperative management methods it will adapt seamlessly to the specific needs of higher education institutions and it will also be the best strategy for

45 Scott/Pasqualoni (n 43) 218 maintain that the way chair appointments were made in Austria in the past may appear "quaint to international readers" as it was the minister for research who made the final decision, choosing the successful candidate from a ranked list (usually of three) drawn up by university internal chair appointments committees. Here, however, it is to be remarked that Austria is a rather small country and the appointment of professors, who thereby became public officials, by a central institution increased transparency and raised the profile of the whole process, thereby making abuses and corruption, at least if they were evident, much more difficult. The minister had to assume political responsibility for his decision (and in particular for any deviation from the ranked list) and in addition this was a legally determined procedure that could be challenged before the Administrative Court in the event of a violation of a law. In contrast, the present appointment procedure takes place exclusively at the local level, with next to no transparency, and the Austrian Courts deny plaintiffs an effective legal remedy – evidently in contrast to Article 47 of the Charter of Fundamental Rights. See Gilbert Gornig/ Paolo Piva, 'Zum Feststellungsinteresse übergangener Bewerberinnen und Bewerber im universitären Berufungsverfahren' (2020) 4 Neue@Hochschulzeitung 131.

46 As was said: "[w]e are at a relatively early stage of understanding lean in the sector [of higher education] and a high level of tailoring for lean to meet the unique contexts of individual institutions currently exists." See Steve Yorkstone, 'Lean Universities' in Torbjorn Netland/Daryl Powell (eds), *The Routledge Companion to Lean Management*, (Routledge/Francis & Taylor: New York 2016), p. 5 of manuscript (on file with author).

reconciling university management with academic freedom, a fundamental principle that universities are usually eager to defend vociferously and which is in many countries constitutionally enshrined.

But there are other approaches, too, that could also be extremely useful from this perspective. One of these newer concepts is the “VUCA approach” that offers particularly interesting elements also for TIL.

5 The VUCA Approach

VUCA stands for the following words: Volatility, Uncertainty, Complexity, and Ambiguity. The acronym was coined by the US military and by political analysts in the late 1980s[47] following the fall of the iron curtain and as a consequence of an international environment that had become extremely dynamic and less predictable and is posing ever more unpredictable challenges, both positive and negative. Soon this term was extended also to the world of business in order to design the new international competition framework individual enterprises have to cope with. It describes the prevailing real-world situation politicians and practitioners have to take into account if they want not only to keep up with present challenges but to persist and to excel in the foreseeable future. For a series of reasons, universities also have to deal with this concept. First of all, in the meantime the VUCA concept has found world-wide acceptance both among political analysts and in the business management community. It has become an instrument that is in itself the object of academic studies as it appears to be a valuable tool to cope with uncertainty and rapidly changing challenges in both politics and the business environment. At the same time, however, the VUCA concept reflects some of the main challenges universities as institutions are confronted with in reciprocal international competition. As shown, the integration of universities into the Public Sector has somewhat softened the “competitive stress” these institutions are exposed to, but in the end this may have created only a temporal lull until the relevant pressure fully sets in. Universities are required to develop expertise in order to soften the impact of these challenges or, preferably, to harness these factors and to transform them into elements of success. In other words, those universities which will best cope with these factors and best anticipate their further development will have a decisive competitive edge in the international academic environment.

47 See U.S. Army Heritage & Education Center, “Who first originated the term VUCA (Volatility, Uncertainty, Complexity and Ambiguity)?” (U.S Army Heritage & Educational Center, 07 May 2019) <https://usawc.libanswers.com/faq/84869> accessed 25 October 2021.

It is interesting to note that up to now, as far as can be seen, the VUCA concept has not been the object of closer analysis from the vantage point of IL even though, from a substantive perspective, close relations between these two subjects can be assumed. In fact, VUCA has been conceived on the basis of developments inherently related to or even based on IL. Their identification has gone in parallel with the shaping of a new view on IL[48] that since then has been characterizing the prevailing view of this discipline of law. There is next to no branch of this discipline in which the VUCA criteria would not be able to offer defining elements in any attempt to assess the status quo of the relevant norms. To take only a few examples, reference can be made to the concept of state (see the discussion about the "Islamic State"),[49] the ever-rising role of NGOs,[50] the growing strength of peoples or sub-state entities seeking autonomy or self-determination,[51] and the growing role of artificial intelligence in IL.[52]

It may be argued that the complexity, ambiguity, and rapid changes in paradigms have always been characterizing traits of IL,[53] and it may even be true that in a bipolar world dominated by the East-West conflict it might have been even harder to identify a common core of generally accepted norms with some degree of stability. At the same time, however, this bi-polarity (or tri-polarity, if the "third world" was also taken into consideration) provided some sort of stability when faced with the lack of agreement as to a large set of norms – with the parallel need to agree on some essential norms to make most

48 Of pivotal importance is Francis Fukuyama, *The End of History and the Last Man* (Free Press 1992) emphasizing, however, first of all, the end of the bipolar world and not yet fully anticipating the ensuing instability. For an early stock-taking on these developments in German see Hanspeter Neuhold/Bruno Simma, *Neues europäisches Völkerrecht nach dem Ende des Ost-West-Konflikts?* (Nomos: Baden-Baden 1996). See also Hans-Joachim Heintze/Pierre Thielbörger, *From Cold War To Cyber War* (Springer: Heidelberg 2016).

49 See Christian Tomuschat, 'The Status of the 'Islamic State' under International Law' (2015) 90 Die Friedens-Warte 223 and Anicée Van Engeland, 'Statehood, Proto States and International Law: New Challenges, Looking at the Case of ISIS' in James Crawford and others (eds), *The international legal order* (2016), 75.

50 See, for example, Pierre-Marie Dupuy, *NGOs in International Law – Efficiency in Flexibility?* (Edward Elgar: Cheltenham 2008).

51 See Peter Hilpold, *Kosovo and International Law* (Brill/Martinus Nijhoff, Leiden/Boston 2012) and Peter Hilpold, *Autonomy and Self-determination – Between Legal Assertions and Utopian Aspirations* (Edward Elgar: Cheltenham 2018).

52 See Ashley Deeks, 'Introduction to the Symposium: How will artificial intelligence affect international law?' (2020) 114 AJIL 138.

53 By the way, it has also been argued that VUCA elements have also always been there in the modern business world. See Michael Skapinger, 'The empty consolation of 'Vuca' and other buzzwords' *Financial Times* (23 October 2018).

essential forms of interaction possible. The VUCA concept would therefore hardly fit into the pre-1989 world, notwithstanding the fact that disagreement and ambiguity had been there since the earliest days of the UN era. For the present world order VUCA provides, instead, a sort of explanatory framework. Though it may be criticized as tautological and simple, it still provides a map with some pivotal elements allowing one to better understand the present IL order. And for the purposes here at the center of interest, it might be useful also to rethink TIL. In the past, it was often strongly knowledge-based so that it was most often "traditional knowledge" drawn from established textbooks. If actual practice did not (or did no longer) correspond to theory, practice was "wrong" or misguided. VUCA, on the contrary, shows that acquired wisdom and purportedly established rules have to be continuously re-examined, and values and central norms of IL, such as the prohibition of the use of force or human rights provisions, need continuous re-affirmation and control of the forces that could undermine them. As to the detection and designation of "ambiguity", the Critical Legal Studies (CLS) approach has somewhat anticipated VUCA.[54]

Some studies have already examined the effects of VUCA on high school education:[55] They have shown that students have to be taught not only to be repositories of knowledge but to deal efficiently with knowledge so that graduates become "independent thinkers, problem solvers, and decision makers".[56] As a consequence, knowledge (as a static element) and dealing with knowledge (knowledge acquirement, selection, elaboration, and assessment) are intertwined,[57] and both have to be given equal attention at universities. As regards TIL, where the wealth of pertinent knowledge is enormous and where at the same time the international framework is subject to relentless change, this challenge is even greater. It has been said that an education system is needed "where students are rooted in content knowledge but also provided

54 On CLS in the field of IL see David Kennedy, 'A New Stream of International Law Scholarship' (1988) 7 Wis Int'L. L.J. 26; See also Anthony Carty, *The Decay of International Law?: A Reappraisal of the Limits of Legal Imagination in International Affairs* (Manchester University Press: Manchester 1986) and Martti Koskenniemi, *From Apology to Utopia: The Structure of International Legal Argument* (Cambridge University Press: Cambridge 1989).

55 See Poh-Sun Seow/Gay Pan/Grace Koh, 'Examining an experimental learning approach to prepare students for the volatile, uncertain, complex and ambiguous (VUCA) work environment' (2019) 17 The International Journal of Management Education 62.

56 Ibid., 62, with reference to Elena Silva, 'Measuring skills for 21st-century learning' (2019) 90 Phi Delta Kapan 630.

57 Ibid.

with 'hands-on learning that mirrors real-world problems and work opportunities in an interdisciplinary way'".[58]

And even more so it becomes extremely important to avoid excessive fragmentation of IL, also in regard to teaching. To "think in boxes" (human rights, environmental rights, UN law, international economic law, and so on) creates the risk of losing sight of the basic ideas undergirding IL and could stand in the way of its further development towards a somewhat coherent order where the lawyer can see law as "enlightenment as responsibility" in the Kantian sense.[59]

This plea for a broader perspective and even interdisciplinarity applies surely to law studies in general, but it seems to be relevant for IL in a particularly pronounced manner. Interdisciplinarity has always been of extreme value for TIL. One might refer to the importance of history for understanding IL's basic developments,[60] to the necessity of economic knowledge to judge questions of International Economic Law appropriately,[61] or to the close relationship between IL and international politics.[62] In the VUCA world it becomes pivotal to understand the broader framework and to prepare for flexible change. From

58 See Seow/Pan/Koh (n 55) 63, referring to "The Economist Intelligence Unit Limited, 2015". See also, in a similar vein, Otto Kimminich, 'Teaching International Law in an Interdisciplinary Context' (1986) 24 AVR 143.

59 See Martti Koskenniemi, 'International Law: Constitutionalism, Managerialism and the Ethos of Legal Education' (2007) 1 EJLS 8. See also, more recently, in a similar vein Anthony Carty, 'International law and nervous states in the age of anger, the collapse of legal formalism and a return to natural law' in Rossana Deplano/Nicholas Tsagourias (eds), *Research Methods of International Law* (Edward Elgar: Cheltenham 2021), 180, emphasizing "individual judgment". As will be revealed towards the end of this contribution, this position is, however, also not without its problems, in particular if this "individual judgment" is made in an exclusively unilateral way.

60 For a recent contribution with ample reference to literature on the "turn to history" see Matilda Arvidsson/ Miriam Bak McKenna, 'The turn to history in international law and the sources doctrine: Critical approaches and methodological imaginaries' (2020) 33 LJIL 37.

61 I have dealt extensively with this question in Peter Hilpold, *Die EU im GATT/WTO-System* (Nomos Verlag 2019).

62 See Anne-Marie Slaughter/Andrew Tulumello/Stepan Wood, 'International Law and International Relations Theory: A New Generation of Interdisciplinary Scholarship' (1998) 92 AJIL 367 who refer to a growing number of cross-citations between the fields of IL and international politics (p 367, note 2).
For a recent analysis of this relationship see Filipe dos Reis/Janis Grzybowski, 'The matrix reloaded: Reconstructing the boundaries between (international) law and politics' (2021) 34 LJIL 547. Manfred Steger 'What is Global Studies' in Mark Juergensmeyer and others (eds), *The Oxford Handbook of Global Studies* (OUP: Oxford 2019), 3, points out that in the United States alone Global Studies now encompass approximately 300 undergraduate and graduate programs. Ibid., 5.

a VUCA perspective it is essential to keep this subject meaningful, of practical relevance.

More and more universities are now in the process of introducing chairs for "Law and information technology (IT)". This appears to be an overdue step, but at the same time care must be taken not to create an isolated subject detached from the other sub-disciplines of law. IT law – with all its possible present and future ramification up to the integration of AI – has rather to be an integral part of all areas of law, and of TIL in particular. In other words, It would make little sense to create another, separate branch of legal research, but all legal sub-disciplines have to fully embrace all relevant aspects of IT.

There can be no doubt that by accepting this new reality that, by the way, has been in the offing for decades university teaching will change profoundly. In relation to TIL the question has to be posed whether classroom teaching in weekly units of 90 minutes as is common at European universities still makes sense, in particular if the lecture consists exclusively of a summary of an IL manual with some additional explanations. To be clear, the conveyance of knowledge will always be an important part of university instruction, especially in the area of TIL, and this form of teaching will most often be "frontal". As was said not long ago, "[F]rontal teaching remains the backbone of offline higher education taught programmes and one of the most effective methods for the transmission of knowledge".[63] In a reality characterized by an over-supply of information and in which information selection and processing are the critical capacities, some expert guidance helping to create the foundations on which further expertise can be based will always be a basic service to be provided by university teaching. The challenge will, however, be to flexibilize this activity with the greater and earlier active involvement of students in this information gathering, selection, and assessment process.[64] The transitional period of the COVID-19 shutdown in physical university teaching has provided an unprecedented opportunity to experiment with new teaching tools in virtual classrooms.[65] The experiences gained in this very particular VUCA

63 See Tarcisio Gazzini, 'A Fresh Look at Teaching International Law – A Few Pedagogical Considerations in the Age of Communications' (2016) 29 LJIL 971.

64 At the business faculties of some universities that have already adopted the VUCA approach such innovative teaching approaches are already in the process of being tried out. See Seow/Pan/Koh (n 55).

65 It is true, that even in the pre-COVID-era university courses, often called as "massive open online courses" (MOOCS), were delivered online. These courses did not always fulfill expectations. See Yorkstone (n 46) 4 of the manuscript, on file with the author. But the COVID period, with its broadly based new experiences and many technological breakthroughs certainly changed the factual situation.

situation should continue and experimented with further in the broader, general VUCA situation representing the post-Covid-19 period.

On the whole, the VUCA model, especially when applied to TIL, confirms pivotal insights gained by the lean management approach and by the experiences had during the COVID-19-pandemic: In a volatile, uncertain, complex, and ambiguous teaching and research environment traditional university hierarchies – unless they are strictly merit-based and permanently assessed – have lost most of their justification, they risk becoming ludicrous. Attempts, as can be noted in some European countries, to even strengthen university hierarchy and to reverse the reforms of the last century are going in the opposing direction to what taking VUCA into consideration would suggest.

And there is yet another aspect that links VUCA to IL: IL is known to be a subject of particular complexity.[66] Even if the student of today will become the lawyer of tomorrow, having little or nothing to do with IL (however improbable this might be), studying IL prepares for any complexity a lawyer will inevitably be confronted with. In this sense, studying IL also has an instrumental function; it prepares students for a VUCA situation that is characterizing the lawyers′ reality in an ever more extensive way.

6 Different Country Situations

6.1 *The Slow Development from Insular Thinking towards Globalization*

This slow but relentless move from insular thinking with sporadic references to International Law to a true globalization of the education program (of at least some prominent law schools) has been described as a process whereby legal education passed from internationalization to transnationalization and was eventually transformed into globalization.[67]

Within this picture, the period of "internationalization", characterized by sporadic, albeit increasing contacts with International Law, lasted until about the end of WW II. It was Philip Jessup who in the 1950s introduced the concept of "transnational law",[68] intended to overcome the national/international divide for the concept of "transnational law" which should cover "all law which regulates actions or events that transcend national frontiers".[69] The perspective

66 See Michael Reisman, 'The Teaching of International Law in the Eighties' (1986) 20 The International Lawyer 987.

67 See Simon Chesterman, 'The Evolution of Legal Education: Internationalisation, Transnationalisation, Globalization' (2009) 10 German Law Journal 879.

68 Philip Jessup, *Transnational Law* (1956).

69 See Chesterman (n 67) 881.

was thereby considerably broadened and awareness raised of the fact that everyday legal reality was determined by developments coming from abroad to a far greater extent than hitherto admitted.[70] In this development, "globalization", starting towards the end of the last century and best epitomized by the creation of the World Trade Organisation (WTO) in 1995, would be the last step in a process of the continuous reshaping of international relations between national jurisdictions which could first be seen as "archipelagos", then develop into a patchwork, and finally present themselves as an intertangled web.[71] Of course, this periodization is nothing more than an abstract model, perhaps apt to give a glimpse of a broader development but hardly suited for strict categorization and to be transferred lock, stock and barrel, to practice. It has also to be further qualified in relation to the situation in different countries and in different regions. This study concentrates on the United States and then, in particular, on the situation in Europe with which this author is most familiar. Notwithstanding these geographic limitations, this author hopes that some relevant insights into theory and practice of TIL resulting from these surely influential academic realities, may be gained.

6.2 *The Situation in the US*

In this study, it has repeatedly been shown that the situation of teachers and teaching varies considerably on a global scale. Law teaching in general is closely related to specific country situations, depending on which "legal family" or "legal tradition"[72] a specific normative system pertains to. At first sight it may be surprising that this holds true even more so as far as International Law is concerned. While international law is in principle and ontologically a unitary order of a uniform nature, on a global level we have, first of all, to reckon with the fact that at the academic level there are different national and

70 As Jessup wrote in 1956: "We may find that some of the problems that we have considered essentially international, inevitable productive of stress and conflict between governments and peoples of two different countries, are after all merely human problems which might arise at any level of human society – individual, corporate, interregional, or international." See Jessup (n 68) 16.

71 For this impressive picture see again Chesterman (n 67) 883.

72 On the concept of „legal families" and "legal tradition" see Patrick Glenn, 'Comparative Legal Families and Comparative Legal Traditions' in Mathias Reimann/Reinhard Zimmermann (eds), *The Oxford Handbook of Comparative Law* (2006). This author points out that the concept of the "legal families", while still in use, is in decline as it is closely associated with the idea of legal nationalism. See also Peter Hilpold, 'What Are and to What Avail Do We Study European International Law Traditions?' in Peter Hilpold (ed), *European International Law Traditions* (Springer: Cham 2021).

regional traditions of and approaches to IL.[73] The political strength and influence of individual countries further contribute enormously to determining their political attitude towards international law, and their preparedness and need to rely on this order to pursue and to implement their goals on the international scene.

For international law teachers these are facts they cannot influence directly; they have rather to accept them as they are. Only by moving into another jurisdiction may they encounter a situation that is perhaps more suitable for them.[74] For a variety of reasons, most often such mobility will not be possible to achieve: Language barriers, private personal relations, professional networks the teacher is already involved in, but also protective measures by other university communities against "foreign" teachers can hinder mobility considerably.[75]

To move from the anecdotal, extensive surveys have been undertaken that should offer a more representative picture of the teaching of international law in the various jurisdictions. The results of these surveys do not lend themselves to an over-simplistic reading; they have rather to be interpreted as context-based in the sense that the role of international law teaching is strongly dependent on a variety of elements, first among them being the structure of legal education as such. It has further to be remarked that to this day no comprehensive world-wide study of the teaching situation in IL has been available.[76] The picture is therefore not complete, but more and more puzzle pieces show up.[77]

---

73 See Peter Hilpold (ed), *European International Law Traditions* (Springer: Berlin/Heidelberg 2021) and Anthea Roberts, *Is International Law International?* (OUP: Oxford 2017).

74 Such reasoning is inspired by thoughts developed in the field of fiscal federalism, a theory based on a large number of different fiscal settings which would be optimized by mobile taxpayers looking for an optimal mix. See Peter Hilpold, *Italienisches Steuerrecht* (Facultas: Vienna 2017), referring to Charles Tiebout, 'A Pure Theory of Local Expenditures' (1956) 64 Journal of Political Economy 416.

75 As will be shown below, even within the European Union the mobility of high school teachers faces substantive barriers, notwithstanding the basic freedom of free movement in accordance with Article 45 TFEU. See Gilbert Gornig/Paolo Piva, 'Freizügigkeit der Hochschullehrer in der EU – der Problemfall Österreich' (2020) 31 EuZW 469.

76 See Ryan Scoville/Milan Markovic, 'How Cosmopolitan are International Law Professors?' (2016) 38 MichJIntL 119: "Much [...] remains unknown" (ibid., 122). As the authors remark, the much-praised study by Anthea Roberts, *Is International Law International?* (OUP: Oxford 2017) had also to concentrate on a handful of countries and schools. Ibid.

77 For an early attempt to undertake a somewhat more comprehensive survey see Bin Cheng, *International Law: Teaching and Practice* (Stevens & Son: London 1982). Many elements of this study are now out of date but they are nonetheless interesting in a historical perspective. Somewhat closer to the present is the (shorter) study by Bengt Broms, 'International Law in the Law School Curriculum' in Ronald Macdonald (ed), *Essay in Honour of Wang*

Many of the relevant studies refer to the United States, and it is American lawyers themselves who have repeatedly taken an interest in the relevance of international law teaching, starting from early in the 20th century and in concomitance with the growing importance of the American legal system on the international scene. This rising weight, being again the consequence of the augmented role of the US on the political, economic, and military level, made it unavoidable to address the question of what role international law should be given in teaching.

In these studies from early on, the surprisingly limited relevance of international law in the curricula of US law schools was attested to. On the one hand, this was surely the result of isolationist tendencies arising in the US after WW I. The most decisive element lies, however, surely in the specific structure of US law school curricula, providing for rather short and condensed instruction if compared with, say, most countries in continental Europe. Six 14-week periods over three years, being the rule for the formation of lawyers in the US,[78] leave little space for subjects that may not be strictly necessary for the bar examination and for the later exercise of the profession of lawyer.[79] In this, law school curricula, relying on the indications of the American Bar Association (ABA), have shown continuity for over a century.[80]

When, towards the end of the last century, the American Society of International Law (ASIL) started to take a closer look at this issue, TIL in the United States again stood at the forefront. From the survey conducted under the direction of Professor John Gamble a dire picture emerged. The role of International Law was rather a marginal one.[81]

Tieya (Kluwer/Martinus Nijhoff: Dordrecht/Boston 1993), 79, comparing the situation in France, the United Kingdom, the United States, and Finland.

78 See Reisman (n 66).

79 See in this sense Edwin Dickinson, 'Teaching of International Law to Law Students' (1923) 17 Am.Pol.Sci-Rev. 464, 465.

80 See Rosa Kim, 'Globalizing the Law Curriculum for Twenty-First-Century Lawyering' (2018) 67 Journal of Legal Education 905, 907. Little more than a century ago, in 1921, the ABA first recommended that admission to practice be linked to the completion of a degree program. See Chesterman (n 67), with reference to James White, 'Rethinking the Program of Legal Education: A New Program for the New Millennium' (2000) 36 Tulsa 397, 400.

81 See John Gamble, *Teaching International Law in the 1990s, Survey of Academic International Law Project of the American Society of International Law under the sponsorship of the Ford Foundation* (1993).

Only a few years before, a renowned US-American IL teacher compared the teaching of IL in the US with that in Great Britain:[82] "While the British approach is quite positivistic, rule-oriented and formally descriptive, the American approach tends to be more process-oriented and contextual".[83] According to Professor Nafziger, IL teaching at US law schools is "highly problem-oriented and technical, relatively untheoretical, and inductive"[84] with a "tendency to diminish the importance of a broad educational background for aspiring international lawyers".[85]

In subsequent years, slowly and mostly inadvertently, some changes oriented towards a broader internationalization of lawyers' instruction have taken place. First of all, since 2015 the amended ABA Standards and Rules of Procedure for Approval of Law Schools have referred to a new "cultural competency" law schools may adopt as a learning outcome.[86] As has been noted,[87] this "cultural competency" could be used as a vehicle to "internationalize" and "globalize" the law schools' curricula. On the more practical level, school curricula were partly adapted in the sense that International Law or Comparative Law or Transnational Law courses were introduced.[88] In other cases, topics traditionally considered as national were supplemented by some international (comparative or transnational) elements.[89]

---

82 See James Nafziger, 'Teaching Public International Law in the United States' (1986) 24 AVR 215.

83 Ibid., 216.

84 Ibid., 217.

85 Ibid., 218. An interesting trait of US law school education, perhaps also worth being considered outside the US, is that access to these studies requires a preliminary set of studies in another field. As Bengt Broms (n 76) 83 remarks, often "entrants to a law school in the United States have a BA in the humanities before entry." Without doubt, such preparation can considerably broaden the perspective of law students.

86 See Kim (n 80) 930ss.

87 Ibid.

88 Ibid., 925ss.

89 Building on this experience Kim (n 80) 947, proposes to create law school that should to do all or the combination of the following in order to globalize the curriculum: "1) Require one course on international, comparative, or transnational law or co-curricular activity for graduation; 2) Expand the menu of skills-focused courses integrating global issues; 3) Encourage faculty development and collaboration on globally focused teaching and scholarship; and 4) Facilitate student engagement with global perspectives in and out of the classroom." In 2000, Philip Trimble drew a fairly optimistic picture of the process the author noticed in the US, according to which international law was to be introduced into the whole domestic law curriculum. Most probably, this vision was too optimistic. See Phillip Trimble, 'The Plight of Academic International Law' (2000) 1 Chic.JIntL 117. For more details about the present-day situation in TIL in the US see Charlotte Ku, U.S. Approaches to Teaching International Law in a Global Environment, in this volume, 82.

From a European perspective all these measures appear to be appallingly limited, and the resulting picture will in many cases stand in clear contrast to the enthralling image of the "Invisible College" conjured up by Oscar Schachter,[90] according to which the community of international lawyers, primarily formed in the United States, would constitute a loosely organized but nonetheless highly effective, influential, and well-coordinated community. One might ask where on earth the members of this community might have been educated if TIL in the US still has only such a comparatively small relevance?

This apparent contradiction can be resolved if we consider that the US law school market is highly segmented with a broad instruction program that caters for pre-eminently national needs and a smaller, highly specialized instruction segment that attracts primarily foreign postgraduate LL.M. students. These programs are often of outstanding quality and peer-certified reputation;[91] for the law schools where these courses have been instituted, and for the US economy as a whole they are, however, also important revenue-generating tools.[92] Hopes that such international programs could have cross-fertilizing effects in the sense that they could spread the globalization idea to students of national J.D. programs have not yet materialized.[93]

90 See Oscar Schachter, 'The Invisible College of International Lawyers' (1977) 72 Northwestern University School of Law Review 217.

91 For a ranking of these schools see US News, Best International Law Programs, 2021, 'Best International Law Programs' (U.S. News, 24 June 2021) <https://www.usnews.com/best-graduate-schools/top-law-schools/international-law-rankings> accessed 25 October 2021.

92 This became clear when former US president Donald Trump in 2017 considered introducing restrictive immigration and travel measures for foreign students. See Paul Caron, 'President Trump Threatens Law Schools' $350 Million Revenue From Foreign LL.M. Students' (TaxProf Blog, 25 October 2021) <https://taxprof.typepad.com/taxprof_blog/2017/04/president-trump-threatens-law-schools-350-million-revenue-from-foreign-llm-students.html> accessed 25 October 2021. "The advanced law degree programs bring in about $350 million annually to the more than 100 U.S. law schools that offer them, with around 10,000 foreign students coming here each year to pursue an LL.M."

93 See Kim (n 80) 946: "interaction among international students and U.S. J.D. students tends to be minimal". Another problem affecting the US university system is the strong divide between "elite universities" and "other universities". There are several, rather expensive, universities of the former group that are very well renowned (also) for their IL courses. Broader access to high-quality courses (or courses that are deemed to be such), not just in the field of IL, is currently a hotly debated issue in the US. See Michael Sandel, *The Tyranny of Merit* (Penguin Press 2020). If Sandel's main contention that access to elite universities is both hereditary and a basic pre-requisite for social advancement were to prove true (at least as a tendency), this would be problematic in general and really serious for IL education in view of the influential positions often obtained by academics educated in this field.

6.3 *The Situation in Europe*

The situation in Europe appears to be extremely heterogeneous, a fact that is all the more surprising in view of the rather narrow geographic borders within which these different approaches are pursued. Different national approaches to international law (for example between the civil law and the common law areas or between Latin countries and German-speaking countries as well as within the German-speaking area) can offer a first explanation for this situation, as can a highly segmented and often extremely protectionist academic reality.

As is obvious, it is not possible here to undertake a comprehensive country-analysis covering all European states,[94] and any selection must therefore be to some extent subjective. Nonetheless, it will be shown that even from the examples chosen a series of conclusions of general application, even beyond Europe, can be drawn.

As for the German-speaking area, the situation with regard to the relevance of international law in university law curricula differs widely between Germany, Austria, and Switzerland. In Germany, international law is not a mandatory subject in the university law curriculum. A law student can complete his/her studies and become – after having acquired some practical experience – a "fully qualified lawyer" (*"Volljurist"*) without having had to study international law as an in independent subject.[95] It is possible to write a dissertation on international law, but the "second dissertation" ("habilitation", *"Habilitationsschrift"*), which qualifies one to teach international law at German universities (as well as at Austrian and Swiss universities) and to apply for a professorial post at

94 See also the contribution by Scoville/Markovic (n 76), cited above, which refers to the study "Who Studies International Law? A Global Survey", of 2015, by one of the two authors named, Robert Scoville. This study has a more limited focus as it concentrates on the question in which regions of the globe international law training is compulsory. The author admits that there is no exhaustive answer even to this rather specific question due to the lack of comprehensive data.

95 The subject touching international and European law in the most immediate way is probably "Staatsrecht III", that is mandatory in most German Bundesländer. As Walter Rudolf wrote in 1986, this situation dates back to the beginnings of the 1970s, when German federal law distinguished between compulsory and optional subjects in the law curricula. IL was not mentioned in the former group as an independent compulsory subject. See Walter Rudolf, 'Die Lehre staatsrechtlicher Bezüge zum Völkerrecht (1986) 24 AVR 163. In this context a "provincial law curriculum" or a "celebrated modernism that is in reality introverted" was spoken of. See Rudolf Bernhardt, 'Vom Provinzialismus deutscher Juristenausbildung' (1971) JZ 581. Michael Reisman qualified optional international law courses as „cosmetic" or „boutique" courses. See Michael Reisman, 'The Teaching of International Law in the Eighties' (1986) 20 The International Law 987.

these universities,[96] has again to focus in practice on issues of public (German) law as there are next to no chairs for international law at German universities. International law is usually presented as no more than an appendix in the job description vacancyies of public law and IL. Competitions for chairs dedicated (*inter alia*) to international law are further biased in favor of applicants who have studied in Germany. One reason for this lies in the fact that law professors from German Universities have to sit in lawyers' examination commissions (*"Staatsexamen"*) where expertise in national law is primarily required. Professors coming from abroad and not having themselves taken both "state examina" would not only often lack the technical expertise to examine German national law but would not even be allowed to do so as they lack the qualifications for becoming judges in Germany in accordance with the "German Judge Law".[97]

Consequently, the burden of these examination activities in the *"Staatsexamen"*, often considered to be rather painstaking, would shift to the members teaching national law subjects.[98] The specific German recruitment process for international law teachers and the institutional combination of international law with public law, with the former in a subsidiary role to the latter, necessarily also influences how international law is understood and taught in Germany. As a consequence, these elements have strongly favored not only the affirmation of the "Constitutional International Law Theory" in this country but also, in a further escalation, the claim that German Legal Scholarship could fulfill a hegemonic role on an international level.[99] The self-perception

96 In theory, such a qualification is not strictly necessary, as other, "equivalent" qualifications can also be offered when applying for such a post. In reality, however, such qualifications have next to no relevance in competitions for such jobs. The Italian University Council (Consiglio Universitario Nazionale) in General Opinion n. 13 of 18 December 2012 expressed a negative opinion as to the possibility to recognize German habilitations in Italy automatically. The reason for the rejection of such a claim was found in the fact that in Germany habilitations are granted by universities (in Italy, l'equivalent, "l'abilitazione", by a central commission), there is no limitation as to the validity (in Italy, at that time, "l'abilitazione" had a validity of four years, now nine) and German habilitations do not distinguish between full professors and associate professors, as "l'abilitazione" does in Italy. At the same time, this Opinion emphasizes the need to create a European university space.

97 See Heribert Hirte, 'Grußwort' in Stephan Hobe/Thilo Marauhn (ed), *Lehre des internationalen Rechts – zeitgemäß?* (C.F. Müller, 2017) referring to § 5 Deutsches Richtergesetz (DRiG).

98 Ibid.

99 This discussion can be traced back to Carl Schmitt's writing: Carl Schmitt, *Die Lage der europäischen Rechtswissenschaft* (Tübingen 1950) and was reintroduced by Armin von Bogdandy in 2021 on the "Verfassungsblog". See Armin von Bogdandy, 'German Legal

of playing a hegemonic role will also influence the way in which international law is taught and eventually how national law is applied to international relations.[100]

In Austria, IL has traditionally had a far greater role both as a teaching subject and on the subsequent professional level. In fact, in all Austrian universities in which studies in law are offered (Vienna, Innsbruck, Graz, Salzburg, and Linz) international law is a mandatory subject. Subsequent professional qualification as a judge, a public prosecutor, a lawyer, or a notary demands evidence of the passing of such an exam as a prerequisite for accession to these professions. The problems and peculiarities of the Austrian university system in general and of law instruction in particular have immediate effects also on instruction in international law. As has been said,[101] the instruction of Austrian

---

Hegemony? (Verfassungsblog, 05 October 2020) <https://verfassungsblog.de/german-legal-hegemony/> accessed 25 October 2021.

Joseph Weiler, however, flatly rejected claims of the superiority of German legal scholarship in a way that might sound disrespectful to the ears of some German lawyers but which, in the end, is not easy to counter: *"Hegemony of German legal scholarship or doctrine perhaps? With the exceptions of some scholarly islands within, say, Spain or Italy, the mainstream of that scholarship is barely known and cited outside Germany and the only contemporary German legal scholars widely admired and referred to outside the Fatherland are for the most part that generation of "Americanized" scholars (meaning mostly those who did an LL.M at Harvard, or Yale or Columbia etc – a fact they never fail to mention in signing any letter or article) writing in English. It's not because German legal scholarship is defective in any way; quite the opposite. Its only "vice" is that it's in German. Likewise, it is not as if all English or American legal scholarship is so breathtaking to explain the attention it gets. But it has the "virtue" of being in English. If you want to talk of Legal Hegemony, put in first place the English Language."* See Joseph Weiler, 'Mirror Mirror on the Wall – Who is the Most Beautiful of All? Legal Hegemony or Legal Hubris?' (Verfassungsblog, 10 October 2020) <https://verfassungsblog.de/mirror-mirror-on-the-wall-who-is-the-most-beautiful-of-all/> accessed 25 October 2021.

100 Consequently, conflicts in relations with other jurisdictions may become unavoidable. One recent example concerns the PSPP judgment of 5 May 2020 of the German Constitutional Court. The psychological circumstances behind this case were analyzed in ironic exaggeration by the CMLRev's Editorial Board as follows: "This is [...] a strongly-worded decision delivered with all the confidence of members of an institution that would very comfortably accept the compliment of being *primus inter pares* among constitutional courts in Europe and, come to think of it, well beyond".

See Editorial Comments, 'Not mastering the Treaties: The German Federal Constitutional Court's PSPP judgment' (2020) 57 CMLRev 965. On this judgment see also Peter Hilpold, 'So long „Solange"? The PSPP judgment by the German Constitutional Court and the conflict between the German and the European "popular spirit"' in John Bell (ed), (Cambridge Yearbook of European Legal Studies 2020).

101 See Willibald Posch, 'The Austrian View of the Bologna Process in Legal Education' (2005) 2 European Journal of Legal Education 67, 68.

lawyers was regulated until the 1970s by an Act dating back to 1893, and therefore to the Austro-Hungarian Empire. This Act was primarily directed at producing lawyers who would defend the legitimacy of the Hapsburg Empire.[102] This basic philosophy went hand in hand with a strong emphasis on history and special regard for this country's international position. To a certain extent, these circumstances gave particular weight to the subject of international law. However, it also had the consequence that considerable, if not excessive, importance was attributed to specific Austrian interests in international law. Thus, in Austrian universities particular attention was paid to neutrality studies, often ignoring the much reduced, if not generally vanishing, importance of this concept in general international law.[103] A conspicuous number of Austrian international law professors obtained tenure by presenting monographs on neutrality.[104] As for the teaching of European Law, for a long period Austrian law faculties were disadvantaged due to that country's rather late accession to the European Union in 1995. As was analyzed elsewhere,[102] European law has in many fields of the Austrian legal reality remained an alien element, not really understood and appreciated even by high-ranking officials. Since the mid-1970s a series of university reform Acts has led to new orientations that have, directly and indirectly, influenced the overall normative (and practical) setting of teaching at Austrian universities. While the University Organization Act of 1975 (*"Firnberg-Refom"*, OJ 1975/258) introduced a modern, liberal university structure with co-decision procedures involving students and younger teachers, the reform of 1993 ("Busek-Reform", OJ 1993/805) signaled the start of some counter-reforms, even though the overall setting remained a progressive one.[105] The University Reform Act of 2002 (*"Universitätsgesetz UG 2002"*, OJ

102 Ibid.

103 See, extensively, Peter Hilpold, *Solidarität und Neutralität im Vertrag von Lissabon* (Nomos: Baden-Baden 2010).

104 Ibid.

In hindsight, of particular interest in this context is the contribution by Konrad Ginther, who held the chair of international law at the University of Graz for quite a long period (1969–2002) and who writes in his contribution to Bin Cheng (ed.), 1982, A Note on the Teaching of International Law in Austria, pp. 199–200 (200) that in Austria "there is nowadays a growing acceptance of a pluralistic approach in teaching and research of international law in so far as distinctive features of a 'Western', 'Soviet' and 'Third World' approach (dominant perspectives) are concerned". See Konrad Ginther, 'A Note on the Teaching of International Law in Austria' in Bin Cheng (ed), *International Law: teaching and practice* (London: Stevens 1982), 199.

105 See Christian Burtscher/Pier-Paolo Pasqualoni/Alan Scott, 'Universities and the Regulatory Framework: The Austrian University System in Transition' (2006) 20 Social Epistemology 241, 246.

2002 I 120) achieved a radical U-turn back to an authoritarian university structure. Co-decision procedures were abolished and University Rectors obtained enormous power, including with regard to the appointment of professors.[106]

The new University Act was understood as a reaction to the previous system of democratic governance, which was held responsible for all the shortcomings of university reality.[107] De-democratization should be the antidote to all these problems.[108] Using grand-sounding rhetoric, it was stated that the Anglo-American model should be copied and Ivy League-type universities created ("Weltklasse-Universität") – but under Austrian conditions and with limited means.[109] The Rector's wide-ranging power to choose university teachers was designed to give utmost expression to hierarchy and to the "manageability" of employees.[110]

In truth, many important teachers and teachings of international law have come from Austria, in proportion perhaps many more than could be expected from a country of this size.[111] Often, however, their academic contributions have emerged from situations of exile, of external and inner emigration, while

106 While the government predicted "World Class Universities" ("Weltklasse-Universitäten"), experienced observers were more cautious and the first assessments of this reform seem to describe very effectively the situation up to today: "These radical changes have caused, and are still causing, a feeling of enormous frustration among the junior members of the law faculties, and prevent many of them from active participation in a new discussion of curriculum reform". See Posch (n 101) 68.

107 See Pier-Paolo Pasqualoni, 'Österreichische Universitäten im Spiegel der Geschichte – Fallstricke einer Reform der Reform' in Österreichische HochschülerInnenschaft/Paulo Freire-Zentrum (eds), *Ökonomisierung der Bildung* (Mandelbaum: Vienna 2005).

108 Ibid.

109 See Burtscher/Pasqualoni (n 107) 251ss. The authors anticipated were sharp-mindedly that this reform was bound to fail: "Good rhetoric does not necessarily produce good governance".

110 Still open is the question to what extent this reform is compatible with EU law, in particular as far systematic ad personam appointments or the denial of any judicial standing of candidates from other EU countries who have been discriminated against is concerned. See, extensively, Gilbert Gornig/Paolo Piva, 'Freizügigkeit der Hochschullehrer in der EU – der Problemfall Österreich' (2020) 31 EuZW 469 and Gilbert Gornig/Paolo Piva, 'Universitäre Berufungsverfahren – eine rechtliche Kritik' *Wiener Zeitung* (Wien, 28 May 2020) 13. See also Waltraud Radau, 'Berufungspraxis in Österreich' (2019) 26 Forschung & Lehre 932 and Gilbert Gornig/Paolo Piva, 'Zum Feststellungsinteresse übergangener Bewerberinnen und Bewerber im universitären Berufungsverfahren – Zugleich eine Replik zu Schweighofer' (2020) 2 N@HZ 48.

111 See Heribert Koeck, 'The 'Austrian School of International Law': The Influence of Austrian International Lawyers on the Formation of the Present International Legal Order' in Peter Hilpold (ed), *European International Law Traditions* (Springer: Heidelberg 2021).

tenured chair-holders celebrated (local) authority, soon falling into oblivion when they reached retirement age.

In Switzerland, also a country with a strong international law tradition, the situation is somewhat more complicated. At first sight, there ideal preconditions seem to be given to enable International Law teaching to flourish. In this country high-quality academic research in the field of international law has a long pedigree. Switzerland is home to important international institutions and the country, being on the one hand rather small in size and population and on the other extremely internationally oriented, must rely heavily on international law to protect and further its interests. And, in fact, nobody can deny that Swiss universities offer a rich panoply of international law courses. At the same time, however, it has been bemoaned that a solid basic instruction in international law is not guaranteed for all law students.[112] According to experts in this field, compulsory training in international law would be needed on a more general basis as early as at the level of bachelor programs.[113] Furthermore, inadequate training of lawyers in English legal terminology, as well as a lack of transparency in the University curricula as to quality and dimension of international law training at the various Swiss universities, was criticized.[114]

In many senses the situation in France is also peculiar, if it is often said that the teaching of international law is of particular importance for smaller countries. The case of France demonstrates that larger European countries may also attribute considerable importance to this subject. As a subject of academic research, IL has been influenced to a considerable extent by French contributions.[115] This influence may have been declining for decades, in particular due to the reduced standing of French both as the lingua franca in international relations and as an academic language for IL, with many international experts in this field no longer reading French texts.[116] Nonetheless French continues to be relevant in IL, in particular in proceedings before international courts.[117] This may be one of the factors (together with the circumstance that

112 See Andreas Ziegler, 'How global should legal education be? Recommendations based on the compulsory teaching in international aspects taught at Swiss law schools' (2020) 1 European Journal of Legal Education 49.

113 Ibid.

114 Ibid. See also Andreas Ziegler, 'Die Entwicklung der Völkerrechtslehre und –wissenschaft in der Schweiz – eine Übersicht' (2016) 26 SZIER 21.

115 See Andrea Hamann, 'The French Tradition of International Law' in Peter Hilpold (ed), *European International Law Traditions* (Springer: Berlin/Heidelberg 2021), 137.

116 As is well known, this situation is even worse with regard to German or Italian texts.

117 See Tomuschat (n 27) 205.

international law generally has a strong position in Latin countries) leading to the prominent curricular position of international law in France. A recent study has, however, shown that this strong position may be only seemingly apparent.[118] In bachelor law studies, international law is, depending on the university, not always compulsory. It is taught, in any case, only in a restricted number of hours and separately from other subjects.[119] Masters' studies in law often offer a rich panoply of specialization courses, but in this context the criticism has been raised that thereby the instruction becomes diffuse, overburdened with detail, and, in particular if the basic course has been avoided, soon obsolete.[120]

International law is of considerable relevance also in Italian law studies. Many globally renowned international lawyers have come from Italy, and without doubt this is also the immediate consequence of the high status the subject of IL has for long enjoyed in Italian university curricula.[121] With regard to teaching in the narrower sense, one of the most characteristic features of the Italian teaching reality has for long been the close connection between public and private international law. Academics having to teach both subjects certainly operate in a very specific environment, with both disciplines reciprocally

118 See Andrea Hamann, 'Die Lehre des Völkerrechts in Frankreich – Überblick und Beobachtungen' (2017) 48 BDGIR 123. On the French University system (with particular reference to the law area) see also Dorothée Perrouin-Verre and Samuel Fulli-Lemaire, 'Career Paths into Legal Academia in France' (2020), 84 RabelsZ 299.

119 Ibid.

120 Ibid.

121 There is some, but not very much literature about TIL in Italy. See, for example, with regard to the "earlier years", Giuseppina De Giudici, 'A cavallo dell'Unità d'Italia. L'insegnamento del Diritto internazionale a Cagliari e l'adesione alla cosiddetta Scuola italiana, in Annali di Storia delle università italiane' (2020) 2 Luglio-Dicembre 213 and Amadeo Giannini, 'Il diritto internazionale in Italia (1851–1948)' (1948) 3–4 15 Rivista di Studi Politici Internazionali 377. For the first years after WW II see, i.a., Manlio Udina, 'Der Beitrag der italienischen Doktrin zur gegenwärtigen Theorie des Völkerrechts' (1969) 29 ZaöRV 331 and Mario Panebianco, 'Tradition und neue Tendenzen in der italienischen Völkerrechtslehre nach 1945' (1987) 25 AVR 387. For the period leading to the present day see Antonio Cassese, in: Cassese, S. (ed.), *Guida alla Facoltà di giurisprudenza* (Il Mulino: Bologna 1994). See also Giulio Bartolini, *A History of International Law in Italy* (OUP: Oxford 2020) as well as Antonio Cassese, Il diritto internazionale in Italia (il Mulino: Bologna 2021). Most recently see also the conference organized by the President of the Italian Society of International Law, Professor Pasquale De Sena, Il ruolo del Diritto internazionale e del Diritto dell'Unione europea nella formazione universitaria e post-universitaria, in Italia: spunti per una riflessione, 17 June 2021, https://www.youtube.com/watch?v=fuFbz-X3aqI, video transcript on file with the author (in the following cited as "SIDI conference June 2021").

influencing their respective academic perspectives. As was said, this close connection between public and private international law is often considered, outside Italy, as an "oddity" or "recognized trademark" of Italian academia.[122] In most other countries after WW I, the teaching of and the research into IL "broke apart institutionally and ideologically and started to develop through their own, autonomous channels".[123]

It was said that this model of teaching and research could again become modern and that the Italian system, prominent for having preserved this unity, could be an example of this.[124] While an explicit return to the "unitary approach" as it is practiced, at least formally, in Italy is rather unlikely – the autonomy of these two disciplines is far too developed – the "Italian tradition" may nonetheless have significantly influenced the present international discussion. It is probably no coincidence that the "Global Administrative Law" (GAL) approach presented below finds qualified support in Italian academia and has been developed to a considerable extent by Italian lawyers. As will be shown, this approach bridges the divide between these two disciplines (and many others) without needing to eliminate the high dogmatic fences that have come to fragment law academia.

What is most awkward in the present situation of IL teaching in Italy is the apparent contradiction between the unitary approach, combining both private and public IL, on the one hand and the highly fragmented situation of research and teaching in this area on the other. In fact, it is not just that most international lawyers in Italy specialize in either the private or public elements of this formally comprehensive discipline. It has rather to be considered that even within these sub-disciplines a further fragmentation has taken place. In the meantime, European Union law as a teaching subject has emancipated itself from that of IL and has been attributed separate teaching hours, separate chairs, separate competitions, and an independent professional organization (Associazione Italiana Studiosi del Diritto Europeo – AISDUE), while in the past the "Società Italiana di Diritto Internazionale e del Diritto dell'Unione Europea" (SIDI) exclusively represented both teaching subjects: IL and EU law. This separation is often not very practicable, with many areas of overlap still in

122 See Pietro Franzina, 'The Integrated Approach to Private and Public International Law – A Distinctive Feature of Italian Legal Thinking' in Giulio Bartolini (ed), *A History of International Law in Italy* (OUP: Oxford 2020), 262.

123 See Martti Koskenniemi 'Nationalism, Universalism, Empire: International Law in 1871 and 1919' (University of Helsinki,) 15, available at https://fdocuments.in/document/nationalism-universalism-empire-international-law-in-.html, cited by Franzina, p. 263.

124 See Franzina (n 122) 282.

place. A further problem concerns the difficulties in separating European Law and IL from constitutional law. Without doubt, these are independent academic disciplines, but the attempt to separate them also creates considerable institutional problems due to the abovementioned many areas of overlap.[125] The alternative would be to create chairs with broader job descriptions, as happens – in a very pronounced way – in Germany. The advantage of this alternative would lie in the opportunity for the teacher to specialize according to his/her preferences and the needs of the respective university without being in danger of entering into competence conflicts with colleagues. The drawback of the "German model" lies, however, in the need to prepare a "habilitation thesis" covering a very broad theme (focused regularly on public law), and in fact that specialization in IL is possible only at a rather late stage of the academic curriculum. Furthermore, according to the German model, international lawyers have usually to continue to dedicate part of their working time to public law.

6.4 *Some Common Challenges for International Law Curricula in Europe (and Beyond)*

Many of the problematic aspects of international law in general and of international law curricula in particular in the various European jurisdictions examined may be, in the specific connotation described, typical for the country situations analyzed. At the same time, however, many of them are also, to a certain extent, expression of problems assailing TIL in general.

This starts with the question whether the subject of international law should be made compulsory even for basic law instruction. It has been rightly observed that a positive answer to this question by representatives of the community of international lawyers may not in any way be decisive, as these advocates for an enhanced role for IL are arguing *pro domo* or are at least not unbiased.[126] Nonetheless, as has been shown throughout this contribution, there are strong arguments in favor of such compulsiveness that should convince any neutral decision-taker.

Similar questions may arise in regard to the issue of how many teaching hours should be dedicated to international law and how those teaching hours should be distributed between compulsory and optional classes. Offering a wide array of optional classes on international law subjects (or sub-subject) like investment arbitration, WTO law, International Competition Law,

125 The ensuing "competence problems" were addressed at the "SIDI conference" of June 2021 (n 121).

126 See Hamann (n 118) 124.

International Criminal Law, International Environmental Law, etc. is appealing. By being offered such classes, further students can be enthused by international law, they can imagine specific professional opportunities, law studies as a whole at the university in question can be rebranded as innovative, future-oriented, and modern. In a certain sense, such specialization takes note only of developments taking place in the legal arena, if we refer to the buzzword of "fragmentation".[127] The fragmentation debate, however, has also revealed the perils of accepting such a continuous further sub-division of the subject. The overall connecting lines between these subjects and the coherence of the system itself may get lost. The same may be true as regards common "legal language" (for example, if general principles are looked for). If dealing, for example, with WTO law, students will be confronted earlier than expected with questions, say, of treaty interpretation or state responsibility to be addressed from the viewpoint of general international law. Sound preparation in that area will therefore be indispensable for any attempt to deal with the special fields of international law indicated.[128]

To focus on "trendy subjects", the attempt continuously to adapt international law curricula to the specific needs of professional activities at the time, which seem to be highly profitable, may therefore be a risky policy. One might remember the popularity of WTO courses in the immediate aftermath of the creation of the WTO, enthusiasm that declined sharply when it became evident that the Doha Round (originally set to be completed in 2005) had ended in failure. International investment arbitration offered no stable shelter for

127 As is well known, the relevant discussion started with the famous statement by the President of the ICJ, Gilbert Guillaume, before the UN General Assembly on 30 October 2001. It continued intensively within the ILC and by the publication of detailed studies by this commission (Study Group of the ILC, Report on the Fragmentation of International Law: Difficulties Arising from the Diversification and Expansion of International Law, finalized by Martti Koskenniemi, U.N. Doc. A/CN.4/L.682 (13 April 2006) with appendix: Draft conclusion of the work of the Study Group, U.N. Doc. A/CN.4/L.682/Add.1 (2 May 2006); Study Group of the ILC, Report on the Fragmentation of International Law: Difficulties Arising from the Diversification and Expansion of International Law, U.N. Doc. A/CN.4/L.702 (18 July 2006). The results of these studies were somewhat inconclusive, and the discussion dragged on despite a series of attempts to declare it closed. The perception that the underlying problems linger on however persists.

128 Andrea Hamann cited in her contribution of 2017 (n 115) 132 the following statement by Robert Jennings which comes straight to the point: "in many universities there are courses in trendy, or politically correct aspects of international law – such as, now, the environment, or human rights; though what those subjects will be in five years' time on, one can only guess, for trendiness by definition changes rapidly". See Sir Robert Jennings, Letter to St. John Macdonald, 15 July 1993, Annuarie de l'Institut de Droit International 67-I (1997), pp. 128–129.

those of the WTO community who attempted to change direction when it became apparent that these institutions and procedures were being met with more and more resistance by states and anti-globalization forces.[129]

6.5 *A Common European University Space?*

As Europe is losing clout in the competition for international knowledge, the idea of fostering the creation of a European university space sounds appealing. Such a space would not be tantamount to the harmonization or reciprocal merger of existing university structures. Competition remains essential for academic excellence in Europe. Such a common space would, on the contrary, even enhance competition, but at the same time allow for more cooperation and for a more efficient investment of resources. In reality, however, such European university space does not seem to be in reach, and this has become particularly clear in the field of international law.

The first issue, we have to deal with here, is the material content of international law teaching. There is little common ground on what should be the basis of an introductory course in international law. This becomes apparent, for example, if law students from, say, a continental European state with no access to the sea take an international law course in another European state with a strong maritime tradition while participating in an Erasmus exchange program. While the students at home had to study the sources of law, human rights, state immunity, and state responsibility, the Erasmus student may return having passed an exam primarily on every detail of the law of the sea. In teaching, perhaps even more so than in research, the question whether international law is really international[130] is of particular importance.

The construction of a European university space in international law is hindered even more by high barriers to the movement of university teachers, also in the field of international law.[131] Some may find justifications for such barriers in history or traditions; others may qualify them as openly protectionist. But in any case, they are often not compatible with pivotal law provisions, in particular with the rules on the free movement of workers in accordance with Article 45 TFEU. In Germany, attaching IL to German Public Law has the evident effect that foreign candidates and candidates without a "habilitation" also

---

129 In part they have become victims of their own success and efficiency, as they lay open the deficiencies of national judicial systems. For an up-dated stock-take on the relationship between arbitration and EU Law see José Mata Dona/Nikos Lavranos, *International Arbitration and EU Law* (Edward Elgar 2021).

130 See Anthea Roberts, *Is International Law International?* (OUP: Oxford 2017).

131 See Gilbert Gornig/Paolo Piva, 'Freizügigkeit der Hochschullehrer in der EU – der Problemfall Österreich' (2020) 31 EuZW 469.

in German Public Law have next to no chance of being considered for a chair in IL at a German university. However, due to the limited importance of international law in German law curricula, the fact that next to no separate international law chairs are provided for can legally be justified. In Austria the main legal problems arise from the fact that candidates applying for a post at an Austrian university have no effective legal remedy in the event of discrimination,[132] with the exception of in the limited cases set out in Article 19 TFEU.[133]

In Italy, after a long experience with cases that have been intensively discussed in the media and have also led to criminal investigations, sophisticated selection mechanisms have been conceived which, however, do not seem to have reached a definitive stage. Central qualifications commissions (*"abilitazione nazionale"*) have been set up whose members are selected by lot. The qualification awarded by these commissions enables successful candidates to apply for a post as an ordinary professor (*abilitazione di prima fascia*) or as an associate professor (*abilitazione di seconda fascia*). Discussions about this system, which continues to be reformed, are ongoing.[134]

132 Here the problem arises how such a situation could be reconciled with Article 47 of the Charter of Fundamental Rights.

133 And also in these cases protection is very limited, as labor contracts concluded in violation of these guarantees are not rescinded but the victorious plaintiff is rather awarded a little compensation.

134 According to a study presented by Emanuele Bajo of 2018 for the "Economic Finance and Economics of Financial Intermediaries" sector there was no difference between the academic impact of candidates that were successful and those who were not, but that candidates of the latter group were in significant number "non-integrated" into the system, for example because they were working abroad. See Emanuele Bajo, 'Commissioni e merito' (il fatto quotidiano, 17 June 2018) <https://www.ilfattoquotidiano.it/2018/06/17/universita-quando-labilitazione-non-e-sinonimo-di-merito/4429044/> accessed 25 October 2021. The ministry for Universities and Research in early 2021 tried to introduce restrictions as to the languages in which candidates could present their research. Candidates undergoing the assessment procedure with written work that was neither in Italian nor in English were required also to file a sworn translation by a certified expert, thereby making access to the *"abilitazione"* for candidates from abroad in many cases also economically unfeasible. Decreto direttoriale 26 February 2021, Article 2 para 4 b). After an outcry by experts in leading national newspapers, this measure had to be withdrawn and the relevant provision was repealed. See decreto direttoriale 5 March 2021, n. 589 "rectifying" art. 2 para. 4 b of the decreto direttoriale of 26 February 2021, n.553 cancelling the reference to the languages in which publications are accepted. On the criticism that prompted this step back see, for example, the contribution by Gian Antonio Stella, in: Corriere della Sera. See Gian Antonio Stella, 'Università, lo strapotere dell'inglese nei bandi: la follia delle traduzioni giurate' *Corriere della Sera* (4 March 2021). Originally, the assessment commissions had also to include members from abroad. This provision was repealed. A further attempt to internationalize Italian universities and to foster merit found expression in a plan to hire 500 renowned professors from Italy and from abroad (*"super-professori"*), to

6.6 *Moving from the "Archipelago" to the Global Level – with a Particular Eye on "Global Administrative Law – GAL"*

The "archipelago perspective" probably currently cohabits with "patchworks" of situations determined by International Law and other situations that appear to have "globalized" characteristics. The "national eye" on everyday legal realities is surely by far the dominant one. The typical practical lawyer still sees himself as a technician prevailingly operating in the national sphere, and this has necessarily to find expression in law school (or university) curricula if they want to respond to the needs of students and professional practice.[135]

Autonomy, rather than dependence or even interdependence, still mainly characterizes the self-perception of national legal orders, of their authors in the Parliaments (as far as democracies are concerned), and of their administrators and executors in the Governments as well as in the broader administration. National pride is often firmly grounded on an idea of national self-determination that emphasizes the uniqueness, if not the superiority, of national traits.

Nonetheless, things are slowly changing.

In fact, nowadays, there are also lawyers dealing principally or even exclusively with International Law on a professional basis. They are probably not as numerous as some euphoric studies may suggest, but they exist. They may not be increasing in number as rapidly as some commentators might declare or hope, but nonetheless their number has been rising over the years.

Furthermore, the above analysis has made clear that any assessment in this field has to consider that situations vary considerably from country to country, depending on a variety of elements among which the size of the "national", the "internal" markets stands out. Confronted with a sizeable internal market for

---

be selected by internationally renowned academics without having to undergo an Italian *"abilitazione"* and selection procedure. See Gianna Fregonara, 'In arrivo le norme sui 500 super-prof. Il premier sceglie i „reclutatori"' *Corriere della Sera* (08 October 2016). This plan was abandoned after strong opposition, in particular from universities. For an overview of the recruitment system in Italian universities (with particular reference to the law sector) see also Francesco Paolo Patti, 'Career Paths into Legal Academia in Italy' (2020), 84 RabelsZ 324.

135 As was well observed by Florian Hoffmann, "Although today's global knowledge exchange makes it increasingly possible to reach intellectual horizons beyond the methodological traditions of one's respective locality, language and (legal) culture, it is the deeply vested expectations of colleagues and students within a specific curricular tradition as much as the teacher's own cognitive horizon that limit the actual choice of teaching method." See Florian Hoffmann, 'Teaching general public international law'in Jörg Kammerhofer and Jean d'Aspremont (eds), *International Legal Positivism in a Post-Modern World* (CUP 2014), 349, 356.

legal assistance and advice like the US one, it stands to reason that lawyers will set a corresponding professional focus on internal law. In small countries like, say, Luxembourg or Liechtenstein, whose economies are far more dependent on international and transnational issues, foreign law expertise has far greater weight.

The situation of the European Union is again unique. EU law, being neither foreign law nor national law in the stricter sense but rather an additional layer of law, in part endowed with direct effect, in part representing an important reference for the interpretation of national law, and in part already transposed into national law as a matter of principle, can no longer be ignored by any lawyer. It has therefore to be part and parcel of everyday legal reasoning and everyday legal practice. Consequently, it has to constitute a mainstay of legal instruction. However, the reality is often quite different.[136]

Globalization is on its own a term with rather uncertain contours. It has long been associated with the factual situation of international markets integrating beyond traditional borders and norm. The law of globalization is considered to have predominantly an International Law character and to be directed at regulating the international economic liberalization process.[137] In recent years, however, a different perspective has arisen which no longer focuses on the legal nature of individual norms characterizing the globalization process, but rather emphasizes their function as the administrative framework of a highly integrated world: Global Administrative Law (GAL). This new approach transcends traditional borders and categorizations. It was said that GAL is not just global, as it also integrates national and local norm-setting and activities; it is not only administrative (at least in the traditional, national sense) as it also includes elements that, according to the traditional perspective, would be qualified as private or constitutional; it is not only law (again according to a traditional, perhaps widely overridden conception)[138] as it also takes into

136 As this author has demonstrated in another study, knowledge of EU law in Austria, after more than 25 years of EU membership, is appallingly low, on both the higher professional and societal levels. See Peter Hilpold, 'Ringen um europäische Werte – Österreich in der EU' in Peter Hilpold/Heinrich Neisser/Walter Steinmair (eds), *Rechtsstaatlichkeit, Grundrechte und Solidarität in Österreich und in Europa – Festgabe zum 85. Geburtstag von Professor Heinrich Neisser, einem europäischen Humanisten* (Facultas: Vienna 2021).

137 For a recent comprehensive study of the phenomenon of globalization see Mark Juergensmeyer and others, *The Oxford Handbook of Global Studies* (OUP: Oxford 2019). On the development of the concept of globalization see in particular the introductory chapter by Manfred Steger, 'What is Global Studies' in Mark Juergensmeyer and others (eds), *The Oxford Handbook of Global Studies* (OUP: Oxford 2019), 3.

138 On the normative power of "soft law" according to a global governance approach see Armin von Bogdandy/Philipp Dann/Matthias Goldmann, 'Developing the Publicness of

consideration soft law and standards.[139] In the more distant past, dissatisfaction with the status (or the traditional understanding) of IL teaching had already led to the plea to override the classic sub-division of legal subjects so as to find the appropriate space for international law, which is in some ways different from all other (national) legal subjects.[140] Especially in business law this necessity was strongly felt. This approach was, however, far more successful in the United States than in Europe. In Europe the attempt was made to adopt a more extensive view of IL and to consider also measures taken by private actors as far as they can be of relevance on the international level. GAL would enlarge this perspective in an even more comprehensive way as it allows one to adopt a fresh view of norm-setting, unconditioned and unrestricted by a source theory based on Article 38 of the ICJ Statute which is no longer able to respond fully to modern needs and reality.[141]

The challenge is to develop an approach that is able to comprehend, to describe, and to analyze "the vast increase in the reach and forms of transgovernmental regulation and administration designed to address the consequences of globalized interdependence in such fields as security, the conditions on development and financial assistance to developing countries, environmental protection, banking and financial regulation, law enforcement, telecommunications, trade in products and services, intellectual property, labor standards, and cross-border movements of populations, including refugees."[142]

It is not yet clear whether GAL will become an autonomous legal discipline, a sub-discipline of IL, or simply a new perspective adopted by some lawyers in order to take a new look at IL issues in a profoundly changed international environment. In any case, it is clear even now that norm-setting in the international

Public International Law: Towards a Legal Framework for Global Governance Activities' (2008) 9 German Law Journal 1375.

139 See Sabino Cassese, 'Global administrative law: where do we stand?', in Philippe Cossalter/ Gilles Guglielmi (eds), *L'internationalisation du droit administrative* (2020), 53. For a recent discussion concerning the legal quality of soft law see Peter Hilpold, 'Opening up a new chapter of law-making in international law: The 2018 Global compacts on Migration and Refugees' (2021) 27 European Law Journal 1.

140 See the „transnational law" approach conceived by Philip Jessup, *Transnational Law* (Yale University Press: New Haven 1956).

141 This does not, of course, mean that Article 38 would no longer fulfill its original function as the primary reference point for the identification of the sources of IL. It needs, however, a series of qualifications and re-interpretations. For a view of Article 38 that is generally positive see i.a. Hugh Thirlway, 'The Sources of International Law' in Malcolm Evans (ed), *International Law* (OUP: Oxford 2010), 95.

142 See Benedict Kingsbury/Nico Krisch/Richard Stewart, 'The Emergence of Global Administrative Law' (2005) 68 Law and Contemporary Problems 15, 16.

reality has undergone thorough modifications, so that the tools developed by traditional IL, almost exclusively centered on the state, meet with the greatest difficulties when trying to deal with this new reality and to explain it. While the state as the primary actor in IL, contrary to many speculations in the past, is still there, it is no longer the monolithic, black box-like unit.[143] Globalized administrative regulation takes the most varied forms where the state remains a prominent actor, but its sub-parts, larger conglomerations of states, their citizens, as well as public and private institutions, to name only a few, are also active norm-setters.[144]

The wide recognition and respect GAL enjoys reflects the fact that this approach is able to consider a far broader spectrum of phenomena that we intuitively associate with the IL order but are difficult to grasp and to explain satisfactorily using traditional IL concepts and tools. Sooner or later these developments will have consequences on the level of teaching, too. At the moment GAL is rather a research subject for senior academics and taught, if at all, in a very limited form: Teachers may make some cursory remarks on GAL in general IL or administrative law courses or will teach GAL in advanced optional courses for a small group of students specializing in the field. In the future, however, this may no longer suffice if teaching in this area is to remain pertinent.

7 The Teacher's Role in Constituting and Developing IL: Promise and Prospect

A closer examination of the teacher's role in this branch of law inevitably leads us to basic questions about the nature of IL, its sources and the methodology to apply to assess its meaning appropriately. But this process also works the other way round. Any inquiry into the meaning and the nature of IL will end up with, or at least lead to, a close encounter with the teacher. In no legal discipline does the lawyer play such a prominent role, and at the same time,

143 See Sabino Cassese, *Global Administrative Law* (Edward Elgar: Cheltenham 2021).

144 Kingsbury/Krisch/Stewart (n 143) 20 distinguish five main types of globalized administrative regulation: "administration by formal international organizations; administration based on collective action by transnational networks of governmental officials; distributed administration conducted by national regulators under treaty regimes, mutual recognition arrangements or cooperative standards; administration by hybrid intergovernmental private arrangements, and administration by private institutions with regulatory functions. In practice many of these layers overlap or combine but we propose this array of ideal types to facilitate further inquiry".

nowhere is he the addressee of so much hope, of such high expectations, of so much delusion. The widespread confusion about the teacher's role and function is associated, first of all, with the enormous changes in the environment in which the teacher has operated over the centuries. These changes have not always been fully realized in the language in which the international lawyer is addressed and are not reflected in the images of the relevant role lawyers themselves and the broader society have in mind.

The law-creating function of the old masters like Vitoria, Grotius, Pufendorf, and Vattel was surely far more pronounced than those of modern international lawyers, as famous and "authoritative" as they may be. Of the many circumstances conducive to this diminishing relevance the most obvious are the enormous rise in the number of academics teaching IL, the loss of the unity of perspective following the end of the Eurocentric approach to IL, and the ever-rising role of treaties as against that of customary IL. The identification of customary IL norms not only requires enormous expert knowledge; it also leaves considerable leeway for individual, competent assessment. The result will be more or less authoritative depending on the name(s) of the experts doing the relevant norm identification act.

When the Statute of the International Court of Justice was drafted back in 1920, "the teaching of the most highly qualified publicists of the various nations" was included in Article 38 paragraph 1 (d) of the Statute as "subsidiary means for the determination of the rules of law". And it was speculated afterwards whether the drafters of this provision included themselves in the "elite professional category they referred to".[145] In 1920, this formulation was a nod to an elitist thinking that by then was already somewhat awkward but still acceptable. In these days, few would believe that such a ranking among IL academics could be feasible or even make any sense. Nonetheless, it deserves preservation as evidence of the past role of individual teachers, who have hitherto influenced the main traits of this order. At the same time it can be seen as an incentive to strive for excellence. While it will not be possible to create a consensual ranking of IL teachers based on their qualifications, this formulation can be seen as a plea for quality, as an invitation to a keen competition of ideas and arguments in this field.

145 See Pierre d'Argent, 'Teachers of International Law' in Jean d'Aspremont and others (eds), *International Law as a Profession* (CUP: Cambridge 2017), 412, pointing out that in 1921 7 out of 11 judges elected to the PCIJ had a very strong academic professional background. In 1946, when the first judges were elected to the International Court of Justice this proportion rose to 11 out of 15. Ibid.

Furthermore, Article 38 para. 1 (d) of the PCIJ Statute (and now the ICJ Statute) marks a compromise: it attributes considerable value to the teachings of international lawyers without elevating them to sources of IL in the formal sense.[146] The "determination of the rules of IL" remains an essential exercise for this order to be effective. As has been said, law in general and IL in particular is "what the generality of its recipients ′believe′ it to be.[147] In this "belief system" teachers of IL have been compared to priests, clergymen, rabbis, imams, or other clerics.[148] If no scientific method were available that would tell us what is the ultimate truth in law: if "legal sciences" cannot even deliver a uncontestable judgement on which of the many conflicting interpretations of IL is the "definite", the "right" one, we have to have recourse to someone who is vested with the authority to decide. It is not only the precariousness and the sketchiness of the international judiciary system that makes the academic teacher of IL so precious as the final arbiter. His lasting aura of enlightenment inherited from the past, his belief, implicit though it may be, of being in touch with the metaphysical, buttresses the international order at the many spots where contradictions and deficiencies risk undermining its authority. The teacher is asked to mend a system continuously anew which is characterized by an often chaotic and inconclusive practice. Teachers have to find a lasting, if not perennial, structure in acts that otherwise could be interpreted as an expression of crude power or mere contingency. As has been said, "belief and hope are a vital part of any law and ultimately sustain justice as the engine for making and unmaking law".[149] The teacher helps to devise techniques of

146 As was shown in the literature, there are many elements indicating that the ICJ relies heavily on scholarly teaching but almost never cites these writings (individual opinions being an exception to this rule). See Sondre Torp Helmersen, *The Application of Teachings by the International Court of Justice* (CUP: Cambridge 2021). A good explanation for this attitude of the ICJ (and of other international tribunals) is given by Gleider Hernández, 'The Responsibility of the International Legal Academic' in Jean d′Aspremont and others (eds), *International Law as a Profession* (CUP: Cambridge 2017): "When a scholarly argument is borrowed by an international tribunal, it is rarely acknowledged explicitly, perhaps to avoid accusations of embracing certain policy preferences. It is also rarely acknowledged out of a desire not to elevate or privilege certain individuals or ′to distribute good or bad marks′". Ibid., with reference to Allain Pellet, 'Article 38' in Andreas Zimmermann and others (eds), *The Statute of the International Court of Justice: A Commentary* (2nd edition, OUP: Oxford 2012).

147 See Carlo Focarelli, *International Law* (Edward Elgar: Cheltenham 2019).

148 See d′Argent (n 145) 418.

149 See Focarelli (n 147) 19.

argumentation vested with the semblance of persuasiveness[150] whereby he or she has to overcome the contradictions of a norm-creating process based both on egoistic state behavior and on values constraining this behavior.[151]

The challenge that the international lawyer has to be value-guided is omnipresent in literature, most obviously as a device to avoid IL becoming an amoral set of rules justifying the vile egoism of the powerful who are not content with oppressing the weak but, in their viciousness, are even looking for a moral justification for their abjection. One example of an attempt to reconcile value-orientation with practice-based positivism is the creation of the figure of the "critical positivist" international lawyer.[152]

That lawyer should adopt basically a positivist approach when looking for international norms and interpreting them. In cases of conflict and indeterminacy he would, however, be empowered to base his judgement on "universal principles of the world community", for example the pursuit of peace, the protection of human rights, or the realization of democratic governance.[153] This approach has been criticized, first of all, because it does not provide any justification for proclaiming the principles stated to be universal.[154]

Both the "critical positivist" approach and the criticism voiced against it need some differentiation. To see in the "pursuit of peace" and the "protection of human rights" pre-eminent values is to some degree justifiable in view of the jus cogens character of the prohibition on the use of force and of at least the core area of human rights.[155] The value of a participative government structure is also more and more recognized; the disruptive effects of authoritarian systems in particular in the field of human rights is also contestable. It

150 See Martti Koskenniemi, 'Methodology of International Law' (2007) MPEPIL online ed <http://www.csil.cn/upFiles/files/International%20Legal%20Theory%20and%20Doctrine.pdf> accessed 25 October 2021.

151 See Martti Koskenniemi, *From Apology to Utopia* (CUP: Cambridge 2006).

152 See Antonio Cassese, *Five Masters of International Law: Conversation with R.J.-Dupuy, E. Jiménez de Aréchaga, R. Jennings, L. Henkin and O. Schachter*, (Oxford and Portland, Oregon: Hart 2011) at 258.

153 See Antonio Cassese, *Five Masters of International Law* (First edition, Bloomsbury Publishing 2011). In "Realizing Utopia" (Oxford: OUP 2012) Cassese writes about his pursuit of the creation of a "realistic utopia". Ibid., p. xxi.

154 See Gleider Hernández, 'The Responsibility of the International Legal Academic – Situating the Grammarian Within the 'Invisible College'', in Jean d'Aspremont and others (eds), *International Law as a Profession* (CUP: Cambridge 2017).

155 See James Crawford, *Brownlie's Principles of Public International Law* (OUP: Oxford 2019), referring to the prohibition of the use of force in Article 2(4) of the Charter, of genocide, of crimes against humanity (including systematic forms of racial discrimination), and the rules prohibiting the slave trade.

would, however, be misleading to look for a neat border between "common" IL norms and "higher-ranking" rules, to search for a clearly determined substantive content for jus cogens.[156] As has been rightly remarked in the literature,[157] the most important value of the acceptance of higher-ranking norms lies in the promotional force of such a belief. The value of these norms is therefore to be found less in a static weighing and balancing of existing IL norms according to their purported greater or lesser impact and importance. It is rather the dynamic aspect that counts, the influence this concept can exert on the further norm-creation and interpretation process.[158] Interpreted in this way, belief in higher-ranking norms and the struggle for their further consolidation brings the "critical positivist" approach best in line with the constraints and the potential of the existing IL order. Thereby, the role of the international lawyer as a teacher is also highlighted. In fact, as has also been underscored in literature,[159] emphasizing the promotional role of jus cogens is closely connected with its educational function.

Seen from a general, abstract vantage point, these considerations might imply a very important role for the teacher, the researcher, the "publicist" of IL. So, the international lawyer is really on the front line when suggestions for a "better" international order are to be made? Is he/she really the "priest" we have to pin all our hopes on? Here again, further qualifications are needed. "The" international lawyer does not exist. There are the judge, the teacher, the practitioner, the litigant, the advisor for governments, corporations, NGOs, to name only a few. And then there is the international lawyer who plays two or more of these roles. More often than not, it is exactly the teacher who wears one or more of these additional hats. Whether IL teachers can really play the leading role many attribute to them will not only depend on their "internal" independence and autonomy as individuals but to a considerable degree also on external circumstances. The position of the teacher/international law publicist

156 On the shortcoming of the „substantive view" in discussions about jus cogens see Robert Kolb, 'Peremptory Norms as a Legal Technique Rather than Substantive Super-Norms' in Dire Tladi (ed), *Peremptory Norms of General International Law (Jus Cogens)* (Brill/Martinus Nijhoff: Leiden/Boston 2021). See also Olivier Corten/Vaios Koutroulis, 'The Jus Cogens Status of the Prohibition on the Use of Force' in Dire Tladi (ed), *Peremptory Norms of General International Law (Jus Cogens)* (Brill/Martinus Nijhoff: Leiden/Boston 2021), 629, citing Ian Brownlie, who compared jus cogens with a vehicle that "does not often leave the garage", and Prosper Weil who compared this concept with a "Rolls Royce that her owner polishes and maintains lovingly but never drives". Ibid., p 631.

157 See Carlo Focarelli, *Trattato di Diritto Internazionale* (Giuffré: Milan 2015).

158 Ibid.

159 Ibid., p 540.

who also plays the role of a government advisor is often discussed. Certainly, examples can be found of renowned international lawyers who have played this role subsequently[160] or even contemporaneously[161] to that of teaching and who represent paradigmatic intellectuals neatly keeping these roles separate. In other cases, however, this works less well, and in some cases there is not even the appearance of such intent (of separation and autonomy). In law practice lawyers are often faced with a problem that may become relevant also for teachers/advisors. Those in situations of conflicting roles and interests are not willing to take notice of this incompatibility as they feel they can move from one role to the other with their integrity unscathed.[162] Thereby, they not only often overestimate their individual autonomy, but, even more basically, ignore the damage they do to their role(s) through the objective appearance of partiality. There is the risk that the advisor becomes "less […] the wise oracle of the international, and more […] an entrapped tin soldier bowing to bureaucratic edict".[163]

Should this analysis be seen as a plea to IL teachers to concentrate on their role as teachers (and researchers) and resist the temptation to be active also in other fields in order to defend their integrity? There are valid arguments for accepting "several hats", for a "cross-over" approach. Thus, there may be egoistic motivations, such as that related to the contention that teachers' wages are too low. Or it may be said that teachers may be motivated by extraordinary self-esteem to accept other jobs too as they feel that their talent would otherwise be (partly) wasted. And then there are more sober considerations such as that the quality of teaching can profit greatly from experience as practitioners and that it is also in the interests of students that their teachers now and again leave the "ivory tower".

On the whole, any final verdict on the role an individual teacher can fulfill will essentially depend on the circumstances of the situation in question. Of decisive importance will be what degree of autonomy the individual institution in which the international lawyers works is prepared to grant/is used to granting. In an authoritarian regime, international lawyers will have scant influence on the overall development of their country's attitude to IL unless

160 As is well known, Martti Koskenniemi and Philip Allot were previously government advisors before becoming professors.

161 See, for example, Sir Michael Wood.

162 See Oscar Schachter, 'The Invisible College of International Lawyers' (1977) 72 NULR 217.

163 See for this formulation Mattew Windsor, 'Consigliere or Conscience? – The Role of the Government Legal Advisor' in Jean d'Aspremont and others (eds), *International Law as a Profession* (CUP: Cambridge 2017) 355, 388.

those lawyers are extremely adept at pushing their agendas without endangering their careers, freedom, or lives. The more a liberal attitude, sensitive to academic freedom, prevails, the more lawyers will develop their role autonomously. Also the climate in which government advisors are working is very different from country to country, with some countries seeing in the advisor a legal expert called on to wrap a pre-determined political decision up in a legal dress that makes it more "sellable" to an internal and an external audience. Other countries have a historic tradition of asking sincerely for independent advice which should then flow into the political decision-making process. The borders between these groups of states are, however, fluid and not always stable over time. In any case, a great deal of prudence is necessary here.

For teachers who also work as advisors to private companies or as counsel to law firms the danger of compromising their independence will be most often less pronounced or, if it exists at all, it will concern specific areas where they could abstain from assuming the role (also) of promotors of law change.

At the end, of decisive importance will be the institutional independence the university/research institution is willing and able to grant to the academic. The word "autonomy" is often misleadingly used in this context. If local universities are independent of governmental control but governed by autocratic institutions without effective control or controlled again by local political forces, then the teacher will hardly enjoy meaningful autonomy. As set out in this contribution, real academic freedom requires a complex system of checks and balances that rewards independent, future-oriented research in a climate of openness to the exchange of ideas. At the same time, these institutions have also to be prepared to take effective measures against academic abuses and lasting unproductivity. What in some regions have been hailed as the "self-cleaning" capacities of universities ("*Selbstreinigungskräfte der Universitäten*") have to operate effectively and forcefully, and to this end both a fostering of talent and strong and genuine competition have to be achieved.

But what of the individual responsibility of international lawyers? Whatever the external circumstances, in most cases a core area will remain where they will have the chance to act autonomously, where their individual will is decisive. On what basis should they act?

Lately it has been argued that the international lawyer should not look for an "already existing consensus among 'reasonable international lawyers', a kind of 'soft law' contractarianism", but an individual judgment is needed which could also be isolated and very costly professionally.[164]

164 See Anthony Carty (n 59) 201, citing, with regard to the "consensus among reasonable international lawyers", Klaus Kreß, *The Crime of Aggression* (CUP: Cambridge 2017).

It is true that the responsibility of the international lawyer is, in the end, an individual one. Past experience of injustice has shown that the individual cannot avoid accepting this responsibility, and even in the cruelest dictatorial regimes like those of fascism in the first half of the 20th century there have been individuals who stood up against terror and oppression. But overemphasizing the role of the individual gives rise, at the same time, to risks that are too great. First of all, there is the danger of pretending too much, of overburdening the individual. Heroes are an important element of society, but they will always constitute a small minority. And a heroic, self-sacrificing attitude can never be pretended. Furthermore, there is the risk that the individual (or a small group of individuals) may misjudge a situation and will, maybe motivated by the best intentions, feel legitimized in imposing his/her will on others, or even on society as a whole. Eventually, in extreme situations these "best intentions" could come close to dictatorship or may serve as a justification for oppression, the violation of rights, or even terrorism. Dialogue with "reasonable international lawyers", on the basis of a "common language" building a platform for some agreed fundamental values,[165] can therefore be an important remedy for such excesses as it may provide direction and correct aberration. The great achievements of civilization, the conviction that the protection of human rights and the prohibition on the use of force without doubt enjoy strong support within the "invisible college" of international lawyers in its world-wide network. There is ample space for the individual international lawyer to contribute within this network to a further improvement in these achievements, but this should happen in dialogue and not unilaterally. The individual international lawyer is only one, though an important, element of a broader system. In order to make his/her work effective, it is essential to fight for academic freedom and the further strengthening of the rule of law in the broader society and also transnationally.

The teacher of IL should, of course, avoid becoming a "tin soldier", however enticing money and "institutional rewards" (such as administrative or political power) may be. Nor is it realistic to aspire to becoming a "priest" of IL. The academic audience may revere some outstandingly successful academics as saints. As long as they do not identify with this label attributed to them by others or openly compete for it, teachers "sanctified" this way can, however, always decline responsibility for this attribution by others. The most meritorious approach would probably be to aspire to a role as a "considerate reformer" attempting, in dialogue with the broader scientific community, to defend and further to develop the values that have become characteristic of this branch of

165 See in this sense also Manfred Lachs (n 5) 228.

law. As was pointed out already at the beginning of this essay, IL and national law now interact closely; in many cases it is no longer possible to tell them apart. At the same time, the great challenges of our time, such as the environment, human rights, and regional conflicts, require answers from IL, to be found in dialogue, not just within the community of international lawyers, but in a truly interdisciplinary fashion. International lawyer stand at the forefront of this, but not as individuals pretending to have better insight or to know the truth. International lawyers have rather to cooperate beyond borders and to operate also as mediators across national perspectives of IL. International lawyers have also to be humble enough to understand that the values they are fighting for are not theirs but those of the community – national and international – of which they are part.[166] To manage this dialogue, to ensure its transparency, continuously to call to mind the basic achievements in this process as they have been enshrined in the Charter of the United Nations and in the core international human rights instruments – these are tasks that are challenging and rewarding enough!

Eventually these endeavors should open the "hidden room of International Law" to the broader public. so that it can be transformed from the gathering place of the aristocratic few to the meeting, debating, and decision-making forum of the informed and responsible democratic public.

Bibliography

Altreiter C, 'Befristete Uni-Stellen: Drei Fehlschlüsse mit gravierenden Folgen' *Der Standard* (23 July).

Antony J, 'Lean Six Sigma for Higher Education' (2015) 32 International Journal of Quality & Reliability Management.

Arvidsson M/McKenna M, 'The turn to history in international law and the sources doctrine: Critical approaches and methodological imaginaries' (2020) 33 LJIL 37.

Bajo E, 'Commissioni e merito' (il fatto quotidiano, 17 June 2018) <https://www.ilfattoquotidiano.it/2018/06/17/universita-quando-labilitazione-non-e-sinonimo-di-merito/4429044/> accessed 25 October 2021.

Bartolini, *A History of International Law in Italy* (OUP: Oxford 2020).

Bernhardt R, 'Vom Provinzialismus deutscher Juristenausbildung' (1971) JZ 581.

166 By the way, also in this context international lawyers will have to struggle to find appropriate compromises. In fact, the "community values" to be pursued will differ considerably depending on the question whether a communitarist or a cosmopolitan perspective is adopted.

Bianchi A, 'Epistemic Community' in Jean d'Aspremont and Sahib Singh (eds), *Concepts for International Law – Contributions to Disciplinary Thought* (Edward Elgar 2018), 251.

Bogdandy A/Dann P/Goldmann M, 'Developing the Publicness of Public International Law: towards a Legal Framework for Global Governance Activities' (2008) 9 German Law Journal 1375.

Broms B, 'International Law in the Law School Curriculum' in Ronald Macdonald (ed), *Essay in Honour of Wang Tieya* (Kluwer/Martinus Nijhoff: Dordrecht/Boston 1993) 79.

Burtscher C/Pasqualoni P/Scott A, 'Universities and the Regulatory Framework: the Austrian University System in Transition' (2006) 20 Social Epistemology 241, 246.

Caron P, 'President Trump Threatens Law Schools' $350 Million Revenue From Foreign LL.M. Students' (TaxProf Blog, 25 October 2021) <https://taxprof.typepad.com/taxprof_blog/2017/04/president-trump-threatens-law-schools-350-million-revenue-from-foreign-llm-students.html> accessed 25 October 2021.

Carty A, 'International law and nervous states in the age of anger, the collapse of legal formalism and a return to natural law' in Rossana Deplano/Nicholas Tsagourias (eds), *Research Methods of International Law* (Edward Elgar: Cheltenham 2021), 180.

Carty A, *The Decay of International Law?: a Reappraisal of the Limits of Legal Imagination in International Affairs* (Manchester University Press: Manchester 1986).

Cassese A, *Five Masters of International Law* (First edition, Bloomsbury Publishing 2011).

Cassese A, *Five Masters of International Law: Conversation with R.J.-Dupuy, E. Jiménez de Aréchaga, R. Jennings, L. Henkin and O. Schachter*, (Oxford and Portland: Hart 2011).

Cassese, A, *Il diritto internazionale in Italia* (il Mulino: Bologna 2021).

Cassese S, *Guida alla Facoltà di giurisprudenza* (Il Mulino: Bologna 1994).

Cassese S, *Global Administrative Law* (Edward Elgar: Cheltenham 2021).

Cassese, S, 'Global administrative law: where do we stand?', in Philippe Cossalter/Gilles Guglielmi (eds), *L'internationalisation du droit administrative* (2020), 53.

Cheng B, *International Law: Teaching and Practice* (Stevens & Son: London 1982).

Chesterman S, 'The Evolution of Legal Education: Internationalisation, Transnationalisation, Globalization' (2009) 10 German Law Journal 879, 880.

Corten O/Koutroulis V, 'The Jus Cogens Status of the Prohibition on the Use of Force' in Dire Tladi (ed), *Peremptory Norms of General International Law (Jus Cogens)* (Brill/Martinus Nijhoff: Leiden/Boston 2021), 629.

Craig P/De Búrca G, *EU Law, Text, Cases and Materials* (6th edition, 2020).

Crawford J, *Brownlie's Principles of Public International Law* (OUP: Oxford 2019).

D'Argent P, 'Teachers of International Law' in Jean d'Aspremont and others (eds), *International Law as a Profession* (CUP: Cambridge 2017), 412.

De Giudici G, 'A cavallo dell'Unità d'Italia. L'insegnamento del Diritto internazionale a Cagliari e l'adesione alla cosiddetta Scuola italiana, in Annali di Storia delle università italiane' (2020) 2 Luglio-Dicembre 213.

Deeks A, 'Introduction to the Symposium: How will artificial intelligence affect international law?' (2020) 114 AJIL 138.

Dickinson E, 'Teaching of International Law to Law Students' (1923) 17 Am.Pol.Sci-Rev. 464.

Do D, 'What is Muda, Mura, and Muri?' (The Lean Way, 5 August 2017) <https://theleanway.net/muda-mura-muri> accessed 25 October 2021.

Dona J/Lavranos N, *International Arbitration and EU Law* (Edward Elgar 2021).

Dupuy P, *NGOs in International Law – Efficiency in Flexibility?* (Edward Elgar: Cheltenham 2008).

Editorial Comments, 'Not mastering the Treaties: the German Federal Constitutional Court's PSPP judgment' (2020) 57 CMLR 965.

Engeland A, 'Statehood, Proto States and International Law: New Challenges, Looking at the Case of ISIS' in James Crawford and others (eds), *The international legal order* (2016), 75.

European Commission, *The Erasmus Impact Study, Effects of mobility on the skills and employability of students and the internationalization of higher education institutions* (2014).

Focarelli C, *International Law* (Edward Elgar: Cheltenham 2019).

Focarelli C, *Trattato di Diritto Internazionale* (Giuffré: Milan 2015).

Franzina P, 'The Integrated Approach to Private and Public International Law – A Distinctive Feature of Italian Legal Thinking' in Giulio Bartolini (ed), *A History of International Law in Italy* (OUP: Oxford 2020), 262.

Fregonara G, 'In arrivo le norme sui 500 super-prof. Il premier sceglie i „reclutatori"' *Corriere della Sera* (08 October 2016).

Fukuyama F, *The End of History and the Last Man* (Free Press 1992).

Gamble J, 'Teaching or Get Off the Lectern: Impediments to Improving International Law Teaching' (2007) 13 ILSA Journal of International & Comparative Law 379.

Gamble J, *Teaching International Law in the 1990s, Survey of Academic International Law Project of the American Society of International Law under the sponsorship of the Ford Foundation* (1993).

Gazzini T, 'A Fresh Look at Teaching International Law – A Few Pedagogical Considerations in the Age of Communications' (2016) 29 LJIL 971.

Giannini A, 'Il diritto internazionale in Italia (1851–1948)' (1948) 3–4 15 Rivista di Studi Politici Internazionali 377.

Ginther K, 'A Note on the Teaching of International Law in Austria' in Bin Cheng (ed), *International Law: teaching and practice* (London: Stevens 1982), 199.

Glenn P, 'Comparative Legal Families and Comparative Legal Traditions' in Mathias Reimann/Reinhard Zimmermann (eds), *The Oxford Handbook of Comparative Law* (2006), 423.

Gornig G/Piva P, 'Freizügigkeit der Hochschullehrer in der EU – der Problemfall Österreich' (2020) 31 EuZW 469.

Gornig G/Piva P, 'Universitäre Berufungsverfahren– eine rechtliche Kritik' *Wiener Zeitung* (Wien, 28 May 2020) 13.

Gornig G/Piva P, 'Zum Feststellungsinteresse übergangener Bewerberinnen und Bewerber im universitären Berufungsverfahren' (2020) 4 Neue@ Hochschulzeitung 131.

Gornig G/Piva P, 'Zum Feststellungsinteresse übergangener Bewerberinnen und Bewerber im universitären Berufungsverfahren – Zugleich eine Replik zu Schweighofer' (2020) 2 N@HZ 48.

Grudowski P/Wisniewska M, 'Lean Management Higher Education Institutions. How to Begin?' (2019) 137 Scientific Papers of Silesian University of Technology, Organization and Management 51.

Hamann A, 'Die Lehre des Völkerrechts in Frankreich – Überblick und Beobachtungen' (2017) 48 BDGIR 123.

Hamann A, 'The French Tradition of International Law' in Peter Hilpold (ed), *European International Law Traditions* (Springer: Berlin/Heidelberg 2021), 137.

Heintze H/Thielbörger P, *From Cold War To Cyber War* (Springer: Heidelberg 2016).

Helmersen S, *The Application of Teachings by the International Court of Justice* (CUP: Cambridge 2021).

Hernández G, 'The Responsibility of the International Legal Academic – Situating the Grammarian Within the 'Invisible College'', in Jean d'Aspremont and others (eds), *International Law as a Profession* (CUP: Cambridge 2017), 160.

Hilpold P, *European International Law Traditions* (Springer: Berlin/Heidelberg 2021).

Hilpold P, 'Maßnahmen zur effektiven Durchsetzung von Menschen-und Arbeitsrechten – Völkerrechtliche Anforderungen' in Nico Krisch and others (eds), *50 Berichte der Deutschen Gesellschaft für Internationales Recht, Unternehmensverantwortung und Internationales Recht* (C.F. Müller 2020), 185.

Hilpold P, 'Opening up a new chapter of law-making in international law: the 2018 Global compacts on Migration and Refugees' (2021) 27 European Law Journal 1.

Hilpold P, 'Ringen um europäische Werte – Österreich in der EU' in Peter Hilpold/ Andreas Raffeiner/Walter Steinmair (eds), *Rechtsstaatlichkeit, Grundrechte und Solidarität in Österreich und in Europa – Festgabe zum 85. Geburtstag von Professor Heinrich Neisser, einem europäischen Humanisten* (Facultas: Wien 2021), 262.

Hilpold P, 'So long „Solange"? The PSPP judgment by the German Constitutional Court and the conflict between the German and the European "popular spirit"' in John Bell (ed), (Cambridge Yearbook of European Legal Studies 2020), 159.

Hilpold P, 'What Are and to What Avail Do We Study European International Law Traditions?' in Peter Hilpold (ed), *European International Law Traditions* (Springer: Cham 2021), 1.

Hilpold P, *Autonomy and Self-determination – Between Legal Assertions and Utopian Aspirations* (Edward Elgar: Cheltenham 2018).

Hilpold P, *Die EU im GATT/WTO-System* (Nomos Verlag 2019).

Hilpold P, *Italienisches Steuerrecht* (Facultas: Vienna 2017).

Hilpold P, *Kosovo and International Law* (Brill/Martinus Nijhoff, Leiden/Boston 2012).

Hilpold P, *Solidarität und Neutralität im Vertrag von Lissabon* (Nomos: Baden-Baden 2010).

Hirte H, 'Grußwort' in Stephan Hobe/Thilo Marauhn (ed), *Lehre des internationalen Rechts – zeitgemäß?* (C.F. Müller, 2017), 7.

Höfer S/Naeve J, 'The Application of Lean Management in Higher Education' (2017) 16 International Journal of Contemporary Management 63.

Hoffmann F, 'Teaching general public international law' in Jörg Kammerhofer and Jean d'Aspremont (eds), *International Legal Positivism in a Post-Modern World* (CUP 2014).

International Law Association (ILA), <www.ila-hq.org/index.php/committees> accessed 25 October 2021.

Jessup P, *Transnational Law* (Yale University Press: New Haven 1956).

Juergensmeyer M and others, *The Oxford Handbook of Global Studies* (OUP: Oxford 2019).

Kennedy D, 'A New Stream of International Law Scholarship' (1988) 7 Wis Int'L. L.J. 26.

Kim R, 'Globalizing the Law Curriculum for Twenty-First-Century Lawyering' (2018) 67 Journal of Legal Education 905.

Kimminich O, 'Teaching International Law in an Interdisciplinary Context' (1986) 24 AVR 143.

Kimminich O, 'The Teacher in International Law by Manfred Lachs' (1986) 24 AVR 238.

Kingsbury B/Krisch N/Stewart R, 'The Emergence of Global Administrative Law' (2005) 68 Law and Contemporary Problems 15, 16.

Koeck H, 'The 'Austrian School of International Law': the Influence of Austrian International Lawyers on the Formation of the Present International Legal Order' in Peter Hilpold (ed), *European International Law Traditions* (Springer: Heidelberg 2021), 61.

Kolb R, 'Peremptory Norms as a Legal Technique Rather than Substantive Super-Norms' in Dire Tladi (ed), *Peremptory Norms of General International Law (Jus Cogens)* (Brill/Martinus Nijhoff: Leiden/Boston 2021), 21.

Koskenniemi M, 'Commitment and Cynicism' in Jean d'Aspremont and others (eds), *International Law as a Profession* (CUP: Cambridge 2017), 38.

Koskenniemi M, 'International Law: Constitutionalism, Managerialism and the Ethos of Legal Education' (2007) 1 EJLS 8.

Koskenniemi M, 'Methodology of International Law' (2007) MPEPIL online ed <http://www.csil.cn/upFiles/files/International%20Legal%20Theory%20and%20Doctrine.pdf> accessed 25 October 2021.

Koskenniemi M, 'Nationalism, Universalism, Empire: International Law in 1871 and 1919' (University of Helsinki,) 15.

Koskenniemi M, *From Apology to Utopia* (CUP: Cambridge 2006).

Koskenniemi M, *From Apology to Utopia: the Structure of International Legal Argument* (Cambridge University Press: Cambridge 1989).

Krafcik J, 'Triumph of the Lean Production System' (1988) 30 Sloan Management Review 41.

Kreß K, *The Crime of Aggression* (CUP: Cambridge 2017).

Lachs M, *The Teacher in International Law* (2nd edition, Martinus Nijhoff: Dordrecht/Boston/Lancaster 1987).

Maciag J, 'Six Sigma as a Method for Improving University Processes: the Case of the Academic Assessment Process' in Stephen Yorkstone (ed), *Global Lean for higher education: a themed anthology of case studies, approaches, and tools* (Routledge/Taylor & Francis: New York 2020), 197.

Mader F, 'Wie viel Elite verträgt Deutschland?' (ARD alpha, 17 July 2019) <https://www.br.de/fernsehen/ard-alpha/sendungen/campus/exzellenz-initiative-foerderung-zeit-100.html> accessed 25 October 2021.

Michael Sandel, *The Tyranny of Merit* (Penguin Press 2020).

Nafziger J, 'Teaching Public International Law in the United States' (1986) 24 AVR 215.

Neuhold H/Simma B, *Neues europäisches Völkerrecht nach dem Ende des Ost-West-Konflikts?* (Nomos: Baden-Baden 1996).

Nicholson A/ Pakgohar A, 'Lean Thinking in a UK University Law Clinic: a Reflective Case Study' (2020) 27 International Journal of Clinical Legal Education 171.

Nicolson A, 'Research-informed teaching: a clinical approach' (2017) 51 The Law Teacher 40, 41.

Panebianco M, 'Tradition und neue Tendenzen in der italienischen Völkerrechtslehre nach 1945' (1987) 25 AVR 387.

Pasqualoni P, 'Österreichische Universitäten im Spiegel der Geschichte – Fallstricke einer Reform der Reform' in Österreichische HochschülerInnenschaft/Paulo Freire-Zentrum (eds), *Ökonomisierung der Bildung* (Mandelbaum: Vienna 2005), 103.

Patti FP, 'Career Paths into Legal Academia in Italy' (2020), 84 RabelsZ 324.

Perrouin-Verre D and Fulli-Lemaire S, 'Career Paths into Legal Academia in France' (2020), 84 RabelsZ 299.

Posch W, 'The Austrian View of the Bologna Process in Legal Education' (2005) 2 European Journal of Legal Education 67.

Radau W, 'Berufungspraxis in Österreich' (2019) 26 Forschung & Lehre 932.

Reis F/Grzybowski J, 'The matrix reloaded: Reconstructing the boundaries between (international) law and politics' (2021) 34 LJIL 547.

Reisman M, 'The Teaching of International Law in the Eighties' (1986) 20 The International Lawyer 987.

Roberts A, *Is International Law International?* (OUP: Oxford 2017).

Rudolf W, 'Die Lehre staatsrechtlicher Bezüge zum Völkerrecht' (1986) 24 AVR 163.

Schachter O, 'The Invisible College of International Lawyers' (1977) 72 NULR 217.

Schmitt C, *Die Lage der europäischen Rechtswissenschaft* (Tübingen 1950).

Scott A/Pasqualoni P, 'Invoking Humboldt – The German model' in James Côté/ Andy Furlong (eds), *Routledge Handbook of the Sociology of Higher Education* (Routledge: London/New York 2016), 211.

Scoville R/Markovic M, 'How Cosmopolitan are International Law Professors?' (2016) 38 MichJIntL 119.

Seow P/Pan G/Koh G, 'Examining an experimental learning approach to prepare students for the volatile, uncertain, complex and ambiguous (VUCA) work environment' (2019) 17 The International Journal of Management Education 62.

Silva E, 'Measuring skills for 21st-century learning' (2019) 90 Phi Delta Kapan 630.

Simpson G, 'On the Magic Mountain: Teaching Public International Law' (1999) 10 EJIL 70.

Skapinger M, 'The empty consolation of 'Vuca' and other buzzwords' *Financial Times* (23 October 2018).

Slaughter A/Tulumello A/Wood S, 'International Law and International Relations Theory: a New Generation of Interdisciplinary Scholarship' (1998) 92 AJIL 367.

Steger M, 'What is Global Studies' in Mark Juergensmeyer and others (eds), *The Oxford Handbook of Global Studies* (OUP: Oxford 2019), 3.

Stella G, 'Università, lo strapotere dell'inglese nei bandi: la follia delle traduzioni giurate' *Corriere della Sera* (4 March 2021).

Thirlway H, 'The Sources of International Law' in Malcolm Evans (ed), *International Law* (OUP: Oxford 2010), 95.

Tiebout C, 'A Pure Theory of Local Expenditures' (1956) 64 Journal of Political Economy 416.

Tomuschat C, 'The (Hegemonic?) Role of the English Language' (2017) 86 NJIL 196.

Tomuschat C, 'The Status of the 'Islamic State' under International Law' (2015) 90 Die Friedens-Warte 223.

Triggs G, 'The Public International Lawyer and the Practice of International Law' (2005) 24 Australian Yearbook of International Law 201.

Trimble P, 'The Plight of Academic International Law' (2000) 1 Chic.JIntL 117.

Udina M, 'Der Beitrag der italienischen Doktrin zur gegenwärtigen Theorie des Völkerrechts' (1969) 29 ZaöRV 331.

U.S. Army Heritage & Education Center, 'Who first originated the term VUCA (Volatility, Uncertainity, Complexity and Ambiguity)?' (U.S Army Heritage & Educational Center, 07 May 2019) <https://usawc.libanswers.com/faq/84869> accessed 25 October 2021.

US News, Best International Law Programs, 2021, 'Best International Law Programs' (U.S. News, 24 June 2021) <https://www.usnews.com/best-graduate-schools/top-law-schools/international-law-rankings> accessed 25 October 2021.

Von Bogdandy A, 'German Legal Hegemony?' (Verfassungsblog, 05 October 2020) <https://verfassungsblog.de/german-legal-hegemony/> accessed 25 October 2021.

Weiler J, 'Mirror Mirror on the Wall – Who is the Most Beautiful of All? Legal Hegemony or Legal Hubris?' (Verfassungsblog, 10 October 2020) <https://verfassungsblog.de/mirror-mirror-on-the-wall-who-is-the-most-beautiful-of-all/> accessed 25 October 2021.

White J, 'Rethinking the Program of Legal Education: a New Program for the New Millennium' (2000) 36 Tulsa 397, 400.

Windsor M, 'Consigliere or Conscience? – The Role of the Government Legal Advisor' in Jean d'Aspremont and others (eds), *International Law as a Profession* (CUP: Cambridge 2017), 355.

Yorkstone S, 'Lean Universities' in Torbjorn Netland/Daryl Powell (eds), *The Routledge Companion to Lean Management*, (Routledge/Francis & Taylor: New York 2016).

Ziegler A, 'Die Entwicklung der Völkerrechtslehre und –wissenschaft in der Schweiz – eine Übersicht' (2016) 26 SZIER 21.

Ziegler A, 'How global should legal education be? Recommendations based on the compulsory teaching in international aspects taught at Swiss law schools' (2020) 1 European Journal of Legal Education 49.

CHAPTER 2

U.S. Approaches to Teaching International Law in a Global Environment

*Charlotte Ku**

July 2021

International Law in a Globalized Environment[1]

On 13 December 2019, I boarded an airplane at London's Heathrow Airport bound for the United States. I carried with me a copy of the *Financial Times* that included a small item on the appearance in China of a novel pneumonia-like disease. I took little notice of what seemed to be just a story about another kind of flu – a common occurrence during winter in the northern hemisphere. A month later, on 30 January 2020, the Director-General of the World Health Organization (WHO) declared the COVID-19 outbreak a Public Health Emergency of International Concern.[2] Two months after that, with the spread of the disease to 114 countries and more than 100,000 cases, COVID-19 was declared a pandemic by WHO on 11 March 2020. As the WHO Independent Panel on Pandemic Preparedness and Response reported in May 2021, "[i]n under four months from the moment when SARS-CoV-2 was first identified as the cause of clusters of unusual pneumonia cases in Wuhan, China, COVID-19 became a global pandemic threatening every country in the world."[3]

While its origins remain under investigation, individual actions and reactions on a personal and public level contributed to creating a global pandemic,

* Professor of Law and Director, Global Programs, Texas A&M University School of Law.

1 Research assistance provided by Kristen Rowlett, Dee J. Kelly Law Library, Texas A&M University School of Law, Adria Stallcup and Sarah Wright, Texas A&M University School of Law is gratefully acknowledged.

2 The Independent Panel for Pandemic Preparedness and Response, "COVID-19: Make It the Last Pandemic" (*The Independent Panel* May 2021) 24 <https://theindependentpanel.org/wp-content/uploads/2021/05/COVID-19-Make-it-the-Last-Pandemic_final.pdf> accessed June 7, 2021.

3 Ibid 8.

 | DOI:10.1163/9789004678880_004

as they will determine the strength of the post-pandemic recovery. The WHO Panel noted:

> The evidence the Panel gathered showed that decisions mattered and had consequences. It also showed that prior conditions mattered – there was much more freedom to act and more choices available in those places where a robust and resilient health system existed, where social and economic protections were solid, and where governments, scientists and citizens trusted one another to do their best.[4]

The need for a global response in early 2020 clashed with an unwillingness in many countries, including the United States, to take the threat seriously and to act accordingly. Reasons for this reluctance varied from country to country but almost always included reluctance to deal with the impact of shutting down entire economies. THE WHO itself was not immune from pressures to understate the need for swift and decisive action to stop the spread of the disease. At the same time, there was a xenophobic and populist response in some countries, including the United States, that fanned the anger of those who felt harmed and left out by globalization. This anger encouraged them to believe that they could build physical barriers against pernicious and now deadly outside forces. The tenor and technical approach used by the WHO did little to instill confidence in people directly affected by the disease or address the socio-economic impacts that resulted.[5] And countries' "selective imposition of travel and trade restrictions"[6] did little to stop the spread of the disease in a globalized world. The need for a more holistic approach in managing health crises and policy was noted in the WHO Independent Panel's report:

> This mega-crisis makes a compelling case for strengthening a true and effective multilateral system which ensures that disease outbreaks do not become pandemics and pandemics are not allowed to escalate into

4 Ibid 6.

5 See for example, WHO guidance that accompanied its finding in January that Covid-19 was a Public Health Emergency of International Concern available at https://www.who.int/publications/m/item/covid-19-public-health-emergency-of-international-concern-(pheic)-global-research-and-innovation-forum and file:///C:/Users/cku/Downloads/global-research-and-innovation-forum-towards-a-research-roadmap%20(1).pdf.

6 The Independent Panel for Pandemic Preparedness and Response, "How an Outbreak Became a Pandemic" (*The Independent Panel* May 2021) 41 <https://theindependentpanel.org/wp-content/uploads/2021/05/How-an-outbreak-became-a-pandemic_final.pdf > accessed June 7, 2021.

> world-wide social, economic, and health crises. ... Understanding the political economy of incentives and barriers to international agreement is a vital task that needs to draw on research disciplines much wider than done today.[7]

But knowing what to do did not mean that governments did what was needed. In mid-2021, they are still lagging behind, but there has been some progress. On 20 May 2021, the Council of the European Union approved a decision "to support the launch of negotiations for an international treaty on the fight against pandemics,"[8] the Framework Convention on Pandemic Preparedness and Response. Negotiations are underway within the World Trade Organization to waive provisions of the Agreement on Trade-Related Aspects of Intellectual Property Rights (TRIPS) to facilitate worldwide equitable access to COVID-19 vaccines. The complex technologies required to produce the vaccine, however, will not make access through manufacturing a quick or easy solution to increase the vaccine supply.[9] After a year of "going it alone," including its announced withdrawal from WHO, the United States, under a new Administration in 2021, reversed its withdrawal announcement and supports this effort.[10] Launched in April 2020, COVAX is one part of the WHO's Access to COVID-19 program to ensure access to vaccines for distribution to low and middle income countries,[11] and the United States announced the purchase and distribution[12] of

---

7 Ibid 45.

8 Council of the EU, "EU Supports Start of WHO Process for Establishment of Pandemic Treaty: Council Decision" (*European Council* May 20, 2021) <https://www.consilium.europa.eu/en/press/press-releases/2021/05/20/eu-supports-start-of-who-process-for-establishment-of-pandemic-treaty-council-decision/#:~:text=The%20Council%20adopted%20today%20a,on%20the%20fight%20against%20pandemics.&text=The%20proposal%20for%20an%20international,Peace%20Forum%20in%20November%202020.> accessed June 7, 2021.

9 ASIL Insight, (*The American Society of International Law* 2021) <https://www.asil.org/insights/volume/25/issue/9> accessed 30 June 2021.

10 "Statement from Ambassador Katherine Tai on the Covid-19 Trips Waiver" (*United States Trade Representative* May 5, 2021) <https://ustr.gov/about-us/policy-offices/press-office/press-releases/2021/may/statement-ambassador-katherine-tai-covid-19-trips-waiver> accessed June 7, 2021.

11 The Independent Panel for Pandemic Preparedness and Response (n 3) 41. See What is COVAX at <https://www.gavi.org/vaccineswork/covax-explained>.

12 "Biden announces US to donate 500M vaccine doses in show of American leadership" (*ABC News* 10 June 2021) <https://abcnews.go.com/Politics/biden-announces-us-donate-500m-vaccine-doses-show/story?id=78201236> accessed 30 June 2021.

500 million doses of vaccines. The European Union has announced similar donations.[13]

The pandemic exposed the many disconnects in mounting a universal response to a global crisis. If it had been a hypothetical scenario in an academic exercise, it would have demonstrated the role of international law and its functions in a globalized world. Unfortunately, it is all too real, and it has revealed how shallow cooperation remains as countries turned inward to protect themselves. It exposed the urgent need to address myriad inequities and mindsets that made common action even within countries impossible. Countries' collective failure to cooperate has resulted so far in the disease infecting at least 150 million people and killing more than three million – more than 600,000 in the U.S. alone.[14] No country on the planet was spared "the worst combined health and socioeconomic crisis in living memory, and a catastrophe at every level."[15] As the WHO Independent Panel noted, "COVID-19 has shown how an infectious disease can sweep the globe in weeks and, in the space of a few months, set back sustainable development by years."[16]

The COVID-19 experience will be an enduring part of teaching international law for some time to come. The work needed to repair the damage done by the pandemic and to develop a better response system will rely (among other resources) on the governance infrastructure provided by international law including forms of obligation, concepts that guide the obligations' implementation, and modes of communication that can direct and motivate action across borders. After World War II, members of the United Nations thought they had both inherited from the League of Nations and developed an adequate system of specialized agencies and functional organizations to deal with a myriad of issues including global health. In the treaties that established the World Health Organization and subsequent agreements, WHO member states

13 "Emmanuel Macron calls on EU to match US' covid vaccine donation" (*Newsweek 10 June 2021*) <https://www.newsweek.com/emmanuel-macron-calls-eu-match-us-covid-vaccine-donations-1599560> accessed 30 June 2021.

14 CDC, "CDC COVID Data Tracker" (*Centers for Disease Control and Prevention* 2021) <https://covid.cdc.gov/covid-data-tracker/#datatracker-home> accessed 7 June 2021.

15 Independent Panel for Pandemic Preparedness and Response (n 3) Preface May 2021.

16 Ibid 10 See details from Independent Panel report:

- US$ 10 trillion of output is expected to be lost by the end of 2021, and US$ 22 trillion in the period 2020–2025 – the deepest shock to the global economy since the Second World War and the largest simultaneous contraction of national economies since the Great Depression of 1930–32;
- At its highest point in 2020, 90% of schoolchildren were unable to attend school;
- 10 million more girls are at risk of early marriage because of the pandemic;
- gender-based violence support services have seen fivefold increases in demand;
- 115–125 million people have been pushed into extreme poverty.

gave it the authority to respond to global pandemics through legally binding international health regulations.[17] However, as we have seen, this authority was not enough to direct states to discharge their individual and collective responsibility to take actions that might have tempered the spread of the disease. Why not?

Answering this question is critical to ensuring a safe and productive global future. The failures of 2020 laid bare the importance of international law and global governance and of expanding the range of students, practitioners, and citizens who understand what happens when these systems break down. The questions of why we teach international law, to whom it should be taught, when and how, and by whom are more compelling in 2021 than they were in 2018 when I delivered portions of this chapter as a conference paper in Innsbruck, Austria on teaching international law.

Equally compelling is the need to understand the environment in which international law functions. As we saw in the COVID-19 response, substantial portions of the response structure seemed not "fit for purpose." How can we teach in a relevant way to those who unexpectedly may find themselves at the front lines of a global challenge requiring collective, orderly, and concerted action? What is the purpose of such teaching? If we say international law now operates in a global environment, what does that mean in concrete terms?

Classic international law focused on *horizontal* state to state relations covering such topics as recognition, state responsibility, diplomatic immunity, and regulation of armed conflict. The global environment – facilitated by international law itself – pushed international law into a *vertical* plane now reaching into a state's domestic legal system down to the local level. As Mayor Yvonne Aki-Sawyerr of Freetown, Sierra Leone, said of local officials dealing with the pandemic, "You are first in the response, but often last in the queue for policy formation" to better address the realities on the ground.[18] Cross-border commercial and personal transactions have introduced new private actors into an international sphere that had previously been the virtually exclusive domain of public officials. Issues like environmental protection engage jurisdictions at multiple levels, including water authorities and municipalities. States are held accountable by other states to international human rights standards for their treatment of those under their jurisdiction. Even in the core international law area of state responsibility, attributing that responsibility may require moving through differing levels of jurisdictions and sectors. This means that

17 "International Health Regulations" (*World Health Organization* 2021) <https://www.who.int/health-topics/international-health-regulations#tab=tab_1> accessed 30 Jun3 2021.

18 Independent Panel (n 7) 52.

TABLE 1 Teaching international law

To Whom	Why	What	When	How	By Whom
Students (Undergraduate)	Essential part of general education	Basic knowledge	Prior to graduation	Classroom; formal interaction with instructor	Academics: local
Students (Professional)	Needed for professional competence and advantage	Basic knowledge; possible focus on how IL interacts with domestic law	Prior to graduation	Classroom: short course or full semester; experiential	Academics, practitioners, officials: local and international
Practitioners	Needed for professional competence and advantage	Updates or basic knowledge	Ongoing throughout professional life	Short courses and professional meetings; through professional associations or standalone	Academics, practitioners, officials: local and international
Public Officials	Needed for professional competence	Updates or basic knowledge	Ongoing throughout professional life	Short courses or professional meetings; through professional associations or standalone	Academics, practitioners, officials: local and international
General Public	Needed for sounder politics and public decision-making	General understanding	Ongoing as part of democratic political process	Social media and other forms of public discourse	Academics, practitioners, occasionally officials: local and occasionally international

international law is no longer the exclusive province of diplomats and foreign ministries, but involves individuals in multiple sectors at multiple levels.

This chapter will explore the multiple and varied audiences we need to reach in international law teaching; the opportunities for such teaching; what our teaching should accomplish; and who will do the teaching. Our audiences include:

1) Students, both undergraduate and professional;
2) Practitioners;
3) Public officials from all levels of government including municipalities;
4) Members of the general public who, as individuals, are subjects of international law, and who, as participants in their respective political processes, affect their governments' commitment to international obligations.

The teaching methods we use and the content we deliver must vary from audience to audience. Table 1 summarizes this information and discussion.

This chapter will look into who is teaching international law in the United States and whether the U.S. international law academy is, in fact, globally minded. It will conclude with some suggestions on how to tackle the multifaceted challenge of teaching international law in a post-COVID-19 global world.

What Will the Post-COVID-19 World Be Like?

In 1919 and 1945, the victorious allies of World War I and World War II were conscious that the postwar era would be, and must be, different in its approach to interstate relations than had been the case before 1914 and in what had been the interwar years, 1919–39. They created a new organization, the League of Nations, in the wake of the Great War of 1914–18; and in 1945, they tried to rectify the failures of the League in the structure and tasks of the new United Nations.

In 2021, the world is again at such a moment, when, despite many successes over the past 75 years, the weaknesses and failures of the post-1945 UN system, specifically of WHO, and the distrust and disinterest in international cooperation of many citizens of democracies worldwide have been revealed. We who are on the front lines of teaching international law must understand "teaching" in the broadest sense, not just of students in a formal academic setting, but as education offered in layman's language to create an informed understanding of the nature of the global environment in the twenty-first century. We must start with the basics.

Global signifies the shrinkage of time and space. A single event in an isolated location such as the eruption of a volcano or the emergence of a new pathogen can have worldwide consequences. The volume and pace of such occurrences with global consequences are increasing as larger numbers of people, goods, and transactions cross and re-cross multiple borders – now including cyber-borders. Although states have facilitated much of this activity by concluding trade and other agreements that have resulted in more open access, borders remain important for law enforcement, regulation, and dispute resolution. The speed with which countries and local jurisdictions within countries closed their borders in response to the pandemic was noteworthy. Not only are multiple types of legal persons now present alongside states and public international institutions in the global arena, but they also perform authoritative actions that shape the form and content of domestic law in specific areas.

Kenneth Abbott and Duncan Snidal provide evidence for this development in their studies of regulation and governance. They noted the proliferation of multinational enterprises, firms, and non-governmental organizations that have appeared in the regulatory and governance space, seeming to supplant the state as the primary regulator. Yet, Abbott and Snidal conclude that:

> the state is not becoming obsolete as a regulator, either domestically or internationally. Instead, in both settings its role is evolving, from the centralized mandatory regulator of tradition (and to some extent of myth) to a more subtle role as catalyst, coordinator, and supporter of diverse regulatory activities.[19]

The state reserves its power to regulate should non-state action fail to ensure adequate order or protection. State institutions, particularly courts, may also serve as places of last resort should conflicts or disputes arise. Nevertheless, the political and regulatory environment of today's global world is more complex than its equivalent at the end of World War II. International law is part of this complexity and international law teaching needs to equip our students for work in this environment.

The changes in what constitutes international law's content are reflected in succeeding editions of leading treatises. Taking just one example, Oppenheim's *International Law,* we can see this development. The first edition published in 1905 focused on issues related almost exclusively to states and their activities,

---

19 Kenneth Abbott and Duncan Snidal, "The Governance Triangle," in Walter Mattli and Ngaire Woods (eds), *The Politics of Global Regulation* (Princeton University Press 2009) 88.

with only a small section titled "unions concerning non-political interests."[20] By the third edition in 1920, a separate section was added for the League of Nations.[21] The 1952–55 edition was further lengthened under the heading of "The Legal Organisation of the International Community."[22] This edition also included a new section on individual human rights. In 2017, two stand-alone volumes, *Oppenheim's International Law: United Nations* were published to supplement the basic treatise.[23]

If one of international law's purposes is to provide a structure for authoritative decision-making, then the pool of decision-makers today has expanded beyond government and public officials. Individual experts and activists in non-governmental organizations can now function as authoritative decision-makers.[24] Having technical experts set standards and procedures can be effective, particularly when they also have the responsibility of implementing the standards. However, as we have seen from the COVID-19 experience, WHO's technical knowledge and effort to coordinate national actors were not adequate to address the crisis, absent political cooperation at multiple levels among and within them.[25] Actions taken in response to a crisis without structure or adequate authority raise questions of accountability and responsibility. The power to decide carries with it the responsibility for the consequences of those decisions, including the ability to remedy any wrongs that may result.

When governments act and damage is done, it is clear whom to hold responsible. When a corporation, an NGO or an international organization acts in a way that harms, the remedy for that harm is less clear. But when others like the United Nations (UN) causes harm, the situation is more complicated. Consider, for example, the effort to claim damages from the UN on behalf of the nearly one million Haitians who suffered, and the 10,000 who died, from cholera,

20 Lassa Oppenheim, *International Law: A Treatise* (1sr edn Longmans, Green and Co.1905).

21 Lassa Oppenheim, *International Law: A Treatise* (3rd edn Longmans, Green and Co. 1920).

22 Lassa Oppenheim, *International Law: A Treatise*, Hersch Lauterpacht (ed), (7th edn, Longmans, Green and Co.1952).

23 Rosalyn Higgins and others, *Oppenheim's International Law, United Nations* (Oxford University Press, 2017).

24 "By authority is meant expectations of appropriateness in regard to the phases of effective decision processes. These expectations specifically related to personnel appropriately endowed with such decision-making power; the objectives they should pursue; the physical, temporal and institutional features of the situations in which lawful decisions are made; the values which may be used to sustain decisions, and so forth." Myres McDougal, Harold Lasswell, and Michael Reisman, "The World Constitutive Process of Authoritative Decision" (1967) 19 *Journal of Legal Education* 256.

25 Eyal Benvenisti, "The WHO – Destined to Fail? Political Cooperation and the Covid-19 Pandemic" (2020) 114 American Journal of International Law 588–97.

brought to Haiti in 2010 by UN peacekeeping troops from Nepal. The class action lawsuits filed in the U.S. in 2013 were dismissed in 2017 because of the immunity under the 1946 Convention on the Privileges and Immunities of the United Nations that the UN enjoys in the United States.[26] In an effort to provide some compensation to the victims, the UN started a voluntary trust fund with contributions from states and private entities, but the fund remains small.[27] Another example of the complexity of seeking relief from damages done by UN operations is outlined in the 2019 Supreme Court of The Netherlands case, *The Netherlands v. Respondents & Stichting Mothers of Srebrenica*.[28] As Kristen Boon summarized:

> The central legal issue in the case was whether the Dutch state, via the acts of Dutchbat, was responsible in whole or in part for the deaths of the Bosnian victims. The plaintiffs were the Stichting Mothers of Srebrenica (Stichting Mothers) who represented the relatives of 6,000 victims. They initiated suit against the Netherlands and the United Nations in 2007. The plaintiffs argued that the defendants should be held responsible for the deaths because they did too little to protect the population of the [UN designated] safe area around Srebrenica and during the evacuation of the refugees, and cooperated in the separation of males from other refugees. The Dutch state argued that the deaths were caused by the acts of the VRS [Army of Republika Srpska].[29]

The Court's finding was a narrow one that focused on the "probabilities of survival of the victims," rather than attributing responsibility.[30] Despite this failure to attribute wrongdoing, the case remains significant as an effort to seek damages for victims from national authorities for actions taken as part of a multinational international operation.

This creates a reliance on courts or some form of dispute resolution to determine the nature of the harm and to prescribe a reasonable remedy for that

---

26 "Court Dismisses Remaining Lawsuit against Haiti cholera" (New York Times, August 24, 2017) <https://www.nytimes.com/2017/08/24/world/americas/haiti-cholera-lawsuit-united-nations.html> accessed 30 June 2021.

27 UN Multi-Partner Trust Fund Office and UN Haiti Cholera Response at <http://mptf.undp.org/factsheet/fund/CLH00> accessed 30 June 2021.

28 "*The Netherlands v. Respondents & Stichting, Mothers of Srebrenic*a No. 17/04567" (Supreme court of The Netherlands July 17, 2019) <https://uitspraken.rechtspraak.nl/inziendocument?id ¼ ECLI:NL: HR:2019:1284> accessed 30 June 2021.

29 Kristen Boon, "Case Note in International Decisions" (2020) 114 *American Journal of International Law* 480.

30 Ibid 485.

harm, including who will provide the resources if financial compensation is involved. In court systems like that of the United States, where judges are generalists, settling such questions increasingly requires some understanding of applicable international standards and obligations. However, in many countries, including the United States, international law is not a required subject in law school or on the bar examination to qualify for practice. Nevertheless, judges and advocates, as well as those involved in private sector mediation and arbitration, are increasingly called on to deal with disputes requiring knowledge of relevant international law that they do not have. To remedy this, the international law academy in a globalized world must teach broadly and concertedly, including in settings outside of the academy.

Who Is the Audience for International Law Teaching?

Students

Although a case can be made for teaching international law at the secondary level, this chapter will focus on students in postsecondary education,[31] with a further distinction between undergraduate students studying law and professional students studying law. Both groups are law students, but their curricula are different. The goal of an undergraduate majoring in law – generally the situation outside the United States – may not be the practice of law as a lawyer or public official. The major can lead to graduate work in another discipline or to professional training at a law school. In the U.S., the professional training is usually a three-year course leading to the Juris Doctor (JD) – a professional doctorate. In many countries outside the U.S., after university study, students are tracked to become judges, prosecutors, or notaries based, on qualifying examinations followed by additional specialized training for those positions.

The majority of U.S. students who graduate from law school have, historically, done so with the goal of private law practice. However, this is changing, and the U.S. academy encourages students to think more broadly about how to use a legal education outside the traditional practice of law in such areas as management or entrepreneurship.[32] This has led to the development of new

---

31 For examples of materials developed for teaching at the secondary level, see "High School Curriculum" (*The American Society of International Law* 2021) https://www.asil.org/education/high-school-curriculum accessed 11 June 2021.

32 Richard Susskind, *Tomorrow's Lawyers: An Introduction to Your Future* (2nd edn Oxford University Press, 2017) Larry Cata Backer, "Toward General Principles of Academic Specialization by Means of Certificate or Concentration Programs: Creating a Certificate

courses such as accounting for lawyers or business for lawyers, but so far, less often to courses in international law, despite its relevance to the private sector. On why law students should study international law, John Sexton, the pioneering dean of a global law school at New York University, wrote twenty years ago:

> There are many levels at which globalization and legal education intersect. Since our graduates will practice in a globalized world, they will have to know how the reality of globalization affects the way legal rules operate, and they must develop a set of techniques for mediating within a much more sovereign system.[33]

Continuing Legal Education for Licensed Practitioners

Due to the growth of domestic subjects that now involve international legal standards or obligations, individuals whose practice started out being completely domestic are likely to find that their subject area of expertise has become an international one. A survey of law practitioners in the Philadelphia area noted that 67.5% of those asked reported they had worked on a legal matter that required them to have some knowledge of international law.[34] For example, in family law, child support payment requirements in the U.S. must be in full compliance with the Hague Convention on the International Recovery of Child Support and Other Forms of Family Maintenance – an international treaty which the U.S. signed in 2007 that entered into force for the U.S. in 2017.[35] In the UK, Rosalyn Higgins reported in 2010 that 45% of cases on appeal to the House of Lords involved some aspect of international law.[36]

In the United States, lawyers must be admitted to the bar of a specific state in order to practice there, and most states require continuing legal education (CLE) for practitioners to maintain their license. As a result, bar associations and universities offer CLE coursework that allows lawyers to build on their

Program in International, Comparative and Foreign Law at Penn State" (2001) 20 Penn State International Law Review 83.

33 John E. Sexton, "Out of the Box: Thinking About the Training of Lawyers in the Next Millennium" (2001) 33 University of Toledo Law Review 191.

34 Susan L. DeJarnatt and Mark C. Rahdert, "Preparing for Globalized Law Practice: The Need to Include International and Comparative Law in the Legal Writing Curriculum" (2010) 17 Legal Writing: Journal of Legal Writing Institute 20.

35 "U.S. Ratification of Hague Child Support Convention" <https://www.acf.hhs.gov/css/policy-guidance/us-ratification-hague-child-support-convention> accessed 30 June 2021.

36 See Rosalyn Higgins, "Teaching and Practicing International Law in a Global Environment: Toward a Common Language of International Law" (2010) 104 American Society of International Law Proceedings 198.

basic legal training throughout their career. Continuing legal education generally focuses on the applied and is less theory-based, but certificate and degree programs are also available. Many of these courses are now offered in intensive, condensed or online forms and are taught by leading practitioners rather than by academics. For a representative sample of international law related CLE programs, see the Events and CLE page of the American Bar Association's Section of International Law.[37]

Public Officials

Given the depth and breadth of international intercourse today, increasing numbers of officials at all levels of government find themselves implementing international law and having to explain its requirements to their constituents, colleagues, and political leaders. For example, the International Organization for Migration provides international law training around the world to border guards, investigators, prosecutors, working-level police and immigration officials, judges, public and government officials in order to combat human trafficking.[38] But few people not engaged professionally with migration issues have heard of the IOM and may wonder why their governments spend money to support it.

The Under2Coalition is an alliance of over 200 subnational jurisdictions from 43 countries committed to fighting climate change by reducing their greenhouse gas emissions to net-zero by 2050.[39] For these officials, understanding and explaining to their constituents both the form and content of relevant international agreements is necessary to facilitate cooperation, networking, and the advancement of their policy agendas. In May 2021 in response to the lower vaccination rates in Mexico, members of the San Diego County Board of Supervisors worked with the Mexican Consulate to provide for a mobile clinic in Baja California to inoculate 10,000 Mexican workers on the Mexican side of the border to keep open the supply chains from the region to the U.S.[40]

---

37 American Bar Association, "Events" (*American Bar Association 2021*) <https://www.americanbar.org/groups/international_law/events_cle.html> accessed 11 June 2021.

38 International Organization for Migration, "Regional Law Enforcement Training" (*International Organization for Migration* June 15, 2016) <https://www.iom.int/news/regional-law-enforcement-training> accessed 11 June 2021.

39 The Climate Group, "Under 2 Coalition" (*The Climate Group 2021*) <http://under2mou.org/coalition/> accessed 11 June 2021.

40 "San Diego County, Mexican Consulate Partner on Cross-Border Vaccines" (San Diego Union Tribune May 25, 2021) https://www.kpbs.org/news/2021/may/25/san-diego-county-mexican-consulate-partner-cross-b/ accessed 30 June 2021.

General Public

The results of the 2016 Presidential election in the United States, like the simultaneous British departure from the European Union (Brexit), reflected the antipathy of voters in many democracies, not only the U.S. and UK, toward what they regard as the negative impact of decades of international cooperation, represented in their eyes by treaty obligations and membership in international organizations that they believe restrict national freedom of action. If WHO cost the U.S. taxpayer money, but could not prevent COVID-19 from reaching the United States, then what good was it? There was little public outcry when President Donald Trump notified the United Nations Secretary-General on 6 July 2020 of the U.S. intention to withdraw from the organization.

Days following his inauguration as U.S. President, Joseph Biden reversed this decision on January 22, 2021, but public antipathy towards an international institution demonstrates the general lack of understanding of what international law and institutions are, how they work, and the range of options they can offer a country and its citizens. As someone once said to me about international law when I worked in the U.S. Senate, "I am not sure what international law is, but I am pretty sure that it is not good for me." To be sure, international organizations can be "held hostage to international rivalries and bogged down in endless negotiation on minor details."[41] But such hostility toward international law and its mutual obligations can impede, as it did in 2020, a concerted response to a deadly global crisis whether COVID-19 or climate change.

International law is not well developed in every aspect and is in need of change and improvement, but it is today as present in our civic and political lives as are the constitutions that govern our countries. This means that a basic understanding of what international law is and how it works needs to be a part of public education to enhance the level of international law literacy. That literacy undoubtedly varies from country to country, but there is little doubt that it is well below public familiarity with domestic institutions. Improving awareness and understanding of international law among the media and thought leaders in countries around the world would help increase public awareness of international law's role in issues as they arise.

What Are the Goals and Objectives of Teaching International Law to These Groups?

In teaching undergraduates, faculty goals are to prepare students for more specialized training and to provide an advanced understanding of civic rights,

41 Independent Panel on Pandemic Responsiveness and Preparedness (n 7) 45.

responsibilities, and duties. The undergraduate course in international law can introduce the idea that multiple systems of law not only exist, but regularly interact with each other. Asking students to write and to think about international law in the context of politics and a domestic legal system can also demonstrate the general limits on all law to provide solutions to policy problems.

For the professional law student, knowledge of international law is an essential part of professional competence to ensure that practitioners are fully aware of the range of possible solutions and remedies available to their clients. Legal education today builds on a basic understanding that there is more than one approach to solving a client's problem and requires students to seek solutions in multiple venues. Professional education should require students to question accepted domestic legal orthodoxy, and in doing so break ground to advance the development of law both international and domestic.[42]

Providing international law training for practitioners as part of CLE enables them to keep up with new developments in subjects and processes that may not even have existed when they were in law school. International regulatory issues concerning virtual currencies and the internet have only emerged in recent years but are now center stage. There have been major international law developments in private law governing family relations, property ownership, business transactions, and legal processes. The list of Conventions, Protocols, and Principles produced by the Hague Conference on International Law provides a representative sample of the subject matters with which legal practitioners now need to be familiar that did not exist sixty years ago.[43] These developments require updating and continuing education.

Public officials at many levels bear the primary responsibility for carrying out numerous international obligations to which their countries have agreed including affording consular protection to foreign nationals, serving legal documents from foreign courts, and enforcing child support arrangements. The training they need to carry out these responsibilities is no different from that required to ensure compliance with domestic law, and the legal academy and practitioners need to provide it. In today's transnational legal environment, cross border actions are regulated by international law, domestic law, or, more likely, a combination of the two. Domestic public officials can provide a bridge to a feedback loop or (recursivity) so that those who set international norms

---

42 Vasuki Nesiah, "A Flat Earth for Lawyers without Borders: Rethinking Current Approaches to the Globalization of Legal Education" (2013) 5 *Drexel Law Review* (2013) 371.

43 "Conventions, Protocols and Principles) (*HCCH* 2021) https://www.hcch.net/en/instruments/conventions accessed 11 June 2021.

and standards can see how these actually perform on the ground to achieve their purposes.[44] In its teaching and writing, the legal academy needs to capture the experiences of local officials in order to further develop international law.

The expansion of international law into new subject areas since World War II has directly affected individuals around the world, but in ways that are not always well understood. International agreements affect jobs, supply chains, marriages, divorce, adoption and other areas of personal conduct, rights, and protection. On a daily basis, the delivery of millions of packages, the arrival and departure of passenger and cargo aircraft and vessels, and the transmission of money and data depend on "functional" treaties, arrangements, and institutions that are some of the oldest in the world. In more politically-charged issue areas such as humanitarian relief, a better-informed public would perhaps have more tolerance for the need to balance sovereignty and intervention.[45] And awareness of the special meaning of refugee status as provided by the 1951 Convention Relating to the Status of Refugees[46] might help the public and political leaders understand the often fraught judgment calls demanded of immigration and border officials. This knowledge might help assuage deep seated feelings of losing control or identity, and at the very least explain why countries chose to enter into such obligations.

It may, indeed, be impossible to sustain support for international obligations without knowledge of the historic reasons for their existence. The result of ignorance can be a visceral and emotionally charged rejection of these obligations by individuals susceptible to demagogic manipulation, rather than a willingness to support a more measured effort to revise and update them. In our teaching, the legal academy has its own responsibility to democratic institutions, requiring us to teach not only to law students and practitioners, but to contribute to a better informed general public. An online presence and a rejection of legal jargon in media and public discussions are necessary to success in this area.

44 Terence Halliday and Gregory Shaffer, *Transnational Legal Orders* (Cambridge University Press, 2010).

45 "Responsibility to Protect" (*International Commission on Intervention and State Sovereignty* (2001) <https://www.globalr2p.org/resources/the-responsibility-to-protect-report-of-the-international-commission-on-intervention-and-state-sovereignty-2001/> accessed 30 June 2021.

46 "1951 Refugee Convention" (*UN High Commissioner for Refugees* 2021) https://www.unhcr.org/en-us/1951-refugee-convention.html accessed 30 June 2021.

What Should Be the Content of International Law Teaching?

Few undergraduate degree programs in the U.S. require international law, although there are notable exceptions. At the United States Military Academy at West Point, international law is part of a core class on law and has been part of cadet education for 200 years. Vattel's *Law of Nations* was adopted as a textbook at the Academy in 1821.[47] Mainly, however, international law undergraduate courses are electives. When I have taught them, the format is usually a large lecture class, and the approach a modified case method with hypothetical exercises. I adopted this approach because many taking an undergraduate class are considering attending law school. The hypothetical case exercises give them a taste of that experience and keeps them actively engaged even in a class of more than 100 students. There is typically a mid-term and a final examination including both short answer and essay questions.

Colleagues teaching undergraduates in the U.S. seem generally to have a mix of these elements in their courses to achieve two principal objectives. The first is to consider the relevance of international law to daily life and to examine how political, social, economic, and historic forces shape international law and how international law in turn shapes and directs those forces. The second objective is to demonstrate how international law enables states, private sector entities, and sub-state actors to deal with issues that transcend functional and physical boundaries. Interactive exercises like simulations and mock trials including use of the problems produced for the Phillip C. Jessup International Law Moot Court Competition, help students engage with these issues. In 2021, the Jessup problem dealt with a pandemic.[48] In countries where the curricular content is more standardized than in the U.S., there may be less scope for innovation beyond the doctrinal presentation of the material to prepare students for required exams.

In teaching international law to professional law students, many different formats and settings reflect the time available in the curriculum to teach international law as well as a variety of views on how best to engage student interest. One approach is to make international law a required short course. One example of this is Georgetown University Law Center's one credit, one-week course required of all students between the first and second semester of the first year. Entitled Week One: Law in a Global Context, the course is designed

---

47 Robert J. Goldstein, "Over There: Teaching International and Comparative Law at West Point," (2014) 20 ILSA Journal of International & Comparative Law 265.

48 "*Aprepluya v. Ranovstayo*" (Jessup International Law Moot Court 2021) with past problems and memorials available at <https://www.ilsa.org/publications/jessup-compendium> accessed 30 June 2021.

to introduce "students to a complex problem that involves not only U.S. law, but also international and/or foreign law in a transnational setting so they can begin to understand how legal problems" increasingly transcend national boundaries and involve more than one legal system.[49]

Another approach is to require a full semester course running 12–14 weeks, but a survey reveals that only 19% of U.S. law schools require a course in international law. More U.S. law schools offer international law as one of a small number of electives available during the otherwise set curriculum of the typical first year.[50] One of them is Harvard Law School, which has made a diverse education with exposure to international legal studies a major priority in the first-year curriculum. In 2008, Harvard Law School offered five three-hour foundational courses from which students were required to select one. The courses were: Public International Law; Law and the International Economy; The Constitution and the International Order; China; and private law systems around the world. In 2021, Harvard Law School has a Spring 1L requirement of a first-year course in international or comparative law. This upper-level requirement provides for the completion of one international and comparative law course with a minimum of 3 classroom credits. In the 2021–22 academic year, there are 16 full term international and comparative courses offered in the course catalog. More specifically, there are now 10 courses offered in Spring 2021 that satisfy the international or comparative law upper-level requirement for first year students. These are Antitrust Law & Economics – Global, Comparative Law: Why Law? Lessons from China, International Human Rights, International Trade Law, Introduction to Islamic Law, Legal Architecture of Globalization: Money, Debt, and Development, Legal History: Continental Legal History, Pathways and Pitfalls: Role of International Human Rights and Constitutional Law in Achieving LGBT Equality, Public International Law, and The International Law of the Sea.[51]

Using international law problems in courses on legal writing or research is an approach that reaches large numbers of students, since writing and

49 "Events" (*Georgetown University* 2021) https://guevents.georgetown.edu/event/week_one_law_in_a_global_context#.WuZo6KqotMs accessed 10 June 2021.

50 DeJarnatt and Rahdert (n 35) 10.

51 "J.D. Requirements Quick Reference Guide" (*Harvard Law School* 2021) <https://hls.harvard.edu/dept/registrar/registration-information/jdreferenceguide/> and "Course Catalog" (*Harvard Law School* 2021) <https://hls.harvard.edu/academics/curriculum/catalog/index.html?year=2021-2022&keywords=&faculty=&term=&subject=International%2C+Comparative+%26+Foreign+Law&otherFilter=International%2FComparative&xtype=Clinic&xtype=Reading+Group&xtype=Seminar&rows=50> accessed 22 June 2021.

research are required of all students in U.S. law schools.[52] Embedding or integrating relevant international law into subject specific topics, so that international law elements are included in the teaching of contracts or criminal law, etc., is yet another approach.[53] In this way, students can see how international law works in contracts or in criminal law in the context of a particular domestic jurisdiction.[54] Some schools offer experiential learning in an applied setting like a clinic or field study to a law firm, business, non-governmental organization or international organization outside of a student's home country to gain exposure to international law.[55] Students can also broaden their understanding of current international law topics and scholarship by serving as student editors of the nearly 100 international law journals now regularly published in the U.S. The oldest such journal is the *Harvard International Law Journal*, first published in 1959. These journals provide students with an intense hands-on experience with scholarly analysis, reference checking, and validation of claims and conclusions.

Moot courts are also a popular way to learn about international law and to interact with international counterparts. Such programs include the Jessup, Vis, and Cassin competitions.[56] Each of these competitions is structured around an international institution or process. The Philip C. Jessup moots a contentious case before the International Court of Justice. The Willem C. Vis moots international commercial arbitration and focuses on the application of the UN Convention on Contracts for the International Sale of Goods and other

52 DeJarnatt and Rahdert, (n 35) 15–8.

53 Franklin A. Gevurtz, *Global Issues in Corporate Law* (1st edn Thomson/West 2006), Marc I. Steinberg, Franklin Gevurtz, and Eric Chaffee, *Global Issues in Securities Law* (1st edn West Academic Publishing 2013), Maxeiner (n 51) 40–1.

54 John A. Barrett, Jr.,; "International Legal Education in the United States: Being Educated for Domestic Practice While Living in a Global Society" (1997) 12 American University Journal of International Law & Policy 997–9.

55 "Foreign Programs" (*American Bar Association 2021*) https://www.americanbar.org/groups/legal_education/resources/foreign_study/foreign_programs/ accessed 30 June 2021. The list, however, may not include short international experiences that are part of global law classes offered at schools like Texas A&M University School of Law. "Global Programs" (*Texas A&M University School of Law 2021*) <https://law.tamu.edu/prospective/academics/centers-clinics-programs/global-programs> accessed 10 June 2021, Andrew Mitchell and others, "Education in the Field: A Case Study of Experiential Learning in International Law" (2011) 21 Legal Education Review 69–95. For a list of representative clinical experiences, see James Cooper, "Punching Above Our Weight: International Legal Studies at California Western School of Law" (2014) 44 California Western International Law Journal 219–21.

56 Carrie Menkel-Meadow, "Why and How to Study Transnational Law" (2011) 1 *University of California Irvine Law Review* 120–8.

international commercial law. The Jessup and Vis competitions are conducted in English. The René Cassin competition is conducted in French and moots a case before the European Court of Human Rights that also conducts a separate competition for English-speaking students.

Marking its 60th anniversary in the 2018–2019 competition year, The Philip C. Jessup International Law Moot Court Competition is the oldest of the student international law competitions, with 680 schools from 100 countries participating annually. Depending on the size of the country, the Jessup can involve students competing initially in a domestic competition to produce a national team that then competes in the international rounds. These take place in Washington, DC during the annual meeting of the American Society of International Law. In 2021, the Global Rounds took place virtually on a custom built competition platform.[57] 550 teams participated from more than 90 countries with 1100 volunteer judges contributing.[58] These volunteer judges come from law faculty, practitioners, national and international judiciaries and coaches, are part of an enduring and wide-ranging network that provides opportunity for outreach in international law.

Held annually since 1994 in Vienna, the Vis Moot attracts more than 300 law schools from around the world. Since 2003, the Willem C. Vis (East) Moot has been held in Hong Kong just before the competition in Vienna to allow students in Asia an opportunity to compete in an international competition without traveling too far from the region.[59] This is a separate competition and Vis (East) competitors do not compete in the Vis rounds in Vienna. The Vis draws approximately 150 teams every year. The René Cassin is the oldest moot in French celebrating its thirtieth anniversary in 2015. This competition draws thirty teams from Europe and Canada. The competition is held in Strasbourg with judges from the European Court of Human Rights participating. Held also at the European Court of Human Rights, English-speaking students compete in the ELSA Moot Court.[60]

One of the most ambitious efforts to integrate international and comparative law teaching into a law school's curriculum is what McGill University in Montreal, Canada calls "transsytemia." Although a completely separate body

---

57 <https://www.ilsa.org/Jessup/Jessup2021/Documents/2021OfficialAnnouncement.pdf> accessed 22 June 2021.

58 <https://www.ilsa.org/Jessup/Jessup2021/Global%20Rounds/Jessup_2021_Commemorative_Program.pdf> accessed 22 June 2021.

59 <https://www.cisgmoot.org/en-US/content/15744> accessed 22 June 2021.

60 "René Cassin Moot Court Competition" (*European Court of Human Rights 2021*) <https://www.echr.coe.int/Pages/home.aspx?p=events/mootcourt&c=> accessed 30 June 2021.

of law, comparative law is sometimes combined with international law as part of introducing students to foreign legal traditions and perspectives. As McGill describes the transsytemic approach initiated in 1999, it:

> [E]nables students, who graduate with both civil law and common law degrees, to study the world's great legal traditions in an integrated fashion. McGill's transsystemic approach is bilingual [English and French] and dialogic. It recognizes legal pluralism as a pervasive phenomenon in the modern world.[61]

This approach was adopted so that students at McGill would acquire knowledge about different legal systems in an integrated rather than sequential manner. Previously, McGill law students studied Common Law Property, Contracts, and Torts and then Civil Law Property and Obligation. The transsystemic approach integrated these classes, not by simply switching back and forth between the common law and the civil law, but working with both systems to explore concepts, practice, and outcomes. It is intellectually demanding for both faculty and students, but over the decades has produced lawyers able to work across multiple legal systems.[62]

For professional law schools in the U.S., the biggest challenge is to find a place to include international law in a curriculum driven by a student's need to secure employment and to pass the bar examination. Job placement objectives discourage students from taking a full course in international law since they often perceive limited employment opportunities in the field. As a program director in charge of international programs first at the University of Illinois and now at Texas A&M University School of Law, I have therefore found it more effective to use shorter applied and problem-focused courses through field study or other forms of international placement to introduce students to the daily applicability of international law. Such courses offer U.S. law students personal encounters with students and practitioners from outside the U.S. who may be better versed in international law and able to share insights through personal experience into the relevance of international law.

Since 2014, Texas A&M University School of Law offers field study courses to the Cayman Islands, Cambodia, Ghana, Israel, Jersey, Scotland, and Iceland. As part of a semester-long Global Lawyering course treating the basics of

61 Paul-André Crépeau Center for Private and Comparative Law, "Transsystemic Legal Education" (*McGill University* 2021) <https://www.mcgill.ca/centre-crepeau/projects/transsystemic>.

62 Rosalie Jukier, "Where Law and Pedagogy Meet in the Transsytemic Contracts Classroom," (2005) 50 McGill Law Journal 790.

international and comparative law, students select a theme for their written projects and travel in small groups with one or two faculty members, to the country/region partnering with the law school in that thematic area. Students have the opportunity to spend time, usually about two weeks, with academics, practitioners, and fellow law students working in their areas of interest. Themes for the field courses are:

Cayman Islands: Financial Regulation
Cambodia: Collaborative Management and Land Use, Human Rights
Ghana: Land Use and Access to Legal Services
Israel: Water Management and Dispute Resolution
Jersey: Financial Regulation
Scotland: Natural Resource Management and Dispute Resolution
Iceland: Comparative Criminal Law Practices.

Field study locations are selected based on a number of criteria: location including the ability to get around a country to experience relevant sites; adequate faculty or other contacts and resources to develop a good program; availability of a good partner to help with local arrangements; and likely internship opportunities for students either immediately following the field study or soon thereafter. Participation in these field course has generated greater interest in both international and comparative law among Texas A&M University School of Law students.[63]

CLE courses in international law for practitioners are generally intensive because of time constraints and cover a specific topic in a single day workshop. Such courses are designed to fulfill mandatory training required either by licensing authorities or by an institutional employer. Typically, bar associations and other legal organizations like the American Society of International Law (ASIL) offer CLE training. Members also receive high quality and up to date information on specific international law topics at ASIL and other associations' annual meetings and ongoing topical programs, both in person and, increasingly, online. Continuing international law education available through professional associations to judges, law enforcement officers, food and drug safety inspectors, customs and agriculture workers, and other public officials offers them information relevant to their daily work.

The legal academy can best engage the general public by participating in open media events in a non-partisan setting. Opening some international law

---

63 "Field Studies: Global Lawyering: Texas A&M School of Law" (*Texas A&M University School of Law* 2021) http://law.tamu.edu/prospective/academics/centers-clinics-programs/global-programs/2021-field-studies accessed 10 June 2021.

programs offered at professional association meetings to public attendance is another promising idea and in use by organizations like the American Foreign Service Association.[64] General public interest in and concern with specific events, including COVID-19, provide opportunities to explain the give and take of international negotiation and the goals and objectives of international obligations to an audience focused, at least for a while, on how to do things better in the future. This was, indeed, the approach used by our international law predecessors during World War II to engage U.S. support for the United Nations. The COVID-19 lockdown pushed institutions like law schools – including the Texas A&M University School of Law – to provide more such programs using webinar formats, thereby expanding their geographic and demographic reach.[65]

What to Teach?

From the standpoint of the international law academic, the broad category of international law encompasses a range of analytical approaches, including comparative law; transnational law; transsystemic law; and the classic international law of Westphalian state to state relations. Each of us generally teaches from our own orientations and academic and professional backgrounds. Does it matter that we take different approaches? I do not believe so, as long as the basic core concepts of international law are covered. We need to be clear in our own minds about what we are doing and why and allow students to see that there are a variety of approaches that are equally valid.

The fundamental challenge in any teaching is to balance breadth and depth. International law is no different, but there are basic concepts that every law student should understand. These are the areas that make international law a distinctive legal system. They will also be the areas that give rise to issues as international legal obligations become part of a country's domestic law. The foundational elements are the *sources* of international law, its *jurisdiction*, and *dispute resolution* as the structural basis, with specific topics included as time permits. Such other topics might include the use of force, human rights, trade, the law of the sea, and the environment. The focus of any foundational teaching will be seeing that students understand how international law shapes

64 "Upcoming and Past Events" (*American Foreign Service Association* 2021) https://www.afsa.org/upcoming-and-past-events accessed 30 June 2021.

65 Texas A&M University System, "Texas A&M Law School to Host Webinar Series on Effects of Coronavirus Relief Package" (*Texas A&M Today* April 3, 2020) <https://today.tamu.edu/2020/04/03/texas-am-law-school-to-host-webinar-series-on-effects-of-coronavirus-relief-package/> accessed 11 June 2021.

international relations and how international and domestic legal systems intersect.

In the case of treaties and custom as sources of international law, the legal effects in a domestic system like that of the U.S. differ. The U.S. Constitution contains specific requirements for the adoption of treaties and their place in the U.S. legal system. With regard to custom, the relevant questions are how widespread a practice is and how much evidence exists that states regard themselves as legally bound by that practice. Students must also understand the core concept of jurisdiction. Domestic authorities may only assert jurisdiction if an act occurs within the territory of the state or through some other link, such as the perpetrator's or victim's nationality.

In the case of universal jurisdiction, a state may prosecute such crimes as genocide should the perpetrator be found in its territory even if there is no other territorial or nationality connection. Understanding the issues of jurisdiction will also flesh out the limits to sovereign immunity, which generally does not apply to commercial activity, even if conducted by the state. International disputes can be resolved in domestic judicial and arbitration bodies, international law now has a set of dispute resolution mechanisms and institutions of its own. These include international and regional courts, arbitral bodies like the International Center for the Settlement of Investment Disputes, and private dispute resolution services offered by Chambers of Commerce around the world.[66]

For the professional law student, application of this foundational content will serve to hone the skills of an effective practitioner in both domestic and international arenas. These include:

- Recognizing that different solutions to a problem might be possible;
- Understanding the limits of the law to solve policy problems;
- Identifying multiple ways to regulate behavior that may not always be through legislated or enacted law;
- Understanding the range of analytical approaches and interpretive strategies available for problem-solving or advocacy through exposure to different legal systems.

By introducing the basic concepts of international law and showing how they interact with concepts of the domestic legal system of the country in which

66 "Arbitration Institute" (*Stockholm Chamber of Commerce* 2021) <https://sccinstitute.com/> accessed 30 June 2021, "Arbitration" (*International Chamber of Commerce* 2021) <https://iccwbo.org/dispute-resolution-services/arbitration/> accessed 30 June 2021, "New York International Arbitration Center" (2021) < https://nyiac.org/> accessed 30 June 2021.

the class is being taught, the classic semester or term-long overview of international law makes international law relevant to the student who will most likely work within his or her domestic legal system. The pitfall of this approach, however, is that it may convey a level of certainty and a tendency to generalize about how international law works, rather than a realization that certain interactions are relevant only to a particular jurisdiction or constitutional framework. Faculty using this approach must therefore find ways to help their students understand the broad range of possibilities available to international law as it interacts with the laws and systems of nearly 200 countries around the world.

The transnational approach to teaching, in contrast, focuses on the interactions that take place among legal systems, rather than focusing only one the domestic with international law.[67] This blend of international and comparative law concepts and methods features particular international and foreign law interactions with domestic law, and focuses on those interactions rather than on the system of international law. It has the virtue of showing how international law works in practice, rather than studying it in the abstract. The approach is also inclusive in terms of recognizing all legal activity, regardless of the source or level, and it educates students to think of law as a continuum, with multiple legal systems working concurrently to offer answers to particular legal questions or problems. Teaching from a transnational perspective allows students to examine a range of topic areas, both public and private, and to focus on the interaction of legal systems, rather than pigeonhole a subject as a matter of public or private law. Professor Mathias Reimann, who pioneered this approach at the University of Michigan, described its advantages:

> The most obvious one is that you are graduating a student body every member of which has at least a minimal knowledge of law beyond American borders. To be sure, that knowledge is often minimal indeed. Still, at least every graduate knows what a treaty is, can read the recent crop of Supreme Court cases dealing with international issues and understand them, has a sense of what the WTO does, and realizes that the UN General Assembly cannot legislate. While that is not much, it is a lot more than what the majority of graduates knew before.[68]

67 Mathias Reimann, "From the Law of Nations to Transnational Law: Why We Need a New Basic Course for the International Curriculum" (2004) 22 Pennsylvania State International Law Review 397–415.

68 Mathias Reimann, "Making Transnational Law Mandatory: Requirements, Costs, Benefits" (2005) 23 Pennsylvania State International Law Review 789.

The advantage to students of short course, experiential, and moot exercises, is that they are motivated to learn the specific law applicable to the course focus or problem, i.e. international human rights law, environmental law, or commercial law. The weakness is that if this is their only exposure to international law, students may not understand the broader legal and political framework within which international law operates. As international law teachers, we need to ensure that our students are exposed to the broad outlines of international law, even if briefly, so that they understand the wider context in which it works. Any time that can be dedicated to introducing the core concepts and operating principles of international law would be beneficial.

The practicing lawyer should have acquired in law school an adequate general understanding of international law to be able to deal with specific subject matters. But in the U.S., historically, this has certainly not been the case for most law school graduates. Judges, senior officials, and senior practitioners often do not understand the role of international law because the foundation was not laid during their formal education. Part of our goal with today's law students is to give them at least a basic knowledge of international law so that this will not be true in the future.

Of the non-specialist and non-lawyer, former International Court of Justice President Rosalyn Higgins said:

> We could regard it as a civic duty that persons everywhere understand that the relations of their country with others, with the United Nations and with other organizations, are governed by a law other than their own national law. To avoid nationalism of the worst sort and ignorant parochialism, it is necessary that the ordinary citizen understand that there is a well-ordered structure for international relations – a structure and a system that all states accept.[69]

Only with this foundational knowledge, Higgins believes, will individual citizens be able to exercise the rights and other entitlements now provided them by international law obligations accepted by their own governments.[70] The desire to instill this level of civic literacy in the United States more than a century ago prompted senior U.S. officials like Secretary of State Elihu Root to found the American Society of International Law in 1906. In the first pages of the first issue of the *American Journal of International Law*, Root wrote:

---

69 Rosalyn Higgins, "Teaching and Practicing International Law in a Global Environment: Toward a Common Language of International Law" (2010) 104 American Society of International Law Proceedings 196.

70 Ibid 197.

> The increase of popular control over national conduct, which marks the political development of our time, makes it constantly more important that the great body of the people in each country should have a just conception of their rights and duties.[71]

Root believed it essential "to increase the general public knowledge of international rights and duties and to promote a popular habit of reading and thinking about international affairs."[72] He understood this to be an ongoing task needed to temper public sentiments that otherwise fail to take into consideration the views of another side.

Root specifically referenced the hostility generated by the Webster-Ashburton Treaty of 1842 that settled a number of outstanding border issues between the United States and Canada. (Root was born near that border, in upstate New York, in 1845). That hostility lingered into the early twentieth century when Root wrote the AJIL article. His plea was that "in every country the people whom negotiators represent and to whom arbitrators must return, shall be able to consider the controversy and judge the action of their representatives in this instructed and reasonable way."[73] Though more than a century has gone by since Root wrote these words and two world wars seemed to educate the American public about international rights and responsibilities, apparently little has changed in the "uncompromising and belligerent attitude" that he saw as obstructing peaceful international relations.[74] Reaching the general public to foster understanding of the give and take of international politics and the role international law plays in facilitating these relations therefore remains an urgent and important aspect of teaching international law.

Who Teaches International Law?

Interest in the question of who teaches international law is growing as the international law academy reflects on who wields influence in its study and practice. It is important to understand what first impression students (and general audiences) receive from their encounters with the subject. Two generations of U.S. students (including my own) had the good fortune to study

---

71 Elihu Root, "The Need of Popular Understanding of International Law" (1907) 1 *American Journal of International Law* 1.

72 Ibid 2.

73 Ibid.

74 Ibid 1.

with international law scholars who had fled Europe to escape Nazi Germany. Refugee status, genocide, and the peaceful settlement of disputes were not abstract issues, but matters of life and death for them and their families.[75] Embryonic international institutions, like the early European Communities and the United Nations, might be imperfect, but they were regarded as worth the effort to avoid another conflict at the scale of World War II.

Since international law has universal applicability, those teaching and studying international law may assume that international law transcends national and other perspectives like economic circumstances, historic experiences, and values. In fact, we see the limits of international law's universality if we consider the backgrounds and experiences of those in the international law academy. Ryan Scoville and Milan Markovic examined the backgrounds of faculty teaching international law at U.S. law schools. What they discovered was that only 66% of those studied had one of the following attributes of international experience:[76]

- at least one year of university study abroad
- practicing law at a foreign office of a law firm
- working for an international organization or NGO outside the U.S.
- serving in a foreign government
- working at a foreign law school.

What these findings revealed is that the strongest resumé for aspiring American law academics includes graduation from a top law school, experience at a major law firm, and a judicial clerkship. This career path leaves little room for meaningful professional experience overseas.[77]

To the extent that U.S. law faculty have overseas experience, it was usually acquired by studying or teaching abroad. Nearly 40% had taught at a foreign university; 35% had an undergraduate or graduate degree from a foreign university. Most with these backgrounds were originally from outside the U.S. Employment outside of academia was far less common. This background encourages an approach to international law that is more theoretical and doctrinal than practical. When faculty have had practical international law experience in the U.S., it tends to be in the Department of State's Office of

75 Elihu Lauterpacht, *The Life of Hersch Lauterpacht* (Cambridge University Press 2012).

76 Anthea Roberts, *Is International Law International?* (Oxford University Press, 2017), Ryan Scoville and Milan Markovic, "How Cosmopolitan Are International Law Professor," (2016) 38 Michigan Journal of International Law 119.

77 Scoville and Markovic (n 73) 126–9, James R. Maxeiner, "Learning from Others: Sustaining the Internationalization and Globalization of U.S. Law School Curriculums" (2008) 32 Fordham International Law Journal 52.

the Legal Adviser. For a student interested in career opportunities outside of academia, job prospects in international law appear limited. Moreover, if the State Department seems to be the only potential employer, students with reservations about U.S. foreign policy may shy away from it.[78]

To the extent that U.S. law professors did have experiences outside the U.S., they were geographically limited. 32% had studied or worked in western Europe, Australia, New Zealand or Canada. Only 19% had experiences exclusively outside those countries, with even fewer who had spent time in both western European and non-western countries. Of countries outside western Europe, the most commonly known were China, Israel, Japan, Russia, and South Africa.[79] Most of Africa, much of Asia, and all of Latin America are virtually unrepresented.

The limits of U.S. experience are not unique. Anthea Roberts's study identifies the narrowness of international engagement among international law academics in several other countries. In Australia and the UK, it is common for academics teaching international law to hold a foreign law degree from the U.S. or UK, but study abroad is less common among academics in Russia and France. Even when there is international experience, looking at the outflow and inflow of students shows that a small number of countries dominate. China and Australia send students abroad, while the U.S. and the UK have historically been the principal recipients of these students. Perceptions of how welcome (and how safe) international students are in the U.S. and the UK and the latter's exit from the European Union may change these flows, redirecting students to Australia and other parts of western Europe, but future, and particularly post-pandemic patterns remain unclear, particularly in the wake of COVID-19.[80]

Without a broader geographic and linguistic exposure, law professors will teach international law from the perspective with which they are most familiar, and that is their domestic legal systems. This may not be overly detrimental for students who principally will be applying international law in particular countries, but others will suffer from faculty who can provide little comparative insight into how another legal system applies the same international law. Students are also not exposed to the views of large parts of the world, with the views of Asia, Africa, and Latin America typically underrepresented.[81] U.S. law schools are attempting to bring broader perspectives into the classroom. Strategies include:

78 Ibid.

79 Ibid.

80 Ibid.

81 Karin Mickelson and others *The Third World and International Order: Law, Politics and Globalization* (Brill Academic Publishers 2004).

- adding foreign professors and visiting academics to the teaching staff
- including international students in the student body
- developing a multi-subject global curriculum for international law
- incorporating materials from less represented areas: Africa, Central and South America, Eastern Europe, Central Asia, the Middle East, Southeast Asia.

Providing the perspectives in the curriculum is useful, but requires student advising and guidance to help students take advantage of the opportunity.

Wrapping Up

In a 1977 article titled "The Invisible College of International Lawyers," Oscar Schachter advanced the proposition that the community of international lawyers could play an important role in serving as "la conscience juridique" of international law. He saw this role fulfilled through scholarly discourse and through the authoritative work judges do when they decide a case. Schachter was not naïve about how states might use international law to advance their interests. Nevertheless, he felt that there were principles and possibly legal values that bound the community of international lawyers together in a way that could advance the development and observance of international law.[82]

What Schachter underestimated was the effect of specialization within international law itself, leading to communities of specialists in human rights, trade law, the environment, and other subfields who do not see themselves as working at the same enterprise. As the International Law Commission (ILC) concluded in 2006,

> such specialized law-making and institution-building tends to take place with relative ignorance of legislative and institutional activities in the adjoining fields and of the general principles and practices of international law. The result is conflicts between rules or rule-systems, deviating institutional practices and, possibly, the loss of overall perspective on the law.[83]

Even as international law facilitated the development of these new bodies of law, their proponents failed to recognize and to promote the structure and

82 Oscar Schachter, "The Invisible College of International Lawyers" (1977) 72 Northwestern University Law Review 217.

83 International Law Commission, *Fragmentation of International Law: Difficulties Arising from the Diversification and Expansion of International Law*, (UN Doc. A/CN.4/L/682 of 13 April 2006) para. 8.

principles that support the overall international legal system.[84] These basic principles provide the basic operating framework of the international legal system and remain constant while the normative content may change as issues and interests shift.[85]

International law in this sense is like a computer's operating system that provides the platform on which specific applications are placed. Without an operating system, the applications will not run. If the operating system is not powerful enough, applications will not run at full capacity. The same is true for international law. The 1948 Convention on the Prevention and Prohibition of the Crime of Genocide could only advance as far as the international system provided it with the means to execute its provisions, including, for example, UN peacekeeping operations; establishment of the International Criminal Court and the specialized courts for the former Yugoslavia and Cambodia; and especially incorporation of its principles into domestic law.[86] State consent to expand the operating international legal system is necessary to develop the content of a norm and assess its effects, and to empower institutions and individuals in the use of the new norm, creating the capacity to implement it.

Teaching international law as a system and process rather than as a set of rules pushes students to see international law, like all law, as including tasks like coordination, facilitation, and standard-setting, rather than judging it by its lack of compliance enforcement mechanisms. Working through the general operating international law structure provides students the ability to determine and to assess the long-term system-wide effects of individual decisions. Four decades after Schachter wrote of the "invisible college," Santiago Villalpando wrote:

> The core intellectual challenges raised by Schachter have also persisted in today's community, including the eternal quest for objectivity and the problem of how to assess the influence of our own value systems and meta-juridical preferences, let alone our national positions, in resolving concrete legal problems. [87]

This remains true for the content of our teaching as well.

Although Rosalyn Higgins described international law as "humdrum stuff,"[88] this humdrum stuff has provided a structure for orderly international

84 Philip Alston, "The Myopia of the Handmaidens: International Lawyers and Globalization" (1977) 3 *European Journal of International Law* 435.

85 Paul F. Diehl and Charlotte Ku, *The Dynamics of International Law* (Cambridge: Cambridge University Press 2010).

86 Ibid.

87 Santiago Villalpando, "The 'Invisible College of International Law Forty Years Later" (2013) European Society of International Law 2013 Research Forum: International Law as a profession Conference Paper Conference Paper 6.

88 Rosalyn Higgins, *The Politics and Process of International Law* (Clarendon Press 1995) 1.

relations for centuries. It is perhaps this humdrum character of international law that makes teaching a challenge, because when things are working (as with the operating system of a computer), the user will not notice it. However, if the system fails to perform, then the user not only notices, but also wants an immediate correction or remedy. The latter can be difficult since international law is generally slow to change, given the level of consensus required among myriad international actors at multiple levels of authority to effect any change. Students who understand this as they move into their professional lives will hopefully be more resourceful and less frustrated global practitioners.

For more than a year, as I write, the world has grappled, incoherently, with a global pandemic that remains a threat to human life, economic stability, and democracy itself. At a time when teaching and awareness of international law cannot be more important, the international legal community needs to grapple with its own fragmentation and incoherence. Both for effective teaching and for the ongoing development of international law, the academy should focus on international law's core concepts to be sure that all law students and professionals are aware of the sources of international law and how these interact with domestic and regional legal systems. Students and practitioners further need to be aware of how international law affects individuals and how it engages with other law in areas of jurisdiction, responsibility, and dispute resolution. Specific issues requiring immediate decisions include a waiver to the intellectual property rights that protect the production of COVID-19 vaccines, as well as climate change and human migration. Are we preparing our law students today, born in the last decade of the twentieth century to practice in the mid-twenty-first century? Or are we sending them into the global environment ill-equipped to handle the tasks at hand?

Although teaching international law will remain the province of the academy, with primary teaching in the United States done in graduate academic institutions, academics should not rebuff the opportunity to disseminate as widely as possible information about international law. Indeed, one of the most far-reaching projects undertaken by the American Society of International Law was its *100 Ways* project, launched during my tenure as ASIL Executive Director to mark the Society's 2006 centennial. It identified 100 ways in which international law affects everyone's daily life. The original booklet and now web material has not only been updated and widely disseminated since 2006, but has been used to teach and to focus discussion of international law at all educational levels.[89] The *ASIL Insights* series was another effort to raise general awareness in the public about the relevance of international law to specific

89 *"International Law: 100 Ways it Shapes Our Lives"* (*American Society of International Law* 2021) <https://www.asil.org/education/100Ways> accessed 11 June 2021.

issues like the effort to ease intellectual property restrictions on manufacturing COVID-19 vaccines.[90]

Teachers of international law can neither afford to forget nor to ignore the responsibility to seize every opportunity to teach and to increase awareness about international law as a central factor not only in the lives of nation-states, but also now in the lives of their citizens. One of the findings of the Independent Panel in Pandemic Preparedness and Response was that the international health system needed to engage with "local communities as key actors in pandemic preparedness and response and as active promoters of pandemic literacy, through the ability of people to identify, understand, analyse, interpret, and communicate about pandemics."[91] This cannot happen effectively without some knowledge, awareness, and understanding of how we are physically bound together on the planet and the legal relationships we have created to manage both the opportunities and challenges of that reality. Not only has international law become a more complex system, it now involves more people in myriad settings who have never previously worked together. To paraphrase Elihu Root, the more aware we are of this complexity, the more effective we will be as practitioners and citizens. As experience with the COVID-19 pandemic has demonstrated, safeguarding lives and livelihoods depends on that awareness.

N.B. As I write the last lines of this chapter, I received news of the passing on May 31, 2021 of James R. Crawford – one of international law's most gifted teachers and jurists whose insightful writings and scores of students stand as a model of the scholar-practitioner dedicated to the sound practice and understanding of international law. With appreciation for his many years of friendship, I dedicate this chapter.

Bibliography

Abbott K and Snidal D, "The Governance Triangle" in Walter Mattli and Ngaire Woods (eds), *The Politics of Global Regulation* (Princeton University Press 2009).

Alston P, "The Myopia of the Handmaidens: International Lawyers and Globalization" (1997) 8 European Journal of International Law.

American Bar Association, "Events" (*American Bar Association* 2021) <https://www.americanbar.org/groups/international_law/events_cle.html> accessed June 11, 2021.

90 "ASIL Insights" (*American Society of International Law* 2021) < https://www.asil.org/insights> accessed 30 June 2021.

91 Independent Panel on Pandemic Preparedness and Response (n 3) 59.

Backer LC, "Toward General Principles of Academic Specialization by Means of Certificate or Concentration Programs: Creating a Certificate Program in International, Comparative and Foreign Law at Penn State" (2001) 20 Penn State International Law Review.

Barrett J, "International Legal Education in the United States: Being Educated for Domestic Practice While Living in a Global Society" (1996) 12 American University Journal of International Law and Policy.

Benvenisti E, "The WHO – Destined to Fail?: Political Cooperation and the COVID-19 Pandemic" (2020) 114 American Journal of International Law.

CDC, "CDC COVID Data Tracker" (*Centers for Disease Control and Prevention* 2021) <https://covid.cdc.gov/covid-data-tracker/#datatracker-home> accessed June 7, 2021.

The Climate Group, "Under2 Coalition" (*The Climate Group* 2021) <http://under2mou.org/coalition/> accessed June 11, 2021.

"Conventions, Protocols and Principles" (*HCCH* 2021) <https://www.hcch.net/en/instruments/conventions> accessed June 10, 2021.

Council of the EU, "EU Supports Start of WHO Process for Establishment of Pandemic Treaty: Council Decision" (*European Council* May 20, 2021) <https://www.consilium.europa.eu/en/press/press-releases/2021/05/20/eu-supports-start-of-who-process-for-establishment-of-pandemic-treaty-council-decision/#:~:text=The%20Council%20adopted%20today%20a,on%20the%20fight%20against%20pandemics.&text=The%20proposal%20for%20an%20international,Peace%20Forum%20in%20November%202020.> accessed June 7, 2021.

"COVID-19 Public Health Emergency of International Concern (PHEIC) Global Research and Innovation Forum" (*World Health Organization* February 12, 2020) <https://www.who.int/publications/m/item/covid-19-public-health-emergency-of-international-concern-(pheic)-global-research-and-innovation-forum> accessed June 7, 2021.

DeJarnatt S and Rahdert M, "Preparing for Globalized Law Practice: the Need to Include International and Comparative Law in the Legal Writing Curriculum" (2010) 17 Legal Writing, The Journal of the Legal Writing Institute.

Diehl PF and Ku C, *The Dynamics of International Law* (Cambridge University Press 2010).

"Events" (*Georgetown University* 2021) <https://guevents.georgetown.edu/event/week_one_law_in_a_global_context#.WuZo6KqotMs> accessed June 10, 2021.

"Field Studies: Global Lawyering: Texas A&M School of Law" (*Texas A&M School of Law* 2021) <http://law.tamu.edu/prospective/academics/centers-clinics-programs/global-programs/2021-field-studies> accessed June 11, 2021.

Gevurtz F, *Global Issues in Corporate Law* (1st edn Thomson/West 2006).

"Global Programs" (*Texas A&M University School of Law* 2021) <https://law.tamu.edu/prospective/academics/centers-clinics-programs/global-programs> accessed June 10, 2021.

Goldstein RJ, "Over There: Teaching International And Comparative Law At West Point" (2014) 20 ILSA Journal of International & Comparative Law.

Halliday T and Shaffer G, *Transnational Legal Orders* (Cambridge University Press 2010).

Higgins R and others, *Oppenheim's International Law: United Nations*, vol 2 (Oxford University Press 2017).

Higgins R, *Problems and Process: International Law and How We Use It* (Clarendon Press 1995).

Higgins R, "Teaching and Practicing International Law in a Global Environment: toward a Common Language of International Law" (2010) 104 Proceedings of the ASIL Annual Meeting.

"High School Curriculum" (*The American Society of International Law* 2021) <https://www.asil.org/education/high-school-curriculum> accessed June 11, 2021.

The Independent Panel for Pandemic Preparedness & Response, "COVID-19: Make It the Last Pandemic" (*The Independent Panel* May 2021) <https://theindependentpanel.org/wp-content/uploads/2021/05/COVID-19-Make-it-the-Last-Pandemic_final.pdf> accessed June 7, 2021.

International Law Commission, *Fragmentation of International Law: Difficulties Arising from the Diversification and Expansion of International Law*, (UN Doc. A/CN.4/L/682, 2006), para 8.

International Organization for Migration, "Regional Law Enforcement Training" (*International Organization for Migration* September 4, 2017) <https://www.iom.int/news/regional-law-enforcement-training> accessed June 11, 2021.

"Int'l Law: 100 Ways It Shapes Our Lives" (*American Society of International Law* 2008) <https://www.asil.org/resources/100Ways> accessed June 11, 2021.

Jukier R, "Where Law and Pedagogy Meet in the Transsystemic Contracts Classroom" (2005) 50 McGill Law Journal.

Mackenzie L and Darnycka Bélizaire M-R, "International Health Regulations" (*World Health Organization* January 1, 2019) <https://www.who.int/health-topics/international-health-regulations#tab=tab_1> accessed June 7, 2021.

Maxeiner J, "Learning from Others: Sustaining the Internationalization and Globalization of U.S. Law School Curriculums" (2008) 32 Fordham International Law Journal.

McDougal M, Lasswell H and Reisman W, "The World Constitutive Process of Authoritative Decision" (1967) 19 Journal of Legal Education.

Menkel-Meadow C, "Why and How to Study 'Transnational' Law" (2011) 1 University of California Irvine Law Review.

Mickelson K and others, *The Third World and International Order: Law, Politics and Globalization* (Brill Academic Publishers 2004).

Mitchell AD and others, "Education in the Field: a Case Study of Experiential Learning in International Law" (2011) 21 Legal Education Review.

Nesiah V, "A Flat Earth for Lawyers Without Borders? Rethinking Current Approaches to the Globalization of Legal Education" (2013) 5 Drexel Law Review.

Oppenheim L, *International Law: a Treatise* (1st edn Longmans, Green and Co 1905).

Oppenheim L, *International Law: a Treatise* (3rd edn Longmans, Green and Co. 1920).

Oppenheim L, *International Law: a Treatise*, (7th edn Longmans, Green and Co. 1952).

Paul-André Crépeau Centre for Private and Comparative Law, "Transsystemic Legal Education" (*McGill University* 2021) <https://www.mcgill.ca/centre-crepeau/projects/transsystemic> accessed June 10, 2021.

Reimann M, "From the Law of Nations to Transnational Law: Why We Need a New Basic Course for the International Curriculum" (2004) 22 Penn State International Law Review.

Reimann M, "Making Transnational Law Mandatory: Requirements, Costs, Benefits" (2005) 23 Penn State International Law Review.

Roberts A, *Is International Law International?* (1st edn Oxford University Press 2017).

Root E, "The Need of Popular Understanding of International Law" (1907) 1 American Journal of International Law.

Schachter O, "The Invisible College of International Lawyers" (1977) 72 Northwestern University Law Review.

Scoville R and Markovic M, "How Cosmopolitan Are International Law Professors?" (2016) 38 Michigan Journal of International Law.

Sexton J, "Out of the Box Thinking about the Training of Lawyers in the Next Millennium" (2001) 33 University of Toledo Law Review.

"Statement from Ambassador Katherine Tai on the Covid-19 Trips Waiver" (*United States Trade Representative* May 5, 2021) <https://ustr.gov/about-us/policy-offices/press-office/press-releases/2021/may/statement-ambassador-katherine-tai-covid-19-trips-waiver> accessed June 7, 2021.

Steinberg MI, Gevurtz F and Chaffee EC, *Global Issues in Securities Law* (1st edn West Academic Publishing 2013).

Susskind R, *Tomorrow's Lawyers: an Introduction to Your Future* (2nd edn Oxford University Press 2017).

Texas A&M University System, "Texas A&M Law School To Host Webinar Series On Effects Of Coronavirus Relief Package" (*Texas A&M Today* April 3, 2020) <https://today.tamu.edu/2020/04/03/texas-am-law-school-to-host-webinar-series-on-effects-of-coronavirus-relief-package/> accessed June 11, 2021.

Villalpando S, "The 'Invisible College of International Lawyers' Forty Years Later" [2013] ESIL 2013 5th Research Forum: International Law as a Profession Conference Paper.

CHAPTER 3

Teaching International Law Today and the Human Person

*Carlo Focarelli**

1 Introduction

A discussion of the 'teaching of international law' requires, first of all, to understand what 'teaching' means. In fact, as this paper will clarify further below, the expression can take several different meanings, including 'to educate' (from the Latin *exducere*, meaning 'to take out', or 'to lead out', or 'to lead forth'), 'to instruct' (from the Latin *instruere*, meaning 'to build into' or 'to build inside' or 'to pile up upon'), 'to train' (meaning 'to skill'), 'to domesticate' (from the Latin *domesticare*, meaning 'to tame' or, literally, 'to make domestic', or 'to dwell in a house') and 'to indoctrinate' (deriving from the Latin *doctrina*, meaning 'to imbue with a doctrine').

In addressing the teaching of international law, this paper places a particular emphasis on what 'teaching' such a discipline means. It does not address the other issues that are typically associated with the subject of teaching international law, namely teaching methods, attention-grabbing techniques or resources. Nor does it touch upon possible reforms of the teaching of international law, including steps towards reaching wider or specific audiences, or ensuring the presence of international law in curricula. Nor does this paper explore international legal scholarship as defined by Article 38(1)(d) of the ICJ Statute, i.e. as 'the teachings of the most highly qualified publicists of the various nations, as subsidiary means for the determination of rules of law'.[1]

* Professor of International Law at Roma Tre University, Rome, Italy. This essay was finalized on 23 August 2019. This is also when the essay was last updated, with the exception of footnotes 51, 63 and 112, which were added or amended thereafter.

1 The International Law Association (ILA), in particular, worked on 'teaching international law' in the period 1999–2010 (for related documents, see <http://www.ila-hq.org/index.php/committees>). The issues mentioned in the main text and which will not be covered by this paper have been widely debated in international legal scholarship, see e.g. Rudolf Bernhardt (ed.), *Das internationale Recht in der Juristenausbildung* (Karlsruhe: C.F. Müller, 1981); Bin Cheng (ed.) *International Law: Teaching and Practice* (London: Stevens and Sons, 1982); Manfred Lachs, *The Teacher in International Law: Teachings and Teaching*

 | DOI:10.1163/9789004678880_005

This is not to underestimate the specific practical issues that international law teachers face every day, nor their tasks and difficulties as professionals who are called upon to form legal professionals in various fields and careers. This paper will focus, in particular, on the teaching of international law *today*, during times – to use the words of Martha Nussbaum, to whom I will return below – of 'a worldwide crisis in education' which has increasingly acquired 'massive proportions', 'grave global significance' and is 'going largely unnoticed like a cancer'.[2]

This paper will start by preliminarily describing four teaching models that have been proposed, since the second half of the 19th century, by intellectuals who were, or are, engaged with teaching in different roles and cultural backgrounds, namely Lev Tolstoj (1828–1910), Edgar Morin (1921–), Robin L. West

(Dordrecht: Nijhoff, 1987); Bengt Broms, 'International Law in the Law School Curriculum', in Ronald St.J. Macdonald (ed.), *Essays in Honour of Wang Tieya* (Dordrecht: Nijhoff, 1994) 79–90; Samuel Bettwy, 'Roundtable on the Teaching of International Law' (1991) 85 *ASIL Proceedings of the Annual Meeting* 102–23; Bin Cheng, 'How Should We Study International Law?' (1994–1995) 13 *Chinese Yearbook of International Law & Affairs* 214; Anne Orford, 'Citizenship, Sovereignty and Globalisation: Teaching International Law in the Post-Soviet Era' (1995) 6 *Legal Education Review* 251; John K. Gamble and Christopher C. Joyner, 'Teaching International Law: Approaches Perspectives' (1997) *ASIL Bulletin* No. 11; Michael W. Reisman, 'The Teaching of International Law in the Eighties' (1996) 20 *International Lawyer* 987; Christopher C. Joyner, 'Teaching International Law: Views from an International Relations Political Scientist' (1999) 5 *ILSA Journal of International & Comparative Law* 377–88; Gerry Simpson, 'On the Magic Mountain: Teaching Public International Law' (1999) 10 *European Journal of International Law* 70–92; Ellen Hey, *Teaching International Law: State Consent As Consent to a Process of Normative Development and Ensuing Problems* (The Hague: Kluwer Law International, 2003); Caroline Starbird, Jenny Pettit and Laurel Singleton, *Teaching International Law* (Denver: CTIR University of Denver, 2004); Thomas Ambrosio, 'Trying Saddam Hussein: Teaching International Law Through an Undergraduate Mock Trial' (2006) 7 *International Studies Perspectives* 159–71; Jan Klabbers and Mortimer Sellers (eds.), *The Internationalization of Law and Legal Education*: Ius Gentium *Perspectives on Law and Justice* (New York: Springer, 2008); Robert J. Beck, 'Teaching International Law as a Partially Online Course: The Hybrid/Blended Approach to Pedagogy' (2010) 11 *International Studies Perspectives* 273–90; Hannah Birkenkötter and Mirka Möldner, 'The Future of Teaching International Law', *Völkerrechtsblog* (19 May 2014) <https://voelkerrechtsblog.org/the-future-of-teaching-international-law>; Tarcisio Gazzini, 'A Fresh Look at Teaching International Law: A Few Pedagogical Considerations in the Age of Communications' (2016) 29 *Leiden Journal of International Law* 971–8; Christine Schwöbel-Patel, 'Teaching International Law Critically: Critical Pedagogy and Bildung as Orientations for Learning and Teaching', in Bart van Klink and Ubaldus de Vries (eds), *Academic Learning in Law* (Cheltenham: Edward Elgar, 2016) 99–120; Christine Schwöbel-Patel, 'Teaching International Law', *Oxford Bibliographies* <http://www.oxfordbibliographies.com/view/document/obo-9780199796953/obo-9780199796953-0166.xml>.

2 See n 31 below.

(1954–) and Anthony Seldon (1953–). The remaining sections will, then, discuss three main questions: (1) what 'teaching' is (ultimately for); (2) whether the teacher's conception of international law and the socio-institutional framework surrounding education in this field are of (what) relevance for international law teaching; and (3) whether the teacher's 'living example' is likewise relevant. Some conclusions will be drawn in the closing section of the paper.

2 Four Introductory Models

By way of introduction, in this section I propose four models or conceptions of teaching, deriving from different backgrounds and times. These may be termed, respectively, 'existentialist', 'co-constructivist', 'professionalist' and 'futurist' conceptions. The intellectuals herein considered are, as suggested above, Lev Tolstoj, Edgar Morin, Robin L. West and Anthony Seldon, and this section's aim is to provide a general background for the following discussion.

(a) *Lev Tolstoj*

In 1882, the Russian writer/novelist Lev Tolstoj – who is regarded as one of the greatest authors of all time and is best known for novels such as *War and Peace* and *Anna Karenina*, short novels (among which *The death of Ivan Illich* is worth mentioning) and pedagogical works – published an autobiography titled *A Confession*.[3] In this book, he made some 'confessions' about, inter alia, his (and others') aspirations to be or become a teacher. Some of his thoughts deserve our attention.

Tolstoj considered himself a priest of the faith in knowledge. In his words, he 'began to write out of vanity, self-interest, and pride'. In particular, he noted, '[a]s an artist and poet I wrote and taught without myself knowing what I was teaching ... This faith in knowledge, poetry, and the evolution of life was indeed a faith, and I was one of its priests'.[4] Nonetheless, soon doubts stemmed from the realisation that the priests of knowledge did not agree among themselves. In this respect, Tolstoj observed: 'The first thing that led me to doubt was that I began to notice that the priests of this faith did not agree among themselves. Some would say, "We are the best and the most useful of teachers, for we teach what is needful while others who teach are in error." Others would say, "No, we are the true teachers; it is you who are in error"'.[5] Moreover, 'there were many

3 Lev Tolstoj, *A Confession* [1882] (New York and London: Norton, 1983).

4 *Ibid*, 18–19.

5 *Ibid*, 19.

among us who were not even concerned about who was right and who was wrong; they simply pursued their own selfish ends'.[6]

He, thus, realized that teaching was carried out without ultimately knowing what was being taught. In his words: 'I naively imagined that... I could teach all men without myself knowing what I was teaching ... I developed a pathological pride and the insane conviction that it was my mission to teach people without knowing what I was teaching them'.[7] Tolstoj informs us that, even at that time, writers felt that they had to publish as much as possible for the benefit of humankind: 'At the time we were all convinced that we had to speak, write, and publish as quickly as possible and as much as possible and that this was necessary for the good of mankind'.[8] He confessed that this occurred 'without taking note of the fact that we knew nothing, that we did not know the answer to the simplest question of life, the question of what is right and what is wrong, we all went on talking without listening to one another'.[9] In particular, '[a]t times we would indulge and praise each other on the condition that we be indulged and praised in return; at other times we would irritate and shout at each other exactly as in a madhouse'.[10] At the time of writing his *Confession*, in his fifties, Tolstoj could conclude: 'It is now clear to me that there was no difference between ourselves and people living in a madhouse; at the time I only vaguely suspected this, and, like all madmen, I thought everyone except myself was mad'.[11]

(b) *Edgar Morin*

In 1999, at the invitation of UNESCO, the French philosopher and sociologist Edgar Morin published *Seven Complex Lessons in Education for the Future*.[12] A succinct summary of this study may be helpful to introduce what might be considered a UN-sponsored 'international view' on education. As the title specifies, Morin made seven key points.

First, he noted '[t]he purpose of education is to transmit knowledge, and yet education is blind to the realities of human knowledge'. To the contrary, in Morin's view, '[k]nowing about knowledge should figure as a primary

6 *Ibid*, 19–20.
7 *Ibid*, 20.
8 *Ibid*.
9 *Ibid*, 21.
10 *Ibid*.
11 *Ibid*., 22.
12 Edgar Morin, *Seven Complex Lessons in Education for the Future* (Paris: UNESCO, 1999), original French: *Les sept savoirs nécessaires à l'éducation du future* (Paris: Seuil, 2000) <https://unesdoc.unesco.org/ark:/48223/pf0000117740_fre>.

requirement to prepare the mind to confront the constant threat of [either individual or collective] error and illusion' (*First Point*: 'Detecting error and illusion').[13] Secondly, he observed that '[t]he predominance of fragmented learning divided up into disciplines often makes us unable to connect parts and wholes' and that '[w]e should teach methods of grasping mutual relations and reciprocal influences between parts and the whole in a complex world' (*Second Point*: 'Knowing the complex whole').[14] Thirdly, he contended that '[h]umans are physical, biological, psychological, cultural, social, historical beings' and '[t]his complex unity of human nature has been so thoroughly disintegrated by education divided into disciplines, that we can no longer learn what human being means'; however, '[t]he human condition should be an essential subject of all education', so as 'to demonstrate the indissoluble connection between the unity and the diversity of all that is human' and to 'become aware of both [every person's] complex identity and shared identity with all other human beings' (*Third Point*: 'Teaching the human condition').[15] Fourthly, Morin emphasized that '[t]he future of the human genre is now situated on a planetary scale' and, '[w]ithout obscuring the ravages of oppression and domination in the past and present, we should show how all parts of the world have become interdependent' (*Fourth Point*: 'Showing planetary interdependence').[16] Fifthly, he noted that '[w]e have acquired many certainties through science but 20th century science has also revealed many areas of uncertainty' and, consequently, '[e]ducation should include the study of uncertainties' so as to 'teach strategic principles for dealing with chance, the unexpected and uncertain', against deterministic predictions of the future (*Fifth Point*: 'Confronting uncertainties').[17] Sixthly, while '[u]nderstanding is both a means and an end in human communication', he claimed that 'we do not teach understanding'. He suggested that '[m]utual understanding among human beings, whether near or far, is henceforth a vital necessity': 'misunderstandings must be studied' thoroughly, and mutual understanding must be taught 'on all educational levels at all ages' (*Sixth Point*: 'Understanding each other').[18]

Finally, Morin proposed an ethics for teaching in the interest of humankind in the 21st century. In his view, '[a] human being is an individual ↔ society ↔

13 *Ibid.*, 1.
14 *Ibid.*, 1–2.
15 *Ibid*, 2.
16 *Ibid.*
17 *Ibid.*
18 *Ibid*, 3.

species' triad, so that 'individual/species ethics requires control of society by the individual and control of the individual by society; in other words, democracy'. However, '[e]thics cannot be taught by moral lessons', it 'must take shape in people's minds through awareness that a human being is at one and the same time an individual, a member of a society, a member of a species', and '[a]ll truly human development must include joint development of individual autonomy, community participation, and awareness of belonging to the human species'. As a result, he proposed 'the two great ethical-political finalities of the new millennium: [the] establishment of a relationship of mutual control between society and individuals by way of democracy, [and the] fulfilment of Humanity as a planetary community'. In this respect, education 'should help this awareness find expression in the will to realize our earth citizenship' (*Seventh Point*: 'Developing an ethics for the human genre').[19]

(c) *Robin L. West*

In 2013, Robin L. West, an American Professor of Law and Philosophy at the Georgetown University Law Center, published a book titled *Teaching Law: Justice, Politics, and the Demands of Professionalism*, on the teaching of law for the legal profession, in which she discusses the alleged current 'crises' of law schools and scholarship.[20] While it essentially deals with US law schools, the book addresses a situation occurring also elsewhere, and it may be helpful to introduce teaching both in the specific field of *law* and from a *professional* perspective.

First of all, West addresses three possible 'crises' of present-day law schools and teaching: an *economic* crisis (in her words, 'law graduates in large numbers are not finding legal jobs' and 'applications to law schools are dropping', just to mention two points she makes),[21] a *professionalism* crisis ('legal education has worsened' and faculties do not adequately fulfil their presumed functions, that is, to train lawyers and to produce scholarship),[22] and an *existential* crisis ('hav[ing] to do with what law schools *are*, and what they *are not*', and at whose roots is 'the simple fact that the professionals that law schools house ... have no shared collective sense of the *reason* for the law schools' existence – the school's teleological purpose').[23] According to West, the economic and professionalism

19 Ibid, 3–4.

20 Robin L. West, *Teaching Law: Justice, Politics, and the Demands of Professionalism* (Cambridge: CUP, 2013).

21 *Ibid*, 1, 4.

22 *Ibid*, 7–11.

23 *Ibid*, 24.

crises (although real) are not decisive, the 'deeper and long-standing problems' being 'existential'.[24]

As a result, she sees three main challenges to law teaching today: a *justice-inspired* challenge, based on the claim that '[l]aw schools produce amoralists ... ready to sell their services as a hired gun to the highest bidder', rather than focus 'on the ideals of justice that law serves', which leads West to suggest that 'the legal professoriate should regard the concept of justice, in addition to truth, as an ideal toward which the legal academy, in both its scholarly and pedagogical missions, should aim';[25] a *politics-inspired* challenge, when considering that 'law students do not learn anything about the causal relation between politics and law', notably the political origins of law, and that they simply take legal 'sources' as given (thus missing not only the teleological *end* of law, i.e. justice, but also its political *cause*, i.e. politics), noting in particular that 'we discredit, in the minds of students, their own capacity to act as moral agents');[26] and a *practice-inspired* challenge deriving, inter alia, from the fact that 'law schools have seemingly no clear sense of their educational obligations to the profession their students will eventually join'.[27]

In light of the foregoing, West's proposal is that law schools' teaching has to be reimagined, so as to 'hold on to the democratic idealism' and to educate students 'in a way that honors their idealism and respects their political agency ... and their budding professionalism', to 'maintain our commitment to high-quality legal scholarship', and to 'reconsider ... students ... not as the operators of a support industry ... but as a detached, albeit interested, and relentlessly critical fellow traveller[s], on a ... path to a more just world'.[28]

(d) *Anthony Seldon*

In September 2017, giving a talk at the British Science Festival in Brighton, Anthony Seldon, a British historian and Vice-Chancellor of the University of Buckingham, made a case for artificial intelligence (AI) to be used as a learning tool in schools for the future. The interview was later expanded and articulated in the book *The Fourth Education Revolution: How Artificial Intelligence is Changing the Face of Learning*, published in 2018.[29] Needless to say, the issue is

24 *Ibid*, 19.
25 *Ibid*, 25–6, 43.
26 *Ibid*, 25, 99.
27 *Ibid*, 35–6.
28 *Ibid*, 42.
29 Anthony Seldon (with Oladimeji Abidoye), *The Fourth Education Revolution: How Artificial Intelligence is Changing the Face of Learning* (Buckingham: The University of Buckingham

highly topical, as proven by several recent stories. For example, on 9 May 2016 it was reported that at the Georgia Institute of Technology '[a] robot has been teaching grad students for 5 months ... and NONE of them realized'.[30]

In his interview, Seldon stated that, thanks to AI robots, '[a]utomated teaching will soon render traditional academic teaching all but redundant'. In fact, '[e]veryone can have the very best teacher and it's completely personalised ... the inspiration in terms of intellectual excitement will come from the lighting-up of the brain which the machines will be superbly well-geared for' and '[t]he machines will know what it is that most excites you and gives you a natural level of challenge that is not too hard or too easy, but just right for you'.

Seldon noted, in particular, that '[e]xperts predict that automated teaching of maths and science will form the vanguard of machine-led learning, but that sophisticated algorithms would soon be devised to teach the humanities'. As for possible objections to the idea of teaching robots, Seldon observed that teachers' reluctance is due to a technological bias, fear of unemployment and uncertainty over the way in which these can be used. He conceded that 'teachers said they were more sceptical of robots being integrated into the classroom' and 'also wanted full control over the robot', but this depends on 'a technological bias associated with their opinions'. In his view, 'this reluctance may have occurred primarily due to an uncertainty of how best to incorporate robots in the class, and a lingering concern that robots may eventually replace teachers'. Finally, he noted that '[t]he students were much more enthusiastic about a robot in their classroom, enjoying the human-like interaction'. This seems to imply that a 'human-like' interaction is better than a 'human' interaction, a point to be discussed in detail below.

3 What Is 'Teaching' (Ultimately For)?

As noted above, it has been observed that '[w]e are in the midst of a silent, massive, worldwide crisis in education'. In particular, national systems of education are said to be about to produce 'generations of useful machines, rather than complete citizens who can think for themselves[, ... since] in order to

---

Press, 2018). It should be noted that the book is much broader and more balanced than the talk reported above.

30 See <https://www.dailymail.co.uk/news/article-3581085/A-robot-teaching-grad-students-5-months-NONE-realized.html>. The story specified that '[r]esponding to questions over email and posted on forums, Jill Watson [an IBM-designed robot] had a casual, colloquial tone, and was able to offer nuanced and accurate responses within minutes'.

stay competitive in the global market ... [nations] prefer to pursue short-term profit-making'.[31] Before examining such crucial challenge to teaching in general, and to the teaching of international law in particular, it is convenient to address a preliminary question: What is 'teaching' (ultimately for)? Clearly, any possible answer to this question hinges on what is meant by 'teaching', a term that can have a variety of (even opposing) meanings. Let us have a look at six of them.

Firstly, teaching may be understood in terms of *providing information*, that is, as far as law and international law are concerned, in terms of describing facts, rules, doctrines, problems and scholarly solutions. This is undoubtedly the least disputed and the most practiced meaning of teaching, at least in democracies.

Secondly, teaching may be seen as *technical training*, that is, as an activity aimed at skilling learners to perform a certain function. Consequently, according to this meaning, teaching is mainly concerned with 'fixing problems', more precisely 'practical' problems, and with transferring the necessary know-how. In this case, typically, the focus is on how the knowledge that the learners acquire can be translated into a job for them to earn a living. In this context, understanding for understanding's sake is secondary at best and, in any event, strictly functional to problem-solving. Understanding as such, or the understanding of the 'root' or 'inner' causes of problems may even be regarded as counter-productive. Teaching, thus, is aimed at forming 'good'(obedient) workers and bureaucrats, according to the adage 'the less critical, the more efficient'.

Thirdly, teaching may be regarded as *an exercise of critique*, that is, as a deconstruction of the knowledge-construction process itself, which, in international law, requires to expose the underlying 'philosophies' of rules and theories (such as Pragmatism, Positivism, Essentialism, Empiricism, Naturalism, Professionalism, Scientism/Rationalism, etc.) and methodologies (such as the predominance of techno-scientific or industrial-like reasoning, and including the 'philosophies' of international 'critical legal studies' themselves).[32] This deconstructing process may occur both ontologically (when pointing to the 'reality' of rules, theories, societies, etc.) and epistemologically (when referring to the way we 'know' such realities).[33] From this perspective, attention tends

31 Martha Nussbaum, *Not for Profit: Why Democracy Needs the Humanities* (Princeton and Oxford: Princeton University Press, 2010) 1–2.

32 Carlo Focarelli, *International Law as Social Construct: The Struggle for Global Justice* (Oxford: OUP 2012) 112–4.

33 See e.g., among the critical theorists of the well-known 'School of Frankfurt', Max Holkheimer, *Eclipse of Reason* [1947] (London: Bloomsbury, 2013) 21, developing the notion that 'thinking itself had been reduced to the level of industrial processes', on

to shift from knowledge to the very process of knowing. Learners are guided to control the process of knowing itself, to unmask others' uses of knowledge, and to become able to reconstruct their own way of knowing. Compared to the second meaning above, teaching as critique may more easily generate 'critics', if not 'rebels', who, for good or ill, can be perceived as dysfunctional in society.

Fourthly, teaching may be regarded as *communication*, that is, as a tool to transmit ideas, and hence to orientate or shape minds. Of course, teaching, in all its possible meanings, always amounts to a communication process, inasmuch as it necessarily involves the transmission of some knowledge. However, one may specifically focus on teaching's communication process itself. In this sense, teaching is particularly significant in our age of global communication, even more so when it is carried out according to a constructivist approach to law and to international law (to which I will return below). It is a fact that, willingly or not, 'informative' teaching is inevitably also 'formative', and does shape people's beliefs. Moreover, besides providing information and deconstructing narratives, teaching is also an endeavour to *engage* and *attune* with learners, involving a *personal responsibility* of the teacher. This goes beyond the mere description or discussion of topics 'as a profession', in exchange for a salary. Teaching also shapes the minds of teachers themselves, inasmuch as it is a form of reasonable communication with an audience.

Fifthly, teaching may be seen as *reinforcement*, that is, as an activity that, for good or ill, legitimizes existing (political, economic, epistemological) power structures. More often than not, teaching serves this end, whether consciously or not. One reason for this is that teachers live on their salaries, which are hardly provided by employers unless the latter's interests are reinforced. This pressure on teachers may be more or less pronounced and may work only indirectly or subliminally, but it is always present to some degree. Law teachers, in particular, risk reinforcing existing power structures not simply by talking about existing rules, but also by their 'legalese' way of reasoning.[34]

Finally, teaching may be understood as *interaction*, that is, as a form of learning while teaching that occurs by 'auscultating' the learners and exchanging one's views with them. Teachers and learners are often focused on the one-way process of teaching – the teacher on one side and the learners on the other side of such process – but the reverse occurs too. And, of course, teachers are

---

which see James Schmidt, 'The Eclipse of Reason and the End of the Frankfurt School in America' (2007) 100 *New German Critique* 47–76, and Theodor Adorno (n 44 below).

34 Schwöbel-Patel, 'Teaching International Law Critically', cit. (n 1), drawing on Antonio Gramsci's work on cultural hegemony and Duncan Kennedy's work proclaiming legal education as an exercise in the reproduction of legal hierarchy.

supposed to learn first, before being allowed to transmit their understanding to other learners.

So, what is 'teaching' (ultimately for)? I believe that all the above meanings *together* contribute to the right answer. In other words, the idea that teaching is, or should be, only or predominantly about one or a few of these things should be dismissed. Teaching in the first meaning mentioned above is the *conditio sine qua non* of teaching. The second meaning is very popular today, especially at the level of universities and with little distinction between different fields of knowledge. The third meaning is key to cultivate critical and active societies. The fourth meaning develops personal responsibility. Teaching in the fifth meaning is ancillary to creating a social common ground, cohesion and comprehension. Teaching in the sixth meaning, finally, is one of the most valuable sources of inspiration for teachers to *learn* and, in so doing, to improve their competence, morality, sense of humanity, and personal responsibility.

4 The Teacher's Conception of International Law and the Socio-Institutional Framework Surrounding International Law Teaching

The second question to be addressed is whether the teacher's conception of what is taught, including his/her conception of international law, and the socio-institutional framework surrounding the teaching of international law matter. My answer to this question is in the affirmative.

(a) *International Law Teaching as a Reflection of One's Own Conception of Law and of International Law*

Teaching international law is inevitably a reflection or a corollary of one's own conception (or lack thereof, at least at the conscious level) of both law and international law as a whole. Even a teacher who has no fondness or intention to express his/her own vision, but wants to maintain him/herself 'neutral', will inevitably communicate *his/her personal way of being neutral*, among many possible (but different) equally neutral attitudes. For example, the teacher may understand the international law discourse as a scientific enterprise or, alternatively, as (*juris*)prudence: clearly, in the latter's sense, the popular 'scientistic' idea that teaching is independent from what the teacher believes is hardly credible. In terms of 'prudence', teaching cannot and should not pretend to be either a logical or mathematical enterprise. Whatever its scientific or logical soundness, it should rather present itself as a tool based on 'good sense', which is necessary in an inherently ambivalent world to help people live together *in practice*. People are very heterogeneous, for good or ill, and law is supposed to let them live together in their ultimate heterogeneity. To this end, logic and more generally 'scientific/efficientistic thinking' and teaching may be in contradiction with the core meaning of law. There is no way to escape from one's own personal view and responsibility, although it is undoubtedly possible (and, in my view, in principle necessary) to be as sober as possible in teaching one's own ideas, unless there are reasons to the contrary. As Rosalyn Higgins noted in reviewing a 'policy-oriented' international law treatise, 'the difference is one of approach and structure' and 'the materials are best systemised to fit the policy-oriented approach'.[35] In this connection, I can only briefly sketch, and account for, my own conception of international law.

I regard law and international law as social constructions within a systemic and realist-constructivist approach.[36] This implies that they are: (a) collective organized violence of the group (*uti universi*) against the violence of its individual members (including the stronger *uti singuli*) on the basis of the motto '*l'union fait la force*'; (b) a collective belief, i.e. what is believed by the addressee group as a whole to be their law (and, as such, worth of obedience), be it divine, natural, positive or other law; (c) supposed to 'work in practice', i.e. to represent a practical tool, rather than a necessarily logical or moral device, enabling people to live together regardless of its 'rational soundness' from the viewpoint of an outsider or of a given theorist; (d) necessarily reflecting the will of the stronger, that is, invariably the outcome of a social struggle, a struggle that is won by the stronger, not necessarily by the wisest or the more just; (e) being ultimately the subject of (juris)prudence rather than of science at its purest, as is typical of natural sciences. This is not to argue that there is no 'objective' law and no 'scientific' merit in studying international law, but only that common beliefs, and the means to shape them in a community, including the international community, are crucial to the existence and objectivity of international law.

Having this in mind, which is the result of my personal research on law and international law, I will teach accordingly.[37] The point is that I cannot escape from myself, even if I should decide (as is actually mostly the case) to describe

35 Rosalyin Higgins, 'On Teaching International Law' (1983) 9 *Yale Journal of International Law* 409, reviewing Myres S. McDougal and W. Michael Reisman, *International Law in Contemporary Perspective: The Public Order of the World Community* (Mineola, New York: Foundation Press, 1981).

36 Focarelli, *International Law as Social Construct*, cit. (n 32).

37 See e.g. Oscar Schachter, 'The Invisible College of International Lawyers' (1977–78) 72 *Northwestern University Law Review* 217, 218, observing that '[i]nternational law is not a scientific discipline in the same sense as physics or chemistry' since '[i]t is not value-free'.

and discuss rules and other scholars' theories as 'facts'.[38] I will obviously present them as modes of *constructing* international law, or as different modes of *defining* 'law' in the first place. In sum, the popular idea that teaching should be 'objective', and be conducted by having students read and discuss papers written by a variety of scholars as a sort of puzzle of articles taken from different contexts and times, makes little sense and, in any event, does not relieve the teacher from developing his/her own vision of what he/she teaches, if only to provide a reasoned connecting thread among the various reading assignments. The 'puzzle' approach conveys the sense that there is no possibility of reducing international law (and indeed reality in general) to some meaningful unity and coherence; or, alternatively, it conveys the message that international law is indeed a 'puzzle', so that it is only with a puzzle technique that its *variety of possible* foundations may be accurately taught (but then this would be in tension with the entire teaching effort to talk about a certain definable object).

If law and international law are conceived of in constructivist terms, as I do, a special consequence will follow, which is worth mentioning. The humanities will be regarded as key to the legal analysis, even where the latter is considered as a scientific endeavour. In such an approach, pure reasoning is necessary but hardly sufficient. Empathy, emotional attuning, common sense, intuition and inspiration are also of utmost importance in order to 'feel' the law that is believed by a community to be their law. While the law thus unearthed needs to be articulated in rational terms, its very identification is not a mere logical operation. One may also say that reason should not be only critical but also *self-critical*, so that 'rational' teaching can include a meta-rational reflection which is capable of mobilizing *intuitive curiosity* and *personal responsibility* in addition to information and knowledge. Scientific hyper-specialisation, although efficient and necessary, leaves the above (that is, what is *systemic*) unthought. In particular, my personal 'systemic' and 'realist-constructivist' approach accommodates these demands by relying on both realism and constructivism. *Realism* is aimed at safeguarding the ability to resist illusory, ill-founded attitudes towards law and justice, building on the humanities-inspired knowledge

38 I subscribe, in principle, to some of the 'objectivist' remarks that Max Weber expressed during a well-known lecture which is believed to have taken place in 1917, entitled *Wissenschaft als Beruf*, in *Geistige Arbeit als Beruf. Vier Vorträge vor dem Freistudentischen Bund* (München: Erster Vortrag, 1919), English translation: *Science as a Vocation*, in *The Vocation Lectures* (Indianapolis/Cambridge: Hackett Publishing, 2004) 1–31. Among these, for instance, that 'opinions on issues of practical politics and the academic analysis of political institutions and party policies are two very different things', and that 'the prophet and the demagogue have no place at the lectern' (at 20).

of human invariants, including the human urge to survive and win the competition with the surrounding (human and non-human) threats. *Constructivism* is aimed at avoiding any hopeless attitude towards law and justice, drawing from vital, invariable human aspirations to build a common ground enabling humans to live together and which, as said, are detectable in the humanities, especially in the world-renowned masterpieces of arts and spirituality of any time, place and culture. Such works express the human world in its complexity, and law, including international law, is supposed to *work in practice* in the human world as it is.

(b) *Teaching in Today's Universities*

The teaching of international law mostly takes place in universities. It is now time to examine this larger environment and see whether and to what extent it exerts a meaningful influence. The point I would like to make is that, despite some timely (but unheard) authoritative critical voices, such as that of Harvard's President Drew Faust in 2009,[39] universities are today 'cultural' shopping malls selling techno-thinking for a profit, according to the business models of multinational enterprises.[40] A second point I would like to make is to show how teachers are deeply affected by such a model, even if their 'academic freedom' is not apparently restricted by censorship or other forms of direct control.

The fact that universities are thought of as sellers of cultural products and prospective jobs, is supported by overwhelming evidence, including the deep cuts implemented in most universities – especially for the humanities and arts' programmes, which are seen as inessential, too costly and providing only low returns – in particular as a consequence of global economic crises that may themselves be *propelled by the same techno-centred thinking*, or the case of 'Oxbridge' secretly investing offshore.[41] A model of 'education for profit' to

39 Drew G. Faust, 'The University's Crisis of Purpose', *The New York Times* (1 September 2009), noting that 'human beings need meaning, understanding, and perspective as well as jobs'.

40 See e.g. Stefan Collini, *What are Universities For?* (London: Penguin, 2012); Gary Hall, *The Uberfication of the University* (Minneapolis: University of Minnesota Press, 2016); Frank Furedi, *What's Happened to the University? A Sociological Exploration of Its Infantilisation* (London and New York: Routledge, 2017); Stefan Collini, *Speaking of Universities* (London and New York: Verso, 2017); Lawrence Busch, *Knowledge for Sale: The Neoliberal Takeover of Higher Education* (Cambridge, MA: The MIT Press, 2017). With specific regard to the United Kingdom, see Andrew McGettigan, *The Great University Gamble: Money, Markets and the Future of Higher Education* (London: PlutoPress, 2013).

41 Luke Harding and Richard Adams, 'Paradise Papers: Oxford and Cambridge Invested Tens of Millions Off-shore', *The Guardian*, 8 November 2017, at

the detriment of 'education for democracy' prevails.[42] Critical thinking's ability to expose such a model is typically perceived as 'dysfunctional' to economic growth and political obedience, dismissed as unnecessarily 'polemic', or simply understood, along with 'creativity', as 'what businesses need for profitability'.[43]

In supermarketized universities, teachers are supposed to be (or progressively tend to become) loyal *clerks* who have to 'sell' international law to students/purchasers. Teachers are compelled to function as cogs in an industrial machine, for the benefit of the machine as a whole. As cogs, they are required to be 'loyal' to the machine rather than to 'truth', to sell their knowledge and

---

<https://www.theguardian.com/news/2017/nov/08/paradise-papers-oxford-cambridge-invest-millions-offshore-funds-oxbridge>, reporting that 'Funds invested in by the universities include a joint venture to develop oil exploration and deep-sea drilling'; Ed Pilkingdon, 'Top US Universities Use Off-shore Funds to Grow their Huge Endowments', *The Guardian*, 8 November 2017, at <https://www.theguardian.com/news/2017/nov/08/us-universities-offshore-funds-endowments-fossil-fuels-paradise-papers>, reporting that 'Paradise Papers show 12 major universities and colleges invest in Cayman Islands hedge fund pumping cash into fossil fuels'.

42 Nussbaum, *Not for Profit*, cit. (n 31), 13–26.

43 *Ibid*, 137. See recently Joseph E. Aoun, *Robot-proof: Higher Education in the Age of Artificial Intelligence* (Cambridge, MA, and London: The MIT Press, 2017), for an updated, perfect illustration – by the incumbent President of an American university – of the university institution as a supermarket, selling knowledge, as well as 'critical thinking', 'creativity' and even empathy ('a *commodity* much in need in our increasingly global and technologically complex era', emphasis added) while chasing global economic changes rather than changing or contributing to develop a sounder global economy. This approach substantially advertises the idea that, in such a model (termed 'humanics'), adopted at this university, students will win the competition with robot workers by learning 'robot-proof' (genuinely 'uniquely human') skills, so as to 'stay relevant in the AI economy'. Unsurprisingly, the conclusions of such analysis are that 'the dichotomy between learning to live and learning to earn a living' is a 'false choice', and it is time 'to move *beyond* the canard that students must choose between an economically rewarding career and a fulfilling, elevated inner life' (*ibid*, 147–9, emphasis added). In short: 'there is no alternative' (TINA). Of course, there is nothing *intrinsically* bad in wishing that schools train future workers in relevant skills, this falling under schools' functions, nor in using AI devices in education. However, the apparently 'human-inspired' model above, excellent for marketing purposes to attract prospective students/clients who are terrorized by the prospects that robots will replace people in the workforce, is designed to form merely 'skilled', 'happy', obedient workers and docile bureaucrats, who are allegedly made able to win the competition with robots in the workplace thanks to their (economically-driven) 'creativity', and to reinforce (without questioning at all) the prevailing *marketized* vision of the human being (i.e. students and future workers and citizens) and the larger conditions in which human beings have to live. This is precisely the way a supermarket typically operates, while 'higher' education is expected to reason and organize itself differently, if only because there is *no* 'higher' institution designed to do so: to have a look from the outside and to be able to propose a (real) way *out* which is 'novel'.

increase the market value of the machine/university, which allows them to earn a living. Moreover, as cogs, they are required to conform to increasingly stricter standards in terms of pure 'performance', which are gradually transforming them into robotized humans, who furthermore are about to lose the competition with 'true' robots. This trend is irresistibly homologating them towards a sort of pseudo-democratic 'collectivization of the world'.[44] Academic 'pluralism' tends to be blended into the illusionistic landscape of advertising. The model is leading universities to assume techno-thinking or industrial-thinking as the optimal way of thinking, as confirmed by current attempts to 'sell' the humanities as techno-science aimed at 'changing the world' (rather than 'understanding' this same change).[45] Teachers are hired and praised to the extent that they 'argue' according to techno-thinking, even when their field of expertise is in the humanities or social science, as is typically the case with jurists. Not only are such developments shaping teachers, who formally remain uncensored; they are also massively shaping *students* – the same students who are then asked by the system to 'evaluate' teachers – and future *societies*.

In sum, university professors are parameterized like robots, and treated as salaried sellers of (international law) pieces of information, as well as compulsory fund-raisers, nothing more or less than (easily replaceable) cogs in the university industrial machine, or 'door-to-door salesmen and profit-makers for vulgarized versions of their increasingly market-oriented products',[46] encouraged 'to go hat in hand to bureaucrats and private companies in search for funds'[47] and progressively proving inadequate (for the very reason of still being 'human') when compared to AI-fuelled robot teachers.[48] Scientific research, which is closely connected to teachers and how they teach, is

44 Theodor Adorno, *Minima Moralia: Reflections from Damages Life* [1951] (London and New York: Verso, 2005), para. 91.

45 See, for example, the 'Health Humanities' research project at the University of Nottingham, at <https://www.nottingham.ac.uk/research/research-areas/health-humanities/index.aspx> ('The arts and humanities do more than hold a mirror up to human nature or give people a voice: they can change the world').

46 Stefan Collini, 'Impact on Humanities: Researchers Must take a Stand Now or be Judged and Rewarded as Salesmen', *The Times Literary Supplement* (13 November 2009), referring to 'humanists in Britain'.

47 Nussbaum, *Not for Profit*, cit. (n 31), 132.

48 On the application of AI, big data and robotics to education, see recently Neil Selwin, *Is Technology Good for Education?* (Cambridge: Polity Press, 2016); Ben Williamson, *Big Data in Education: The Digital Future of Learning, Policy and Practice* (London: Sage Publications, 2017); Rosemary Luckin (ed.), *Enhancing Learning and Teaching with Technology: What the Research Says* (London: IOE Press, 2018); Rosemary Luckin, *Machine Learning and Human Intelligence: The Future of Education for the 21st Century* (London: IOE Press, 2018).

equally parameterized and funded only inasmuch as it constitutes a practical problem-solving tool, that is, as a strategic means for power which is functional to competitive political, economic, epistemic and epistemological prevalence. For example, research funding agencies do not provide resources for research aimed at questioning this model itself, and place 'impact' at centre stage. Impact means, to first approximation, 'economic impact' and, ultimately, political impact/power. This trend is witnessed at many levels, notably:

(a) by the organizational approach taken in all institutions (including for example, in addition to research and educational institutions, also health care, policing, and social work institutions) which are transformed into markets and corporation-like agencies;
(b) by students being transformed into customers/consumers of knowledge 'products' and treated as investors of 'human capital' seeking a monetary return in the form of higher salaries, with the entire system shifting to a 'user pays'-'user punishes' model;
(c) by an increased effort to improve student 'satisfaction' and teaching assessment based on student evaluations;
(d) by the general simplification of higher education standards according to the requirements of the market and the infantilization of universities;
(e) by unbridled students' plagiarism and ghost authoring, made even easier by the internet, as a result of the shift of university education from citizenship and culture to preparation for a well-paid job;
(f) by universities' obsession with annual rankings, which are similar to quarterly profits, and notoriously largely flawed, illusory, poorly designed and entirely focused on the natural science and engineering, and with metrics accepted at face value;
(g) by outputs and speed requirements which ultimately encourage mediocrity rather than excellence, and conformity rather than diversity, with scholars and university administrators being concerned only with meeting such requirements;
(h) by the ubiquitous emphasis on audits, i.e. with mechanisms traditionally associated with gaining information about financial systems and the financial records of businesses;
(i) by critical thinking being reduced to either useless speculation/polemics or to outright implied self-recognition of one's inability to meet the standards, and being replaced by performance scores and skill learning, or alternatively 'sold' as just another commodity;

(j) by education techniques entirely focused on creating trained automated workers who will be able to perform 'competently' in a given job, rather than educated citizens and autonomous thinkers;
(k) by welfare programs being cut by the (currently 'bossy') *state* against the 'nanny' *state*;
(l) by science and engineering teaching and research being hailed for efficiency and profits, while the humanities and the arts are cut away as 'old-fashioned' and inefficient;
(m) by higher education being managerially controlled by the state on grounds of an efficient use of public funds, through largely opaque and unaccountable bureaucrats, in parallel with 'free market' rhetoric 'against' the state;
(n) by the entire educational system being focused on national economic gain (with the university as a growth machine based on new, generally proprietary, knowledge) subject to a 'teach to the test' exercise;
(o) by research being evaluated on the basis of its estimated (market) value, with its 'quality' being 'measured' and researchers being scored, with rewards and penalties, through the count of publications (hence, the proliferation of academic journals, with the activity of scholars being much more focused on the 'production' of as many published writings as possible than on reading what others have written); the count of citations (though everybody knows, inter alia, that a researcher may be endlessly cited for erroneous or even fraudulent findings); journal rankings, in particular for English-language journals (with declining incentives to publish books, as is most typical in the humanities); the competition for grants (requiring, inter alia, the development of complex, at times strikingly unreliable, bureaucracies for peer review); and an assessment of research in terms of (short-term) future impact (though on such standards most, if not all, acclaimed works of human creativity would have never seen the light, such as Schopenhauer's *The World as Will and Representation*);
(p) by the enormous pressure of the system on research fraud, including plagiarism, ghost and honorary authorship and forced citations by journal editors aimed at gaming the system itself;
(q) by the pervasive conflicts of interest that exist in research funding, development, as well as scholarly governmental and intergovernmental assistance;

(r) by an overflowing epistemological, methodological and linguistic Anglo-American bias;
(s) by higher education institutions' funds being massively used for advertising and marketing to 'sell' universities to prospective students, faculty, research funding agencies, private corporations and donors.

Somewhat surprisingly, academic freedom is still generally viewed as just a matter of 'institutional coercion' or censorship by state or hierarchically superior authorities, rather than a matter of pervasive, 'bottom-up', structural managerialism, at a time when the state itself and politics have undergone a mutation into corporation-like entities.[49] The UN Committee on Economic Social and Cultural rights still views academic freedom as a matter of state obligations to 'ensure' it by taking positive measures, without daring to enter the minefield of economics, and without addressing the question about the reduction of universities (and their staff) to corporations and their manifest dependence on the market (and, in the end, on the state itself that subjects them to the market).[50] Today, the threat is not only the (traditional) political influence on *individual* teachers or scholars by individual institutions (including ministries of higher education, universities, research centres, publishing houses, journals, and so on) but also, and more significantly, the *systemic condition* of virtually all teachers and scholars, who are nowadays 'ruled' by what may be called a market pan-logicism.[51]

49 See Joanna Williams, *Academic Freedom in an Age of Conformity: Confronting the Fear of Knowledge* (Houndmills: Palgrave Macmillan, 2016); Cheryl Hudson and Joanna Williams, *Why Academic Freedom Matters: A Response to Current Challenges* (London: Civitas, 2016). For an analysis of academic freedom as a human right, extending to international law, in particular as part of the rights to free expression and education, see Balakrishnan Rajagopal, 'Defending Academic Freedom as a Human Right: An Internationalist Perspective' (2003) 89 *Academe* 25–8; Jogchum Vrielink, Paul Lemmens, Stephan Parmentier and the LERU Working Group on Human Rights, 'Academic Freedom as a Fundamental Right' (2011) 13 *Procedia – Social and Behavioural Sciences* 117, available online at <https://www.sciencedirect.com/science/article/pii/S1877042811001790>.

50 UN CESCR, 'No. 13: The Right to Education (Art. 13)' of 8 December 1999, UN Doc. E/C.12/1999/10, paras 38–40, stating that 'the right to education can only be enjoyed if accompanied by the academic freedom of staff and students' and that 'staff and students in higher education are especially vulnerable to political and other pressures which undermine academic freedom'. Moreover, according to the Committee, '[t]he enjoyment of academic freedom requires the autonomy of institutions of higher education' consistently 'with systems of public accountability, especially in respect of funding provided by the State'.

51 Carlo Focarelli, *International Law* (Cheltenham and Northampton, MA: Edward Elgar Publishing, 2019), para. 85.9; Carlo Focarelli, 'International Human Rights "in Crisis" and

The system, in fact, is anything but immune from criticism. It has been said, for example, that the 'standards movement' – which 'favors direct instruction of factual information … [i]t is sceptical about creativity, personal expression, and nonverbal, nonmathematical modes of work' – has failed 'the objectives it has set for itself' when considering, inter alia, that 'youth unemployment around the world is at record levels', many graduates are 'saddled with debt', 'there is an ever-widening gap between what schools are teaching and what the economy actually needs', 'few if any of the abilities that the entrepreneurs need are facilitated' by the strategy that movement values so much, and catastrophic consequences have emerged 'on student engagement and teacher morale'. In a word, the movement 'is largely failing by its own terms and creating more problems than it is solving'.[52]

(c) *A Few Examples*

The above picture may be further analysed through a few examples in two countries (United Kingdom and, in particular, Italy).

(1) Research Excellence Framework (REF) in the United Kingdom

It seems that in many British universities departments are anxious about the 2021 Research Excellence Framework (REF). The criteria of evaluations include 'outputs (e.g. publications, performances, and exhibitions)' – a typical industrial term – and the 'environment that supports research'. Those most concerned, apparently, are the humanities departments, especially with regard to the criterion of 'impact beyond academia'. As a result, an 'Impact accelerator' has been devised. Scholars are actually 'encouraged' to highlight and promote their research on social media, and to track the likes they receive, one of the possible parameters to measure impact. The system is said to be either defective but with no plausible alternative, or vastly flawed.[53]

---

the Neoliberalization of the Human Person' (2020) 19 *Chinese Journal of International Law* 53–100.

52 Ken Robinson and Lou Aronica, *Creative Schools* (New York: Penguin Books, 2015) 12–25.

53 For criticism of REF 2014, see Peter Scott, 'Why Research Assessment is Out of Control' (4 November 2013) <https://www.theguardian.com/education/2013/nov/04/peter-scott-research-excellence-framework>, characterising REF as 'a monster, a Minotaur that must be appeased by bloody sacrifices'; Derek Sayer, 'Five reasons why the REF is not fit for purpose' (15 December, 2014) <https://www.theguardian.com/higher-education-network/2014/dec/15/research-excellence-framework-five-reasons-not-fit-for-purpose>. Noteworthy is Derek Sayer's appeal against his inclusion in REF on grounds that excluded colleagues were discriminated against, see <https://www.timeshighereducation.com/news/lancaster-historian-appeals-against-his-inclusion-in-ref/2008570.article>.

(2) Evaluation of Research Quality ('Valutazione della qualità della ricerca', VQR) in Italy

A rough 'replica' of REF in Italy is represented by the 'Evaluation of the Quality of Research' ('Valutazione della qualità della ricerca', VQR).[54] The system is abundantly flawed in many respects. I will point only to a few of them.

The last VQR required teachers/researchers to select 'no more' (rather than 'no less'!) than two 'outputs', i.e. two research works which had been published in the period 2011–2014.[55] A national public body within the Ministry of Education, Universities and Research ('Ministero dell'educazione, dell'università e della ricerca', MIUR), called 'Italian National Agency for the Evaluation of Universities and Research Institutes' ('Agenzia nazionale di valutazione del sistema universitario e della ricerca', ANVUR'), may forward the outputs to reviewers who are selected among 'peers' who have specifically applied for this purpose.[56] The criteria for the selection of reviewers are such that there are no guarantees against the possibility that certain reviewers may be much less competent than the researchers they will review.[57] Even the membership criteria

54 For the Call for Participation approved by the ANVUR's Board of Directors on 11 November 2015 in English, see <http://www.anvur.it/wp-content/uploads/2015/12/Call%20VQR_2011_2014_11nov_~.pdf>.

55 Article 4(3) of the MIUR 'Guidelines VQR 2011–2014' adopted by Ministerial Decree of 27 June 2015 (at <http://www.anvur.it/wp-content/uploads/2015/07/dm_27_06_2015_vqr_11-14.pdf>) specifies that researchers have to 'submit a number of outputs which does not exceed 4 and is not inferior to 2' ('presentano un numero non inferiore a 2 e non superiore a 4') to their respective departments, while it is up to departments to select for any of their researchers 2 outputs to be forwarded to the ANVUR for the evaluation process. Article 5(3) of the Guidelines adds that researchers may submit only 'one research monograph or similar output' rather than two outputs, in which case 'the evaluation of the output will weigh twice' ('Quanto al numero dei prodotti, l'art. 5, comma 3, della Linee-Guida prevede che: al posto di due prodotti si può presentare una monografia di ricerca o prodotto assimilato fermo restando che in tal caso la valutazione attribuita al prodotto peserà il doppio'). In practice, departments have mostly selected the two outputs indicated by researchers as a priority. That is to say, outputs are fundamentally chosen by researchers, who must submit at least two of them but no more than four, and in any event no more than two outputs will undergo the evaluation process (or only one in case of a 'research monograph').

56 Article 5(1) Guidelines (n 55 above) specifies that it is up to the ANVUR 'Groups of Experts of the Evaluation' ('Gruppi di esperti della valutazione', GEV) to forward the outputs to peer reviewers.

57 Article 5(1)(b) of the Guidelines (n 55 above) only states that 'peer-review is attributed to external experts who are independent from one another and jointly chosen by the GEV, as a rule two for each publication [that is, one is also fine], and who are tasked with anonymously pronouncing on the quality of the publications selected' ('peer-review affidata a esperti esterni fra loro indipendenti scelti collegialmente dal GEV, di norma due per

for the 'Group of Evaluation Experts' ('Gruppo di Esperti della Valutazione', GEV) are far from reassuring that their 'quality' will be higher than that of either the reviewers or the scholars being reviewed.[58]

As mentioned, only *two* outputs are required, and there is no difference among 'outputs', nor does it make any difference the total actual number of works published by a scholar, nor, at least in principle, his/her research area (whether it is, for example, physics, sociology or law), which nonetheless has relevance for patterns of research and publication.[59] As a result, the system does not differentiate between, for example, a researcher who may have written two 10-page articles, and another researcher who has written five 400-page books and ten 40-pages articles published in high-profile journals in the relevant timeframe. Of course, the first researcher may well be better than the second one, especially when it comes to 'natural sciences' and related disciplines, in which seminal articles are typically short. However, the difference is

---

ciascuna pubblicazione, cui è affidato il compito di esprimersi, in modo autonomo, sulla qualità delle pubblicazioni selezionate').

58 Article 3 of the Call for serving as experts in the Groups of Experts of Evaluation of 5 May 2015 ('Avviso per la presentazione di manifestazioni di interesse a ricoprire l'incarico di esperto nei Gruppi di Esperti della Valutazione (GEV) per l'esercizio di Valutazione della Qualità della Ricerca (VQR) 2011–2014') (see <http://www.anvur.it/wp-content/uploads/2015/05/call%20GEV%20finale%205_5_2015.pdf>) broadly states that 'scholars, including foreigners, of high scientific qualification who are experts in the field of evaluation and endowed with research experience at the international level may apply' to serve as reviewers ('Possono presentare la propria candidatura studiosi, anche stranieri, di elevata qualificazione scientifica, esperti nel campo della valutazione e dotati di esperienza di ricerca in campo internazionale'). Article 8 specifies that 'in order to establish the membership of the Groups of Experts of the Evaluation, ANVUR will ascertain with priority, albeit not exclusive, candidates to the present call, and will select those who best meet the following criteria' ('Al fine di definire la composizione dei Gruppi di Esperti della Valutazione l'ANVUR valuterà in via prioritaria, ma non esclusiva, i candidati al presente invito, scegliendo coloro che meglio rispondono ai seguenti criteri'): 'Scientific indicators, notably bibliometric indicators where available and appropriate, or indicators of the quality of scientific research, with special regard to the last five years; experience in the direction of research; experience in the evaluation of research; international scientific experience' ('Indicatori scientifici, e in particolare indicatori bibliometrici se disponibili e appropriati, o indicatori della qualità della ricerca scientifica, con particolare riferimento agli ultimi cinque anni; Esperienza nella direzione della ricerca; Esperienza nella valutazione della ricerca; Esperienza scientifica internazionale'). For the components of the GEV with respect to area 12 ('Law'), see <http://www.anvur.it/attivita/vqr/vqr-2011-2014/gev/area-12-scienze-giuridiche>.

59 Point 2.3 of the Call of 11 November 2015 (n 54 above) points out that 'each GEV can further detail the description of the outputs, or limit the list of outputs being eligible for evaluation on the basis of the scientific characteristics of each sector, motivating their choices in the evaluation criteria report'.

generally significant in the humanities and legal studies. In practice, a 'difference' is potentially witnessed only by the second researcher, who must *choose* among the many 'outputs' that he/she has written and generally has no idea about the criteria according to which he/she will be reviewed, or about the identity of the reviewers (who remain anonymous). He/she may thus 'wrongly' choose his/her two outputs based on his/her own perception of his/her work, but his/her 'mistake' will become apparent only at the end of the process, when of course he/she has no more the option to 'change' the low-score outputs with others that are equally eligible and might have scored higher.[60] By contrast, this preoccupation remains alien to the first researcher, who has no choice to make. For the system the two researchers are simply identical, in that both have submitted two outputs. The fact that the second researcher has written many other 'outputs' whereas the first one only the two that he/she submitted, is totally irrelevant.

However, one may suppose that the system will somehow encourage a responsible behaviour on the part of the reviewers. Not at all. They have no obligation to give a motivation and may confine themselves to give a grade (corresponding to excellent, good, fair, acceptable, limited, or not eligible for evaluation, which respectively weigh 1, 0.7, 0.4, 0.1, 0 and 0) and 'a synthetic final evaluation'.[61] Quite foreseeably, a grade without a detailed motivation can be given even without reading the 'output' under review, if only to save time. In addition, the ANVUR sends the two submitted outputs to two different reviewers or couples of reviewers, who have no idea of the other output of the same researcher that is being reviewed by the other, let alone of the entire 'output' or 'production' of the scholar under revision in the relevant period. At the same time, while the reviewers remain anonymous, they know, instead, who is the

60 In fact, Article 5(2) Guidelines (n 55 above) provides for certain criteria that the GEV has to consider for evaluation purposes, including originality, methodological soundness, actual or potential impact in the international scientific community, with regard to international standards of research quality ('originalità, rigore metodologico e impatto attestato o potenziale nella comunità scientifica internazionale, con riferimento a standard internazionali di qualità della ricerca'). These criteria may in the abstract orientate the choice of the outputs to be submitted in order not to make 'mistakes'. However, the possibility of 'mistakes' is never totally ruled out in any field, given that the choice is based on a subjective inferential process. Moreover, the reliability of the above criteria varies considerably with the research area in issue and is notoriously lower in the area of social sciences, in particular in the field of law, than in 'hard sciences'.

61 Under Point 2.6.1. of the Call of 11 November 2015 (n 54 above) 'each peer reviewer will have to write a synthetic final evaluation'.

author that they are reviewing.[62] Needless to say, any kind of *extra ordinem* evaluation is then possible among 'peer' researchers who are in fierce competition with one another. There exists a strong incentive to become a member of the GEV, or at least a reviewer, in order to gain academic power and career opportunities. In other words, the reviewed scholar is accountable for his/her 'bad' outputs, while the reviewers are not for their scores. An essay that has a certain meaning within the larger research activities of a specific scholar may appear less important, or plainly meaningless, when read alone. As a result, the system steers (rather than merely 'evaluate') research and researchers to avoid works that make sense only in a larger (arguably more complex) research project, which may engage the whole academic life of the researcher. The system does not detect this failure.

Despite such flaws, the system goes on as if it were infallible. Critics are regularly discredited simply as people who 'fear' to be tested, so there is no way to express criticism and be taken seriously.[63] The system of 'grades' itself assumes that there is an error-proof graduation of *objective* merit.[64] Flaws are, if ever,

62 See n 57 above. Under Point 3.5 of the Call of 11 November 2015 (n 54 above) '[e]valuation results of single research outputs and the names of their specific reviewers will not be disclosed' but '[a] list of the reviewers will be published within 30 days from the publication of the final VQR Report'. As to Area 12 ('Law'), see <http://www.anvur.it/attivita/vqr/vqr-2011-2014/gev/area-12-scienze-giuridiche>.

63 For sake of clarity, the present writer has 'got' the maximum score at the latest VQR process and may well have an interest and truth in the system described in the text (this footnote was added on 21 October 2022, while the book was in press).

64 The issue of 'meritocracy' has been recently critically discussed by Michael J. Sandel, *The Tyranny of Merit: What's Become of the Common Good?* (London: Allen Lane, 2020). The main thesis of the book is that meritocracy 'is a justification for inequality' (p. 122). The book has been harshly criticised, *inter alia*, for being 'anti-American', as it questions the structural competitive 'ethics' of the United States. However, despite arguing that the tyranny of merit is detrimental to a just society and democracy – to the extent that it promotes 'hubris among the winners and humiliation among the losers' (p. 150) and it fuels populism – the book keeps insisting on 'success in life' (thus proving to be, at least in this very respect, still very 'American' in spirit). It also fails to discuss a key aspect of every meritocratic thesis, that is, what does 'merit' itself means. Throughout history, 'merit' has been regularly (mis)used by certain social groups against others in order to gain or to maintain supremacy, by defining the concept in terms of what those groups simply were better at doing, so as to prevail. Consequently, for Christians, for instance, prayer may have been a 'merit', for capitalists 'money-making', for Communists social equalization, and for Nazis 'not being a Jew'. For engineers, merit may mean 'intelligence' as calculating ability, for poets, instead, 'intelligence' as an intuitive sense able to capture the essence of life beyond any calculations and sophistic rationalizations, and so on. The main gate of Buchenwald's concentration camp displayed the 'meritocratic' motto *Jedem das Seine* ('To each their own'), meaning 'to each what they deserve', i.e. in practice, *according to the Nazis, inter alia* that 'it is right to exterminate the Jews', and 'it is right that the Arians/

explained in terms of practicalities: if all the products of a scholar were admitted for assessment, if the reviewers' motivations were required, etc., the system 'would not work'. Briefly, it is assumed that a failing system is better than nothing, although in certain circumstances 'nothing' (i.e. non-action or a different conception of action) might indeed prove better than arbitrary action based on alleged 'practical' reasons. The pragmatist 'better-than-nothing' approach, in other words, takes for granted that action is invariably better than non-action and that the concept itself of 'action' is to be understood in such a way that it reasonably appears as better than (correlatively defined) non-action. The reason why valuable research was carried out in the past without such a system remains a mystery. Be that as it may, the point is that people *must* believe in the 'objectivity' of the system against 'arbitrary' subjective assessments or self-assessments. In fact, pragmatism is not only a means to adapt to the market, or more generally to the circumstances, it is also a strategy to ban any alternative from the point of conception.

(3) Departments of Excellence in Italy

In 2017, MIUR decided that 180 university departments, out of a ranking list of 352 departments preliminarily admitted to the selection procedure (out of a total of 800 existing departments), should be elevated to the rank of 'Departments of Excellence' and benefit from higher public funding for a five-year period (2018–2022). Departments all over Italy were asked to submit a development research project. Given the scarcity of universities' resources, all departments were very eager to submit their project. They chose the disciplinary area in which they were 'stronger', that is, the area in which they had scored higher than average according to the above-mentioned VQR, and an ad hoc Committee was set up to evaluate the projects.

Nazis dominate the world'. Therefore, Sandel's book seems to fail discussing the very core of the question, beyond the obvious need in any society for a certain degree of differentiation according to merit: the *definition* of 'merit' and of *who* controls it in order to *prevail*, and whether such definition is acceptable or not. The issue captures the very heart of the current 'ethics of success' as the 'right' (in fact, the *predatory*) idol to be believed in (and actually believed in) globally. It is in these terms that, in recent decades, the school and higher education institutions have been recast everywhere (by both right-and left-wing parties) as a system to teach how to become as predatory as possible, including by brandishing 'justice' or 'ethics' or 'human rights' and the like for that purpose. Such predatory behaviour is tacitly the only subject that is taught in practice (underpinning the relatively insignificant variety of officially taught subjects, such as international law) and the only message that is imparted to 'form' the new generations.

As a result, departments were forced, in practice, to specialize in the disciplinary area in which they were 'stronger' *at that moment*, according to the VQR evaluations. This specialization process has inevitably changed departments overnight beyond recognition, with a view to winning resources. In the meanwhile, after the process ended on 31 December 2017, the 180 winning Departments of Excellence have been left to compete on the market with all the other departments.[65] They all highlighted their top-ranking status on their websites as an extraordinary achievement. This would make sense, perhaps, if the VQR were well-founded, but this is not the case, as discussed above. In short, half of the existing departments have become stronger and stronger on the market while the others tend to become weaker and weaker. This 'meritocratic' situation is based on an extemporaneous evaluation carried out by an extemporaneous committee and concerning an extemporaneous 'promise' of possibly ground-breaking research results, rather than being the result of actual accomplishments realized by universities over decades or centuries. Consequently, now in Italy there are 180 *artificially-created* Departments of Excellence, which have been forced to 'specialize' in one subject-area mainly with a view to obtaining the funds necessary to survive, at a time when all departments, over the last decades, *have been progressively substantially deprived* of resources. At best, the process will be repeated in the near future for a further five-year period, and the former Departments of Excellence may be 'downgraded' on account of an 'inadequate' new research project, or simply because of the different membership of the evaluating committee, and compelled to change once again their strategic plans, while *other* (currently less fortunate) departments may be 'upgraded' to 'excellence' and have their day of glory and sufficient funding. At worst, the process will not be repeated, for one reason or another or for no reason at all, so that the present situation will be in fact perpetuated for good (that is, in practice, until a future government once again makes a subverting 'reform' of the system).[66]

Clearly, the mechanisms of both the VQR and the Departments of Excellence affect teachers, including international law teachers. For example, international law may fall among the disciplines which deserve less attention or outright deletion. Perhaps, to contain such 'threats', international law teachers will try their best to 'adjust' their teaching, in order not to be dismissed or treated badly in the departments where they work. The way teaching is carried out

65 For the list of the 180 winning departments see <http://www.anvur.it/attachments/article/1205/All6DElenco180Ammessi.pdf>.

66 The issue has been much debated, see e.g.<https://www.roars.it/online/dipartimenti-di-eccellenza-anvur-secreta-i-calcoli-cantone-se-ci-sei-batti-un-colpo>.

may be informally constrained, or formally forced by departments into a specific mode, as a condition for the department to remain competitive on the market, to grow 'stronger', and to pursue the 'excellence' research project that allows it and its staff to survive and possibly prosper. One may even imagine that 'honest' (or 'idealist') researchers will stay as far away as possible from such a system, so that the system will be actually led by the worst (or the most 'down-to-earth') and most career-oriented.[67]

(4) Vacancy Adverts

University vacancy adverts tend today to be surprisingly similar worldwide, whatever the university and the discipline, parallel to the homologation of universities themselves. By way of illustration, let us take one advert and try to imagine a sort of 'counterpoint' to each one of its main points. I will do so by inserting in square brackets the possible comments (or the underlying rationale) of a highly (but not so unlikely) critical reader or prospective applicant. The advert presented here is 'real' and appeared in January 2018 on the well-known <jobs.ac.uk> website. I will not mention the (British) Law School concerned and call it '*X*' for privacy reasons; in contrast, comments in brackets are invented. As is obvious, in principle such an advert would not pose any significant problem *if* the university were a business, selling, for instance, apples or cars. The comments in square brackets below, on the contrary, reflect the thoughts of a hypothetical applicant who believes that the 'culture' that universities are supposed to promote does not compare to apples or cars, and should not engage people in the same way. The emphasis in the advert's text is added.

At the very outset, the prospective employer praises itself. '*X* Law School … has a distinctive mission – the provision of *commercially intelligent* legal education and research – reflecting our position in a leading international business school and in *a university focused on maximising the employability of its students*' [such self-praising implies that you, the applicant in quest for a job to survive, would be really lucky if selected and would enjoy the honour to be salaried by *X* Law School]. On this premise, the advert goes on as follows: 'We seek an *inspirational* Chair to lead the School's research activities [needless to say, there are many different ways to understand what is 'inspirational', which can also include to be inspired and to inspire others to make money through

67 For a Bartlebian 'I-would-prefer-not-to' reply to the invitation by the ANVUR President extended to lots of university professors to be available to serve as VQR reviewers and the promise to 'receive a nominal fee of 30 Euro including taxes for each item you will review', see <https://www.roars.it/online/vuoi-essere-revisore-vqr-preferirei-di-no>.

selling the notions of a discipline], building on *our* successes in learning and teaching [it is only *us* and *our* successes that matter here; the teacher is only a cog in the wheel, although he/she has to be an 'inspirational' one]. The ideal candidate will be able to develop further the international research and enterprise profile *of the School* [the teacher's only aim must be to expand *our* profile, while her/his *own* profile must be functional/complementary to that of the School; if he/she wants to work, in order to score high in our rankings, according to our criteria, he/she must side-line his/her existence as an autonomous individual; we are simply informing potential applicants, in a transparent and fair way]. According to the advert, '[t]he Professor will be expected to provide academic and thought leadership – based on substantial prior experience in Higher Education – in their area of expertise and will be required to take a significant role in driving the continuing development of Law at *X* [if that was not clear enough, let us remind you: you are nothing]. They will contribute to developing and enhancing the Law and Business Schools' research and external business/professional and policy engagement in law. They will contribute to developing and enhancing *our* engagement activities [*us* again, not you] (with business, the professions and policy makers) and in shaping the impact of *the Law School's* activities [you won't be hired to contemplate the world, but – while still being nothing – you will increase our impact, which means, more funding and control over the students. Forget about studying, researching and teaching for the sake of it]'. The advert continues by noting that 'Applicants should have an *outstanding* record of research publications' in their field of expertise [again: you are and must be no one, and yet you have to be 'inspirational' and 'outstanding']. They should be able to demonstrate *success* (as appropriate to subject specialism) *in attracting funding* from research funding bodies or commercial sources [you also have to be 'successful' in selling yourself to gain funds for *us*; the same funds, moreover, that we are not able to raise in order to pay you], and in supervising and supporting PhD students and research teams. They should have *a strong international profile and network* and the *ambition* to develop that profile within a committed and commercially-focused Law School [if that wasn't enough – and again, remaining a nothingness – you must have not only an international profile, but also the ambition to develop it further; we want you acquiescent, but passionate]. The advert ended with these reassuring words: 'We value your feedback on the *quality* of our adverts. If you have a comment to make about the overall quality of this advert, or its categorisation then please send us your feedback [considering the relevance that this School attributes to the 'quality' of their advert – besides that attributed to the 'quality' of the School itself – how would they take my comment were I to send it? They would find it not pertinent, because what they mean for 'quality' of the advert is whether it is technically clear, etc. My comment would be immediately turned down, with the utmost ease and indifference. This is a typical way to clarify power relations and to say to the person sending his/her feedback, once again, 'you do not exist'. Let us be clear: if we ask you for feedback, it is only *in our interest*]'.

It is now possible to imagine a situation in which virtually all professors of virtually all universities in the world are recruited on the basis of the above rationale and what kind of 'teaching' students will receive. Will such 'teaching' still be worthy of this name? Or, rather, will a very different activity be carried out substantially while 'teaching'? Under such circumstances, would not 'teaching' be just a pretext to make money? Would not this be, in the end, the only true, core purpose of the enterprise? Would not students capture this all-encompassing purpose as the *key message*, whatever the details (such as this or that knowledge of, or this or that piece of information about 'international law')? One could also take a further step and try to conjecture what kind of larger society will 'flow' from such a pervasive 'teaching' and teaching environment. Finally, we could ask ourselves whether we would be happy to live in that society.

Be that as it may, one point seems uncontroversial: this 'system' affects teachers *at root*, driving them in one sole direction, not only *during* their teaching activities but *even before they become teachers*. Clearly, once that this 'global' selection process has been passed, teachers will be very satisfied with the system, for the simple reason that this has co-opted them and they are the 'winners'. Those who disagree are simply deleted as underserving, if not dysfunctional 'rebels', whose only goal is to sabotage an efficient system designed to benefit all. One may also believe that the system is 'pluralistic', and that a deserving applicant who is not hired here may well be hired elsewhere, so that the end result is that all 'good' teachers find a job. However, as said above, all vacancy adverts are very similar worldwide, which occurs because the entire world system places universities in such conditions that they cannot afford to behave otherwise. *This is exactly the opposite of pluralism*. Pluralism is, thus, a sham or, more accurately, just another commodity to be sold on the market. Someone who is critical of the system, such as the imaginary commentator above, will be considered, at best, to be someone who 'exaggerates' things, at worst, a saboteur, if not a terrorist and, in fact, he/she will *never* find a job anywhere unless he/she converts to the only path capable of ensuring a job. Under the circumstances, the 'satisfaction' expressed in surveys by the 'actual' teachers who have been hired, or the students who attend their 'inspirational' lectures, is scientifically quite irrelevant and, once again, a commodity to be sold on the market. Fairness would suggest that also the excluded should be surveyed, but no one knows who and where they are. Nor the 'practical' reasons supporting the system can tolerate different reasons, and this very statistical methodology *itself* is practical. In sum, 'data' will confirm that the system is right and enjoys massive support, with possibly some (ultimately negligible) data apparently going in the opposite direction, so as to reinforce the 'neutrality' (and hence the overall reliability) of the system. Critical voices have no merit by definition. Of course, one may suppose that those excluded are not 'victims' of a bad system but, rather, simply undeserving aspirant teachers. However, even assuming that this were true, it can be safely said that, in any event, those who are hired are 'better' only according to the market parameters expressed in the advert, including their ability to sell their discipline to the greatest possible advantage of the university and its departments.

(d) Education and the Media in International Law

One may ask what international law does to 'correct' the above picture or at least its most extreme effects on learners, and hence on societies and on those who, willingly or not, are engaged in 'constructing' the law, including international law itself. In fact, the media have largely replaced the school as key shaping-mind agencies, and the school, on its part, has been mediatized. One would expect that international law should address the issue of 'just' knowledge and media operating worldwide, but this is hardly the case. International law (lightly) steers and is (strongly) steered by the reality-construction process that occurs through knowledge, education, the media and culture.

Generally speaking, if law depends on what people believe and beliefs depend on what people know, then the reliability of the knowledge available to people is critical to international law.[68] At the same time people expect the law to control the media, rather than the other way around. Knowledge – understood here in broad terms to include information provided by education systems and the media – is today more critical than ever. Both states and global non-state actors compete to shape people's beliefs. Sellers and purchasers of 'truths' naturally abound, while the ability to detect what is fabricated dwindles. What matters is who controls global media, including the internet, and hence global reality. This section provides a few succinct insights into education and the media by discussing the international law rules on the rights to education and to freedom of expression.

---

68 The question addressed here, although related, is different from that concerning the communication of international law through the media, on which see Focarelli, *International Law as Social Construct*, cit. (n 32) 132–9.

(1) *Education*

Education plays a key role in shaping the beliefs of people, and hence has an influence on what they are prepared to struggle for. Whoever controls education also controls, to a significant extent, the behaviour of the mass of people and its impact on local and global affairs. What really matters is not only information, or technical information, but rather the capacity for critical judgment on the information that is available. Information and critical judgment on information are not only distinct, they may even be opposed when the former is allowed to flow, or more precisely to overflow, and actually impede the latter. Elites and businesses in the education sector have little or no interest at all in people who are capable of critical judgment. They prefer people who are flooded by information beyond their capacity to control its flow, including its apparent diversification.

Historically, it was with the advent of the modern secular state in Europe, concomitant with the Enlightenment, that education became a matter of state responsibility. Today, all major human rights treaties establish the right to education, and impose on the states parties a number of obligations.[69] They generally require states to provide free and compulsory primary education, as well as progressive access to secondary and higher education on the basis of merit or capacity. A basic principle in this context is that of equality of opportunity for all in education, including the marginalized and underprivileged such as girls, tribal and indigenous peoples, cultural and linguistic minorities, disadvantaged groups and persons with disabilities, both in developed and developing countries.[70] States not only have a negative obligation not to impair the right to education, but also positive obligations to take steps towards promoting education and, in particular, a duty to protect people's right to education from being impaired by private persons and entities.[71] However, it has been noted that 'Governments are failing to address the root causes of marginalization in education'.[72] The prospects of achieving by 2030 the Millennium Development

69 Klaus D. Beiter, *The Protection of the Right to Education by International Law: Including a Systematic Analysis of Article 13 of the International Covenant on Economic, Social and Cultural Rights* (Nijhoff: Leiden, 2006).

70 See UNESCO Convention against Discrimination in Education (adopted 14 December 1960, entered into force 22 May 1962) 429 UNTS 93.

71 UNHRC, 'The Promotion of Equality of Opportunity in Education', Report of 18 April 2011, UN Doc A/HRC/17/29, paras 19, 46–47, at <http://www2.ohchr.org/english/issues/education/rapporteur>, pointing out that states have obligations not only to respect, but also to protect, and to fulfil (i.e. to facilitate and to provide).

72 UNESCO, *EFA Global Monitoring Report 2010: Reaching the Marginalized* (Paris: Unesco, 2010) 5 (Summary).

Goal No. 4 on 'Quality Education' are up for debate[73] and the 'Education for All' project (EFA) is falling behind.[74] The same applies to the idea to ground education on human rights as stated in the Universal Declaration of Human Rights (UDHR) and in subsequent resolutions of the UN General Assembly, UNESCO recommendations, and the works of the Council of Europe.[75] States are proving either unwilling or simply unable to reach minimum thresholds of equal access to education, let alone advancing critical judgment.

The current worldwide trend towards the commodification of knowledge, under the pressure of international economic institutions and rules, has shifted from pursuing 'truth' in good conscience, to pursuing 'profit' deliberately. In the quest for profit, the system is destined to reproduce itself uncritically without being able to see its own functioning and ultimate direction.[76] The structural adjustment policies promoted by international financial institutions have required the privatization of social services, including education, often causing an increase in school fees and the transfer of costs (from the community, in particular the wealthier) to families. While enrolment in schools in many countries is expanding, fewer and fewer resources are provided by states to ensure the right to education. The inclusion of education (notably higher education as far as critical judgment is concerned) in the services which are subject to liberalization under the GATS has reinforced this trend, despite the flexibility of the GATS.[77] The pursuit of 'efficiency', whether purely economic

---

73 See <https://www.un.org/sustainabledevelopment/education>.

74 UNHRC, 'The Promotion of Equality of Opportunity in Education' (n 71).

75 In the preamble of the UDHR, the UN General Assembly proclaimed the Declaration 'as a common standard of achievement for all peoples and all nations, to the end that every individual and every organ of society, keeping this Declaration constantly in mind, shall strive by *teaching and education* to promote respect for these rights and freedoms' (emphasis added). Paragraph 33(1) of the 1993 Vienna Declaration and Programme of Action reaffirmed that 'States are duty-bound ... to ensure that education is aimed at strengthening the respect of human rights and fundamental freedoms'. Noteworthy is also UNESCO's 1974 Recommendation concerning Education for International Understanding, Cooperation and Peace, and Education Relating to Human Rights and Fundamental Freedoms. With regard to the Council of Europe, it is worth recalling the Charter on Education for Democratic Citizenship and Human Rights Education adopted in the framework of Recommendation CM/Rec(2010)7.

76 See Nussbaum, *Not for Profit*, cit. (n 31).

77 See e.g. Luc E. Weber and James J. Duderstadt (eds), *The Globalization of Higher Education* (London, Paris, and Geneva: Economica, 2008); Vinay V. Mishra, 'Liberalisation of Higher Education Services under the GATS Regime: Implications for a Developing Country' (2009) 42 *Comparative and International Law Journal of Southern Africa* 387–421; Antoni Verger, *WTO/GATS and the Global Politics of Higher Education* (New York and Abingdon: Routledge, 2010).

or of other kinds, in educational matters is often disruptive, and actually meets stiff resistance.[78] It constrains the intellectual and emotional development of a mass of people according to standards (and increasingly to 'global' standards which reflect the cultural traditions and preferences of the global stronger) suited to match the demands of the market, i.e. the purchasing power of the wealthier (who are not necessarily the wiser, let alone the most vulnerable), thereby taking for granted the world 'as it is' as the best of all possible worlds. It is, in fact, the task of education, knowledge, and critical judgment to imagine new (previously completely unimaginable) better worlds, however good the present world may be, and all the more so where the present world is not so good for too many people. Under the present circumstances, the humanities are deemed valuable only in so far as they are able to 'sell' thought and art on the market, without taking seriously that sales hinge on strong demand from purchasers and that it may be precisely the purchasers (among others) who need to take a more critical glimpse at life. Masses of uncritical people, including people who are 'well-educated' according to uncritical global standards or to standards encouraging the sale of 'critical' attitudes to uncritical purchasers, may prove efficient at the workplace, just as slaves may be for the master, but there can be no real democracy when the 'demos' apparently managing the 'cratos' is actually unable (and even left to feel unwilling) to unmask constantly the strategies of the elite in power, whether this remains quite stable over time or changes through elections.

Human rights treaties and monitoring bodies are still pre-eminently construed as being based on states' willingness to comply with existing treaties.[79] They place several obligations on states, including a duty to protect, without providing for powers to meet with their positive obligations. For example, a UN Comment on the right to education has suggested that states are, inter alia, under an obligation to ensure the 'academic freedom of staff and students',[80] without considering that this freedom may actually be largely contingent on private financing and that the alternative to less freedom is no freedom at all. Moreover, the right to education is systematically limited to the individual, and

78 See Dave Hill (ed.), *Contesting Neoliberal Education Public Resistance and Collective Advance* (New York and Abingdon: Routledge, 2008); Mario Novelli and Anibel Ferus-Comelo (eds), *Globalization, Knowledge and Labour: Education for Solidarity within Spaces of Resistance* (New York and Abingdon: Routledge, 2009).

79 See Katarina Tomasevski, 'Globalizing What: Education as a Human Right or as a Traded Service?' (2005) 12 *Indiana Journal of Global Legal Studies* 1–78.

80 See CESCR, 'General Comment No. 13: The Right to Education (Art 13 of the Covenant)' of 8 December 1999, UN Doc. E/C.12/1999/10, para. 38.

the social benefits of education are confined within local and national communities, especially in terms of informed political participation,[81] with little attention being paid to what is to be done to ensure critical judgment in assessing global realities. The content of education is generally left unaddressed.[82] It is also difficult to see how critical knowledge may be subject to 'quality standards', which are tailored to train and obtain information for specific ends, such as how a job is to be done efficiently, according to the standard 'the less critical, the more efficient'.

(2) *Media*

The well-known MacBride Report, approved by UNESCO in 1980 for a New World Information and Communication Order (NWICO), introduced information-and communication-related issues to the global agenda for the first time.[83] The eighty-two recommendations thereby included, which were insisting on the democratization of communications, were favourably received by Third World countries but not by Western states. The former denounced the distortions of Third World realities by the world information system controlled by the West, which was thereby perpetuating inequality and dependence, whereas the latter complained about the use of national or local media by Third World leaders to divert attention from abuse of power and atrocities. Western states contended that their media were free from political power, and thus necessary in order to 'free' oppressed people in the Third World. In fact, the report remained dead letter.

Media power is today concentrated in the hands of few large multinational corporations, as a result of the convergence of both media (newspapers, magazines, books, radio, broadcast television, cable systems and programming, movies, music recordings, video recordings and online services, etc.) and technologies (satellite, cable, the internet, bandwidth, fixed and mobile networks, content digitalization, etc.), as well as of the vertical integration, mergers

81 *Ibid*, para. 1, referring to the education of people as something that gives them a 'means to participate fully in their community', 'one of the best financial investments States can make', and 'one of the joys and rewards of human existence'.

82 UNHRC, 'The Promotion of Equality of Opportunity in Education' (n 71). See para. 6, for the idea that 'the form and substance of education, including curricula and teaching methods, have to be acceptable (e.g. relevant, culturally appropriate and of good quality) to students and, in appropriate cases, parents'. Nowhere does the Comment specify what is meant by 'acceptable' or from whose viewpoint the assessment is to be made.

83 At <http://unesdoc.unesco.org/images/0004/000400/040066eb.pdf>.

and acquisitions that have occurred over the last two decades.[84] Few doubt that Western corporations and states, led by the United States, dominate the world's entertainment and information networks, and that the Western lifestyle is in the process of becoming globalized.[85] Risks of manufactured consent and fabricated information,[86] including scientific information, as well as risks that public attention is diverted away from sensitive issues through convenient entertainment policies, along the lines of the Roman *panem et circenses* ('bread and circuses')[87] are very likely and difficult to keep under control. Those who control information and entertainment also control the psychology and the expectations of workers, consumers, taxpayers, investors and speculators, in short of households, markets and stock exchanges. Self-fulfilling prophecies may be triggered relatively easily to manufacture realities on the basis of any news, whether true or untrue. In international law, the worldwide broadcasting of manipulated information on alleged acts of brutal repression by a given government may be used to mobilize people and trigger the action of international bodies, such as a mandate from the UN Security Council to use military force.

No doubt all states work hard to control the hearts and minds of people in other states. States use the media both to shield information within their own boundaries and to protect their national identity and cohesion, as well as to influence information in other states.[88] Media liberalization entails the fall of national borders with regard to information in-and outflows, and the comparative advantage of those states that have greater opportunities and power to affect the information policy of others, in particular by profiting from their language (today English) as the world's lingua franca. Such liberalization also entails the massive appearance of private media conglomerates on the market. As a result, the states in which these conglomerates are based have an additional (indirect) source of control of the internal cohesion of other states, and all 'messages' (whether private or public) are forced to pass through and be filtered by one or another private conglomerate. The net result is that a few

84 See C. Edwin Baker, *Media Concentration and Democracy: Why Ownership Matters* (Cambridge: CUP, 2007).

85 Daya K. Thussu, *International Communication* (London: Hodder Education, 2nd edn, 2006) 111, 141.

86 Edward S. Herman and Noam Chomsky, *Manufacturing Consent: The Political Economy of the Mass Media* (New York: Pantheon, new edn, 2002).

87 Juvenal, *Satires*, 10, 77–81.

88 Monroe E. Price, *Media and Sovereignty: The Global Information Revolution and the Challenge to State Power* (Cambridge, MA: The MIT Press, 2002) 3–29.

states and the private conglomerates linked to these states, tend to control all knowledge on the planet, and what is in the minds of people worldwide.

The right to freedom of expression and information set out in all major human rights treaties places on the states parties not only an obligation not to control information through monopolies or oligopolies and to ensure pluralism of the sources, but also a positive obligation to prevent excessive concentration of media ownership in private media conglomerates.[89] National and regional antitrust regulations are, indeed, in place, but prove hardly capable of keeping the issue at bay, while a global, legitimate, and effective anti-trust authority is missing. The prevention of concentrations of media ownership should be attained through the adoption of measures aimed at ensuring the 'impartial allocation of resources as well as equitable access to such media', and 'anti-trust legislation regulating mass media'.[90] In 2011, the UN Human Rights Committee referred to the obligation of states 'to ensure that persons are protected from any acts of private persons or entities that would impair the enjoyment of the freedoms of opinion and expression' and 'to prevent undue media dominance or concentration by privately controlled media groups in monopolistic situations that may be harmful to a diversity of sources and view'.[91]

Typical measures contrary to the right to freedom of expression and information are the impairment of basic rights on the basis of someone's actual, perceived, or supposed opinions, be these political, scientific, historic, moral, or religious in nature; the criminalization of the holding of a given opinion; the harassment, intimidation, or stigmatization of persons, including their arrest, detention, trial or imprisonment, because of the opinions they hold; and any kind of effort to coerce people to hold or reject certain opinions. States are required to ensure the free communication of information and ideas about public and political issues between citizens, candidates, and elected representatives.[92] A free and uncensored press or other media is of 'paramount importance' in a democratic society, as is 'the right of individuals to criticize or

89 IACtHR, *Compulsory Membership in an Association Prescribed by Law for the Practice of Journalism (Articles 13 and 29 American Convention on Human Rights)*, Advisory Opinion of 13 November 1985 No OC-5/85, IACtHR Series A No. 5, para. 56; COE, Parliamentary Assembly, Resolution 428 (1970) containing a 'Declaration on Mass Communication Media and Human Rights', para. 8.

90 See UNHRC, 'Concluding Observations on Italy of 3 August 1994', UN Doc. CCPR/C/79/Add.37, paras. 10, 17.

91 UNHRC, 'General comment No. 34 (Article 19: Freedoms of opinion and expression)' of 21 July 2011, in UN Doc. CCPR/C/GC/34, 21 July 2011, paras. 7, 14, 40.

92 *Ibid*, paras. 9–11.

openly and publicly evaluate their Governments without fear of interference or punishment'.[93] Freedom of expression and information covers, in principle, all forms of expression and all means for the dissemination of information, including spoken, written and sign language, and such non-verbal expressions as images and art, books, newspapers, pamphlets, posters, banners, dress, and legal submissions.[94] States are also required to take all necessary steps to foster the independence of the new mass media intermediaries, including internet-and mobile-based electronic information dissemination systems, and to ensure individuals' access to these means.[95] They must ensure that public broadcasting services operate in an independent manner by guaranteeing, in particular, their independence and editorial freedom.[96] All of these obligations are limited only by two sets of legitimate restrictions (nonetheless, to be construed narrowly), i.e. (a) the safeguarding of the rights or reputation of others, and (b) the protection of national security, public order (*ordre public*) or public health or morals.[97]

This legal regime is largely unsatisfactory in terms of what is needed to promote and protect critical knowledge at the global level. First, existing rules focus on limiting state power, but at the same time, quite schizophrenically, require states to do everything in their power to prevent private actors from abusing freedom of expression. What states could do against private abuse is often prohibited by the same rules. Secondly, no provision is made to combat the form of censorship that is inherent in the functioning of the free market itself. In a free market environment, the best goods and services are those which are sold, i.e. which are purchased by those who can afford it, and these are the wealthier, i.e. the stronger. All goods and services which do not attract 'sufficient' purchasers to cover their costs and make a profit, are 'censored'. When media service providers select what information is to be given (in the news, in advertisements,[98] etc.), they cannot but choose what consumers want to be told and, since the media firms basically sell media products to audiences and sell audiences to advertisers, the greater the number of purchasers of

93 UNHRC, *Marques de Morais v Angola* Views of 18 April 2005, Comm. No. 1128/2002, paras. 6.7, 6.8, UN Doc. CCPR/C/83/D/1128/2002.

94 UNHRC, General comment No. 34 (n 91), para. 12.

95 *Ibid*, para. 15.

96 *Ibid*, para. 16.

97 *Ibid*, paras. 21–36.

98 For the view that freedom of expression can in principle be restricted to prevent untrustworthy or misleading advertising, see ECtHR, *Casado Coca v Spain* Judgment of 24 February 1994, App. 15450/89, Series A No 285-A, 18 (1994) EHRR 1, para. 51.

entertainment and information, the higher the profits from the sale of advertising.[99] This 'upstream', hidden censorship, which profoundly affects people's beliefs, is rarely explicitly discussed. What is extensively debated is the need for pluralism within the market environment in which today the state also finds itself. Thirdly, human rights rules do not provide the means to counter the fabrication of an idea of pluralism that resembles any commercial strategy of product diversification by the same covert firm. Today, perhaps, there are less opportunities for overt monopolies, but hidden monopolies abound behind apparent pluralism. Pluralism itself can be sold on the market as a 'brand', like any other. Finally, the private actors operating in the media correspond to a few global conglomerates, and existing rules do not adequately address the impact of their dimension and the resulting effects on local communities.[100]

5 Teaching as 'Living Example' and the 'Human Person'

The third question to address is whether 'living by example' is relevant for the teaching of international law. Here, again, my answer is in the affirmative. Professionalism is of course necessary[101] but hardly sufficient, especially in teaching law and international law.[102] For a teacher who regards law and international law as social constructions, law is basically (empathy towards perceived) justice, and empathy is inextricably linked to personal experience. Empathy is also part of legal reasoning, much more than it is generally believed. For example, many judgments of the European Court of Human Rights may be explained in terms of reasoned empathy, especially when the Court has to define up to what point an evolutionary interpretation of the European Convention on Human Rights (ECHR) is warranted.[103] To teach law requires

99 For the 'special nature' of media products and the view that the standard model of economics (whatever the validity of general critiques thereof) applies particularly badly to such products, see C. Edwin Baker, *Media, Markets, and Democracy* (Cambridge: CUP, 2002) 7–14.

100 For an extensive survey of the ECtHR and comparative (especially British) case law, see Andrew Nicol, Gavin Millar and Andrew Sharland, *Media Law and Human Rights* (Oxford: OUP, 2009, 2nd edn).

101 James R. Crawford, 'International Law as Discipline and Profession' (2012) 106 *American Journal of International Law* 471–86; Jean d'Aspremont, Tarcisio Gazzini, André Nollkaemper and Wouter Werner (eds), *International Law as a Profession* (Cambridge: CUP 2017).

102 Focarelli, *International Law*, cit. (n 51), paras. 1.16, 1.19, 33.7, 85, 236.3.

103 For a nice illustration, see ECtHR, *Oliari et al. v. Italy* judgment of 21 July 2015, Apps. 18766/11 and 36030/11, establishing a positive obligation upon the states parties under Article 8

the teacher to feel in real-time what living together means, and to 'attune' with his/her students and with society at large.

(a) *Teaching International Law as a Profession*

Strict professionalism is a by-product of the prevailing techno-scientific approach to human life, morality, education and law, and focuses on how to be 'a good cog in the machine'. What really matters is the machine and the performance of its functions, ideally for the benefit of all of its cogs, whatever its 'direction' or 'sense'. Both direction and sense are rather understood as 'specific' subjects of 'other' disciplines and professions. As noted earlier, teaching should not be limited to training young people for the job market. Similarly, international law should not be seen only 'as discipline and profession', as though this were the only 'certainties' among endless ambiguities. International law should be presented, inter alia, as a complex and challenging tool aimed at better *understanding* the living together of all human beings on Earth.

It is a fact that nobody can teach more or better than what he/she is. Teachers cannot avoid coming to terms with who they are, and with how they have understood their discipline. To suppose that teaching is a set of methods or techniques that can be applied without any interference of the teacher's particularities, is a dream. The discourse on the teaching of international law based on 'methods and techniques' assumed as valid *regardless of the teacher* makes little sense and ends up relieving both teachers and learners of their responsibilities. There is no optimal abstract way of teaching. Any teaching implies a certain view of the substance. The 'regardless-of-the-teacher' approach is just another industrialist endeavour.

Living by example implies a sense of responsibility, of the 'delicacy and fragility of thinking' and the awareness that 'the self-criticism of reason is its truest morality',[104] with a view to: (a) *feeling* empathy towards all those with whom we have to live together under common legal rules, (b) *acting* rather than just only 'arguing' this or that thesis, and (c) acknowledging the *living* tension and *ambivalence* that underlie any international law theoretical position.

ECHR (right to respect for private and family life) to provide legal recognition for same-sex couples, but without arriving at admitting a similar positive obligation to open marriage to same-sex couple under Article 12 ECHR (right to marry). In other words, the judges of the Court seem to have 'felt' that an evolutionary interpretation of Article 12 ECHR in favour of same-sex marriages was too remote to the general perception at the moment, whereas the broadening of the meaning of Article 8 ECHR so as to cover legal recognition of same-sex couples was not as much remote.

104 Adorno, *Minima Moralia*, cit. (n 44), paras. 81–2.

(b) *The 'Human Person'*

In the teaching process two 'persons' interact, the teacher and the learner, and the ultimate purpose is to shape a better society. Does the teacher see him/herself and the learner as a 'person'? Does the learner see him/herself and the teacher as a 'person'? In this respect, it seems promising to look at the teaching process in terms of the 'human person'.[105]

The meaning of the 'human person' as a general value or, more specifically, as the key foundation of human rights, is much debated, especially in the current of philosophical and theological 'personalism'.[106] The term has been particularly worked out in the Christian theological conception of the human being as an image of the Trinity, which conceives the human as something 'more' than what is revealed by the measurable parameters of the physical sciences. This notion ultimately points to what it means to be human. Thus defined, the term 'human person' is not redundant since it is opposed to the Divine

105 The term 'person' comes from the Latin *persona*, meaning 'mask' and, by implication, the 'character' played by an actor on stage, or, more broadly in colloquial English 'the particular type of character that a person seems to have and that is often different from their real or private character' (*Cambridge English Dictionary*) or 'the aspect of someone's character that is presented to or perceived by others' (*Oxford English Dictionary*). This meaning partly differs from the deeper meaning of *human* person pointing to what it means to be human described in the text. Carl Jung defined it as 'a kind of mask, designed on the one hand to make a definite impression upon others, and, on the other, to conceal the true nature of the individual' (see Carl G. Jung, *Two Essays on Analytical Psychology* (London: Pantheon Books, 1953) 190). In the Italian literature, Luigi Pirandello emphasized that all human beings wear a 'mask' which hides their multiple identities (see Ali Jamali Nesari, Shadi Shahraz, Nabieh Filinezhad and Shamsaldin Jamali Nesarid, 'A Study of the Lack of Identity in Luigi Pirandello's *Six Characters in Search of an Author* and *Henry IV*' (2011) 28 *Procedia – Social and Behavioral Sciences* 896–9). In the movie *Persona* (1966), one of the most enigmatic and enduring masterpieces of the world-renowned Swedish director Ingmar Bergman, the concept of *persona* is deeply represented at many different levels and in virtually all of its implications (see, for an in-depth analysis, Emanuel Levy, 'Persona: Ingmar Bergman's 1966 Masterpiece is among the Films that Made Me Want to Become Critic' (28 May 2016) <http://emanuellevy.com/review/featured-review/persona-1966-ingmar-bergmans-masterpiece-starring-liv-ullmann-and-bibi-andersson>). In marketing and advertising a *persona* is defined as a group or segment of customers (see Bonnie Rind, 'The Power of the Persona' <https://www.pragmaticmarketing.com/resources/articles/The-Power-of-the-Persona>). Of particular interest here are the uses of the verbs 'depersonalize' and 'personalize', the former being relevant in the context of criminals capable of committing crimes through a psychological depersonalization of the victim and the latter being relevant especially in the marketized form of 'customization', which is typical of the 'massified individual' discussed in the text as a further form of depersonalization.

106 See, e.g., Cheikh Mbacke Gueye (ed.), *Ethical Personalism* (Frankfurt/Paris/Lancaster Ontos Verlag, New Brunswick, 2011).

Person. However, beyond its philosophical and theological underpinnings, the term is found – typically together with the expressions 'inherent dignity' and/or 'worth', not further specified – in a number of international instruments, such as in the preambles of the UN Charter (affirming its 'faith in fundamental human rights, in the dignity and worth of the human person, in the equal rights of men and women and of nations large and small') and the UDHR, in the preamble and in Article 10 ICCPR, and in the preamble of the ICESCR, in the 'Martens Clause',[107] and in the 1986 UN Declaration on the (human) right to development.[108] The term has also been used by the ICJ, for instance in its 1970 *Barcelona Traction* judgment[109] and 1996 *Nuclear Weapons* Advisory Opinion.[110] Despite its relative frequency in the international law jargon, the term 'human person' has been poorly analysed by international scholars, who seem to take it for granted, including a few who tend to use it very broadly to defend every possible 'human' cause.[111] It is, therefore, in a secular and legal sense that it will be addressed here.

The 'human person' can be defined as *a limit to any kind of massification*, whether political (either dictatorial or democratic), economic, epistemological, psychic, religious or technological. *Human rights are against (industrial-like) massification*, that is, homologation (and in fact negation) of the individual as such. This is not necessarily to imply that human rights thus defined are 'individualistic' as a product of Western liberalism or, more broadly, civilization. The human person is typically associated with the protection of the

107 The 1977 Geneva Protocol (II), additional to the four 1949 Geneva Conventions on the protection of the victims of war, contains in the preamble the following Martens Clause: 'In cases not covered by the law in force, the *human person* remains under the protection of the principles of humanity and the dictates of the public conscience' (emphasis added).

108 The Declaration, annexed to Resolution 41/128 of the UN General Assembly of 4 December 1986, defines the right to development as 'an inalienable human right' by virtue of which 'every *human person* and all peoples' are entitled to 'participate in, contribute to, and enjoy economic, social, cultural and political development, in which all human rights and fundamental freedoms can be fully realized'.

109 ICJ, *Barcelona Traction, Light and Power Co Ltd (Belgium v. Spain) (Second Phase)* Judgment of 5 February 1970, [1970] ICJ Rep. 3, para 34.

110 ICJ, *Legality of the Threat or Use of Nuclear Weapons*, Advisory Opinion of 8 July 1996 [1996] ICJ Rep. 66, para. 79 ('a great many rules of humanitarian law applicable in armed conflict are so fundamental to the respect of the *human person* and "elementary considerations of humanity"' that 'are to be observed by all States whether or not they have ratified the conventions that contain them, because they constitute intransgressible principles of international customary law', emphasis added).

111 See Antônio Augusto Cançado Trindade, 'The Historical Recovery of the Human Person as Subject of the Law of Nations' (2012) *Cambridge Journal of International and Comparative Law* 8–59.

individual, but much depends on what is meant by 'individual', and individualism may be defended on the basis of very different, even opposite, conceptions of the individual. One has to distinguish the 'massified individual' from the 'individual in his/her uniqueness'.

The former may be intended as the individual acknowledged as a commodity in psychological terms, or as an entity that can always be exchanged with someone else to carry out a function and that is today increasingly driven by artificial intelligence (AI) and mass data (that is, data *massively collected* from a *mass of data* for a *mass of people*), ultimately as (a variable of) an algorithm. In terms of human rights, this massification process and the negation of any distinctiveness beyond the functions that individuals perform amount to the 'inhuman', and to treating human beings as a thing or, more specifically, a cog in the machine. His/her value is equal to his/her ability to perform a function. Nothing else is recognized as relevant and, rather, relegated to the (publicly insignificant) 'private' sphere. Of course, this notion of the individual does not exclude but rather ostensibly welcomes the 'uniqueness' of any individual. However, this same uniqueness is commodified, sold and massified by having people believe that they are unique. It is not uniqueness but the idea of uniqueness that becomes relevant, as long as it can be sold and there are consumers willing to buy it. This process is today culminating in the results of AI and in the global automation that it is leading to,[112] raising inter alia 'moral' issues.[113]

112 A number of interesting (non-binding) instruments on AI and its impact on both the economy and human rights have been recently released by international organizations, including the 'Guidelines on Artificial Intelligence and Data Protection' adopted on 25 January 2019 by the Consultative Committee of the Council of Europe's Convention for the Protection of Individuals with regard to Automatic Processing of Personal Data of 28 January 1981 (so-called 'Convention 108'), <https://rm.coe.int/guidelines-on-artificial-intelligence-and-data-protection/168091f9d8> (accessed 20 July 2019); the Resolution on a 'Comprehensive European Industrial Policy on Artificial Intelligence and Robotic', adopted by the European Parliament on 12 February 2019, <http://www.europarl.europa.eu/doceo/document/TA-8-2019-0081_EN.html?redirect> (accessed 20 July 2019); the Recommendation on Artificial Intelligence, adopted on 22 May 2019 by the OECD Council, <https://legalinstruments.oecd.org/en/instruments/OECD-LEGAL-0449> (accessed 20 July 2019). On 21 April 2021 the EU Commission adopted a Proposal for a Regulation of the European Parliament and of the Council laying down harmonised rules on artificial intelligence, at <https://eur-lex.europa.eu/legal-content/EN/TXT/HTML/?uri=CELEX:52021PC0206&from=EN>). On AI in general see, e.g., Matt Carter, *An Introduction to the Philosophy of Artificial Intelligence* (Edinburgh: Edinburgh University Press, 2007); Keith Frankish and William M. Ramsey (eds), *The Cambridge Handbook of Artificial Intelligence* (Cambridge: CUP 2014); Stuart Russell and Norvig Peter, *Artificial Intelligence: A Modern Approach* (Harlow: Pearson, 2016, 3rd edn).

113 For a recent experiment on 'quantifying societal expectations about the ethical principles that should guide machine behaviour' in making 'moral decisions', see Edmond Awad,

AI requires and *at the same time shapes* the automaton-human: rather than making robots as similar as possible to humans, as it is commonly believed, AI actually makes humans as similar as possible to robots, since it is only in this way AI can work. For example, users of artificially intelligent sex-dolls enthusiastically say that their (silicon-made) 'skin' is incredibly 'almost equal' to that of 'true' women. The process transforms users in beings who appreciate silicon skin more than 'real' (old-fashioned, that is, out-of-market) skin.[114] This is not of course to imply that AI is in itself troubling. A trouble arises only when it becomes impossible to assess, from the outside, AI and its possible flaws in particular circumstances or in certain respects, with particular regard to its intrinsically gregarious logic of functioning.

On the contrary, given 'their uniqueness', individuals are not interchangeable; once an individual is lost, for instance when he/she dies, he/she is lost forever, although others may replace him/her in one function he/she used to perform. Such individual does not equate to a set of functions; he/she feels and conveys a sense of humanity. It seems that this is the true 'weak' that human rights are designed to protect, the individual who is *alone and helpless*. This individual represents both me when I talk (alone, without a category to side ideally with me) and my interlocutor (alone as well, here and now, without an ideal and abstract category to support him/her). The point is how I understand, first of all, *myself* as a human person and, *by reflection*, if and how I understand others as human persons, irrespective of their social (or, more appropriately, mechanical) functions.

The focus on the human person as defined above should be distinguished from other notions that often accompany it, such as 'dignity' or 'worth'. These are culturally-biased and of limited relevance. It has been noted for example that, while all societies possess a conception of human dignity, human rights

---

Sohan Dsouza, Richiard Kim, Joseph Schulzm Azim Shariff, Jean-François Bonnefon and Iyad Rahwan, 'The Moral Machine Experiment' (2018) 563 *Nature* 59–64 (surveying '40 million decisions from millions of people in 233 countries and territories' concerning 'moral dilemmas faced by autonomous vehicles'). Similar studies may be understood as (involuntary) self-fulling prophecies: a mass of people inform the scientists on how they expect machines to make moral decisions, then such expectations are authoritatively published and become 'scientific', hence: (a) people will end expecting what science dictates, and (b) machines will be designed accordingly. The process of analysis is scientific, but the source and the effects of the data are not, when considering that data are collected from masses of people (ultimately) to shape masses of people. It seems, thus, that what is actually at stake is what must count as ethics for *humans* as an aggregate, rather than for machines and the machine discourse is a sham.

114 John Danaher and Nail McArthur, *Robot Sex: Social and Ethical Implications* (Cambridge, MA, and London: The MIT Press, 2018).

specifically express a (Western) 'liberal' conception of life, and that communitarian societies, by giving priority to the community over the individual, 'regard their members as worthy of concern and respect, but only as members of society performing prescribed roles'.[115] In Kant, dignity amounts to treating others as ends rather than means.[116] This is a rational and abstract position, while the human person as defined above goes beyond rationality and embraces empathy.[117] This empathy does not amount to irrationality either, but can be attained especially through the humanities, in particular through widely recognized masterpieces of art and spirituality of all cultures and times.

Clearly, a world where all human beings conceive of themselves and all others as human persons in absolute terms is impossible. To the very least, society requires organizational forms and these reduce the possibility of treating people as human persons in the above terms. Moreover, the human person, as it is understood here, has nothing to do with a Christian-grounded, or romantic, or even anti-technological or anti-organizational vision of how individuals should be expected to behave towards others. Attention drawn on the human person does not necessarily preclude social action, planning and organization. To the contrary, it provides a foundation and a direction to every human action, including the foundation and direction of (international) human rights. So, in what sense is the human person relevant to our purposes? My answer is that, in order not to risk losing the sense of human rights, we have to keep the human person *at centre stage*. This may enable us to see efficiency,

---

115 See Rhoda E. Howard-Hassmann and Jack Donnelly, 'Human Dignity, Human Rights, and Political Regimes' (1986) 80 *American Political Science Review* 801, 808.

116 Focarelli, *International Law as Social Construct*, cit. (n 32) 381.

117 See e.g. Simon Baron-Cohen, *The Science of Evil: On Empathy and the Origins of Cruelty* (New York: Basic Books, 2001) (arguing that 'empathy erosion [this terms is deliberately designed to replace 'the unscientific term "evil"'] is necessary but not sufficient for cruelty to take place'); Martin L. Hoffman, *Empathy and Moral Development: Implications for Caring and Justice* (Cambridge: CUP, 2002, 2nd edn); Michael Slote, *The Ethics of Care and Empathy* (Abingdon: Routledge, 2007); Giacomo Rizzolatti and Corrado Sinigaglia, *Mirrors in the Brain: How Our Minds Share Actions, Emotions, and Experience* (Oxford and New York: OUP, 2008); Frans De Waal, *The Age of Empathy: Nature's Lessons for a Kinder Society* (New York: Harmony Books, 2009); Jeremy Rifkin, *The Empathic Civilization: The Race to Global Consciousness in a World in Crisis* (Cambridge: Polity Press, 2010); Amy Coplan and Peter Goldie (eds), *Empathy: Philosophical and Psychological Perspectives* (Oxford: OUP, 2011); Patricia S. Churchland, *Braintrust: What Neuroscience Tells Us About Morality* (Princeton, N.J.: Princeton University Press, 2012); John C. Gibbs, *Moral Development and Reality: Beyond the Theories of Kohlberg, Hoffman, and Haidt* (Oxford and New York: OUP, 2013). For a discussion of empathy in connection with law and international law, see *International Law as Social Construct*, cit. (n 32) 78–80, 85, 493.

organization, economy, politics, etc. *from the outside* and to keep a 'human' safeguard *constantly alive* and *potentially trumping* other considerations.

(c) *Placing the Human Person, Empathy, and the School at the Centre Stage*

In line with my general approach to international law as a social construction,[118] I would like to indicate how to construct a better law and international law rather than describing the best international law ever. This is not a 'solution', nor a remedy. It is only an invitation to those (including voters and members of international human rights monitoring bodies) who share the above analysis, to struggle for what seems to be a more convenient path to follow. I assume that international law is a process of which we are part. In this context, the key question is: towards which direction should I lean, including in my *plainly scientific* work (as opposed to militant action or idiosyncratic inclinations), once that I have realized that, by expressing my interpretation of the law according to my scientific analysis, I exert some pressure on this process, even when I believe that I do not?

Three elements appear key to correct the system. First, I would place at centre stage the human person as defined above, that is, the 'true' weak, in contrast to the massified individual. I am aware that in a world of 'strong' competitors such as ours, the promotion of 'weak' attitudes amounts to a pious, actually hardly acceptable and ultimately impracticable illusion. I fail nonetheless to see other really credible paths, and we all know that when, in the past, certain attitudes have changed (such as when the previously 'natural' practice of slavery or of racial discrimination/segregation were prohibited), this has occurred as a result of someone's different thinking and acting differently, at the cost of losing (rather than gaining) advantages in the prevailing system as it stood.

Secondly, I would place at centre stage empathy, that is, empathic self-containment, in contrast to massified reason. By 'empathic self-containment', I refer to the capacity of *feeling* (rather than only reasoning about) the hunger of another as equal to my hunger, and consequently my *factual* incapacity, just to give an example, to rush and eat the only piece of bread that is available before us both. Empathy is part of the endowment of the human person and may be used to different ends: either for neoliberalism-driven advertising or omnipresent pressure on competitiveness, with the aim to overwhelm people in their psychic processes; or for dictatorship's practices of torture through 'feeling' and performing the most unbearable acts towards the tortured, in

118 See n 36 above, and the accompanying text.

order to overwhelm people in their body and mind; or, on the contrary, to make people and their relationships become more intimate and meaningful. This same paper is designed as a different narrative of international law teaching. It is an experiment of 'weak' or 'empathically self-containing' writing (i.e. not intended to provide 'strong' reasons to which the interlocutor is invited to adhere, because of their perceived inherent logical irresistibility) which is at the same time 'inspirational' (i.e. not intended to convince, and yet susceptible of inspiring others' thinking and acting) and 'open to rational empathy'. It is, thus, intentionally constructed in such a way that readers attracted to strong 'reasons' will find it *too weak* and possibly guiding them to this weakness. Its underlying assumption is that the form is part of the message: a weak, empathically self-containing message cannot be conveyed by a strong argument, since the end result would simply be, against the intentions, a strong message. This form of expression is best conveyed by the *living example* of the human person and the possibility that it can *inspire* others more than words and reasons (and this same paper) can do.

Thirdly, I would place at centre stage the school, at any level, in contrast to the massified 'cookbooks' now in vogue. A school that is not 'supermarketized' as it is today, this being one of the most abhorrent operations having been conducted in the last decades and still in progress, against which rebellion, in my view, is fully justified. Indeed, the school has always been used by any kind of dominant or totalitarian regimes to shape the minds of current and future societies. Today, the 'old' mind-shaping function of the school has been largely replaced by profit-driven media, and schools themselves, including their staff, have been mostly commodified and mediatized. However, much more than elsewhere, it is in the school as an institution that people are educated to cultivate rational thinking and 'inner eyes' – as opposed to being overwhelmed by the emotions of the moment – to compare and to objectively discuss an endless variety of different perspectives, both synchronically and diachronically. Within a person-centred school, teachers can hardly avoid to ask themselves: if I behave as the current globally marketized system requires me to do, am I still 'human' as I expect others to be towards me? If the answer is no, then teachers should behave differently, i.e. retrieve the human and inspire learners accordingly, especially by their living example, in order to be credible in the first place.[119] A humanities-based school where people are educated on the

119 For a more balanced and still illuminating humanistic vision of education, see Harvard Committee, *General Education in a Free Society* [1945] (Cambridge, MA: Harvard University Press, 1945) (regarding 'the cultivation of the mind as the chief function of the school' while viewing 'reason as a means to the mastery of life' and defining 'wisdom as

basis of data and ideas to comprehend (that is, to progress in the ability of the mind to hold *together*) both *complexity* (that is, the circumstance that one and the same thing can be seen from many, even opposing, points of view at the same time) and *ambivalence* (that is, the circumstance that one and the same thing may have many, even opposing, meanings at the same time), two circumstances surrounding every human aspiration, expression, craftwork and accomplishment.

6 Conclusion

My conclusion is that in teaching international law we should reclaim the human person, referring to both the teacher and the learner, and be able to abandon any industrialist sense of ourselves and the other. I would articulate this as follows.

First, any teacher can and does teach his/her view of international law, or his/her way to see international law's objective data, whatever his/her intentions. The best teaching methods, techniques, goals, strategies, etc. *follow* one's own view (or lack thereof) of the topic to be taught, including international law or a certain view of international law as a whole, not the other way around. Teaching cannot be 'neutrally' the same at any place and time, and whatever the audience may be. Its standardization/automatization risks aligning students, teachers and society at large to hegemonic forms of influence and control against critical thinking. The same discourse on the 'teaching' of international law, and its optimal 'best' standardization, may become itself an instrument of dominating international law 'as discipline and profession'. Language is also important. The adoption of English (or any other dominant language) often forces the use of thoughts and reasoning refrains that automatically distort the perception of non-native-speaking audiences.

Secondly, as a 'human person', the proper teacher is he/she who constantly learns. Teaching is ultimately tantamount to learning, which is inspired by curiosity for life *as a whole*, although it may also be (and indeed is) a profession aimed at forming professionals. What a teacher really teaches is basically how he/she learns.

Thirdly, teaching's 'quality standards' make no sense, especially in the field of law when law is thought of as a 'social construction'. The motto 'teaching to

---

the art of living', as well as pointing to '[r]easonableness [which] does not lead to exciting conclusions because it aims to do justice to the whole truth in all its shadings', at 176).

the test' is said to increasingly produce 'student passivity and teacher routinization'.[120] Standardization tests are demanded by economic growth, but this is poorly correlated with education.[121] In light of the above discussion, it is very difficult to say what should be meant by the 'quality' of teaching. Depending on the circumstances, the 'best' teaching may well be the 'worst' teaching at the same time, and vice versa. The best 'quality' teaching is that which ties the discipline, with its entire toolkit, to the core problems of life, but there are endless (not necessarily in contradiction) approaches to what this core is about, as the humanities testify, and no reliable standards worthy of trumping/censuring others.

Fourthly, teaching is never only equal to 'transmitting', but also to 'reinforcing'. Teachers who 'confine' themselves to transmitting 'realities' as 'givens' and to provide students with 'abilities', end up *reinforcing* current practices and their underlying theoretical underpinnings and interests. One should rather wonder whether the system *itself* is adequate, to what end, and if necessary how it can be reasonably changed. This is to imply that the teaching of international law should include if and how international law changes, and if and how it can change the world for the better.

Finally, living by example is never overrated. Teaching is basically an attempt to shape/inspire other human beings. Hence, (a) the responsibility of teachers against the risk of their de-responsibilization induced by a blind faith in either objectivity or authorities that reward them when they act 'objectively' in the guise of robots; and (b) the absurdity of the very idea of human teachers being 'replaced' by robot teachers and entailing a transformation of human teachers in parameterized 'pseudo-human' robots in such a way that over time nobody is able to 'notice' the difference. The 'human' should remain at centre stage against the 'human-like'. Teachers are called upon to make sense of this very difference simply by their living example.

Bibliography

Adorno Theodor, *Minima Moralia: Reflections from Damages Life* [1951] (London and New York: Verso, 2005).

Ambrosio Thomas, 'Trying Saddam Hussein: Teaching International Law Through an Undergraduate Mock Trial' (2006) 7 *International Studies Perspectives* 159–71.

120 Nussbaum, *Not for Profit*, cit. (n 31), 25, 134.

121 *Ibid.*

Aoun Joseph E., *Robot-proof: Higher Education in the Age of Artificial Intelligence* (Cambridge, MA, and London: The MIT Press, 2017).

Awad Edmond, Sohan Dsouza, Richiard Kim, Joseph Schulzm Azim Shariff, Jean-François Bonnefon and Iyad Rahwan, 'The Moral Machine Experiment' (2018) 563 *Nature* 59–64.

Baker C. Edwin, *Media Concentration and Democracy: Why Ownership Matters* (Cambridge: CUP, 2007).

Baker C. Edwin, *Media, Markets, and Democracy* (Cambridge: CUP 2002).

Baron-Cohen Simon, *The Science of Evil: On Empathy and the Origins of Cruelty* (New York: Basic Books, 2001).

Beck Robert J., 'Teaching International Law as a Partially Online Course: the Hybrid/Blended Approach to Pedagogy' (2010) 11 *International Studies Perspectives* 273–90.

Beiter Klaus D., *The Protection of the Right to Education by International Law: Including a Systematic Analysis of Article 13 of the International Covenant on Economic, Social and Cultural Rights* (Nijhoff: Leiden, 2006).

Bernhardt Rudolf (ed.), *Das internationale Recht in der Juristenausbildung* (Karlsruhe: C.F. Müller, 1981).

Bettwy Samuel, 'Roundtable on the Teaching of International Law' (1991) 85 *ASIL Proceedings of the Annual Meeting* 102–23.

Birkenkötter Hannah and Mirka Möldner, 'The Future of Teaching International Law', *Völkerrechtsblog* (19 May 2014) <https://voelkerrechtsblog.org/the-future-of-teaching-international-law>.

Broms Bengt, 'International Law in the Law School Curriculum', in Ronald St.J. Macdonald (ed.), *Essays in Honour of Wang Tieya* (Dordrecht: Nijhoff, 1994) 79–90.

Busch Lawrence, *Knowledge for Sale: the Neoliberal Takeover of Higher Education* (Cambridge, MA: The MIT Press 2017).

Cançado Trindade Antônio Augusto, 'The Historical Recovery of the Human Person as Subject of the Law of Nations' (2012) *Cambridge Journal of International and Comparative Law* 8–59.

Carter Matt, *An Introduction to the Philosophy of Artificial Intelligence* (Edinburgh: Edinburgh University Press, 2007).

Cheng Bin (ed.) *International Law: Teaching and Practice* (London: Stevens and Sons, 1982).

Cheng Bin, 'How Should We Study International Law?' (1994–1995) 13 *Chinese Yearbook of International Law & Affairs* 214.

Churchland Patricia S., *Braintrust: What Neuroscience Tells Us About Morality* (Princeton, N.J.: Princeton University Press, 2012).

Collini Stefan, 'Impact on Humanities: Researchers Must take a Stand Now or be Judged and Rewarded as Salesmen', *The Times Literary Supplement* (13 November 2009).

Collini Stefan, *Speaking of Universities* (London and New York: Verso, 2017).

Collini Stefan, *What are Universities For?* (London: Penguin, 2012).

Coplan Amy and Peter Goldie (eds), *Empathy: Philosophical and Psychological Perspectives* (Oxford: OUP 2011).

Crawford James R., 'International Law as Discipline and Profession' (2012) 106 *American Journal of International Law* 471–86.

d'Aspremont Jean, Tarcisio Gazzini, André Nollkaemper and Wouter Werner (eds), *International Law as a Profession* (Cambridge: CUP 2017).

Danaher John and Nail McArthur, *Robot Sex: Social and Ethical Implications* (Cambridge, MA, and London: The MIT Press, 2018).

De Waal Frans, *The Age of Empathy: Nature's Lessons for a Kinder Society* (New York: Harmony Books, 2009).

Faust Drew G., 'The University's Crisis of Purpose', *The New York Times* (1 September 2009).

Focarelli Carlo, 'International Human Rights "in Crisis" and the Neoliberalization of the Human Person' (2020) 19 *Chinese Journal of International Law* 53–100.

Focarelli Carlo, *International Law* (Cheltenham and Northampton, MA: Edward Elgar Publishing, 2019).

Focarelli Carlo, *International Law as Social Construct: the Struggle for Global Justice* (Oxford: OUP 2012).

Frankish Keith and William M. Ramsey (eds), *The Cambridge Handbook of Artificial Intelligence* (Cambridge: CUP 2014).

Furedi Frank, *What's Happened to the University? A Sociological Exploration of Its Infantilisation* (London and New York: Routledge, 2017).

Gamble John K. and Christopher C. Joyner, 'Teaching International Law: Approaches Perspectives' (1997) *ASIL Bulletin* No. 11.

Gazzini Tarcisio, 'A Fresh Look at Teaching International Law: a Few Pedagogical Considerations in the Age of Communications' (2016) 29 *Leiden Journal of International Law* 971–8.

Gibbs John C., *Moral Development and Reality: beyond the Theories of Kohlberg, Hoffman, and Haidt* (Oxford and New York: OUP 2013).

Hall Gary, *The Uberfication of the University* (Minneapolis: University of Minnesota Press, 2016).

Harding Luke and Richard Adams, 'Paradise Papers: Oxford and Cambridge Invested Tens of Millions Off-shore', *The Guardian*, 8 November 2017, at <https://www.theguardian.com/news/2017/nov/08/paradise-papers-oxford-cambridge-invest-millions-offshore-funds-oxbridge>.

Herman Edward S. and Noam Chomsky, *Manufacturing Consent: the Political Economy of the Mass Media* (New York: Pantheon, new edn, 2002).

Hey Ellen, *Teaching International Law: State Consent As Consent to a Process of Normative Development and Ensuing Problems* (The Hague: Kluwer Law International, 2003).

Higgins Rosalyin, 'On Teaching International Law' (1983) 9 *Yale Journal of International Law* 409.

Hill Dave (ed.), *Contesting Neoliberal Education Public Resistance and Collective Advance* (New York and Abingdon: Routledge, 2008).

Hoffman Martin L., *Empathy and Moral Development: Implications for Caring and Justice* (Cambridge: CUP 2002, 2nd edn).

Holkheimer Max, *Eclipse of Reason* [1947] (London: Bloomsbury, 2013).

Howard-Hassmann Rhoda E. and Jack Donnelly, 'Human Dignity, Human Rights, and Political Regimes' (1986) 80 *American Political Science Review* 801.

Hudson Cheryl and Joanna Williams, *Why Academic Freedom Matters: a Response to Current Challenges* (London: Civitas, 2016).

Jamali Nesari Ali, Shadi Shahraz, Nabieh Filinezhad and Shamsaldin Jamali Nesarid, 'A Study of the Lack of Identity in Luigi Pirandello's *Six Characters in Search of an Author* and *Henry IV*' (2011) 28 *Procedia – Social and Behavioral Sciences* 896–9.

Joyner Christopher C., 'Teaching International Law: Views from an International Relations Political Scientist' (1999) 5 *ILSA Journal of International & Comparative Law* 377–88.

Jung Carl G., *Two Essays on Analytical Psychology* (London: Pantheon Books, 1953).

Klabbers Jan and Mortimer Sellers (eds.), *The Internationalization of Law and Legal Education*: Ius Gentium *Perspectives on Law and Justice* (New York: Springer, 2008).

Lachs Manfred, *The Teacher in International Law: Teachings and Teaching* (Dordrecht: Nijhoff, 1987).

Levy Emanuel, 'Persona: Ingmar Bergman's 1966 Masterpiece is among the Films that Made Me Want to Become Critic' (28 May 2016) <http://emanuellevy.com/review/featured-review/persona-1966-ingmar-bergmans-masterpiece-starring-liv-ullmann-and-bibi-andersson>.

Luckin Rosemary (ed.), *Enhancing Learning and Teaching with Technology: What the Research Says* (London: IOE Press, 2018).

Luckin Rosemary, *Machine Learning and Human Intelligence: the Future of Education for the 21st Century* (London: IOE Press, 2018).

Mbacke Gueye Cheikh (ed.), *Ethical Personalism* (Frankfurt/Paris/Lancaster Ontos Verlag, New Brunswick, 2011).

McDougal Myres S. and W. Michael Reisman, *International Law in Contemporary Perspective: the Public Order of the World Community* (Mineola, New York: Foundation Press, 1981).

McGettigan Andrew, *The Great University Gamble: Money, Markets and the Future of Higher Education* (London: PlutoPress, 2013).

Mishra Vinay V., 'Liberalisation of Higher Education Services under the GATS Regime: Implications for a Developing Country' (2009) 42 *Comparative and International Law Journal of Southern Africa* 387–4215.

Morin Edgar, *Seven Complex Lessons in Education for the Future* (Paris: UNESCO, 1999), original French: *Les sept savoirs nécessaires à l'éducation du future* (Paris: Seuil, 2000) <https://unesdoc.unesco.org/ark:/48223/pf0000117740_fre>.

Nicol Andrew, Gavin Millar and Andrew Sharland, *Media Law and Human Rights* (Oxford: OUP, 2009, 2nd edn).

Novelli Mario and Anibel Ferus-Comelo (eds), *Globalization, Knowledge and Labour: Education for Solidarity within Spaces of Resistance* (New York and Abingdon: Routledge, 2009).

Nussbaum Martha, *Not for Profit: Why Democracy Needs the Humanities* (Princeton and Oxford: Princeton University Press, 2010).

Orford Anne, 'Citizenship, Sovereignty and Globalisation: Teaching International Law in the Post-Soviet Era' (1995) 6 *Legal Education Review* 251.

Pilkingdon Ed, 'Top US Universities Use Off-shore Funds to Grow their Huge Endowments', *The Guardian*, 8 November 2017, at <https://www.theguardian.com/news/2017/nov/08/us-universities-offshore-funds-endowments-fossil-fuels-paradise-papers>.

Price Monroe E., *Media and Sovereignty: the Global Information Revolution and the Challenge to State Power* (Cambridge, MA: The MIT Press, 2002).

Rajagopal Balakrishnan, 'Defending Academic Freedom as a Human Right: an Internationalist Perspective' (2003) 89 *Academe* 25–8.

Reisman Michael W., 'The Teaching of International Law in the Eighties' (1996) 20 *International Lawyer* 987.

Rifkin Jeremy, *The Empathic Civilization: the Race to Global Consciousness in a World in Crisis* (Cambridge: Polity Press, 2010).

Rizzolatti Giacomo and Corrado Sinigaglia, *Mirrors in the Brain: How Our Minds Share Actions, Emotions, and Experience* (Oxford and New York: OUP 2008).

Robinson Ken and Lou Aronica, *Creative Schools* (New York: Penguin Books, 2015).

Russell Stuart and Norvig Peter, *Artificial Intelligence: a Modern Approach* (Harlow: Pearson, 2016, 3rd edn).

Sandel Michael J., *The Tyranny of Merit: What's Become of the Common Good?* (London: Allen Lane, 2020).

Sayer Derek, 'Five reasons why the REF is not fit for purpose' (15 December, 2014) <https://www.theguardian.com/higher-education-network/2014/dec/15/research-excellence-framework-five-reasons-not-fit-for-purpose>.

Schachter Oscar, 'The Invisible College of International Lawyers' (1977–78) 72 *Northwestern University Law Review* 217.

Schmidt James, 'The Eclipse of Reason and the End of the Frankfurt School in America' (2007) 100 *New German Critique* 47–76.

Schwöbel-Patel Christine, 'Teaching International Law Critically: Critical Pedagogy and Bildung as Orientations for Learning and Teaching', in Bart van Klink and Ubaldus de Vries (eds), *Academic Learning in Law* (Cheltenham: Edward Elgar, 2016) 99–120.

Schwöbel-Patel Christine, 'Teaching International Law', *Oxford Bibliographies* <http://www.oxfordbibliographies.com/view/document/obo-9780199796953/obo-9780199796953-0166.xml>.

Scott Peter, 'Why Research Assessment is Out of Control' (4 November 2013) <https://www.theguardian.com/education/2013/nov/04/peter-scott-research-excellence-framework>.

Seldon Anthony (with Oladimeji Abidoye), *The Fourth Education Revolution: How Artificial Intelligence is Changing the Face of Learning* (Buckingham: The University of Buckingham Press, 2018).

Selwin Neil, *Is Technology Good for Education?* (Cambridge: Polity Press, 2016).

Simpson Gerry, 'On the Magic Mountain: Teaching Public International Law' (1999) 10 *European Journal of International Law* 70–92.

Slote Michael, *The Ethics of Care and Empathy* (Abingdon: Routledge, 2007).

Starbird Caroline, Jenny Pettit and Laurel Singleton, *Teaching International Law* (Denver: CTIR University of Denver, 2004).

Thussu Daya K., *International Communication* (London: Hodder Education, 2nd edn, 2006).

Tolstoj Lev, *A Confession* [1882] (New York and London: Norton, 1983).

Tomasevski Katarina, 'Globalizing What: Education as a Human Right or as a Traded Service?' (2005) 12 *Indiana Journal of Global Legal Studies* 1–78.

Verger Antoni, *WTO/GATS and the Global Politics of Higher Education* (New York and Abingdon: Routledge, 2010).

Vrielink Jogchum, Paul Lemmens, Stephan Parmentier and the LERU Working Group on Human Rights, 'Academic Freedom as a Fundamental Right' (2011) 13 *Procedia – Social and Behavioural Sciences* 117, available online at <https://www.sciencedirect.com/science/article/pii/S1877042811001790>.

Weber Luc E. and James J. Duderstadt (eds), *The Globalization of Higher Education* (London, Paris, and Geneva: Economica, 2008).

West Robin L., *Teaching Law: Justice, Politics, and the Demands of Professionalism* (Cambridge: CUP 2013).

Williams Joanna, *Academic Freedom in an Age of Conformity: Confronting the Fear of Knowledge* (Houndmills: Palgrave Macmillan, 2016).

Williamson Ben, *Big Data in Education: the Digital Future of Learning, Policy and Practice* (London: Sage Publications, 2017).

CHAPTER 4

What Is a Good International Law Teacher?

Natalino Ronzitti

1. As early as in 1982, Judge Lachs in his book on "The Teacher in International Law"[1] pointed out that international law should be understood not only by students, but also by a much broader public. He was absolutely right. There are issues of international law that are very technical (like, for instance, immunities or the principle of domestic jurisdiction), and others that should be dealt with in a less technical way (such as the prohibition of the use of force and aggression). They are of common concern and are employed by public opinion to take a position on a situation.

The study of what is a good law teacher has engaged both writers and learned societies. One can count a number of books on the subject, for instance the book by Michael Hunter Schwartz et al.[2] As far as learned societies are concerned, both ASIL (American Society of International Law) and ILA (International Law Association) deserve to be mentioned. ASIL has instituted an "interest group" on Teaching International Law, and in 2014 a joint ASIL/ILA panel on teaching took place during the annual ASIL meeting. The ILA established a Committee on the teaching of international law (1998–2010) and thereafter continued its work on the topic trough a Study Group.

Should the instructions in this article be valid for every law teacher or does international law possess special features in comparison to domestic law which require more targeted recommendations? The following elements should be taken into consideration by an international law professor when dealing with the relationship between international and domestic law:

- A better relation between international law and domestic law is essential for the implementation of international law.
- If international law is ignored by domestic courts, there is the possibility that the state will commit an internationally wrongful act, for instance if the international norm on state immunity is not applied or human rights are not enforced.

---

1 Manfred Lachs, *The Teacher in International Law* (Springer, 1982).

2 Michael Hunter Schwartz et al., *Assessing Students Book: What the Best Law Teachers Do* (Harvard University Press, 2013).

 | DOI:10.1163/9789004678880_006

- A further possible consequence of international law ignorance at the domestic level is that sometimes international judgments are not executed at the domestic level.
- However, non-application of international law is often due not to the ignorance of the international community legal order, but to the fact that domestic law in a given case prevails over international law, for instance because of the particular strength of some principles of a domestic Constitution. This is what happened in the case of the ICJ judgment in Germany *v.* Italy,[3] where the Italian Constitutional Court stated that the judgment was not enforceable in Italy. This was not due to disregard for international law, but to the fact that the ICJ judgment violated some fundamental principles of the Italian Constitution, first of all the provisions on human rights protection.[4]
- Students who aspire to practise before domestic courts should be aware of the importance of international law as implemented into national systems. There are a number of provisions they are called upon to apply, for instance state immunity from the jurisdiction of local courts.

2. A teacher of international law cannot limit him/herself to lecture only on the formal part of an international law programme such as sources of international law, subjects, settlement of disputes and international responsibility. He/she is confronted day by day with reality and the practice of states that are often at variance with international law as it is written in the textbooks. Usually international relations scholars refer to the world order, a notion which does not necessarily coincide with the international community as understood by lawyers or with the United Nations. International lawyers, too, are not in agreement in identifying the international community with the United Nations.

A very distinctive feature is that the international legal system is more conservative than the world order discussed in international relations theory. While rules of international law change over time and are slow in adapting to new realities and exigencies, the world order, as appraised by international relations scholars, changes more quickly and its governing political rules are promptly adapted to the new reality. This is true not only for customary norms, but also for treaties. Universality as regards important treaties is often a chimera and the United Nations are adopting, more and more, legislative resolutions as a way to circumvent treaty-based rules.

3 *International Immunities of the State (Germany* v. *Italy: Greece Intervening)*, ICJ Reports, 2012.

4 Italian Constitutional Court, 22 October 2014, No. 238. For the English translation see <www.cortecostituzionale.it/documenti/download/doc/recent_judgments/ S238_2013_en.pdf.

The main problem is that often international law norms and international relations rules contradict each other. Take, for example, the US strikes against Syria in 2017 and 2018 (the second time with the participation of France and the UK).[5] From the standpoint of international law they were illegal since they were a kind of armed reprisal prohibited by international law. From the standpoint of international relations one may arrive at a different conclusion: they were a laudable effort against a bloody dictatorship that resorted to the use of chemical weapons and the intervening states put into practice the doctrine of "responsibility to protect". Other examples may be made.

What should a good teacher do in the event of contradiction or inconsistency between a rule of international law and conduct dictated by the world order that allows more prompt and realistic behaviour? Should he/she limit him/herself to pointing out the difference between the two systems? Or, on the contrary, may he/she take a position? Another view that the present author does not share, is to say that a given conduct is legitimate, even though it is not legal, a conclusion endorsed by many lawyers to justify, for instance, the NATO intervention in Kosovo.

De lege ferenda considerations are also important. An international relations approach should be an incentive for taking into account the possibility of reforming the international system.

3. For a long time ethical considerations have been absent from law discourse. Ethics could be the foundation of several norms. However, they cannot be taken into consideration unless the ethical principles are transformed into a rule of law in accordance with the normal process of law production, i.e. custom, treaty and general principles of law of (civilised) nations. The positivist approach was too tight and was an obstacle to the transformation of international law and to its adaptation to new exigencies. It is true that moral principles can find a place in the law-making process, but they have only a residual character. The best example is given by the Martens clause, which was enshrined in the Hague Convention of 1899 No II on respect to the law of war on land and the Preamble to the Hague Convention No IV of 1907 and was restated in subsequent treaties: Protocol I Additional to 1949 Four Geneva Conventions, 1981 Convention on Certain Conventional Weapons, 2008 Convention on Cluster Weapons. According to that clause (as set out in the Hague Convention of 1907):

5 Contemporary Practice of the United States "United States Bombs Syrian Government Facilities in Response to Chemical Weapons Use", (2018) AJIL, 522–527.

"Until a more complete code of the laws of war has been issued, the High Contracting Parties deem it expedient to declare that, in cases not included in the Regulations adopted by them, the inhabitants and the belligerents remain under the protection and the rule of the principles of the law of nations, as they result from the usages established among civilized peoples, from the laws of humanity, and the dictates of the public conscience".

As has been stated by an eminent writer,[6] through the Martens clause moral principles were elevated to the rank of international law norm, and the clause became a kind of process for creating new international law.

Both the general theory and the philosophy of law may contribute to softening the positivist approach and to giving legal relevance to ethical considerations. The instruments are manifold in the UN era and there is the possibility that ethical principles will be substantiated in soft-law provisions before transmigrating into hard-law norms. For instance, the fight against colonialism and the obligation to give independence to colonial peoples were inserted into a series of UN GA resolutions before becoming norms of international law and a principle of *ius cogens* prohibiting the resurrection of foreign/colonial domination.

Other examples may be extracted from the prohibition of genocide and the protection of human rights. Genocide, which was unfortunately perpetrated on a large scale before and during World War II, was the object of the 1948 Convention on the prohibition of genocide and may now be considered to have been endorsed by a norm of peremptory international law, as stated by the ICJ.[7]

Another candidate for transmigration from moral principles to those of law is the notion of responsibility to protect (R2P). The imperative that a state has the duty to protect its own population is already stated in a norm of international law, but a state is not empowered to intervene abroad in order to protect a population or a minority object of persecution by the properly constituted government. Humanitarian intervention is nowadays allowed only if authorised by a UNSC resolution. Nevertheless it is not excluded that this rule be changed and, as many Western governments assert, intervention without SC authorisation could become legal in the future.

The best example of a connection between ethical principles and law norms is given by the human rights movement. Firstly, human rights have been affirmed at the philosophical level; they were then enshrined in a soft-law

6 Giuseppe Sperduti, *Lezioni di Diritto Internazionale*, 68–74 (Dott. A. Giuffrè Editore 1958).

7 ICJ *Armed Activities on the Territory of the Congo (New Application: 2002) (Democratic Republic of the Congo v. Rwanda)*, Judgment, 3 February 2006.

instrument, the 1948 Universal Declaration on Human Rights. Subsequently they have been codified in treaties of both a universal and a regional character. A number of principles established by the Universal Declaration have since been transformed into customary international law.

The examples cited above show that ethical considerations cannot be ignored by a teacher of international law. He/she should only distinguish between what is ethics and what is law, pointing out that often ethical principles can transform into norms of international law of a customary or conventional nature.

4. The academic skill and ability to present a topic should be indispensable qualities of a good teacher. The problem is whether a law teacher should only have doctrinal knowledge or whether expertise based on practising international law is also necessary. It is argued that he/she should have both.

(a) Doctrinal Knowledge

A good teacher should know the relevant literature and keep his/her knowledge up to date. He/she should have a knowledge of most reliable authors and inquire into contending interpretations, taking into account also the minority doctrine. To this end, a good teacher should rely not only on the doctrine of his/her own country, but also on foreign authors. It should be remembered that Article 38 (1) (d) of the ICJ refers to "the teaching of the most highly qualified publicists of the various nations" as a subsidiary means for the determination of the rule of law. Good examples of doctrinal knowledge (or a source of doctrinal knowledge) are the *travaux* of the International Law Commission. The problem with the knowledge of foreign literature is often that books and articles are written in languages that many western students may not be familiar with, such as Russian or Chinese. However, referring to these examples, today more and more Russian and Chinese authors write in English. One is obliged to point out that some common law lawyers prefer to refer only to English literature and common law authors, with the consequence that this narrow approach tends to overlook continental lawyers. For instance, French literature is often ignored by common law scholars. There are journals in English which collect articles written not only by English lawyers but also by French, German and Italian scholars. While this is still not enough to understand the variety of different schools of law and achieve universality it does help one to have a more complete understanding of the discipline.

(b) Practice

Doctrinal knowledge is not enough for one to be a good international law teacher. Desirable expertise can and should be acquired by the practice of international law. It easier for samebody teaching domestic law to practise than it is for someone teaching international law. On the contrary, for international law the opportunities are few and far between. First of all, an international lawyer can give his advice in domestic courts, for example in litigation involving immunities of foreign states and other affairs. The chance to act as arbitrator or counsel before an arbitral tribunal is far more difficult and very few lawyers have the chance to appear in interstate litigation before the ICJ. Regional human rights courts provide a more concrete possibility For instance, many international law professors appear before the European Court on Human Rights or simply advise the parties. Note that a number of judges of the Strasbourg Court are law professors, and that often they resume teaching at the end of their mandates.

Practice may be carried out as an advisor to the Ministry of foreign affairs and other ministries with an international outlook, such as, for instance, the Ministry of defence. Often professors are appointed as members of their national delegations to international conferences. It is even possible that professors are requested to advise Parliament on whether it is necessary to adopt specific legislation to ensure the implementation of a treaty. This can be a very important task, particularly when treaty implementation requires the enactment of criminal legislation.

NGOs can also provide an opportunity for practice. For instance, nowadays mass migration has become a hot issue, including rescuing people on the high seas, often carried out by NGOs' vessels.

Last but not least, the issue of originality deserves a few words. Fresh and original thinking is welcomed and a good and experienced professor may have his/her own vision of the international legal system or parts of it. A good professor is free to present his/her vision and doctrines, especially to postgraduate students. However, he/she should also introduce theories and doctrines he/she does not share. Students should be educated to form their own critical assessments.

A few words follow on practitioners as adjunct professors. They may be very useful to teach a specialised course or part of a general course. In this case, experience is the paramount criterion and all the requirements for a "regular" professor are not strictly necessary.

5. As already pointed out, international law is made up not only of the main formal architecture of the system, i.e. sources, subjects, settlement of

disputes, international responsibility and relations between international law and domestic law. It is also made up of substantive parts, such as the law of the sea, international economic law and human rights/humanitarian law. It is impossible to teach all the issues and solve all the problems in one course. In a general course it is possible only to give an overview of the most important parts of the legal order. If more courses are available, students may follow a specialised course.

The good teacher should teach students the way to solve a problem that they are dealing with, teaching them how to find the relevant literature and case law. Legal clinics are of paramount importance in this connection.

Method is therefore very important. It should provide the key to solving a problem and to reaching a conclusion. More refined methodology may be employed in a specialized course. In such a course it is possible to teach students how to solve a case when practising before a domestic tribunal or an international court or how to behave as an advisor to an international conference.

6. Should a teacher be "conservative" or try to present innovative solutions? Such solutions may help to create new treaty law or even new directions for judges. Take, for instance, the issue of foreign state immunity from domestic jurisdiction. An innovative solution has been proposed by the Italian Court of Cassation[8] and endorsed by the Constitutional Court. It was held that state immunity may be disregarded if a war crime amounting to a violation of a peremptory norm of international law has been committed. The problem is whether the innovative solution is followed by a substantial number of jurisdictions. In the case in question, the Court of Cassation's reasoning was not upheld by the ICJ or by the domestic courts of other states. Only recently a few exceptions can be counted due to the courts of Greece, Brazil, South Korea and Ukraine

That said, we believe that prospecting innovative solutions is very important for stimulating students, namely those who will become members of Parliament, judges or diplomats. Obviously, an innovative solution should be put forward which points out the pros and cons of its adoption. Innovative solutions are often *de lege ferenda* assessments of a case.

7. Academic freedom should be a "must" for a teacher and for teaching. It is at the same time a right and a duty. Unfortunately, academic freedom is a value that cannot always be enjoyed. International law is strictly connected

8 *Ferrini* v. *Federal Republic of Germany*, Court of Cassation, 11 March 2004, (2005) AJIL, 242–248. For the ICJ and the Italian Constitutional Court judgments see *supra* notes 3 and 4.

with international relations and international politics and is not "neutral". For professors of more technical fields, for instance civil procedure, it is easier to maintain academic freedom since their topic does not in principle impact on politics, as happens for international law.

Authoritarian regimes do not permit or protect academic freedom. Democracies, on the other hand, allow it and both free writing and free speech are guaranteed. However, this privilege is often disregarded by law professors for a number of reasons, some of which could even be labelled opportunistic. Take the case of a professor teaching and at the same time practising on behalf of his/her government. How is he/she supposed to criticise his/her government and present a different position to the classroom?

A further problem originates from teaching at universities located in non-democratic (or even dictatorial) countries. Local teachers may be obliged to espouse the policy of the authoritarian regime as far as governmental claims are concerned. Otherwise they run the risk of being fired. What about a foreign teacher coming from a democratic country? If he/she is obliged to endorse tthe view of the authoritarian regime, the invitation to teach should be declined. The same is true if serious critical review is not allowed. Nevertheless, there is always a chance of finding a middle ground. For instance, the topic of human rights cannot be ignored in a general course. The teacher is by no means obliged to assess the conduct of the hosting state according to human rights parameters, a task that can be undertaken by his/her students once they have understood the basis of the course and are in command of the relevant instruments (the Universal Declaration on Human Rights, the two Covenants, applicable regional treaties, etc.).

The extreme situation happens when an oath to the government is required by the regime in power. This happened in Italy during Fascism. Those who refused were fired. Nowadays professors are still civil servants, but they are no longer obliged to take an oath of loyalty to the government like other civil servants.

8. A list of tips is given for obtaining and hopefully keeping the attention of students. Obviously, the list is not exhaustive and other recommendations may be put forward.

Examples are as follows:

(a) Teachers should prepare their lectures according to the requirements of each class (for instance beginners' or postgraduate courses);
(b) Teachers should declare from the beginning what they expect from their students;
(c) Teachers should explain why international law is important:
  - for finding a job;

– for dealing with international law cases that a domestic lawyer is also occasionally called upon to decide (for instance state immunity).

(d) Teachers should explain that international law is an obligatory subject for admission to the bar (this depends on the state/region where admission is sought); international law is a subject of paramount importance for some international professionals, for instance diplomats, members of international law firms, legal advisors to government or to international organisations, etc.

(e) A good teacher should provide/indicate teaching materials for students, a task facilitated by the modern techniques of communication. Textbooks are also important since they help students to grasp the basic principles. A good textbook should perform the task of being an easily available reference work. Not every teacher is asked to write a textbook. However, he/she may give a critical assessment of solutions given in the works of others.

(f) Inviting guest speakers is recommended, in particular for those topics that are highly specialised. The same is true for workshops, which are necessary to test the preparedness of students and help them to critical appraisals. Moot Court competitions, for instance, are a common law experience to be adopted.

9. Teaching experience should be acquired domestically and abroad. Comparisons are important and the experience obtained abroad could be a way to improve lectures at one's own university. Teaching abroad also means exchanging views with colleagues and foreign students. Mention should also be made of courses at the Hague Academy of International Law. This is a unique institution, since students from every part of the world attend courses there. The teaching is very challenging and enriches the experience of the lecturers, which may be used at their own universities. Note that at the Hague Academy a professor is called on to give formal lectures as well as to direct seminars. This means that discussions are open to students coming from all regions of the world.

In a provocative opinion recently published by the New York Times and entitled "Those Who Can Do, Can't Teach", Adam Grant[9] cites the example of Albert Einstein, the father of relativity, who was never considered "an inspired teacher" and whose lectures "tended to be regarded as disorganized". He

9 New York Times 2018/08/25 (https://www.nytimes.com/2018/08/25/opinion/sunday/college-professors-experts-advice.html).

therefore proposes that a good teacher have fresh knowledge of his/her material and be able to master and communicate it, a talent possessed by young people and not just by experienced teachers. However, an international law teacher is usually able to communicate, since in many cases he/she practises before a Court or acts as a delegate to international conferences. It is thus to be admitted that practice and teaching are mutually reinforcing.

10. The teaching of postgraduate students may have distinctive features. I will choose two examples of where it may take place: (a) schools of public administration (civil servants) and (b) military academies.

(a) It is assumed that civil servants have a degree in law. A good teacher should focus on those principles and provisions which help civil servants solve problems that have an international aspect. This implies, for instance, that the techniques for implementing international law into domestic law must be assessed with examples drawn from treaties relevant to the country. The same is true for customary international law. A further relevant topic is related to the technique of treaty negotiation, how to draft a MOU, etc. Human rights and state responsibility are also important. Human rights should be implemented and applied in the domestic legal order and decision-makers should be informed about conduct that may possibly violate international law.

(b) The main courses that an international law professor teaches in military academies pertain to international humanitarian law and the law of armed conflict, a task that has become very important with the evolution and complexities of the latter. It requires a knowledge of the law of war on land, naval warfare and air warfare. Developments need to be kept in view, for instance as far as cyberwarfare is concerned. A good teacher should single out not only treaties, but also those provisions which have become customary international law. This is very relevant for countries that are not party to important treaties of international humanitarian law. For instance, the US is not a party to Protocols I and II additional to the 1949 Geneva Conventions. It is important for states parties to those Protocols to assess which norms have to be considered to be customary international law. In multinational operations (for instance NATO operations), military action may give rise to the international responsibility of the states which are party to a humanitarian treaty, while those which are not cannot be held responsible. The same is true for the use of weapons forbidden by treaties not ratified by all the parties to the same military action.

A teacher should maintain his/her academic freedom even if he/she teaches military students and should not abstain from criticising actions that he/she holds to be at variance with international law.

11. Finally, something must be said about student international law journals. They are a characteristic of US universities, but are also gaining ground in Europe, mainly through online journals. Student journals are a good way of deepening knowledge of international law and of helping students to grow accustomed to writing. Writing is important for a variety of reasons: first of all for students' future careers as judges, practising lawyers and diplomats. Reviewing articles submitted to journals stimulates the students' critical approach. Contributors may be experienced professors, students, especially postgraduate students, and alumni.

12. I say a few words by way of conclusion. Identifying a good international law teacher cannot be encapsulated in a formula. I have given a number of tips. First of all, academic freedom is to be considered paramount. Competence, obviously, is a *sine qua non* element of a good professor, who should have a vast knowledge of all subjects of international law. He/she should also have experience, which means experience in teaching and practising. For younger professors, however, expertise is achieved day by day and may be acquired over time. Finally, I think that dedication to the classroom is a paramount virtue that professors should show by preparing their lectures and paying attention to the questions of students. Dispensing appropriate knowledge and preparing students to approach the real world are challenging tasks that a good teacher should never ignore. Teaching has been put under strain by these hard times and the pandemic emergency (Covid 19). Good teachers have had the opportunity to show their ability in lecturing online and organizing webinars, tasks which strongly hint at the type of skills they may have to refine in the future.

Bibliography

Broms, Bengt International Law in the Law School Curriculun, Ronald St. John Mc Donald (ed.), *Essays in Honour if Wang Teya* (Brill, 1994), 79–90.

D'Apremont, Jean *International Law as a Profession* (Cambridge, 2017).

Gamble, John King Teaching International Law in the 1990s (ASIL, 1993).

Gazzini, Tarcisio A Fresh Look at Teaching I*nternational Law. A Few Pedagogical Considerations in the Age of Communications*, (2016) Leiden Journal of International Law, 941–978.

International Law Association, Committee on Teaching of International Law (1998–2010), https://www-ila-hq.org/en/committees/index.cjd/Icfm/cid/I009.

Klabbers Jan and Mortimer Sellers, The *Internationalization of Law and Legal Education,* (Springer, 2009).

Lachs, Manfred *The Teacher in International Law* (Springer, 1982).

Nienaber, Annelize A Presumptuous Beginner; Some Thoughts on Teaching International Law at Undergraduate Level for the First Time, (2012) South African Yearbook of International Law, 301–313.

Roberts, Anthea *Is International Law Internat*ional?(Oxford, 2017).

Schwartz Michael Hunter et al., *Assessing Students Book: What the Best Law Teachers Do* (Harvard University Press, 2013).

CHAPTER 5

Is There an Art of Teaching International Law?

Pierre-Marie Dupuy

I will give here a few considerations the merit of which is, by definition, relative. This is only a personal view, necessarily subjective, no more. Now, in law as elsewhere, as a general rule, as Blaise Pascal said, "the self is hateful". If I am led to make an exception here, it is precisely because the authors of this book have asked me to report on the conclusions that I draw from my own experience in teaching international law. This is also the reason why reference is made in this chapter to works of a number of which I am myself the author, and I apologize in advance for this. My experience may have been considered of some interest in that my career has been conducted in different academic settings, in different languages, before different audiences, in relation to each of the main areas of international law, and often in direct relation to my own practice of international law as State counsel or as an international arbitrator.

I was trained in the teaching of public law and political sciences, in particular constitutional, administrative, and international law, in the French tradition according to rather strict and codified canons, allowing me to pass, after writing an in-depth thesis, the "Concours d'agrégation des facultés de droit". I also taught in Spanish at the Complutense University in Madrid, in English at Michigan University (Ann Arbor Law School), in German at the Ludwig Maximilian University in Munich, before teaching in French, English, and sometimes even Italian at the European University Institute in Florence. I was on leave at my request from my own university, the University of Paris (Panthéon-Assas), to which in every sense of the word I remain attached. I staid in Florence for eight years as a professor and PhD supervisor before finishing my academic career in Geneva at the "Graduate Institute of International and Development Studies".

The foregoing indicates in passing two elements which, in my opinion, are of importance in order to appreciate the teaching of a branch of the law which, in principle, aims at universality. The first is that one teaches in part in a different way depending on the legal tradition in which one has been trained but also depending on the academic framework within which one expresses oneself.[1] A French professor addressing a German audience will have to adapt and

1 Even within Europe, the diversity of legal cultures should not be underestimated as demonstrated in particular in Peter Hilpold (Edt.) *European International Law Traditions*, Springer, 2021.

 | DOI:10.1163/9789004678880_007

try to take into account, as far as his or her means allow, the academic tradition specific to the environment in which he or she is speaking. The second element is today partly (but only partly) eroded by the fact that English as a language has become the *lingua franca* of international law almost everywhere in the world. Whatever the case may be, the fact remains that the language which one speaks has a direct impact on the conceptual baggage that one uses to transmit a particular piece of knowledge. However, in addition to the fact that the concepts used in this discipline are not necessarily the same from one language (and legal tradition) to another, not all professors are equally multilingual. This contributes to the fact that everyone tends to use, even in a foreign language, the legal (or philosophical) concepts with which they are most familiar.[2]

Yet, to take only a few examples, "legal system" is only a rather approximate equivalent of "ordinamento juridico" in Italian or "ordinamiento juridico" in Spanish; moreover, "principe de légalité" is not really identical to obedience to the "rule of law", just as the latter does not exactly cover the concept of "Rechtsstaat". As was experienced in contentious cases before the ICJ, the best authors trained in the common law tradition will not hesitate to speak spontaneously of "mitigation of damages" without bothering to check systematically whether this notion is truly received in international law in the same way as it is in the tradition to which they belong, starting implicitly from the viewpoint that international law is for a good part merely an extension of common law (which, with due respect, it is not)!

Although this tends to diminish greatly depending on the generation to which the authors belong, many are still aware, in Europe in particular, of the distinctions or nuances that exist between many of the legal concepts used from one language to another. Similar scruples are more rarely found in the United States. Such an attitude is not always the expression of a lack of comparative law culture; but the use of a language – especially English, because of its contemporary diffusion – naturally leads those who have spoken it from childhood to believe that it is their way of thinking that has triumphed and takes precedence over all others. I have been able to observe this in particular during my teaching of and discussions with students, but also with, at least, some of my colleagues in the United States. I also saw it in the conception and drafting of their pleadings by lawyers and government counsel from various backgrounds with whom I teamed up to defend the interests of a particular State before the International Court of Justice. The same remark could, *mutatis*

2 E. Roucounas, A Landscape of Contemporary Theories of International Law, Brill/Nijhoff,(2020), in particular at 100–133.

mutandis, be made on the occasion of the deliberations of arbitral tribunals in which I have participated and still participate.

In general, one should be aware that everyone tends to start implicitly from the intimate conviction that he or she has learned law from the strongest, richest, and most rigorous legal tradition: one's own! Nevertheless, attendance at academic institutions and/or teams or academic associations involving internationalists from very different backgrounds help to combat this unfortunate conviction. The same applies to reading works written in different languages and traditions. One challenge for the doctrine and teaching of international law is that the universality of international law can be truly guaranteed only if the diversity of the intellectual modalities of its practice and teaching is maintained, even if all those interested in it should be able to understand each other to a large extent.! A good part of some impassioned discussions in international colloquia thus stems from the persistence of conceptual misunderstandings: for example, whether there is a "constitution" of public internal law [3]!

How should one teach international law? This is, of course, the question facing all those whose task it is to impart a discipline that is often poorly perceived by the student public, which remains influenced by the tenacious belief that international law either does not really exist as such or is affected by intrinsic weaknesses of such importance that they radically undermine its application. The first objective of any teaching in this field, whether it concerns the presentation of the main features of international law or whether it focuses on a particular area (e.g. human rights, environmental law, law of the sea, investment law), is therefore to make the audience understand that it is a true "legal order"; an order whose technical means are on the whole as elaborate as those of a domestic law and whose character and functioning are reflected in the way it is applied.

At least two requirements result from what has just been said: the first is that, in one way or another, any teaching of international law presupposes, depending on the case, a systematic exposition or simple reminder of what a "legal order" is, as defined by authors such as Triepel, Anzilotti, Kelsen, Santi Romano, Duguit, Geny, Scelle, Lauterpacht, Hart, and a few others.[4] The second consequence is that the study of international law is first and foremost the study of the law as it is in force: with regard to each question

3 See CEDIN-Paris X, *La Charte des Nations Unies, constitution mondiale ?* (2006), 267p. ; P.M.Dupuy, The Constitutional Dimension of the Charter of the United Nations Revisited, *Max Planck Yearbook of United Nations Law*, (1997) vol. 1, 1–33.

4 See P.M.Dupuy, RdC, Hague Academy of International Law, L'Unité de l'ordre juridique international, Cours général de droit international public, (2002),Vol.297, 59–77.

under consideration, the examination of positive law remains indispensable. This seems to be true whatever the limits are of legal positivism as a doctrinal school, one of the ordinary shortcomings of which consists in cultivating the fantasy that it is itself free of all ideological and political a-priorioriousness, which is obviously inaccurate.[5]

After having taken up these two points, legal order and positive law, we will always conclude that certain current tendencies encourage us to think that the teaching of international law can react against certain doctrinal tendencies that we might have thought for a moment mislead it.

1 International Law as a Legal Order

The proportion to be accorded in a course to the demonstration that international law is a legal order depends, of course, on the general subject matter of the course, depending on whether it is general or specialized.

What is important, in my view, is to make students understand from the outset that international law is not simply a more or less chaotic accumulation of norms, each of which can only be envisaged in itself, regardless of the normative context and the connecting techniques that link it to others within international law. To use Jean Combacau's very telling expression in an article that has unfortunately remained unknown to too many readers, international law is not a "junk shop" but a normative system organized by "rules of the game" and "rules within the game."[6] It is a set in which, whatever one's starting options, there are pre-established types of relationships between norms, which Herbert Hart has defined particularly well, even if he was then clearly caught off guard by the specificity of international law itself, in which he did not know or did not want to see a legal order.[7] A mistake commensurate with the talent of this remarkable author, since this law, like other laws, has "primary norms", setting out obligations "to do" or "not to do", empowerments as well as substantial prohibitions, just as it has "secondary norms" whose function is precisely to enable the management of primary rules, whether it be to recognize them,

5 Ibid., 25–38.

6 See J. Combacau, Le droit international, bric-à-brac ou système ? (1986) *Archives de philosophie du droit* 85.

7 See H. Hart, *The Concept of Law,* Oxford, Clarendon Law Series, 5th Ed.,1984, 77f ; see also Norberto Bobbio, Nouvelles réflexions sur les normes primaires et secondaires, *Essais de théorie du droit,* Bruylant/LGDJ (1998), 159f. ; Comandi e consigli, in *Studi per una teoria générale del diritto,* Torino, Giappichelli (1970) 49.

create them, transform them, abolish them, or draw normative consequences from their violation.

In other words, little can be understood about the system of sources in international law or, even more so, among other examples, the law of the international responsibility of States if one has not understood how a legal order is composed and "how it works". But, particularly through the theory of norms of recognition, it is also from the perception of what such a normative order is that one can grasp the question of the relationship between domestic law and international law or that of the differences between public and private international law.

Moreover, from the point of view of the philosophy of international law and the identification of what "law" itself is or, more broadly still, what a normative phenomenon is, it is again necessary to have recourse to the central notion of a legal order whose theoretical extensions are manifold.[8] Finally, last but not least, the question of the birth of an international legal order or several international legal orders is itself directly linked to the history of international law; it is also central, in particular to understanding the phenomenology of this law in the very sense that Husserl gave to this expression.[9] In short, to teach international law without resorting to the concept of a legal order would be tantamount to wanting to teach music without studying harmony. The score to be deciphered would then become difficult to understand, with the consequences that one can imagine for its execution!

To be even more precise, one can understand in part how much the question of the so-called "fragmentation" of international law may have occupied so many good minds for at least twenty years by the fact that the theory or theories of law are insufficiently taught, particularly in certain academic traditions which it is useless to name here.[10] It is also in connection with this state of affairs that many talented young people specialize too soon in this or that field of international law, designating their chosen field by reference to the freedom of their choice. Here we see the link, both fundamental and more complex than it seems, between "general international law" and "specialized international law".

8 See D. Alland, De l'ordre juridique international, *Droits,*(2002), Vol. 35, 79f.

9 See P. Amselek, *Le monde du droit et des règles en général,* Paris, Armand Colin, (2012), 674 p [???].

10 ILC, 'Conclusions of the work of the Study Group on the Fragmentation of International Law: Difficulties arising from the Diversification and Expansion of International Law' in Yearbook of the International Law Commission (2006) Vol II, Part Two, UN Doc A/61/10, 177–184.

We will take this opportunity to point out how certain problems of interpretation of the rule of law require particular attention, in connection with the question of what gives normative coherence to international law as a legal order. Of particular interest here is the place to be given to the rule laid down in Article 31(3)(c) of the Vienna Convention on the Law of Treaties that any treaty obligation of a State must be interpreted in the light of its other relevant obligations under other treaty instruments or customary international law.[11] This provision may be seen as a general principle of integration of the law or as a mere measure of interpretation. The second is probably, partly for functional reasons, how the International Court of Justice will most probably continue to see it, which could be decisive for its influence in the years to come. In any event, as a matter of teaching, consideration of this rule and its theoretical and practical implications will make it possible to address the question of the correlation and coordination of obligations in respect of separate subjects in the international legal order.

The question of the relationship between general law and particular areas is in any case far from neutral. It is linked in particular to the theory of the sources of international law, one of the main elements of the legal order to which it belongs. Thus, many narrowly specialized internationalists will tend to be convinced that there is ultimately some sort of implicit hierarchy between treaties and custom, some even going so far as to reduce the latter to the bare essentials, or even to a source in danger of extinction! However, while it is true, as is also explained elsewhere, that a functional hierarchy can be found between one source and the other, particularly within Article 38 of the Statute of the International Court of Justice, the contemporary dynamism of custom should not be underestimated.[12] It will be reiterated later that many of these doctrinal trends are also partly related to the distance of their authors from any contentious practice of international law.

In general, it is important, as far as possible, to relate certain fundamental theoretical issues to their practical extensions. It is true that law must be based on a thorough knowledge of legal theory, but it can only be defined, explained, and commented on on the basis of a rigorous analysis of positive law, as it is in force and actually practiced.

---

11 See Campbell McLachlan, The Principle of Systemic Integration and Article 31, 3 , c of the Vienna Convention, in *The International and Comparative Law Quarterly*, Vol. 54, N°2, (2005) 279–319 ; P.M.Dupuy, *2000–2020: twenty years later, where are we in terms of the unity of international law? Cambridge International Law Journal*, July 2020.

12 See P.M.Dupuy *op.cit. supra* fn 1, at 121.

II International Law as Practice

Without going into in-depth developments here, even if the notion lends itself to it, it is important to list a few reminders concerning the notion of "positive law".[13] In the general theory of law, it can be approached in various ways but, generally speaking, its origins can be found in Emer de Vattel, who already stated in his Principles of the Law of Nations that "these three species of law of nations, voluntary, conventional and customary, together make up positive law of nations. For they all derive from the will of Nations: voluntary law, from their presumed consent; conventional law, from express consent; and customary law, from tacit consent. And, since there can be no other way to infer any right from the will of Nations, there are only these three kinds of positive people's law. »[14]

Even if this Vattelian conception can only be understood by reference to "natural law", it already highlights the linkage of a definition of positive law both with its sources and with the will of States. Subsequently, the distinction between positive law and natural law was particularly stressed by Dionisio Anzilotti;[15] then, following him, internationalists of strict voluntarist obedience such as Proper Weil had to return to the importance of the notion, to distinguish it from what they designated as not directly binding and, in fact, fundamentally indeterminate as to its legal value, namely what has been called "soft law".[16]

The link between "positive law" and "legal order" is no longer to be stressed, since positive law is also traditionally defined as "the law actually in force within a given legal order, following a process of creation or modification established by that legal order".[17] It is so true, as we have seen above, that it is useful to return periodically to the concept of "positive law" in the light of successive developments in its practice.

---

13 Klaus F. Röhl, Hans Christian Röhl: *Allgemeine Rechtslehre.* 3. Auflage, C. Heymanns, Köln (2008) § 34 I, 291.

14 See E. de Vattel, *Le droit des Gens ou principes de la loi naturelle,* Paris, Guillaumin (1863) Préliminaires, paragraphe 27, 105–106 ; see V.Chetail &P.Haggenmacher, *Vattel's International Law in z XXIst Century Perspective/Le droit international de Vattel vu du XXI°siècle,* The Graduate Institute/Geneva, Martinus Nijhoff Publishers, (2011), notamment P.M.Dupuy, Vattel et le droit des traités, 151–166.

15 See D. Anzilotti, *Cours de droit international,* premier vol. Introduction, Théorie générale, Traduction Gidel, Paris, Sirey (1929) 181.

16 On P.Weil's article see https://www.cambridge.org/core/journals/american-journal-of-international-law.

17 See J.Salmon (Edt.), Dictionnaire de droit international public, Bruylant/AUF,(2001) 391.

Another illustration of the direct link between "legal order", "positive law" and the theory of the sources of international law is of course perpetually illustrated by any teaching on the origins and characteristics of customary international law.[18] Contrary to what some people claim, international non-treaty law has lost none of its force, despite the very considerable increase in the number of treaties and, moreover, the uncertainties surrounding the "opinio juris sive necessitatis" in the present era.

The question of the definition of "positive law" is in any case both distinct from and closely related to that of the conditions for its creation. Thus, in the contemporary era, the question of the impact of "international civil society" and non-governmental organizations on the creation of international law remains linked to that of the inevitable recourse to the final manifestation of the assent of States to the consecration of a new rule of positive law.[19] Thus, far from being abstract, the unavoidable study of positive law also provides an opportunity to return to demanding theoretical and technical questions which it would be wrong to believe can be overcome by remaining in a more or less controlled conceptual vagueness.

This is the case, among many other examples, with the study of the international law of State responsibility.[20] From the latter point of view, as from that of all the other areas which have been the subject of codification efforts within the United Nations framework as a result of the work of the International Law Commission, it is obviously particularly interesting, following the various Special Rapporteurs concerned, to compare, on the one hand, the conduct of States with regard to the rule of law and the interpretation they give to it with, on the other hand, international case law as commented upon and explained by the doctrine.

Judicial practice is in many respects as decisive as that of States, inasmuch as the role of the judge proceeds from their assent. The study of the evolution or even the ruptures or contradictions of international jurisprudence is particularly stimulating for the study of any question of international law and the richness of the contribution of the Permanent Court of International Justice as

18 See P.M.Dupuy &V.Chetail (edts.), *The Roots of International Law/Les fondements du droit international, Liber Amicorum Peter Haggenmacher,* Martinus Nijhoff (2014) 764p. notamment P.M. Dupuy, Quelques observations sur les origines de l'ordre juridique international, 389–404.

19 See P.M.Dupuy, Le concept de société civile internationale : identification et genèse, in P.M.Dupuy, *Ordre juridique et désordre international,* Paris, Pedone (2018), 311–326.

20 See P.M.Dupuy, Quarante ans de codification du droit de la responsabilité internationale des Etats, Un bilan, in Ordre juridique et désordre international, *op.cit. supra,* 215–263.

well as that of the ICJ, today supplemented by that of many other international courts or tribunals, offers a particularly attractive breeding ground. From this point of view, and insofar as it is of interest for the teaching of international law, I would like to make a few comments on the value, as a professor, of being able to benefit at the same time from experience drawn from the practice of international law.

To focus on one of these activities, I have been privileged to be able to draw on international jurisprudence as my career as a litigator before the International Court of Justice began shortly after my career as a professor, and I have since been active in many proceedings.[21] I found it particularly useful to explain to students the theoretical, technical, and practical issues involved in a case before the ICJ. This is particularly so with respect to disputes in which one has been involved. In such cases, the audience can be shown the strategic and tactical directions that lead a State to choose a particular type of argument. However, the dangers inherent in this kind of exercise are immediately apparent: it is not all about "telling a good story"! We must avoid falling into anecdote and subjectivism, and know how to take the necessary distance in order to state, among others, the strong points but also the weaknesses of each of the lines of argument involved, including those that we have defended. One must also be careful not to reduce the decisions taken by the Court to the attitude and personal influence that one believes can be attributed to a particular judge *intuitu personae*. On the other hand, the legal-political context in which a case takes place is not necessarily always to be ignored. If one manages, at the cost of real vigilance with regard to oneself, to avoid these various pitfalls, it remains of particular interest to be able to show students how, beyond the myth of "international justice", it really works, with its greatness as well as its constraints.

The concrete stakes of an often technical legal question, in particular concerning the international responsibility of a State, can also be highlighted in this way. More generally, the famous question about the "role of the judge" in the dynamics of international law and the question of knowing, beyond the very theoretical affirmation of its neutrality, to what extent it participates in the creation (in principle proscribed) and the evolutionary interpretation of the rule of law can gain much from the analysis of the jurisprudential dynamics in this or that species, at least in compliance with the strict conditions recalled above.

21 See P.M.Dupuy, The Judicial Policy of the International Court of Justice, in F.Salerno (Edt.) *Il ruolo del judicie internazionale nell'evoluzione del diritto internazionale e communitario*, CEDAM (1995) 61–82.

The same is sometimes true for correcting the academic presentation of the legal arguments of each of the parties, sometimes stated too superficially or allusively by some commentators. However, a judgment or, even more so, an arbitral award is first constructed on the basis of what the parties have argued. Everything, once again, is however a question of imbalance, mastery as well as of rigor for the one who cumulates the functions of teacher and practitioner. With the exception of questions relating to the determination of the jurisdiction of a court or arbitral tribunal, most of the time purely legal in nature, it is also important to be able to illustrate to students the decisive role played by facts in any contentious case, which is also an opportunity to make them understand what a "legal fact" is. One cannot go so far as to say that facts take precedence over law, but it is only on the basis of the different aspects of their reality that one can understand how the judge "says the law". It is also on the basis of this observation that it is easier to understand the importance of giving reasons for judicial decisions. This is obviously legal, but it is based on the facts that the judge has chosen to select and present as determining factors. However, in a certain number of cases, this selection is not neutral: it may also result from the judge's determination of the results he has set out to achieve. Several illustrations could be given from the ICJ case law itself, but this would be outside the limited scope of this article.

Of course, it is not only litigation practice that is relevant to the teaching of international law. Anyone who has seen a large international intergovernmental organization from the inside can thus contribute greatly to the understanding of the respective roles of the national delegations and the permanent secretariat of an organization, whether at the universal or regional level, the institutions of the European Union being of particular interest in this respect but in the context of the specific problems of that organization. That said, the proportion of teachers of international law with experience of its practice remains relatively small. Even if this is regrettable, it should also be borne in mind that this discipline can very well be taught without this empirical input, the use of which, once again, needs to be weighed up in order to avoid one falling into an ineffective subjectivism.

The dialectical relationship between theory and practice in some respects also makes it possible to put in its place the concrete influence of the doctrine on State practice.[22] The doctrinal effort remains in a way the nobility of the profession of professor of international law and, if I may take my own example,

22 See E. Roucounas, A Landscape of Contemporary Theories of International Law, Brill/Nijhoff,(2020) in particular at 137f.

I did not hesitate in my general course at the Academy of International Law to present a general theory of international law. In any case, attending courts and chancelleries should also make an academic feel very modest. As a general rule, even if there may be exceptions, authors are consulted only to the strict extent that the judge or legal adviser believes that in their work they can find precise and usable answers to the question to which they must find a concrete solution. Conversely, generally speaking, consultation of major theoretical constructs is considered in the chancelleries or during the Court's deliberations to be of only incidental interest. One should not exclude the possibility that the judge or arbitrator will ignore the analysis of the doctrinal debates between the authors on the meaning to be given to a particular conception of law or, more closely, to the technical analysis of a particular legal institution; however, the judge or arbitrator will be guided by them only if the substance of such debates can shed some light on the meaning or scope of that technique or legal institution as related to the facts of the case. In other words, the doctrine realistically retains in most cases the ancillary or complementary role assigned to it by the drafters of article 38 of the Statute of the International Court of Justice. Nor are the commentaries on case law established in the academic world any exception to the rule. It follows that the teaching of law should not be confined to the presentation of doctrinal debates. Thus, the foregoing remarks converge with those made above with regard to the primacy to be accorded to the analysis of positive or settled law.

This does not necessarily exclude developments directly inspired by the philosophy of law and even philosophy itself, starting with that of the great authors, from Plato and Aristotle to Marx, including of course Descartes, Spinoza, and Kant. On the other hand, I must admit to a certain skepticism with regard to the gloss of commentators, however scholarly they may be. Very concretely, in many cases, the quarrels between such and such supporters of the *Critical legal studies* often interest only themselves and it is decidedly vain to reduce the doctrinal debate to questions that often confusingly mix political philosophy, sociology, and ideology more or less distilled by a certain "political correctness" to the analysis of legal problems that are not always very rigorously defined.[23] That said, even if, in practice, the role of doctrine should not be overestimated, it remains of primary importance in the teaching of law. It is crucial for students to understand the different conceptions of law that have clashed over a long period of time and continue to do so. This must be done

23 Some Reflections on Contemporary International Law and the Appeal to Universal Values : a Response to Martti Koskeniemmi, EJIL,(2005) Vol. 16, 1, 131–137 http://www.ejil.org/pdfs/16/1/281.pdf.

without dogmatism and with a sense of relativity as well as of the intellectual and sometimes political stakes of the option for one or the other doctrine or the combination of several of them.

It is by no means forbidden to take sides, possibly taking the opportunity to propose one's own conception and justify it. The presentation of doctrinal debates is undoubtedly one of the best ways of animating the teaching of all or part of international law, but on the condition, to return to what was said earlier, that the law would not be reduced to the presentation of academic jousting. The confrontation of the different doctrines of international law with their practical effectiveness thus remains a test to which the theories developed by the authors are subjected.

It would be wrong, however, to end on a pessimistic note that some might consider inspired by nostalgia for a bygone past. On the contrary, it can be seen that recent initiatives show an awareness of the attention to be paid to international legal issues as they arise in practice, which does not exclude consideration of their theoretical dimension at all. Quite the contrary. A very favourable element is the constant increase in exchanges between internationalists, at both the European and interregional levels. In this respect, as in others, digitalization offers hitherto unsuspected possibilities also in terms of access to information in all its different forms. A recent example of this phenomenon is the publication of the *Blog: talk*,[24] which now appears several times a week under the aegis of the *European Journal of International Law*. It has already become, over a short period of time, an extremely useful and well-documented tool for learning about the issues raised by the most immediate international legal news, without, however, lacking in its contributions, which are usually rigorous, the evocation of some of the theoretical as well as technical issues raised in practice and case law as mentioned above. This attention to the legal analysis of current events has long had certain precedents in national international law journals, but because of its frequency of publication it is particularly stimulating in the form it takes under the responsibility of the EJIL, also in that it allows for the expression of the author's own points of view.

In a different vein, among so many other excellent publications let me note here two recent books which offer the possibility of revisiting certain referencial texts, both illustrative of the political context in which they were adopted and sufficiently out of step with the contemporary practice of those involved in international relations to reflect on their concrete extensions and

24 https://www.ejiltalk.org/.

the conditions for their updating. Particular mention should be made here of the book devoted to the *Rio Declaration on the Human Environment* adopted at the 1992 Earth Summit[25] and the collection of studies examining the topicality of the *United Nations Declaration on Friendly Relations among States* adopted in 1972.[26] Both of these collective works make it possible to measure contemporary developments in international law and the durability of certain cardinal principles that should always govern relations between States. These publications also make it possible to underline, always in connection with the teaching of international law, the role to be given to the *context* in the analysis of the norms or conduct in question. The political, strategic, economic, ecological, and social contexts, as the case may be, is all the more necessary to mention since the audiences concerned are not necessarily made up of people who are always plainly familiar with the history of contemporary international relations.

Legal norms must be studied both on their own and "*in situ*" in order to understand their drafting, their connotations, as well as their scope and implications. To take one example, the historically very marked notion of "*peaceful coexistence*" has been decisive in explaining the normative developments that have taken place, particularly within the United Nations General Assembly, during three of the last four decades of the twentieth century. However, I have observed that this notion remains poorly perceived by current student audiences, partly because, for political reasons, the idea that the "Cold War" lasted until the collapse of the Soviet Union has been pushed through, which is very approximate. In reality, one has to distinguish between the hard tensions phase taking place between 1947 and 1963 wich was the true period of « Cold war » in the proper sense of the term from the period which came after the Cuban Crisis (i.e. after October 1962). This period was, on the contrary, particularly beneficial for the development of modern international law (1963–1991), announcing the last decade of the XXth Century which constituted not the last but the most recent time during which one could speak in the positive sense of the term of a « progress » in the development of international law, in particular with the expansion of the law of the maintainance of peace, the creation of the WTO, and that of international criminal law.

---

25 See J. Vinuales (Edt.), *The Rio Declaration on Environment and Development,* Oxford University Press (2015), 665p.

26 See J.Vinuales (Edt.), *The UN Friendly Relations Declaration at 50, An Assessment of the Fundamental Principles of International Law* (2020), Cambridge University Press.

The last word on the teaching of international law is undoubtedly to try to capture its movement, developments, tensions, and contradictions. It is not an inert discipline. Its technique itself evolves and its goals, although always centered on peaceful relations between states, are constantly being broadened. This is what makes this subject matter so exciting to share with a student audience.

CHAPTER 6

Teaching International Law

The Added Value of Working as a Diplomat-Jurist

Giuseppe Nesi[1]

JEL Classification: K33; I23; I28.
Suggested Citation:
Nesi, Giuseppe, **Teaching International Law: The added value of working as a diplomat-jurist** (XYXYX, YXY, 2023). Available at SSRN:

1 Introduction

While I usually refrain from making any reference in writing to personal experiences, in the following pages I will make an exception in order to describe the impact of practicing international law on teaching it. Namely, I will go through my personal experience as a scholar "on loan" to diplomacy, a path that started accidentally thirty years ago and had many phases and different configurations. My aim is to illustrate what being involved in international diplomacy means for an academic and how this experience can be useful in teaching international law. I will touch upon how working in a diplomatic multilateral environment has allowed me to learn more about international law and its relationship with other aspects of international relations. This in turn provided both a deeper understanding of international law and – I hope – a greater capacity to explain it to my students.

Before explaining the structure of the present paper, I would like to make some preliminary remarks. First, my task here is writing about the importance of the experience of an academic as a practitioner in *teaching* international law; thus, I will touch only marginally upon the implications for an academic of being the legal adviser of a State in multilateral diplomacy.[2] However, I do

1 University of Trento, Italy (forthcoming in: Peter Hilpold/Giuseppe Nesi (eds.), Teaching International Law, Brill/Martinus Nijhoff: Leiden/Boston 2022).

2 Several in-depth studies have been conducted on the role of legal advisers in international law. For the most recent one, that refers to pertinent previous literature, see M. Windsor, "Consigliere or Conscience? The Role of the Government Legal Adviser", in *International*

 | DOI:10.1163/9789004678880_008

not intend to dodge the question regarding the role of the academic as a practitioner at the crossroad between international law and international politics, or to avoid address the dichotomy "commitment-cynicism". As these pages will hopefully clarify, I greatly favour commitment over cynicism.[3] Second, as regards the term "teaching", I cannot dwell here on its different meanings; I rather make a *renvoi* to very interesting contributions present in this volume and elsewhere.[4] Finally, the international law I will refer to is the so-called "public international law" because this is the international law I have predominantly practiced and taught.

The structure of this contribution will follow that of my personal experiences. I will start with the beginning of my practice in the diplomatic environment, which actually came before I officially began working as an assistant professor at University. The negotiations within the Conference on Security and Cooperation in Europe (CSCE) were an extraordinary "training ground" where I was able to learn a lot in the field of international law and politics (Section 2). While I was dealing with both the diplomatic and academic aspects of the CSCE, I became interested in international criminal justice and namely in the creation of international criminal tribunals that culminated in the establishment of the International Criminal Court and its aftermath (Section 3). The preparatory works for the International Criminal Court, together with unexpected tragic events such as those of 9/11 were the reasons for which I started a new path as the legal adviser at the Permanent Mission of Italy to the United Nations (UN) in New York, and then as a UN officer, serving the President of the General Assembly (Section 4), leaving the University life for almost ten years. The return to University allowed me to give back, so to say, what I had learnt in the diplomatic world and to reflect upon the relationship between University and inter-State practice, what I will refer to in the last part of these short notes (Section 5).

Law as a Profession, J. d'Aspremont, T. Gazzini, A. Nollkaemper and W. Werner (eds.), CUP, Cambridge, 2017, 355–411.

3 I borrow the dichotomy commitment-cynicism from a famous practitioner and academic, Martti Koskenniemi, who knows very well both worlds. "Between Commitment and Cynicism. Outline for a Theory of International Law as Practice", first published as Chapter 11 in Martti Koskenniemi, *The Politics of International Law* (Hart Publishing 2011), and republished in *International Law as a Profession*, cit., 38–66.

4 E.g, see the paper by C. Focarelli, in this volume, and in particular par. 3. See also P. d'Argent, "Teachers of International Law", in *International Law as a Profession*, cit., 412–427.

2 The CSCE and the OSCE

Both in professional and personal terms 1992 was undoubtedly a revolutionary year for me. In 1992, after different steps of education in legal and political matters, including a Laurea Magistrale in Law, a Master of Arts in International Affairs, and a PhD in International Law, only a few days before my wedding, I won a competition to work as an assistant professor in International Law at the University of Trento.

During my PhD studies, between 1987 and 1990, in parallel with my dissertation research I had the chance to teach, assist and tutor students at the University of Rome "La Sapienza". This was greatly rewarding, but it was also a meaningful responsibility which prepared me to further commitments.

After the PhD, in the absence of any opportunity to start an academic career I thought about working in a law firm, perhaps one specialized in international affairs. Instead, in January 1992, the Head of the Legal Service of the Italian Ministry of Foreign Affairs, a renowned academic and a brilliant practitioner of international law such as Luigi Ferrari Bravo, offered me the opportunity to serve as legal *attaché* of the Italian diplomatic delegation to the Follow-Up Meeting of the Helsinki Process, that took place in Helsinki between March and July 1992. That was a real turning point, as mentioned above, and not only for my academic pursuits.

My early propensity towards international affairs, (i.e. international law but also international politics, international relations, international history and international economics) made the prospect of participating in international negotiations particularly exciting. I gladly accepted that offer and spent almost four months in Helsinki, a place I had never visited before and where I felt immediately at home. On the eve of my departure, Luigi Ferrari Bravo called me to his office at the Ministry of Foreign Affairs. After a very interesting conversation on the working program for the Helsinki Follow-up meeting and what working with diplomats could have amount to, he gave me his International Law Handbook and wrote on it: "A Giuseppe Nesi, che sto tentando di trasformare in diplomatico-giurista" ("To Giuseppe Nesi, who I am trying to transform in a diplomat-jurist").

While participating in the interminable negotiations on the various legal aspects that were on the agenda I reflected on my studies and came to the following conclusions. On the one side, I thought about the role and impact of international law in intergovernmental relations; on the other side, I began to perceive how important it is to learn and to try to have a good knowledge of all the other components of theory and practice of other aspects of international affairs in order to understand their "essence". With the term "essence", I allude not only to the knowledge of different topics studied at Universities and institutions; I refer mainly to how those topics are combined in practical issues, something that you do not find in any book, article, or encyclopaedia.

In that extraordinary period of mutation of the international legal and political system, I dealt with topics ranging from self-determination and minority rights to peacekeeping, from issues of territorial delimitations and armed conflicts in the former Yugoslavia and elsewhere to the settlement of international disputes and disarmament, to name just a few. In parallel, the idea of transforming an intergovernmental conference in a fully-fledged international organization was fledgling together with all the institutional aspects that it embroiled. In Helsinki, I was required to give advice on many of those topics, sometimes on very short notice. Quite often, the Head of the Italian Delegation, Ambassador Antonio Armellini would ask on short notice for assistance him in a meeting or in conversations with his counterparts. From time to time he would also request some talking points on the spot. I could never thank him and the other diplomats enough for their trust and courage (or perhaps foolishness?) in relying on the advice of a young international law scholar.

Needless to say, in many situations my expectations that there would be a clear-cut national position with instructions coming from Rome on the single issues was not satisfied. I was often obliged to offer a legal interpretation of certain questions at stake, and I was very pleased to discuss them with the rest of the Delegation or during the negotiations. Participating in Helsinki meetings was – as I said – a sort of "training ground" where I had the chance to use the many tools I had at my disposal and I was familiar with but had never used before in practice. Even more important, this experience provided an opportunity to look at international law not as a topic to be taught to goodwill and patient students in isolation from the real world, but as a tool essential to relations between people and States all over the world.

Thus, the first lesson I learnt from this early diplomatic experience was an awareness of the impact my legal advice could have on international relation. On the one hand, I had to give complete and correct advice. On the other, I had to remain conscious of the deference my superiors would give to the word of the law and the repercussions this could have also on the rest of the negotiations. This implies the need to be quick and clear in giving advice on different international law issues at any moment of the day, since the final stage of negotiations can come early in the day or late into the night.

The second lesson was that international law does matter in international relations; maybe not as much as it seems from reading pertinent books and articles, but surely more than what one is often led to believe.[5] In this regard, I experienced an interesting phenomenon that has had repercussions in my way of teaching international law: on the one side, there are concepts and notions of international law that could appear theoretically simple but reveal their intricacies in the real world; on the other side, something that is difficult to explain could be quite straightforward in practice, if you know in advance what you are talking about.

Examples of the former could be found in self-determination and minority rights: if you look at them in isolation it could be easy to explain them; but when we tried to combine them in a written text, it became difficult to reconcile this task with States' obligations towards minorities and minority rights. This can become extremely complex in multilateral negotiations where different States' approaches and sensitivities to the issue must be considered. On the other side, dealing with peacekeeping, something that was a *première* in the CSCE environment, appeared at first sight to be a gargantuan task. However, knowing the main features of peacekeeping in the UN environment, although at that time only theoretically, gave me the possibility of clarifying the essential elements of peacekeeping in general terms, paving the way to diplomatic solutions to the relationship between the CSCE and the UN in conformity with Chapter VIII of the UN Charter. The most important consequence of these considerations in teaching international law is that you must always prepare your lectures carefully and any type of scholarly intervention, since you must always be keenly aware of the issues that are going to be presented and never forget the practical implications of notions and theories of international law.

My "association" with the CSCE continued in the years following the Helsinki Follow-up meeting and I was invited to participate in several activities and negotiations including the meetings that established the Court of Conciliation and Arbitration of the CSCE, the Human Dimension meetings in Warsaw, all the Review meetings until the year 2000 (Budapest, Lisbon, Oslo, Vienna), where I had the chance to follow the evolution of an intergovernmental diplomatic conference and its transformation into an unusual international organization.[6]

5 "Almost all nations observe almost all principles of international law and almost all of their obligations almost all the time" (L. Henkin, *How Nations Behave*, 1979, 2nd ed., Columbia University Press, New York, 47).

6 After attending the CSCE/OSCE meetings I thought it would have been useful to write pertinent articles for specialized journals and reviews. Those articles are available at: https://webapps.unitn.it/du/it/Persona/PER0004357/Pubblicazioni.

These experiences were another important brick in my legal and political education and had repercussions on my way of teaching international law. In 1994, the CSCE changed its denomination to the Organization for Security and Cooperation in Europe (OSCE), while discussions on the legal status continued mainly in Vienna. At the University of Trento, after every meeting I organized a lecture on the main features of these negotiations; it was a sort of debriefing to clarify, sometimes also to myself, the essential components of those intergovernmental negotiations. Meanwhile, motivated students were invited to organize a sort of legal clinic where they reproduced the negotiations. These were very fruitful experiences and the students adhered enthusiastically and with full commitment.

3 The International Criminal Court negotiations

As we all know, the 1990s were years of tragic and important events in Europe. The international crimes committed in the former Yugoslavia and Rwanda brought the Security Council to establish *ad hoc* international criminal tribunals, something that was unthinkable just a few years before. In the early 1990s I was living and working between Rome and Trento. In Rome, I was still working with Professor Ferrari Bravo, at the Ministry of Foreign Affairs. The events in former Yugoslavia and Rwanda and the decisions by the Security Council revitalized the idea of prosecuting those responsible for international crimes and even breathed life in the idea that a permanent international criminal court could be established.

In those years I was also working, from time to time, with the legal adviser at the Permanent Mission of Italy to the United Nations in New York, my friend and colleague Mauro Politi. He was very active, together with other friends and colleagues, in promoting the initiative to establish a permanent international criminal court. This initiative was so starkly supported by the Ministry of Foreign Affairs of Italy that, when an international conference for the establishment of the International Criminal Court was proposed, Italy offered Rome as the seat for the conference. I had the opportunity to participate in an historical event that, while I was very active at University, offered me another occasion to be fully involved in international multilateral negotiations. I lived in Rome, until July 17, 1998, when the text of the Rome Statute was formally adopted at the Campidoglio. This was a challenging time since, by then, my family had already moved to Trento.

Less than one year later, in May 1999, together with Mauro, we organized the "Trento Conference" on the International Criminal Court. It was attended by the main negotiators of the Rome Conference, including the non-governmental organizations officers that played a decisive role in Rome. The aim of the Trento meeting was, on the one side, to sum up the main results obtained thus far with the Rome Statute; on the other, to prepare the ground for the follow-up meetings of the preparatory committee and speed up the process of ratification of the Statute. This meeting also gave students the unique opportunity to meet and talk with some of the protagonists of the process that led to the Rome Statute, and with some of those who were going to be the first judges and officers of the International Criminal Court, but also with several NGOs experts who actively participated in the negotiations within the delegations of States that required their assistance (in the framework of the International Coalition for the ICC). It is worth recalling that "No Peace without Justice" was co-sponsoring the Trento Conference.

The extraordinary interactions between students, diplomats, United Nations and NGO officers, that took place at the Trento Conference made it one of the most fruitful synergies of my academic and diplomatic activities. From that moment on, Trento University and its Law School were recognized and renowned as important academic institutions in the field of the repression of international crimes; a reputation that persists to this day.

4 The United Nations

Working in diplomacy I sharpened certain key skills including, providing balanced advice in a matter of minutes or hours, clarity and the ability to propose viable and realistic options, and most importantly listening closely to all parties involved. This is the toolkit I constantly turned to during my eight years working as the legal adviser at the Permanent Mission of Italy to the United Nations in New York.

Since 1998, at the request of the Ministry of Foreign Affairs, I had been following the work of the Sixth Committee of the General Assembly. In this capacity, I participated in several meetings at the UN Headquarters in New York. At the beginning of the summer of 2001, I was invited to attend the meetings of the preparatory committee for the establishment of the International Criminal Court.

In September of that year the international order was upended by the terrorist attacks on the World Trade Centre. Weeks later, against the protests of my wife and children and with a sizable dose of fear swelling within me, I flew to New York to attend a meeting. Shortly after my arrival, the Italian Ambassador asked whether I was interested in becoming the legal adviser at the Permanent Mission.

I had recently been promoted to Full Professor at the University of Trento and had to explain to my colleagues since this new job would have required that I move to New York. Recognizing that this was not just an opportunity for me but also for the University of Trento, they encouraged me to accept the offer. This was in fact the continuation of a tradition that started in the 1980s according to which a professor of international law is seconded to the Permanent Mission of Italy to the United Nations as its legal adviser.[7]

Although I already knew the UN environment, living and working "permanently" in New York was a new and exciting prospect. As the legal adviser I was glad to assist the Permanent Representative and collaborate with the rest of the Italian Mission on any legal issue. In my new function, I had to attend all pertinent meetings, ranging from the Sixth Committee to those related, for instance, to international criminal tribunals and to the law of the sea or specialized meetings of the United Nations Commission on International Trade Law (UNCITRAL). There were also regular meetings with the EU partners, and special meetings on the reform of the Security Council. When Italy was elected in the Security Council, in 2007–08, I ensured my colleagues at the permanent mission were aware of all the relevant substantive and procedural issues.

These were all occasions in which, while accomplishing my duties, I had the opportunity to research and draft notes and reports that served useful in my academic life. In preparing these notes, reports, draft statements I strengthened my knowledge of several topics. The work aimed at providing legal elements on specific issues and the necessity to "deliver" forced me to be exhaustive but also quick and to the point in the outcome of my research, skills that are also useful in teaching and researching in an academic context. My tenure as legal adviser at the Mission also included some fascinating conflicts between international law and politics. For instance, granting observer status in the General Assembly to the International Olympic Committee, a proposal made by the Italian Government that presented some perplexities from the legal point of view. Nevertheless, through a combination or technical legal work and persistent lobbying it was eventually supported by the entire membership and finalized in the adoption of a pertinent resolution in October 2009.[8]

7 I was preceded in this job by Luigi Ferrari Bravo (1981–1984), Tullio Treves (1984–1992), Mauro Politi (1992–2000), and followed by Salvatore Zappalà (2010–2018) and Enrico Milano since 2018.

8 For a detailed recount of what happened and other interesting issues in the General Assembly and the relationship between law and politics at the U.N., see G. Nesi, "Brevi note su diritto e politica all'ONU. Ammissione, accreditamento, rappresentanza e status di osservatore in

All the while, I did not forget everything that had led me to become an academic. I missed teaching and interacting with students on a daily basis. I mitigated this by hosting several groups of students who came to New York to learn more about the United Nations. In addition, I was often invited to deliver lectures or attend seminars at different Universities and institutions, both in and around New York. Thus, I had several opportunities to meet and work with friends and colleagues and reflect upon the role of international law within international organizations. In this regard, I was provided with platforms to express my opinion on difficult topics that were on the agenda of the UN, which included: the fight against international terrorism and the role of the Security Council, the attempts to reform the United Nations that culminated in the Summit Outcome Document, the negotiations on the crime of aggression in the framework of the Rome Statute that took place mainly at Princeton, the completion strategy of the *ad hoc* international criminal tribunals, the ban of human cloning.

Among various tasks, I also coordinated the participation of Italy in the periodic debate on the report of the International Law Commission (ILC). This event took place annually during the International Law week when all the legal advisers came from their respective capitals. I loved this experience for two reasons. First, it reminded me of my early days as researcher of international law, in the 1980s of last century, when I had the pleasure of assisting one of the members of the ILC, Professor Gaetano Arangio-Ruiz, Special Rapporteur on State Responsibility for Internationally Wrongful Acts, and one of my early mentors. Second, studying and commenting the report of the ILC was an opportunity to reflect upon the impact practice has on the codification and progressive development of international law.[9] Those sessions convinced me to integrate more critical thinking skills into my teaching activities, as I came to better understand the decisive role they would play in the careers of my students.

Assemblea Generale", in M. Vellano (a cura di), *Il futuro delle organizzazioni internazionali. Prospettive giuridiche*, Atti del XIX Convegno S.I.D.I., Courmayeur, 26–28 giugno 2014, Napoli, Editoriale Scientifica, 2015, 601–619.

9 In this regard another famous professor who is also a practitioner of international law, Alain Pellet, observed: "C'est certainement mon activité comme membre de la Commission du droit international qui marque le mieux la transition entre la vie universitaire et la pratique pure – ou impure – du droit. En effet, l'essentiel du travail de la CDI consiste bien à dégager de la pratique (…) des règles de droit international et à la codifier", in Société Française pour le droit international, *Enseignement du droit international. Recherche et pratique*, Pedone, Paris, 1997, 126.

One way of doing this was organizing international meetings in Trento on some of the topics I tackled during my experience as practitioner at the UN. On these occasions, colleagues from New York provided informed perspectives on international terrorism and the crime of aggression.[10] While I felt free to present my personal positions on these very delicate issues, I cannot deny that being the legal adviser at the Mission of Italy obliged me also to think twice before talking for fear that my ideas could be confounded with the positions of the Republic of Italy. This was different from the freedom I had known in academia.

At the end of my tenure as the legal adviser at the Mission of Italy, when I was planning to resume my full-time University life in Trento, I received a proposal to work as the legal adviser to the President of the 65th session of the General Assembly (PGA). This was an opportunity to look at the UN from "the other side of the fence", being a UN officer and not as a delegate of a member State. In that period (2010–11) I had to advise on Arab Springs, and in particular on the crisis in Libya and the position of the Security Council on the issue. In this regard it was noteworthy that "responsibility to protect", that was first referred to in a UN official document in 2005 (Summit Outcome Document), was included for the first time in a Security Council resolution in February 2011 (Resolution 1970/2011). These events provided the opportunity, during the staff meetings with the PGA and in other meetings, to dwell on the legal and political implications of what was happening; to reflect on the use of armed force and the principle of non-intervention in internal affairs; to elaborate on the Security Council prerogatives in the maintenance of international peace and security and the meaning of sanctions; to reflect upon the relevance of a deferral to the International Criminal Court. On those occasions, as a UN officer (and not a delegate by a member State) I felt obliged to recall that while nobody can doubt that international law principles and norms have a unitary content, there are many and different ways to look at them. These different approaches may depend on the positions of those who interpret and apply those principles and rules in multilateral diplomacy, but also on other factors linked to international politics and national interests.

10 The proceedings of the meeting on the crime of aggression were published in 2004 (*The International Criminal Court and the crime of aggression*, M. POLITI and G. NESI (eds.), Aldershot, Ashgate, 2004); those on the meeting on international cooperation in the fight against terrorism, were published in 2006 (G. Nesi (ed.), *International co-operation in counter-terrorism: the United Nations and regional organizations in the fight against terrorism*, Aldershot, Ashgate, 2006).

5 Final Remarks

Laws can be followed or they can be used, or abused. As a practitioner one learns to do the first two and tries to steer clear of the third. Practical experience often translates into an understanding of the limits of the law. These limits can look different depending on the profession one inhabits. In my years with the Ministry of Foreign Affairs and later with the UN, I represented different (and sometimes divergent) views. Working as a legal adviser for a State is profoundly different to doing the same job for an international institution. When facing difficult problems, one should look at international law norms and principles as they are and at their impact on the specific case; but one should also try to see the same norms and principles through the eyes of others and evaluate their impact. This broadmindedness is something that will be essential for future generations. In my lessons, I always work to make clear how the discursive method of international law implies that we represent interests to the best of our abilities to ensure the best outcome prevails. The best for one may not always be the best for all, but when representing questionable interests, we must hope that the sensibility of the law will prevail. In other words, we should choose commitment over cynicism.[11] It may be the harder route, but it is certainly more worthwhile.

To share the experience of practicing as an academic "on loan" to diplomacy, I went through the various moments in which my academic life intertwined with diplomatic experience. In my case, university and diplomacy as practice ran in parallel for the last thirty years. As we have seen, running in parallel in this case does not mean that those tracks cannot be connected; indeed, the opposite is true. Practicing international law has been a highly enriching experience with important repercussions on my teaching. Practicing and teaching are mutually reinforcing. I always tried to take advantage, as a teacher, of my diplomatic experience, and to offer my expertise of international law to diplomacy, knowing that international law is but one of the tools that matters in international relations. Acknowledging the limits of international law and tackling them with commitment as opposed to cynicism, provides the most rewarding way to both practice and teach.[12]

---

11 See note 2.

12 Ibidem.

Bibliography

d'Argent P., "Teachers of International Law", in *International Law as a Profession*, J. d'Aspremont, T. Gazzini, A. Nollkaemper and W. Werner (eds.), CUP, Cambridge, 2017.

Henkin L., *How Nations Behave*, 1979, 2nd ed., Columbia University Press, New York.

Koskenniemi M., "Between Commitment and Cynicism. Outline for a Theory of International Law as Practice", in *International Law as a Profession*, J. d'Aspremont, T. Gazzini, A. Nollkaemper and W. Werner (eds.), CUP, Cambridge, 2017.

Nesi G., "Brevi note su diritto e politica all'ONU. Ammissione, accreditamento, rappresentanza e status di osservatore in Assemblea Generale", in M. Vellano (a cura di), *Il futuro delle organizzazioni internazionali. Prospettive giuridiche*, Atti del XIX Convegno S.I.D.I., Courmayeur, 26–28 giugno 2014, Napoli, Editoriale Scientifica, 2015.

Nesi G, "Il divieto di clonazione di esseri umani: recenti dibattiti in ambito Nazioni Unite", in *Ordine internazionale e valori etici*, Atti dell'VIII Convegno S.I.D.I, Verona, 26–27 giugno 2003, Napoli, Editoriale scientifica, 2004.

Société Française pour le droit international, *Enseignement du droit international. Recherche et pratique*, Pedone, Paris, 1997.

Windsor M., "Consigliere or Conscience? The Role of the Government Legal Adviser", in *International Law as a Profession*, J. d'Aspremont, T. Gazzini, A. Nollkaemper and W. Werner (eds.), CUP, Cambridge, 2017.

PART III

National and Regional Perspectives, New Methodological Approaches

CHAPTER 7

Teaching International Law from a European Perspective

Jan Wouters

1 Introduction

Isn't there an inherent bias, even some kind of bigotry, in the view that international law should be taught from a European perspective in teaching programmes on European soil? Nevertheless, this is precisely the thesis that will be ardently defended in this chapter. The argument will not be made *in abstracto* but *in concreto*, with reference to a textbook which was published by the present author and three colleagues in December 2018.[1]

Let us first formulate the thesis in a more extensive manner and clarify the underlying assumptions. It is submitted that any form of teaching of international law in Europe, especially within the European Union (EU or Union), should ideally incorporate a "European perspective". This has to do, in the first place, with the massive "europeanisation" process that all the legal systems of the EU Member States have undergone and continue to undergo.[2] As will be elaborated upon here below, the practice of international law in Europe is also becoming to an important extent "europeanised". The thesis can be generalised to the teaching of other branches of the law in Europe: how can one still teach administrative (or public),[3]

1 J. Wouters, C. Ryngaert, T. Ruys and G. De Baere, *International Law: a European Perspective*, Oxford, Hart Publishing, 2018, xcv + 1038 p. Certain parts of the present text are based, with adaptations, on the introduction of this book (pp. 1–5).

2 See *inter alia* W. Heun and V. Lipp (eds.), *Europäisierung des Rechts*, Deutsch-Ungarisches Kolloquium Budapest 2007, Göttingen, Universitätsverlag Göttingen, 2008; H.-W. Rengeling (ed.), *Europäisierung des Rechts*, Cologne – Berlin – Bonn, Carl Heymanns Verlag, 1996; H. Roth (ed.), *Europäisierung des Rechts: Ringvorlesung der Juristischen Fakultät der Universität Regensburg*, Tübingen, Mohr Siebeck, 2010; F. Snyder (ed.), *The Europeanisation of Law: The Legal Effects of European Integration*, Oxford, Hart Publishing, 2000; T.G. Watkin (ed.), *The Europeanisation of Law*, Cardiff, United Kingdom National Committee of Comparative Law, 1998.

3 See *inter alia* M. Eliantonio, 'Europeanisation of Administrative Justice? The Influence of the ECJ's Case Law in Italy, Germany and England', 22 *Revue européenne de droit public*, 2010, 681–733; J. H. Jans, S. Prechal and R.J.G.M. Widdershoven (eds.), *Europeanisation of Public Law*, Groningen, Europa Law Publishing, 2015, 2nd ed.; R. Wahl, 'Die Zweite Phase

 | DOI:10.1163/9789004678880_009

commercial,[4] company,[5] competition,[6] constitutional,[7] criminal,[8] intellectual property,[9] labour,[10] social,[11] and private international law,[12] or even more traditional areas of private law,[13] such as contract,[14] family,[15] and tort

des Öffentlichen Rechts in Deutschland. Die Europäsierung des Öffentlichen Rechts, 38 *Der Staat* 1999,495.

4 See, e.g., D. Krimphove, 'The Europeanization of Commercial Agency Law', in *Europeización del Derecho Privado: Cuestiones Actuales*, Madric, Marcial Pons, 2016, 129.

5 See *inter alia* J. Wouters, 'European Company Law: Quo Vadis?', 37 *Common Market Law Review* 2000, 257; M. Blauberger and R.U. Krämer, 'Europeanisation with Many Unknowns: National Company Law Reforms after Centros' 37 *West European Politics* 2014, 786.

6 See *inter alia* N. Green and A. Robertson (eds.), *The Europeanisation of United Kingdom Competition Law*, Oxford, Hart Publishing, 1999.

7 See, e.g., M. Claes, 'The Europeanisation of National Constitutions in the Constitutionalisation of Europe: Some Observations against the Background of the Constitutional Experience of the EU-15, 3 *Croatian Yearbook of European Law & Policy* 2007, 1.

8 Although with difficulties: see, e.g., J. Ouwerkerk, 'Criminal Justice beyond National Sovereignty. An Alternative Perspective on the Europeanisation of Criminal Law' 23 *European Journal of Crime, Criminal Law and Criminal Justice* 2015, 11.

9 See *inter alia* A. Ohly and J. Pila (eds.), *The Europeanization of Intellectual Property Law: Towards a European Legal Methodology*, Oxford, OUP, 2013.

10 See, e.g., R.L. Zahn, 'The "Europeanization" of Labour Law: Can Comparative Labour Law Solve the Problem?" 61 *Northern Ireland Legal Quarterly* 2020, 79.

11 See, e.g., M. Stolleis, Chapter on 'Europeanization of Social Law' in the author's *History of Social law in Germany*, Heidelberg, Springer, 2013, 235.

12 See already N.A. Baarsma, *The Europeanisation of International Family Law*, The Hague, T.M.C. Asser Press, 2011. See also, with strong attention for the Europeanisation process, J.D. McClean and V.R Abou-Nigm, Morris Conflict of Laws, London, Sweet & Maxwell, 2016, 9th ed. Compare J. von Hein, E.-M. Kieninger and G. Rühl (eds.), *How European Is European Private International Law? Sources, Court Practice, Academic Discourse*, Cambridge, Intersentia, 2019.

13 See *inter alia* E. Kristoffersson and A.H. Persson (eds.), *Swedish Perspectives on Private Law Europeanisation*, Portland, Hart Publishing, 2017; K. Riesenhuber (ed.), *Die Europäisierung des Privatrechts,* Berlin – Boston, De Gruyter, 2006; R. Zimmermann, 'Le droit comparé et l'européanisation du droit privé', 2007, 451; id., 'Comparative Law and the Europeanization of Private Law', in M. Reimann and R. Zimmermann (eds.), *The Oxford Handbook of Comparative Law,* Oxford, OUP, 2012, 539. Compare, however, L. Niglia, 'The Non-Europeanization of Private Law', 9 *European Review of Private Law* 2001, 575, and J. M. Smits, 'What Do Nationalists Maximise? A Public Choice Perspective on the (Non-) Europeanization of Private Law', 8 *European Review of Private Law* 2012, 296. See further also C. Twigg-Flesner, *The Europeanisation of Contract Law: Current Controversies in Law*, Abingdon, Routledge, 2008.

14 See *inter alia* P.A. MacDermott, 'The Europeanisation of Contract Law', in M.C. Lucey and C. Keville (eds.), *Irish Perspectives on EC Law*, Dublin, Thomson Round Hall, 2003, 173–196.

15 See, e.g., W. Pintens, 'Europeanisation of Family Law', in K. Boele-Woelki (ed.), *Perspectives for the Unification and Harmonisation of Family Law in Europe*, Antwerp, Intersentia, 2003, 3.

law,[16] within the EU without paying proper attention to the influence of, and many interactions with, Union law?

Certainly, some will argue that the situation of public international law is fundamentally different from that of the branches of the law belonging to "national" legal systems. We beg to differ on this for the reasons indicated below (*infra*, Section 3).[17]

Here below it is explained first of all what is exactly meant by "a European perspective" on the teaching of international law (Section 2). It will then be explained why a lecturer teaching international law in programmes in Europe (or at least in the EU) should pay proper attention to the Union's international law practice (Section 3). Some concluding observations round up this contribution (Section 4).

2 What Is Teaching International Law "from a European Perspective"?

Before responding to the question what the teaching of international law from a "European perspective" exactly entails, it is useful to explain the rationale for a textbook as the one referred to in the introduction of this chapter. The thinking about it mounts back almost a quarter of a century, to 1998 to be precise, when the present author was appointed chair in public international law at KU Leuven. Looking for English language teaching materials, a plethora of excellent English language textbooks and treatises was available, but nearly all were written for common law jurisdictions. Inevitably and understandably, these textbooks focused principally on practice from common law countries, particularly from the United States of America (U.S.) and the United Kingdom (UK). Very few, if any, paid attention to the international law practice of continental European States, the EU, and the Council of Europe. In Leuven, where one is just a stone' s throw away from Brussels, the heart of the EU, and which has a long tradition of comparative law, the need was felt to study international law through the multiple layers of transnational legal engagement that European countries have developed in the past 70 years: that is, with sufficient attention to the international law practice of a wide number of European

16 See *inter alia* P. Giliker, *The Europeanisation of English Tort Law*, Oxford, Hart Publishing, 2014.

17 See for earlier explorations on this subject J. Wouters, A. Nollkaemper and E. De Wet (eds.), *The Europeanisation of International Law. The Status of International Law in the EU and its Member States*, The Hague, T.M.C. Asser Press, 2008.

countries – both civil and common law – and the EU institutions and the Council of Europe, in particular the 'supreme courts ' of both organisations, i.e., the Court of Justice of the EU (CJEU) and the European Court of Human Rights (ECtHR).

By now, this need must be felt all over Europe. Indeed, in these past 20 years, often as part of the Sorbonne-Bologna reforms and the rapidly evolving internationalisation of curricula, ever more law faculties in Europe have introduced courses in public international law in English, both at bachelor and master levels.

A textbook as the one referred to in the introduction aims to fill this gap by taking a comprehensive European perspective when discussing the classic doctrines and the main sub-branches of public international law. That perspective notably includes the EU, the Council of Europe, and their respective Member States. Throughout the book, special attention is devoted to the reception of international law in the Union legal order and the EU's international legal action, and to the dialectical relationship between general international law and the European Convention on Human Rights (ECHR), as applied by the ECtHR.

The European perspective is informed by a substantial amount of practice at the level of EU Member States, including, at the time, the UK. This includes the treaty practice of these States: it is systematically indicated which international law treaties have been adhered to by which Member States. There are abundant references to domestic case-law on international law from the Member States.

The book also refers to practice at the diplomatic and executive level, which includes EU coordinated positions and statements on issues of international law. Indeed, in most international organisations and international conferences, EU Member States coordinate their positions and actions through the EU, making for a fascinating phenomenon of collective international practice.[18]

---

18 For earlier work, see *inter alia* J. Wouters, 'The European Union as an Actor within the United Nations General Assembly' in V. Kronenberger (ed.), *The EU and the International Legal Order: Discord or Harmony?*, The Hague, T.M.C. Asser Press, 2001, 375; J Wouters, 'The United Nations, the EU and Conflict Prevention: Interconnecting the Global and Regional Levels' in V. Kronenberger and J. Wouters (eds.), *The European Union and Conflict Prevention: Policy and Legal Aspects*, The Hague, T.M.C. Asser Press, 2004, 369; J. Wouters, F. Hoffmeister and T. Ruys (eds.), *The United Nations and the European Union: An Ever Stronger Partnership*, The Hague, T.M.C. Asser Press, 2006; M. Emerson, R. Balfour, T. Corthaut, J. Wouters, P.M. Kaczynski and T. Renard, *Upgrading the EU's Role as Global Actor: Institutions, Law and the Restructuring of European Diplomacy*, Brussels, Centre for European Policy Studies, 2011; J. Wouters, H. Bruyninckx, S. Basu and S. Schunz (eds.), *The European Union and Multilateral Governance: Assessing EU Participation in United Nations*

It should be stressed that this book constitutes by no means a textbook on EU law or even on the EU's practice in international law. It is completely an international law textbook. The book therefore follows a typical textbook structure, tackling the main tenets of international law, as will be explained below. Crucially, what differentiates this textbook from the existing literature is that, as an international law textbook, it devotes considerable attention to both EU and the broader 'European' practice in public international law. In particular, the book explores, on the one hand, the dynamics of international law in Europe on the basis of the practice of European States (including non-EU Member States, such as, for instance, Switzerland), the EU, and the Council of Europe, as well as of other organisations, for example the United Nations Economic Commission for Europe ('UNECE') and the European Space Agency ('ESA'). On the other hand, the book examines European practice in a broad range of international organisations, including within the United Nations ('UN') and the UN system, the World Trade Organization ('WTO') and the International Criminal Court ('ICC').

More specifically, this book refers to practice of continental European 'civil law' jurisdictions, European common law practice (as noted, including the UK), as well as practice of EU institutions and the Council of Europe. However, it also discusses relevant non-European practice regarding international law – for example with a view to comparing it to parallel European practice – as well as the main cases brought before international dispute-settlement mechanisms, in particular the International Court of Justice ('ICJ').

As a textbook of public international law, the book aims to give a comprehensive overview of international law, with attention to all the 'classics' that form the core of any international law textbook: the sources (Chapters 2 and 3), the subjects (Chapters 5, 6, 7 and 8), jurisdiction (Chapter 9), diplomatic relations (Chapter 10), immunities (Chapter 11), State responsibility (Chapter 12), and the peaceful settlement of disputes (Chapter 13). But it goes beyond that core by entering into various sub-fields of international law, notably the law on the

---

Human Rights and Environmental Fora, Basingstoke, Palgrave Macmillan, 2012; B. Van Vooren, S. Blockmans and J. Wouters (eds.), *The EU's Role in Global Governance: The Legal Dimension*, Oxford, OUP, 2013; J. Wouters, J. Odermatt and T. Ramopoulos, 'The Status of the European Union at the United Nations General Assembly', in I. Govaere, P. Van Elsuwege, E. Lannon and S. Adam (eds.), *Liber Amicorum Marc Maresceau*, Leiden, Brill, 2013, 211; J. Wouters and A.-L. Chané, 'Brussels Meets Westphalia: The European Union and the United Nations', in P. Eeckhout and M. Lopez-Escudero (eds.), *The European Union's External Action in Times of Crisis*, Oxford, Hart, 2016, 299; A.-L. Chané and J. Wouters, 'The European Union in United Nations Economic Governance Fora' 8 *European Yearbook of International Economic Law* 2017, 541.

use of force (Chapter 14), the law of armed conflict (Chapter 15), human rights law (Chapter 16), international criminal law (Chapter 17), the law of the sea and global commons (Chapter 18), international economic law (Chapter 19), and international environmental law (Chapter 20). The book also covers, at least with broad brushstrokes, the law of international organisations, paying attention to both global (Chapter 6) and regional organisations (Chapter 7), in Europe and in other continents.

In all these areas the book endeavours to pay attention to European contributions to, and engagement with, these fields and/or organisations. This includes *inter alia* EU treaty practice (see notably Chapter 2); European (EU and national) case law on the effects of international law in the domestic legal order, which includes both the EU legal order and the legal orders of European countries (Chapter 4); European practice on the recognition of States (Chapter 5, Section IV(A)); EU practice with regard to the UN and its most important bodies, including the UN Human Rights Council; EU cooperation with non-European regional organisations; European conventions and case law (including both from national courts and the ECtHR) on immunities (Chapter 11); the EU and the International Law Commission ('ILC')'s work on the responsibility of international organisations and ECtHR case law on attribution of State responsibility (Chapter 12, Section VII); European practice on the peaceful settlement of disputes (including with regard to the acceptance of the jurisdiction of the ICJ); practice in Europe regarding (collective) self-defence; European dimensions (both under the ECHR and the Charter of Fundamental Rights of the EU) of human rights protection (including on social rights, minorities and torture prevention); European practice on the law of the sea (from port State control to naval operations and the EU common fisheries policy) and global commons (e.g. under the United Nations Convention on the Law of the Sea ('UNCLOS'), on the Arctic and outer space, be it through the EU or ESA); the EU in the WTO, the EU's rich record of international trade agreements, the relationship between WTO law and the EU legal order, and European practice on international investment protection including the Commission's proposals for a World Investment Court; European dynamics of international environmental law, including the EU's participation in many international environmental treaties, such as the Convention on International Trade in Endangered Species of Wild Fauna and Flora ('CITES') and the Convention on Access to Information, Public Participation in Decision-Making and Access to Justice in Environmental Matters (the Aarhus Convention), and the most prominent EU instruments for environmental and wildlife protection.

Last but not least, it is important to emphasise what a textbook like the one referred to in the introduction of this chapter does *not* do. It does not put forward a 'provincial' European perspective on international law. It does not suggest a conception of the EU or of Europe more generally as the world centre of political virtue. It is not built on a conception of European identity based on the negation of the 'non-European otherness' – to use the expression of Koskenniemi in his book *The Gentle Civilizer of Nations*[19] – of the wider world, which arguably constituted part of Europe's identity during its past of colonialism and imperialism. Narratives of international law depicting progress in terms of a unified international community have also been described as speaking 'a thoroughly Eurocentric language',[20] with Europe imagining its values as universal.[21] The textbook does not put forward such a narrative. Rather, it critically engages with the role of Europe in international law, including from a historical perspective.

Furthermore, in the book at hand it is acknowledged that history demonstrates that international law 'has been as Asian or African as it has been European',[22] and that the first instruments and institutions of international

19 M. Koskenniemi, *The Gentle Civilizer of Nations: The Rise and Fall of International law, 1870–1960*, Cambridge, Cambridge University Press, 2001.

20 Several strategies have been put forward to address the challenge of Eurocentrism in international law. Koskenniemi suggests four ways: first, a careful demonstration of the 'colonial origins' of a particular international legal rule or institution; second, focusing on encounters between the European and non-European world as a crucial moment in the history of international law; third, examining the hybridisation of international legal concepts as they are transferred between the coloniser and the colonies; and fourth, what Koskenniemi calls 'exotising' or 'provincialising' Europe and European laws: M. Koskenniemi, 'Histories of International Law: Dealing with Eurocentrism' 9 *Rechtsgeschichte*, 2011, 152, 170–175. Lorca, in turn, suggests three trends followed by historians of international law aware of potential Eurocentric distortions: first, histories have been written in which international law both reflects the interests of powerful Western sovereigns and enables weaker actors to resist by using the universal language of rights; second, Koskenniemi's *Gentle Civilizer of Nations* represents a turning point in the historiography of international law in recounting the history of international law as an intellectual history, thereby showing a way beyond realist and post-colonial structuralism, as well as beyond histories of ideas committed to a narrative of progress; third, a number of legal scholars have explored the dynamics between centre and periphery as a heuristic to retrieve the history of international law in its global rather than solely Western dimensions: A.B. Lorca, 'Eurocentrism in the History of International Law', in B. Fassbender and A. Peters (eds.), *The Oxford Handbook of the History of International Law*, Oxford, OUP, 2012, 1055–1056.

21 M. Koskenniemi, *supra* note 10, at 160.

22 See, e.g., T.O. Elias, *Africa and the Development of International Law*, Dordrecht, Nijhoff, 1988, 2dd ed.

law identified to date probably originate outside Europe.[23] At the same time, to the extent that some of the central precepts of current international law have their origins in early modern European political thought and practice, the book acknowledges that this fact may create tensions for any claims with respect to the universality of international law.[24]

The book's prime value, however, it is submitted, lies in presenting European contemporary practice and doctrine of international law. It enables the reader to better grasp the contemporary 'European' approach to international law, which will in turn enrich the debate on the truly universal character of international law. Indeed, knowledge of the various approaches to international law is key to apprehend how international law events and arguments are globally understood, whether or not the reader or practitioner ultimately accepts all these approaches as valid.[25] Accordingly, the book is a starting point for, rather than the conclusion of, an international conversation on the content and meaning of international law, taking place in a diverse world with different power and knowledge centres – one of them being Europe.

In sum, the book aims to complement the existing literature by providing a comprehensive European perspective that takes European practice into account next to relevant practice from across the international legal order, including from the EU, the Council of Europe, and a great number of European States, without understanding this practice to be 'standard' or paradigmatic.

3 Why So Much Attention to the EU?

When teaching international law in European programmes, a lecturer should be aware that large parts of the international law practice of EU Member States have essentially been taken over by the EU, or, are at the very least practised by these Member States and the Union in a coordinated manner.

First of all, the EU has been conferred unique competences by its Member States in the EU Treaties. Thus, the Union has exclusive powers – meaning that

---

23 See A. Orakhelashvili, 'The Idea of European International Law' 17 *EJIL*, 2006, 315, 329 and 339, citing as an example the system of treaty law and diplomatic immunities in Sumerian cities in the third and second millennia BC.

24 J. Crawford, *Chance, Order, Change: The Course of International Law, General Course on Public International* Law, The Hague, Hague Academy of International Law, 2014, 311–314. See also M. Koskenniemi, 'International Law in Europe: Between Tradition and Renewal' 16 *EJIL*, 2005, 113.

25 See further A. Roberts, *Is International Law International?*, Oxford, OUP, 2017.

it alone can act, and the Member States themselves no longer – in the areas of international economic relations (competition, customs, investment, trade), international monetary relations (monetary policy)[26] and international maritime relations (conservation of marine biological resources).[27] The implications for international law should be clearly understood here. Instead of 27 States negotiating and concluding their own multilateral and bilateral treaties in these areas, only the Union can do so. And it has done so extensively, creating a dense network of increasingly deep and comprehensive international association, cooperation, trade and – more recently – investment treaties with a large number of third countries.[28] Furthermore, in these areas of exclusive competence, only the EU can adopt unilateral acts, such as autonomous trade measures, unilateral decisions on customs, monetary policy, and marine conservation.

As in areas of exclusive competence the Union has essentially replaced its Member States as an international actor, this has implications for the question of practice under customary international law. Tullio Treves put it in the following manner in pre-Lisbon Treaty times:

> When, as in the case of the European Communities, the international organization replaces, in whole or in part, its Member States in international relations, its practice may be relevant in broader areas. Thus it is that the practice of the European Community is relevant in fields such as economic relations, the law of human rights, the law of the sea, and environmental law. The European Court of Justice (and the Court of First Instance) have on many occasions referred to customary international law rules.[29]

More recently, Sir Michael Wood confirmed this in his work as ILC special rapporteur:

---

26 On this topic, see recently *inter alia* S. Lütz, T. Leeg, D. Otto and V. Woyames Dreher, *The European Union as a Global Actor: Trade, Finance and Climate Policy*, Cham, Springer, 2021.

27 See Article 3(1) Treaty on the Functioning of the European Union (TFEU).

28 See recently *inter alia* M.J. Hahn and G. Van der Loo (eds.), *Law and Practice of the Common Commercial Policy: The First 10 Years after the Treaty of Lisbon*, Leiden – Boston, Brill Nijhoff, 2021; B.A. Melo Araujo, *The EU Deep Trade Agenda: Law and Policy*, Oxford, OUP, 2016. See, more broadly, A. Bakardjieva, E. Niklas Bremberg, A. Michalski and L. Oxelheim (eds.), *The European Union in a Changing World Order. Interdisciplinary European Studies*, Cham, Palgrave MacMillan, 2020.

29 T. Treves, "Customary International Law", in Max Planck Encyclopedia of Public International Law (2006), para. 52.

> The practice of those international organizations (such as the European Union) to which member States sometimes have transferred exclusive competences, may be equated with that of States, since in particular fields such organizations act in place of the member States. This applies to the actions of such organizations, whatever forms they take, whether executive, legislative or judicial. If one were not to equate the practice of such international organizations with that of States, it would in fact mean that, not only would the organization's practice not count for State practice, but its Member States would be deprived or reduced of their ability to contribute to State practice in cases where the Member States have conferred some of their public powers to the organization.[30]

There seems to be broad agreement on this idea, at least from European States,[31] although it has been emphasised that the EU is in a rather unique position in this regard, compared to other international organisations.[32]

It should be added that the importance of EU practice for teaching international law in Europe is definitely *not* limited to areas of EU exclusive competence. Almost as important are the areas where the Union acts internationally together with its Member States, such as in cases of shared competences and of the common foreign and security policy (CFSP). There are many more areas of shared competence than exclusive competence of the EU.[33] Particularly noteworthy for international law are areas such as the environment,[34] fisheries, health, social policy and transport. In the international arena, although

30 Second Report, para. 44. See also Fourth Report, para. 20.

31 See *inter alia* the positive endorsement by the representative of Germany during the Sixth Committee meeting of 25 October 2016, https://undocs.org/A/C.6/71/SR.21, para. 116; and the joint Nordic written comments referred to in the Fifth Report of Sir Michael Wood, para. 36.

32 See *inter alia* the position of New Zealand, Fifth Report of Sir Michael Wood, para. 39; Sean D Murphy, 'Identification of customary international law and other topics: the sixty-seventh session of the International Law Commission', 109 American Journal of International Law (2015), 822 and 828, who suggests that, while references to the EU "may well be valid", the organisation "may not be exemplary of international organizations generally".

33 See the enumeration in Article 4(2) TFEU.

34 See, e.g., C. Adelle, K. Biedenkopf and D. Torney (eds.), *European Union External Environmental Policy: Rules, Regulation and Govenance,* Cham, Palgrave Macmillan, 2018; J. Auvret-Finck (ed.), *La dimension environnementale de l'action extérieure de l'Union européenne: actes du colloque de Nice des 6 et 7 avril 2017,* Paris, Pedone, 2018 ; E. Lerum Boasson and J. Wettestad, *EU Climate Policy: Industry, Policy Interaction and External Environment,* Farnham – Burlington, Ashgate, 2013; S. Minas and V. Ntousas, *EU Climate Diplomacy: Politics, Law and Negotiations,* Abingdon – New York, Routledge, 2018.

its competences are shared with the Member States, it is often the EU that expresses common positions in international organizations and at international conferences,[35] conducts international negotiations and becomes – alongside its Member States – a contracting party to international agreements where such agreements allow for it.[36] Important examples include a great variety of multilateral environmental treaties (from the UN Framework Convention on Climate Change to the Paris Agreement), the UN Framework Convention on Tobacco Control, the UN Convention against Transnational Organized Crime (or 'Palermo Convention'), the UN Convention against Corruption, the UN Convention on the Rights of Disabled Persons. Even if a multilateral treaty does not contain such a clause and is formally only open to signature and ratification by States, but falls within the scope of EU law, the Council of the EU has developed the interesting practice under which EU Member States are authorized to ratify such treaties "in the interests of the Union".[37]

Even when outside the "integrated" policymaking fields of the EU – i.e., the areas in which the "Community method" of decision-making is followed[38] – the joint practice of the EU and its Member States in international law is highly relevant. The CFSP is the area in which most EU declarations, positions and statements are made, either autonomously or within international organisations like the UN. Since the beginning of European Political Cooperation, and in an increasing number of cases since the CFSP was established under the

35 See *inter alia* R.A. Wessel and J. Odermatt (eds.), *Research Handbook on the European Union and International Organizations*, Cheltenham, Edward Elgar Publishing, 2019; K. Joergensen (ed.), *Routledge Handbook on the European Union and International Institutions: Performance, Policy, Power*, London, Routledge, 2013. For the UN context, see, apart from the publications mentioned *supra* note 18, S. Blavoukos and D. Bourantonis (eds.), *The EU in UN Politics: Actors, Processes and Performances*, London, Palgrave Macmillan, 2017.

36 This is typically on the basis of a 'regional economic integration organization' (REIO) or a 'regional integration organization' (RIO) clause: see G. De Baere, 'EU Status in Other International Organizations', in R. Schütze and T. Tridimas (eds.), *Oxford Principles of European Union Law*, Vol 1: The European Union Legal Order, Oxford, OUP, 2018, 1241.

37 See, for instance, Council Decision 2014/165/EU of 3 March 2014 authorising Member States to ratify, in the interests of the European Union, the Arms Trade Treaty, O.J. 2014, L89/44; Council Decision of 11 September 2018 authorising Member States to ratify, in the interest of the European Union, the Protocol amending the Council of Europe Convention for the Protection of Individuals with regard to Automatic Processing of Personal Data (10923/18).

38 On the specificity of the "Community method" as opposed to intergovernmental decision-making, see Y. Devuyst, 'The European Union's Institutional Balance after the Treaty of Lisbon: Community Method and Democratic Deficit Reassessed', 39 *Georgetown Journal of International Law*, 2008, 247.

1992 Maastricht Treaty, countless declarations have been made on behalf of the EU or on behalf of the EU and its Member States on matters of public international law. This number and the gremia in which such statements are made has only intensified in recent years, from the UN General Assembly[39] to the UN Human Rights Council[40] and a great number of other international organizations and conferences. With the Russian military aggression in 2022, the EU has even developed an operational strategy for dealing with Russia (and Belarus) in international organizations.[41] In terms of international law related statements one recent example, out of many, can be given from the field of international humanitarian law (IHL): the 2021 report of COJUR, the Council's Working Party on Public International Law,[42] on the EU's Guidelines for the Compliance with International Humanitarian Law, provides an overview in its annex of all EU conclusions and declarations on IHL during the year 2020, arriving at a total of 38 (not counting resolutions of the European Parliament) and 35 statements within the UN.[43] For the purposes of establishing customary international law,

39 On the EU at the UN General Assembly, see *inter alia*, apart from various contributions in S. Blavoukos and D. Bourantonis (eds.), *The EU in UN Politics: Actors, Processes and Performances, supra* note 35, E. Paasivirta and T. Ramopoulos, 'UN General Assembly, UN Security Council and UN Human Rights Council: The EU in State-Centred Multilateral Frameworks', in R.A. Wessel and J. Odermatt (eds.), *Research Handbook on the European Union and International Organizations, supra* note 35, 58; J. Wouters, 'The European Union as an actor within the United Nations General Assembly', in V. Kronenberger (ed.), *The EU and the International Legal Order: Discord or Harmony?*, The Hague, T.M.C. Asser Press, 2001, 375.

40 See, on the EU's actorness at the UN Human Rights Council, *inter alia* I. Lakatos, 'External Human Rights Diplomacy of the European Union: Has the EU Become a Decisive Human Rights Actor in Multilateral Fora?' *European Human Rights Law Review* 2020, 49; J. Wouters and K. Meuwissen, 'The European Union at the UN Human Rights Council. Multilateral Human Rights Protection Coming of Age?', *European Journal of Human Rights – Journal européen des droits de l'homme* 2–2014, 135. Importantly, the activity of the EU at the UN Human Rights Council has not impeded the EU Member States themselves to play an increasingly active role on the Council: see K.E. Smith, 'EU Member States at the UN: A Case of Europeanization Arrested?', 55 *Journal of Common Market Studies* 2017, 628.

41 See Council of the EU, *Principles regarding Russia and Belarus in multilateral fora following the Russian aggression against Ukraine*, 16 March 2022, 7261/22.

42 On COJUR, see Frank Hoffmeister, 'Public International law Working Group (Comité Juridique (COJUR))', *Max Planck Encyclopedia of International Law*, 2019.

43 Working Party on Public International Law (COJUR), *Report on the EU Guidelines on Promoting Compliance with International Humanitarian Law January 2020 – December 2020*, June 2021, https://www.consilium.europa.eu/media/51415/ihl-report-en-2021.pdf.

such statements have been referred to by international courts, such as in the 1995 *Tadić* judgment of the ICTY.[44]

A very interesting new development in this regard are media stakeouts held by permanent representatives of EU Member States sitting on the UN Security Council, which often involve statements on issues of international law.[45]

At the crossroads of the integrated and intergovernmental policies of the EU is the very important arena of international sanctions – or, in EU parlance, "restrictive measures" – adopted by the EU autonomously or in order to implement UNSC resolutions.[46] Here too, one faces an area in which the public international law practice of the Member States and of the EU have largely become unified since at least three decades. The EU has adopted a great variety of sanction schemes against third countries – more than 40[47] – and all Member States are bound, as a matter of EU law, to apply and implement these sanctions. Especially with its "Blocking Statute", the EU has adopted an important instrument dealing with extraterritorial sanctions.[48]

The EU's sanctions arsenal has recently been enriched by other instruments, such as the cyber sanctions regime,[49] the EU's 'Magnitzky Act', i.e. the

44 Prosecutor v. Tadić, Case No. IT-94-1, Decision on the Defence Motion for Interlocutory Appeal on Jurisdiction (Appeals Chamber of the International Tribunal for the Former Yugoslavia), 2 October 1995, para. 115, where reference is made to two declarations of the Council of January 1995 on international humanitarian law.

45 See, for instance, Stakeout following the AOB on the situation in Belarus, 11 November 2021, https://www.dfa.ie/pmun/newyork/news-and-speeches/securitycouncilstatements/statementsarchive/stakeout-following-the-aob-on-the-situation-in-belarus.html; Stakeout on the Middle East, 8 November 2021, https://www.dfa.ie/pmun/newyork/news-and-speeches/securitycouncilstatements/statementsarchive/joint-stakeout-by-eu-members-of-the-council-as-well-as-norway-and-albania-on-the-middle-east.html; Stakeout on DPRK, 20 October 2021, https://www.dfa.ie/pmun/newyork/news-and-speeches/securitycouncilstatements/statementsarchive/stakeout-of-eu-members-on-dprk.html; Stakeout on Ukraine, 17 February 2022, https://media.un.org/en/asset/k12/k12c1orih3; Stakeout on the Middle East, 26 May 2022, https://media.un.org/en/asset/k12/k12pm77fyt.

46 See *inter alia* K. Urbanski, *The European Union and International Sanctions: A Model of Emerging Actorness*, Cheltenham, Edward Elgar Publishing, 2020.

47 For an up-to-date overview, see the EU Sanctions Map: https://sanctionsmap.eu/#/main.

48 See Council Regulation (EC) No 2271/96 of 22 November 1996 protecting against the effects of the extra-territorial application of legislation adopted by a third country, and actions based thereon or resulting therefrom (O.J. 1996, L309/1), as amended by Regulation (EU) No 37/2014 of 15 January 2014 (O.J. 2015 L18/1) and Commission Delegated Regulation (EU) 2018/1100 of 6 June 2018 (O.J. 2018, L199I/1).

49 See Council Decision (CFSP) 2019/797 of 17 May 2019 concerning restrictive measures against cyber-attacks threatening the Union or its Member States (O.J. 2019 L129I/13) and Council Regulation (EU) 2019/796 of 17 May 2019 concerning restrictive measures against

Union's instrument to sanction human rights offenders,[50] and its proposed anti-Coercion Instrument.[51] Truly impressive are the eleven sanctions packages which the EU has adopted time against Russia because of the latter's military aggression against Ukraine.[52]

4 Concluding Observations

The present contribution has made the case to not teach and study international law "in clinical isolation"[53] in Europe, especially within the EU, but

cyber-attacks threatening the Union or its Member States (O.J. L129I/1). See *inter alia* A. Verhelst and J. Wouters, 'Filling Global Governance Gaps in Cybersecurity: International and European Legal Perspectives', 15 *International Organisations Research Journal* 2020, 105–124; A. Verhelst, M. Ruelens and J. Wouters, 'Het EU-cybersanctieregime en zijn verenigbaarheid met de grondrechten', *Rechtskundig Weekblad* 2021–22, 43–52.

50 Council Decision (CFSP) 2020/1999 of 7 December 2020 concerning restrictive measures against serious human rights violations and abuses (O.J. 2020, L410I/13), as amended by Council Decision (CFSP) 2021/372 of 2 March 2021 (O.J. 2021, L71I/6), Council Decision (CFSP) 2021/481 of 22 March 2021 (O.J. 2021, L99I/25), Council Decision (CFSP) 2021/2160 of 6 December 2021 (O.J., 2021, L436/40), Council Decision (CFSP) 2021/2197 of 13 December 2021 (O.J. 2021, L410I/17); Council Regulation (EU) 2020/1998 of 7 December 2020 concerning restrictive measures against serious human rights violations and abuses (O.J. 2020, L410I/1), as amended by Council Implementing Regulation (EU) 2021/371 of 2 March 2021 (O.J. 2021, L71I/1), Council Implementing Regulation (EU) 2021/478 of 22 March 2021 (O.J. 2021, L99I/1), Council Implementing Regulation (EU) 2021/2151 of 6 December 2021 (O.J. 2021, L436/1), Council Implementing Regulation (EU) 2021/2195 of 13 December 2021 (O.J. 2021, L445I/10), and Commission Implementing Regulation (EU) 2022/595 of 11 April 2022 (O.J. 2022, L114/60). See *inter alia* C. Eckes, 'EU Global Human Rights Sanctions Regime: Is the Genie Out of the Bottle?' 30 *Journal of Contemporary European Studies* 2022, 255.

51 See European Commission, proposal for a Regulation of the European Parliament and of the Council on the protection of the Union and its Member States from economic coercion by third countries, 8 December 2021, COM(2021) 775 final.

52 For an overview, see https://ec.europa.eu/info/business-economy-euro/banking-and-finance/international-relations/restrictive-measures-sanctions/sanctions-adopted-following-russias-military-aggression-against-ukraine_en. For an overview of the EU's sanctions legal practice, see C. Eckes, 'The Law and Practice of EU Sanctions', in S. Blockmans and P. Koutrakos (eds.), *Research Handbook on the EU's Common Foreign and Security Policy*, Elgar, 2018, 206.

53 This is the well-known expression used by the WTO's Standing Appellate Body about the interpretation of WTO law in its first report: *United States: Standards for Reformulated and Conventional Gasoline–Report of the Appellate Body* (20 May 1996) WT/DS2/AB/R, 17, where it held that "the General Agreement is not to be read in clinical isolation from public international law."

rather to do this while taking the European dimensions fully into account. More than in any other continent, international law in Europe is an integral part of a multi-layered legal order which does not only comprise national legal systems but notably also the two European legal orders which find their origins in international law, i.e. the law of the EU and of the European Convention on Human Rights, as shaped by Europe's two supreme courts, i.e. the Court of Justice of the EU and the European Court of Human Rights. For sure, this adds to the complexity of the learning process, but without such an approach, one risks not conveying an adequate picture of the international law practice in Europe to students. In short: to come to a proper understanding of international law when teaching and studying – and practicing – it in Europe, it is essential to consider its constant interactions with both national and European legal developments.

Bibliography

Adelle C, Biedenkopf K and Torney D (eds.), *European Union External Environmental Policy: Rules, Regulation and Govenance* (Palgrave Macmillan: Cham 2018).

Auvret-Finck J (ed.), *La dimension environnementale de l'action extérieure de l'Union européenne: actes du colloque de Nice des 6 et 7 avril 2017* (Pedone: Paris 2018).

Baarsma NA, *The Europeanisation of International Family Law* (T.M.C. Asser Press: The Hague 2011).

Bakardjieva A, Niklas Bremberg E, Michalski A and Oxelheim L (eds.), *The European Union in a Changing World Order. Interdisciplinary European Studies* (Palgrave MacMillan: Cham 2020).

Blauberger M and Krämer RU, 'Europeanisation with Many Unknowns: National Company Law Reforms after Centros' (2014) 37 *West European Politics* 786.

Blavoukos S and Bourantonis D (eds.), *The EU in UN Politics: Actors, Processes and Performances* (Palgrave Macmillan: London 2017).

Chané A-L and Wouters J, 'The European Union in United Nations Economic Governance Fora' (2017) 8 *European Yearbook of International Economic Law* 541.

Claes M, 'The Europeanisation of National Constitutions in the Constitutionalisation of Europe: Some Observations against the Background of the Constitutional Experience of the EU-15' (2007) 3 *Croatian Yearbook of European Law & Policy* 1.

Crawford J, *Chance, Order, Change: the Course of International Law, General Course on Public International Law* (Hague Academy of International Law: The Hague 2014).

De Baere G, 'EU Status in Other International Organizations' in Schütze R and Tridimas T (eds.), *Oxford Principles of European Union Law, Vol 1: the European Union Legal Order* (OUP: Oxford 2018).

Devuyst Y, 'The European Union's Institutional Balance after the Treaty of Lisbon: Community Method and Democratic Deficit Reassessed' (2008) 39 *Georgetown Journal of International Law* 247.

Eckes C, 'EU Global Human Rights Sanctions Regime: Is the Genie Out of the Bottle?' (2022) 30 *Journal of Contemporary European Studies* 255.

Eckes C, 'The Law and Practice of EU Sanctions' in Blockmans S and Koutrakos P (eds.), *Research Handbook on the EU's Common Foreign and Security Policy* (Elgar: 2018).

Eliantonio M, 'Europeanisation of Administrative Justice? The Influence of the ECJ's Case Law in Italy, Germany and England' (2010) 22 *Revue européenne de droit public* 681.

Elias TO, *Africa and the Development of International Law* (Nijhoff: Dordrecht 1988).

Emerson M, Balfour R, Corthaut T, Wouters J, Kaczynski PM and Renard T, *Upgrading the EU's Role as Global Actor: Institutions, Law and the Restructuring of European Diplomacy* (Centre for European Policy Studies: Brussels 2011).

Giliker P, *The Europeanisation of English Tort Law* (Hart Publishing: Oxford 2014).

Green N and Robertson A (eds.), *The Europeanisation of United Kingdom Competition Law* (Hart Publishing: Oxford 1999).

Hahn MJ and Van der Loo G (eds.), *Law and Practice of the Common Commercial Policy: the First 10 Years after the Treaty of Lisbon* (Brill Nijhoff: Leiden – Boston 2021).

von Hein J, Kieninger E-M and Rühl G (eds.), *How European Is European Private International Law? Sources, Court Practice, Academic Discourse* (Intersentia: Cambridge 2019).

Heun W and Lipp V (eds.), *Europäisierung des Rechts* (Universitätsverlag Göttingen: Göttingen 2008).

Hoffmeister F, 'Public International law Working Group (Comité Juridique (COJUR))' (2019) *Max Planck Encyclopedia of International Law*.

Jans JH, Prechal S and Widdershoven RJGM (eds.), *Europeanisation of Public Law* (Europa Law Publishing: Groningen 2015).

Joergensen K (ed.), *Routledge Handbook on the European Union and International Institutions: Performance, Policy, Power* (Routledge: London 2013).

Koskenniemi M, 'Histories of International Law: Dealing with Eurocentrism' (2011) 9 *Rechtsgeschichte* 152, 170.

Koskenniemi M, 'International Law in Europe: Between Tradition and Renewal' (2005) 16 *EJIL* 113.

Koskenniemi M, *The Gentle Civilizer of Nations: the Rise and Fall of International law, 1870–1960* (Cambridge University Press: Cambridge 2001).

Krimphove D, 'The Europeanization of Commercial Agency Law' (2016) *Europeización del Derecho Privado: Cuestiones Actuales*, Madric, Marcial Pons 129.

Kristoffersson E and Persson AH (eds.), *Swedish Perspectives on Private Law Europeanisation* (Hart Publishing: Portland 2017).

Lakatos I, 'External Human Rights Diplomacy of the European Union: Has the EU Become a Decisive Human Rights Actor in Multilateral Fora?' (2020) *European Human Rights Law Review* 49.

Lerum Boasson E and Wettestad J, *EU Climate Policy: Industry, Policy Interaction and External Environment* (Ashgate: Farnham – Burlington 2013).

Lorca AB, 'Eurocentrism in the History of International Law' in Fassbender B and Peters A (eds.), *The Oxford Handbook of the History of International Law* (OUP: Oxford 2012).

Lütz S, Leeg T, Otto D and Woyames Dreher V, *The European Union as a Global Actor: Trade, Finance and Climate Policy* (Springer: Cham 2021).

MacDermott PA, 'The Europeanisation of Contract Law' in Lucey MC and Keville C (eds.), *Irish Perspectives on EC Law* (Thomson Round Hall: Dublin 2003).

McClean JD and Abou-Nigm VR, *Morris Conflict of Laws* (Sweet & Maxwell: London 2016).

Melo Araujo BA, *The EU Deep Trade Agenda: Law and Policy* (OUP: Oxford 2016).

Minas S and Ntousas V, *EU Climate Diplomacy: Politics, Law and Negotiations* (Routledge: Abingdon – New York 2018).

Murphy SD, 'Identification of customary international law and other topics: the sixty-seventh session of the International Law Commission' (2015) 109 American Journal of International Law 822 and 828.

Niglia L, 'The Non-Europeanization of Private Law' (2001) 9 European Review of Private Law 575.

Ohly A and Pila J (eds.), *The Europeanization of Intellectual Property Law: towards a European Legal Methodology* (OUP: Oxford 2013).

Orakhelashvili A, 'The Idea of European International Law' (2006) 17 *EJIL* 315, 329 and 339.

Ouwerkerk J, 'Criminal Justice beyond National Sovereignty. An Alternative Perspective on the Europeanisation of Criminal Law' (2015) 23 *European Journal of Crime, Criminal Law and Criminal Justice* 11.

Paasivirta E and Ramopoulos T, 'UN General Assembly, UN Security Council and UN Human Rights Council: the EU in State-Centred Multilateral Frameworks' in Wessel RA and Odermatt J (eds.), *Research Handbook on the European Union and International Organizations* (Edward Elgar Publishing: Cheltenham 2019).

Pintens W, 'Europeanisation of Family Law' in Boele-Woelki K (ed.), *Perspectives for the Unification and Harmonisation of Family Law in Europe* (Intersentia: Antwerp 2003).

Rengeling H-W (ed.), *Europäisierung des Rechts* (Carl Heymanns Verlag: Cologne – Berlin – Bonn 1996).

Riesenhuber K (ed.), *Die Europäisierung des Privatrechts* (De Gruyter: Berlin – Boston 2006).

Roberts A, *Is International Law International?* (OUP: Oxford 2017).

Roth H (ed.), *Europäisierung des Rechts: Ringvorlesung der Juristischen Fakultät der Universität Regensburg* (Mohr Siebeck: Tübingen 2010).

Smith KE, 'EU Member States at the UN: a Case of Europeanization Arrested?' (2017) 55 *Journal of Common Market Studies* 628.

Smits JM, 'What Do Nationalists Maximise? A Public Choice Perspective on the (Non-) Europeanization of Private Law' (2012) 8 *European Review of Private Law* 296.

Snyder F (ed.), *The Europeanisation of Law: the Legal Effects of European Integration* (Hart Publishing: Oxford 2000).

Stolleis M, 'Europeanization of Social Law' in Stolleis M (ed.), *History of Social law in Germany* (Springer: Heidelberg 2013).

Treves T, "Customary International Law" in Max Planck Encyclopedia of Public International Law (2006).

Twigg-Flesner C, *The Europeanisation of Contract Law: Current Controversies in Law* (Routledge: Abingdon 2008).

Urbanski K, *The European Union and International Sanctions: a Model of Emerging Actorness* (Edward Elgar Publishing: Cheltenham 2020).

Van Vooren B, Blockmans S and Wouters J (eds.), *The EU's Role in Global Governance: the Legal Dimension* (OUP: Oxford 2013).

Verhelst A and Wouters J, 'Filling Global Governance Gaps in Cybersecurity: International and European Legal Perspectives' (2020) 15 *International Organisations Research Journal* 105.

Verhelst A, Ruelens M and Wouters J, 'Het EU-cybersanctieregime en zijn verenigbaarheid met de grondrechten' (2021–2022) *Rechtskundig Weekblad* 43.

Wahl R, 'Die Zweite Phase des Öffentlichen Rechts in Deutschland. Die Europaisierung des Offentlichen Rechts' (1999) 38 *Der Staat* 495.

Watkin TG (ed.), *The Europeanisation of Law* (United Kingdom National Committee of Comparative Law: Cardiff 1998).

Wessel RA and Odermatt J (eds.), *Research Handbook on the European Union and International Organizations* (Edward Elgar Publishing: Cheltenham 2019).

Working Party on Public International Law (COJUR), *Report on the EU Guidelines on Promoting Compliance with International Humanitarian Law January 2020 – December 2020* (June 2021).

Wouters J and Chané A-L, 'Brussels Meets Westphalia: the European Union and the United Nations' in Eeckhout P and Lopez-Escudero M (eds.), *The European Union's External Action in Times of Crisis* (Hart: Oxford 2016).

Wouters J and Meuwissen K, 'The European Union at the UN Human Rights Council. Multilateral Human Rights Protection Coming of Age?' (2014) 2 *European Journal of Human Rights – Journal européen des droits de l'homme* 135.

Wouters J, 'European Company Law: Quo Vadis?' (2000) 37 *Common Market Law Review* 257.

Wouters J, 'The European Union as an Actor within the United Nations General Assembly' in Kronenberger V (ed.), *The EU and the International Legal Order: Discord or Harmony?* (T.M.C. Asser Press: The Hague 2001).

Wouters J, 'The European Union as an actor within the United Nations General Assembly' in Kronenberger V (ed.), *The EU and the International Legal Order: Discord or Harmony?* (T.M.C. Asser Press: The Hague 2001).

Wouters J, 'The United Nations, the EU and Conflict Prevention: Interconnecting the Global and Regional Levels' in Kronenberger V and Wouters J (eds.), *The European Union and Conflict Prevention: Policy and Legal Aspects* (T.M.C. Asser Press: The Hague 2004).

Wouters J, Bruyninckx H, Basu S and Schunz S (eds.), *The European Union and Multilateral Governance: Assessing EU Participation in United Nations Human Rights and Environmental Fora* (Palgrave Macmillan: Basingstoke 2012).

Wouters J, Hoffmeister F and Ruys T (eds.), *The United Nations and the European Union: an Ever Stronger Partnership* (T.M.C. Asser Press: The Hague 2006).

Wouters J, Nollkaemper A and De Wet E (eds.), *The Europeanisation of International Law. The Status of International Law in the EU and its Member States* (T.M.C. Asser Press: The Hague 2008).

Wouters J, Odermatt J and Ramopoulos T, 'The Status of the European Union at the United Nations General Assembly' in Govaere I, Van Elsuwege P, Lannon E and Adam S (eds.), *Liber Amicorum Marc Maresceau* (Brill: Leiden 2013).

Wouters J, Ryngaert C, Ruys T and De Baere G, *International Law: a European Perspective* (Hart Publishing: Oxford 2018).

Zahn RL, 'The "Europeanization" of Labour Law: Can Comparative Labour Law Solve the Problem?" (2020) 61 *Northern Ireland Legal Quarterly* 79.

Zimmermann R, 'Comparative Law and the Europeanization of Private Law' in Reimann M and Zimmermann R (eds.), *The Oxford Handbook of Comparative Law* (OUP: Oxford 2012).

Zimmermann R, 'Le droit comparé et l'européanisation du droit privé' (2007) 451.

CHAPTER 8

Teaching Global Administrative Law

A New Domain for Administrative Law?

Barbara Marchetti

1 Introduction

The international landscape has radically changed in the last 40 years. Many public functions, traditionally exercised by national authorities, are now governed at the international (and supranational) level. Above and beyond the EU Institutions, a variety of bodies and organizations have been created globally: they are often different from the traditional International Organizations (IOs) because of their memberships, their mission, their regulatory powers, and their tools. Every single area of life, from sport to the environment, from health to trade, from food to culture, from labor to transportation, has new global regulatory regimes which produce norms, enact decisions, manage procedures, and settle disputes. These developments are the natural product of economic globalization and of the consequent need to take care of public interests at the international level.

Many of these regulatory regimes overlap. Furthermore, they live in an environment which lacks a Constitution and a Parliament. They are not always the result of multilateral agreements among member States, but have different origins.[1] ICANN, for example, is a private US company, but its decisions spread all over the world. Again, global regulatory regimes can be of a private or public nature and can use a variety of tools and instruments, such as standards, guidelines, private regulation, infra-institutional rules, and soft law. It is the case of the World Bank's operational policies; of the International Labor

1 Sabino Cassese, *'Lo spazio giuridico globale'*, Roma-Bari, Laterza, 2003; Sabino Cassese, *'Il diritto globale. Giustizia e democrazia oltre lo Stato'*, Torino, Einaudi, 2009; Lorenzo Casini, *'Potere globale. Regole e decisioni oltre lo Stato'*, Bologna, Il Mulino, 2018; Eyal Benvenisti, *'The Law of Global Governance'*, Hague Academy of International Law 2014; Benedict Kingsbury, Nico Krisch, Richard B. Stewart, *'The emergence of Global Administrative Law'*, Law and Contemporary problems, 2005, 68, 15; Benedict Kingsbury, *'The Concept of Law in Global Administrative Law'*, Eur. J. Intern. L, 2009, vol. 20, 29; Maria Rosaria Ferrarese, *'Prima lezione di diritto globale'*, Roma-Bari, Laterza, 2012.

 | DOI:10.1163/9789004678880_010

Organization's (ILO) standards; of the WADA's antidoping code, and so on. Sometimes they even have their own dispute settlement system, other times no Courts or Tribunals are instituted inside them. Their decisions affect not only national States, but also civil society, NGOs, national administrative authorities, and private corporations.

Their variety explains why, when we are confronted with this reality, it is necessary to use a different lens. The international law lens continues to be necessary and important: it can explain the relationships between a global regulatory regime and the national States or clarify whether we are before a public classic international organization or something different, or if a dispute settlement system is of a dyadic or triadic nature. But for a more comprehensive look at these new regulatory bodies, we also need other lens: the administrative law lens, for example, can help us understand how they adopt their decisions, how these public powers can be made accountable, how they enforce their decisions, how to force them to open their procedure to participation, and how to demand transparency in their actions.

The more lenses we have, the more we can understand the complexity of this new landscape and its implications in terms of justice: a constitutional law approach, in this discourse, is useful too, because global constitutionalism addresses the foundations and limitations of the principles of political order in the global context, which is essential for discussing democracy and fundamental rights before global powers and institutions. But also sociological and economic analyses are important in understanding the causes of their institution, comprehend effects and consequences on civil society and States' legal orders and adjust or modify them. As Lorenzo Casini says, "indeed, GAL scholarship owes several insights to political science and sociological studies on globalization, as well as to works in economics, history, and anthropology, that have been crucial in enabling GAL to understand complex concepts such as regulatory regimes, accountability, legitimacy, and governance more generally".[2]

2 Why the Global Order Is Complex and Why It Could Become a Global Disorder

The creation of numerous global bodies and Institutions taking care of different public interests above and beyond the national level generates many

2 Lorenzo Casini, *'Global Administrative Law',* in Jeffrey L. Dunoff, Mark A. Pollack (eds), *'International Legal Theory: Foundations and Frontiers',* Cambridge University Press, 2019.

problems, which concern their democratic legitimacy, their mutual relations, the need to build judicial protection mechanisms and remedies, and the necessity to limit abuse of powers.

One of the problems is related to their plural, varied and composite nature: the fact that many different actors have arisen beyond the State for environment, trade, food safety, health, and work regulations means there is a risk that the rules produced by a specific sectoral regime, for example by the World Trade Organization, conflict with those of other sectoral regimes or international regional organizations carrying out the same public functions and taking care of the same interests. The fragmentation of this myriad of regulatory bodies, in fact, generates overlaps and requires rules that can ensure their cohabitation.[3]

These rules of coexistence are not easy to identify and an important role in determining when and to what extent a norm or a decision produced in a given regulatory regime can penetrate a different sectoral regime, or impose itself and prevail over it, is often played by Courts, which are called upon to build the stepping stones between the different regulations.

A significant case is the well-known Kadi decision, in which a Court of an international regional system (the European Union Court of Justice) checked a decision made by an international organization (the United Nation Security Council) to safeguard fundamental rights and founding values recognized at the European level, denying access to its system to UNSC decisions.

The fact that Courts act as guardians of the different regulatory systems, however, can highlight another problem: in particular, if international Courts adopt the choices on the cohabitation of the different regulatory regimes and decide how to balance the many interests at stake, it is necessary to question who the global judges are and what funds their legitimacy for making these choices.

It is the case of Art. XX of the GATT agreements: it establishes that restrictive measures for international trade can be justified to ensure human, animal and plant life and health. When a State imposes a restriction on the trade of a product using this standard, the Dispute Settlement System of the World Trade Organization can establish, applying a proportionality test – in a similar way to those used by administrative Courts in reviewing administrative decisions – what should be the correct balance between trade interests and health interests. In the well-known *Thai Cigarettes* case of 1990, for instance,

3 Sabino Cassese, '*I Tribunali di Babele. I giudici alla ricerca di un nuovo ordine globale*,' Donzelli editore, 2009.

the Appellate Body (AB) of the WTO decided that the value at stake, health, could be protected with a less incisive measure on the freedom of trade of cigarettes, concluding that the restrictive measures imposed by the State were illegal and unjustified.

The WTO dispute settlement system, composed of first instance bodies and a Court of Appeal (the panels and the Appellate Body), is considered an advanced judicial system after the juridification process following the Uruguay Round. But, if we look at the procedural rules governing its functioning, we might wonder whether it really is a judicial system in the traditional meaning of the word. If one examines its fundamental features, one may have some doubts: the negotiating-diplomatic component remains significant in the composition and functioning of its adjudication bodies, the procedures are still partially secret, and non-governmental organizations (NGOs) have limited access to procedure. We should ask, therefore, which is the source of its legitimacy and why its decisions – that affect not only States but also civil society, commercial corporations and private citizens – should be accepted and considered legally binding.

More generally, we should consider that different global courts could have different problems of legitimacy depending on their legal regime and source, and that should make their decisions more or less acceptable or binding.

Global Courts are an extremely heterogeneous category:[4] it is necessary not only to distinguish between inter-state Tribunals, as instances for resolving conflicts between States, and supranational Tribunals, as instances for the protection of citizens against the States, but also to recognize that the different judges could have varying degrees of independence regarding the governmental bodies, different compositions, diverse evolution layers, diplomatic or legal traits in defining the dispute, different legal training of their judges and so on.[5]

Some identify three characteristics that international Courts must possess in order to be considered democratically accountable: they should base their decisions on legal arguments (in particular articles 31 and 32 of the Vienna Convention on the Law of Treaties); they should be independent and impartial judges; they should decide through procedures possibly open to third-party participation. At the international level, these traits are often lacking in dispute

4 Laurence R. Helfer – Anne-Marie Slaughter, '*Why States Create International Tribunals: A Response to Professors Posner and Yoo*', Calif. L.R., 2005, vol. 93, 3.

5 Joseph H.H. Weiler, '*The geology of International Law – governance, democracy and legitimacy*,' J. Int. Law, 64, 2004, 547. On supranational and International Courts see also Edoardo Chiti, Bernardo G. Mattarella (eds.), '*Global Administrative Law and EU Administrative Law*', Relationships, Legal Issues, and Comparison, Springer, 2011.

settlement bodies. Diplomatic thinking often prevails over the legal one, and independence is not firmly guaranteed, due to both the systems of appointment and the proximity to the interests of the executives; the procedures are often secret, in order to favor negotiation practices and resolutions based on agreements between the parties.[6]

Another factor of complexity – and potential disorder – derives from the variety of the constitutive and organizational structures of the global regimes. Their genesis can be very different, as well as their memberships, with important consequences on the accountability deficit.

Furthermore, they are also heterogeneous from the point of view of their public or private nature and their consequent course of action. Beyond the common drive that generated them – namely economic globalization – regulation beyond the state did not follow a unitary constitutive model, giving birth to public international organizations or private bodies, using tools of the public sphere or exclusively private modules, giving rise to binding or soft law measures.[7]

With regard to their organizational features, for example, we find not only classical international organizations but also transnational bodies made up of administrations (governmental networks), mixed public-private bodies and private institutions. Each global entity corresponds to different accountability regimes and sometimes different forms of action, not necessarily corresponding and symmetrical to the public or private nature of the bodies using them.

Furthermore, they can have different relations with the States, with civil society, with the sectoral national administrations, and with NGOs.

That raises further problems: it is necessary to ensure that a national administration, which is a member of a mixed global network that produces standards or guidelines regulating a specific sector, can be held responsible and accountable for its choices; or again it implies the need to find accountability mechanisms suitable for the action of a private body whose technical rules have legal effects on States, national administrations, and civil society. And it is necessary to understand whether or not the way in which a rule is generated can influence its ability to enter into other legal regimes.

The transnational "networks", which constitute one of the best suited institutional solutions for coordinating the global action of national administrations,

---

6 Armin Von Bogdandy – Ingo Venzke, '*On the democratic legitimation of International Judicial Lawmaking*', German, Law Journal, 2011, vol. 12.

7 Benedict Kingsbury, '*The Concept of Law in Global Administrative Law*', (n 1), 29; Sabino Cassese, '*Oltre lo Stato*', Roma-Bari, Laterza, 2007; Lorenzo Casini, '*Potere globale. Regole e decisioni oltre lo Stato*', (n 1).

are based not on top-of-the-line logic but on the horizontality of relations and can be of both a public and mixed nature. In the first case, the nodes of the network are made up of representatives of national governments or administrations who agree – often through soft law – on the policies and actions which will then be implemented, through binding legal acts, at the national level. The regulation that is produced through the network therefore enters and influences the national systems, and determines the contents of the national law.

For this type of network, accountability mechanisms must be guaranteed, but it is not clear how. If we consider the action produced by a national administration, as it is known, legitimacy can be assured through participatory mechanisms that allow the representation of stakeholders' interests in decision-making procedures; furthermore, a judicial review of the administrative decisions constitutes another important remedy for people who are affected in their legal interests.

On the contrary, when the same national administration participates in a transnational network, the stakeholders have little or no ability to influence the results of the global decision-making process and, usually, there are no remedies available for challenging the final network's action before a judge. The circumstance, therefore, that the position of the national administration is expressed in the network determines a decrease in the power of stakeholders, to the point that some legal systems, such as the United States, impose on their own authority (this is the case, for example, of the Federal Drug Administration in the context of its participation in the International Conference of Harmonization) to open a national participatory procedure in which interested parties can represent their interests and influence the public authority position in the global network.

The problems are even more delicate when the transnational network is mixed public/private. Again, the International Conference on Harmonization (ICH), set up to develop the technical standards for the registration of medicinal products, allows the participation, in addition to some governmental agencies, also of some associations that bring together the main multinational pharmaceutical products. Thus constituted, however, these networks can generate various problems, ranging from the exclusion of subjects representing categories or countries on which their action nevertheless falls, to the capture of regulators by those being regulated, to conflict of interest, to the impossibility of effective control over their action.

Then, again, there is another flaw related to the effectiveness of global powers: it concerns the enforcement of their decisions. The enforcement mechanisms for standards and decisions adopted at a global level continue to be anchored to a negotiation-diplomatic logic, which refers to the bargaining power of States. Even though the juridification process has led to the institution of Courts and dispute resolution systems, as was the case in the World Trade Organization with the creation of the Dispute Settlement System,[8] the sovereignty of States is still an obstacle to effective global justice, because it imposes a largely power-based logic. Therefore, also in this aspect, it is necessary to recognize the limits of juridification: in other words, if it is true that "the creation of adjudication procedures entrusts the assessment of violations to third parties, and sometimes also recognizes to civil society and individuals a role of promoters of monitoring compliance", however, "the Contracting States reaffirm the principle of sovereign immunity and the right of equality during the enforcement phase, which remains dominated by the rule of consensus and by horizontal logic".[9]

With respect to the accountability and enforcement problems generated by global bodies, Global Administrative Law scholars are trying, with some success, to transfer to the action of global powers the typical guarantees and principles existing at the national level in order to increase the democratic legitimacy of the Institutions, to make decision-making procedures more fair and just, to strengthen rationality, proportionality and publicity of final decisions,[10] and to build administrative and judicial review mechanisms.

Obviously, the contribution from administrative law still remains insufficient if we look at the substantial data, since it does not solve the problem of the starting inequality of the parties, particularly evident in the functioning of some regulatory regimes, but it constitutes, together with the instruments of private law, international law and constitutional law, an important key for understanding, rationalizing, and legalizing the global legal space.

8 R.E. Hudec, *'The Role of GATT Secretariat in the Evolution of WTO Dispute Settlement Procedure'*, in AAVV, *'The Uruguay Round and Beyond: Essays in Honor of Arthur Dunkel, J. Bhagwati and M. Hirsch, Berlin'*, 1998, 109; Barbara Marchetti, *'The WTO Dispure Settlement System: Administration, Court or Tertium Genus?*, Suffolk Transnational L.R., 2009, vol. XXXII, 3, 567.

9 Barbara Marchetti, *'The enforcement of global decisions'*, Sabino Cassese (ed.), *'Research Handbook on Global Administrative Law'*, Edward Elgar, 2016; Thomas Nagel, *'The problem of global justice'*, Philosophy and Public Affair, 2005, 33, 113; Joseph H.H. Weiler, *'The geology of International Law – governance, democracy and legitimacy*; (n 5), 547.

10 Sabino Cassese, *'Chi governa il mondo?'*, Bologna, Il Mulino, 2012; Carol Harlow, *'Global Administrative Law: the Quest for Principles and Values'*, Eur. Journal Int. Law, 2006, vol. 17, 1, 187.

3 How to Study a Fragmentated Global Order

As we have already said, in the global order we have a lot of fragmentation and variations in actors, procedures, decisions, relations with State and civil society, accountability mechanisms, and review mechanisms (Courts, dispute settlement system, arbitration). In regulating this institutional scenario, the role of Global Administrative law can be to limit powers.

If we examine the different national administrative law traditions, from civil law to common law countries, there is a common denominator that brings them together: it is the core of rules and principles which governs and limits powers and procedures of the administrative authorities, when they are called upon to ensure the multiple responsibilities of the Modern State. In any administrative law system, there are limits placed on administrative power, which are bound both substantially and procedurally, and there are tools and remedies given to citizens to enforce these rules and to protect their interests.

This nucleus is also fundamental in the newborn global administrative law. In particular, GAL tries to develop procedural guarantees and review mechanisms to ensure legal accountability of international administrations, particularly because these bodies and Institutions exist in a legal space in which – as we highlighted before – neither a Parliament nor a Constitution can effectively limit them.

If global powers cannot be limited through the traditional channel of representative democracy, participatory democracy can partially assure some degree of accountability. The aim is to build decision-making procedures to make them transparent, reasonable, accountable, and open to participation. More specifically, guarantees and principles of administrative law, like the notice and comment procedure, the right to be heard, the duty to give reasons, the impartiality principle, the proportionality principle, the right to access documents, and the transparency principle can counterbalance the lack of representative democracy, contributing to decrease the accountability deficit that characterizes many of these global bodies.

From a methodological point of view, that means, first of all, to go into a deep analysis of different global regulatory regimes, to recognize their features, and to apply mechanisms and general principles to make them accountable and just. But also trying to find common guarantees and rules applicable to all the global administrations to assure a minimum standard of rule of law and global justice.

4 How to Teach GAL?

For many reasons, teaching Global Administrative Law is not an easy task. When we teach national administrative law, or comparative administrative law, we start from an idea of public administration, we examine the public authorities which carry out public functions in a given national system, then we explain the rules and principles that govern their organization and actions, we analyze them from a structural and functional point of view; again, we study the legal regime of administrative decisions, the grounds for their review before the Courts, their contractual activity, their civil liability and, at least broadly, their administrative justice. All these elements differ from State to State, but they are generally supported by a tendentially stable and certain ground: there may be border issues, in identifying what "public authority" is or is not, but the dividing line between administrative function, on the one hand, and judicial and legislative functions, on the other, is quite clear; as well defined is, in its essential core, the object to be investigated.

A stable and certain background is lacking, on the contrary, when we study and teach global administrative law. First of all, it is not easy to draw the same dividing line between the executive function, on the one hand, and the judicial and legislative functions, on the other; secondly, it is not clear, in the global context, "who makes what", identifying offices and competences.

Furthermore, among the various bodies and Institutions existing beyond the State, we must distinguish between formal treaty-based international or intergovernmental organizations (such as the WTO, the Security Council, the World Bank), transnational networks of domestic regulatory officials (such as the Basel Committee on Banking Supervision), hybrid public/private regulatory bodies (such as the ICH, the World Anti-Doping Agency, ICANN, the Global Fund to Fight Aids, Tuberculosis and Malaria – Global Fund) and private regulatory bodies (such as International Sport Federations, the Society for Worldwide Interbank Financial Telecommunications) to understand to what extent principles and guarantees of Global Administrative Law can be applied.

Teaching global administrative law therefore means, first of all, to analyze and distinguish between the different global regulators, to know how to trace their origins and constitutive powers, to examine their public or private traits, to discover their tools and instruments of action, to understand their relationships with States or national regulators, and to know their sources of law and procedural rules.

It also means to verify how the fundamental principles of administrative law – the duty to give reasons, the principle of transparency and publicity, the right to be heard, and proportionality and reasonableness principles – can help to make bodies not democratically elected more accountable.

In this perspective, many global administrative law courses have been instituted around the world, not only at the New York University (Institute for International Law and Justice), where this discipline was born (and taught for the first time), but in several Italian Universities like Tor Vergata in Rome, Bocconi in Milan, La Tuscia in Viterbo, Palermo and Trento.

Teaching Global Administrative Law means, conclusively, to analyze the global rule of law and its implications for global powers, through the analysis of the different regulatory regimes and their features. The International Organization for Standardization (ISO), the Codex Alimentarius Commission and the International Conference on Harmonization (ICH) can be considered three useful and paradigmatic case studies for our discussion.

5 The International Organization for Standardization (ISO) and the Codex Alimentarius Commission as Global Standard-Setting Bodies

The ISO is probably the most important standard-setting organization operating in the global space. It is an independent non-governmental Institution which adopts non-binding standards which are subsequently transposed in national binding norms because of the World Trade Organization TBT (Technical Barriers to Trade) Agreement. Because this agreement strongly encourages Member States to base their regulations and measures on international standards (mostly from ISO) as a means to facilitate trade, these standards become *de facto* binding. ISO has 164 national members and three membership categories: the member bodies, which are considered the most representative standard body in each country and the only members that have voting rights; correspondent members, which do not participate in standards promulgation but are informed of the work of ISO, even if they do not have their own standard organization; and subscriber members, which are countries with small economies which can only follow the development of standards.

The National standards bodies can be private or public: in western industrial countries they are generally private (like the American National Standards Institute), but consist of members from both the private sector (such as businesses, professional societies, and trade associations) and federal agencies, while in most other countries they are governmental, especially in developing countries. Because of this mixed membership, ISO is a hybrid public-private organization whose publicness has become more and more pronounced.[11] This increase in the dimension of public law has required more accountability mechanisms, open decision-making procedures, and cooperation with other standardization bodies and institutions like the ILO.

In particular, the study of ISO confirms that much in international standardization involves a balancing of interests. These can be interests of the same kind, like commercial interests of different manufacturers or industries, or interests of different stakeholder groups (such as consumers, environmentalists, or governments). But if standards setting has public policy implications, the way in which these standards are established is crucial; particularly, it becomes fundamental to wonder if all the relevant actors are sitting at the negotiating table, if there is a way to assure reasonable and proportionate decisions and to make the decision-making process transparent; if there is some possibility of reviewing the outcome of the standard-setting procedure by people affected by ISO decisions, and so on.

The same problem can arise with the Codex Alimentarius Commission (CAC). This institution was established in 1963 by FAO and the World Health Organization to establish food standards, guidelines and codes of practice to promote fair practice in food trade and to protect consumer health. These standards constitute a formally non-binding law, but their importance has grown enormously due to the express reference in the international agreements on phytosanitary measures adopted within the WTO. Since these standards constitute for developing countries a condition for trading their products (which otherwise could be rejected for health protection reasons), they are *de facto* binding.

In the formulation of these standards, the participation of numerous stakeholders is established and encouraged, in order to make decisions open, participatory, and accountable.

But, for many reasons, while the industries of rich and developed countries actively participate in the formulation of standards, consumers and environmental protection associations have limited ability to influence the Codex Alimentarius Commission's decision-making procedure. In particular, environmental and consumer associations in poor and developing countries do not have the economic resources or skills needed to exercise effectively their

---

11 Eran Shamir Borer, '*Legitimacy without Authority in Global Standardization Governance: the Case of the International Organization for Standardization* (ISO)', in Sabino Cassese, Bruno Carotti, Lorenzo Casini, Eleonora Cavalieri, Euan MacDonald (eds.), '*Global Administrative Law: the Casebook*', 3rd ed., IRPA, Institute for International Law and Justice, NYU School of Law, 2012, 162.

participation rights. Trivially, these actors cannot afford to pay travel expenses to attend Commission meetings, nor are they able to compete in terms of the expertise necessary to effectively exert some influence on the decision-making process.

An attempt to face this initial imbalance was made by setting up a Fund (the Codex Trust Fund) to encourage the participation of developing countries, but this reform is still not enough to guarantee the effectiveness of participation rights. Furthermore, the tendentially irreversible nature of these standards (once approved according to the consensus principle) makes subsequent changes difficult, even if future greater participation of developing countries had been guaranteed.

Establishing participatory rights and due process can therefore result in an empty and formal exercise of guarantees if the starting position of the Member States (or of the interested parties) is so unequal that it does not allow an effective possibility of influencing the decision-making process. From this point of view, therefore, the traditional guarantees and principles of administrative law, while producing some results, prove to be insufficient and require further efforts to reduce the substantial inequality between rich and poor countries.

6 The International Conference on Harmonization (ICH)

The International Conference on Harmonization of Technical Requirements for Registration of Pharmaceuticals for Human Use (ICH) was set up in 1991 and was initially composed of three drug regulation authorities (from the US, the EU, and Japan) and R&D pharmaceutical industry associations from the same regions. The purpose of the ICH is to harmonize the technical requirements of drug registration rules concerning the quality, efficacy, and safety of drugs: it has issued more than 50 guidelines so far, which have become *de facto* global standards, adopted not only by its members, but by many companies and countries beyond the ICH regions.

This public-private harmonization network has grown in the last 20 years: its membership consists now of 50 different entities as founding members, regulating members, and observers. Among them, regulating members are now the regulatory authorities of Canada, Switzerland, China, Brazil, Singapore, South Korea, and Turkey.

In adopting its guidelines, the ICH conducts a five-step procedure. In the first step, the expert working group develops a draft guideline, which is released for consultation. Consultations have to take place in each of the regions, according to the rules established for any regulatory authority, but comments may also be submitted directly to the ICH Secretariat. After all comments have been transferred to the working group, a consensus-building process takes place. If a consensus is reached, the guideline will be submitted to the regulatory members of the Assembly, who have to reach a sufficient consensus. After that, the harmonized guideline moves immediately to the final step of the process, which is regulatory implementation. They are legally non-binding, but they all have to be implemented domestically by the member regulatory authorities.

In her research on ICH, Berman highlights three different critical aspects in ICH functioning. The first issue is related to the (in)adequacy of the guideline development procedure: even though the (regional) consultation procedures can assure participatory rights, and hence some accountability, nothing is established about how input can influence output, in the absence of any duty to give reasons for the acceptance or rejection of comments, and with the lack of appeal mechanisms at the transnational level.

A second issue concerns the inclusion of the pharmaceutical industry in the harmonization process: while its inclusion can create advantages for the effectiveness of the process, also because of expertise brought by these private actors, on the other hand, it can also raise concerns around regulatory capture: Berman observes that "while public interest stakeholders, such as patients organizations, may comment on drafts, they are not at the table with the pharmaceutical industry and the regulators when these drafts are being developed in the working group sessions. Indeed, according to some accounts, ICH guidelines promote faster and cheaper drug development that benefits the industry, but do so at the expense of patient security. This raises the question of whether NGOs representing patients (or other public interests) should be allowed at the table".

A third issue is related to the global effects produced by ICH guidelines. They do not affect only the ICH countries, but have become *de facto* global standards that are adopted or relied on by non-ICH members. Their impact goes beyond the ICH membership and their content reflects the interests of developed and rich countries (and of their industries) without taking into account the interests of poor and developing countries. More specifically, as Berman stresses, "the problem manifests itself when local industries in non-ICH countries follow these guidelines that were never tailored to their needs" because "the guidelines often reflect a standard that is unattainable or unaffordable, while their high or complicated requirements are not necessarily justified from a public health perspective".[12]

12 Ayelet Berman, '*Public-private Harmonization Networks: the Case of the International Conference on Harmonization* (ICH)', Sabino Cassese, Bruno Carotti, Lorenzo Casini,

Addressing this problem of "regulatory capture" and participatory rights of non-ICH countries and stakeholders means to find new solutions in relation to governance mechanisms and guideline development procedure: in doing this, global administrative law principles and guarantees can offer some help to make global powers more just and legitimate. But it is not enough.

As Nagel observed in *The problem of global justice*, "If we look at the historical development of conceptions of justice and legitimacy for the nation-state, it appears that sovereignty usually precedes legitimacy. First there is the concentration of power; then, gradually, there grows a demand for consideration of the interests of the governed, and for giving them a greater voice in the exercise of power. It is the existence of concentrated sovereign power that prompts the demand, and makes legitimacy an issue".[13]

7 Global Powers, Juridification Process and Rule of Law

From what has been said above, it can be concluded that the composition and identity of the decision-maker tell us a lot about the global institution, its functioning and its logic dynamics: they reflect, in other words, the forces at play and the technical or political nature of the regulator. Of course, the question of its independence is also fundamental, looking at the independence from both the Member States and the regulated parties.

Even the appointment mechanisms and the background – diplomatic or legal – of officials sitting in the Boards or panels shows the degree of juridification of the international organization or, on the contrary, the prevalence of diplomatic logic:[14] if the dispute settlement mechanism, for example, has a dyadic structure and operates on a diplomatic basis, the final decision escapes the sphere of legal dimension and remains anchored to negotiation between the parties, privileging the contractual powers of the conflicting parties.

If, on the contrary, the settlement of the dispute between the contracting parties is entrusted to third parties (triadic model), the latter will tend to be impartial and will seek the right and just solution according to law.

The constant demand for predictability and certainty in international relations, especially in trade, has strengthened and incremented – as is well

---

Eleonora Cavalieri, Euan MacDonald (eds.), '*Global Administrative Law: the Casebook*', 3rd ed., IRPA, Institute for International Law and Justice, NYU School of Law, 2012, 228.

13 Thomas Nagel, '*The problem of global justice*', (n 8), 113.

14 Joseph H.H. Weiler, '*The geology of International Law – governance, democracy and legitimacy*', (n 5), 547.

known – the juridification and judicialization of the global space, producing in sectoral regulatory regimes a division of tasks between those who make decisions (with the rule of consensus or according to more informal procedures) and those who review these decisions, whether with the more developed features of a real Court or with those of a compliance committee.

Equally important in understanding the nature of the global institution or organization is the presence or absence of rules governing the decision-making procedure: however, it remains difficult, at the international level, to obtain information on what is about to be decided, to guarantee transparency for the stakeholders, to ensure that interested parties have a right to be heard, and to have adequate investigations before the final decision. On the one hand, it is difficult because many procedures are de-formalized and do not lead to formal and individual decisions, as the regulatory authorities use much more frequent informal negotiation and diplomatic agreements.

On the other hand, transparency and publicity of decision-making processes and judicial control are lacking in a context of extreme technical complexity.

Consider once again the International Conference on Harmonization: even though private citizens and NGOs have the standing to do so, it is clear what difficulties these subjects would face in controlling information or making effective participation within the standard-setting procedure of the transnational network. Or in influencing the outcome of the procedure approved by the Basel Committee for setting financial or commercial standards with highly specialized content.

Looking at these global regulators, an effort is needed to adapt the traditional rules and principles of administrative law to a reality which, due to its complexity, cannot be read according only to traditional categories or a specific legal discipline. This is why the Global Administrative law approach cannot be – as we already said at the beginning of this article – exclusive but has to be inclusive.[15] Through the GAL lens, global regulators have first of all to be described and analyzed, and then form the ground for a more general theory. But such approach has to be combined with analysis conducted also through the lens of international and private law, together with historical, economic and sociological perspectives.

As Lorenzo Casini highlights, "GAL and its scholarship may continue to fruitfully face challenges launched by globalization if they remain inclusive and consistent with its origins, and do not claim to offer solutions or responses,

15 L. Casini, *'Global Administrative Law,'* (n 2).

but rather frame problems and raise questions that are able to illustrate and unpack such ambiguities".[16]

Teaching GAL means, first of all, moving from this methodological premise.

Bibliography

Benvenisti, Eyal *'The Law of Global Governance'*, Hague Academy of International Law 2014.

Berman, Ayelet 'Public-private Harmonization Networks: the Case of the International Conference on Harmonization (ICH)', Sabino Cassese, Bruno Carotti, Lorenzo Casini, Eleonora Cavalieri, Euan MacDonald (eds.), *'Global Administrative Law: the Casebook'*, 3rd ed., IRPA, Institute for International Law and Justice, NYU School of Law, 2012, 228.

Casini, Lorenzo 'Global Administrative Law', in Jeffrey L. Dunoff, Mark A. Pollack (eds), *'International Legal Theory: Foundations and Frontiers'*, Cambridge University Press, 2019.

Casini, Lorenzo *'Potere globale. Regole e decisioni oltre lo Stato'*, Bologna, Il Mulino, 2018.

Cassese, Sabino *'Chi governa il mondo?'*, Bologna, Il Mulino, 2012.

Cassese, Sabino *'I Tribunali di Babele. I giudici alla ricerca di un nuovo ordine globale'*, Donzelli editore, 2009.

Cassese, Sabino *'Il diritto globale. Giustizia e democrazia oltre lo Stato'*, Torino, Einaudi, 2009.

Cassese, Sabino *'Lo spazio giuridico globale'*, Roma-Bari, Laterza, 2003.

Chiti, Edoardo Bernardo G. Mattarella (eds.), *'Global Administrative Law and EU Administrative Law'*, Relationships, Legal Issues, and Comparison, Springer, 2011.

Ferrarese, Maria Rosaria *'Prima lezione di diritto globale'*, Roma-Bari, Laterza, 2012.

Harlow, Carol *'Global Administrative Law: the Quest for Principles and Values'*, Eur. Journal Int. Law, 2006, vol. 17, 1, 187.

Helfer, Laurence R. – Anne-Marie Slaughter, *'Why States Create International Tribunals: a Response to Professors Posner and Yoo'*, Calif. L.R., 2005, vol. 93, 3.

Hudec, R.E. *'The Role of GATT Secretariat in the Evolution of WTO Dispute Settlement Procedure'*, in AAVV, *'The Uruguay Round and Beyond: Essays in Honor of Arthur Dunkel, J. Bhagwati and M. Hirsch, Berlin'*, 1998, 109.

Kingsbury, Benedict *'The Concept of Law in Global Administrative Law'*, Eur. J. Intern. L, 2009, vol. 20, 29.

16 L. Casini, *'Global Administrative Law',* (n 2).

Kingsbury, Benedict Nico Krisch, Richard B. Stewart, *'The emergence of Global Administrative Law'*, Law and Contemporary problems, 2005, 68, 15.

Marchetti, Barbara *'The enforcement of global decisions'*, Sabino Cassese (ed.), *'Research Handbook on Global Administrative Law'*, Edward Elgar, 2016;.

Marchetti, Barbara *'The WTO Dispure Settlement System: Administration, Court or Tertium Genus?'*, Suffolk Transnational L.R., 2009, vol. XXXII, 3, 567.

Nagel, Thomas *'The problem of global justice'*, Philosophy and Public Affair, 2005, 33, 113.

Shamir Borer, Eran 'Legitimacy without Authority in Global Standardization Governance: the Case of the International Organization for Standardization (ISO)', in Sabino Cassese, Bruno Carotti, Lorenzo Casini, Eleonora Cavalieri, Euan MacDonald (eds.), *'Global Administrative Law: the Casebook'*, 3rd ed., IRPA, Institute for International Law and Justice, NYU School of Law, 2012, 162.

Von Bogdandy Armin – Ingo Venzke, *'On the democratic legitimation of International Judicial Lawmaking'*, German, Law Journal, 2011, vol. 12.

Weiler, Joseph H.H. *'The geology of International Law – governance, democracy and legitimacy'*, J. Int. Law, 64, 2004, 547.

CHAPTER 9

International Law and Interdisciplinarity

*Sergio Dellavalle**

1 Three Reasons for Interdisciplinarity

Presently, almost all disciplines are caught in a curious contradiction. On the one hand, their languages have become increasingly specialistic, making each of them into an exclusive field for experts, thus excluding even well-educated laymen from participating in the discourse. On the other hand, the reference to interdisciplinarity has surged to the status of a kind of mantra, bearing the traits of a *conditio sine qua non* for academic recognition and research funding. International law is no exception to this rule. Only a couple of decades ago, its *corpus juris* was essentially made of a manageable number of inter-state treaties, whose validity was limited to the signing parties. This *corpus* of inter-state legal agreements was completed through an essential body of norms – to be led back, initially, to natural law, and later laid down in written covenants and treaties – which was assumed to have a worldwide and almost all-encompassing validity. In recent years, however, some new phenomena have triggered a significant increase in complexity. Among them were – just to make a few examples – the fragmentation of international law into distinct legal sub-systems, the establishment of an impressive number of international courts, the creation of a system of global governance through international organizations, the emergence of global administrative law, the strengthening of private international law and the involvement of powerful private actors as subjects of international agreements, as well as, finally, the introduction of new categories of norms, such as the codes of conduct. We can generally assume that a society, to perform its tasks, has to differentiate itself into specialized social subsystems and that each social subsystem tends to increase the specificity of its own flow of internal information on the basis of its idiosyncratic rationality in order to implement its social function properly. Consequently, the language of each legal subsystem – which itself is a social subsystem – becomes more

* Professor of Public Law and State Theory at the University of Turin (Italy), Department of Law; senior research affiliate of the Max Planck Institute for Comparative Public Law and International Law, Heidelberg (Germany); email: sergio.dellavalle@unito.it; dellavalle.affiliate@mpil.de.

 | DOI:10.1163/9789004678880_011

and more the matter for highly trained professionals. Teaching international law, therefore, must comprise specialized courses in which the language of the legal discipline (or disciplines) is properly introduced and the students are trained in the use of its (or their) instruments.

Nonetheless, the other side – namely the side of interdisciplinarity – should not be neglected either, both in research and teaching. There are three main arguments that speak in favour of an interdisciplinary opening of international law: the first deals with a change in international law's *scope* which occurred in the last decades, the second with the *content* of law in general and of international law in particular, and the third with the *overall rationale* of law. Starting with the first argument, it should be kept in mind that traditional international law has been, for a long time, either a law between states or a law that aspired to supersede nation states. Yet, in both cases it was assumed to maintain the internal unity and coherence of the legal system, regardless of whether the system whose unity had to be preserved was referred to national law, to international law, or to some kind of cosmopolitan law. With the transition from traditional international law to *transnational law* – as a result of two driving forces, namely globalization and the inherent tendency of national social subsystems to expand beyond the borders of the state – we are confronted, for the first time in modern Western history, with specialized legal systems that, by overcoming the boundaries of nation states and by making themselves independent of the pyramidal structure of the constitutional order, increasingly tend to overlap one another. In the transnational sphere, therefore, we essentially have a significant intersection of competences, so that international lawyers cannot do their job appropriately without having a substantial expertise in fields that transcend the usual understanding of international law, such as constitutional law, administrative law, cyberlaw, investment law, law of the financial markets, and so on.

After having highlighted, in Section 2, some aspects of the emergence of transnational law and the increase in interdisciplinarity triggered by this new development, Section 3 will focus on the content of law as a driving force of a parallel strengthening of interdisciplinarity. At this point, our gaze extends from international law to law in general. Indeed, it is the analysis of the content of any kind of law that requires an interdisciplinary approach. This becomes evident if we consider both the achievements and the failures of that strand of legal theory which, like no other, advocates the independence and self-reliance of the law as a system, thus explicitly rejecting any recourse to interdisciplinarity, namely legal positivism. Regardless of the different accents highlighted by its exponents, legal positivism always focused on the formal requisites for a sentence to be justifiably considered a legal norm. Yet, legal propositions are not only characterized by a specific form but also by a content that is expected to be properly channelled by those formal requirements and is ultimately based on a specific dimension of the social function of the law. In other words, inasmuch as a set of norms fulfils the task of stabilizing the normative expectations that are generated within the social subsystems,[1] it inevitably incorporates the kind of rationality that characterizes the functioning of that same subsystem.[2] As a result, if we want to understand how a legal subsystem works, we have to take into due account the fundamental constituents of that kind of rationality which makes up the rules of interaction within the social subsystem related to that particular set of norms. In plain words, this means – for instance – that teaching law and artificial intelligence or cyberlaw cannot refrain from giving sufficient information about what artificial intelligence is or about how information technology operates. In the same vein, human rights law is not only about the formal principles and rules that are thought to protect the fundamental entitlements of human beings but also presupposes a sufficiently sophisticated awareness of the ways in which those entitlements are justified as well as of which claims are arguably to be regarded as binding human rights. Only this way can the interpretation of the existing norms as well as their further development be properly substantiated.

Yet, the rationality of the law – regardless of whether in its general meaning or, more specifically, as international law – cannot only be limited to its functional dimension. Indeed, beyond the functional rationality that the legal norms acquire insofar as they fulfil the task of stabilizing the normative expectations generated within specialized social subsystems, the law also expresses and enshrines a more inclusive understanding of a metasystemic rationality, namely a comprehensive *idea of social order*. In other words, law is to be interpreted, too, as the system of formal propositions that lay down the rules and principles that govern human interaction according to a specific view of how the "well-ordered society" should be defined. While law's relation to the specialized subsystems is the expression of its functional rationale, its link to the idea of how the "well-ordered society" is understood manifests its more encompassing social rationality. However, if we try to define what the "well-ordered society" is, we will easily find out that it cannot be limited either to inner-state interactions or to inter-state relations. Rather, it covers both the national and the international dimensions at the same time, so that studying

---

1 Niklas Luhmann, *Das Recht der Gesellschaft* (Suhrkamp 1993; English: *Law as a Social System*, Fatima Kastner *et al.* eds., OUP 2004), 125ff (English: 142ff).

2 Andreas Fischer-Lescano and Gunther Teubner, 'Regime Collisions: The Vain Search for Legal Unity in the Fragmentation of Global Law' (2003–2004) 25 MichJIntIL 999, 1004ff.

and teaching international law from the perspective of a comprehensive idea of social order must include references to traditional issues of constitutional and administrative law. Furthermore, an encompassing idea of social order entails assumptions with reference to both public and private law, as well as to their relation. As a result, the disciplines of public and private international law cannot be kept separated as they were assumed to be following the traditional doctrine, but have rather to be analysed in their mutual balance and interactions. For instance, private actors can supposedly shape global social order in a way that refrains from the usual resort to public law, thus undertaking tasks traditionally allocated to public power. Accordingly, research and teaching must consider whether goals usually referred to common interests can be properly accomplished by private law systems, or whether the "well-ordered society" necessarily needs, on the contrary, public power institutions to foster what the civic debate comes to define as shared purposes. Finally – and most importantly – if the law is to be understood as the formal expression of a certain idea of social order, then those disciplines should be taken into consideration, such as political philosophy as well as social and political sciences, which have the specific task of highlighting the main features of the fundamental patterns of order. Basically, insofar as the different forms of legal order – to be better understood – are to be connected with general and distinct paradigms of social order, we can perform this operation in the best way by resorting to the intellectual instruments and to the knowledge put at disposal by fields of study other than the law. The connection and interdependence between the law and the general paradigms of social order – together with the advantages for research and teaching that can be drawn from them – are addressed in Section 4. A short conclusion – in Section 5 – will draw the strands together, while also outlining the consequences that an interdisciplinary turn might have for the approach to international law teaching.

2 Interdisciplinarity and the Change in International Law's Scope

The first reference to interdisciplinarity in international law refers to a deep-going reshape of its scope. Until only a few decades ago, international law was essentially seen – as advocated by the exponents of dualism – as a system of norms, beside domestic law, to regulate the interactions between nation states, or, according to the rather marginal monist approach, as the normative dome located above domestic law and due to encompass the worldwide domain of human behaviour with the aim to guarantee universal peace (2.1.). With the emergence of transnational law, the legal order beyond nation states profoundly changed its form and field of application. In particular, legal systems which had developed within the national domain and under the rule of constitutional public power expanded beyond the boundaries of individual states, broke the former dominance of domestic public law and created a new landscape of specialized and globalized regimes tending to overlap with one another (2.2.). Against this background, different dimensions or variants of transnational law have been outlined, including legal pluralism, the regimes of globalized markets, international public authority and global constitutionalism (2.3.). Within the context of transnational law, the coexistence of overlapping legal regimes, with no established normative priority accorded to anyone of them, not only generates frequent conflicts but makes them also difficult to resolve by traditional means. In fact, the new constellation renders it impossible to resort to the old-fashioned strategy of conflict solution, based on a generally recognized hierarchy of norms and institutions. Since this instrument is unavailable, unprecedented forms of conflict management have been introduced and successfully pioneered (2.4.).

2.1 *Monism and Dualism*

Historically, the relationship of national and international law has been interpreted along the line of the dichotomy between two powerful narrations: dualism and monism. Dualism – by far the approach with the most supporters – maintains that domestic and international law are two distinct legal systems, which apply to different and largely incommensurable fields of social interaction. The most striking argument in favour of dualism consists in the evidence of conflicts between the two systems of norms. For instance, if a state issues a law that contrasts with international norms, this law is ordinarily assumed to be valid despite the violation. In his defence of monism, Hans Kelsen dismissed the argument by establishing a similarity between this case and a domestic situation in which a constitutional order does not provide for a mechanism to abolish an unconstitutional statute: the statute remains valid, although no doubt can be raised that it has been illegally issued. Even, "certain organs may be tried in court personally for their part in the establishment of the 'unconstitutional' statute."[3] Analogously, it may be true that a national law that runs against international norms is nonetheless to be considered valid within the domestic order; yet, it is illegal, and international institutions are justifiably required to create a mechanism to abolish it and to make accountable those

3 Hans Kelsen, *Pure Theory of Law* (English translation by Max Knight of *Reine Rechtslehre*, from the Second German Edition of 1960, University of California Press 1967) 331; Hans Kelsen, *Reine Rechtslehre. Einleitung in die rechtswissenschaftliche Problematik* (Deuticke 1934).

responsible for the violation. On the opposite side of dualism, H. L. A. Hart criticized Kelsen's analysis not primarily because of logical inconsistency, excessive abstraction or lack of evidence, but rather because of a fundamental assumption regarding the validity of law. Indeed, while from the monist point of view law has essentially only one fundament, dualists assume that the fundaments are two: domestic law is grounded on the constitutional order, and international law is based on the agreements between states.[4]

On the opposite side, monism generally assumes that the whole worldwide legal system – in all its international and domestic implementations – has to be considered as a normative unity. The logical consequence of this assumption is that international law, as the most inclusive component of the cosmopolitan legal system, should be granted superiority over every kind of domestic law, be it constitutional or statutory. At this point, it is worth being noticed that Kelsen himself – undoubtedly the most powerful defender of monism – gave two quite significantly different justifications of why the worldwide system of laws should be regarded as a unity with international law at its apex. The most radical interpretation can be found in the first German edition of his *Reine Rechtslehre* (*Pure Theory of Law*) of 1934, in which no validation of the superiority of international law by the sovereign state is required. Rather, it is international law itself, as the most inclusive legal order, that specifies the range of competences on which the individual state can legally legislate. Indeed – Kelsen argued – a contradiction would arise if we had to admit that the priority of international law should be sanctioned by the domestic constitutional organs. Since we have a large number of individual states, if international law were depending for the specification of its normative range on sovereign decisions taken by each of those single states, then we would also have as many different international law systems as we have sovereign states – with the consequence that no binding law beyond the domestic context would exist. No less incongruous is the circumstance that, given that international law provides for the mutual recognition of states as equal actors in the international arena, exactly this mutual acknowledgment, which is fundamental for the very functioning of the international system, would have to rely upon the free and arbitrary will of each individual state. The result would be that the recognition of every state as equal actor of international law would lie in the hands of every other single state, as well as that each individual state would decide on the international recognition of all other states.[5] The confusing consequences that would be

4 H. L. A. Hart, 'Kelsen's Doctrine of the Unity of Law' in H. L. A. Hart, *Essays in Jurisprudence and Philosophy* (Clarendon 1983) 309–342.

5 Kelsen, *Reine Rechtslehre* (n 3) 142ff.

generated by such an assumption are hardly contestable – and thus Kelsen's radical solution seems to be, indeed, the most rational outcome. Nonetheless, in the second edition of 1960 – which is better known to the English-speaking readers due to its translation of 1967 – he considerably watered down his position, probably in order to make his theory more realistic and acceptable by taking into due account that, as a matter of fact, international law *is* created by sovereign states. According to the later interpretation, it is ultimately secondary – if not from the conceptual point of view, at least with reference to the results – whether the obligations that derive from international law are validated by the individual states, or international law itself is self-validating. Either assumption guarantees, first, that international law "determines ... the reason and sphere of validity of the national legal order,"[6] thus ensuring a paramount hierarchical position to the supra-state order, and, secondly, that the whole legal system has a monist character.

From a positivistic perspective, the difference between monism and dualism essentially consists in whether international treaties are directly applicable by domestic courts. Indeed, according to the monist understanding, international law has immediate validity within the national legal order without any intervention by national constitutional organs – more specifically, by the legislature. On the contrary, in dualist systems international treaties – to be recognized as valid law of the country and to be applicable by domestic courts – must be transposed into the domestic legal system by a parliamentary act. This distinction, which seems to be clear and evident at first sight, blurs if faced with a more deep-going analysis. In fact, most countries – at least in the Western world – combine some aspects of monism (for example, the possibility of an immediate reference by domestic courts to international law as a valid law of the country) with features deriving from a dualist interpretation of the legal system (for instance, the introduction of some kind of intervention by a legislative organ in order to grant an overall internal validity to the treaty, or the differentiation between some parts of international law, which do not need any intervention by the domestic legislature, and others which require them to be regarded as valid). Ultimately, most countries seem to have adopted, from a formal point of view, a mixture of monist and dualist attributes.

Yet, what Kelsen and Hart hint at in their contributions is not the formalistic difference between procedures of validation, but something more profound, namely the contraposition of two opposite views as regards the foundation of the legitimacy of law. Following Kelsen's monism, the ultimate legitimacy of

---

6 Kelsen, *Pure Theory of Law* (n 3) 340.

the law lies in the most inclusive legal community. In front of this fundamental assumption, it is substantially marginal – even if not formally irrelevant – whether rules and principles that govern this most inclusive legal community of international law are immediately self-executing or whether a parliamentary act is necessary to insert them into the domestic legal order. In fact, by binding it to international norms, even the parliamentary act simply acknowledges that no proper legitimacy of public power is given without taking into account the interrelations within the worldwide community of states, peoples and individuals. Furthermore, since the individual state *is* unquestionably part of this international community, the parliamentary act that binds the individual state to international law is *normatively* due and *factually* realistic. On the contrary, Hart lays the fundament of the legitimacy of the individual legal community in the norms and procedures of every single state.[7] According to his view, the direct or self-committed obligation towards international law is no necessary condition for a full-fledged internal legitimacy. Going a step beyond what Hart explicitly claims, but arguably not unduly forcing his thought, since it is the internal order that factually creates international law and guarantees its effectiveness, and not vice versa, the legitimacy of international law is based on the free decisions of the single states, while the legitimacy of the domestic legal order does not depend on the recognition of the normative superiority of international law. Therefore, the contraposition between Kelsen's monism and Hart's dualism basically moves along the line of the distinction between *universalism* and *particularism* as the fundamental categories related to the extension of social, political and legal order. This distinction will be further analysed while discussing the relationship between the interdisciplinarity of international law and law's overall social rationale.[8]

Despite their much-discussed opposition, monism and dualism nonetheless share a fundamental assumption, namely that it is not acceptable that two not hierarchically related norms, which derive from two independent legal systems, are both valid if applied at the same time to the same matter. This assumption is quite evident in the monist context: indeed, if all legal norms are worldwide part of a unitary pyramidal system, every conflict that may arise between them can arguably be brought to a solution by clarifying their respective position within the overall hierarchy. In the end, this is the reason why, from the monist perspective, normative conflict is always an illness which, however, can in any event be cured. The question is more complicated from

7 Hart (n 4) 317ff.

8 See *infra*, Section 4.

the dualist point of view: here, it is doubtlessly accepted that norms can be trapped in a conflict which cannot find a solution within a shared hierarchy. More specifically, Hart explicitly admitted that international law can contrast with domestic law.[9] Since the two systems are independent of one another, the way out of the conflict consists, in this case, in giving up on the idea of a common legal order and in identifying to which legal order the norms in question respectively and primarily belong. In other words, if they both belong to the domestic – or to the international – order, their conflict can be resolved by resorting to the hierarchy of their system of reference. But, if they belong to two different systems, we have to understand which rule of recognition applies to which norm, to that each of them can be led back to its context and be interpreted accordingly. Ultimately, in both monism and dualism no normative conflict is irresolvable – and in both of them the main instrument for conflict solution is the resort to hierarchy – simply because no overlapping of legal systems is assumed to exist as a non-pathological condition. It is precisely on this point that the emergence of transnational law intervenes by introducing a groundbreaking novelty.

2.2 *What Is Transnational Law?*

The definition of transnational law is highly contested – and there are even scholars who deny that there is something like transnational law. For instance, Franz Werro expresses doubts that a body of norms can be singled out with so unique features that the creation of a specific concept would be justified. Rather, transnational law would identify a *method* to approach some legal developments beyond the nation state with quite diverse and non-systemic characteristics. In contrast to international law, these norms do not build a consistent *corpus juris*; nonetheless, they cannot be led back to the domestic legal order either. Therefore, what methodologically distinguishes the discipline of transnational law studies – and not of transnational law as a legal system – is that, first, the analytic view must concentrate neither on domestic law nor on traditional international law, but on the space between them, and, secondly, that lawyers must rely on non-legal competences in order to understand the specific rationality of the most recent developments in their field of expertise.[10] Here we have the first hint to the necessity to take interdisciplinarity seriously while studying contemporary non-domestic law, more specifically

9 Hart (n. 4) 324ff.

10 Franz Werro, 'Is There Such a Thing as Transnational Law? Suggestions for defining the Object of Transnational Legal Studies' in Marc Amstutz, Stefan Keller and Stefan Wiprächtiger (eds.), *Recht zwischen Dogmatik und Theorie* (Dike/Nomos 2012) 311–328.

with reference to the inevitable relation between law's contents and extra-legal knowledge. I will come back to this point in the next Section. Returning, now, to the possible meaning of transnational law, Werro's low-profile preference had been already voiced, a couple of years before and in an even more radical form, by Claudio Grossman. In his view, "transnationalization" means nothing more than the advisable opening up of legal education, within the programs of law schools and as a result of the globalization process, to both international law – which is quite not obvious, in particular in the US system – and to foreign legal traditions.[11] Finally, the turn to transnationalism in legal practice and studies has been accused of being nothing else than an instrument created – during the "decade of greed", namely the 1990s – by hegemonic Western states and companies to foster the interests of the few and to the detriment of the many.[12]

To find an unapologetically positive assessment of transnational law in both its dimensions – namely, first, as a method to understand recent legal phenomena which, secondly, led to the establishment of a body of laws with unique features – it seems to be necessary to go back as far as to the first author who introduced the concept, i.e., to Philip C. Jessup. According to his definition, transnational law includes "all law which regulates actions or events that transcend national frontiers."[13] Going more into detail, it comprises "both public and private international law …, as … other rules which do not wholly fit into such standard categories."[14] On a more philosophical note, Jessup specifies that "in spite of the vast organizational and procedural differences between the national and the international stage, … there are common elements in the domestic and the international drama", that are lastly rooted in "merely human problems which might arise at any level of human society."[15] Put this way, transnational law appears to be the quintessential realization of a system of norms for the whole humankind and for the protection of its shared interests. Apart from Jessup's overtly optimistic tone, the question remains as to what the novelty of transnational law really consists of. Frankly, this novelty

11 Claudio Grossman, 'Building the World Community through Legal Education' in Jan Klabbers and Mortimer Sellers (eds.), *The Internationalization of Law and Legal Education* (Springer 2008), 21–35.

12 Muthucumaraswamy Sornarajah, 'Why "No" to Transnational Legal Studies' in Cornelia T. L. Pillard et al., *Why Transnational Legal Education* (Center for Transnational Legal Studies 2018) 20–25, <https://www.law.georgetown.edu/ctls/wp-content/uploads/sites/33/2018/01/CTLS-Why-Transnational-Education.pdf> accessed 2 January 2020.

13 Philip C. Jessup, *Transnational Law* (Yale University Press 1956), 2.

14 ibid.

15 ibid 15ff.

cannot be sought in its universalistic scope since international law itself no less emphatically claims – at least in its monist understanding – to be the system of rules for the whole humanity. Nor is the opening up of the law beyond the nation states to new subjects like individuals, private companies, NGOs, and so on, really something unprecedented, as can be proved by having a look at the most recent and post-traditional handbooks of otherwise quite traditionally defined international law. Moreover, transnational law is not the first system to overcome the principle of state consent by giving, in some cases, higher and normatively binding authority to supra-state institutions: indeed, the same outcome has already been advocated by the most uncompromising versions of monism. Finally, also the coexistence of private and public law in the domain beyond the nation states – far from being something unheard of – is a generally accepted component of the discipline of international law. Therefore, once having noticed that none of these elements accounts for the novelty of transnational law, we definitely have to look at something different to find a convincing answer to the questions of what the notion stands for and why its use can be reasonably regarded as a heuristic step forward.

By adopting a new theoretical perspective, we can see transnational law as the result – unprecedented indeed – of the processes of disaggregation that affected the nation states following globalization. According to the point of view of the contemporary neo-liberal theory of international law and relations, the individual state should never be seen as a "billiard ball", but rather as a conjunction of different social groups with distinct interests and priorities.[16] As soon as the grip of the central public power loosened as a consequence of the international economic interconnections that increasingly built up starting in the last decades of the last century, the public and private components of the domestic fabric found themselves empowered as new actors of the international arena. On the other hand, as pointed out by systems theory, the domestic social and legal subsystems always possess an inherent tendency to become independent from central regulation and to grow globally in order to properly implement their specific functional rationality.[17] In other words, the larger the field of implementation of every single social subsystem is, the likelier it is for each of them – as the doctrine of the economy of scale teaches us – to perform

16 Andrew Moravcsik, 'Taking Preferences Seriously: A Liberal Theory of International Politics' (1997) 51 International Organization 513; Anne-Marie Slaughter, *A New World Order* (Princeton University Press 2004) 12ff.

17 Niklas Luhmann, *Die Gesellschaft der Gesellschaft* (Suhrkamp 1997) Vol. 1, 125ff (English translation by Rhodes Barrette: *Theory of Society*, Stanford University Press 2012, Vol. 1, 142ff).

its specific social function in the most rational and successful way. Regardless of which theoretical approach we may prefer – neo-liberalism or systems theory – the outcome is largely the same: recently, we have seen domestic social subsystems – politics, administration, economy, financial sector, and many others – become self-reliant actors in the space beyond nation states. Since the activities of these social subsystems generally need to be regulated by law, also the legal subsystems respectively related to them have gone global. For instance, administrative law has become *global* administrative law, constitutional law has become *global* constitutionalism, and so on. This is precisely the field where transnational law as a new phenomenon in the world of law can be located and conceptually identified. Thus, from this point of view, transnational law is the non-unitary *corpus juris* made of different legal subsystems which, originally located in the domestic sphere, overcame the boundaries of the nation state as a result of globalization. It is almost superfluous to underline that, understood this way, transnational law is indeed something different from traditional international law: while the latter is the law *between* states or the law of the global *civitas maxima*, the former is the law of the specialized legal subsystems *beyond* the nation states. More specifically, transnational law overcomes both monism and dualism. It overcomes monism because it does not maintain that law, to be consistent, has to form a unitary and hierarchical system, but presupposes that law is made of different interacting systems. On the other hand, transnational law also overcomes dualism because it does not identify two clearly separate legal systems, but a plurality of overlapping systems.

Yet, there is a second, no less important distinction between international and transnational law. Since the domestic control and the strive for normative consistency that was guaranteed by the nation states have not been replaced by any comparable or even just functionally equivalent mechanism, the specialized legal subsystems that have become self-reliant tend to overlap with one another. Therefore, we have here, as a condition of normality, what was generally assumed to be a dangerous illness of the whole system of laws, namely the contemporary validity of two distinct and even contradictory norms, which originate from two different sources, but are applied to the same matter. Put this way, transnational law is the field of unprecedented horizontal conflicts, the solution of which requires a high-profile intellectual creativity. We can find here a robust justification for the interdisciplinary turn in studying and teaching non-domestic law: insofar as this is now made of a mixture of traditional norms of international law with regulations that were typical for specialized domestic legal systems and are now applied beyond the national domain, legal professionals and experts of post-domestic law must not only be well-versed in the conventional international law doctrine but also possess adequate knowledge of the other fields of law. Inevitably, international law must be studied and taught in combination with constitutional law, with administrative law, with law and finance, with economic law, with private law, and so on. Inasmuch as such a huge task is almost impossible to be undertaken by a single person or course, the teaching of international law must be split into specialized classes.

2.3 *Facets of Transnational Law*

Transnational law is a quite diverse and multifaceted phenomenon, so that its representation takes different shapes, depending on which aspect prevails. Basically, we have four versions of what transnational law is essentially assumed to be.

2.3.1 Legal Pluralism

The main novelty introduced by transnational law – and, thus, also the most innovative label that has been used to describe it – is *legal pluralism*. The novelty introduced by the approach of legal pluralism into legal theory is underlined by Nico Krisch. In his passionate and eloquent plea, pluralism is presented as a "break",[18] thus – in epistemological terms – as a paradigmatic revolution which overcomes the old-fashioned idea of the unity of the legal system,[19] paving the way to the acknowledgement of diversity.[20] National constitutionalism is criticized because it "not only fails to include but also fails to deliver."[21] As regards the first issue, "domestic constitutionalism, which places the national community at the centre of the legal and political universe [...] cannot reflect [the] broader constituency" that "goes well beyond the national community": therefore, "on transboundary issues, it remains underinclusive."[22] And, referring to the second point, "domestic constitutionalism [...] would require us to withdraw from, rather than extend, effective postnational decision-making structures in order to safeguard control by domestic political processes."[23] Yet, the criticism is broadened to comprehend cosmopolitan or postnational constitutionalism as well, insofar as it is accused "to provide continuity with the domestic constitutionalist tradition by construing an overarching legal framework that determines the relationships of the different levels

18 Nico Krisch, *Beyond Constitutionalism* (OUP 2010) 16, 23 and 68.
19 ibid 305.
20 ibid 303.
21 ibid 21.
22 ibid.
23 ibid.

of law and the distribution of power among their institutions."[24] On contrast, pluralism is adaptable and enables us to adopt a highly flexible system of checks and balances which can fit into the postnational legal system with its heterarchical character.[25] Last but not least, legal pluralism not only defines a theoretical instrument able to describe the present state of the art but also depicts what can be regarded as a normatively attractive perspective.[26]

By welcoming the coexistence of distinct and non-hierarchically connected legal systems in a sphere that comprises the domestic as well as the international domain, the theory of legal pluralism also acknowledges that these postnational legal systems interact and even overlap with one another. More concretely, "using pluralism, we can conceive of a legal system as both autonomous and permeable; outside norms (both state and nonstate) affect the system but do not dominate it fully."[27] This creates a new phenomenon, which Paul Schiff Berman defines as "jurisdictional hybridity",[28] i.e., a plurality of normative spaces in which norms from different sources – all claiming to be valid and applicable at the same time and to the same cases – contend with one another for priority. Within the context of jurisdictional hybridity, no resort to hierarchy is possible in order to clarify the respective rank of norms, so that the outcome must be seen as the always contestable result of an open-ended exchange of arguments. Berman refers to four examples of the phenomenon, the first of which are the "state versus state conflicts of norms".[29] Unlike the traditional jurisdictional disputes between states, contemporary inter-state conflicts – due to globalization and to the development of the cyberspace – have a much broader and more deep-going mutual impact on internal forms of interaction and regulation. The problems related to the territorial reach of free speech regulations – as shown by the cases referring to the removal of contents from the internet – demonstrate that solutions cannot easily be found by drawing boundaries between legal systems, but require an innovative approach that mutually takes into due account the position of the counterpart. The second example is the "state versus international conflicts of norms", where the international dimension – as in the case of the International Court of Justice (ICJ) or, even more, of the European Court of Human Rights (ECHR) scheme – is understood in a way that "may have impact on various entities within a nation

24 ibid 23.
25 ibid 78.
26 ibid 103.
27 Paul Schiff Berman, *Global Legal Pluralism* (CUP 2012) 25.
28 ibid 23 ff.
29 ibid 27ff.

state", so that "the international forums can provide a source of alternative norms that people then use as leverage in their local settings."[30] Thirdly, Berman introduces the "nation states versus substate conflicts of norms", in which tensions between regional unities and the central state – in particular in fields such as environmental regulation, foreign affairs and immigration – are characterized by an increasing assertiveness of the former, even to the point of bypassing the latter.[31] The last form of jurisdictional hybridity referred to by Berman are the "state versus nonstate conflicts of norms",[32] which seem to blur – arguably for the first time in modern Western legal history – the well-established distinction between formal laws and non-formal social norms.[33]

2.3.2 The Legal Regimes of the Globalized Markets

Of all specialized legal systems that have developed independently of a central regulation, the most socially powerful and influential are probably the legal regimes that specify the norms for global trade and economic transactions. Two distinct transnational regimes have emerged in this field: the first concentrates on the legal framework and on the praxis of the World Trade Organization (WTO),[34] while the second refers to the normative self-organization of private economic actors on global scale, i.e., to the so-called new Lex mercatoria.[35] What typifies the transnational nature of both regimes is, first, their transfer of regulations that were traditionally under the control of domestic law to the space beyond the state; secondly, their mixture of private and public dimensions; and, thirdly, their export of concepts that were typical for the domestic discourse – more specifically, elements of constitutional – from the statist to the transnational level.

As regards the first aspect, the domain of economic transactions and the freedom of initiative that was granted to its agents were traditionally limited by the decisions taken by domestic public organs as well as by laws and regulations issued by them, according to the principles that public interest must have priority over private preferences and that public interests can be sorted out best at the level of the individual political and legal community. Within the context

30 ibid 36ff.

31 ibid 37ff.

32 ibid 41ff.

33 H. Patrick Glenn, *Legal Traditions of the World* (OUP 2010) 61ff.

34 Peter-Tobias Stoll, 'World Trade Organization (WTO)', *Max Planck Encyclopedia of Public International Law* (2014).

35 Gunther Teubner, 'Global Private Regimes: Neo-spontaneous Law and Dual Constitution of Autonomous Sectors in World Society?' in Karl-Heinz Ladeur (ed.), *Globalization and Public Governance* (Ashgate 2004) 71–87.

of transnational law, the regulation has either been passed over to an international organization, as in the case of the WTO, or it has been left downright to the private actors, insofar as they undertake activities that go beyond national borders, as for the Lex mercatoria. With reference to the second transnational dimension of the regimes of the globalized markets, the mixture of public and private elements takes different forms in the two regimes. Being part of public international law – i.e., having been signed by public entities, which are the member states – the WTO has an essentially public core. Nevertheless, while the WTO allows, to a certain extent, waivers from the principle of free trade, especially "non-discriminatory national regulation of protection of human health, the environment, and other public interests,"[36] it nonetheless firmly assumes that "international trade liberalization tends to increase the economic welfare of every trading nation, e.g. by reducing the prices of consumer goods, enhancing productivity through specialization, creating new job opportunities, and enabling governments to redistribute part of the 'gains from trade' for helping the poor, assisting workers to shift from import-competing to export sectors of the economy, or protecting the environment."[37] In the end, the public dimension is largely overruled by the predominance of private interests, and the incapacity to find a well-balanced solution for the conflict between private and public might be seen as one of the most relevant reasons for the current crisis of the WTO regime.[38] In the case of the Lex mercatoria, the search for a balance between public and private went the opposite way. The starting point, here, is undoubtedly private, being located in the transnational activities of private agents. However, since the legal system of the spontaneous agreements between private actors aims at being self-reliant and independent of any external source of authority, it has to incorporate some defining features of public law in order to become self-validating, such as the establishment of a hierarchy of norms, the standardization of contracts and the creation of a judiciary *sui generis* in form of arbitration.[39]

---

36 Ernst-Ulrich Petersmann, 'Principles of World Trade', *Max Planck Encyclopedia of Public International Law* (2010) 5.

37 ibid 3.

38 The Guardian, 'WTO Faces Crisis over Disputes Settlement unless Trump Backs off' (2019) <https://www.theguardian.com/world/2019/dec/08/wto-faces-crisis-over-settlement-disputes-unless-trump-backs-off> accessed 4 January 2020; SWP, 'Ways Out of the WTO's December Crisis' (2019) <https://www.swp-berlin.org/10.18449/2019C46> accessed 4 January 2020.

39 Gunther Teubner, '"Global Bukowina": Legal Pluralism in the World Society' in Gunther Teubner (ed.), *Global Law Without a State* (Dartmouth 1997) 3–28.

Finally, as regards the use of constitutional language, this has been introduced into the legal regimes of the globalized markets only at the high price of a significant – and highly questionable – semantic reduction of the concept of constitution. Indeed, it is quite undisputed that the legal regimes of the globalized markets lack most of the essential contents of a full-fledged notion of constitution, such as a comprehensive bill of rights or the guarantee that the hereby established power is democratically legitimated. To grant those regimes nevertheless a constitutional rank, it is therefore necessary to presuppose an extremely narrow definition of constitution, namely as the legal document that contains the rules for the production of secondary norms.[40] As a result, constitutional law is understood exclusively in its *functional* dimension, or, more concretely, as the legal document that (a) enables the production of norms by specifying the procedures which govern the issuing of valid rules; (b) restrains this production by clarifying in which fields no rule-making should take place; and (c) fills the gaps, in the contexts where rule-making is allowed, which may arise from disparate norm-issuing actions at the transnational level, thus guaranteeing sufficient homogeneity to the legal regime.[41] However, even if we assumed this point of view, some questions would remain unresolved. Starting with the allegedly constitutional regime of the WTO, its most fundamental assumption that the legal documents that lie at the basis of the WTO regime take on the role of a functional constitution insofar as they govern the making of secondary rules is highly contestable. Indeed, it is not by chance that in many circumstances, due to the lack of norms regulating rule-making in the WTO agreements, the tasks of a functional constitutionalization – i.e., enabling, constraining and homogenizing rule-making – have been assumed by the Appellate Body.[42] However, while on the one hand the intervention of the Appellate Body has covered only singular cases, missing therefore the inherently general scope of constitutional rule-making, on the other hand it could be easily argued that precisely the necessity of this kind of intervention rather proves the absence of a truly constitutional framework.

40 Gunther Teubner, *Constitutional Fragments* (OUP 2012).

41 Jeffrey L. Dunoff and Joel P. Trachtmann, 'A Functional Approach to International Constitutionalization' in Jeffrey L. Dunoff and Joel P. Trachtmann (eds.), *Ruling the World? Constitutionalism, International Law, and Global Governance* (CUP 2009) 9.

42 Jeffrey L. Dunoff, 'The Politics of International Constitutions: The Curious Case of the World Trade Organization' in Dunoff and Trachtmann, *Ruling the World?* (n 41) 189; Joel P. Trachtmann, 'Constitutional Economics of the World Trade Organization' in Dunoff and Trachtmann, *Ruling the World?* (n 41) 216.

With reference to the alleged constitutional character of the new Lex mercatoria – apart from any other consideration regarding the deficits of an exclusively functional definition of constitution – it remains controversial whether mechanisms for self-validation are really suitable for the task. Furthermore, insofar as the Lex mercatoria is undergoing a process of codification, elements are necessarily introduced into its *corpus* which are derived from national codes of private law and through these, due to the usual interconnection of private and public law at national level, also from the national systems of public law.[43]

2.3.3 Global Governance and Public International Authority (IPA)

While the legal regimes of the globalized markets emphasize the private dimension of the turn to transnational law, its third variant highlights precisely the opposite aspect, namely its *publicness*. In other words, transnational law is not only – or not primarily – the expression of the more or less spontaneous regulation of private interactions going global but also the way in which shared interests of the worldwide community are identified and protected. The initial assumption, here, is that global processes like labor and financial markets, migration, ecological crises, terrorism, organized crime, technological and scientific innovation, exploitation of natural resources, etc., need to be met by establishing executive networks composed of members of national governments and of international organizations. In plain words, this means that the world of globalized interactions can only address its most urgent challenges by introducing more *global governance*.[44] Transnational governance also triggers the development of what has been defined as "global administrative law"[45] which – not unlike the task of administrative law in the domestic realm – establishes at the same time the legal framework for the measures that transnational executive organizations take in order to guarantee the control of relevant phenomena, and prevents them from overstepping their competences by asserting the principle of the rule of law.[46]

43 Armin von Bogdandy and Sergio Dellavalle, 'The Lex Mercatoria of Systems Theory: Localisation, Reconstruction and Criticism from a Public Law Perspective' (2013) 4 Transnational Legal Theory 59.

44 Slaughter (n 16).

45 Benedict Kingsbury, Nico Krisch and Richard B. Stewart, 'The Emergence of Global Administrative Law' (2005) 68 Law and Contemporary Problems 15.

46 Eyal Benvenisti, *The Law of Global Governance* (Hague Academy of International Law 2014).

Some authors – with Anne-Marie Slaughter as arguably the most prominent amongst them – see the transnational law of global governance as a mixture of regulations issued by public agents, such as representatives of national governments acting within the context of international organizations,[47] and rules emerging from agreements taken by private actors, like those at the basis of the Lex mercatoria, whereas the line that should separate the two dimensions is not always clear-cut.[48] Other exponents of this strand, instead, focus unequivocally on the *public* dimension of global governance, which is expressed, in particular, by international public authorities (IPA).[49] In this case, the "publicness" of the policies that lie at the basis of transnational law is assumed to be guaranteed by the fact that IPAs are expected to pursue shared interests and the common good.[50] Here, however, the question arises about the definition of the common good and the ways of its realization. Although the theorists of IPA also refer to substantial criteria like freedom or the rule of law, the most relevant feature to ensure the "publicness" of the IPA policies is lastly just formal, namely the very fact that IPAs are endowed with a public mandate, derived from public power, to act for the common good.[51] Insofar as they do so, the acceptance of their policies by at least the majority of individuals and populations involved leads to a sort of output legitimacy, whereas hardly any attention is paid to deliberative and democratic procedures of legitimation of international organizations. Yet, it has also been argued that scaling down the expectations – by giving up on a full-fledged democratic input legitimation, such as the one that is enshrined in domestic democratic constitutions, while concentrating on the form of accountability that can be achieved through global administrative law – is actually the only affective way to convincingly address the legitimacy deficit in the transnational realm.[52]

47 Slaughter (n 16) 36ff.

48 Anne-Marie Slaughter, 'A Liberal Theory of International Law' (2000) 94 American Society of International Law 240.

49 Armin von Bogdandy, Philipp Dann and Matthias Goldmann, 'Developing the Publicness of Public International Law: Towards a Legal Framework for Global Governance Activities' (2008) 9 German Law Journal 1375.

50 Armin von Bogdandy, Matthias Goldmann and Ingo Venzke, 'From Public International Law to International Public Law: Translating World Public Opinion into International Public Authority' (2017) 28 EJIL 115, 134.

51 ibid 138ff.

52 Nico Krisch, 'Global Administrative Law and the Constitutional Ambition' in Petra Dobner and Martin Loughlin (eds.), *The Twilight of Constitutionalism* (OUP 2010) 245–266.

2.3.4 Global Constitutionalism

The fragmentation of the legal framework of transnational law and the limitation of its legitimacy claims to the guarantee of an efficient governance or the rule of law – and, therefore, far below the usual standards in democratic political systems – are two of its most relevant problems. The fourth strand of transnational law – generally known as global or transnational constitutionalism – puts their resolution at the top of its agenda.

As far as the question of legal fragmentation is concerned, global constitutionalism responds to the challenge by carrying the promise that "there is something which helps keep the systems together."[53] At this point, however, the problem arises on what this "something" could be and where it is to be located. Substantially, it can be assumed that this role is to be taken on by a conjunction of *jus cogens*, general principles of international law, *erga omnes* principles and human rights,[54] as they have been laid down in international treaties – in particular in the UN Charter,[55] in the UN Conventions and in the Vienna Convention on the Law of Treaties – as well as in the jurisprudence of the international courts, most prominently in the ICJ *Barcelona Traction* judgement of 1970. Global constitutionalism also builds a fence against an unfettered privatization of the international sphere "by carving out a protected public realm."[56] However, it is quite evident that the elements that should set up the core of global constitutionalism are either customary law – thus, anything but formal and generally recognized norms laid down in treaties, in the way in which the norms of domestic constitutions are usually understood – or, if they are enshrined in treaties or judgements,[57] their content is widely subject to diverging interpretation. In this sense, it is undoubtable that – as Jan Klabbers puts it – "constitutionalization is an intensely political process."[58] Consequently, even if we assume, following the premises of global constitutionalism, that "a constitutional world order is one which has a centre of authority,"[59] it has nonetheless to be acknowledged that this "authority" is not one issuing binding decisions through top-down processes, but one that, while claiming normative superiority, always attempts to make it concrete through

---

53 Jan Klabbers, 'Setting the Scene' in Jan Klabbers, Anne Peters and Geir Ulfstein (eds.), *The Constitutionalization of International Law* (OUP 2009) 18.

54 ibid 16ff.

55 Bardo Fassbender, 'Rediscovering a Forgotten Constitution' in Dunoff and Trachtmann, *Ruling the World?* (n 41) 133–147.

56 Klabbers (n 53) 18ff.

57 Geir Ulfstein, 'Institutions and Competences' in Klabbers, Peters and Ulfstein (n 53) 45–80.

58 Klabbers (n 53) 18.

59 ibid.

horizontal interactions, open contestation and dialogue. In fact, while hierarchical domestic constitutionalism aims at curbing the plurality of legal systems through the imposition of a centralized legal and institutional structure, global constitutionalism unequivocally recognizes the positive and ineliminable value of pluralism. Put differently, pluralism in the international realm is something which *cannot* and *should not* be reduced to unity, first because such an endeavour would hardly be crowned by success, at least currently, and secondly because even if success were possible, it would not be desirable due to the values – or to the specific and irreducibly different ideas of the "good life" – that are enshrined in national social, political and legal orders.

"In the absence of a unitary world state – Klabbers maintains – ... a constitutional order must somehow find ways of dealing with relations between the whole and its parts."[60] Here, the concept of multilevel constitutionalism comes to the aid. Although essentially conceived for an application to the constitutional framework of the European Union, it bears some traits that can also be highly useful if implemented in the context of transnational law.[61] Notoriously, unlike truly federal constitutional orders, the legal framework of global constitutionalism might be regarded, in the most favourable case, as normatively superior – at least in some fields – to national legal orders, but does not enjoy any recognized overall hierarchical supremacy. Therefore, while in the federal tradition a general priority of the law of the federation over that of the federated units is recognized, in multilevel constitutionalism this priority is only partial and always heavily contested. The rationale of this deep-going difference lies in the different roles that individuals play in the multilevel setting, as opposed to the federal one, when it comes to the legitimation of the more inclusive legal framework. Indeed, in a traditional federal system the legitimation of central public authorities is guaranteed by the citizens of the federation *exclusively in this function*. In other words, insofar as they are called to give legitimacy to the central public power, the citizens of the federation suspend their status as citizens of the member states and come into action only in their political identity related to the central unit. In doing so, they are indeed the source of two forms of legitimacy – that of the federation and that of the federated state of which they are also citizens – but the two procedures of legitimation are strictly independent. In contrast, individuals within the cosmopolitan

60 ibid 31.

61 Jürgen Habermas, *Zur Verfassung Europas* (Suhrkamp 2011); Jürgen Habermas, *Im Sog der Technokratie* (Suhrkamp 2013); Jürgen Habermas, 'Democracy in Europe: Why the Development of the EU into a Transnational Democracy Is Necessary and How It Is Possible' (2015) 21 ELJ 546.

setting never suspend their status as citizens of the individual states when called to legitimize cosmopolitan institutions and norms. As a result, the legitimacy of cosmopolitan constitutionalism is inherently twofold, coming at the same time from two distinct sources: the cosmopolitan community and the individual states. The epistemological fundament, here, is the communicative understanding of society, according to which this is constituted by different contexts of interaction. The most general and inclusive among these is the one in which human beings are involved transnationally and irrespective of their citizenships and belongings. In accordance with this understanding, world – or, to be precise, "cosmopolitan" – constitutionalism is the political project that aims at regulating this kind of transnational interactions with principles and rules in order to make them predictable, inclusive and just.[62] In a multilayered and stratified, but also horizontally intertwined legal and institutional system, which is characterized by the non-hierarchical coexistence of two legitimacy strands, conflicts between norms cannot be resolved by resorting to a pyramid of sources that is presently missing and should not be established in the future, but only through dialogue between institutions and, in particular, between courts.[63]

The considerations about the way in which the balance between the whole and its parts could be guaranteed in a cosmopolitan setting lead us directly to the second main issue of global constitutionalism, namely to the question of the conditions under which its norms and institutions can be considered legitimate. In particular, we have to address the problem of what kind of legitimacy should be arguably envisaged in the cosmopolitan context and which mechanism can support it. Essentially, the debate offers three solutions. The first one refers to the use of the concept of "reasonableness".[64] Leaning on Ronald Dworkin's work,[65] Mattias Kumm introduces the notion with the aim to separate, in the field of cosmopolitan constitutionalism, the concept of legitimacy from the praxis of democracy, i.e., from the direct or indirect, but always reflexive involvement of all those concerned. In his view, legitimacy is sufficiently guaranteed, in cosmopolitan perspective, if standards of "public reasonableness" are respected. Consequently, active involvement of the

62 Sergio Dellavalle, 'Addressing Diversity in Post-unitary Theories of Order' (2020) 40 OJLS 347.

63 See *infra*, Section 2.4.

64 Mattias Kumm, 'On the Cosmopolitan Turn in Constitutionalism: On the Relationship between Constitutionalism in and beyond the State' in Dunoff and Trachtmann, *Ruling the World?* (n 41) 269, 273, 290, 301, and 312.

65 Ronald Dworkin, *Law's Empire* (Belknap Press of Harvard University Press 1986).

citizens can be substituted by the safeguard of fundamental rights as the main content of public reasonableness.[66] Apart from the nebulous content of the notion, it remains unclear how the centrality of "the free and equal" – also advocated by Kumm – [67] can be preserved in front of such a far-going concession to that kind of technocratic paternalism that colonizes a large part of the debate on governance beyond the nation state. Indeed, it is difficult to ascertain who the legitimate holders and guardians of public reasonableness should be – if not those citizens or, in general, fellow humans who are affected by the consequences of the decisions.

The second solution to the question of the legitimacy of a cosmopolitan constitutional order, quite on the contrary, explores bottom-up forms of non-representative and inclusive empowerment of stakeholders, aiming at the safeguard of the social and ecological conditions of life.[68] On the basis of the hardly contestable assumption that modern constitutionalism has been a bottom-up political project, the purpose of this second approach basically consists in identifying chances for the development of locally based forms of direct democracy. The third and last solution lies somehow between the first and the second – though slightly more on the side of the second due to its specific attention to the direct involvement of citizens in guaranteeing the legitimacy of institutions and norms. Unlike both the reference to "reasonableness" – which seems to favour the institutional point of view of the international organizations – and the appeal to the worldwide and largely unformalized self-determination of the stakeholders, the third solution strives for a balance between the whole and its part in the form of a double two-tier approach. The first leg of the two-tier approach focuses on the institutional setting of cosmopolitan constitutionalism. Taking a two-level perspective, it assumes that cosmopolitan constitutionalism is based on two pillars: a thin layer of international organizations – largely comprised of institutions under the aegis of a reformed UN – with the limited task to protect peace and fundamental human rights,[69] and the nation states which make up the international community. However, in contrast with the present situation and with any kind of technocratic idea of governance, *both* pillars should be endowed

66 Kumm (n 64) 303.

67 ibid 322.

68 James Tully, Jeffrey L. Dunoff, Anthony F. Lang Jr., Mattias Kumm and Antje Wiener, 'Introducing Global Integral Constitutionalism' (2016) 5 Global Constitutionalism 1.

69 Jürgen Habermas, *Der gespaltene Westen* (Suhrkamp 2001; English translation by Ciaran Cronin: *The Divided West*, Polity Press 2006); Stefan Kadelbach and Thomas Kleinlein, 'Überstaatliches Verfassungsrecht' (2006) 44 Archiv des Völkerrechts 235.

with adequate democratic legitimation. This implies – on the side of the whole of the international organization – a serious effort towards the parliamentarization of as many institutions of the international community as possible,[70] and on the other hand a no less heartfelt commitment to the development of democracy inside the individual states. It cannot be denied, however, that this sort of "dual democracy"[71] is severely hampered by the undemocratic nature of many national regimes: indeed, it is difficult to imagine how the institutions of the international community can be made more democratic if a significant number of member states violate the most fundamental democratic rules. Under these circumstances, the role of the democratic representation of the worldwide community of citizens might provisionally and putatively be taken on by a permanent assembly of NGOs, characterized by precise deliberative rules and unequivocally endowed with the right to be heard. The second leg of the two-tier approach aims at building an equilibrium between the participation of the stakeholders and the institutional competence of international organizations. Unlike the plea for a diffuse cosmopolitan direct democracy, dual democracy combines two different levels: first by counterbalancing participation with representation, and secondly by integrating – admittedly, more openly and far-going than in the democratic nation state – the bottom-up source of legitimacy with the expertise and knowledge that settled over time, both nationally and internationally, in the institutions of the executive power. In fact, the legitimacy of the international organizations is ultimately guaranteed not only by the citizens of the cosmopolitan community but also by its member states.

2.4 *How to Manage Transnational Legal Conflicts*

Transnational law is characterized by the presence of a number of horizontally coexisting legal systems which overlap with one another, while not being hierarchically bound to one another. Taken together, these two aspects account for both the increase of legal conflicts and – even more importantly – the impossibility to resolve them by resorting to the usual procedure, namely by clarifying which norm or institution is superior. Thus, three substantially new strategies have been developed in order to manage transnational conflicts of law. The first one aims at creating "interface norms" and practices, with the essential purpose to "embrace hybridity",[72] i.e., to establish a post-hierarchical system of mutual

70 Daniele Archibugi, *The Global Commonwealth of Citizens: Toward Cosmopolitan Democracy* (Princeton University Press 2008).

71 Anne Peters, 'Dual Democracy' in Klabbers, Peters and Ulfstein (n 53) 263–341.

72 Berman (n 27) 141ff.

recognition of an almost unlimited equal normative dignity of all involved legal systems, as well as of their substantial self-reliance and independence.[73] This approach comprehends mechanisms like the acknowledgement of margins of appreciation[74] or of subsidiarity schemes,[75] the acceptance of "limited autonomy regimes",[76] "mutual recognition regimes",[77] and "conditional recognition" – such as the *Solange II* decision of the German Federal Constitutional Court of 1986 – [78] as well as, finally, the recognition of judgements.[79] This last mechanism – namely the recognition of judgements issued by a court belonging to a different legal system – also constitutes one of the ways in which the second strategy operates. This focuses, indeed, on the dialogue between courts of distinct legal regimes – or, as it has been specified, on the "engagement with foreign precedents", since the courts' actions are in many cases one-sided and do not imply any interaction with the counterpart.[80] The category comprises both the cases in which a domestic court (in most cases a constitutional court) refers to a decision taken by a foreign court (generally, also a constitutional court), and the situations in which – giving a broad meaning to the definition of "foreign" – a domestic court vertically interacts with a supranational court such as the European Court of Justice (ECJ) or the European Court of Human Rights (ECtHR). Regarded by some as a limited and rather marginal phenomenon[81] while utterly praised by others as a fundamental step towards a cosmopolitan jurisprudence[82] and as a significant contribution "to enhance democracy and inclusion",[83] transnational activities of courts are undeniably growing in numbers and becoming increasingly influential. The third strategy makes the otherwise informal interaction between transnational institutions and, in

73 Krisch (n 18) 285ff.
74 Berman (n 27) 161ff.
75 ibid 168ff.
76 ibid 163ff.
77 ibid 179ff.
78 Krisch (n 18) 287ff.
79 Berman (n 27) 294ff.
80 Vicki C. Jackson, *Constitutional Engagement in a Transnational Era* (OUP 2010).
81 Tania Groppi and Marie-Claire Ponthoreau, 'The Use of Foreign Precedents by Constitutional Judges: A Limited Practice, An Uncertain Future' in Tania Groppi and Marie-Claire Ponthoreau (eds.), *The Use of Foreign Precedents by Constitutional Judges* (Hart 2013) 411–431.
82 Clara Marsan-Raventós, 'From Judicial Dialogue to Cosmopolitan Norms: Enhancing Democracy in Globalised States' in Amrei Müller (ed.), *Judicial Dialogue and Human Rights* (CUP 2017) 435–466.
83 Eyal Benvenisti and George W. Downs, *Between Fragmentation and Democracy. The Role of National and International Courts* (CUP 2017).

particular, courts to a formalized procedure by establishing mechanisms of consultation and dialogue. While being the most ambitious of the three strategies, since it institutionalizes dialogue by making it sometimes mandatory and always advisable, it is – probably exactly because of its ambition – also the less broadly developed and applied. Basically we have, indeed, only one example as regards constitutional law – i.e., Art. 39 of the Constitution of the Republic of South Africa – and the same limited number of applications with reference to the interactions between domestic and supranational courts, namely the "preliminary ruling" procedure ex Art. 267 of the Treaty on the Functioning of the European Union (TFEU). Nonetheless, this third strategy is arguably the best way to deal with transnational conflicts of norms in case that we have in mind an overall system of norms and institutions which, albeit non-hierarchical, strives nonetheless for as much consistency as possible.

This last remark anticipates a second question related to how transnational conflicts of norms are addressed, namely its most essential rationale. In other words, which are the rationalities that come into play while dealing, in different forms, with conflicts of norms against a transnational background? And what are their final purposes? Substantially, we can distinguish three understandings of rationality and purposes when we take up the managing of transnational conflicts – which, quite tellingly, correspond to the three post-unitary paradigms of social order.[84] Considered from this perspective, the managing of transnational conflicts unveils the connection between legal discourse and a specific weltanschaaung, or a way to define knowledge and justify action. The first understanding takes up the epistemology of systems theory, regardless of whether explicitly or implicitly. It applies if external elements are taken into account only with the purpose of adapting the internal operations of one's own legal system to the challenges coming from outside so as to maintain its original functional rationality. In this sense, law-making happens "through mutual irritation, observation and reflexivity of autonomous legal orders,"[85] and the rationality of the external system is only interesting insofar as it impacts on the internal procedures. Instead, if the logic that inspires the interaction originates from postmodern thinking, the main aim of the dialogue will be the establishment of positive comity and tolerance, finally leading to a broad acknowledgement of foreign judgements.[86] In this case, the rationality of the external system is fully recognized as having the same value, although it is also considered incommensurably different since no overarching and

84 See *infra*, Section 4.3.
85 Fischer-Lescano and Teubner (n 2) 1018.
86 See *supra* n 79.

all-encompassing rationality is assumed to be possible. Precisely this kind of assumption that an overarching rationality is both arguably identifiable and desirable imbues the third understanding of the rationale of transnational interaction. Indeed, if the epistemological background is the communicative paradigm of order, the goal of transnational interaction arguably consists in the implementation of the normative contents of intersubjective rationality. Because an all-encompassing rationality is presumed to exist, its correct application through horizontal dialogue is likely to lead to consistent solutions of conflicts. Even though no resort to top-down hierarchies is accepted, a relative normative superiority of certain legal regimes is nonetheless recognized, in particular when their internal contents – as in the case of human rights law – more reliably embody the principles of communicative rationality.[87]

3 Interdisciplinarity and International Law's Content

The case against the interdisciplinarity of international law was most powerfully advocated by those authors who claimed that the law constitutes a self-contained and self-reliant system. Given this premise, the legal system may be assumed to have a truth content in itself – i.e., without any resort to truth sources located in extra-legal discourses – or to be a mere instrument for the realization of individual preferences, thus being devoid of any truth content. Starting with the first variant – namely with the interpretation that recognizes that the law has a truth content, but denies that this is to be sought outside the realm of legal sentences – the first point of reference cannot but be Hans Kelsen's legal philosophy.

One of the central aims of Kelsen's work – probably the most central at all – was the attempt to lay down the epistemological presuppositions for considering the legal system an object of *scientific* research. In this sense, legal theory had to become "legal science" (*Rechtswissenschaft*). To achieve his goal, he had to find out both the specific form of legal sentences and their ultimate foundation, which, if legal science had to be self-sufficient, could not be sought in extra-legal disciplines, such as morals, philosophy, religion, sociology or political science.[88] As for the form of legal sentences, Kelsen claimed that they are shaped as hypothetical propositions, according to the structure "Z = if Z_1, then Z_2". In this kind of sentence, Z_2 is validated by Z_1, which is therefore vested with

87 Geir Ulfstein, 'The International Judiciary' in Klabbers, Peters and Ulfstein (n 53) 126–152.

88 Kelsen, *Reine Rechtslehre* (n 3) 21.

the function to act as a foundation of Z_2. However, the proposition does not say anything about the possible foundation of Z_1, so that the overall validity of Z cannot be seen as guaranteed. As a result, we need a higher norm which establishes the rules for the valid production of Z. Such a norm has the form "if X, then Z", where "X = if X_1, then X_2". At this point, Z is validated by X and, within X, X_2 is validated by X_1; yet, once again, to find a foundation for X_1 and for X as a whole, we have to climb a step higher, up to the norm "if Y, then X", where "Y = if Y_1, then Y_2" – but only with the result of being confronted with the same problem as in the previous steps. Indeed, since in the formal pyramid of legal positivism the validity of any proposition is founded on the validity of a norm located at a hierarchically higher level, the whole process runs the risk of a regression ad infinitum, with the consequence that no reliable foundation can be established for the legal system. Kelsen proposed to stop the upward climbing at a certain point, at which the whole system of legal propositions was thought to find its last validation in what he called the "basic norm" (*Grundnorm*).[89] Following his view, we have to put at the last stage of our regression in the search of the last fundament of the legal system the proposition "if A, then B", where "B = if B_1, then B_2". What is remarkable, here, is that A – as the *Grundnorm* – does not have the usual form "if A_1, then A_2". Indeed, in order to stop the backward process, A cannot display the structure of a hypothetical sentence – which would imply a further regression – but of an apodictic proposition. Put differently, the "basic norm" cannot be – as legal propositions generally are – a sentence formulated and declared as valid on the basis of a hierarchically higher located procedure, or a *lex posita*. Instead of being a set, "posed" (*gesetzt*) or positive norm, it has to be, to stand on its own, a "pre-posed" (*vorgesetzt*) or presupposed assumption. Concretely, the content of the assumption at the basis of a legal system varies from case to case. For instance, the *Grundnorm* can maintain that "all power derives from the people", or – quite to the contrary – that "all power derives from the monarch" or even from "God"; the only condition is that the pre-positive principle of the whole legal system has to be strong and well-accepted enough to secure effectiveness.[90]

Substantially, Kelsen's ultimate source of the validity of the legal system neither meets the criteria that generally characterize legal propositions, nor does its content properly belong to the legal discourse. Rather, it seems to take inevitably the form of a general assumption about the extra-legal – i.e., social and political, or even moral and philosophical – fundament of the "order of human

89 ibid 67ff; Kelsen, *Pure Theory of Law* (n 3) 193ff; Hans Kelsen, *General Theory of Law and State* (Harvard University Press 1949; 1st ed. 1945) at 115ff.

90 Kelsen, *General Theory of Law and State* (n 89) 120.

behaviour". On that basis, the conclusion cannot but be that the legal system is not capable of sustaining itself on its own, but requires the resort to an extra-legal *content*. The same problem is shared by the other major exponent of legal positivism, this time from the English-speaking intellectual tradition, namely H. L. A. Hart. In fact, Hart tried to avoid Kelsen's somehow obscure and explicitly metalegal foundation of the legal system by introducing the notion of the "rule of recognition".[91] In his theory, the "rule of recognition" is understood as the principle that allows us to identify the context for the valid application of a certain legal norm. For example, it should enable us to "recognize" a norm as belonging to the domestic legal order or, instead, to the international legal system, due to the fact that the norm is produced, in the first case, according to the rules laid down in the national constitution, or is the result, in the second case, of an inter-state treaty. Consequently, the "rule of recognition" is assumed to guarantee the validity of the norms within a specific system, while identifying their scope of application. Thus, Hart's theory attempted to overcome the quite evident extra-legal connotation of Kelsen's *Grundnorm* by including the source of validity – which was presumed to be itself a "rule" and not a general assumption – into the system of legal norms. Moreover, it concentrated more on the conditions for the validity of a norm than on its content. However, it was Hart himself who admitted that the "rule of recognition" is lastly not a rule of the legal system in the full meaning of the term since "in the day-to-day life of a legal system its rule of recognition is very seldom expressly formulated as a rule."[92] If not a proper norm, then the "rule of recognition" must be a non-positive and in the most cases implicit presumption concerning the range of validity of a legal proposition, which provides "both private persons and officials ... with authoritative criteria for identifying primary rules of obligation."[93] From this point of view, therefore, the difference from Kelsen's approach tends to vanish away. Moreover, putting "recognition" at the basis of the legal system implies that the validity of a norm has to be *acknowledged* by the social community in charge of applying it – and the acknowledgement of the binding character of a normative proposition is always a social process which inevitably goes far beyond the boundaries of the formal system of laws.

Legal positivism denies interdisciplinarity by claiming that the legal system is a self-reliant hierarchical set of normative propositions, characterized by a specific formal structure and an autonomous truth content. This truth content has been identified, by the two main exponents of legal positivism,

91 H. L. A. Hart, *The Concept of Law* (Clarendon Press 1994; first published 1961) 100ff.

92 ibid 101.

93 ibid 100.

respectively with the *Grundnorm* or with the "rule of recognition". However, we can consistently argue that the truth content of the legal system is precisely what links it to extra-legal discourses, thus reintroducing that element of interdisciplinarity which should have been purged from jurisprudence. Faced with the substantial failure of the most essential tasks undertaken by legal positivists and with the evidence that this shortcoming is related to the truth content of the legal system as the Trojan horse of interdisciplinarity and extra-legal discourses, we must now turn to the question on whether a better result in favour of the self-reliance of the legal system could be achieved if we assume that the formalism of the law goes along with the rejection of any kind of truth content, be it inherent or external to the system. In other words, could a legal system without aspiration to possess a truth content be effectively self-sufficient, thus definitively silencing the request for interdisciplinarity? This is precisely the claim made by Martti Koskenniemi, one of the most influential legal theorists of his generation. Koskenniemi's influences can essentially be traced back to three sources: the Critical Legal Studies, from which he draws the conviction that law is intrinsically linked to power; postmodern thinking, from which he takes up the idea that no universal rationality can be discovered in human knowledge and action, either in the law or elsewhere; and a sort of Wittgensteinian epistemology, according to which propositions do not have a truth content in themselves – be it intrinsic or object-related – but derive their meaning from the context in which they are uttered.[94] Following along those intellectual paths – in particular the epistemological scepticism of Wittgenstein's *Philosophical Investigations* – Koskenniemi maintains that legal norms and notions, i.e., legal propositions and their main substantive components, neither contain an inherent truth nor unequivocally refer to external facts.[95] Having no rationality in its own right, law is regarded by Koskenniemi as a set of formal sentences[96] that can be used to foster the priorities of the individual legal professionals.[97] In the light of the rejection of any truth content of the law, the only task of the schools of law would consist in training

94 Ludwig Wittgenstein, 'Philosophische Untersuchungen' in Ludwig Wittgenstein, *Werkausgabe* (Suhrkamp 1984; first published 1953) Vol. 1, 225–580 (English translation by G. E. M. Anscombe et al.: *Philosophical Investigations*, Wiley-Blackwell 2009, first published 1953).

95 Martti Koskenniemi, *The Politics of International Law* (Hart 2011) 298ff; Martti Koskenniemi, *From Apology to Utopia: The Structure of International Legal Argument* CUP 2005) 478ff, 513ff.

96 Martti Koskenniemi, *The Gentle Civilizer of Nation: The Rise and fall of International Law 1870–1960* (CUP 2001) 500ff.

97 Koskenniemi, *From Apology to Utopia* (n 95) 536ff, 615ff.

the students in the application of legal technicalities in order to acquire the instruments to push forwards in the best way their idiosyncratic preferences. It is almost superfluous to say that, under those circumstances, any reference to interdisciplinarity would be meaningless.

Koskenniemi's position, however, turns out to be rather unconvincing for two main reasons.[98] First, insofar as the law relies, for its interpretation and application, on individual convictions, these are themselves something that goes beyond the formal character of legal propositions. Consequently, even if we adopt Koskenniemi's perspective, we have to admit that the legal system inevitably finds its meaning in a world outside the overall set of legal norms – and this should always be taken into account while studying and teaching law. Secondly, the interpretation of legal propositions should not be considered as arbitrary as Koskenniemi is prone to assume. In fact, Wittgenstein's radical idea of a language devoid of objective references and, thus, without falsifiable truth content never became mainstream among philosophers of language and epistemologists. Rather, in order to avoid a cognitive scepticism that would prove disruptive, in particular for natural sciences, and to prevent a moral neutralism that would permanently weaken the normative content of human sciences, the post-Wittgensteinian philosophy of language and theory of knowledge were rather committed to mend the rift and to bridge the gap between language and objective reality again.[99] The most recent linguistic and epistemological research suggests, indeed, that legal propositions – as any other sort of propositions too – should be assumed to have a truth content that research and teaching are committed to explore accordingly.

Yet, what is this truth content that lies at the basis of the legal system and should be properly considered while analyzing the law as well as in the context of legal education? We can get a first hint at a possible answer from Niklas Luhmann's sociology of law. According to his version of systems theory, society necessarily differentiates itself into different social subsystems, the rationale

98 Sergio Dellavalle, 'Law as a Linguistic Instrument without Truth Content? On the Epistemology of Koskenniemi's Understanding of Law' (2017) ZaöRV 199.

99 Donald Davidson, *Problems of Rationality* (Clarendon 2004); Donald Davidson, *Subjective, Intersubjective, Objective* (Clarendon 2001); Robert Brandom, *Making It Explicit* (Harvard University Press 1998; first published 1994); Jürgen Habermas, *Vorstudien und Ergänzungen zur Theorie des kommunikativen Handelns* (Suhrkamp 1984; English translation by Barbara Fultner: *On the Pragmatics of Social Interaction*, The MIT Press 2001); J. Habermas, *Nachmetaphysisches Denken* (Suhrkamp 1988; English translation by William Mark Hohengarten: *Postmetaphysical Thinking*, The MIT Press 1992); Jürgen Habermas, *Wahrheit und Rechtfertigung* (first published 1999; Suhrkamp 2004; English translation by Barbara Fultner: *Truth and Justification*, The MIT Press 2003).

of which is to deliver in the most efficient way the functions whose fulfillment the society as a whole needs in order to persist and thrive. Against this background, every social subsystem is characterized by its own rationality, depending on the priorities and choices of action that guarantee the most effective outcome with reference to the function to be fulfilled.[100] While performing its function, each subsystem inevitably produces expectations in those interaction participants who come into contact with it. In order to prevent the disruptive effects that could arise from the pretensions formulated by social actors, their legitimate expectations are expressed in the form of norms, and the claims appealing to these norms are dealt with through formal procedures following the principles laid down by law. Therefore, law's function lastly consists in stabilizing the normative expectations deriving from other social subsystems.[101] Two further aspects are relevant here. First, like society is made of distinct social subsystems, also the whole of the system of legal norms divides itself into specialized legal subsystems, each of them typified by the task of stabilizing the normative expectations of a specific social context. For example, we have the administrative social system and, related to it, we have also a specialized administrative law; analogously, we have internet and the law of internet, financial markets and the law of finance, and so on. Secondly, every social subsystem organizes the flow of communication within its range of influence on the basis of its own rationality, i.e., following the rational criteria which autonomously emerge as the most appropriate in order to achieve the functional goal of the subsystem. To make once again an example, the rationality of the administration has to be different from the rationality that governs the financial markets. On that basis, every specialized legal subsystem has to make that specific rationality to its own, which shapes the flow of communication of the social subsystem whose normative expectations it has to regulate.

At this point, the second argument in favour of interdisciplinarity – which is applicable not only to international law, but to law in general – stands out with the force of evidence: since every specialized system of legal norms is necessarily imbued by the very same rational principles that we may find in the social subsystem of reference, the analysis and teaching of law cannot refrain from dealing with the systemic rationalities that create the functional horizon of society. In other words, if we want to know why a legal subsystem operates in a certain way, then we have to be aware of the logics that underlie that particular

100 Niklas Luhmann, *Die Gesellschaft der Gesellschaft* (Suhrkamp 1997; English translation by Rhodes Barrette: *Theory of Society*, Stanford University Press 2012).

101 Niklas Luhmann, *Das Recht der Gesellschaft* (Suhrkamp 1993; English translation: *Law as a Social System*, Fatima Kastner *et al.* eds., OUP 2004).

flow of subsystemic communication. As a matter of fact, in the legal sentence "if Z_1, then Z_2", the second element – namely Z_2 – is determined not only by the formal structure of the proposition but also by the content of Z_1, i.e., by the social rationale that shapes it. Resorting to an example again, the law of international organizations cannot be understood without knowing their rationality and operating mode. Far from being self-reliant as the *Rechtswissenschaft* wanted to believe, the law is deeply embedded in social processes. It should be the task of research and teaching to take them into due account.

4 Interdisciplinarity and Law's Overall Social Rationale

In the last section the interdisciplinary approach to legal research and education has been justified by referring to the essential link between the legal system and the different forms of functional rationality that characterize the social subsystems respectively regulated by the distinct legal subsystems. Yet, there is a further justification, which relies on a broader and intersubjective concept of rationality. Indeed, beyond functional rationality, which focuses on the instruments and procedures that make possible to fulfil fundamental social services in the most efficient way, we can detect a non-systemic or supra-systemic rationality, the task of which consists in determining the conditions for the social life as a whole to be considered ethically justifiable. In other words, the supra-systemic rationality is shaped, in epistemological terms, by the intersubjective exchange of arguments about what a "good social life" is assumed to be. At the basis of the "good social life" are rules which are considered ethically qualified and advantageous by a sufficiently large part of the members of the community. Since the law plays a major role – at least in modern societies – in defining those rules, we can infer that the system of legal norms is directly connected to the way in which the idea of the "good life" is understood in a specific society.

4.1 *Paradigms of Order and Paradigmatic Revolutions*

To clarify the content of the legal system, we have to address the question of the overall rationality that imbues the society whose interactions are regulated by that system. However, we can only undertake this task if we can rely on a notion that enables us to build a conceptual bridge between the two dimensions, i.e., between the system of norms and social rationality. I claim that this role is to be taken up by the notion of *order*. "Order" is the condition in which social interactions are effectively directed by rules that make them predictable, peaceful and, in the most favourable cases, also cooperative. On that basis, the connection between the concept of "order" and the first of the above-mentioned dimensions – namely, norms in general, as well as legal norms in particular – is quite immediate. Yet, the notion of "order" also has a normative qualification: to be accepted, the norms that create the "ordered society" must correspond to the predominant idea of what a social and political community assumes to be a "good social life". Put differently, the "ordered society", to persist and thrive, has to qualify as a "well-ordered society" in the eyes of the majority of its members. We have, here, the connection of "order" with the second above-mentioned dimension, i.e., with a general idea of social rationality. Indeed, we can detect different ideas of social rationality and, therefore, as many conceptions of the "well-ordered society" as well as of the legal system based on it. We can draw a map of the distinct understandings of "order" by resorting to the essential components of any idea of "order". I will come back to this point in short. But, first, it is important to pay attention to the further advantages that can be derived from the use of the notion of "order".

Beside the advantage of building a bridge between the legal system and overall social rationality, the concept of "order" can be applied – secondly – to a very large number of social, political, legal and economic institutions, making possible to find out at a very abstract level the invariables that bind them, or the differences that divide them. This aspect is of paramount importance in a time in which, as it has been highlighted above,[102] the traditional distinctions – such as between public and private, national and international, and so on – are increasingly blurred and urgently need a redefinition. A third advantage in using the concept of "order" is connected to the relation between the different disciplines of human science. Although they are, to a certain extent, all correlated to each other, and often share a common origin, they have been suffering, in the last decades, from a loss of mutual communication. Yet, dialogue allows the transfer of knowledge deriving from related sciences into the language of one's own discipline, improving this way also the research results in this field. This leads to the third argument in favour of interdisciplinarity in legal research and education – once again an argument that is not limited to international law, but can be expanded to law in general. In fact, legal theory – but also legal praxis, to some extent – can highly benefit from the knowledge developed by political science, sociology, economy and political theory. More concretely, the engagement with non-legal discourses, often due to their more innovative approaches, helps legal professionals to better understand the society in which law operates. This process does not have only a practical

102 See *supra*, Section 2.

dimension – in the sense that enables legal professionals to be more successful because of their more profound understanding of the reality – but also makes it possible for the law and for those who work with it to become self-reflexive inasmuch as the legal discourse and the preferences of those who use it can be located against a more ambitious background regarding how the society as a whole should be organized. Interdisciplinary dialogue, however, needs some conceptual elements in common, which build the bridges of communication and guarantee that the scholars on each side have a chance to understand each other. The notion of "order" is one of such conceptual bridges. Indeed, "order" is a concept that is familiar to philosophers and political scientists, lawyers and sociologists, theologians and economists – and some other categories of experts of human sciences could be added.

We can detect, in the history of human thought, different ideas of the "well-ordered society". I propose to define them as the *paradigms of order*.[103] More specifically, a "paradigm of order" is a set of concepts and abstract claims as definitions of those concepts, which shape, according to certain parameters, the contours of what a "well-ordered society" is assumed to be. These parameters correspond to three claims regarding how a well-ordered social interaction should be organized, which are necessarily contained in every paradigm of order. The first claim addresses the extension of order, namely whether this is inevitably limited to a homogeneous social community, or can potentially be extended to the whole humankind. The second claim is related to the ontological foundation of order, i.e., whether some kind of organic community builds the basis of social order, or rather the individuals are at the centre of society. The third claim, finally, is about whether a well-ordered society has to be necessarily unitary and hierarchical, with no overlapping and horizontal interaction of norms and institutions, or a pluralist society with a heterarchical normative and institutional system can also be seen as "well-ordered".

To use a metaphor, we always see the world – and the possible actions that we can carry out in it – through the glasses that the specific culture of that time puts at our disposal. But, glasses must be changed over time. And paradigms change, too. This happens through what we can call *paradigmatic revolutions*. A "paradigmatic revolution" is a huge change of perspective – or, to put more correctly, of the conceptual pre-conditions of knowledge and action – following which our understanding of the world and of the possibility to act in it is

103 Armin von Bogdandy and Sergio Dellavalle, 'Universalism Renewed. Habermas' Theory of International Order in Light of Competing Paradigms' (2009) 10 German Law Journal 5; Sergio Dellavalle, *Paradigms of Social Order. From Holism to Pluralism and Beyond* (Palgrave Macmillan 2021).

profoundly reshaped. We see the world differently, we explain phenomena differently, and we discover new chances for our activities. Put very simply, we get a new idea of what is true and what is right. If applied to the patterns of social order, this means that in every period of human history our understanding of the "well-ordered society" has been shaped by a sufficiently coherent vision containing assumption on all three above-mentioned claims. However, when social changes occurred, making some of those assumptions obsolete, a new paradigm eventually emerged, which was better suited to the new situation, in the sense that it provided a more useful conceptual instrument to understand it and more valuable advice for action. Nevertheless, paradigms of social order – contrary to the paradigms of natural sciences – seem never to die, but only to spend times, even long periods, of recovery, just to reappear in a shape which is thought to be more adequate to meet the challenges of the new era. As a result, even the most ancient paradigms of order are still present in our time, offering an interpretation of society that, even though to some extent old-fashioned, is still capable of deeply influencing the debate.

4.2 *The Unitary Paradigms of Order*

Going through the history of political thought, we become aware of the presence of three historical paradigms of order, characterized by an evolution that lasted many hundred – or even a few thousand – years. Furthermore, we can detect three more recent paradigms, which developed only a couple of decades ago as a result of the last paradigmatic revolution. The most ancient of all paradigms of order maintains – with reference to the claims that essentially characterize each paradigm of order – that, first, a well-ordered society cannot but be limited in range, while between territorially constrained well-ordered communities only containment of dis-order is feasible. Thus, it is *particularistic* and not *universalistic*. Secondly, its supporters generally assume that a community, to be well-ordered, must be largely homogeneous, i.e., a *holon*. Accordingly, the first paradigm of order is *holistic* and not *individualistic*. Thirdly, the well-ordered society must be organized as a *unitary* structure, as opposed to a *pluralist* one, since it is not accepted that conflicting norms and institutions of different origins can be valid or have authority at the same time and in the same place. The basic assumptions of this first paradigm of order – which we can call *holistic particularism* – were already laid down for the first time in the Western history of ideas as far back in time as in ancient Greece,[104] to pass then through different stages of development, determined

104 Thucydides, 'The Peloponnesian War' in *Hobbes's Thucydides*, Richard Schlatter ed. (Rutgers University Press 1975); Plato, *The Republic* (Benjamin Jowett tr., Collier 1901); Aristotle, *Politics* (H. Rackham tr., Harvard University Press 1959).

by the respective predominance of concepts such as territorial sovereignty,[105] national identity[106] and continental hegemony.[107]

The first paradigmatic revolution addressed the content of the first assertion that distinguishes every paradigm of order, namely the assertion concerning the extension of order. That means that conceptions of order were developed, for the first time, according to which the well-ordered society can extend so far as to comprise the entire humankind. This marked the transition from a *particularistic* to a *universalistic* understanding of order. Nothing changed, on the contrary, as regards the other contents of the paradigm: social order was still based on the assumption of an organic ontological fundament, and order had to be unitary. Due to its characteristics, this second paradigm of order can be defined as *holistic universalism*. Probably, the idea that order can be universal was formulated for the first time in the Buddhist philosophy through the concept of *dharma*.[108] In the Western world, instead, it was the Stoic philosophy that took this step.[109] Later, Stoic universalism was taken up by the upcoming Christian philosophy.[110] In fact, the idea of order of Christianity is, in principle, universalistic, since the message of the Gospel is directed to all human beings. Yet, a significant problem arose with Christian universalism: indeed, if the universality of social, political and legal order is grounded on religion, there is an undeniable threat of discrimination, or even of persecution of the "infidels", who are actually excluded from the order of peace.[111] Thus, given that the religion-based universalism is always curtailed and incomplete, the attempt was made – in particular by thinkers influenced by the theology of Reformation – to ground holistic universalism on purely rational arguments.[112]

105 Jean Bodin, *Six livres de la république* (first published 1576, Imprimerie de Jean de Tournes 1579; English transl. by M.J. Tooley, Blackwell 1955).

106 Adam H. Müller, *Die Elemente der Staatskunst* (first published 1809, Fischer 1922).

107 Carl Schmitt, 'Der Begriff des Politischen' (1932) in Carl Schmitt, *Der Begriff des Politischen. Text von 1932 mit einem Vorwort und drei Corollarien* (Duncker & Humblot 1963) 20–78 (English transl. by George Schwab, The University of Chicago Press 2007); Carl Schmitt, *Der Nomos der Erde im Völkerrecht des Jus Publicum Europeum* (Greven 1950; English transl. by G. L. Ulmen, Telos 2006).

108 Rebecca Redwood French and Mark A. Nathan (eds.), *Buddhism and Law* (CUP 2014).

109 Johannes von Arnim, *Stoicorum veterum fragmenta* (Teubneri 1905), Vol. I and Vol.

110 Aurelius Augustinus, *De civitate Dei* (413–426) (Moretus 1600; English translation by Philip Schaff, The Christian Literature Publishing Co. 1890); Thomas Aquinas, *Summa theologica* (1265–1273) (W. Benton-Encyclopedia Britannica 1980); Thomas Aquinas, *Political Writings* (R. W. Dyson ed., CUP 2004); Francisco Suárez, 'De legibus, ac Deo legislatore' (1612) in Francisco Suárez, *Selections from three Works* (Clarendon 1944).

111 Francisco de Vitoria, *De Indis et De Jure Belli Relectiones* (Oceana, 1964).

112 Alberico Gentili, *De Jure Belli Libri Tres* (1589) (Typographeo Clarendoniano 1877; English: Clarendon 1933); Hugo Grotius, *De Jure Belli ac Pacis* (1625) (English: *The Rights*

Interestingly, to avoid religion-based biases, they justified the possibility to establish a cosmopolitan social order by resorting to an old Stoic argument, namely to the areligious and allegedly purely rational assumption of the universal sociability of humans. In continuity with the past, the belief in the holistic, universalistic and unitary essence of social rationality is still a defining character of contemporary natural law theory.[113]

The third paradigm of order was the result of the second paradigmatic revolution, which did not affect – like the first one – the extension of order, but what had to be regarded as the ontological basis of the "well-ordered society". In the first two paradigms of order this ontological basis was always holistic or organic, in the sense that a community (of more or less broad extension) was assumed to exist which was regarded as axiologically superior to the sum of all its members. Put in a simpler way, the totality of the community was located above the individuals. It was Thomas Hobbes who took the first step on the way to the paradigmatic revolution from holism to individualism in political philosophy. In his view, the logical starting point of social order was not the existing community, but the individuals with their endowment of rights, reason and interests. With the second paradigmatic revolution the hierarchy was thus reversed: the individuals were located above the community, which was presumed to exist only on the basis of their free act of will and in order to protect their rights.[114] Accordingly, society was established by a contract stipulated by free and equal individuals – whence the definition of this strand of political philosophy as *contractualism*. Depending on how many rights the individuals, then united to form a society, agreed to transfer to the public power that had been created by the contract, the *individualistic paradigm of order* developed into two different strands: *liberal* contractualism, in which only the right to persecute offenders is handed over to the public power and the parliament is

---

of War and Peace, Richard Tuck ed., Liberty Fund 2005); Johannes Althusius, *Politica Methodice Digesta* (1603) (English transl. of the 1614 ed.: Johannes Althusius, *Politica*, Frederick S. Carney ed., Liberty Fund 1995); Samuel Pufendorf, *De jure naturae et gentium libri octo* (1672) (complete English translation by Basil Kennet, Lichfield et al. 1703; partial English translation by Michael J. Seidler, in: Samuel Pufendorf, *The Political Writings*, Craig L. Carr ed., OUP 1994).

113 John Finnis, *Natural Law and Natural Rights* (Clarendon 1980); Germain Grisez, Joseph Boyle and John Finnis, *Practical Principles, Moral Truth, and Ultimate Ends* (1987) 32 The American Journal of Jurisprudence 99; Nigel Biggar and Rufus Black (eds.), *The Revival of Natural Law* (Ashgate 2000).

114 Thomas Hobbes, *Elementa philosophica de Cive* (first published 1642; Johan. Jac. Flick 1782; English translation by Richard Tuck and Michael Silverthorne: *On the Citizen*, CUP 1998); Thomas Hobbes, *Leviathan, or the Matter, Form, and Power of a Commonwealth Ecclesiastical and Civil* (first published 1651, Clarendon 1929).

entrusted with strong legislative and control competences;[115] and *democratic* contractualism, in which actually all rights are alienated, yet not to the institutions of public power, but to the citizens themselves as a whole, who are now joined to form a political community.[116]

At first, the supporters of the individualistic paradigm of order had little interest in international relations, so that the question regarding how this paradigm dealt with the extension of order remained unanswered for long time. However, since the individualistic paradigm put at the centre of its idea of order the individuals with their most abstract features – i.e., as holders of rights, interests and reason – it is difficult to imagine how limits could be set to the extension of the well-ordered society. As a result, individualism is implicitly *universalistic*, so that we can properly define the third paradigm of social order as *universalistic individualism*. The first author who became aware of the intrinsically cosmopolitan nature of individualism was Immanuel Kant. Indeed, he not only upheld the idea of the centrality of the individuals in his understanding of social, political and legal order but also explicitly took position in favour of a cosmopolitan framework for order. More specifically, he introduced for the first time a cosmopolitan law (*jus cosmopoliticum*) as one of the three parts of public law – along with state law (constitutional law, especially) and traditional international law (*jus gentium*).[117] While traditional international law is a legal framework that governs the relations *among* states, cosmopolitan law is *supra-state law*. More than a century after Kant, Hans Kelsen drew the most radical consequence from the idea of cosmopolitan law by locating international law – and in particular that part of it which has *erga omnes* validity – at the top of his still rigorously unitary and hierarchical system of legal norms.[118] His legally shaped *civitas maxima* can be regarded as

115 John Locke, *Two Treatises on Government* (first published 1690, Yale University Press 2003).

116 Jean-Jacques Rousseau, *Du contract social, ou principes du droit politique* (first published 1762; Garnier-Flammarion 1966; English translation: 'The Social Contract' in Rousseau, *The Social Contract and the First and Second Discourses*, Susan Dunn ed., Yale University Press 2002, 149–254).

117 Immanuel Kant, 'Zum ewigen Frieden. Ein philosophischer Entwurf' in Immanuel Kant, *Werkausgabe* (Wilhelm Weischedel ed., Suhrkamp 1977; first published 1795) Vol. XI, 193–251, 203 (English translation by H. B. Nisbet: 'Perpetual Peace: A Philosophical Sketch in Immanuel Kant, *Political Writingsm*, CUP 1991, 93–130, 98ff); Immanuel Kant, 'Die Metaphysik der Sitten' (first published 1797) in Kant, *Werkausgabe* (n 117), Vol. VIII, 309–634, Part I/II, § 62, 475ff (English translation by Mary J. Gregor: *The Metaphysics of Morals*, CUP 1991, 158ff).

118 See *supra* n. 5.

the most ambitious blueprint for a strongly centralized cosmopolitan order centred on the priority of individual rights.

4.3 *The Post-unitary or Pluralist Paradigms of Order*

The *third paradigmatic revolution* involved what has been described as the third element that is always present in a paradigm of order, namely the assertion concerning the unitary or non-unitary character of a well-ordered society. Regardless of whether they were particularistic or universalistic on the one hand, holistic or individualistic on the other, the paradigms of order before the third paradigmatic revolutions were all characterized by a *unitary* idea of order. This means that, in all these previous paradigms, the institutional structure and the system of norms are considered "well-ordered" only if they are organized as coherent, vertical and hierarchical unity, as a pyramid in which conflicts between different institutions and norms have to be resolved by defining which institution or norm, respectively, has priority over the conflicting one. Instead, the third paradigmatic revolution has paved the way for an understanding of order in which the well-ordered society is conceived of as a polyarchic, horizontal and interconnected structure that reminds us more of a network than of a pyramid. In this social, political and legal configuration of interrelated decision-makers, conflicts of institutions and norms are not a dangerous threat for order; rather, they can be operationalized in discursive procedures aiming at reaching consent and not at establishing – or re-establishing – hierarchies.

The first contemporary post-unitary paradigm of order is based on the epistemological approach of *systems theory* and has already been introduced before while addressing the question of the truth content of the specialized legal subsystems.[119] Resuming its main conceptual tenet, it can concisely be said that, insofar as the law has the function to guarantee the internal order of different social subsystems, the legal system itself loses its unity and develops distinct legal *sub*systems, each of them characterized by the rationality, expressed in legal terms, that underlies the implementation of the subsystemic functions.

The second post-unitary paradigm of order has essentially developed as a result of the sceptical philosophy of language of the later Wittgenstein[120] and, even more, as a consequence of the transfer of Michel Foucault's postmodern critical approach into political philosophy and legal theory. The explicit target of postmodern criticism is the modern concept of subjectivity, as expressed

119 See *supra* Section 3., n 100ff.

120 See *supra* n 94.

by the context of the universalistic-individualistic paradigm.[121] In particular, the modern subject is accused to be nothing less than an artificial construct imposed to constrain human experience and action capabilities into a forced and oppressive unity. Therefore, actual human individualities have to realize themselves beyond the boundaries of a unitary – and lastly tyrannical – idea of order, enforced by a diffuse power aiming at the full control over bodies and minds. The specific feature of the paradigm of order that derives from the postmodern criticism of modern individualism, consists in the assumption – made, in such explicit terms and with such a large influence, for the first time in Western thinking – that order, in the sense of rules that the society in its totality has to follow, is in principle a threat to the self-realization of the concrete individualities. At this point, two different strands of the postmodern approach develop, both applying the critical look at the world of social, political and legal interactions. The first variant picks up the most radical interpretation of postmodern criticism, maintaining that, insofar as order is in its essence oppressive, the only possibility to make the society more "human" would consist in opposing, if necessary with violence, the established rules and in substituting them with spontaneous form of self-expression of subjectivity. The second variant is by far less extreme and relies on the more moderate dimension of postmodern critical analysis of the modern society: order in its absoluteness remains threatening, but it does not need to be radically denied and subverted. Rather, it has just to be de-structured as a whole and split into a plurality of *orders* – in plural. Given the context of plurality, order loses its all-embracing, tyrannical comprehensiveness, and the individuals gain a new and better chance to realize their plans according to their priorities in the spaces generated by the break of the former rigid texture.

According to the *communicative paradigm* as the third post-unitary paradigm of order, society is made of a plurality of interactions, each of them

---

121 Michel Foucault, *L'ordre du discours* (first published 1970; Gallimard 1971; English translation in : Robert Young (ed.), *Untying the Text : A Post-Structuralist Reader*, Routledge & Kegal Paul 1981, 48–78); Michel Foucault, *Histoire de la folie à l'âge classique* (Gallimard 1961; English translation by Jonathan Murphy and Jean Khalfa: *History of Madness*, Routlegde 2006); Michel Foucault, *Les mots et les choses* (Gallimard 1966; English translation : *The Order of Things*, Routledge 1989, first published 1970); Michel Foucault, *Surveiller et punir* (Gallimard 1975; English translation by Alan Sheridan: *Discipline and Punish*, Vintage Books 1995, first published 1977); Michel Foucault, *Histoire de la sexualité, 1 : La volonté de savoir* (Gallimard 1976; English translation by Robert Hurley: *The History of Sexuality. Volume 1: An Introduction*, Pantheon Books 1978); Michel Foucault, 'The Subject and Power' in Hubert L. Dreyfus and Paul Rabinow (eds.), *Michel Foucault: Beyond Structuralism and Hermeneutics* (Chicago University Press 1982) 208.

characterized by a specific aim that influences decisively the discursive contents of the interaction.[122] Yet, although the aim of the social interaction is essential to determine the contents of the discourse, the rationality embodied in the communication is, from the perspective of the communicative paradigm, not exclusively and even not primarily functional.[123] Rather, the communicative rationality – right from the understanding of communication that is here presupposed – has always a normative core.[124] Precisely this normative core is what makes communicative rationality universal – and therefore different from the purely systemic rationalities. As regards the legal system, communicative rationality paves the way to a conception in which the manifold articulation of the legal system is recognized, but in a quite different way than in the post-unitary approaches described before. Here, plurality is embedded into an overarching structure, held together by the implementation of communicative reason as a counterpart of systemic rationality – a counterpart that is operating not only from outside the social subsystems but also inside each of them.

4.4 *How to Locate the Concepts of Legal Theory within the Context of the Paradigms of Order*

Drawing the map of the paradigms of order enables us to understand which social rationality lies at the basis of a system of legal norms as well as of the most relevant legal concepts. Furthermore, it allows us to recognize the reasons why a concept has changed its meaning during time in order to adapt to the way in which the "well-ordered society" was then conceived. Finally, it makes it easier to identify similarities – or differences – between concepts insofar as their contents refer to the same paradigms or to different ideas of order. Let us make some examples of how the procedure works.

a) Originally, the concept of *sovereignty* was undoubtedly part of the conceptual construct of holistic particularism inasmuch as it reinforced the idea that political power had to be necessarily hierarchical, organic and

122 Karl-Otto Apel, *Transformation der Philosophie* (Suhrkamp 1973); Karl-Otto Apel, *Diskurs und Verantwortung* (Suhrkamp 1990); Karl-Otto Apel, *Selected Essays* (Eduardo Mendieta ed., Humanities Press 1996); Jürgen Habermas, *Theorie des kommunikativen Handelns* (Suhrkamp 1981; English translation by Thomas McCarthy: *The Theory of Communicative Action*, Beacon Press, 3rd ed.).

123 Jürgen Habermas, *Erläuterungen zur Diskursethik* (Suhrkamp 1991; English translation by Ciaran Cronin: *Justification and Application*, MIT Press 2001, first published 1993).

124 Habermas, *Nachmetaphysisches Denken* (n 99); Habermas, *Vorstudien und Ergänzungen zur Theorie des kommunikativen Handelns* (n 99); Habermas, *Wahrheit und Rechtfertigung* (n 99).

limited in extension. To some extent, this interpretation – though partially softened – is still influential.[125] However, the transition to the individualistic paradigm – and therefore to the idea that individuals have to be put at the centre of the political community – also transformed the notion of sovereign power in the sense that, from then on, this had to be understood as "power of the people", or "popular sovereignty". Moreover, the emergence of a universalistic conception of order requires from sovereign powers to qualify as "trustees of humanity".[126] In addition, the turn to pluralism introduced the possibility to conceive of sovereignty as a multilayered structure, in which the identity of the single polity coexists with cosmopolitan responsibility.[127]

b) The second pillar of holistic particularism is the conviction of the central importance of *national identity*.[128] While some authors still maintain that national identity is the bulwark of constitutionalism,[129] the supporters of any conception of social order beyond holistic particularism claim that we have entered a post-national constellation – which they explicitly welcome as an important step towards the realization of international peace and social justice.[130]

c) A further support for holistic particularism originates from *religious identity*, which is seen by some as the ideological element that can weld together social communities more diverse and larger than nations, while preparing them for the inevitable existential struggle against other, similarly shaped communities.[131] Yet, from a universalistic point of view the

125 Martin Loughlin, 'What Is Constitutionalisation' in Dobner and Loughlin (n 52) 47–69; Martin Loughlin, *The Foundations of Public Law* (OUP 2010) 209–237.

126 Eyal Benvenisti, 'Sovereigns as Trustees of Humanity: On the Accountability of States to Foreign Stakeholders' (2013) 107 AJIL 295.

127 Sergio Dellavalle, 'On Sovereignty, Legitimacy, and Solidarity: Or: How Can a Solidaristic Idea of Legitimate Sovereignty Be Justified?' (2015) 16 Theoretical Inquiries in Law 367; Sergio Dellavalle, 'Squaring the Circle: How the Right to Refuge Can Be Reconciled with the Right to Political Identity' (2018) 16 ICON 776.

128 Anthony D. Smith, *National Identity* (Penguin 1991).

129 Dieter Grimm, 'The Achievement of Constitutionalism and its Prospects in a Changed World' in Dobner and Loughlin (n 52) 3–22; Dieter Grimm, *Sovereignty* (Columbia University Press 2015).

130 Jürgen Habermas, *Die postnationale Konstellation* (Suhrkamp 1998; English translation by Max Pensky: *The Postnational Constellation*, MIT Press 2001).

131 Samuel P. Huntington, *The Clash of Civilizations and the Remaking of World Order* (Simon & Schuster 1996).

very same religious faith can undertake the opposite task, i.e., it can contribute to forge a cosmopolitan sense of solidarity.[132]

d) The fourth and last conceptual instrument of holistic universalism is the application of the theory of *rational choice* to international law and relations, according to which only selfish preferences of national states are rationally justifiable.[133] However, if we adopt any other understanding of rational behaviour – which does not regard behaviour as rational inasmuch as it increases particularistic payoffs, but rather insofar as it aims, for example, at reaching the largest possible consensus – then the most rational option will take the shape of the strengthening of international cooperation.[134]

e) The claim of the contemporary *Lex mercatoria* to be a self-reliant subsystem of legal norms is much better understandable if we become aware of the social rationality on which it is grounded, namely systems theory.[135] Indeed, since each subsystem – characterized by a specific functional rationality – is self-referential and independent of the environment made by all other subsystems, it is possible to conceive of the corpus of norms that regulates the interaction of private economic agents as a self-regulating order, and therefore as an autonomous paradigm of order. From the perspective of communicative rationality, on the contrary, the self-reliance of the Lex mercatoria appears to be quite questionable.[136]

f) *Legal pluralism*[137] and *global governance*[138] are expressions of the post-modern idea of social rationality since both of them reject – explicitly in the first case, implicitly in the second – the existence of an all-encompassing suprasystemic rationality. However, they are subject to criticism not only from the supporters of the communicative rationality: indeed, from the point of view of the non-pluralist conception of

132 Parliament of the World Religions, *Declaration Toward a Global Ethic* (Chicago (IL) 1993); Foundation Global Ethic, *World Religions – Universal Peace – Global Ethic* (Global Ethic Foundation 2008).

133 Jack L. Goldsmith and Eric A. Posner, *The Limits of International Law* (OUP 2005).

134 Thomas Risse, '"Let's Argue!": Communicative Action in World Politics' (2000) 54 International Organization 1; Sergio Dellavalle, 'Opening the Forum to the "Others": Is There an Obligation to Take Non-National Interests into Account within National Political and Juridical Decision-Making-Processes?' (2014) 6 Göttinger Journal of International Law 217.

135 See *supra* n 39.

136 See *supra* n 43.

137 See *supra*, Section 2.3.1.

138 See *supra*, Section 2.3.3.

rationality, both approaches are simply undermining the true meaning of law as the manifestation of a particularistic sovereign power.[139]

g) In its most radical variant, postmodern thinking radically dismisses the very idea of social order as a positive phenomenon – at least in the form in which we have traditionally known it – denouncing it as an instrument of the diffuse oppression that characterizes the "society of control".[140] Some other authors use the postmodern deconstruction of modern subjectivity, as the bulwark of a centralized, Western-biased, patriarchal and ultimately authoritarian notion of the "well-ordered society", not to reject order entirely, but to restructure it so as to make it more receptive to the claims raised by non-Western scholars[141] and feminist theorists.[142]

h) Cosmopolitan constitutionalism is a central goal of all universalistic paradigms of order. Nonetheless, we can detect different proposals with quite distinct features, depending on their respective epistemological background. Authors who can be led back to holistic universalism, for example, tend to assume a natural law fundament for world constitutionalism, implicitly refer to an alleged sociability of all humans, which would urge them to build a universal community of shared values and interests, and finally assign to the international judiciary the most relevant role in defending world order.[143] On the contrary, individualistic universalism puts – in Kant's and Kelsen's vein – individual rights and freedom of agency at the centre, without postulating any kind of predetermined universal community which would pre-exist the legal shaping of world order.[144] The universalism of the communicative paradigm,

139 Alexander Somek, 'Administration without Sovereignty' in Dobner and Loughlin (n 52) 267–287.

140 Michael Hardt and Antonio Negri, *Empire* (Harvard University Press 2001).

141 B. S. Chimni, 'Third World Approaches to International Law: A Manifesto' (2006) 8 International Community Law Review 3.

142 Catharine A. MacKinnon, *Toward a Feminist Theory of the State* (Harvard University Press 1991; 1st ed. 1989); Hilary Charlesworth, 'Feminists Critiques of International Law and Their Critics' (1995) 13 Third World Legal Studies 1.

143 Christian Tomuschat, *International Law: Ensuring the Survival of Mankind on the Eve of a New Century*, (Collected Courses of The Hague Academy of International Law, Vol. 281, Nijhoff 1999) 56–90; Bardo Fassbender, 'Rediscovering a Forgotten Constitution' in Dunoff and Trachtmann (n 41) 133–147; Mehrdad Payandeh, *Internationales Gemeinschaftsrecht* (Springer 2010). For a critique, *see* Andreas L. Paulus, 'The International Legal System as a Constitution' in Dunoff and Trachtmann (n 41) 69–109.

144 Otfried Höffe, *Demokratie im Zeitalter der Globalisierung* (first published 1999; Beck 2002; English translation by Dirk Haubrich and Michael Ludwig: *Democracy in an Age of Globalization*, Springer 2007).

lastly, takes the pluralist turn into due account by locating cosmopolitan cosmopolitanism into a multilayered setting.[145] Furthermore, it emphasizes – much more than its holistic counterpart – the necessity of an adequate democratic legitimacy of cosmopolitan institutions.[146]

5 The Roads to Interdisciplinarity and the International Law Teacher: Epistemic, Curricular and Pratical Obstacles for Interdisciplinarity

The analysis has shown that, to understand the legal phenomenon in our times and to keep pace with it, the interdisciplinary approach to the law with its many disciplines should be developed along three main lines. The first dimension of interdisciplinarity is internal to the law and refers to the overlapping of the different legal disciplines in the context of law's transnationalization. The second refers to the extra-legal rationality that impacts upon legal norms which regulate specific social interactions. The third dimension, finally, connects legal subsystems to broader ideas of the "well-ordered society" and, through these, to extra-legal knowledge. Opening up to interdisciplinarity does not mean that the positive and unique contents of legal disciplines should be neglected in research and teaching. Rather, it implies that their analysis in scholarly works has to be integrated by a more focused attention on transnational law and on how, in that context, specialized legal disciplines interact with one another. Furthermore, on a more theoretical level, the ways should be explored in which the positive contents of legal disciplines are imbued by the functional rationalities of the social subsystems to which they are related, as well as by the suprasystemic claims about how a "well-ordered society" is assumed to look like.

Yet, how can these findings – which have essentially been analysed, so far, from the conceptual point of view – be transferred into the practice of international law teaching? Before we shortly address this dimension, however,

145 Habermas, *Der gespaltene Westen* (n 69); Jürgen Habermas, 'Eine politische Verfassung für die pluralistische Weltgesellschaft?' (2005) 38 Kritische Justiz 222; Jürgen Habermas, 'Kommunikative Rationalität und grenzüberschreitende Politik: eine Replik' in Peter Niesen and Benjamin Herborth (eds.), *Anarchie der kommunikativen Freiheit* (Suhrkamp 2007) 439ff; Jürgen Habermas, 'Konstitutionalisierung des Völkerrechts und die Legitimationsprobleme einer verfassten Weltgemeinschaft' in Winfried Brugger, Ulfried Neumann and Stephan Kirste (eds.), *Rechtsphilosophie im 21. Jahrhundert* (Suhrkamp 2008) 368ff; Kumm (n 64).

146 Peters, 'Dual Democracy' (n 71).

another question should be answered first: Which are the consequences of the turn to interdisciplinarity in all its facets for the law students? Or, put in a more explicit way, is there the danger that the legal professionals who are educated in the spirit of interdisciplinarity might find more difficulties in the development of their careers? I think that the answers to these questions can be highly reassuring. Far from being at a professional disadvantage, lawyers with interdisciplinary competences are an important asset for a large number of employers, public and private. Legal professionals working in the public sector might profit from an expertise that, going beyond the knowledge of the constitutional and administrative rules that apply in their specific environment, also draws from the study of social and political sciences. In the same vein, private lawyers who possess a basic know-how in economics or informatics can bring an added value to their employers. The same can be said with reference to international law: to navigate an increasingly complex and transnational world, the combination of competence in legal technicalities with skills deriving from other educational contexts – from the field of economics to linguistic proficiency, from the knowledge of cultural backgrounds to ethical awareness, and from informatics to social and political science – might prove essential.

If interdisciplinarity is arguably a benefit for legal professionals, the question is much more difficult to settle with reference to how it could be inserted into the curricula of laws schools. Apart from the deplorable fact that international law plays a marginal role in some quite relevant academic systems of the Western world – among them, for instance, the US and Germany – the second most important problem is directly related to the methodology of the recruitment of the academic staff. The most immediate solution for the inclusion of interdisciplinarity into the curricula would consist, indeed, in creating faculty positions for scholars who have acquired specific interdisciplinary competences during their scientific career, for instance for international law scholars who have distinguished themselves through publications that address the overlapping fields between law and other disciplines. According to this ambitious approach, the expertise on legal technicalities should be integrated with the knowledge of the social processes that these technicalities are going to regulate and with an encompassing idea of the well-ordered society, which the legal system is assumed to stabilize and its operators are presumed to serve. Apart from these changes, the interdisciplinary turn in international law would affect the research agenda of legal scholars and the curricula of law students rather peripherally, since the core of legal research and teaching would largely remain concentrated on the specific contents of the respective legal fields.

Nonetheless, considering how academic recruitment works in almost any country, this plan could turn out to be utterly unrealistic: in fact, the criteria for recruitment are completely in the hand of a rather traditional academic community, in which the only competence that is evaluated is generally the one that refers to the most particular legal dimension of the discipline. In other words the most relevant, if not the only, criterion for a successful academic career in international law as well as in all other legal disciplines seems to be – at least presently – the valuable knowledge of their technical and positive aspects. Given these premises, young scholars who should concentrate on the new frontiers of their discipline risk to be left behind in any evaluation procedure. As a result, the best way to insert a sufficient interdisciplinary dimension into at least some curricula necessarily goes through the creation of specific courses of study with an explicit interdisciplinary vocation. Within those academic contexts, each course unit might also remain rather traditional and be taught by staff with only sectorial competences. Yet, without much of a revolution in the way in which the faculty is recruited, the interdisciplinary added value would be generated by the synergy between the different course units. In the most favourable of cases, such an environment would also lead to more co-taught courses addressing the overlapping fields between law and non-legal disciplines, whose essential presupposition necessarily consists in an increase of mutual interest and recognition. Although this is not the best of all programs to foster interdisciplinarity within the academic context, it is probably the most feasible proposal for the time being.

Given the traditional closure of the disciplines, generally justified by referring to the high specialization of their contents, the transition of interdisciplinarity from a distant promise to a real praxis has still a long way to go. Yet, our day-to-day experience, not least as a result of the Covid-19 pandemic, teaches us that well-established legal notions – from the balancing of individual rights, to the protection of intellectual property, and to the role of international organizations – must be re-adjusted in the face of new situations, whereas these re-adjustments are the more credible and successful, the more they are guided by falsifiable knowledge and based on an open as well as properly informed public debate on the kind of society in which we want to live. Surely, the interdisciplinary opening up of law, in general, and international law in particular, represents a challenge for all those who operate in the sector. The beneficial effects of such a move, however, would be anything but irrelevant: in fact, by meeting the challenge of interdisciplinarity legal research and teaching would prove their capacity to take the most recent social developments into account, while being self-aware of the social role of legal norms as well as of how this has to be constantly redefined in a rapidly changing world.

References

Althusius, Johannes, *Politica Methodice Digesta* (first published 1603; English transl. of the 1614 ed.: Johannes Althusius, *Politica*, Frederick S. Carney ed., Liberty Fund 1995).

Apel, Karl-Otto, *Diskurs und Verantwortung* (Suhrkamp 1990).

Apel, Karl-Otto, *Selected Essays* (Eduardo Mendieta ed., Humanities Press 1996).

Apel, Karl-Otto, *Transformation der Philosophie* (Suhrkamp 1973).

Aquinas, Thomas *Political Writings* (R. W. Dyson ed., CUP 2004).

Aquinas, Thomas *Summa theologica* (1265–1273) (W. Benton-Encyclopedia Britannica 1980).

Archibugi, Daniele, *The Global Commonwealth of Citizens: toward Cosmopolitan Democracy* (Princeton University Press 2008).

Aristotle, *Politics* (H. Rackham tr., Harvard University Press 1959).

Arnim, Johannes von, *Stoicorum veterum fragmenta* (Teubneri 1905), Vol. I and Vol. III.

Augustinus, Aurelius, *De civitate Dei* (413–426; Moretus 1600; English translation by Philip Schaff, The Christian Literature Publishing Co. 1890).

Benvenisti, Eyal, 'Sovereigns as Trustees of Humanity: On the Accountability of States to Foreign Stakeholders' (2013) 107 AJIL 295.

Benvenisti, Eyal, *The Law of Global Governance* (Hague Academy of International Law, The Hague 2014).

Benvenisti, Eyal; Downs, George W., *Between Fragmentation and Democracy. The Role of National and International Courts* (CUP 2017).

Berman, Paul Schiff, *Global Legal Pluralism* (CUP 2012).

Biggar, Nigel, and Black, Rufus (eds.), *The Revival of Natural Law* (Ashgate 2000).

Bodin, Jean, *Six livres de la république* (first published 1576; Imprimerie de Jean de Tournes 1579 ; English transl. by M.J. Tooley, Blackwell 1955).

Bogdandy, Armin von, and Dellavalle, Sergio, 'The Lex Mercatoria of Systems Theory: Localisation, Reconstruction and Criticism from a Public Law Perspective' (2013) 4 Transnational Legal Theory 59.

Bogdandy, Armin von, and Dellavalle, Sergio, 'Universalism Renewed. Habermas' Theory of International Order in Light of Competing Paradigms' (2009) 10 German Law Journal 5.

Bogdandy, Armin von, Dann, Philipp, and Goldmann, Matthias, 'Developing the Publicness of Public International Law: towards a Legal Framework for Global Governance Activities' (2008) 9 German Law Journal 1375.

Bogdandy, Armin von, Goldmann, Matthias, and Venzke, Ingo, 'From Public International Law to International Public Law: Translating World Public Opinion into International Public Authority' (2017) 28 EJIL 115.

Brandom, Robert, *Making It Explicit* (first published 1994; Harvard University Press 1998).

Charlesworth, Hilary, 'Feminists Critiques of International Law and Their Critics' (1995) 13 Third World Legal Studies 1.

Chimni, B. S., 'Third World Approaches to International Law: a Manifesto' (2006) 8 International Community Law Review 3.

Davidson, Donald, *Problems of Rationality* (Clarendon 2004).

Davidson, Donald, *Subjective, Intersubjective, Objective* (Clarendon 2001).

Dellavalle, Sergio, 'Addressing Diversity in Post-unitary Theories of Order' (2020) 40 OJLS 347.

Dellavalle, Sergio, 'Law as a Linguistic Instrument without Truth Content? On the Epistemology of Koskenniemi's Understanding of Law' (2017) 77 ZaöRV 199.

Dellavalle, Sergio, 'On Sovereignty, Legitimacy, and Solidarity: Or: How Can a Solidaristic Idea of Legitimate Sovereignty Be Justified?' (2015) 16 Theoretical Inquiries in Law 367.

Dellavalle, Sergio, 'Opening the Forum to the "Others": Is There an Obligation to Take Non-National Interests into Account within National Political and Juridical Decision-Making-Processes?' (2014) 6 Göttinger Journal of International Law 217.

Dellavalle, Sergio, 'Squaring the Circle: How the Right to Refuge Can Be Reconciled with the Right to Political Identity' (2018) 16 ICON 776.

Dellavalle, Sergio, *Paradigms of Social Order. From Holism to Pluralism and Beyond* (Palgrave Macmillan 2021).

Dunoff, Jeffrey L., 'The Politics of International Constitutions: the Curious Case of the World Trade Organization' in Jeffrey L. Dunoff and Joel P. Trachtmann (eds.), *Ruling the World? Constitutionalism, International Law, and Global Governance* (CUP 2009) 178–205.

Dunoff, Jeffrey L., and Trachtmann, Joel P., 'A Functional Approach to International Constitutionalization' in Jeffrey L. Dunoff and Joel P. Trachtmann (eds.), *Ruling the World? Constitutionalism, International Law, and Global Governance* (CUP 2009) 3–35.

Dworkin, Ronald, *Law's Empire* (Belknap Press of Harvard University Press 1986).

Fassbender, Bardo, 'Rediscovering a Forgotten Constitution' in Jeffrey L. Dunoff and Joel P. Trachtmann (eds.), *Ruling the World? Constitutionalism, International Law, and Global Governance* (CUP 2009) 133–147.

Finnis, John, *Natural Law and Natural Rights* (Clarendon Press 1980).

Fischer-Lescano, Andreas and Teubner, Gunther, 'Regime Collisions: the Vain Search for Legal Unity in the Fragmentation of Global Law' (2003–2004) 25 MichJIntIl 999.

Foucault, Michel, 'The Subject and Power' in Hubert L. Dreyfus and Paul Rabinow (eds.), *Michel Foucault: Beyond Structuralism and Hermeneutics* (Chicago University Press 1982, 208ff).

Foucault, Michel, *Histoire de la folie à l'âge Classique* (Gallimard 1961; English translation by Jonathan Murphy and Jean Khalfa: *History of Madness*, Routlegde 2006).

Foucault, Michel, *Histoire de la sexualité, I : La volonté de savoir* (Gallimard 1976 ; English translation by Robert Hurley: *the History of Sexuality. Volume 1: an Introduction*, Pantheon Books 1978).

Foucault, Michel, *L'ordre du discours* (Gallimard 1970; English translation in: Robert Young (ed.), *Untying the Text: a Post-Structuralist Reader*, Routledge & Kegal Paul 1981, 48–78).

Foucault, Michel, *Les mots et les choses* (Gallimard 1966; English translation : *the Order of Things*, Routledge 1989; first published 1970).

Foucault, Michel, *Surveiller et punir* (Gallimard 1975; English translation by Alan Sheridan: *Discipline and Punish*, Vintage Books 1995; first published 1977).

Foundation Global Ethic, *World Religions – Universal Peace – Global Ethic* (Global Ethic Foundation 2008).

French, Rebecca Redwood, and Nathan, Mark A. (eds.), *Buddhism and Law* (CUP 2014).

Gentili, Alberico, *De Jure Belli Libri Tres* (first published 1589; Typographeo Clarendoniano 1877; English: Clarendon 1933).

Glenn, H. Patrick, *Legal Traditions of the World* (OUP 2010).

Goldsmith, Jack L., and Posner, Eric A., *The Limits of International Law* (OUP 2005).

Grimm, Dieter, 'The Achievement of Constitutionalism and its Prospects in a Changed World' in Petra Dobner and Martin Loughlin (eds.), *The Twilight of Constitutionalism* (OUP 2010) 3–22.

Grimm, Dieter, *Sovereignty* (Columbia University Press 2015).

Grisez, Germain, Boyle, Joseph, and Finnis, John, 'Practical Principles, Moral Truth, and Ultimate Ends' (1987) 32 The American Journal of Jurisprudence 99.

Groppi, Tania, and Ponthoreau, Marie-Claire, 'The Use of Foreign Precedents by Constitutional Judges: a Limited Practice, An Uncertain Future' in Tania Groppi and Marie-Claire Ponthoreau (eds.), *The Use of Foreign Precedents by Constitutional Judges* (Hart 2013) 411–431.

Grossman, Claudio, 'Building the World Community through Legal Education' in Jan Klabbers and Mortimer Sellers (eds.), *The Internationalization of Law and Legal Education* (Springer 2008) 21–35.

Grotius, Hugo, *De Jure Belli ac Pacis* (first published 1625; English: *the Rights of War and Peace*, Richard Tuck ed., Liberty Fund 2005).

Habermas, Jürgen, 'Democracy in Europe: Why the Development of the EU into a Transnational Democracy Is Necessary and How It Is Possible' (2015) in 21 European Law Journal 546.

Habermas, Jürgen, 'Eine politische Verfassung für die pluralistische Weltgesellschaft?' (2005) 38 Kritische Justiz 222.

Habermas, Jürgen, 'Kommunikative Rationalität und grenzüberschreitende Politik: eine Replik' in Peter Niesen and Benjamin Herborth (eds.), *Anarchie der kommunikativen Freiheit* (Suhrkamp 2007) 406–459.

Habermas, Jürgen, 'Konstitutionalisierung des Völkerrechts und die Legitimationsprobleme einer verfassten Weltgemeinschaft' in Winfried Brugger, Ulfried Neumann and Stephan Kirste (eds.), *Rechtsphilosophie im 21. Jahrhundert* (Suhrkamp 2008) 360–379.

Habermas, Jürgen, *Der gespaltene Westen* (Suhrkamp 2001; English translation by Ciaran Cronin: *the Divided West*, Polity Press 2006).

Habermas, Jürgen, *Die postnationale Konstellation* (Suhrkamp 1998; English translation by Max Pensky: *the Postnational Constellation*, MIT Press 2001).

Habermas, Jürgen, *Erläuterungen zur Diskursethik*, (Suhrkamp 1991; English translation by Ciaran Cronin: *Justification and Application*, MIT Press 2001, first published 1993).

Habermas, Jürgen, *Im Sog der Technokratie* (Suhrkamp 2013).

Habermas, Jürgen, *Nachmetaphysisches Denken* (Suhrkamp 1988; English translation by William Mark Hohengarten: *Postmetaphysical Thinking*, The MIT Press 1992).

Habermas, Jürgen, *Theorie des kommunikativen Handelns* (Suhrkamp 1981; English translation by Thomas McCarthy: *the Theory of Communicative Action*, Beacon Press 1987, 3rd ed.).

Habermas, Jürgen, *Vorstudien und Ergänzungen zur Theorie des kommunikativen Handelns* (Suhrkamp 1984; English translation by Barbara Fultner: *On the Pragmatics of Social Interaction*, The MIT Press 2001).

Habermas, Jürgen, *Wahrheit und Rechtfertigung* (first published 1999; Suhrkamp 2004; English translation by Barbara Fultner: *Truth and Justification*, The MIT Press 2003).

Habermas, Jürgen, *Zur Verfassung Europas* (Suhrkamp 2011).

Hardt, Michael, and Negri, Antonio, *Empire* (Harvard University Press 2001).

Hart, H. L. A., 'Kelsen's Doctrine of the Unity of Law' in H. L. A. Hart, *Essays in Jurisprudence and Philosophy* (Clarendon 1983) 309–342.

Hart, H. L. A., *The Concept of Law* (first published 1961; Clarendon 1994).

Hobbes, Thomas, *Elementa philosophica de Cive* (first published 1642; Johan. Jac. Flick 1782; English translation by Richard Tuck and Michael Silverthorne: *On the Citizen*, CUP 1998).

Hobbes, Thomas, *Leviathan, or the Matter, Form, and Power of a Commonwealth Ecclesiastical and Civil* (first published 1651; Clarendon 1929).

Höffe, Otfried, *Demokratie im Zeitalter der Globalisierung* (first published 1999; Beck 2002; English translation by Dirk Haubrich and Michael Ludwig: *Democracy in an Age of Globalization*, Springer 2007).

Huntington, Samuel P., *The Clash of Civilizations and the Remaking of World Order* (Simon & Schuster 1996.

Jackson, Vicki C., *Constitutional Engagement in a Transnational Era* (OUP 2010).

Jessup, Philip C., *Transnational Law* (Yale University Press 1956).

Kadelbach, Stefan, and Kleinlein, Thomas, 'Überstaatliches Verfassungsrecht' (2006) 44 Archiv des Völkerrechts 235.

Kant, Immanuel, ‚Zum ewigen Frieden. Ein philosophischer Entwurf‘ (1795) in Immanuel Kant, *Werkausgabe* (Wilhelm Weischedel ed., Suhrkamp 1977) Vol. XI, 193–251 (English translation by H. B. Nisbet: 'Perpetual Peace: a Philosophical Sketch' in Immanuel Kant, *Political Writings*, CUP 1991, 93–130).

Kant, Immanuel, 'Die Metaphysik der Sitten' (1797) in Immanuel Kant, *Werkausgabe* (Wilhelm Weischedel ed., Suhrkamp 1977) Vol. VIII, 309–634 (English translation by Mary J. Gregor: *the Metaphysics of Morals*, CUP 1991).

Kelsen, Hans, *General Theory of Law and State* (first published 1945; Harvard University Press 1949).

Kelsen, Hans, *Pure Theory of Law* (English translation by Max Knight of *Reine Rechtslehre*, from the Second German Edition of 1960, University of California Press 1967).

Kelsen, Hans, *Reine Rechtslehre. Einleitung in die rechtswissenschaftliche Problematik* (Deuticke 1934).

Kingsbury, Benedict, Krisch, Nico, and Stewart, Richard B., 'The Emergence of Global Administrative Law' (2005) 68 Law and Contemporary Problems 15.

Klabbers, Jan, 'Setting the Scene' in Jan Klabbers, Anne Peters, and Geir Ulfstein (eds.), *The Constitutionalization of International Law* (OUP 2009) 1–44.

Koskenniemi, Martti, *From Apology to Utopia: the Structure of International Legal Argument* (CUP 2005).

Koskenniemi, Martti, *The Gentle Civilizer of Nation: the Rise and fall of International Law 1870–1960* (CUP 2001).

Koskenniemi, Martti, *The Politics of International Law* (Hart 2011).

Krisch, Nico, 'Global Administrative Law and the Constitutional Ambition' in Petra Dobner and Martin Loughlin (eds.), *The Twilight of Constitutionalism* (OUP 2010) 245–266.

Krisch, Nico, *Beyond Constitutionalism* (OUP 2010).

Kumm, Mattias, 'On the Cosmopolitan Turn in Constitutionalism: On the Relationship between Constitutionalism in and beyond the State' in Jeffrey L. Dunoff and Joel P. Trachtmann (eds.), *Ruling the World? Constitutionalism, International Law, and Global Governance* (CUP 2009) 258–324.

Locke, John, *Two Treatises on Government* (first published 1690; Yale University Press 2003).

Loughlin, Martin, 'What Is Constitutionalisation' in Petra Dobner and Martin Loughlin (eds.), *The Twilight of Constitutionalism* (OUP 2010) 47–69.

Loughlin, Martin, *The Foundations of Public Law* (OUP 2010).

Luhmann, Niklas, *Das Recht der Gesellschaft* (Suhrkamp 1993; English: *Law as a Social System*, Fatima Kastner *et al.* eds., OUP 2004).

Luhmann, Niklas, *Die Gesellschaft der Gesellschaft* (Suhrkamp 1997; English translation by Rhodes Barrette: *Theory of Society*, Stanford University Press 2012).

MacKinnon, Catharine A., *Toward a Feminist Theory of the State* (first published 1989; Harvard University Press 1991).

Marsan-Raventós, Clara, 'From Judicial Dialogue to Cosmopolitan Norms: Enhancing Democracy in Globalised States' in Amrei Müller (ed.), *Judicial Dialogue and Human Rights* (CUP 2017) 435–466.

Moravcsik, Andrew, 'Taking Preferences Seriously: a Liberal Theory of International Politics' (1997) 51 International Organization 513.

Müller, Adam H., *Die Elemente der Staatskunst* (first published 1809; Fischer 1922).

Parliament of the World Religions, *Declaration Toward a Global Ethic* (Chicago 1993).

Paulus, Andreas L., 1993, 'The International Legal System as a Constitution' in Jeffrey L. Dunoff and Joel P. Trachtmann (eds.), *Ruling the World? Constitutionalism, International Law, and Global Governance* (CUP 1993) 69–109.

Payandeh, Mehrdad, *Internationales Gemeinschaftsrecht* (Springer 2010).

Peters, Anne, 'Dual Democracy' in Jan Klabbers, Anne Peters and Geir Ulfstein (eds.), *The Constitutionalization of International Law* (OUP 2009) 263–341.

Petersmann, Ernst-Ulrich, 'Principles of World Trade' (2010) in *Max Planck Encyclopedia of Public International Law*, Oxford Public International Law, <https://opil.ouplaw.com/view/10.1093/law:epil/9780199231690/law-9780199231690-e1558?prd=EPIL> accessed 15 June 2021.

Plato, *The Republic* (Benjamin Jowett tr.; Collier 1901).

Pufendorf, Samuel, *De jure naturae et gentium libri octo* (first published 1672; complete English translation by Basil Kennet, Lichfield et al., Oxford 1703; partial English translation by Michael J. Seidler, in Samuel Pufendorf, *The Political Writings*, Craig L. Carr ed., OUP 1994).

Risse, Thomas, '"Let's Argue!": Communicative Action in World Politics' (2000) 54 International Organization 1.

Rousseau, Jean-Jacques, *Du contract social, ou principes du droit politique* (first published 1762; Garnier-Flammarion 1966; English translation: *the Social Contract*, in Rousseau, *The Social Contract and the First and Second Discourses*, Susan Dunn ed., Yale University Press 2002, 149–254).

Schmitt, Carl, *Der Begriff des Politischen* (1932) in Carl Schmitt, *Der Begriff des Politischen. Text von 1932 mit einem Vorwort und drei Corollarien* (Duncker & Humblot 1963) 20–78 (English transl. by George Schwab, The University of Chicago Press 2007).

Schmitt, Carl, *Der Nomos der Erde im Völkerrecht des Jus Publicum Europeum* (Greven 1950; English transl. by G. L. Ulmen, Telos 2006).

Slaughter, Anne-Marie, 'A Liberal Theory of International Law' (2000) 94 American Society of International Law 240.

Slaughter, Anne-Marie, *A New World Order* (Princeton University Press 2004).

Smith, Anthony D., *National Identity* (Penguin 1991).

Somek, Alexander, 'Administration without Sovereignty' in Petra Dobner and Martin Loughlin (eds.), *The Twilight of Constitutionalism* (OUP 2010) 267–287.

Sornarajah, M., 'Why "No" to Transnational Legal Studies' in Cornelia T. L. Pillard et al., *Why Transnational Legal Education* (Center for Transnational Legal Studies 2018) 20–25 <https://www.law.georgetown.edu/ctls/wp-content/uploads/sites/33/2018/01/CTLS-Why-Transnational-Education.pdf> accessed 15 June 2021.

Stoll, Peter-Tobias, 'World Trade Organization (WTO)' (2014) in *Max Planck Encyclopedia of Public International Law*, Oxford Public International Law, <https://opil.ouplaw.com/view/10.1093/law:epil/9780199231690/law-9780199231690-e1555?prd=EPIL> accessed 15 June 2021.

Suárez, Francisco, 'De legibus, ac Deo legislatore' (1612) in Francisco Suarez, *Selections from three Works* (Clarendon 1944).

SWP, 'Ways Out of the WTO's December Crisis' (2019) <https://www.swp-berlin.org/10.18449/2019C46> accessed 4 January 2020.

Teubner, Gunther, '"Global Bukowina": Legal Pluralism in the World Society' in Gunther Teubner (ed.), *Global Law Without a State* (Dartmouth 1997) 3–28.

Teubner, Gunther, 'Global Private Regimes: Neo-spontaneous Law and Dual Constitution of Autonomous Sectors in World Society?' in Karl-Heinz Ladeur (ed.), *Globalization and Public Governance* (Ashgate 2004) 71–87.

Teubner, Gunther, *Constitutional Fragments* (OUP 2012).

The Guardian, 'WTO Faces Crisis over Disputes Settlement unless Trump Backs off' (2019) <https://www.theguardian.com/world/2019/dec/08/wto-faces-crisis-over-settlement-disputes-unless-trump-backs-off> accessed 4 January 2020.

Thucydides, 'The Peloponnesian War' in *Hobbes's Thucydides* (Richard Schlatter ed.; Rutgers University Press 1975).

Tomuschat, Christian, *International Law: Ensuring the Survival of Mankind on the Eve of a New Century* ("Collected Courses of The Hague Academy of International Law", Vol. 281, Nijhoff 1999).

Trachtmann, Joel P., 'Constitutional Economics of the World Trade Organization' in Jeffrey L. Dunoff and Joel P. Trachtmann (eds.), *Ruling the World? Constitutionalism, International Law, and Global Governance* (CUP 2009) 206–229.

Tully, James, Dunoff, Jeffrey L., Lang, Anthony F. Jr. Kumm, Mattias, and Wiener, Antje, 'Introducing Global Integral Constitutionalism' (2016) 5 Global Constitutionalism 1.

Ulfstein, Geir, 'Institutions and Competences' in Jan Klabbers, Anne Peters and Geir Ulfstein (eds.), *The Constitutionalization of International Law* (OUP 2009) 45–80.

Ulfstein, Geir, 'The International Judiciary' in Jan Klabbers, Anne Peters and Geir Ulfstein (eds.), *The Constitutionalization of International Law* (OUP 2009) 126–152.

Vitoria, Francisco de, *De Indis et De Jure Belli Relectiones* (1532) (Oceana 1964).

Werro, Franz, 'Is There Such a Thing as Transnational Law? Suggestions for defining the Object of Transnational Legal Studies' in Marc Amstuzt, Stefan Keller and Stefan

Wiprächtiger (eds.), *Recht zwischen Dogmatik und Theorie* (Dike/Nomos 2012) 311–328.

Wittgenstein, Ludwig, 'Philosophische Untersuchungen' (1953) in Ludwig Wittgenstein, *Werkausgabe* (Suhrkamp 1984) Vol. 1, 225–580 (English translation by G. E. M. Anscombe et al.: *Philosophical Investigations*, Wiley-Blackwell 2009, first published 1953).

CHAPTER 10

Teaching International Law as "Law of the Land"

Taking into Account the Domestic Nexus

*Andreas R. Ziegler**

Introduction

International aspects play an immense role in the work of most lawyers today. One can even go further and say in order to understand most current challenges most people would need a better understanding of global problems and the potential (and limitations) of (international) law to deal with them. Nevertheless, in this contribution I shall focus on the specific requirements with regard to the training of future lawyers - irrespective of whether they will work as attorneys, judges, prosecutors, notaries, civil servants or as employees of companies, associations, NGOs, or international organizations.

In my view, knowledge of how to deal with these aspects is of fundamental importance for the goal-oriented and high-quality training of lawyers. Ideally, these aspects should always be an essential part of the training, but this is only possible if sufficient basic knowledge and skills are guaranteed.[1] Unfortunately, it is still very common that no compulsory courses of international law are taught to future lawyers. This is particularly common for larger countries where many legal transactions seem to be solely governed by domestic facts and law (though this is obviously most of the times a wrong assessment).[2]

---

* Professor at the University of Lausanne, Switzerland, the President of the Swiss Society of International Law (SSDI/SVIR), the Swiss Branch of the International Law Association (ILA Suisse), and a Member of the Board of the European Law Faculties Association (ELFA).

1 See Andreas R. Ziegler, How global should legal education be? – Recommendations based on the compulsory teaching in international aspects taught at Swiss law schools, European Journal of Legal Education (EJLE) 2020, 1 (1), ISSN: 17504686 pp. 49–82, online at: https://ejle.eu/index.php/EJLE/article/view/8.

2 See, for example, Rudolf Bernhardt (eds.), Das internationale Recht in der Juristenausbildung – Materialien einer Kommission der Deutschen Gesellschaft für Völkerrecht, Heidelberg 1981 or for an empirical analysis Ryan Scoville / Mark Berlin, Who Studies International Law? Explaining Cross-National Variation in Compulsory International Legal Education, EJIL 30/2019, 481–508 (also available online: Political Science Faculty Research and Publications. 72, https://epublications.marquette.edu/polisci_fac/72). More recently also: Stephan Hobe / Thilo Marauhn (eds.), Lehre des internationalen Rechts im deutschsprachigen

 | DOI:10.1163/9789004678880_012

Smaller legal systems are often considered more exposed to foreign elements in the normal course of affairs, and this is nowadays often reflected in their law school curricula.[3]

In view of the long tradition of European integration and close cooperation between European States, one might think that in Europe international law plays a more important role in the education of lawyers. This is astonishingly not entirely true. Many of these States have long traditions of nation-building that also influence the legal culture. The idea that the typically German or English system in training lawyers should be preserved and that the domestic legal systems needs to be protected often leads to a focus on outdated syllabi and a reluctance to integrate international law into the teaching. In this respect, even the importance of European Union (EU) law has not changed much in teaching and makes the problems described in this contribution as relevant to Europe as to most legal systems around the world. A recent study[4] holds that legal tradition and regional geography predict variation undermine accounts that attribute all differences to national needs or socio-political conditions, suggest a variety of new research questions and indicate that, in at least one area, inter-traditional and inter-regional socialization might be the most effective mechanism for harmonizing national practices and perspectives.

This is not a new finding, but it is surprising that we have never taught so much international law (and published in this field) and at the same time, we still do not ensure that every graduate in law has a sound understanding of international law. A very comprehensive study was recently undertaken for Asian countries taking into account their geopolitical position and the importance of English sources for their teaching needs (TRILA Report, 2020).[5] The

---

Raum – Herausforderungen und Entwicklungspotentiale, in: Hobe / Marauhn (eds.), Lehre des internationalen Rechts – zeitgemäß? Heidelberg 2017, 11–34; this volume contains various contributions on the topic, namely, Andrea Hamann, Die Lehre des Völkerrechts in Frankreich – Überblick und Beobachtungen, 123–138; Lauri Mälksoo, Die Lehre des Völkerrechts: ein Blick aus Estland, 139–142; Volker Röben, Die Lehre des Internationalen Rechts in Großbritannien, 143–150. For an older appraisal of the situation in France see L'enseignement du droit international public en France, Annuaire Français de Droit International Année 1/1955, 816–818.

3 For the example of Switzerland see Andreas R. Ziegler, Von den Anfängen des Unterrichts des internationalen Rechts in der Schweiz, in: Franco Lorandi / Daniel Staehelin (eds.), Innovative Recht – Festschrift für Ivo Schwander, Zürich 2011, 125–140 and Andreas R. Ziegler, Die Entwicklung der Völkerrechtslehre und -wissenschaft in der Schweiz – eine Übersicht, Swiss Review of International and European Law (RSIEL / SZIER) 1/2016, 21–53.

4 See Scoville/Berlin, op. cit.

5 See Antony Anghie and JAR Robert G Real, Teaching and Researching International Law in Asia (TRILA) Project – 2020 Report, NUS Centre for International Law, 2020, online

following recommendations have been tested also for Switzerland in a more extensive analysis.

A proper understanding of the complexities we face today relies – especially for lawyers – also on an understanding (concepts, language) of international and foreign law. In addition, universities must teach the skills to (quickly) find the information and assess it. This is best done through a good introduction to the foundations of international, European, and comparative law, the respective skills (languages, research tools etc.), and the integration into all other courses in order to apply said skills and understand the specific international aspects of the various areas of law (private law, public law, criminal law etc.). This seems particularly important for the teaching of public law, which is often less developed, especially when it comes to administrative law (in the broad sense) such as taxation, health law, environmental law, migration law, economic law, financial law, etc.

National societies for international law or regional law as well as all branches of the International Law Association (ILA) should urgently address the minimum requirements in this area and make appropriate recommendations to the relevant institutions.[6] This is probably true for many university systems at this point. The German Society for International Law and its resolutions of 2016[7] could serve as examples. It calls upon all those responsible in the German-speaking world to work towards ensuring that the basic elements of international law, private international law and comparative law become an integral part of basic legal training. At the regional level, the respective organizations like the Asian Academy of International Law (AAIL), the American Society of International Law (ASIL), the European Society of International Law (ESIL), etc. could consider a joint initiative. Of course, it would also be welcome to involve practioners like attorneys, judges, arbitrators etc. (e.g., the International Bar Association – IBA or the International Association of Judges – IAJ). The International Law Association (ILA) has undertaken such efforts in the past.[8] Nowadays, the Global Network for International Law, a relatively recent informal body, could also be a good forum. For Europe, the European Law Faculties Association (ELFA) has called upon members to improve their curricula.[9]

at: https://cil.nus.edu.sg/publication/teaching-and-researching-international-law-in-asia-trila-project-2020-report/.

6 See below for the activities undertaken so far.

7 See Resolution of the German Society for International Law, online at: http://www.dgfir.de/veranstaltungen/archiv/lehre-des-internationalen-rechts-zeitgemaess/.

8 See below.

9 See ELFA, Resolution adopted at the Annual General Meeting in Turin (11 and 12 April 2019), https://elfa-edu.org/event/turin-2019/#b1bc8f2aee6683ea3.

Here are my suggestions for making international law reach a larger number of students and improving the way how we contribute to the education of lawyers (and others) with regard to the importance of international law for their work and understanding of society at large.[10]

1 Every Law Student Needs a Sound Introduction to International Law

There are considerable differences in the compulsory training in international aspects between law graduates around the world. There is certainly no need for total harmonization, but certain institutions should urgently reconsider their minimum requirements. I would strongly recommend introducing adequate compulsory teachings of international law (public and private), as well as European law (or other regional systems where applicable) during the early years of legal education (Bachelor where applicable).

This is the only way to make sure that students understand the challenges and connections in all areas of law while studying them in a more detailed way. In addition, it is the only way to guarantee student mobility (between institutions, programs, and even university systems) without risking that some students never acquire the necessary skills and tools (as it can even be the case within a system, as shown for Switzerland). It becomes even more problematic if students move globally and lack sufficient foundations to understand the legal problems and challenges when studying the specialized field of international or foreign law.

In view of the increasing influence of international and regional developments on most legal systems one could easily think of integrating these transnational elements into existing thematic course. For example, an introduction to law or methodology course could integrate the sources of law, the various actors (subjects of law but also non-state actors) and the basic notions of dispute settlement at the international level. The course on the history of law should ideally include the relevant aspects of the history of international law and the basic introduction to public law should also look at the role of

10 As to reach larger public, I have put forward these proposals in a shorter form in a blog entry in: Andreas R. Ziegler, Don't Let International Law Become an Exotic Field Irrelevant for Lawyers ... Seven Demands, in: AfronomicsLaw Blog, Symposium: Teaching and Researching International Law – Global Perspectives, September 18, 2020: https://www.afronomicslaw.org/2020/09/18/dont-let-international-law-become-an-exotic-field-irrelevant-for-lawyersseven-demands/#.

the state in international organisations and state responsibility at the international level, etc.

This idea has (at least) partly been taken up by colleagues in certain systems and sometimes led to specialized courses like international private law, international criminal law, international tax law, etc. In these cases, one can at least recognize dealing with international aspects as a logical continuation of the relevant teaching of the domestic aspects. In Germany, public law is often taught in three different courses, whereby the first two focus on the basic concepts and organization of the state, the second on fundamental rights, and the third (normally under the title "Staatsrecht III") adds international and European aspects regarding the role of the state and the national constitution.[11] In principle this could be a very interesting approach to show immediately that we do not talk about different legal systems but one integrated system. At the same time, this should not lead to a narrower focus of the respective teaching of international and regional (e.g., European) aspects – a risk that obviously exists. The same is true for the courses in private and criminal law of specialized areas like tax law, economic law, human rights protection, etc. At this time, many colleagues have warned me that it is not realistic that such an integration of international (global and regional) aspects into the existing subject-related courses is not realistic and would lower the level of ambition with regard to the teaching of the international aspects. Until this can be achieved, one could therefore envisage that a basic introduction is maintained (e.g., a basic course in public international law) and that the international elements in the other courses are systematically increased, in order to demonstrate the presence of international elements in all areas of law (although there may be specific differences given the situation of a particular legal system).

2 Public International and Regional Integration Law Must Always Be a Compulsory Subject, and Students Must Acquire This Expertise in Order to Graduate

While most universities offer courses in international law, too often they are electives. At these institutions, this can very easily lead to students not acquiring any knowledge at all during their education in this field (because, as has been shown, there is no guarantee at Master level either or they may change

11 See the existing textbooks, eg as one of the oldest ones Rudolf Geiger, Grundgesetz und Völkerrecht mit Europarecht, 7th edn., Munich 2018.

institutions before they get to the respective compulsory training). University systems that provide a full-length education leading to a final professional degree may have more flexibility in this respect. University systems have introduced the option of easily switching institutions after obtaining a first degree (e.g., Bachelor) before obtaining a second compulsory degree (e.g., Master), as is the case under the so-called Bologna system for many European States, must make sure there is guaranteed teaching in international law at some point (ideally at the beginner's level). It should be recalled, however, that this mobility has many advantages, in particular, it allows students to spend more time in another legal system. Therefore, the general introduction of compulsory international law courses at the Bachelor level certainly ensures better compatibility and allows students to take advanced courses at the Master's degree level.

Under this section, I would like to reiterate that ideally, we would not need these separate courses on international (global and regional) elements but in practice, few law curricula will otherwise guarantee the necessary level of understanding of these aspects. The worst outcome one can imagine is certainly that no specific introductions are taught and that no foreign and international elements are taught in the subject-specific courses. Ideally, professors of international law should therefore coordinate with their colleagues to what extent they repeat and integrate concepts stemming from international law in their courses and what elements are of particular relevance to their courses. E.g., the professor of family law and the professor of international law could both use specific treaties relating to child abduction or alimonies.[12] It may be true, that some of these treaties are very specific, but they can be used to show the type of international cooperation that becomes increasingly important and relates to certain basic problems also present at the purely domestic level.

In many legal systems, the university education is conceived (or at least strongly centered on) the preparation of students for the bar exam (or an equivalent exam administered by the state of a body responsible for this professional qualification. Historically, these exams are not taking into account the growing number of international aspects (often due to the education of the examiners themselves). This is another problem for the education of future attorneys and other professions where this type of admission or exam is seen as compulsory access control. It would therefore be of interest to change in the long run also these exams and the way they are handled. What we said for the teaching of international law at universities or in academic settings is in

12 Like the Convention on the Recovery Abroad of Maintenance, New York, 20 June 1956, United Nations, Treaty Series, vol. 268, 3, and vol. 649, 330.

principle also applicable to these exams. This may prove to be even more challenging. Related problems are whether those working in more international settings really need the domestic bar exam and ultimately to what extent one could influence these professional bodies and/or state examiners to take into account the necessary understanding of international and regional law. Such a debate seems not to take place in many systems, and I would therefore strongly advocate that all those interested in a generally better understanding of international law also think of how the preparation of attorneys and/or judges,[13] notaries, etc. could benefit from reforms in this respect. This would obviously reinforce the acceptance of better preparation in this respect at the university level.

3 Private International Law and Comparative Law Should Also Be Compulsory Subjects at an Early Stage (at Least as an Overview in General Introductions to Private Law)

It would be desirable for international aspects to be integrated into the bachelor's degree in private law. This should take into account aspects of private international law and possibly also comparative law. Where this does not take place in a separate course, it should be ensured that compliance with these aspects is reported transparently and verifiably in the existing units. It seems that failure to do so is rather common in most university systems, and therefore this recommendation could be taken up again by the respective associations at the national or international level. Comparative Law helps to improve analytical skills and can thus be integrated into an introduction to legal sciences.

While this approach was more common in the past, the proliferation of very specific statutory solutions at the national level has often led to the elimination of general courses on comparative law and the (partial integration) of private international law into the general courses on civil or private law. While this is not negative in itself, the same risk that we had identified before exists: students never really understand the specific added elements relating to the international nature of a specific legal situation. It would therefore again be ideal to give students the tools and concepts that are understanding comparative law and private international law and then regularly repeat and apply them in the specific courses (family law, criminal law, tort law, arbitration, etc.). This

13 Such as the German State exam, the English Legal Practice Course and Bar Practice Course etc.

approach can often also improve the understanding of the specific underlying problems of an area of law as such and the comparative approach separates the analysis of the problem from the specific solution chosen in a legal system (which may evolve over time).

4 English or Specific English Legal Terminology Should Be Included in Compulsory Training

All institutions should consider ensuring that students have a knowledge of legal English. As for teaching legal terminology in a second national official language, this should not be seen as an additional obstacle to studying law but as a necessary requirement to understand law (in a globalized) world as such. Of course, where possible, we should teach more languages, and in legal systems where important legal documents and academic writings are only available in several national languages, this should be taken into account. At the same time, this should not be understood as refraining from publishing in languages other than English as this contributes to the lack of diversity that could endanger the system by itself.[14]

At too many law schools, the knowledge of a second or third language (in particular where already an important second national language is involved) is still considered outside of the responsibility of the universities. Some legal systems have used recent reforms (often necessary as part of a political transition of the country) to strengthen the understanding of English (and possibly even other important languages in the global context but many systems seem totally immune to change. This is particularly true for big countries with a certain importance of their legal tradition at the global level, most importantly former colonial powers, and their former colonies (such as the UK, France, the US, etc.) but also other European countries with a long tradition in this respect (Germany, Italy, Spain, etc.). One often hears that students and lawyers are responsible for themselves to acquire the necessary language skills (sometimes even through voluntary courses taught at universities). However, it must be remembered that students have limited time and financial resources to acquire these skills and that, in particular when it comes to legal terminology and writing, the guidance of law professors may prove particularly useful and even necessary. When it comes to business law, certain law schools and

14 See e.g., Jacqueline Mowbray, The future of international law: shaped by English, Völkerrechtsblog, 18 June 2014, doi: 10.17176/20170104-165855.

programs have understood this already while in other fields the developments seem not satisfactory at this stage in most countries. The understanding of at least one other language obviously helps also to better grasp the real meaning of foreign law (comparative approach) and to understand the relevance of culture and language for the very conceptualization of law and legal norms as such.

5 Don't Let International Law Become an Exotic Subject Only Taken by Those Already Interested

It would be advisable to make better use of the resources tied up in optional courses by diverting them to compulsory areas and to ensure that international aspects are guaranteed as a fundamental part of the basic training (Bachelor) of all lawyers. There is a risk that most resources available are used for a small group of interested students and do not reach most students. This is particularly true when these resources are mostly used for exchange programs with foreign students and courses taken by students lacking knowledge of domestic law. This is not to say that these offers are not important, but it seems wasteful not to make sure these offers are also used to assure the understanding of international aspects by those students who will be shaping the domestic legal environment, i.e., judges, prosecutors, attorneys, notaries, and civil servants in general. In too many countries (in particular big ones like the United States, France, or Germany) international aspects remain somewhat exotic and irrelevant to the examinations organized by the State. While not a new trend, this problem should be addressed again with more vigour.

This does not mean that the proliferation of international programs and specializations is not welcome. But this has not the necessary effects on the general understanding of international law by legal professionals but rather leads to the education of specialists for specific fields (diplomacy, international organizations, international business lawyers etc.). It should be possible to use the often-impressive resources for these programs and courses also to provide every law student (and maybe even other students with a sufficient introduction). Here again the worst outcome is if the existing staff teaching international law is only used to give highly specialized courses that are voluntary or intended for a small group of international and specializing students and leave the general law programs entirely to teachers focusing on domestic (positive) law.

6 The Concretization of International Aspects in Relation to Domestic Law Must Be Better Addressed

A particular problem is that the international aspects of the law must be specified in concrete terms with regard to their significance for domestic politics and the administration of justice. This is not always ensured. On the one hand, this can happen if the reference to the positive law of a State – and in particular the case law of the highest courts – is not made in the respective teaching. Furthermore, although the acquisition of international aspects of law abroad is, in principle, highly desirable and positive, it also does not guarantee an understanding of how the domestic legal system exactly deals (or should deal) with international law or regional integration law (hierarchy, direct applicability, consideration of the case law of the regional courts, etc.), or how the domestic private international law is presented (e.g., public order in the case law of the courts or questions of sufficient internal reference in the recognition of foreign decisions or arbitral awards).

It must be ensured that the international aspects are concretized in relation to domestic law, such as by using examples in torts, criminal, or family law that involve international law questions. The TRILA Report suggests that international law is indeed compulsory in many Asian countries, but students still do not acquire the needed skills.[15] I argue that by teaching the essentials early on in education, one should later integrate more international aspects into all specialized areas and thereby constantly apply more theoretical concepts and train students to use them. The training institutions must also ensure that this problem is taken into account in teaching and in the recognition of legal skills acquired abroad. The example of Germany, where the international and European aspects and their interrelationship with German law are usually only taught in a compulsory course as a continuation of the teaching of domestic public law (*Staatsrecht III*)[16] could be used as an inspiration (though it should not replace the more comprehensive compulsory teaching of international aspects, as is the case in this country).

In principle, this approach is related to the more general desire to educate lawyers who see the (domestic) positive law in the wider context. It can be achieved by better coordinating the various courses and assuring that they are not simply seen as separate areas (in view of a specific exam that is passed for the assessment of the course) but that students acquire analytical skills that

15 See above.

16 See above.

enable them (at a later stage of their education) to understand more complicated legal situations that involve various fields of law and the applicability (or influence) of rules with different origins (multi-layered governance). With regard to European law (predominantly EU law) that seems to be happening in certain EU member states, but not everywhere, let alone in other areas of international (or internationalized) law.

7 Quality and Transparency with regard to International Aspects, or Even the Existence of a Conceptual Approach, Must Be Guaranteed

Traditionally, most university systems and law schools (and rightly so) place great emphasis on academic freedom. In the case of traditional universities, the quality of teaching is normally assured by reputation and informal peer review. Normally, it is the national and international professional associations that are particularly challenged in this respect. The management of the institutions concerned should be interested in ensuring their own quality in this way. Due to the many new actors and new forms of legal education, this is not always possible today. Academic associations would be well advised to ensure that they are interesting and relevant to all lecturers in the subjects concerned. Where to make access to education easier, the threshold is lowered. This should not be done at the price of eliminating international topics. All educational institutions must ensure that the subjects concerned are adequately taught, with clear responsibilities and transparency. It would be desirable for accredited institutions to develop a concept not only of their training as a whole or for individual courses but also about the appropriate consideration of international aspects. It could be worthwhile to ensure that national or international accreditation systems of law schools and programs take this aspect into due account. Potentially, the development of a label could be such a means to increase awareness and transparency.

Here international associations and national learned societies should get more involved. This is not to say that they have not done so in the past. But it seems to me that this was often crowned with limited success and should be intensified given current challenges. Organisations like the International Law Association (ILA) or the European Law Faculties Association (ELFA) may be particularly well placed to approach their members to use their positions to improve the curricula in their universities and institutions. In addition, national societies for the promotion of the fields that interest us here have a responsibility to also keep an eye on the general education at law schools and not only specialize in doctrinal questions and research of a very small group of highly specialized international law specialists. The mentioned examples of the ELFA Resolution of 2019[17] or the German Society of International Law of 2016 seem to have remained without much effect. At the same time, some think "that professional associations like the ILA and ASIL tend to under-emphasize teaching."[18]

A particularly noteworthy experience is the fate of the ILA Committee on Teaching international law. Upon the initiative of the ILA's Director of Studies of the time (Professor Fred Soons), a special session on this topic had been organized at the 1998 Taiwan Regional Meeting of the ILA that resulted in the establishment of the Committee on the Teaching of International Law in 2000. The Committee was active for ten years and was dissolved in 2010 despite the finding in its final report that "the need for the ILA to address teaching remains pressing".[19] Among other things, its members asked: "Should we advocate actively for a more prominent role for international law courses within curricula?"

One thing the members of the ILA Committee in 2010 were able to agree upon was the idea that the creation of a website on teaching international law would be very beneficial. This has never happened. One such initiative, however, focusing on Switzerland is a blog I run in my function as a professor teaching a basic introduction to public international law to first-year students. I see it also as a service to the community in my role as President of both the Swiss Society for International Law and the Swiss Branch of the International Law Association. The basic idea is to provide first-year law students with easy access to information about international legal developments, in particular, related to the national legal system in which most of them work. I observed that for non-specialists, it is increasingly difficult to see how international law affects their daily lives and that the focus on particularly complex problems sometimes leads to forgetting the plethora of decisions and instruments that are negotiated and applied without major difficulties as a matter of routine. This focus on controversial issues leads to the perception that international law is always controversial in itself and not clear enough for application by lawyers, judges, the authorities, or even lawmakers. The blog has the name

17 See above.

18 International Law Association, The Hague Conference (2010), Committee on the Teaching of International Law, Conclusions, 12 online: https://www.ila-hq.org/index.php/committees.

19 International Law Association, The Hague Conference (2010), Committee on the Teaching Of International Law, Conclusions, 12 online: https://www.ila-hq.org/index.php/committees.

"International Law in Switzerland". It is primarily a tool related to the teaching of public international law (at the Law Faculty of the University of Lausanne) and it tries to provide reliable information regarding public international law (PIL) that I consider of interest to my students. I try to cover Switzerland comprehensively and the rest of the world to the extent possible. Thereby, I have discovered that it is often subscribed to by my students (even after they finish the course) but also others who want easy access and a way to update their knowledge of international law. It is heavily based on the argument I tried to make in this article that the nexus between international law and local reality (also in the form of domestic law) has to be shown more clearly.

Conclusion

The main finding of this contribution is that most universities offer enough courses on international aspects of law but do not ensure all their students get the minimum necessary, i.e., a sound introduction to the principles of public and private international law as well as ideally the skills to compare legal solutions in various jurisdictions (comparative law).

In addition, the language skills so necessary on the job market and to reading international sources are too often left to the students and not guaranteed by the university when delivering a degree. This certainly contributes to the claim that universities do not prepare students well for the actual needs of employers and the challenges facing the world. It is also unfair when no free language education is available at the universities (or elsewhere in the education system).

A third finding is, that it is not easy for students to find out which universities are more diligent concerning the adequate teaching of international aspects. The need for more transparency in this respect and the setting of certain minimum standards is being reinforced by new forms of education and new institutions (distance universities, universities of applied sciences, etc.). Personally, I would advocate for an accreditation or label that improves awareness and transparency regarding this aspect.

Ideally, the integration of foreign and international (including European) law would take place in all areas today. Such an integrated approach is, however, more difficult to achieve and it will take time before in all courses all levels of regulation can be integrated. Without a thorough introduction to the basic foundations and the skills necessary to find and apply non-domestic sources, this cannot work. This contribution, therefore, focuses on the existing situation where specific knowledge on the international aspects (or at least the foundations and skills/tools) are taught in separate courses. Modern techniques should be used to keep students interested in developments in international law that are relevant to their work and/or life in general (also as citizens, voters, political activists, etc.). This can include blogs, social media newsletters, etc. in addition to the more sophisticated specialized courses and academic writings and textbooks.

Bibliography

Anghie, Antony / Real, J.R. Robert G., Teaching and Researching International Law in Asia (TRILA) Project – 2020 Report, NUS Centre for International Law, 2020, online at: https://cil.nus.edu.sg/publication/teaching-and-researching-international-law-in-asia-trila-project-2020-report/.

Bernhardt, Rudolf (eds.), Das internationale Recht in der Juristenausbildung – Materialien einer Kommission der Deutschen Gesellschaft für Völkerrecht, Heidelberg 1981.

Geiger, Rudolf, Grundgesetz und Völkerrecht mit Europarecht, 7th edn., Munich 2018.

Hamann, Andrea, Die Lehre des Völkerrechts in Frankreich – Überblick und Beobachtungen, in: Stephan Hobe / Thilo Marauhn (eds.), Lehre des internationalen Rechts – zeitgemäß? Heidelberg 2017, 123–138.

Hobe, Stephan / Marauhn, Thilo (eds.), Lehre des internationalen Rechts im deutschsprachigen Raum – Herausforderungen und Entwicklungspotentiale, in: Stephan Hobe / Thilo Marauhn (eds.), Lehre des internationalen Rechts – zeitgemäß? Heidelberg 2017, 11–34.

International Law Association, The Hague Conference (2010), Committee on the Teaching of International Law, Conclusions, 12 online: https://www.ila-hq.org/index.php/committees.

Mälksoo, Lauri, Die Lehre des Völkerrechts: ein Blick aus Estland, in: Stephan Hobe / Thilo Marauhn (eds.), Lehre des internationalen Rechts – zeitgemäß? Heidelberg 2017, 139–142.

Mowbray, Jacqueline The future of international law: shaped by English, Völkerrechtsblog, 18 June 2014, doi: 10.17176/20170104-165855.

NN, L'enseignement du droit international public en France, Annuaire Français de Droit International Année 1/1955, 816–818.

Röben, Volker, Die Lehre des Internationalen Rechts in Großbritannien, in: Stephan Hobe / Thilo Marauhn (eds.), Lehre des internationalen Rechts – zeitgemäß? Heidelberg 2017, 143–150.

Scoville, Ryan / Berlin, Mark, Who Studies International Law? Explaining Cross-National Variation in Compulsory International Legal Education, EJIL 30/2019,

481–508 (also available online: Political Science Faculty Research and Publications. 72, https://epublications.marquette.edu/polisci_fac/72).

Ziegler, Andreas R., Von den Anfängen des Unterrichts des internationalen Rechts in der Schweiz, in: Franco Lorandi / Daniel Staehelin (eds.), Innovative Recht – Festschrift für Ivo Schwander, Zürich 2011, 125–140.

Ziegler, Andreas R., Die Entwicklung der Völkerrechtslehre und-wissenschaft in der Schweiz – eine Übersicht, Swiss Review of International and European Law (RSIEL/SZIER) 1/2016, 21–53.

Ziegler, Andreas R., Don't Let International Law Become an Exotic Field Irrelevant for Lawyers ... Seven Demands, in AfronomicsLaw Blog, Symposium: Teaching and Researching International Law – Global Perspectives, September 18, 2020: https://www.afronomicslaw.org/2020/09/18/dont-let-international-law-become-an-exotic-field-irrelevant-for-lawyersseven-demands/#.

Ziegler, Andreas R., How global should legal education be? – Recommendations based on the compulsory teaching in international aspects taught at Swiss law schools, European Journal of Legal Education (EJLE) 2020, 1 (1), ISSN: 17504686 pp. 49–82, online at: https://ejle.eu/index.php/EJLE/article/view/8.

CHAPTER 11A

Teaching International Law in Germany

Is the Legal Regime on Teaching Law Still Adequate?

Rüdiger Wolfrum

I Introduction

The issue I am meant to write about has been dealt with intensively in a study edited by Stephan Hobe and Thilo Marahn under the auspices of the Deutsche Gesellschaft für Völkerrecht.[1] This study is quite pragmatic, and so will be my presentation. I do not intend to develop a new theory on international law, deconstructive or otherwise, but shall deal with the teaching of public international law as embedded in the culture of legal studies as practiced in Germany. To do so I will briefly address the status of international law in the German legal system from the theoretical point of view and in practice. The two perspectives do not match. Whether the jurisprudential practice has influenced the teaching or the teaching of international law has had, as I may say already here, a negative influence on the jurisprudence is an open question. At the end, I will cautiously address where I see deficits and how they may be amended.

II Basics on the Legal Training in Germany

1 *Some Historic Considerations*

When Samuel von Pufendorf was teaching in Heidelberg – I mention him since he held the first chair on international law in Germany dedicated to the teaching of international law as developed by Hugo Grotius – the teaching of law was undertaken in two phases – undergraduate and postgraduate phases one may say – dividing the teaching between philosophy and the teaching of law. Samuel Pufendorfs's chair belonged to the philosophy level and was less paid then the chairs held by the professors teaching law. Pufendorf tried to become

1 Hobe/ Marauhn, Lehre des internationalen Rechts – zeitgemäß?, with contributions by Hobe/Marauhn/Weller/Benicke/Beham/Fink/Janik/Haumer/Schöberl//Reißmann/Gössl/Junker/Hamann/Mälksoo/Röben. Apart from more generic contributions the situation prevailing in Germany, France, Estonia and the United Kingdom is being covered.

 | DOI:10.1163/9789004678880_013

member of the law faculty properly speaking but failed. He left Heidelberg in a disagreement with the law faculty. One has to consider his book on the status of the Holy Roman Empire (1667) in which he claimed that the latter was an 'irregulare aliquod corpus e monstro simile' in this context.

2 *The Status of International Law in the German Legal System*

As far as the integration of public international into the national German legal system is concerned, the German legal system follows neither a monistic nor a dualistic approach – or – one might say – it follows both. There is a clear distinction between 'general rules of international law' according to Article 25 Basic Law (German Constitution)[2] and international treaties referred to in Article 59 (2) Basic Law.[3] The former reflects monism and the latter dualism. Apart from that, these two provisions of the Basic Law reflect an openness towards international law. Such openness has been frequently referred to by the jurisprudence of the Federal Constitutional Court but not always been honored. It is generally be accepted that international treaties have nationally the rank of acts of parliament.[4] However, it is disputed whether they may be overruled by a later act of parliament or not.

There are two dogmatic approaches towards the status of acts of parliament, which provide for the applicability of international treaties in the German legal system. The first one interprets the act of parliament concerned as transforming the international treaty into German law. This means that, for example, the national rules on the interpretation of legal norms would apply. The second approach, since several years now dominant in the jurisprudence of the Federal Constitutional Court, considers the act of parliament concerned as the permission to apply the treaty in question as international law in the

2 Article 25 reads: The general rules of international law shall be an integral part of federal law. They shall override laws and directly establish rights and obligations for the inhabitants of the federal territory.
This provision is meant to be enforced by Article 100 (2) Basic Law which reads: Where in the course of litigation doubts exists whether a rule of international law is an integral part of federal law and whether such rule directly establishes rights or obligations for the individual (Article 25), the court shall seek the ruling from the Federal Constitutional Court.

3 Article 59 (2) reads in part: Treaties which regulate the political relations of the Federation or relate to matters of federal legislation shall require the approval or participation of the appropriate legislative body in the form of a federal law.

4 See on that Volker Röben, Außenverfassungsrecht, 2007, p. 92 et seq.; Siljy Vöneky, Verfassungsrecht und völkerrechtliche Verträge, in: Handbuch des Staatsrechts, 3rd ed, vol. XI, 2013, (Isensee/ Kirchhof, eds.), p. 413 at at 417 et seq.

German legal system.[5] This has for consequence, for example, that the international rules on the interpretation remain applicable.

It is a matter of fact, that neither general rules of international law (which includes customary international law nor general principles of law (articles 38 (1)(b) and (c) Statute of the International Court of Justice play a significant role in the jurisprudence of German courts. If, for example, human rights are invoked German courts will first consider the Basic Law. The situation may be different in respect of environmental law. As far as international criminal law is concerned, the reference to international law is dominant. However, relevant cases have been rare, so far, before German Courts.

3 *Objective of Legal Training as Traditionally Understood*

Traditionally the teaching at the universities in Germany is being perceived – following the philosophy of Humboldt – as the means to enrich the knowledge of students in general, to form their character but not to prepare them necessarily for a certain profession. Although this ideal is still being upheld and celebrated, the reality has become different, in particular for the teaching of law. Nevertheless, this approach is still of significance. The teaching of international law is covered by Article 5 para. 3 Basic Law which states,

> Art and scholarship, research and *teaching* shall be free. Freedom of teaching shall not absolve anybody from loyalty to the constitution. (Emphasis added)

The relevance of Article 5 para 3 Basic Law is essential. It means the academic teaching cannot be limited easily. Such limitation is only possible if overarching constitutional principles are at stake. In comparison training for a particular job falls under Article 12 Basic Law. Such training can be limited and is being limited if such limits are pursue an objective, which justifies the limitations concerned. The proportionality check (Verhältnismäßigkeitsprinzip) comes into play. Already here it should be mentioned that the legal training in Germany covers two phases: the one undertaken in the universities and the other outside thereof in various courts, in the administration, with attorneys and prosecution. Only the former are to be considered as university teaching with the consequence of being protected by Article 5, para. 3 Basic Law.[6] I shall

5 Vöneky (note 4) at MN 9–11. Andreas von Arnauld, Völkerrecht 2012, MN 499.

6 There has been the attempt to combine university teaching with the teaching in the traditional second phase of the German legal training. This approach, considered by some as having been successful was never adopted by the majority of the laws schools.

return to this issue in the assessment the practice concerning the training of lawyers and in my conclusions).

Apart from that, different from the situation in the United States, the teaching of law is not considered as postgraduate studies. Students enter law schools coming directly from the Gymnasium (technically equivalent to high school or junior college). Depending upon the school system, the students enrolled in law school will have gone through four years of primary school and eight or nine years in Gymnasium. In these twelve or thirteen years, the students are hardly confronted with law as a subject matter if at all. This is not only true for the studying of law. The development of the high school curricula is the responsibility of the Länder and differ significantly. In only few of them, the law plays a role, often addressed from a historical or a socio-political perspective. International law is only rarely touched upon and, if so, by referring to an international organization such as the United Nations Organization. The information students receive evidently cannot go into details and certainly will not prepare for studying law.

One has also take into account that the universities are under the jurisdiction of the Länder. Accordingly, the curriculum of the various law schools differ although attempts have been made to harmonize the law studies. The teaching of law at the universities is the responsibility of professors, in some law schools attorneys and judges may teach special courses.

The curriculum for the teaching of law is not being decided by each single law faculty but by the 'Justizausbildungsordnung' issued by the each Land (state). Applicable in Baden-Württemberg are the Gesetz über die Juristischen Prüfungen und den Juristischen Vorbereitungsdienst and a Regulation oft he Minister of Justice.[7] The law faculties have certain flexibility to add special courses, which give the students the possibility to specialize (so-called Schwerpunktbereiche).[8] Thus, there exists a mandatory canon of legal courses (which also include courses on legal philosophy, legal history and sometimes sociology) and non-mandatory courses. Students have to engage in the study of one cluster of non-mandatory courses. The mandatory canon of courses does not contain public international law; it contains, though, European Law.

7 Law concerning the examinantions on law and the preparation phase, as amended 17 December 2020(GBl. 2021, p.1) and the Verordnung des Justizministers über die Ausbildung und Prüfungen der Juristinnen und Juristen, 2019 as amended 6 December 2021(Gbl. P. 993) (Regulation concerning the training and examination of Lawyers).

8 See on that Christoph Benicke, Die Lehre des internationalen Rechts in den Schwerpunktbereichen, in: Hobe Marauhn (note 1), p. 49 et seq.

International law is part of the curriculum if the law faculty concerned so provides as a non-mandatory cluster (it is frequently combined with international private law and sometimes also with European law); the examination of the issues which are covered by the 'Schwerpunktbereiche' (focal areas) rests fully in the authority of the law faculty concerned. The grades received by the students are added to the grades of the state examination. The cluster among the non-mandatory courses containing international law is less sought after than other clusters. This is due to the fact that this cluster is considered particularly complex and demands that students are able to master apart from English one further foreign language. Apart from that, students do not see while studying the professional potential they see in other subject matters such as labor law. Therefore, one may say that studying international law (may it be private or public) is closer to the Humboldt ideal than other law studies. The effect is, to make it quite clear, that the majority of students studying law at the German law schools do not intensively and sometimes not even marginally get into contact with public international law and private international law. They are, however, taught in European law. This is already indicative for the priorities pursued in the academic legal training.

The emphasis on European law may be guided by two considerations. European law is by its structure and content closer to national public law than is public international law. Apart from that, those who in their professional life have dealt with national public law and mostly with administrative law have problems in accepting public international law as law properly speaking. This tendency does exist also in other national legal systems. It has become quite dominant when facing the Russian aggression against Ukraine. Public forums speaking on the decline of relevance of public international law are quite common in Germany nowadays. They totally overlook that law, not only international public law, may be violated. It is astonishing though that in case of murder nobody would speak about the decline of criminal law. Law does anticipates of being violated and have reactions in reserve – in international public law these are sanctions.

One should not and one cannot criticize the treatment of public or private international law as non-mandatory courses from the point of Article 5 para. 3, referred to above. Every professor may teach public of private international law and may freely choose whether to teach a general course or specific course such as on international environmental law or the law on dispute settlement. Every student may freely decide whether to join such classes or not. One has to accept though that students are pragmatic. They concentrate on the subjects which are of relevance for the examinations or – as they perceive it – their later job. One has to take into account that the issues to be covered for the examination are vast. It is the particularity of the German system on legal training requires students to cover the information received from the first to the last days at the university. There is no possibility to invoke examinations done at the end of each semester in university.

Every professor may teach public of private international law and may freely choose whether to teach a general course or specific course such as on international environmental law or the law on dispute settlement.

In general, the studies in law at the German law schools do not end with a university degree – the bachelor degree is being accepted by only very few law schools in Germany – but by a state examination under the auspices of an appeal court. Examiners are law school professors, judges and attorneys, which means the examination is controlled at least in part by persons, which are not involved in teaching. This system applies only to the mandatory curriculum mentioned above.

The examination concerning the non-mandatory curriculum takes place under the authority of the law faculty and there under the authority of those professors who teach the relevant courses. This perfectly meets the demands of Article 5 para. 3 Basic Law.

This is the factual situation. However, this situation is cemented by the state examinations, which finalize the academic legal training. Object and purpose of the state examinations as well as the issues, which may be part of these examinations, determine not only what students will learn but also what professors will teach in the mandatory part of the curriculum. It is equally determinative whom the faculties will accept in the case of vacancies.

III Specifics on Legal Training in Germany

1 *The 'State Examination'* [*Erste/Zweite Juristische Prüfung*] *as the Compass for the Legal Training*

The object and purpose of the state examination (in fact, these are two (first and second) so as to become a 'full lawyer' is being defined by, for example, in § 1 Justizausbildungsordnung Baden-Württemberg which states:[9] (2) The

9 Regulation, see note 6; § 1 (1)…(2) Das Universitätsstudium wird mit der Ersten juristischen Prüfung abgeschlossen. Die Erste juristische Prüfung dient der Feststellung, ob das rechtswissenschaftliche Studienziel erreicht und die fachliche Eignung für den juristischen Vorbereitungsdienst vorhanden ist. Die Erste juristische Prüfung umfasst eine staatliche Pflichtfachprüfung (Staatsprüfung) und eine universitäre Schwerpunktbereichsprüfung (Universitätsprüfung). (3) Die Ausbildung im Vorbereitungsdienst wird mit der Zweiten

University studies are concluded with the First State Examination. Its object and purpose is to ascertain whether the student has successfully reached the goal of legal studies and has gained the qualification to enter into the juridical preparation phase (Vorbereitungsdienst). The First State Examination embraces a State examination (Staatsprüfung) concerning the mandatory curriculum and an examination concerning the non-mandatory curriculum (university examination). Further of relevance is § 3 of the Regulation, which defines what students are meant to study or – respectively what faculties have to offer.[10] This provision is quite detailed as far as the form and the substance of the teaching is concerned. However, it is significant that the law faculties are obliged to provide supplementary courses to civil, criminal and public law concerning philosophy, etc whereas international law is only covered by the reference to 'international references'.

Let us briefly consider the curriculum of one law faculty, the one of Heidelberg. The courses offered in summer 2021 were divided in groups – introduction and basics, covering history of law, such as Roman law and philosophy of law; civil law covering the subject matter comprehensively in about

---

juristischen *Staatsprüfung abgeschlossen. Die Prüfung dient der Feststellung, ob die Befähigung zum Richteramt, für die Rechtsanwaltschaft und für den höheren allgemeinen Verwaltungsdienst vorliegt.* (*emphasis added*).

10 See note 6; para. 3 reads: (1) Im Studium sollen sich die Studierenden in wissenschaftlicher Vertiefung exemplarisch mit den wichtigsten Gebieten des Zivilrechts, des Strafrechts und des Öffentlichen Rechts sowie mit einem Schwerpunktbereich, jeweils unter Einschluss internationaler, insbesondere europarechtlicher, sowie verfahrensrechtlicher Bezüge, befassen. Grundlagenfächer (Rechtsgeschichte, Rechtsphilosophie, Rechtssoziologie, Juristische Methodenlehre, Rechtsvergleichung, Allgemeine Staatslehre) sind angemessen zu berücksichtigen. (2) Die Inhalte des Studiums berücksichtigen die praktische Bedeutung und Anwendung des Rechts einschließlich der Rechtsgestaltung und Rechtsberatung. Sie erfassen auch die zunehmende Bedeutung der Digitalisierung. Am Ende des Studiums sollen die Studierenden die inneren Zusammenhänge der Rechtsordnung erkennen und das Recht mit Verständnis für wirtschaftliche, soziale und gesellschaftliche Fragen anwenden können. (3) Die Vorlesungen in den Pflichtfächern werden durch Lehrveranstaltungen begleitet und ergänzt, in denen in Kleingruppen der behandelte Lehrstoff aufbereitet wird (Fallbesprechungen). (4) Die Universitäten bieten außerdem Lehrveranstaltungen an, in denen aus Sicht der beruflichen Praxis der Lehrstoff in Kleingruppen exemplarisch aufbereitet wird. (5) Die Universitäten bieten Lehrveranstaltungen an zur exemplarischen Vermittlung interdisziplinärer Schlüsselqualifikationen wie Grundkenntnisse in Wirtschafts-und Sozialwissenschaften, Verhandlungsmanagement, Gesprächsführung, Streitschlichtung, Mediation, Rhetorik, Vernehmungslehre, Kommunikationsfähigkeit und digitale Kompetenzen. Ferner werden fremdsprachige rechtswissenschaftliche Veranstaltungen oder rechtswissenschaftlich ausgerichtete Sprachkurse angeboten. (6) Die Regelstudienzeit bestimmt sich nach § 5d Absatz 2 Satz 1 des Deutschen Richtergesetzes (DRiG).

twenty different courses; criminal law in 11 different courses and national public in 13 different courses with an emphasis on tax law. The Heidelberg Law Faculty describes the objective of its courses at its website as follows: "The aim of the Law course is set out in § 3 I of the JAPro:[11] "With the requisite academic thoroughness, students engage with the most important sectors of Civil Law, Criminal Law and Public Law as well as a focal subject with due concern for international (notably European) and procedural perspectives. Appropriate attention is paid to the foundational subjects (History of Law, Philosophy of Law, Sociology of Law, Legal Methodology, Comparative Law, General Constitutional Law)." The Law course as described here is designed to establish the basis for admission to preparatory (judicial) service and the later practice of a legal profession."[12] There is no particular mentioning of public international law, neither as a particular subject nor as a subject, which might inspire the understanding and interpretation of the national legal system side by side with legal philosophy. What has been taught in public international law in summer 2021 was comprehensive though. The curriculum included general courses on public international law and on private international law, a course on international organizations, a course on WTO law and a course on international protection of data. However, these courses were not mandatory to take not even the courses on public and on private international law. Therefore it all depends upon the students whether they take advantage of what was offered in the curriculum.

As indicated above the universities studies end with the first state examination, which is undertaken under the jurisdiction of an appellate court. As far as the Focal Areas (Schwerpunktbereiche) are concerned – which may include public international law – the examination is undertaken by the law faculties.[13]

The legal training is concluded with the Second State Examination. The object and purpose of this examination is to ascertain whether the student is being qualified as judge, as attorney or as higher civil service.[14]

---

11 See note 6.

12 See https://www.uni-heidelberg.de/courses/prospective/academic/programs/law-en.htm (last visited 31. December 2021.

13 The Heidelberg Law Faculty offers the following Focal Areas: History of Law and Historical Comparative Law; Criminology; Law of Industrial Relations and Social Law; Fiscal Law; German and European Administrative law; Company (Enterprise) Law; Economic Law and European Law; Law of Civil Procedure; International Private and Procedural Law; International Law; Medical Law and Health Law; European and International Law on Capital Markets and Financial Services.

14 The majority of students enter the preparatory phase which confronts students with the work of judges, (in courts at different levels focusing on different subjects) prosecutors and attorneys. That students undergo this practical training period and a second

Considering the object and purpose of the two examinations, it becomes apparent that academic legal training in Germany principally means to train students to become judges, attorneys or member of the civil service. The Humboldt ideal is still upheld but less and less relevant in reality of studying law. The focus of such training is on civil law, followed by national public and European law and by criminal law. This is reflected in the composition of most law faculties. In the majority of law faculties in Germany up to 50 per cent of the faculty members teach civil law, including the relevant classes on legal philosophy and history of law. Only roughly, 30 percent teach national public law and about 10 percent criminal law. This is meant to reflect what is needed from the perspective of the object and purpose of academic legal studies in Germany. The teaching in the Focal Areas will in most cases not amount to more than 20 per cent of the teaching load.

Those students who participate in a focal area, which includes public international law, will be trained mostly in what is considered the essentials. What is 'essential' is difficult to determine. It may mean two different issues, namely that very specific areas of public international law are not covered. This is the reason why courses concerning law of the sea or international humanitarian law are not taught or that the course on, let us say the United Nations does not go into details. Depending upon the expertise of the person teaching public international law the classes may provide some insight into practice.

The objective of legal studies as described above is still being pursued albeit the fact that only a small fraction of students which have finished the academic legal training including the 'Vorbereitungsdienst' successfully become judges. Many of them join the corps of attorneys, go into industry, or find an occupation unrelated to their expertise in law. The labor market for students with a law background is still quite good since the standard of legal studies is considered to be high and demanding. The good chances lawyers have at the job market outside the traditional jobs for lawyers may be interpreted that the legal training is still believed to meet the demands of Humboldt that university studies should be designed to form the personality of students rather the prepare them for a particular job.

2 *Who is Teaching International Law?*

At the moment, there is hardly any professor in Germany who is teaching public international law only. This is due to the fact already referred to that

---

examination executed mainly by judges is due to the fact that without the second examination one is not considered to be a fully qualified lawyer and the opining for jobs are limited and in general not well paid.

public international is occupying only a small segment of the curriculum of law schools. Most of those who teach public international law and European law cover public international law as well as national public law (mostly concentrating de facto on constitutional law). The rules concerning the Habilitation (second academic qualification after the PhD) require the qualification in national public law as well as in public international law to get the most desirable venia legendi on public law. Without such qualification to teach national public law one may not become a member in the Deutsche Staatsrechtslehrervereinigung (association of German professors teaching national public law) which will be essential for the professional career.

The hiring practice of law faculties matches this pattern. They prefer colleagues who can teach national public law as well as one or the other issues taught in the focal areas, such as public international law, since the classes concerning the mandatory curriculum are much bigger and more numerous than classes in the focal areas. As already indicated teaching on courses of the focal areas, mostly do not cover more than 20 per cent of the overall teaching load. The hiring practices of Law Schools match this fact. To hire lecturers who cover courses, which are mandatory is essential, otherwise the teaching load within the faculty cannot be distributed equally.

The fact that professors teaching public international also have an expertise in national public law (mostly on constitutional law) has certainly an influence on how public international law is being perceived, taught and researched in Germany. The approach to and the interpretation of public international law is often comparable to the approach in dealing with constitutional law. This distinguishes the teaching of and the research on public international law from the teaching in the United States for example where often professors have an additional background in political science or history or economics. However, the situation is changing in this respect. More and more law school professors in Germany have spent an extended period for research in the United States and keep their established contacts. This leads to an approximation of approaches.

If interdisciplinary connections are being sought, the focus is mostly on philosophy, political science, economy and may be ethics. However, public international is more and more covering issues where an expertise from natural science is useful or even warranted. This is particularly true for the law of the sea, international environmental law, including the rules concerning climate change. The necessity of background knowledge renders teaching more demanding on the side of the lecturer as well on the side of the students.

3 *Which Students Choose International Law?*

The student body in a class on public international law is often somewhat different from the student body in let us say specialized classes on national administrative law. The student body in the former is mostly more internationally composed since most foreign LLM students will enlist in a public international law class rather than in some of the classes on a typical German legal issue. This has an influence on the discussion in such a class. German student are frequently confronted by interventions from foreign students with attitudes towards public international law, which have a flavor of the region where they come from.

German students who choose the international law classes are motivated to do so for several reasons. Many of them would like to find an appointment at some or other international organization. If asked, most of them indicate that this is where they want to go after having finished law studies. Others consider the possibility to join the German Foreign Office and finally, others want to study abroad (LLM in the US or in the United Kingdom) or seek an affiliation with a NGO. The subject matters they are interested in mostly is human rights and the protection of the environment. The fascination in international criminal law has declined recently. Only few consider a career in an international law firm on the basis of public international law. Those who wish to retain such an option often chose economic or trade law. Many of them who choose a specialization do so via an LLM on either US American or British law schools. The special composition of classes on international law must be reflected in the teaching mode. The teaching has to be particularly interactive and should be flexible as far as the language used is concerned.

IV Some Tentative Conclusions

Compared to the years when I entered law school (1964 – 1968) public international law has changed significantly. In these years, only classes on public international law and classes on the interrelationship of public international law and national public law were delivered. The term environmental law was never mentioned in international law classes. By the way, it was only hardly mentioned in national law. The curriculum is richer today reflecting the development of public international law. However, this plurality carries with it the danger that the view on public international law is getting lost. Specialists on law of the sea, international economic law and international environmental law seem to forget that these issues are part of public international law. One has to concede that due to the proliferation of international law it has become difficult to master teaching international law in its entirety.

Although public international law has changed, the mode of its teaching has not. Students are still confronted mostly with lectures and seminars, which have a tendency of being rather abstract.

This does not meet the expectations of students of today. They would like to hear more about the relevance of public international law. They raise questions concerning migration, for example, on climate change, the export of weapons and the war in Syria. Under most circumstances the professor asked, may not have the full factual background to answer the questions in a way expected. All these issue are utterly complex and the public international law question is very often just an element and not necessarily a dominant one.

What could and should be done to remedy this situation. It may be recommendable that practitioners take over supplementary classes to enrich the curriculum. Some law schools have implemented such course of action by inviting retired diplomats or international judges to teach.

Additionally, it would be recommendable that students are increasingly faced with moot courts. This approach to teaching is still at an infant stage in Germany compared to what is common in the United States or in Singapore.

Another option is to visit international courts with the class and to listen through a full hearing. I must confess this may be burdensome for students. They would need an introduction to the subject matter from the court in question. This is for many reasons impossible.

All this would give the students the feeling that public international law is and remains a reality although it may not always be sufficiently respected.

However, what is essential that German students, even those who have no interest in international public law get a basic feeling what international public is all about, its methodology, its approach and in particular its connection with constitutional law. They should at least be aware of the existence of international public law and its relevance. This would benefit students in two respects. They would be basically informed about the existence of the impact international public law has on their daily life. To be more concrete they might understand the legal intricacies of mass migration in a somewhat more balanced fashion. Second, being informed about a legal system, which is of relevance in the whole world may open the mind of students to think more in alternatives. This may be irrelevant for the daily professional life later but it would bring student back to the ideals of Humboldt referred to above. The status international law according to the Basic Law is not reflected in the legal training as of today. The Länder should make every effort to close the gap between the constitutional status of international law Germany and the way it is being taught.

However, the deeper problem may be the changes public international law is undergoing and whether these changes require a modified approach concerning its teaching. The changes public international law is undergoing have been well described elsewhere. These are that public international law touching on more and more issues, including constitutional law issues, which formerly were under the jurisdiction of States and considered as internal affairs (Article 2 para. 7 UN Charter). Another development of a more recent origin is that an increasing number of issues are treated as issues, the management of which should respect not only particular States but also the international community, including future generations.[15] The protection of the world climate is a telling example.[16] Finally, it should be mentioned that States have enriched the international normative system by accepting non-legally binding commitments. The International Compact for Safe Orderly and Regularly Migration is such a norm.[17] These challenges might render it necessary to undertake the training of international in a close connection with the national law. This being accepted in respect of the law of the European Union and it might be necessary to pursue the same approach as far as public international law is concerned. Perhaps in one time a course on 'National and International Administrative Law' might be the only appropriate means in dealing with administrative law reflecting the ever growing interdependence between public international law and national law.

15 See on that more comprehensively Rüdiger Wolfrum, Solidarity and Community Interests: Driving Forces for the Interpretation and Development of International Law, General Course on Public International Law, RdC vol. 416, 2021,p. 26 at 179 et seq, with further references.

16 Another example is the fight against the Corona 19 Pandemic. The challenges the WHO has been facing may lead to the development of a new form of international administrative law.

17 A/RES/73/195 of 19 December 2018.

CHAPTER 11B

Teaching International Law in Germany

Some Additional Remarks by a Former Parliamentarian, Practitioner and Teacher

Heribert Hirte

Teaching International Law – is the subject of this book. And for a lawyer this is already a title subject to interpretation and uncertainty: Since, what is „International Law“? Is it the (truly) international law that governs the relationship between states, i.e. public international law? Does this include European Law (and if so, is this because of the fact that the European Union is not (yet?) a state)? And does it include the teaching of national law with taking account of comparative law aspects and/or the teaching of national laws by focusing on the generalized common principles, an approach taken by the U.S. law schools regarding their states‘ laws (and which is not necessarily restricted to the genuine common law). There are so many questions in this regard and this book aims at answering quite a few of them.

My Perspective

In this regard, I am happy to have the opportunity to add some of my thoughts to the very topic of the book.[1] I am doing this in my capacity as a member of the Standing Committee of the German Law Faculties Association (i.e., the Executive Board), and in this context certainly also as a former board member and temporary chairman of the *European Law Faculties Association* (ELFA).

But then also as a former member of the German Bundestag, which was also responsible for questions of legal education in the Legal Affairs Committee of the Bundestag and in the CDU/CSU parliamentary group-internal working group on Legal Affairs – and whose constituency then also includes the local university and my own *alma mater*, the University of Cologne.

1 The following is in part based on the author's *Grußwort* (address), in: Hobe/Marauhn (Eds.), Lehre des internationalen Rechts – zeitgemäß? Berichte der Deutschen Gesellschaft für Internationales Recht, vol. 48, Heidelberg 2017, pp. 7–9.

 | DOI:10.1163/9789004678880_014

And finally, of course – perhaps most importantly – as a university professor who was particularly concerned about the internationality and internationalization of law.

To the point a few words, necessarily from a German perspective:

International Law as a Contribution to a more Peaceful World

First of all, it is good and important to hold up the flag of international law at a time when the return to nation states, national law and national borders determines the discussion. Teaching International Law and/or teaching law internationally (which is not the same), first of all, is a clear statement against law being completely determined by the national (sovereign) state (see on this point also *Carlo Focarelli*, in this volume).

In this regard, the debate taken up in this book is reflected by the struggle of the German *Bundesverfassungsgericht* (Federal Constitutional Court),[2] just recently followed by the Polish Constitutional Tribunal,[3] and the European Court of Justice on the question on how far European law prevails over the EU states' national laws.

However, this also includes – especially from my point of view as a former politician – the need for a stronger analysis of the political process. Here I have repeatedly experienced great ignorance about even elementary questions of the formation of political decisions and laws. Scholarly work in law – and the teaching based on it – also implies showing where the "ideal" solutions found by a scholar are limited and why.[4]

Accordingly, the focus should also be on the sources of law, which extend far beyond the "scholarly law review article", especially in international law. Anyone who deals a little more intensively with the influences and interests that underlie legal and political decisions quickly realizes that there is neither

2 See particularly the BVerfG's PSPP judgment of 5 May 2020 (2 BvR 859/15) E 154, 17 = NJW 2020, 1647; for the author's view on this decision *Hirte*, Die Ultra Vires-Kontrolle des Bundesverfassungsgerichts nach PSPP. Wie die umstrittene Ultra Vires-Kontrolle des BVerfG im Deutschen Bundestag aufgenommen wurde, AnwBl 2021, pp. 214 215.

3 Polish Constitutional Tribunal, judgment of 7 October 2021; see on this decision and the (non-) comparability with the BVerfG's approach *Thiele*, Whoever equates Karlsruhe to Warsaw is wildly mistaken, Verfassungsblog of 10 October 2021 (available at https://verfassungsblog.de/whoever-equals-karlsruhe-to-warsaw-is-wildly-mistaken/).

4 See, in detail, on the legislative process from the point of view of a parliamentarian *Hirte*, in: Recht und Gesetz. Festschrift für Ulrich Seibert. Zum 65. Geburtstag (Köln 2019), pp. 345-357.

a clear demarcation between law and politics, nor is (legal) scholarship free of lobbying influences.[5]

The Importance of Legal Training

This brings us to legal training in the field of International Law. Here I do not believe that a solution – as is often claimed – lies in the introduction of a two-step education system (Bachelor and Master).[6] Because this is only a question of structuring the training, not the content and not the examination. And that is why I remain convinced that it was right to prevent the introduction of "Bologna" for jurisprudence, not least because it was one of the topics that brought me into active politics … It should therefore also be mentioned that there is no initiative known to me at the German federal political level to change this. The last relevant German law in this field, the "Gesetz zur Modernisierung des notariellen Berufsrechts und zur Änderung weiterer Vorschriften" of 25 June 2021[7] explicitly rejected attempts by the German *Länder*[8] to move to some extent in this direction (by abolishing the overall grade in the legal examination, as currently provided for in the Deutsches Richtergesetz [DRiG] which includes state and university part of the examination).[9]

That's why it's about the content and the examination. As far as the content is concerned, we still lack sufficient "common European teaching material", as

5 See on this point in more detail *Hirte*, in: Festschrift für Thomas Heidel (Baden-Baden 2021), pp. 57-77.

6 From the author's point of view at a glance *Hirte*, „Bologna" und die deutsche Juristenausbildung – Zu den Schwierigkeiten Deutschlands bei der Übernahme des Bachelor-/Master-Modells in die Rechtswissenschaft-, ZSR 2008 I, pp. 253–267; previously *Hirte/Mock*, Die Juristenausbildung in Europa vor dem Hintergrund des Bologna-Prozesses, JuS 2005, Beilage zu Heft 12; *id.*, Auswirkungen des Bologna-Prozesses auf die Juristenausbildung. Überlegungen aus deutscher Sicht, EJLE (European Journal of Legal Education) 2005, pp. 141–147; *id.*., Auswirkungen des Bologna-Prozesses auf die Juristenausbildung – Überlegungen aus rechtsvergleichender Perspektive – in: Deutscher Juristen-Fakultätentag (Hrsg.), Der „Bologna-Prozess" und die Juristenausbildung in Deutschland, Stuttgart 2007, pp. 43–51; on the integration of "practice" into the training of lawyers, moreover *id.*, The Role of Practice in Legal Education, in: Jürgen Basedow, Uwe Kischel and Ulrich Sieber (Eds.), German National Reports to the 18th International Congress on Comparative Law (Washington 2010), Tübingen 2010, pp. 19–38.

7 BGBl. I, p. 2154.

8 Stellungnahme des Bundesrates zum Entwurf eines Gesetzes zur Modernisierung des notariellen Berufsrechts und zur Änderung weiterer Vorschriften, BT-Drucks. 19/26828 p. 251.

9 Deutscher Bundestag, Beschlussempfehlung und Bericht des Ausschusses für Recht und Verbraucherschutz, BT-Drucks. 19/30503, p. 14.

I suggested and proposed years ago as chairman of ELFA. However, this material and this approach must then also be included in the examination on equal *footing*.

The Recruitment of the Judiciary

And here lies perhaps the more central problem: because our judiciary (which carries the state examinations) is, unlike the legal profession, to a much lesser extent internationally oriented and internationally experienced (see, more extensively, on legal education in our context *Rüdiger Wolfrum*, in this volume). The needs of the (German) judiciary determine the state examination concerning the way students are being examined (writing from the judge's perspective) and its contents (mainly national law). International Law, therefore, only plays a role as elective course. Since it is a self-referential system, it will be difficult to change this situation. However, this is necessary in central points: If foreign legal scholars can – for example – teach at German universities, but on the other hand cannot test in the context of the state examination due to a lack of "qualification for the [German] judicial office" (§ 5 DRiG), the cat bites its tail to a certain extent. This is because in Germany appointments of foreign (and certainly not German-speaking) legal scholars fail in advance, because they cannot participate in the state examination – with the result that the corresponding burdens have to be borne by other colleagues, which in turn significantly reduces the willingness to appoint foreign colleagues (which I can confirm from my own experience). It is therefore not surprising that the willingness to teach courses with an international connection is greater than the need: and this need is determined by the requirements for taking state examinations which are essentially determined by national law and the national judiciary.

The Recruitment of Members of Parliament

Ultimately – and here, I speak from my view as a former member of the Bundestag – the root of this problem lies even deeper: Because even in Parliament, which elects the judges of the federal courts (but this of course also has indirect influence on the attitude of the judges in the initial instance), experience in international law is rather rare. They are therefore – usually rather intuitively – not tended to be important in selection decisions. Conversely, the "defense" of the German judiciary (and sometimes even more so of the German legal profession) against foreign influences is sometimes much more central.

And it is therefore not surprising to consider that, in order to report from my experience as rapporteur for the Transatlantic Trade and Investment Partnership (TTIP) in the Committee on European Affairs, the German Association of Judges was one of the sharpest critics of the (possible) arbitration provisions of this agreement, ultimately because it rejects "cross-border national courts".[10] The fact that some things could still have be improved there, and some things have already been improved (particularly in the Comprehensive Economic and Trade Agreement with Canada [CETA]), is another matter.[11]

And in other areas too – namely in the debate on the introduction of class actions or the reform of the Small Claims Regulation[12] – it was quite noticeable that we in Parliament have a more reserved attitude towards questions of international law or of cross-border enforcement – as soon as it leaves the familiar paths of national law.[13]

Anyone who wants to change this must therefore start earlier – namely ensure that international experience and internationality are also present in the parliaments, which unfortunately often fails because those who demand this orientation and could do so do not want to participate themselves. Noteworthy in this context, for example, is the approach of French law (and some other states) to have the French living abroad represented by their own deputies in parliament – which automatically leads to a stronger consideration of international references. Some parties similarly have "local associations" of their party members living abroad. Whether such a strengthening of international law, which would ultimately only be possible through a change in the

10 Deutscher Richterbund (Association of German Judges), Stellungnahme zur Errichtung eines Investitionsgerichts für TTIP – Vorschlag der Europäischen Kommission vom 16.09.2015 und 12.11.2015, Stellungnahme 4/16 vom Februar 2016 (available at www.drb.de).

11 For the author's demands and proposals, see *Hirte*, Beteiligung des Deutschen Bundestages oder des Europäischen Parlaments bei der Auswahl von Schiedsrichtern in Investor-Staat-Schiedsverfahren (ISDS), in: Privatrecht, Wirtschaftsrecht, Verfassungsrecht. Privatinitiative und Gemeinwohlhorizonte in der europäischen Integration. Festschrift für Peter-Christian Müller-Graff (Baden-Baden 2015), pp. 876–884; shorter also *id.*, Beteiligung des Deutschen Bundestages oder des Europäischen Parlaments bei der Auswahl von Schiedsrichtern in Investor-Staat-Schiedsverfahren (ISDS), Audit Quarterly Review I/2015, pp. 38–40.

12 Regulation (EC) No 861/2007 of the European Parliament and of the Council of 11 July 2007 establishing a European Small Claims Procedure; OJ EU No. L 199 of 31.7.2007, p. 1.

13 On the political consequence (parliamentary reservation): *Hirte*, Small Claims: „Kleine" Forderungen und große Auswirkungen. Zum Parlamentsvorbehalt des Deutschen Bundestages bei der Änderung der Verordnung (EG) Nr. 861/2007 des Europäischen Parlaments und des Rates vom 11. Juli 2007 zur Einführung eines europäischen Verfahrens für geringfügige Forderungen, in: Festschrift für Heinz Vallender zum 65. Geburtstag (Köln 2015), pp. 247–259.

electoral law, would also be possible in my country is a constitutional question that I can only touch on here.

The German-French Parliamentary Assembly (Deutsch-Französische Parlamentarische Versammlung [DFPV])

In this context, however, attention should in any case be paid to the German-French Parliamentary Assembly, in particular its Working Group on the "Harmonization of German and French Economic and Insolvency law" („Harmonisierung des deutschen und des französischen Wirtschafts-und Insolvenzrechts" (AG HWIR).

First of all, some explanations:[14] The German-French Parliamentary Assembly is composed of 100 members, including 50 members of the German *Bundestag* and 50 members of the *Assemblée nationale*, who are to meet at least twice a year alternately in Germany and France. The constituent meeting took place on Monday, 25 March 2019, in Paris under the leadership of *Bundestag* President Dr. *Wolfgang Schäuble* and the President of the *Assemblée nationale*, *Richard Ferrand*. The basis of this institutionalized cooperation at parliament level is the German-French Parliamentary Agreement, which was adopted by the *Assemblée nationale* on 11 March 2019 and by the German *Bundestag* on 20 March 2019. The parliamentary agreement is the result of intensive discussions by the German-French Working Group, which was set up for this purpose on 22 January 2018 on the occasion of the 55th anniversary of the signing of the Treaty on German-French Cooperation (Élysée Treaty).

The Working Group "Harmonization of German and French Economic and Insolvency Law" (AG HWIR) was set up by decision of the German-French Parliamentary Assembly on 6 February 2020[15] in Strasbourg. It consists of voting and advisory members from the German *Bundestag* and the *Assemblée nationale*. On the part of the German *Bundestag*, all parliamentary groups, on the part of the *Assemblée nationale* six out of nine parliamentary groups participated in the work of the working group. This was coordinated by the deputies Prof. Dr. *Heribert Hirte* (CDU/CSU) and *Liliana Tanguy* (LaREM). The task of the working group was to identify gaps in the current economic and insolvency law of Germany and France and to develop proposals for a German-French harmonization of these areas of law.

14 Based on the information on the DFPV on the homepage of the German *Bundestag* (available at https://www.bundestag.de/dfpv).

15 DFPV, Dokument Nr. 2020.5 (available at https://www.bundestag.de/resource/blob/682444/c10b7f6beef5a92290ef1049dbc11ad5/2020_5_wirtschafts_insolvenzrecht-data.pdf).

The members of the working group met for four meetings, which took place exclusively virtually as a result of the corona pandemic, and dealt with draft regulations of the *Association Henri Capitant* on the legal areas of corporate law, banking and financial market law, insolvency law and market law[16] and heard the following experts: Professor *Philippe Dupichot* (University of Panthéon-Sorbonne), Professor Dr. *Urs Gruber* (University of Mainz), Professor *Philippe Roussel Galle* (Universität Réné Descartes), Professor *Martine Behar-Touchais* (University of Panthéon-Sorbonne), Professor Dr. *Matthias Lehmann* (University of Vienna), Professor *Louis Vogel* (University of Panthéon-Assas), Professor Dr. *Rüdiger Veil* (Ludwig-Maximilians-Universität München), Professor and Attorney at Law *Hubert de Vauplane* (Institut d'études politiques de Paris / Rechtsanwälte Kramer Levin LLP), Department Director *Julia Thomas* (Bundesverband Deutscher Banken e.V.), Attorney at Law Dr. *Hans-Jürgen Meyer-Lindemann* (Attorneys at Law Pinsent Masons), Professor Dr. *Katja Langenbucher* (Goethe University Frankfurt a.M.), Professor Dr. *Christian Kersting* (Heinrich Heine University Düsseldorf) and Attorney at Law *Dominique Heintz* (Attorneys at Law Hertslet Wolfer & Heintz).

The work of the working group was the basis for a decision of the German-French Parliamentary Assembly of 28 June 2021,[17] which was reproduced and appreciated elsewhere.[18] It was introduced by the following members of the DFPV: *Patrice Anato, Valérie Gomez-Bassac, Buon Tan, Liliana Tanguy* (LaREM); Prof. Dr. *Heribert Hirte*, Dr. *Volker Ullrich* (CDU/CSU); Dr. *Karl-Heinz Brunner, Christian Petry* (SPD); Dr. *Jürgen Martens* (FDP); *Sabine Thillaye, Sylvain Waserman* (Dem); *Cécile Untermaier* (SOC); *Jean-Michel Clément* (LT). For our present context, it is important that the project is not exclusive, but exemplary – and that all other EU states are therefore called upon to cooperate. In this respect, the considerations also represent a first step towards a European Economic Code.[19] For the *teaching* which is in the focus here, the work is important insofar as it broadens the number of those in politics and legal academia who – so to speak inevitably – deal with comparative law and international law – with the repercussions described above.

---

16 Detailed presentation by *Gruber/Herrmann/Lehmann(Schulze/Teichmann*, EuZW 2021, pp. 413 *et seq*.

17 DFPV, Dokument Nr. 2021.4 (available, in German and French, at https://www.bundestag.de/resource/blob/850826/176527fc1731dc43d8dabfee7418d592/2021_4_hwir-data.pdf).

18 See, e.g., the partial reprints in ZInsO 2021, pp. 1716 *et seq*. and at *Hirte*, in: Festschrift für Christoph Paulus zum 70. Geburtstag (München 2022), pp. 345-357.

19 See, *ibidem* (note 18).

CHAPTER 11C

Teaching International Law in Germany

Constitutional Safeguards for the Freedom of Research and Teaching

Gerd Morgenthaler

I Teaching Law

When we teach law as an academic subject, we are fully aware of the fact that we are not simply instructing our students of how to use a mere technique. We know that our discipline's heart beats well below the surface of statutes and conventions, doctrines and dogmatic figures. But it would still not go far enough to interpret the given legal system as an accidental compromise between more or less selfish interests and more or less convincing ideas. Instead, we only advance to the very core of the law if we also consider and try to understand the reality and impacts of the underlying civilizational system, a system that consists of cultural paradigms which are deeply rooted but largely unconscious, and of institutions which effectively drive the development but have themselves evolved over time, usually and mostly without rational planning.

The philosophers of the Enlightenment were convinced that there is a deeper sense, a *telos*, in history, that mankind is on a path of progress towards freedom and reason, and that, consequently, our whole civilizational system has a mission. In this view the legal system was seen as needing constant improvement in democracies of free citizens, but it was also realized that the legal system stored up a wisdom accumulated by generations reaching far beyond the individual's understanding. Western-style constitutions and legal systems, international and national, were strongly influenced by this conviction and the ethics connected with it during the last centuries. Therefore, if we want to analyze and teach the law in its full meaning, instead of just scratching the surface in a positivistic way, we must do research into the paradigmatic and institutional foundations of our constitutions and treaties, of statutes and customary law, and we should encourage our students to do the same. But this constant quest for the deeper sources and the spirit of our law can only be successful if we are able to distance ourselves from vested political, economic or social interests and from the prevalent ideologies as far as possible, and endeavor to take an objective, purely academic and "jurisprudent" standpoint.

 | DOI:10.1163/9789004678880_015

In other words: we have to be free.

II The Guarantee of Free Research and Teaching in the German Basic Law

Article 5 III 1 of the German Basic Law (BL) states that "research and teaching shall be free". Like all rights and liberties guaranteed by the Constitution, this provision must be interpreted in the light of the ideas of Enlightenment with special regard to the "idealistic" philosophy of German Classicism, as represented by thinkers like Immanuel Kant and Georg Wilhelm Friedrich Hegel. For them, 'civic freedom' (*bürgerliche Freiheit*) meant the individual's competence – under general laws – to determine his or her own thinking autonomously and to act creatively and responsibly according to his or her independent will. It is also important to note that this idea of civic freedom was always connected with the conviction that only free individuals will be able to develop their personalities (cf., Article 2 I BL) and thereby become capable to act in full 'moral freedom' (*sittliche Freiheit*).[1]

The guarantee of free research and teaching must be seen in the context of this underlying concept. According to the German Federal Constitutional Court, Article 5 III 1 BL protects all "processes, actions and decisions based on the autonomous laws of science which are thought to contribute to the quest for knowledge, its interpretation and communication".[2] For the individual, this includes the free choice of research questions and methodology, the entire practical implementation of a research project and the evaluation and dispersal of its results.[3] As generally the guarantee of 'civic freedom' is connected with the expectation that free individuals will develop the capacity to act in 'moral freedom', the special guarantee of free research and teaching is linked with the conviction that the ensuing process of methodically disciplined and critically reflected thinking in combination with unhindered communication and publicity can best contribute to the generation of knowledge in the never-ending scientific debate and in the quest for truth.[4] In this sense, the Federal Constitutional Court expressed its confidence that free research and teaching

1 Cf., Gerd Morgenthaler, *Freiheit durch Gesetz. Der parlamentarische Gesetzgeber als Erstadressat der Freiheitsgrundrechte* (Mohr Siebeck: Tübingen 1999) 106 et seq.

2 BVerfGE [=Decisions of the Federal Constitutional Court] 111, 333 (354); 122, 89 (105).

3 BVerfGE 35, 79 (113).

4 Cf., BVerfGE 90, 1 (13).

will serve society most if they are "pure", i.e. free of considerations of practical usefulness and political correctness.[5]

Like many other European countries, Germany has a long tradition of universities, dating back to the Middle Ages. Their specific concept of research and teaching, connected with the name of Wilhelm von Humboldt,[6] was conceived in the same epoque of "idealistic" philosophy of German Classicism that was mentioned before. We owe to this philosophy: firstly, the guiding ideas – that universities should be places for pure research and teaching, and that they should primarily aim at the formation of the personality (*Bildung*) by encouraging the students to make use of their capacity to think independently instead of merely offering practical professional training (*Ausbildung*) – and secondly, the tradition of organizing the universities, not as private, profit-oriented enterprises, but as public corporations, installed, financed and supervised by the state and at the same time enjoying the full guarantee of the freedom of research and teaching.

Evidently, if the state oversees the universities, this means that they can generally enjoy strong support and even a privileged position. On the other hand, state control can also pose a threat to the freedom of research and teaching if the state forgets about what the "idealistic" philosophers called a *Kulturstaat's* civilizational mission. It is therefore important to emphasize the fact that, despite their organization in the forms of public law, universities are part not of the state apparatus but of society, i.e., the sphere of freedom. The Federal Constitutional Court has repeatedly emphasized the state's obligation to form out the universities as functional institutions and to provide them with sufficient personnel and financial resources for a free academic process.[7] The state administrations managing the universities and even the university institutions themselves are not allowed to interfere with the free research and teaching of the individual members of the universities, neither directly or indirectly, e.g., by means of withholding personnel or resources, preventing publications or publicly commenting on the academic output of individual scientists.[8] Furthermore, they have to protect the university members against any attempts, from outside or inside, to disrupt their free research and teaching.[9]

5 BVerfGE 127, 87 (115); 128, 1 (87); 136, 338 para. 56.

6 For an excellent introduction into Humboldt's guiding ideas, see: Helmut Schelsky, *Einsamkeit und Freiheit* (Rowohlt: Reinbek bei Hamburg 1963).

7 BVerfGE 35, 79 (114); 88, 129 (136); 94, 268 (285); 136, 338 para. 55; 139, 148 para. 44, 68.

8 BVerfGE 102, 304 (312); Friedhelm Hufen, Wissenschaftsfreiheit: 13 Thesen zur Klarstellung. In: Wilhelm Hopf (ed.), Die Freiheit der Wissenschaft und ihre Feinde. Berlin 2019, pp. 3 et seq.

9 BVerfGE 55, 37 (68).

In Germany, professors in state-run universities traditionally enjoy the status of a civil servant. But this does not mean that they are integrated in the state apparatus like genuine civil servants endowed with administrative competences. Instead, this peculiar legal construction must be interpreted as a kind of "borrowed" concept intending to make sure that the university professors are alimented for lifetime, thus empowering them to do research and teaching in full independence and with the only aim of serving the truth. Consequently, the Federal Constitutional Court has emphasized that the legislator may not simply subject university professors to the general regulations concerning civil servants but must consider the peculiarities of academic life, including the fact that Article 5 III BL is the decisive scale for any legal arrangements in this field.[10]

III European and International Law

The freedom of research and teaching as protected under Article 5 III 1 of the German Basic Law is backed, reinforced and supplemented by some parallel guarantees in European and international law.[11] Article 13 of the EU Charter of Fundamental Rights states that "scientific research shall be free of constraint. Academic freedom shall be respected."[12] Although the European Convention on Human Rights does not contain an explicit provision on the freedom of research and teaching, the European Court of Human Rights considers it as included in the guarantee of the freedom of speech (Article 10).[13] Similarly, on the global level, the International Covenant on Civil and Political Rights is of importance for the issue as it guarantees the right to hold opinions and the freedom of expression (Article 19), and the International Covenant on

10 BVerfGE 35, 23 (30); 43, 242 (277); 67, 1 (14); 122, 89 (106); 130, 263 (299).

11 Cf., Jogchum Vrielink/Paul Lemmens/Stephan Parmentier et.al., *Academic Freedom as a Fundamental Right* (2010) LERU Advice Paper No. 6, 6–8 <https://www.leru.org/publications/academic-freedom-as-a-fundamental-right>, accessed 19 December 2022.

12 For the interpretation of this provision in literature (and for an overview of the still very rudimentary jurisprudence), see Norbert Bernsdorff, in: Jürgen Meyer/Sven Hölscheidt (eds), *Charta der Grundrechte der Europäischen Union. Kommentar* (Nomos: 5th ed, Baden-Baden 2019), Art. 13; Hans D. Jarass, in: Hans D. Jarass (ed), *Charta der Grundrechte der EU. Kommentar* (CH Beck: 4th ed, München 2021), Art. 13.

13 ECtHR, Sapan v. Turkey, 8 June 2010 (application no. 44102/04); Birgit Daiber, in: Jens Meyer-Ladewig/Martin Nettesheim/Stefan von Raumer (eds), *Europäische Menschenrechtskonvention. Kommentar* (Nomos: 4th ed, Baden-Baden 2017), Art. 10, no. 21.

Economic, Social and Cultural Rights calls up the State Parties "to respect the freedom indispensable for scientific research and creative activity" (Article 15).

Beside these sources of European and international law, the – legally non-binding[14] – UNESCO Recommendation concerning the Status of Higher-Education Teaching Personnel[15] deserves to be mentioned in this context because it expresses the basic idea and the various dimensions of the freedom of research and teaching very well. This recommendation affirms that "the right to education, teaching and research can only be fully enjoyed in an atmosphere of academic freedom" and that "open communication of findings, hypotheses and opinions lies at the very heart of higher education and provides the strongest guarantee of the accuracy and objectivity of scholarship and research". It then emphasize, *inter alia*, the importance of institutional autonomy with "that degree of self-governance necessary for effective decision-making by institutions of higher education regarding their academic work, standards, management and related activities" (no. 17–21), the fact that free research and teaching are individual rights and have to include "the right, without constriction by prescribed doctrine, to freedom of teaching and discussion, freedom in carrying out research and disseminating and publishing the results thereof, freedom to express freely their opinion about the institution or system in which they work, freedom from institutional censorship and freedom to participate in professional or representative academic bodies" (no. 25–30), the principles of self-governance and collegiality including "the right to elect a majority of representatives to academic bodies" (no. 31–32), and the importance of tenure or a functional equivalent as a safeguard of academic freedom and against arbitrary decisions (no. 45–46).

IV Threats to Free Research and Teaching

In the face of these constitutional, European and international guarantees two recent developments must be considered with worry because they threaten to deprive the university and its members of their specific spirit: the technocratic

14 Even though this Recommendations is not legally binding, it does "reveal a certain international consensus on the meaning of academic freedom and its corresponding responsibilities, as well as on the link between academic freedom and collegial self-government" – as pointed out by Jogchum Vrielink/Paul Lemmens/Stephan Parmentier et.al. (n 11) 6–8.

15 Recommendation adopted by the UNESCO General Conference in 1997; for the full text, see <https://unesdoc.unesco.org/ark:/48223/pf0000160495>, accessed 19 December 2022.

concept of a new "Managerialism"[16] on the one side, and an increasing ideological pressure culminating in what has been called "Cancel Culture"[17] on the other side.

Based on New Public Management theories the German *Länder* have introduced very hierarchical models of university administrations which endow the presidents with far-reaching competences but limit the possibilitics of the senates and other institutions of academic self-administration to exercise control. At the same time, they open the universities for a decisive influence exerted by newly installed university boards partly or totally composed of external members who usually represent certain interest groups in society but are in no way formally made responsible for the fate of "their" universities. Another dangerous trend is the tendency to employ young (and not so young) researchers under temporary contracts instead of granting them the traditional lifetime position of a civil servant. This is combined with a new policy of curbing the researchers' basic endowments with financial resources, thereby forcing them to permanently endeavor for external funds. Evidently, all these tendencies involve the danger that all university research, including the formulation

16 For the general debate see, e.g.: Rosemary Deem/Kevin J. Brehony, 'Management as Ideology: The Case of 'New Managerialism' in Higher Education' (2005) 31 Oxford Review of Education 217–235; Eckhart Schröter, 'Modernisierung des Hochschulmanagements. Herausforderungen und Reformtrends in vergleichender Perspektive' (2008) 14 Verwaltung und Management 175–179; Sanne Smeenk/Christine Teelken/Rob Eisinga/Hans Doorewaard, Managerialism, Organizational Commitment, and Quality of Job Performances among European University Employees' (2009) 50 Research in Higher Education 589–607; Richard Münch, *Akademischer Kapitalismus. Zur Politischen Ökonomie der Hochschulreform* (Suhrkamp: Berlin 2011); Otto Hüther/Georg Krücken, 'Wissenschaftliche Karriere und Beschäftigungsbedingungen: Organisationssoziologische Überlegungen zu den Grenzen neuer Steuerungsmodelle an deutschen Hochschulen' (2011) 62 Soziale Welt 303–325; Nilgun Massih-Tehrani/Christian Baier/Vincent Gengnagel, 'EU-Forschungsförderung im deutschen Hochschulraum: Universitäten zwischen Wissensökonomie und akademischer Selbstbestimmung' (2015) 66 Soziale Welt 55–74; Christian Johann Schmid/Uwe Wilkesmann, 'Ansichtssache Managerialismus an deutschen Hochschulen. Ein empirisches Stimmungsbild und Erklärungen' (2015) 37 Beiträge zur Hochschulforschung 56–87; Richard Joseph, 'The cost of managerialism in the university: an autoethnographical account of an academic redundancy process' (2015) 33 Prometheus 139–163.

17 Christian von Coelln, 'Beschneidet die 'Cancel Culture' die Freiheit der Wissenschaft?' (Forschung und Lehre 12/2021), <https://www.forschung-und-lehre.de/recht/beschneidet-cancel-culture-die-wissenschaftsfreiheit-4237>, accessed 19 December 2022. – For an overview about the situation in Germany, Austria and Switzerland, see Wilhelm Hopf (ed.), *Die Freiheit der Wissenschaft und ihre ‚Feinde'* (LIT: Berlin 2019), and the documentation of cases regularly updated by the Netzwerk Wissenschaftsfreiheit: <https://www.netzwerk-wissenschaftsfreiheit.de/dokumentation/>, accessed 19 December 2022.

of research questions, the choice of methods and the presentation of results, becomes more dependent on private stakeholders outside academia. State funds are also more and more confined to certain topics of current mainstream political interest, and the policy regulations and questionnaires often arouse the suspicion that the applicant should from the outset avoid certain hypotheses, approaches, or outcomes if he or she wants to be successful in procedures of this kind.

The new Managerialism may have intended to increase the universities' output, and the rising influence exercised by agenda-setting groups outside and inside the universities is often justified by the needs of modern society to cope with certain global challenges. But do we really believe that "governance" principles developed for business enterprises with predominantly quantitative parameters for measuring performance can really improve the quality of research and teaching? Do we really expect that the permanent pressure of economic competition combined with an atmosphere that demands 'political correctness' will create the intrinsic passion and professional ethics needed in the never-ending quest for scientific truth? In fact, we don't. The decisive question is therefore how to reform the universities in a way to make them the places for pure and independent thinking again. This is important not only for the sciences and the humanities, but for all academic disciplines including the more "practical" or "applied" subjects like our's: Teaching law, international and national, means to teach the law as a concept in its own right, with its own "logic" and a very long tradition of refined ideas and practical experience, a concept that should not bow to group interests or current ideologies but understand and cherish the cultural asset it has developed over centuries and the *ethos* it represents. As we said it earlier: academic legal studies should not only offer practical professional training but aim at the formation of the personality by encouraging the students to make use of their own capacity to think.

Bibliography

Deem R/Brehony KJ., 'Management as Ideology: the Case of 'New Managerialism' in Higher Education' (2005) 31 Oxford Review of Education 217.

Hopf W (ed), *Die Freiheit der Wissenschaft und ihre ,Feinde'* (LIT: Berlin 2019).

Hufen F, 'Wissenschaftsfreiheit: 13 Thesen zur Klarstellung' in Wilhelm Hopf (ed), *Die Freiheit der Wissenschaft und ihre ,Feinde'* (LIT: Berlin 2019) 3.

Hüther O/Krücken G, 'Wissenschaftliche Karriere und Beschäftigungsbedingungen: Organisationssoziologische Überlegungen zu den Grenzen neuer Steuerungsmodelle an deutschen Hochschulen' (2011) 62 Soziale Welt 303.

Jarass HD (ed), *Charta der Grundrechte der EU. Kommentar* (CH Beck: 4th ed, München 2021).

Joseph R, 'The cost of managerialism in the university: an autoethnographical account of an academic redundancy process' (2015) 33 Prometheus 139.

Massih-Tehrani N/Baier C/Gengnagel V, 'EU-Forschungsförderung im deutschen Hochschulraum: Universitäten zwischen Wissensökonomie und akademischer Selbstbestimmung' (2015) 66 Soziale Welt 55.

Meyer J/Hölscheidt S (eds), *Charta der Grundrechte der Europäischen Union. Kommentar* (Nomos: 5th ed, Baden-Baden 2019).

Meyer-Ladewig J/Nettesheim M/von Raumer S (eds), *Europäische Menschenrechtskonvention. Kommentar* (Nomos: 4th ed, Baden-Baden 2017).

Morgenthaler G, *Freiheit durch Gesetz. Der parlamentarische Gesetzgeber als Erstadressat der Freiheitsgrundrechte* (Mohr Siebeck: Tübingen 1999).

Münch R, *Akademischer Kapitalismus. Zur Politischen Ökonomie der Hochschulreform* (Suhrkamp: Berlin 2011).

Schelsky H, *Einsamkeit und Freiheit* (Rowohlt: Reinbek bei Hamburg 1963).

Schmid CJ/Wilkesmann U, 'Ansichtssache Managerialismus an deutschen Hochschulen. Ein empirisches Stimmungsbild und Erklärungen' (2015) 37 Beiträge zur Hochschulforschung 56.

Schröter E, 'Modernisierung des Hochschulmanagements. Herausforderungen und Reformtrends in vergleichender Perspektive' (2008) 14 Verwaltung und Management 175.

Smeenk S/Teelken C/Eisinga R/Doorewaard H, 'Managerialism, Organizational Commitment, and Quality of Job Performances among European University Employees' (2009) 50 Research in Higher Education 589.

Von Coelln C, 'Beschneidet die 'Cancel Culture' die Freiheit der Wissenschaft?' (Forschung und Lehre 12/2021), <https://www.forschung-und-lehre.de/recht/beschneidet-cancel-culture-die-wissenschaftsfreiheit-4237>, accessed 19 December 2022.

Vrielink J/Lemmens P/Parmentier S et.al., *Academic Freedom as a Fundamental Right* (2010) LERU Advice Paper No. 6, <https://www.leru.org/publications/academic-freedom-as-a-fundamental-right>, accessed 19 December 2022.

PART IV

Teaching Different Sub-disciplines of International Law

CHAPTER 12

Teaching International Economic Law in the 21st Century

*Ernst-Ulrich Petersmann**

Russian wars of aggression and related economic sanctions, health pandemics, climate change and its impact on the global economy and on individual 'life chances' (eg of poor people in less-developed island states that risk being submerged by rising sea levels) illustrate how economic, political, legal, social, biological, chemical and physical systems interact in complex ways. Different people are likely to perceive the legal regulation of these interactions differently depending on their 'human condition' and situated perspective, for example as a healthy citizen of the European Union (EU) compared with a poor citizen in Africa or in dictatorships like Belarus, North Korea and Cuba. Just as individuals (like Sisyphus) draw diverse conclusions from their existential 'human condition', so do human societies organize themselves – and regulate their economies – through law and politics in response to diverse social conditions and democratic preferences. For instance, neo-liberal interest group politics in industrialized Anglo-Saxon countries, totalitarian control over the economy in China and other authoritarian states, multilevel constitutional protection of the EU's common market freedoms and common trade and investment policies, and insistence by less-developed countries on 'special and differential treatment' often give rise to conflicting conceptions of international economic law (IEL). European democracies committed to normative individualism (using individual welfare as relevant normative standard) and to methodological individualism (explaining social phenomena in terms of the interplay of individual actions) tend to acknowledge economic 'consumer sovereignty', democratic

* Emeritus professor for international and European law, European University Institute Florence (Italy). Dr. Petersmann taught constitutional law, international law and European law at numerous Universities in Germany, Switzerland, Italy, the USA, Latin-America, South-Africa, China, India and Singapore. He published more than 30 books and 350 contributions to books and journals focusing on international law, European law and comparative constitutional law. He represented Germany in European and UN institutions and worked as legal counsel in GATT, legal consultant for the EU, WTO and UNCTAD, as secretary, member or chairman of GATT and WTO dispute settlement panels, and as chairman of the International Trade Law Committee of the International Law Association (1999–2014).

 DOI:10.1163/9789004678880_016

'citizen sovereignty', and voluntary, mutually beneficial agreements among citizens with informed, individual consent as ultimate source of values – at least as normative ideals even if, in majoritarian political practices, political compromises may be dominated by common self-interests of citizens or protectionist group interests. Authoritarian rulers, by contrast, tend to advocate collective and state-centered values (like making 'America great again', conquering historically Russian territories in sovereign neighboring states like Ukraine, regaining Chinese control over the South-China Sea in violation of the UN Convention on the Law of the Sea (UNCLOS)). Money-driven politics and business-driven market regulation in neoliberal countries aim at maximizing power, business income and macroeconomic efficiencies even if they involve considerable social costs like environmental pollution and social inequalities.

1 Perspectivism and Existentialism in International Economic Law

Perspectivism is an existential problem of all social and legal systems. Just as individuals grow up in unique social contexts with particular worldviews, so do legal cultures evolve in unique political contexts with particular value traditions. Similar to religions proceeding from 'original sin' (eg requiring the expulsion of Adam and Eve from paradise and justifying God's punishment of Cain for having murdered his brother Abel by condemning Cain to become a 'restless wanderer on earth'), legal philosophers perceive the unruly nature of human beings (T. Hobbes: '*homo homini lupus est*') and their 'unsocial sociability' (I. Kant) as the main justification of law and of the need for 'justice' (eg in the sense of reasonable justification of law), 'social contracts' and for 'institutionalizing public reason' (J. Rawls). For instance, from the perspective of industrialized countries, protecting patent rights for pharmaceutical products as incentive and compensation for private research and inventions of medicines may appear reasonable – even if it may be viewed as a 'death sentence' from the perspective of poor countries that cannot afford paying monopoly prices for newly developed vaccines offered and sold initially in developed country markets.[1] The examples of 'climate refugees', patent protection for medicines, or of unnecessary famines (eg in dictatorships like North Korea) illustrate how economic regulation may involve existential questions that may be answered differently from different perspectives: What kind of limitations

1 Cf Peter Drahos, Public lies and public goods: ten lessons from when patents and pandemics meet, in *European University Institute Law Working Paper* 2021–5.

of intellectual property rights do human rights of individual access to public health protection require? Are human rights to education and to freedom of opinion compatible with governmental instructions (eg in authoritarian countries like China) to avoid discussing the importance of human and constitutional rights for designing IEL? Authoritarian and democratic governments offer different answers to many 'existential questions' like whether, and how, the 'human condition' of 'social conflicts' (eg due to different conceptions of the good) can be overcome by reasonable political conceptions of justice in non-homogeneous societies where unreasonable people risk preventing social peace and justice by transforming politics into fights against 'political enemies' or 'religious infidels'. Similar to the 'Heisenberg principle' in quantum physics, the mere fact of observation from different perspectives risks changing realities: individual, communitarian, national, international or cosmopolitan social perspectives may call for diverse regulatory understandings and responses.

The diversity of textbooks on IEL – defined as the private and public, national and international law regulating transnational economic relations – illustrates how IEL is taught in different ways. Textbooks on IEL written from 'third world perspectives' often discuss past constitutional failures and structural biases of economic regulation (eg during centuries of colonial exploitation, slave trade and opium trade),[2] which IEL textbooks written from neo-liberal United States (US) perspectives (eg focusing on the post-1945 'embedded liberalism' and US-led neo-liberal economic order based on the 1944 Bretton Woods Agreements and the 1947 General Agreement on Tariffs and Trade: GATT) or from ordo-liberal European perspectives (eg focusing on Europe's common market and the external relations law of the EU) often neglect. Commercially oriented business and law schools prefer using IEL textbooks prioritizing professional training and an interdisciplinary understanding of the complex interactions between economic, political and legal orders, rather than textbooks criticizing the positively existing IEL for failing to protect human rights and other 'principles of justice'. Teaching IEL must acknowledge such 'perspectivism', diverse needs and demands of IEL students. This contribution proceeds from the normative premise that human right law (HRL) and the 2030 UN Sustainable Development Agenda require placing individual human beings and their human rights, basic needs, democratic and cosmopolitan responsibilities at the center of IEL teaching, research and regulation. This normative premise

2 Cf Leila Choukroune/James J Nedumpara, *International Economic Law: Text, Cases and Materials* (CUP 2021), at 3f. For a fascinating case-study see: William Dalrymple, *The Anarchy: The East India Company, Corporate Violence and the Pillage of an Empire* (Bloomsbury 2019).

remains ignored by many authoritarian governments in many UN member states as well as in many intergovernmental institutions like the International Monetary Fund (IMF), the World Bank and the World Trade Organization (WTO). From a normative citizen perspective, challenging socially unjust government and business practices (like the fact that so many billionaires pay hardly any taxes) must be a central part of teaching IEL. The human rights and environmental litigation for holding governments and business accountable for abuses of public and private power (like pollution) confirms the practical relevance of IEL approaches focusing on civil societies as democratic principal of government agents with limited, delegated powers. Without empowerment of civil societies and of democratic and judicial institutions, the central regulatory challenge of IEL and sustainable development – ie the ubiquity of market failures and governance failures – cannot be effectively addressed.

The regulatory challenges of IEL constantly change in response to technological, environmental and political changes and global governance crises (like financial and migration crises, geopolitical rivalries, 'green' and 'digital revolutions'). Hence, no textbook of IEL can offer a 'complete overview' of all areas of IEL. Their selection of IEL subjects is influenced by their often diverse, methodological premises such as

- intergovernmentalism (eg enhancing national interests through intergovernmental negotiations);
- functionalism (eg promoting national interests though multilevel governance in international organizations protecting transnational public goods);
- constitutionalism (eg democratic self-limitation of policy discretion by rights of citizens, rules and institutions of a higher legal rank); and
- 'law and economics' (eg promoting economic efficiency of law and governance).

The methodological choices often entail prioritization of diverse values and regulatory approaches like using 'intergovernmental alliances' and 'functional spillovers' (eg in China's bilateral 'Belt and Road networks') rather than markets as citizen-driven information, coordination and sanctioning mechanisms. In order to avoid getting lost in the jungle of multilevel economic regulation and economic transactions at national, regional and worldwide levels of governance, teaching IEL should focus on both (II) regulatory challenges common to all countries in order to realize their universally agreed 'sustainable development goals' (SDGs); (III) the regulatory diversity among national and regional IEL traditions; and (IV) on policy lessons from the historical evolution of IEL and from the close interrelationships between economic, political, legal and social orders.

II What Is International Economic Law? What Are Its Objectives and Regulatory Challenges?

Textbooks and classes on IEL should clarify (1) how to define IEL; (2) the goals and instruments of economic regulation; and (3) the main regulatory and methodological challenges. Access to – and processing of – all relevant information (eg on tax evasion, cybercrimes, global warming) turns out to remain a major frontier of IEL and of its democratic regulation, notwithstanding information and communication technology (ICT) 'revolutions' and artificial intelligence. A human rights-approach to IEL requires encouraging students to challenge the existing, power-oriented UN and WTO legal practices from the perspectives of their individual conceptions of justice and democratic responsibilities – notwithstanding the fact that the existing 'positive IEL' tends to be construed by most governments as justifying intergovernmental power politics. If law depends on the legal opinions of people and 'justice is the first virtue of social institutions',[3] legal education should be based on theories of justice – also in IEL. Yet, teachers should inform their IEL students about the professional risks which 'human rights advocacy' may entail for professional careers in power-oriented governance and money-driven business institutions. As discussed below, legal systems – including IEL – remain highly imperfect constructs dominated by social, political and economic struggles for power that are too often won by profit-seeking interest groups rather than by advocates for justice and human rights protection.

1 *Diverse Conceptions of International Economic Law*

Since ancient times, the human desire for more, better and a larger variety of goods and services has given rise to trade, division of labor and regulation of markets.[4] This human desire for increasing individual welfare through trade interacts – as illustrated by millennia of feudalism and colonial and imperial conquests – with the human hunger to possess land and natural resources: 'if goods can't cross borders, soldiers will'.[5] International trade and investment agreements (eg among city republics around the Mediterranean Sea) and regulation of currencies, property and commercial contracts have been recorded since ancient times (eg in the Code of Hammurabi ca 1772 BCE). IEL courses

3 John Rawls, *A Theory of Justice* (OUP revised edition 1999), at 3.

4 Cf Philip Coggan, *More: The 10,000 Year Rise of the World Economy* (Profile Books 2020).

5 The quotation reflects the trade and investment agreements and colonial policies since ancient time (eg the practice of the republic of Venice to protect its foreign trading posts by military force, if necessary).

should explain the economic logic underlying IEL. For instance, as market-driven trade and investments depend on stable currencies and responsive market prices, the post-WWII efforts at recreating a multilateral international economic order began with the 1944 Bretton Woods Agreements establishing:

- the IMF for promoting stability and convertibility of national currencies, liberalization of international payments and balance-of-payments assistance; as well as
- the World Bank Group for providing financial assistance for the reconstruction of war-torn countries and development assistance for less-developed countries.

Following the US Congress' refusal to ratify the 1948 Havana Charter for an International Trade Organization, GATT 1947 provided the legal basis for the progressive liberalization of tariffs, regulation of non-tariff trade barriers, multilateral dispute settlement procedures and eight 'GATT Rounds' of multilateral trade negotiations extending trade liberalization and trade regulation to additional barriers for trade in goods, services, trade-related investments and intellectual property rights. The international monetary, financial and trade agreements were supplemented by the UN legal system based on the 1945 UN Charter and 15 UN Specialized Agencies, eg for liberalization of international air transports, maritime transports, postal services, telecommunications services, health and tourism services, educational, scientific and cultural cooperation, agricultural and industrial cooperation, and intellectual property rights. The UN also provided institutional frameworks for negotiating hundreds of additional multilateral agreements (like the 1982 UNCLOS and international commodity agreements) and institutions (like the 1964 UN Conference on Trade and Development: UNCTAD) for regulating and monitoring particular areas of international economic relations.

There are two central path-dependent fields of IEL: (1) private commercial law (based on national private law and conflict-of-law rules, and international agreements that coordinate contract law principles and provide for mutual recognition and enforcement of commercial arbitration), and (2) international public law (based on treaties, customary law and generally recognized principles of law). These fields were progressively supplemented by (3) multilevel economic regulation (eg multilevel cooperation among national and international monetary and competition authorities inside the EU, the International Competition Policy Network) that coordinate and implement agreed economic policies; (4) global administrative law conceptions that emphasize the legal constraints of international economic organizations by constitutional law principles like transparent policy-making, conferral of limited powers, legal and judicial accountability; and (5) regional constitutional approaches to economic regulation based on common market freedoms, fundamental rights, multilevel parliamentary control and multilevel judicial protection of transnational rule-of-law, national and regional constitutional rights, human rights and economic courts.[6] New regulatory challenges (like the 'green' and 'digital revolutions' aimed at decarbonizing and digitalizing the global economy) give rise to the emergence of new fields of IEL (like electronic commerce, governance of the internet and the use of artificial intelligence, or the commercial use of outer space). Different textbooks draw different borderlines of IEL, for instance regarding labor and business law, HRL, environmental law, air and space law.

Many regulatory challenges of IEL (such as protection of human and intellectual property rights in IEL, WTO appellate review, investment arbitration, social inequalities) remain contested. Teaching IEL should enable students to understand why the regulatory approaches to IEL continue to differ and to coexist. One explanation relates to the diversity of values pursued by private and public economic actors like:

- *private autonomy* advocated by private traders, producers and investors, as illustrated by the pursuit of utility-and profit-maximization strategies of commercial companies and rent-seeking industries;
- *public autonomy* ('sovereignty', power, policy discretion) advocated by governments representing states even if the same governments often threaten the autonomy of other governments by international power politics;
- *economic efficiency* and consumer welfare emphasized by consumers;
- *democratic input-legitimacy* of governments and regulation emphasized by citizens and their democratic institutions (eg challenging the legitimacy of allowing military rulers to represent states like Myanmar);
- *republican output-legitimacy* emphasized by counter-majoritarian, republican institutions (like central banks, competition, health, environmental and other regulatory agencies, international organizations); or
- *transnational rule of law* and equal individual rights protected by national and international courts of justice.

This fact of legal pluralism underlying IEL reflects the reality of political disagreements on whether law and governance need to be justified vis-à-vis citizens by prioritizing private autonomy (eg human rights), public autonomy (eg democratic governance, representative and deliberative democracy), social

6 On these five competing conceptions of IEL and the need for their integration see Ernst Ulrich Petersmann, *International Economic Law in the 21st Century. Constitutional Pluralism and Multilevel Governance of Interdependent Public Goods* (Hart Publishing 2012), 78ff.

responsibilities (eg limiting abuses of public and private power), or authoritarian power politics (eg prioritizing 'law and order'). For instance, the UN Charter prioritizes 'sovereign equality' of member states and veto powers of the five victorious powers in WWII; UN HRL prioritizes individual and democratic self-determination as 'inalienable' rights; and the 2015 UN Sustainable Development Agenda aims at reconciling protection of private and public autonomy of individuals (human rights) and of peoples (democracy) with sovereign equality of states and human rights-oriented SDGs, including also democratic governance, access to justice and rule-of-law.

2 *Changing Functions, Structures and Regulatory Paradigms of IEL*

If 'justice is the first virtue of social institutions' and of social sciences (like law, economics and politics) as distinguished from the search for objective truth in the natural sciences studying physical, chemical or biological facts, this raises the question: What kind of 'basic structures' of IEL, of law-making, and of procedural and substantive 'principles of justice' does justice require? How to reconcile justice for states, people, and for all men, women and children? Does the 'Anthropocene' require also 'justice for animals and other natural organisms' since human 'rule of law' interacts inevitably with 'the rule of nature' (as manifested through climate change), and considering that the interactions between law and nature require duties of care?

Procedural, constitutional, distributive, corrective, commutative principles of justice and equity for justifying 'basic structures' of legal systems are much older than the post-1945 universal recognition of 'inalienable' human and democratic rights and modern conceptions of 'justice as economic efficiency' in a world of scarce resources. The 'embedded liberalism compromise' underlying UN law (eg UN HRL) and WTO law protects national sovereignty and legitimate diversity of national legal, political and economic systems.[7] The EU's multilevel democratic constitutionalism extends nationally agreed 'constitutional principles of justice' to the EU's common market and to multilevel governance of transnational public goods (PGs). In September 2015, 170 heads of governments adopted the UN 2030 Agenda for Sustainable Development specifying 17 SDGs and 169 policy targets as an integrated framework for guiding national and global development actions up to 2030. In contrast to the Millennium Development Goals adopted by the UN in 2000, the 2030 Agenda is grounded more in HRL as a means for 'localizing' sustainable development.

---

7 For a discussion of the historical evolution of 'embedded liberalism' and the need for its 'greening' see Ernst Ulrich Petersmann, *Transforming World Trade and Investment Law for Sustainable Development* (OUP 2022), chapters 3 and 8.

Almost all of the 17 SDGs relate to human rights values like ending poverty in all its forms everywhere (SDG 1); ending hunger and achieving food security (SDG 2); ensuring healthy lives (SDG 3) and inclusive, equitable quality education (SDG 4); achieving gender equality (SDG 5); availability of water and sanitation for all (SDG 6); access to affordable and sustainable energy for all (SDG 7); promoting economic growth and decent work for all (SDG 8); sustainable industrialization (SDG 9); reducing inequality within and among countries (SDG 10) and promoting sustainable development (SDGs 11–17), including combatting climate change (SDG 13) and promoting peaceful societies with access to justice and accountable, inclusive institutions for all (SDG 16). The SDGs 'seek to realize the human rights of all' and 'balance the three dimensions of sustainable development: the economic, social and environmental'.[8] The Agenda describes itself as being

> guided by the purposes and principles of the Charter of the United Nations, including full respect for international law. It is grounded in the Universal Declaration of Human Rights, in international human rights treaties, the Millennium Declaration and the 2005 World Summit Outcome.[9]

Arguably, the universal endorsement of the 2030 Agenda is relevant legal context also for interpreting and implementing the WTO 'sustainable development' commitments. Teaching IEL should prompt students to discuss the impact of the UN human and labor rights systems and of the SDGs on interpreting and developing IEL. The UN Guiding Principles for Business and Human Rights, as endorsed by the UN Human Rights Council on 16 June 2011 and increasingly invoked in litigation on 'corporate responsibilities' (eg to reduce the carbon emissions of oil companies like Shell), confirm

- *state duties* to protect against human rights abuses by third parties, including business, through appropriate policies, regulation and adjudication;

8 United Nations, *Transforming our World: the 2030 Sustainable Development Agenda*, UN General Assembly Resolution A/RES/70/1 of 25 September 2015.

9 UN Resolution A/RES/70/1 (n 8), para. 10. On interpreting 'sustainable development' commitments in conformity with HRL in the sense of A Sen's 'development as freedom' protecting basic needs and human capacities for individual and social self-development see Petersmann (2012), at 190, 340, 374ff.

- *corporate responsibilities* to respect human rights, which means to avoid infringing on the rights of others and to address adverse impacts with which a business is involved; and the need for
- *access to effective remedies for rights-holders* when abuse has occurred, through both judicial and non-judicial grievance mechanisms.[10]

IEL students must be taught why financial and debt crises, climate change, global health pandemics and geopolitical rivalries focusing on 'friends or enemies' are undermining the neo-liberal, business-driven economic order. Likewise, 'executive emergency governance' without effective parliamentary and judicial controls threatens democracy, rule of law, human rights and the realization of the SDGs, as illustrated by US President Trump's abuses of executive powers and 'national security exceptions' (like Section 301 of the US trade legislation) for starting discriminatory trade wars against China and NATO allies, disrupting multilateral treaty systems, rejecting democratic election results and fighting political critics as enemies of his 'republican creed'.[11] It is often only by incorporating the non-binding UN Resolutions on SDGs into domestic legal systems and treaty obligations like the 2015 Paris Agreement on Climate Change Mitigation and free trade agreements (eg FTAs of the EU) that the SDGs can actually change the dialectic tensions between normative orders (based on agreed rules, principles and institutions recognized as law and social facts) and subjective legal claims, practices and politics dominating legal practices. Can – and should – this 'politics of legal systems' be limited by 'constitutional restraints' based on 'pre-commitments' to constitutional rules, 'principles of justice' and institutions of a higher legal rank constraining abuses of legislative, executive, judicial, non-governmental and private powers (eg in IEL), as it has been successfully realized in European economic integration law since the 1950s?[12] Why is it that the 'Washington consensus' for a neo-liberal

10 Cf. *Guiding Principles on Business and Human Rights. Implementing the UN 'Respect, Protect and Remedy' Framework* (UN 2011).

11 IEL courses should also discuss the obvious similarities between the politics of former US President Donald Trump and Carl Schmitt's justification, in the 1930s, of 'charismatic legitimacy' of authoritarian leaders abusing 'emergency powers' and anti-liberal, ethnic 'identity politics', perceiving politics as existential struggles between 'friends and foes', contesting the legitimacy of their 'political enemies', rejecting courts as 'defenders of the Constitution', defending illiberal cultures and undermining democratic constitutionalism by 'political religions' justifying 'big lies' (eg about democratic election results); cf Ellen Kennedy, *Constitutional Failure. Carl Schmitt in Weimar* (Duke University Press 2004); Ernst Ulrich Petersmann, The 2018 Trade Wars as a Threat to the World Trading System and to Constitutional Democracies, in: *Trade, Law and Development* X (2018), 179–225.

12 Cf Ernst Ulrich Petersmann, *Multilevel Constitutionalism for Multilevel Governance of Public Goods – Methodology Problems in International Law* (Hart Publishing 2017).

design of the international economic order has become progressively challenged by a more human rights-based 'Geneva consensus',[13] as it is confirmed in the universally agreed 2015 UN Sustainable Development Agenda? Will the 'new nationalism' (as illustrated by the 'Brexit', the disruption of multilateral treaties by former US President Trump, and Russia's imperial wars) and the rise in authoritarian governments undermine democracies and lead to a new 'geopolitical economic order' characterized by bilateral power politics (eg in the trade wars initiated by former US President Trump and by China)? Will the collective countermeasures against Russia's wars of aggression and China's threats of military aggression against WTO members (like Taiwan) lead to a second 'deglobalisation' similar to the first deglobalisation provoked by World Wars I and II and the great depression during the 1930s?

3 *Regulatory and Methodological Challenges*

Constitutional and institutional economics and public choice theories explain the failures of IEL (eg to protect human rights and related SDGs) in terms of 'market failures', 'governance failures' and 'constitutional failures' of multilevel governance of PGs.[14] The predominance of intergovernmental power politics and of insufficient democratic and judicial remedies inside worldwide and many regional organizations reflects prioritization of 'state sovereignty' and disregard for human rights inside many UN member states. Since the 1950s, European integration law demonstrated how 'constitutional approaches' to IEL can transform intergovernmental power politics and periodic wars – as they devastated the welfare of European citizens during centuries – into mutually beneficial economic, political, social and legal cooperation promoting more than 70 years of 'democratic peace' among EU member states. The interactions between economic, political, social and legal orders – and the need for 'constitutionalizing' foreign policies in order to better protect the SDGs – should be a central part of teaching IEL. For example, students of IEL should understand why democratic struggles for input-legitimacy and republican output-legitimacy of IEL are driven by 'constitutional insights' that 'state duties' must be legally defined in terms of equal rights and judicial remedies of all citizens rather than in terms of policy discretion of rulers. By focusing on reasonable self-interests and common rights of citizens rather than on conflicting 'state interests', the SDGs can promote cooperation and 'democratic peace'.

13 Cf Pascal Lamy, *The Geneva Consensus. Making Trade Work for All* (CUP 2013). Already before the neo-liberal politics by UK Prime Minister Thatcher and US President Reagan, US trade policies insisted on numerous exceptions and 'waivers' from GATT 1947.

14 Cf Petersmann (n 7), chapter 4.

The 2019 'Sustainable Development Goals Report' identified climate change (the need to cut 'record-high greenhouse gas emissions now' so as to prevent displacement of up to 140 million people by 2050) and 'increasing inequality among and within countries' as the two most challenging issues of our time.[15] Intensifying climate-, health-, migration-and social crises are prompting ever more governments to resort to executive 'emergency governance', for example by imposing 'lockdowns' aimed at reducing Covid-19 infections. Did the collapse of the health infrastructures in India's capital New Delhi in response to India's more than 400'000 daily Covid-19 infections in May 2021 confirm the prediction by Peter Drahos that the authoritarian Chinese government might be better capable of 'survival governance' and of decarbonizing national economies than democratic countries?[16] Can 'survival governance' justify empowering totalitarian rulers to disregard human rights and democratic governance (eg by abusing facial recognition technologies for 'smart cities' in China)? Does the US destruction of the WTO dispute settlement system undermine the rule-of-law objectives of the SDGs? What are the lessons from the historical experiences that empowerment of dictatorial regimes has led to economic misery and famines, genocides, military aggressions, and disregard for human rights time and again?

Law as a democratic self-restraint on human freedom reflects the psychological insight that human beings act like social animals – in their private as well as public lives – out of a mix of unconscious instincts, senses, passions, rational self-interests, morality and reasonableness. Hence, understanding legal, economic, political and social interactions requires combining (1) *rules-based legal* with (2) *utilitarian economic*, (3) *power-oriented political*, (4) *ethical communitarian* and (5) *natural science* methodologies in addition to (6) philosophical and psychological theories of justice.[17] All human societies use 'rule by law' for ordering civil, political, economic, social and cultural cooperation. Constitutional limitations of rulers by 'rule of law', however, depend on 'struggles for justice' and remain contested in the 'politics of law'. The interactions among local and national societies, economies, polities and legal systems vary

15 *The Sustainable Development Goals Report 2019* (UN 2019), 3, 42, 48.

16 Cf. Peter Drahos, *Survival Governance: Energy and Climate Change in the Chinese Century* (OUP 2021).

17 This relates to the distinction between four basic forms of human regulatory systems that engage with the practical and moral senses of the regulated human beings: legal (hierarchical), social (self-regulatory), economic (market) and technological (architectural). See Lawrence Lessig, *Code: Version 2.0* (Basic Books 2006). This work has been criticized, however, for neglecting genetic, geo-and climate-engineering technologies that are closer to natural regulatory systems than to intentional human regulation.

among countries depending on their democratic preferences and political and legal cultures. The history of colonialism, slave trade and imperial conquests illustrates how the evolution of IEL was also shaped by power politics. It is thanks to democratic and anti-colonial struggles that, today, 'positive law' tends to be defined not only by (1) 'primary rules of conduct' and (2) 'secondary rules of recognition, change and adjudication', but also includes (3) ever larger numbers of constitutional and human rights protecting 'principles of justice' and SDGs as integral parts of legislation and 'secondary law' adopted by administrative, regulatory or judicial institutions.[18] Path-dependent legal positivism continues being challenged by human rights and democratic revolutions resulting in social challenges of power-oriented international law practices and of social injustices (eg regarding the unequal distribution of power, money and social welfare inside and among states). IEL students should be taught why normative *legal orders* reflecting the 'public reason' and rationality of their legal subjects and governments dynamically evolve through politicized *legal practices* and 'dynamic interpretations' of indeterminate rules and principles. This occurs, for instance, where citizens, governments or courts of justice invoke – as in the case of the SDGs and related climate litigation – human rights for justifying 'new interpretations' or citizen-oriented rules in order to respond to abuses of public and private power. In addition, regional economic integration law also confirms the empirical fact that democratic constitutionalism has been comparatively more successful in 'institutionalizing public reason' and maintaining 'democratic, peaceful cooperation' than authoritarian power politics (eg prior to World Wars I and II, in postwar politics among Eurasian countries).

'Critical legal positivism' acknowledges this 'dual nature' of modern legal systems, which include 'inalienable' human rights and 'principles of justice' that empower citizens to resist unjust legal practices and path-dependent rules of positive law.[19] Due to the constant tensions between reason and will (power), and the interactions between the surface level of positive law and the sub-surface level of legal and political cultures and social psychologies (or pathologies) influencing law-making and adjudication of legal rules and principles, positive IEL constantly interacts with institutionally framed *legal practices* shaped by political cultures, politics, self-interests and the will (power) of legal actors. Together, the *legal orders* and the *legal practices* constitute *legal systems* developing in response to dialectic interactions between law (reason,

18 For details see Petersmann (n 12), 59ff.

19 Cf Robert Alexy, *The Argument from Injustice: Reply to Legal Positivism* (Clarendon Press 2002); Karlo Tuori, *Critical Legal Positivism* (Routledge 2016).

rationality) and practices (political choices, psychology).[20] Conceptions of today's 'IEL system' remain highly contested. Teaching IEL cannot be 'neutral' in a world of vast social inequalities and injustices (like tax evasion by multinational companies) vis-à-vis billions of poor people. If the young generation of today does not succeed in changing IEL by 'institutionalizing public reason', environmental, health and governance crises risk destroying the human welfare of billions of people.

III Diversity of National and Regional Approaches to IEL

The emergence of world order treaties depends on either hegemonic leadership (eg by the USA for the UN and Bretton Woods legal systems) or on treaty provisions reconciling the diverse national and regional interests of countries with their common global interests (eg the WTO provisions protecting national sovereignty, regional free trade areas and customs unions, special and differential treatment of less-developed countries). In the 21st century, the coexistence of Anglo-Saxon neo-liberalism (as illustrated by the 'Brexit' and US disregard for WTO law), authoritarian state-capitalism (eg in China and many formerly communist countries), ordo-liberal European economic constitutionalism (notably in the EU and the European Economic Area: EEA) and diverse 'third world conceptions' of economic regulation, transforms the post-1945 neo-liberal Bretton Woods system into a new 'geo-economic security order' with politically motivated economic sanctions disrupting multilateral treaty systems (eg the WTO dispute settlement system).[21] The political domination of 'GATT politics' (1948–1994) by what was called the 'Quad' (ie the USA, the EU, Japan and Canada) has become replaced by geopolitical power rivalries among WTO members prioritizing diverse values like hegemonic neo-liberalism (eg dominating the money-and market-driven 'Washington consensus' on interest-group driven trade policies), authoritarianism (eg prioritizing power monopolies in 'one political party states' like China), multilevel economic constitutionalism (eg in the EU prioritizing human, constitutional, common market rights and social rights of EU citizens) or 'UN political idealism' without effective implementation inside many UN member states (eg disregard for UN HRL in many non-democratic countries in Africa, Asia and Latin America). The 'UN politics' was reflected also in the joint statement of the heads of the

20 For this dialectic conception of legal systems and IEL see Petersmann (n 7), chapters 2.1 and 3.

21 Cf. Petersmann (n 7), chapter 3.

IMF, the World Bank, the World Health Organization (WHO) and the WTO of 1 June 2021 on 'A new commitment for vaccine equity and defeating the pandemic', which called for a 'coordinated strategy ... to vaccinate the world' based on (1) financing the COVAX global vaccine access programme; (2) investments into vaccine production capacity; and (3) calling for accelerated negotiations for a 'pragmatic solution around intellectual property'. This occurred without reference to human rights and the anti-competitive distortions of business-driven, pharmaceutical patent protection.[22]

The regional and functionally limited 'human rights constitution', 'common market constitution', incomplete monetary constitution and 'foreign policy constitution' of the EU and its member countries have embedded national, democratic constitutionalism and intergovernmental cooperation into multilevel constitutionalism, which offers unique protection of civil, political, economic, social and cultural rights that EU citizens never enjoyed before on this European scale.[23] The EU's 'New Green Deal' (2019) and European climate legislation (2021), the EU's leadership in the Covid-19 health pandemic for securing access to vaccines inside and outside the EU, the EU's 'Recovery and Resilience Facility' and 'Next Generation EU investment program' financed through EU loans/bonds of up to €750 bn (2020/21), and the EU's digital economy, digital common market legislation and global reach of regulatory standards (eg for chemical industry standards), illustrate how European economic constitutionalism has enabled the EU countries to respond more effectively to global environmental, health and governance crises and regulatory challenges (like climate change, the 'digital revolution') than other regional economic communities in Africa, Asia and the Americas. Yet, the business-driven focus – in the 2022 US Inflation Reduction Act – on investing more than $370 bn for decarbonizing the economy may ultimately prove more effective for climate change mitigation than Europe's environmental constitutionalism and related climate litigation.

Comparing national and regional economic integration systems should be an integral part of teaching IEL in order to explain why some legal and economic systems have led to famines and economic poverty (eg in communist

22 Cf the criticism by Diane A Desierto, The IMF, WTO, World Bank, and WHO all come around? Multilateral Unity Against Inequitable Global COVID Vaccine Distribution, but still without Human Rights, in *EJIL Talk* of 3 June 2021. On the distortions of health governance by business-driven interest group politics and the shortcomings of the patent system for responding to global health pandemics see: Drahos (n 1), at 7: 'the patent system itself has become a source of pandemic risk'.

23 Cf Karlo Tuori, *European Constitutionalism* (CUP 2015); Petersmann (n 7), chapter 5.5.

China before its progressive economic liberalization since 1978) and fail to protect human rights and the SDGs. The constitutional values underlying national and regional systems often explain their 'public choices' of diverse economic policy instruments. For instance, industrialized democracies protect patent systems for pharmaceutical products as incentives for decentralized research and protection of private property rights, national health and industrial interests, with populations capable of paying high prices for patented pharmaceutical products. But patent protection for pharmaceuticals may be less appropriate for less-developed, low-income countries, notably in global health pandemics where public health requires providing vaccines to everybody everywhere. Globalization (eg of health pandemics and climate change) requires multilevel governance of PGs responding to the diverse 'collective action problems' of diverse kinds of PGs, for instance by international stock-piling of scarce resources and emergency aid and national promotion of manufacturing know-how for generic medicines (eg in Brazil and India).[24] IEL courses should compare and explain the law, regulatory instruments and practices of the 15 UN Specialized Agencies in order to help students understand why only some of them (like the WHO, ILO, FAO, UNESCO) are based on 'constitutions' (*sic*) that commit member states to the protection of human rights (like health rights, labor rights, rights to food and education) and provide for inclusive forms of multilevel governance (like the 'tripartite' composition of ILO bodies by government, worker and employer representatives). IEL students should know why the GATT/WTO legal system continues being deliberately kept out of the more politicized UN legal system.

Contrary to the post-1945 'cold war' between the economically dysfunctional Soviet Union and Western democracies, the cultural value differences underlying Anglo-Saxon neo-liberalism (eg prioritizing money-driven market mechanisms dominated by the *homo economicus*), authoritarian state-capitalism (eg prioritizing power monopolies of authoritarian governments) and of Europe's ordo-liberal, economic constitutionalism (eg protecting common market rights and constitutional rights of EU citizens) are likely to persist for a long time. In the coming decades, China and India are expected to resume their centuries-old status as the two largest national economies. Hence, the future international economic order is likely to become shaped by 'competing

24 See Petersmann (n 12); Drahos (n 1) at 17f: 'Under the current global patent regime developing countries cannot expect to be given any priority in the times of pandemics' ... 'developing countries should continue to build networks of collaboration among themselves' ... 'Without a manufacturing knowledge base, developing countries will find it hard to escape the deadly consequences of a patent-mediated response to pandemics'.

regionalism' (eg between African, Asian and North-American FTAs, the state-centered bilateralism of China's 'Belt and Road' infrastructure and communication networks, the EU and EEA). The likely decentralization of IEL may require more flexible re-interpretations of the WTO provisions for trade remedies, general and security exceptions, regional and plurilateral agreements, and special and differential treatment for less-developed WTO member countries. IEL courses should invite students to reflect on the impact of the increasing geopolitical rivalries among business-driven Anglo-Saxon neo-liberalism, China's totalitarian state-capitalism and Europe's ordo-liberal, economic constitutionalism on worldwide economic treaties and institutions. For instance, why does the US Biden administration find it politically so difficult to re-commit to the WTO Appellate Body system after its arbitrary destruction by the US Trump administration? Climate change necessitating de-carbonization of the global economy, the 'digital revolution' requiring new regulations of ICT services (eg regarding 'cyber security', data privacy, use of artificial intelligence), global health pandemics requiring global supply of vaccines, and the realization of other SDGs and related PGs illustrate the need for IEL courses to explore new fields of IEL and their impact on the existing UN and WTO legal systems.

IV The Historical Evolution of IEL: Policy Lessons?

IEL textbooks and seminars should explore also 'foundational problems' of IEL like (1) the changing paradigms of 'embedded liberalism' underlying IEL, (2) 'law and economics', and (3) human rights dimensions of IEL. What are their policy lessons for the 2030 UN Agenda for 'transforming our world' in order to realize the citizen-oriented SDGs and related PGs like 'digitalization', 'de-carbonization' and 'humanization' of the global economy?

1 *Need for Adjusting 'Embedded Liberalism'?*

Trade liberalization before World War I reflected 'dis-embedded liberalism' based on *laissez faire*-attitudes in most countries vis-à-vis the social adjustment problems created by colonialism, the first industrial revolution (based on machines driven by steam power) and by the first 'imperial globalization' during the second half of the 19th century. The post-war second industrial revolution (based on mass assembly line production driven by electricity) was embedded into domestic economic regulation, competition and social policies in most industrialized countries, notwithstanding the 'social dis-embedding' resulting from the global financial crises and economic disintegration since

1929. The 'embedded liberalism'[25] underlying GATT 1947 *acknowledged* sovereign rights to regulate 'market failures', related 'governance failures' and constitutional problems. It further also *enabled* and *promoted* welfare states through reciprocal trade liberalization that enhanced mutually beneficial division of labour and economic and legal cooperation in producing private and public goods.

WTO law responded to the third industrial revolution of computers and telecommunications by additional, multilateral harmonization of product and production standards, competition and trade remedy rules, liberalization and regulation of services trade, protection of intellectual property rights, and of transnational rule of law through compulsory jurisdiction for the settlement of trade disputes through domestic judicial remedies and WTO dispute settlement procedures. WTO law changed the embedded liberalism underlying GATT 1947 in ways reflecting both neo-liberal Anglo-Saxon interest-group politics (eg resulting in the WTO Anti-dumping and TRIPS Agreements),[26] and ordo-liberal insistence on rule compliance (eg through the compulsory jurisdiction of the WTO dispute settlement system and the (quasi)automatic adoption of more than 420 WTO panel, appellate and arbitration reports). WTO law also promoted non-discriminatory conditions of competition (as reflected by the non-discrimination and 'necessity' requirements in the WTO Agreements on technical barriers to trade and (phyto)sanitary standards, and the phasing-out of the Agreement on Textiles and Clothing), and 'sustainable development' commitments. Compared with the 'provisional application', lack of parliamentary ratification and 'grandfather exceptions' of the intergovernmental GATT 1947, the WTO Agreement strengthened the 'constitutional dimensions' of WTO law, as illustrated by parliamentary approvals of the WTO Agreement, its incorporation into the domestic legal systems of many WTO members, the separation of legislative, administrative and judicial powers of WTO institutions (*cf.* Article III WTO Agreement), provisions for majority voting (cf Article IX)

---

25 Cf John G Ruggie, International regimes, transactions and change: Embedded liberalism in the postwar economic order, in: *International Organization* 36 (1982), 379–415; Ernst Ulrich Petersmann, Neo-liberalism, Ordo-liberalism and the Future of Economic Governance, in: *Journal of International Economic Law* 26 (2023), issue 4.

26 The inconsistencies of anti-dumping laws and practices with non-discriminatory competition rules are widely recognized; they prevented WTO negotiators from agreeing on a Preamble text explaining the economic rationale of the WTO Anti-dumping Agreement. Many competition lawyers express concerns that some anti-dumping and TRIPS rules – whose drafting was dominated by industry lobbyists – offer too much protection stifling competition and innovation. See, for example, Hanns Ullrich *et alii*, eds, *TRIPS Plus 20. From Trade Rules to Market Principles*, Springer, 2016.

and for domestic implementation of WTO rules (Article XVI.4), and the compulsory WTO dispute settlement system.

The progressive adjustment of the 'embedded liberalism' underlying GATT/WTO law – to the emergence of social welfare states,[27] decolonization,[28] European economic integration,[29] and to China's WTO membership subject to 'WTO plus commitments' incorporated into WTO law through China's Accession Protocol – needs to be continued in order to render WTO law consistent with the regulatory challenges of globalization, climate change and other SDGs. The insufficient WTO competition and environmental rules entail that the prices of many internationally traded goods do not reflect their social costs so that the welfare effects of WTO rules are largely unknown. The macroeconomic Kaldor-Hicks-justification of WTO rules reflects also utilitarian cost-benefit analyses, which are often abused for neglecting market failures (like pollution costs, social inequalities) and alternative definitions of welfare (eg by 'constitutional economics' focusing on informed, voluntary consent to Pareto-efficient rules like equal freedoms and human rights enabling individuals to develop their 'human capacities'). WTO law does not explicitly refer to climate change. Decisions on greenhouse gas (GHG) emission reductions have to be coordinated in the specialized UN bodies (like the UN Framework Convention on Climate Change: UNFCCC, the International Maritime Organization, or the International Civil Aviation Organization), as well as regional and national institutions outside the WTO. Yet, trade and climate rules inevitably interact and must remain consistent and mutually supportive.

The 2015 Paris Agreement on climate change mitigation entered into force in November 2016, and was ratified by 190 Parties (2021). 182 countries plus the EU notified their 'nationally determined contributions' (NDCs) by 2019. These voluntary contributions to reduce GHGs differ enormously and remain insufficient. President Trump's withdrawal of the USA – as the largest economy and second-largest emitter of GHGs – from the Agreement entailed that, during the UN climate conference in Madrid in December 2019 focusing on 'carbon market systems', other major emitters of GHGs (like China, India, Australia) avoided committing to ambitious limitations of GHGs. In January 2021, US

---

27 Eg by providing for GATT-consistency of social policies under Articles III, XVI, XIX, XX GATT.

28 Eg by providing in GATT Article XXVI:5,c for easy transition from 'dependent' to 'independent' GATT membership, Part IV GATT on 'Trade and Development', 'special and differential treatment' provided for in many WTO provisions.

29 Eg by recognizing sovereign rights to form customs unions and admitting EU membership in the WTO.

President Biden recommitted the USA to join the Paris Agreement and to transform the US into a carbon-neutral economy by 2050. Yet, the lack of effective legal disciplines for NDCs, for the WTO-consistent application of 'climate change mitigation measures' or, in case of inconsistencies with WTO law, for WTO exemptions (eg 'waivers' granted by the WTO Ministerial Conference), WTO surveillance measures (eg by the WTO Trade Policy Review Mechanism) and for mutually consistent dispute settlement procedures (eg in the context of the UNFCCC and the WTO), risk provoking legal conflicts between WTO rules and climate mitigation policies. It remains uncertain whether WTO members can agree on a 'peace clause' for climate actions, or on how to determine the 'likeness' of competing products based on the amount of carbons used in producing them, and on standards for calculating 'carbon border adjustments measures' (CBAMs like border tax adjustments) on the basis of carbon use, carbon emissions, agreed carbon prices and an agreed framework for emissions trading. The 2022 WTO Agreement on limitation of fishery subsidies will have to be followed by, *inter alia*, WTO negotiations on limiting fossil fuel subsidies, non-discriminatory CBAMs and emission trading systems aimed at reducing GHG emissions.[30] IEL courses should teach students the regulatory challenges of de-carbonizing the global economy by 2050, for instance why CBAMs will be necessary so as to (1) increase carbon prices, (2) reduce carbon emissions, (3) prevent 'carbon leakage', (4) induce polluting industries (like steel, aluminum, cement, plastics, aviation, maritime and road transports) and 'free-riding countries' to participate in climate mitigation (eg by waiving CBAMs among members of the same 'carbon club'), and (5) maintain non-discriminatory conditions of competition ('trade neutrality').

The needed adaptations of WTO rules are facilitated by the 'systemic interpretation requirement' of customary international law (as codified in Article 31.3(c) VCLT) and by the compulsory WTO dispute settlement system. These both call for clarification of the WTO's sustainable development objectives in conformity with the 17 SDGs accepted by UN member states. The 2030 Agenda for Sustainable Development aims at implementing its 17 SDGs (like overcoming poverty, hunger and global warming, protecting health, education, gender equality, access to water, sanitation and clean energy, urbanization, the environment, human rights and social justice) by 'localizing the SDGs' so as to empower local institutions, actors and civil society support. As the SDGs aim at reconciling 'climate mitigation measures' with other sustainable development

30 For details see: James Munro, *Emission Trading Schemes under International Economic Law* (OUP 2018); Petersmann (n 7), chapter 9.3.

objectives (like poverty reduction, sustainable agriculture, sustainable use of marine resources and terrestrial ecosystems) and with trade rules, they may offer 'relevant context' for interpreting WTO rules, for 'balancing' competing policy measures, for evaluating NDCs under the Paris Agreement, and for citizen-oriented WTO governance reforms. This is confirmed by the recent climate litigation against governments and oil companies (like the Anglo-Dutch Shell company) which prompts national courts (eg in Germany, France and the Netherlands) to hold governments and corporations accountable for reducing carbon dioxide emissions and recognizing human and constitutional rights to protection of the environment.[31] The SDGs and related 'social corporate responsibilities' are also influencing investor-state arbitration (eg under the Energy Charter Treaty) and related constitutional concerns that the 'outsourcing' of investor-states disputes to commercial arbitrators risks undermining the public law dimensions of such investment disputes. The US disruption of the WTO dispute settlement system also disrupts compliance with WTO law. It enhances the risks of future 'trade wars' caused by unilateral introduction of CBAMs and related disputes.

2 *IEL and Economics: 'Enlightenment Now'?*

Many areas of IEL (like trade and competition laws) are strongly influenced by economics like the 'theory of optimal intervention'. This justifies GATT's legal ranking of alternative trade policy instruments and subsidies in terms of their economic efficiency to promote mutually welfare-enhancing legal harmonization which reduces transaction costs and political conflicts without limiting national sovereignty over non-discriminatory domestic regulation of the economy and polity. IEL cannot be understood without good knowledge of economics. Yet, some politicians (like former US President Trump) and 'critical legal theorists' refuse to engage with economic theories (eg on why trade has been instrumental for lifting billions of people out of poverty over the past decades), for instance based on their mercantilist beliefs, self-interests or claims that the correctness of economists' models always 'depends on a number of assumptions not directly addressed in them'.[32] The claim of 'critical legal

31 Cf Petersmann (n 7), chapter 9.3.

32 Martti Koskenniemi, International Law and the Far Right: Reflections on Law and Cynicism (Asser Institute 2020), at 17. According to Koskenniemi, 'the cynicism of the "system" lies in its insufficient scepticism' (at 31). Yet Koskenniemi's radical skepticism about values and reform proposals – apart from pleading for 'truthfulness' and emancipation – can also be seen as a refusal to clarify public reason and change harmful practices by engaging with the social and natural sciences underlying the SDGs.

theories' (eg as represented by Koskenniemi) 'that law is incapable of providing convincing justifications to the solution of normative problems',[33] cannot be derived from descriptions of 'the politics of indeterminate international law' transforming lawyers into moralists, nor from Koskenniemi's critique of liberalism, human rights and economics:[34]

- The ethical commitment (eg underlying UN HRL, the 17 SDGs and their 169 agreed policy targets) to inclusive reasoning, humanism and emancipation requires refining ('falsifying') our understanding of the world through evidence-based science (eg open debates with 'conjectures and refutations' as explained by K. Popper) which accept our cosmopolitan responsibilities for 'transforming our world' in order to realize the agreed SDGs. The past technological, economic and 'human rights revolutions' enabled progress in realizing the American revolutionary ideals of 'life, liberty and pursuit of happiness' and the French revolutionary ideals of '*liberté, égalité et fraternité*'. The remaining social injustices (like unequal distribution of power and wealth) are reminders of the imperfections of all political and legal struggles.
- Empirical evidence confirms that democratic constitutionalism, deliberative democracy and 'institutionalization of public reason' (eg in independent regulatory agencies like central banks, competition, public health and environmental agencies) not only enable, but also require going beyond Koskenniemi's semantic and interpretative

33 Cf Marti Koskenniemi, *From Apology to Utopia. The Structure of International Legal Argument* (CUP 2005), at 69. Koskenniemi's focus on discretionary political decision-making – and his contempt for liberal theories of justice ('the liberals are my enemies') justifying the need for democratic 'institutionalization of public reason' (J. Rawls) and of human rights – resemble the reasoning of Carl Schmitt for political decision-makers in 'exceptional situations'. For a criticism see: Jeff L Dunoff, From Interdisciplinarity to Counterdisciplinarity: Is there Madness in Marti's Method? in *Temple International & Comparative Law Journal* 27 (2013), 309–338.

34 Koskenniemi's emphasis on the open-ended nature of international legal discourse and of the purposes and meaning of legal rules, and his endless criticism of 'false universalism' (like human rights and the fight against impunity which he describes as 'hegemonic maneuvers') present themselves as 'Socratic dialogues' without an academic theory of justice, doctrinal or institutional reform proposals, or practical proposals for improving social justice. Koskenniemi's emphasis on the inescapably situated, contextual and contested nature and politics of legal claims, arguments and related structural biases favouring certain actors and outcomes, and his proposed 'culture of legal formalism' are less about finding 'correct answers' in legal doctrine and professional practices than about protecting adversarial processes of legal argumentation among juridical equals.

'argumentative games' with indeterminate legal rules. Competing legal and social science doctrines may remain controversial. Yet, such controversies can be reduced by democratic, legislative, administrative, judicial and other agreed procedures providing for authoritative decision-making, including multilevel constitutionalism protecting human rights, multilevel governance and third-party adjudication of disputes among member states. If 'entropy, evolution and information' can be identified as the 'enlightenment challenges' of our modern human condition,[35] the SDG of a 'global partnership for sustainable development … with the participation of all countries, all stakeholders and all people' deserves support as a humanitarian 'enlightenment strategy' aimed at reducing social injustices, intergovernmental abuses of power and non-inclusive bad faith governance in authoritarian UN member states.

– Like other social sciences, the history of economic thought has evolved enormously, eg from mercantilist focus on the welfare of rulers and of merchants to welfare economics aimed at maximizing general consumer welfare, and to constitutional economics aimed at protecting 'development as freedom' and empowerment of human capacities. In order to promote the SDGs, lawyers should accept moral responsibilities for criticizing the hegemonic purposes of US neo-liberalism and totalitarian state-capitalism and the status quo bias of intergovernmental power politics. European economic integration law offers empirical evidence for how 'multilevel economic constitutionalism' can promote human rights, social welfare and 'democratic peace' and serve as a model for realizing SDGs also beyond Europe. The acceptance of the compulsory WTO dispute settlement system by China and Russia confirmed that 'constitutional reforms' (like independent

35 Cf Steven Pinker, *Enlightenment Now. The Case for Science, Reason, Humanism and Progress* (Penguin 2018), at 14ff. Entropy (eg disorder in closed systems) can be transformed into more orderly, open systems through evolution and better information: 'for all the flaws in human nature, it contains the seeds of its own improvement, as long as it comes up with norms and institutions that channel parochial interests into universal benefits' (at 28). Ordoliberals emphasize the necessary 'international embedding' of 'competitive orders', the legal construction of international order composed of nation states, 'open societies' and 'open regionalism', 'economic constitutionalism' as a method for decentralizing, dispersing and 'constitutionalizing' power and special interest groups, and multilateral economic agreements as 'second line of constitutional entrenchment' of equal liberties, rule-of-law and non-discriminatory conditions of competition.

third-party adjudication of economic disputes) can successfully constrain intergovernmental power politics.

IEL classes should encourage students to explore why the UN SDGs offer more coherent benchmarks for evaluating economic, environmental and social policy measures than the neo-liberal focus on Kaldor-Hicks efficiency. Should the WTO 'sustainable development' objectives and related WTO exceptions (eg for national health and environmental protection measures) be interpreted in conformity with the universally accepted SDGs for evaluating whether national human rights protection, climate change mitigation measures, 'green subsidies', regulatory restrictions of GHG emissions and other 'NDCs' under the 2015 Paris Agreement are consistent with world trade rules and with the 'proportionality balancing' of competing policy objectives required under Article XX GATT?

3 *Are Human Rights Part of IEL?*

As the reality of 'regulatory competition' is driven by conflicting value preferences, IEL researchers should discuss which values can justify IEL. Adam Smith's formulation of liberal economics in his *Inquiry into the Nature and the Causes of the Wealth of Nations* (1776) was preceded by his *Theory of Moral Sentiments* (1759), in which Smith explored the human nature of seeking mutually beneficial exchanges in social interactions. Smith's justification of mutually beneficial trade by the advantages of specialization and division of labor has been supplemented by numerous additional theories (focusing on 'comparative' rather than 'absolute advantages', accumulation of financial and human capital, scientific inventions, legal preconditions for social welfare states, market competition as decentralized information, coordination and sanctioning mechanisms). The social inequalities inside and among states demonstrate that macro-economic Kaldor-Hicks efficiencies do not ensure social justice: economic markets remain *instruments* (eg for efficient production of goods, services and wages demanded by consumers and workers) in order to enable people to pursue also non-market goals like social well-being and PGs. As globalization promotes interdependencies, governments increasingly emphasize the need for diversifying or 'de-risking' global supply chains and for balancing efficiency gains against 'strategic vulnerabilities' enhanced by globalization (eg due to concentration of production of rare earth materials in China) and 'weaponization' of energy and food supplies by Russia under President Putin.

European economic law recognizes common market freedoms and civil, political, economic, social and cultural rights as constitutional foundations of

European economies. Arguably, HRL and the SDGs prioritize respect for human dignity by satisfying basic human needs so as to enable 'development as freedom' (A. Sen) and self-realization of one's human capacities.[36] The ordo-liberal arguments for limiting 'market failures',[37] 'governance failures',[38] and 'constitutional failures'[39] are likewise grounded in human rights arguments for protecting equal liberties, social justice and transnational rule of law as 'principles of justice' justifying the 'basic structures' of legal systems.[40] Democratic self-limitation of abuses of public and private power by means of constitutional rules of a higher legal rank and institutional 'checks and balances' respond to the insights of behavioral economics: bounded rationality can be reduced by changing the legal incentives for decision-making and encouraging ('nudging') individual economic and social actors to autonomously do things that are good for them and for society without governments compelling them to do so.

IEL confirms the methodological insight that social sciences exploring autonomous, social behavior motivated by ideas, beliefs and passions are confronted with much more uncertainty than natural sciences studying physical, chemical and biological facts. The democratic objective of institutionalizing inclusive 'public reason' to protect the human rights of all is different from natural science conceptions of 'truth' open to 'falsification'. Ordoliberalism explains why economic systems cannot be understood without the humanities and anthropology explaining the close interactions between social, economic, political and legal orders. The perennial human struggles for procedural and substantive 'justice principles' – as illustrated by statues of *justitia*, the blindfolded Roman goddess of law and justice (armed with a sword symbolizing power and will, and with a balance symbolizing reason and justice for peaceful settlement of disputes) in courthouses all over the world – offer empirical evidence that utility maximization based on cost-benefit analyses is only one among other motivations for social conduct.[41] The 2030 UN Sustainable

36 Cf Petersmann (n 7), chapter 4.

37 Like abuses of power, cartel agreements, adverse external effects, social injustices and information asymmetries.

38 Like wasteful and discriminatory trade protectionism and inflationary money policies leading to unjust redistribution of domestic revenue.

39 Like totalitarian disregard for human rights in China and Russia and US President Trump's initiation of illegal trade wars and executive 'emergency governance' without effective parliamentary and judicial review.

40 Cf Petersmann (n 7), chapter 4; Petersmann (n 6), chapters II and III.

41 For example, constitutionalism and human rights are reasonable responses to the facts of 'bounded rationality' of human beings, their 'unsocial sociability' (I.Kant) and their psychological need for moral pre-commitments (cf. Neal S Rubin, ed, *The Cambridge Handbook on Psychology and Human Rights*, CUP 2020).

Development Agenda reflects universal rejection of a money-driven, neo-liberal 'Washington consensus' in favor of a human rights-centered 'Geneva consensus', even if it does not openly embrace the ordo-liberal 'Brussels consensus' on embedding economic markets into multilevel democratic constitutionalism (as in European economic law) in order to constrain selfish legal and economic practices. Most UN and WTO diplomats prioritize state-centered intergovernmentalism, just as economists (like D. Rodrik's claims concerning a 'globalization paradox')[42] and politicians outside Europe disregard the 'constitutional failures' necessitating multilevel constitutionalism.

The future relationships between the bilateral management approaches characteristic for China's Belt and Road networks, the neo-liberal economic multilateralism dominating many US trade agreements concluded by republican US Presidents (like the US-Mexico-Canada FTA), Europe's regional economic constitutionalism, and regional FTAs in Africa, Asia and Latin-America are bound to evolve dynamically through 'regulatory competition', 'trial and error' (in coping with climate change and global health pandemics), and power politics (like hegemonic 'trade wars' between China and the USA, military aggression by Russia). Teaching IEL should help researchers to better understand why non-discriminatory 'regulatory competition' is consistent with the 'embedded liberalism compromise' underlying UN and WTO law as long as UN and WTO legal obligations are respected. As both China's disregard for arbitration under the UNCLOS[43] and the US destruction of the WTO Appellate Body were legally arbitrary, explaining the systemic importance of 'access to justice', independent third-party adjudication of economic disputes and multilevel judicial protection of transnational rule of law for realizing the SDGs must remain a central task of teaching IEL and of preventing further 'governance failures' and 'constitutional failures'.

42 Cf Dany Rodrik, *The Globalization Paradox. Democracy and the Future of the World Economy* (WW Norton & Company 2011) and his unconvincing 'incompatibility proposition' that we cannot have national sovereignty, democratic politics and global economic integration at once (cf pp 200–201). The EU's multilevel democratic constitutionalism does protect national sovereignty (eg in terms of democratic capacity to protect national and international PGs), democratic politics and rules-based, global economic integration at once, as discussed in Petersmann (n 7), chapter 5.

43 China's rejection of the arbitration award of 12 July 2016 under UNCLOS Annex VII was driven by China's maritime expansion disregarding its legal and judicial obligations under the UNCLOS; see the Permanent Court of Arbitration Case No 2013–19 in the matter of the South China Sea Arbitration (*The Republic of the Philippines v The Peoples Republic of China*). The award is published on the PCA website at www.pcacases.com/web/view/7.

Explaining the need (as recognized in the UN Sustainable Development Agenda) for developing IEL and HRL in mutually supportive and legally consistent ways can also contribute to educating non-lawyers about the systemic importance of IEL for realizing the universally agreed SDGs in a world of scarce resources, of short-sighted power struggles and the Anthropocene – our new global context of humans having become a geophysical force provoking climate change, massive biodiversity losses and other geological changes that risk running out of human control. Arguably, the global climate change, health pandemics and related governance crises confirm the need for global constitutional approaches limiting 'governance failures' so as to prevent the human destruction of our environmental system.[44] European law illustrates why the 'normative pull' of human rights depends on their 'normative push': their effective legal implementation through (1) constitutional law, (2) legislation, (3) administration, (4) adjudication, (5) democratic support and 'public reason', (6) international treaties, (7) international institutions and (8) 'secondary law' of international institutions. In multilevel governance of PGs, domestic governance failures (in protecting human rights and rule-of-law, 'moral hazards' prompting opportunistic rulers to default on international debt obligations) can often more easily be overcome if adversely affected citizens can invoke and enforce precise international rules inside states and thereby constrain power politics (eg by judicial remedies of citizens in national and European courts). Such multilevel legal, democratic and judicial remedies have no equivalent in many authoritarian UN member states (like China and Russia) which invoke UN principles (like 'sovereign equality of states', 'non-intervention' into domestic affairs) as 'shields' against external criticism of their domestic suppression of human rights (eg of political critics in Russia) and minority rights (eg of Uighur and Tibetan minorities in China, people in Hong Kong).

44 Cf Louis J Kotzé, *Global Environmental Constitutionalism in the Anthropocene* (Hart 2016). While transition to a net-zero carbon emissions economy by 2050 appears technologically possible, it requires far-reaching changes also in agricultural, food, environmental, political and social policies; cf. *Making Mission Possible: Delivering a Net-Zero Economy* (Energy Transition Commission September 2020). In contrast to the preceding 'Holocene epoch', which was characterized by relative stability in ecological conditions, the Anthropocene risks disrupting the 'Earth system' and international legal regulation of socio-ecological issues. Do the interactions between human 'rule of law' and 'rule of nature' (eg through natural catastrophes) require not only 'duties of care', but also more inclusive decision-making procedures, as proposed by advocates for 'constitutionalizing the anthropocene'? Should legal duties to protect human rights have priority over legal duties to protect non-human parts of nature, especially in legal systems (like UN law) which fail to protect human rights effectively?

The decrease in the number of constitutional democracies suggests that 'constitutionalizing' the UN system may remain a political utopia. Yet, 'democratic alliances' of countries should continue their 'normative push' for constitutional reforms, eg following the successful introduction of worldwide compulsory settlement of disputes through the 1994 WTO Agreement and its Dispute Settlement Understanding for multilevel third-party adjudication. IEL courses should explain why 'interdisciplinary agnosticism' by 'critical legal theories' impedes legal responses to the technological transformations of the international economy and to the perennial tasks of legally limiting 'market failures' (eg through competition, social and environmental rules) and 'governance failures' (eg through tax reforms, protection of PGs and related human rights).

4. *'Transforming Our World' through IEL?*

Since 1950, European law was progressively transformed through regional HRL and economic integration law which created ever more 'spillovers' for additional cooperation among the now 46 member states of the Council of Europe. The 2030 UN Agenda for Sustainable Development aims at 'transforming our world' through multilevel protection of human rights and the SDGs. Realizing the SDGs also requires 'transforming' the UN and WTO legal systems and strengthening trade, investment and human rights adjudication as preconditions for maintaining transnational rule of law in the transformative processes that are bound to provoke economic, humanitarian, legal and governance conflicts (eg over protecting future 'climate refugees' and endangered environmental resources). Without empowerment and participation of civil societies, implementation of the SDGs through legislative, administrative, judicial, economic, democratic and technological reforms in the 193 UN member states risks lacking 'political drivers', democratic support, vigilant guardians and self-interested defenders of rule of law and of 'enlightenment now'. Citizen-driven 'struggles for justice' and their protection by democratic and judicial institutions remain the most powerful driver for democratic reforms.

Yet, will rules-based UN, WTO and other IEL reforms be possible in the 'Asian century' with an increasingly authoritarian government in China resisting protection of human rights, suppressing transparent information (eg on the outbreak of the Covid-19 health pandemic in the city of Wuhan in 2019), supporting authoritarian dictatorships also outside China (like Iran, North Korea and Myanmar), and with China's aggressive sanctions in response to human rights criticism (eg prompting the European Parliament to 'freeze' ratification of the 2020 EU-China Agreement on Investments)? Will neo-liberal interest group politics push Anglo-Saxon countries to pursue more nationalist foreign policy agendas disregarding multilateral treaties protecting PGs? Will the African FTA among 54 African countries succeed in expanding mutually beneficial trade and rule of law inside Africa? Can the transpacific and Asian FTAs, and China's bilateral Belt & Road agreements without references to human rights, promote the necessary decarbonization and digitalization of the global economy without disrupting multilateral treaty systems if multilateral dispute settlement systems are increasingly disregarded? Can public health systems continue to rely on private pharmaceutical companies without stricter controls of abuses of patent rights and without better protection of public health as a global PG also in poor countries without proper infrastructures (like local capacities to produce pharmaceuticals for tropical diseases)?

Future textbooks and university classes on IEL will be faced with many new regulatory challenges that cannot be exhaustively discussed in one single textbook or seminar. In order to show students the 'wood behind the trees' and explain the 'constitutional problems' undermining UN and WTO governance, teaching IEL should focus on the 'basic legal structures' of IEL and of multilevel governance aimed at protecting the SDGs, including the universal recognition in the 2030 UN Sustainable Development Agenda (eg para. 9) that 'democracy, good governance and the rule of law ... are essential for sustainable development'. Yet, is cosmopolitan democracy a politically realistic strategy beyond Europe? Is it undermined by the 'rational ignorance' of local citizens rejecting – also inside democracies like the United Kingdom and Switzerland – multilevel governance in European institutions protecting European PGs (like a rules-based common market, European courts protecting human rights and rule of law throughout Europe)? Does artificial intelligence reduce the information problems of economic markets and democracies by enabling 'global internet governance' based not only on 'public reason' of local citizens, but incorporating also additional information flows (eg from global biological and environmental systems)? Which communities are relevant and legitimated for answering such 'IEL challenges'? Teaching IEL should conclude with 'Socratic questions' rather than with 'pretense of knowledge'. It should emphasize the need for protecting human rights and 'open societies' designing IEL in humane and cosmopolitan ways without justifying dictatorial regimes for 'survival governance'.

Bibliography

Alexy A, *The Argument from Injustice: Reply to Legal Positivism* (Clarendon Press 2002).

Choukroune L/Nedumpara JJ, *International Economic Law: Text, Cases and Materials* (CUP 2021).

Coggan P, *More: the 10,000 Year Rise of the World Economy* (Profile Books 2020).

Dalrymple W, *The Anarchy: the East India Company, Corporate Violence and the Pillage of an Empire* (Bloomsbury 2019).

Desierto DA, The IMF, WTO, World Bank, and WHO all come around? Multilateral Unity Against Inequitable Global COVID Vaccine Distribution, but still without Human Rights, in *EJIL Talk* of 3 June 2021.

Drahos P, *Survival Governance: Energy and Climate Change in the Chinese Century* (OUP 2021).

Drahos P, Public lies and public goods: ten lessons from when patents and pandemics meet, in *European University Institute Law Working Paper* 2021–5.

Dunoff JL, From Interdisciplinarity to Counterdisciplinarity: Is there Madness in Marti's Method? in *Temple International & Comparative Law Journal* 27 (2013), 309–338.

Kennedy E, *Constitutional Failure. Carl Schmitt in Weimar* (Duke University Press 2004).

Koskenniemi M, *From Apology to Utopia. The Structure of International Legal Argument* (CUP 2005).

Koskenniemi M, *International Law and the Far Right: Reflections on Law and Cynicism* (Asser Institute 2020).

Kotzé LJ, *Global Environmental Constitutionalism in the Anthropocene* (Hart 2016).

Lamy P, *The Geneva Consensus. Making Trade Work For All* (CUP 2013).

Lessig L, *Code: Version 2.0* (Basic Books 2006).

Munro J, *Emission Trading Schemes under International Economic Law* (OUP 2018).

Petersmann EU, *International Economic Law in the 21st Century. Constitutional Pluralism and Multilevel Governance of Interdependent Public Goods* (Hart Publishing 2012).

Petersmann EU, *Multilevel Constitutionalism for Multilevel Governance of Public Goods – Methodology Problems in International Law* (Hart Publishing 2017).

Petersmann EU, The 2018 Trade Wars as a Threat to the World Trading System and to Constitutional Democracies, in: *Trade, Law and Development* X (2018), 179–225.

Petersmann EU, *Transforming World Trade and Investment Law for Sustainable Development* (OUP 2022).

Pinker S, *Enlightenment Now. The Case for Science, Reason, Humanism and Progress* (Penguin 2018).

Rawls J, *A Theory of Justice* (OUP revised edition 1999).

Rodrik D, *The Globalization Paradox. Democracy and the Future of the World Economy* (WW Norton & Company 2011).

Rubin NS (ed), *The Cambridge Handbook on Psychology and Human Rights* (CUP 2020).

Ruggie JG, International regimes, transactions and change: Embedded liberalism in the postwar economic order, in: *International Organization* 36 (1982), 379–415.

Tuori K, *European Constitutionalism* (CUP 2015).
Tuori K, *Critical Legal Positivism* (Routledge 2016).
Ullrich H *et alii*, eds, *TRIPS Plus 20. From Trade Rules to Market Principles*, (Springer 2016).

CHAPTER 13

Teaching International Investment Law Requires a Holistic Approach

*Nikos Lavranos**

1 The Right Historic Starting Point

Most books on international investment law start with the first bilateral investment treaty (BIT) that was signed between Germany and Pakistan in 1959.[1] Consequently, most courses on international investment law also start with this BIT.

However, the truth is that the promotion, regulation and hence also the protection of trade and investment flows goes many centuries back.

Indeed, trading and investing is arguably one of the most fundamental activities of human beings as is evidenced by, for example, the original Silk Road[2] (and the new Silk Road), the extensive network of trading cities in the Greek and Roman Empire, Hugo Grotius book *Mare Liberum*[3] on the freedom of the seas, which developed the new legal principle that the sea was international territory and all nations were free to use it for seafaring trade, which in turn paved the way for the ruthless expansion of the Dutch and English East and West India Companies.

Also, as the example of the United States of America (USA) and the States of the African continent shows, the creation of new States or the achievement of independence of States required free trade and foreign investments. Therefore, the USA immediately after obtaining independence from the British Empire concluded so-called Treaties of Amity and Commerce, which were later

* Visiting Professor Vienna University; Guest Professor Leiden University; Secretary General of EFILA; Co-Editor-in-Chief of the European Investment Law and Arbitration Review; founder of NL-Investmentconsulting.

1 Germany-Pakistan BIT (1959), the text is available at: https://investmentpolicy.unctad.org/international-investment-agreements/treaty-files/1387/download.

2 See for a short history of the original Silk Road, Joshua J. Mark, https://www.worldhistory.org/Silk_Road/.

3 Hugo Grotius, *Mare Liberum* (1609), a digital version is available at the Dutch Royal Library at: https://galerij.kb.nl/kb.html#/nl/mareliberum/page/4/zoom/3/lat/3.601142320158735/lng/-127.79296875.

 | DOI:10.1163/9789004678880_017

renamed Friendship, Commerce and Navigation (FCN) agreements, which are the precursors of the BITs.[4] Similarly, in the 1960s and 1970s, when African States became independent, they all massively signed BITs in order to promote foreign direct investments (FDI).

In fact, the idea of creating a level playing field for unhindered trade and investment flows goes back to Adam Smith [1723–1790] who laid the foundations of classical free market economic theory. In his book on *The Wealth of Nations*,[5] he developed the concept of division of labour and expounded upon how rational self-interest and competition can lead to economic prosperity.

However, all freedom of trade and investment is useless if it cannot be effectively protected. This does not only apply to the protection of *international* trade and investment but equally for the protection of *domestic* trade and investment or, more generally speaking, the protection of property.

2 The Central Importance of the Rule of Law

Indeed, it is no coincident that the protection of property is a fundamental or even constitutional right that can also be traced back many centuries. For example, in Europe, Roman law defined property as "the right to use and abuse one's own within the limits of the law". The notion of private property and property rights was elaborated further in the Renaissance as international trade by merchants gave rise to mercantilist ideas. In 16th-century Europe, Lutheranism and the Protestant Reformation advanced property rights using biblical terminology. The Protestant work ethic and views on man's destiny came to underline social views in emerging capitalist economies in early modern Europe. The right to private property emerged as a radical demand for human rights vis-à-vis the State in 17th-century revolutionary Europe and the USA.

Accordingly, French revolutionaries recognised property rights in Article 17 of the Declaration of the Rights of Man and of the Citizen (1791), which stated that no one "may be deprived of property rights unless a legally established public necessity required it and upon condition of a just and previous indemnity".[6] In fact, Article 17 already encapsulates one of the most fundamental

4 Kenneth J. Vandevelde, *The First Bilateral Investment Treaties: US Postwar Friendship, Commerce, and Navigation Treaties* (Oxford University Press, 2017).

5 Adam Smith, *Inquiry into the Nature and Causes of the Wealth of Nations* (1776), a digital version is available at: http://files.libertyfund.org/files/220/0141-02_Bk.pdf.

6 See here for the text of the Declaration of the Rights and of the Citizen: https://www.elysee.fr/en/french-presidency/the-declaration-of-the-rights-of-man-and-of-the-citizen.

principles of modern international investment law, namely, that expropriation for public purposes must be accompanied by adequate compensation.

Thus, the protection of property is essentially a protection against an unrestrained State, which points exactly to Thomas Hobbes' *Leviathan.*[7] In Leviathan, he sets out his doctrine of the foundation of States and legitimate governments and creating an objective science of morality. Much of the book is occupied with demonstrating the necessity of a strong central authority to avoid the evil of discord and civil war. Beginning from a mechanistic understanding of human beings and their passions, Hobbes postulates what life would be like without government, a condition which he calls the "state of nature". In that state, each person would have a right, or license, to everything in the world. This, Hobbes argues, would lead to a "war of all against all" (bel lum omnium contra omnes). The description contains what has been called one of the best-known passages in English philosophy, which describes the natural state humankind would be in, were it not for political community:

> In such condition, there is no place for industry; because the fruit thereof is uncertain: and consequently no culture of the earth; no navigation, nor use of the commodities that may be imported by sea; no commodious building; no instruments of moving, and removing, such things as require much force; no knowledge of the face of the earth; no account of time; no arts; no letters; no society; and which is worst of all, continual fear, and danger of violent death; and the life of man, solitary, poor, nasty, brutish, and short.[8]

In such states, people fear death and lack both the things necessary to commodious living, and the hope of being able to obtain them. So, in order to avoid it, people accede to a social contract and establish a civil society. According to Hobbes, society is a population and a sovereign authority, to whom all individuals in that society cede some right for the sake of protection. Power exercised by this authority cannot be resisted, because the protector's sovereign power derives from individuals' surrendering their own sovereign power for protection. The individuals are thereby the authors of all decisions made by the sovereign.

---

7 Thomas Hobbes, *Leviathan* (1651), a digital version is available at: https://www.gutenberg.org/files/3207/3207-h/3207-h.htm.

8 Thomas Hobbes, *Leviathan*, "Chapter XIII.: Of the Natural Condition of Mankind As Concerning Their Felicity, and Misery."

Hence, this boils down to what is nowadays termed as the Rule of Law.[9] Accordingly, the effective protection of property (including investments) against unfair measures by the State is a central part of the protection of the Rule of Law, which in turn is part of any modern constitutional law system.

3 The New Tension between EU Law and International Investment Law

As such the protection of investments at both international and national level cannot be taught and studied in "clinical isolation"[10] but must be done in a holistic way as it interacts with many other branches of public international law. For example, since the EU has obtained exclusive competence regarding FDI (Art. 207 TFEU) with the entering into force of the Lisbon Treaty on 1 December 2009, the EU has become a very active driver in reforming international investment law, such as through introduction of an investment court system (ICS) in its new trade and investment agreements with Canada (CETA), Singapore and Vietnam and the proposal for a similar multilateral investment court (MIC) in the UNCITRAL Working Group III.

Internally, the EU and its Member States go even one step further by actually demolishing international investment law the termination of intra-EU BITs and the announced common withdrawal from the Energy Charter Treaty (ECT), thereby effectively banning arbitration proceedings of investors against States within the EU – whether based on intra-EU BITs or the ECT.[11]

While this approach may be understandable from the perspective of preserving the supremacy of EU law and the final authority of the Court of Justice of the EU (CJEU), it comes with a high price, namely, the backsliding of the Rule of Law in several EU Member States – notably, but not exclusively regarding Poland, Hungary, Rumania, and Bulgaria.[12]

9 See for short historic overview regarding the concept of the Rule of Law: Stanford Encyclopaedia of Philosophy, https://plato.stanford.edu/entries/rule-of-law/. See also the 20021 Rule of Law index by the World Justice Project, available at: https://worldjustice project.org/our-work/publications/rule-law-index-reports/world-justice-project-rule-law -index-2021.

10 This is in analogy to the call not to look at WTO law in clinical isolation when WTO law started to develop in the late 1990s, see: Gabrielle Marceau, A Call for Coherence in International Law – Praises for the Prohibition Against "Clinical Isolation" in WTO Dispute Settlement, Journal of World Trade, Volume 33, Issue 5 (1999) pp. 87 – 152.

11 As per the CJEU's *Achmea* and *Komstroy* judgments.

12 See for a detailed analysis: D. Kochenov and N. Lavranos, *Achmea versus the Rule of Law: CJEU's Dogmatic Dismissal of Investors' Rights in Backsliding Member States of the*

Thus, it seems that the EU has created a new tension between EU law and international investment law, which did not exist previously, but which needs to be explained to students, in particular those who do not have a background in EU law.

4 Outside the Brussel's Bubble

In contrast, if we leave the Brussel's bubble and take a more global perspective, it appears that in other regions of the world, notably in Asia, the benefits of investment protection and treaty arbitration are still considered very important as is evidenced by the recent conclusions of mega trade and investment agreements such as the Comprehensive and Progressive Trans Pacific Partnership (CPTPP) agreement and the Regional Comprehensive Economic Partnership (RCEP, signed in November 2020).

But also the transformation of a State's economy from a capital importing into a capital exporting country is an important driver for concluding BITs in order to protect those capital exporting investments. For example, Turkey is becoming an important regional economic power and thus has been actively signing BITs in recent times.[13]

At the same time, developments in Latin America and Africa illustrate new trends away from classic investment protection towards investment facilitation agreements. Notably, Brazil has become driver in this regard by signing several investment facilitation agreements with African States, such as with Angola and Mozambique.[14]

Indeed, also the EU is following this trend and recently started its first negotiations for an investment facilitation agreement with Angola.[15]

European Union, Hague J Rule Law (2021), freely available at: https://link.springer.com/content/pdf/10.1007/s40803-021-00153-7.pdf.

13 Between 2018 and 2021 alone Turkey has signed 12 BITs, according to UNCTAD: https://investmentpolicy.unctad.org/international-investment-agreements/countries/214/turkey.

14 Natali Cinelli Moreira, Cooperation and Facilitation Investment Agreements in Brazil: The Path for Host State Development, Kluwer Arbitration Blog, September 13, 2018, http://arbitrationblog.kluwerarbitration.com/2018/09/13/cooperation-and-facilitation-investment-agreements-in-brazil-the-path-for-host-state-development/.

15 Press release: EU and Republic of Angola launch negotiations for a first-ever Sustainable Investment Facilitation Agreement, 22 June 2021, https://trade.ec.europa.eu/doclib/press/index.cfm?id=2278.

Moreover, other branches of law are also increasingly interacting and thus influencing international investment law as well. For example, the protection of the environment, most notably, the fight against climate change with ever-more ambitious targets agreed by States, will inevitably have a negative impact on investments. In addition, the growing attention for Corporate Social Responsibility (CSR) obligations for investors and their increasingly effective enforcement through domestic courts and naming and shaming through social media means that CSR obligations are taken more seriously by States and investors.

Also, the COVID 19 pandemic resulted in the adoption of drastic measures by States, such as lock downs and travel restrictions, which directly affect investors for example in the tourism-related sectors.[16]

5 A Call for a Holistic Approach in Teaching International Investment Law

This short overview attempted to underline the main point, namely, that the teaching and studying of International Investment Law requires a true holistic approach in various dimensions.

First, regarding the historic and temporal dimension, the appreciation that trading and investing has been considered an essential motor for social and economic development, which in turn requires effective protection and in case of expropriation adequate compensation. This fundamental concept was already recognized centuries before the first modern German-Pakistan BIT in 1959.

Second, it is important to convey the understanding that the protection of foreign investments or, more generally speaking, the protection of property, is nothing particular or special but rather identical to the protection of property guaranteed by modern constitutional law. In other words, the protection of foreign investments is not a special right but part of the Rule of Law.

Third, the emergence of EU law and its special characteristics of its autonomous legal order and the particular role played by the CJEU, must now also be taught as an integral part of international investment law courses. The impact of EU law on international investment law is simply too big that it could be ignored – even if you are teaching and studying outside the EU.

16 N. Lavranos and A. Mazlom, *The Investment Treaty Implications of Covid-19 Responses by States*, European Investment Law and Arbitration Review 2021, pp. 3–57.

At the same time, it is important not to remain stuck in the Brussel's bubble but to take a more global geographical approach by taking into account the developments in international investment law that take place in other parts of the world.

Fourthly, the interaction between international investment law and other branches of law, such environmental law is becoming increasingly important, and thus more attention must be paid to this interaction.

Fifthly, it is also crucial to recognize that international investment law is part of the economy and therefore students need a good understanding of economics in order to appreciate also the important economic impact of foreign direct investments.

Since most law professors lack the necessary knowledge of economics, it is necessary to closely collaborate with business and economic faculties and to ensure that basic economics is an integral part also of the international investment law curriculum.

6 Using Multiple Teaching and Learning Tools

International investment law is particularly suitable for using multiple teaching and learning tools in order to strengthen the holistic approach as outlined above. For example, encouraging students to participate in one of the many international arbitration moot courts, such as the FDI moot court, the Vis moot court etc., and guiding and supporting them has proven to be an excellent opportunity for students to apply their law knowledge as well as developing their writing and oral presentation skills. In addition, moot courts can also serve as an opportunity to network with senior practitioners.

Another useful tool is to occasionally invite practitioners from the ministries, the European Commission, arbitrators or lawyers to tell students what is actually happening on the ground. They can also advise students about their career path and how to enter the field of arbitration.

In this context, post graduate arbitration courses and Arbitration Academies have proven to be particularly useful for students. They enable students to further specialize in the various fields of arbitration, such as investment treaty arbitration, commercial arbitration, sports arbitration etc.

However, at the end of the day, arbitration needs to be learned on the job. Therefore, it is highly important that universities and their lecturers have developed a network with relevant law firms, which facilitates the training-on-the-job through internships and other short term work engagements.

All this of course requires flexibility in the law curricula of the universities, which in turn need to be opened up in order to allow university lecturer to be able to fully use all these multiple teaching and learning tools, while at the same time they are fully recognized.

In conclusion, as international investment law remains an evolutionary discipline open to the fast changes in broader human society, the predominant focus on bilateral investment treaties and investor-State arbitration dispute resolution is not enough any longer.

All these factors, and many more, call for a true holistic approach in the teaching and studying of international investment law.

List of Literature

Grotius, Hugo *Mare Liberum* (1609), a digital version is available at the Dutch Royal Library at: https://galerij.kb.nl/kb.html#/nl/mareliberum/page/4/zoom/3/lat/3.6011423201587 35/lng/-127.79296875.

Hobbes, Thomas *Leviathan* (1651), a digital version is available at: https://www.gutenberg.org/files/3207/3207-h/3207-h.htm.

Kochenov D. and N. Lavranos, *Achmea versus the Rule of Law: CJEU's Dogmatic Dismissal of Investors' Rights in Backsliding Member States of the European Union*, Hague J Rule Law (2021), freely available at: https://link.springer.com/content/pdf/10.1007/s40803-021-00153-7.pdf.

Marceau, Gabrielle *A Call for Coherence in International Law – Praises for the Prohibition Against "Clinical Isolation" in WTO Dispute Settlement*, Journal of World Trade, Volume 33, Issue 5 (1999) pp. 87–152.

Lavranos N. and A. Mazlom, *The Investment Treaty Implications of Covid-19 Responses by States*, European Investment Law and Arbitration Review 2021, pp. 3–57.

Mark, Joshua J. Short history of the original Silk Road, https://www.worldhistory.org/Silk_Road/.

Moreira, Natali Cinelli *Cooperation and Facilitation Investment Agreements in Brazil: the Path for Host State Development*, Kluwer Arbitration Blog, September 13, 2018, http://arbitrationblog.kluwerarbitration.com/2018/09/13/cooperation-and-facilitation-investment-agreements-in-brazil-the-path-for-host-state-development/.

Smith, Adam *Inquiry into the Nature and Causes of the Wealth of Nations* (1776), a digital version is available at: http://files.libertyfund.org/files/220/0141-02_Bk.pdf.

Vandevelde, Kenneth J. *The First Bilateral Investment Treaties: US Postwar Friendship, Commerce, and Navigation Treaties* (Oxford University Press, 2017).

PART V

Tools, Instruments, Resources

CHAPTER 14

Visualising International Law

Movies and Image References in Teaching International Law

*Markus Beham, Melanie Fink and Ralph Janik**
ORCID: 0009-0006-0075-8796

1 Introduction

Discussions concerning the visualisation of international law are nothing new. The last couple of years have seen films discussed across the international law blogsphere.[1] The 2014 European Society of International Law Anniversary Conference in Vienna even dedicated a full Agora to "International Law and Film: The Power of Pictures", convened by Andreas von Arnauld and Carlos Esposito. We have been equally engaged, contributing to a conference held in Cologne in 2016 on the future of international law in German academia in general and new methods of teaching international law in particular,[2] along with a teaser blog post on the German *Völkerrechtsblog*.[3] Our contribution and impressions from the debate – which oscillated between a more traditional approach of teaching international law and the need to adapt to changed

* Markus Beham is an Associate Professor at the University of Passau, Germany. Melanie Fink is Assistant Professor at Leiden University (Europa Institute) and APART-GSK Fellow of the Austrian Academy of Sciences at the Central European University. Ralph Janik is an Adjunct Lecturer at the University of Vienna. They are authors of the public international law textbook „Völkerrecht verstehen" [„Understanding public international law"], now in its third edition with Facultas publishers. The chapter includes developments until the end of 2019.

1 See, exemplary, Marko Milanović, "Eye in the Sky", *EJIL: Talk!* (9.5.2016) <http://www.ejiltalk.org/eye-in-the-sky>; Kristen Boon, "International Law Movies", *Opinio Juris* (10.2.2016) <http://opiniojuris.org/2016/02/10/international-law-movies/>; Marko Milanović, "House of Cards and International Law", *EJIL: Talk!* (11.3.2015) <http://www.ejiltalk.org/house-of-cards-and-international-law/>; Kevin Jon Heller, "The Problem with 'Crossing Lines'", *Opinio Iuris* (24.6.2013) <http://opiniojuris.org/2013/06/24/the-problem-with-crossing-lines/>.

2 "Die Lehre des internationalen Rechts – zeitgemäß?!", University of Cologne, 16 March 2016, conference programme available <http://www.dgfir.de/workspace/media/documents/2016-03-16flyer-programm-tagung-koeln.pdf>.

3 Markus Beham, Melanie Fink, Ralph Janik, "Völkerrecht verstehen – Wie gewinnen wir die anderen 99%?", *Völkerrechtsblog* (9 March 2016) <https://voelkerrechtsblog.org/volkerrecht-verstehen-wie-gewinnen-wir-die-anderen-99/>.

 | DOI:10.1163/9789004678880_018

realities in classrooms where every student has a smartphone or tablet ready – were since published in a conference volume[4] and provide the starting point for our elaborations.

While we previously focused on the contextualisation of the use of image and film as a didactical tool and the need to open up the Germanophone tradition to more progressive teaching methods, the present contribution serves as a retrospective account of how this has worked out for us, sharing personal experiences in teaching both actively in the classroom and passively through textbooks (a joint effort that brought us together as a team of authors in the first place).[5] We have included an English version of the annex first drawn up for our Cologne contribution suggesting possible film materials for use within the classroom.

II General Considerations

While the possibilities for the use of film and image references in teaching international law are boundless, there are a number of important considerations to keep in mind. Three particularly pressing issues that we have been confronted with in our past teaching careers involved the timeliness of cultural references, the boundaries stretched by the use of innovative teaching methods, and copyright considerations.

All of these issues are exacerbated by the necessity of almost exclusively teaching online classes throughout the Covid-19 pandemic (such as preserving any use of film and image references to eternity through recording sessions). For all the benefits resulting from the visualisation of international law through images: Whenever there is doubt, there is probably a good reason not to use a particular reference. Visualisation should never be the end in itself. Notwithstanding the importance to engage and stimulate students by using content they can relate to emotionally – we are teachers, not entertainers.

1 *Cultural References and Credibility*

Cultural references add a timestamp that may become dated quickly. A tip of the hat to the TV series *Homeland* may have been timely in 2015 but may be

4 Markus Beham, Melanie Fink, Ralph Janik, "Völkerrecht und Film: Von A wie 'Argo' bis Z wie 'Zero Dark Thirty', in: Georg Nolte and Stephan Hobe (eds.), *Lehre des internationalen Rechts – zeitgemäß?!* (C.F. Müller 2017) 63–68.

5 Markus Beham, Melanie Fink, and Ralph Janik, *Völkerrecht verstehen* (Facultas 2015; 2nd edn. 2019; 3rd edn. 2021).

met without triggering effect just a few years later. We have already been called out and for mentioning *Terminator 2: Judgment Day*[6] or Sean Connery James Bond movies, what we would have thought as timeless classics. In reworking the second edition of our textbook we ended up editing out the one or other example.

It is equally important to remain credible in the use of such film and image references. An inevitable fact of academic life is the increasing age gap between student and teacher as the latter progresses along his or her career. The issue lies less in the age gap itself than the fact that it is only the teacher that gets older.[7] The use of a particular cultural reference may simply no longer be appreciated by a new generation of students or, in the worst case, appear as an inappropriate attempt at youthfulness. This leads to a second consideration.

2 *Drawing Boundaries*

The use of progressive teaching methods may create a more open teaching atmosphere but may equally necessitate drawing the boundaries more carefully. While it is a personal choice, how much of one's personal life and interests – think cultural references – flow into teaching, one should be aware that this reduces the distance between teachers and students. The use of progressive teaching methods should be grounded in their didactical value, not (primarily) in amusement. What is the image one wishes to project? This is a fine line that each and every teacher needs to draw for herself.

3 *Copyright Issues*

Educational and research establishments, such as universities, are increasingly aware of the complexities surrounding the use of copyright-protected materials in teaching activities, especially in the digital realm. Whereas some universities have clearer guidelines for such use and have put in place the required licenses for different teaching uses, that is not always the case. Even then, it is sometimes unclear what types of use are allowed for teachers in different contexts.

The result is that universities (explicitly or implicitly) pass the burden of clarifying rights clearance to teachers. These then have to, typically on a

---

6 The reference was used to show that debates on artificial intelligence and killer robots are not new; according to a spontaneous poll in my (Ralph) classes, only about a fifth of the students had seen the movie. Some two years later, the number had even decreased to 3 out of approximately 80 students (!).

7 See also the various references to the age gap between teacher and student throughout the contributions of this volume.

case-by-case basis, assess which restrictions apply before making available educational materials that include third-party content online. For instance, making such materials available will generally be allowed if three conditions are met: it must be for the sole purpose of illustration for teaching, take place under the responsibility of an educational establishment, and be accompanied by the indication of the source, including the author's name, unless this turns out to be impossible. In many cases, the university must also pay compensation to rights holders for these uses trough a licensing agreement.

For a teacher, it is burdensome to check these conditions. The alternative approach of using solely publicly available materials with open content licenses that allow educational re-use is equally laborious given the time restraints attached to the preparation for courses as part of the academic schedule.

The best approach is generally to contact the university library or competent service to clarify the type of educational licenses agreed upon with rights holders' representatives (usually collective rights management organisations) and clarify the applicable guidelines in your establishment. Usually these will involve allowing the posting of copyright-protected materials through a secure electronic environment accessible only by the educational establishment's students and teaching staff (Moodle, Canvas, or Blackboard, for example). For the hobby photographers among us, we recommend building up a personal photo stock of public international law imagery for teaching purposes (from a visit to an international organisation, a trip to a *de facto* state, or a glass of shōchū).

III Images

One of the first conscious confrontations with the use of images for teaching law came for me (Markus, pursuing his LL.M. degree) during a seminar on international investment law at Columbia Law School held by adjunct professor Oliver Thomas Johnson, judge at the Iran-US Claims Tribunal. After brief introductions and a presentation of the overall syllabus, he handed out a Peanuts comic strip to which he had added the heading "All you need to remember about fair and equitable treatment". It featured the recurring scenario in which Lucy van Pelt pulls a football away from Charlie Brown shortly before he kicks it, leading him to trip and fall over. In the present scenario, suspicious Charlie Brown already knows better than to try and kick the ball again. So Lucy offers a signed document testifying that she will not pull the ball away. Checking the document, Charlie Brown is reassured, and – how else could it be – runs straight into his usual misfortune. Picking up the document,

Lucy marvels: "Peculiar thing about this document.. It was never notarized!" What started off as a humorous gimmick ends up in a long-term anchor for the concept of fair and equitable treatment – arguably a "you know it when you see it" standard, often difficult for students to grasp at first.

Of course, the use of images is neither novel nor uncommon. Textbooks and PowerPoint slides around the world are dotted with anything from clipart to pictures to any other imaginable visualisations. The distinction lies in the respective purpose: Should the image simply refresh student's attention, should it make an otherwise dry and abstract topic more colourful, or does it serve to prove a point in itself (as was the case with the Peanuts comic strip)? Each of these are equally useful in different situations.

An image that has stood the test of time in defining international law at the outset of any general or specialised course, is a collage or potpourri of multiple images encapsulating international law, from diplomatic relations (any images of heads of state) to the use of force, from land and sea to air and space, from international crimes (Joseph Kony and the then-viral video from 2012 about his crimes[8] comes to mind) and terrorism to liberal democracy and multilateralism (a picture of the UN headquarters, for example). What at first might appear overwhelming, allows students to embrace the broad scope of international regulation that spans way beyond any domestic legal field they will have usually been confronted with in their curriculum.

When dealing with the sources of international law or international organisations, it is oftentimes useful to show a picture, ideally taken oneself to add to the overall credibility. A picture of the "Non-Violence" sculpture, commonly referred to as "the knotted gun", in front of the Secretariat Building of the United Nations in New York may quickly engrain the main purposes and principles of the UN Charter in the minds of students. A picture of the fireproof safe stacked up with international treaties at the Treaty Section of the United Nations Office of Legal Affairs can illustrate that the sources are neither abstract nor just available as PDF documents online: they lead a physical existence just as any private law contract. A picture of the observer seat of the Sovereign Military Order of Malta in the General Assembly of the United Nations makes both international organisations and subjects of international law *sui generis* immediately relatable.

But the idea of images is not just restricted to pictures. Images may be created in the minds of students by simple descriptions. In our textbook, we oftentimes included brief depictions of movie or TV series sequences featuring

8 Wikipedia, "Kony 2012" <https://en.wikipedia.org/wiki/Kony_2012>.

international law to serve as anchors. Similarly, passing out the playlist of songs which supposedly drove Manuel Noriega out of the Apostolic Nunciature in Panama City,[9] may serve as a humorous anchor in a class on diplomatic law.

A final topic we broadly discussed in Cologne was that of internet memes[10] with international law references – of course, more topical then than now – easily available for use through the procrastination Tumblr site "Internationally Wrongful Memes"[11] or the "Apologetic Internat'l Law Memes for Utopian Teens Twitter Account" (@IntLawMemes). Here, the line between didactical use and mere amusement is particularly narrow with the danger of drawing upon images that may since have acquired a negative connotation – think "Pepe the Frog" – for being overall offensive. To close the circle here to the preliminary considerations above: when in doubt, do not use.

IV Film

As indicated above, short clips from movies or TV series may also serve as an introduction into specific topics. I (Ralph, also pursuing his LL.M. degree) remember well how Martijn Keeman, who was my coach back when I was part of the University of Amsterdam's team participating in the Frits Kalshoven International Humanitarian Law competition, showed us a number of key scenes from *Saving Private Ryan* to discuss them from a legal point of view – assuming the Geneva Conventions and the Additional Protocols had already existed during World War II. The movie contains numerous questions for a class on International Humanitarian Law to kick off a discussion: Is a soldier picking up an apple when entering a foreign village engaging in pillage? What is the law on targeting (the sniper scene)[12]? Do surrendered soldiers enjoy Prisoner of War status and what shall be done with them if they cannot be detained on the spot?[13] Some of these scenes are available on YouTube and can thus be used effortlessly.

In general, IMDb's list of war movies contains countless suggestions for movies suitable for teaching International Humanitarian Law ranging from *Apocalypse Now*, *Full Metal Jacket*, or *Platoon*, to more recent ones such as

9 http://nsarchive.gwu.edu/nsa/DOCUMENT/950206.htm.

10 A term borrowed from Richard Dawkins, *The Selfish Gene* (Oxford: Oxford University Press, 1976) to describe ideas spreading through popular culture.

11 http://memecogens.tumblr.com/.

12 https://www.youtube.com/watch?v=wgHRj2-vvs8.

13 https://www.youtube.com/watch?v=3QspU7uDDM8.

Inglorious Basterds and *Eye in the Sky* (which, strictly speaking, discusses targeted killings outside of armed conflicts and may thus be used to illustrate the difference between International Humanitarian Law with its principle of distinction and law enforcement operations). However, since these movies inevitably contain drastic depictions of violence and other explicit content, one should warn students before clicking the play-button (at the same time, students signing up for International Humanitarian Law classes might be aware of and prepared for the subject matter; the situation may be different in general international law classes).

Another topic easily enriched with short clips is diplomatic law, a long-time fascination for movie producers starting with Alfred Hitchcock's classic *The Man Who Knew Too Much*.[14] More recently, the first minutes of Ben Affleck's 2012 thriller *Argo* contain an apt summary of the background and facts of the *Tehran Hostages* case.[15] In TV, the Columbo episode *A Case of Immunity* ends with a somewhat absurd scene where the murderer "declares" to waive his immunity in order to avoid prosecution in his home state, having realized that his head of state has heard his confession. On top of that, the head of state announces that he will bow to the decision of Inspector Columbo – who is, as a reminder, a homicide detective with the Los Angeles Police Department.[16] The scene provides a perfect occasion to ask students to identify legal and policy issues and how these might actually play out in practice. Other TV series such as *Homeland* provide more thoroughly researched scenes on diplomatic law, including the special status of a diplomatic bag (Season 2, Episode 3) and the inviolability of diplomats (Season 1, Episode 10).

These are just two examples of international law featuring prominently on screen – either directly by explicitly mentioning international law or indirectly by featuring situations regulated by international law. Movie buffs might come up with countless other scenes suited to be shown and discussed in class.

Aside from fiction, there is an increasing number of documentaries. To name just a few examples: International Criminal Law and the International

14 Confusingly enough, Hitchcock produced two movies with the same name; we are talking about the one from 1956.

15 *Case Concerning United States Diplomatic and Consular Staff in Tehran* (*United States of America v. Iran*), Judgment of 24 May 1980, ICJ Reports 1980, 3.

16 For an analysis of this episode from an international law point of view see Maxime Didat, "Columbo (Ted Post,1975, saison 5, épisode 2): un diplomate peut-il renoncer à son immunité diplomatique?", *Centre de droit international, Université Libre de Bruxelles* <http://cdi.ulb.ac.be/columbo-ted-post1975-saison-5-episode-2-un-diplomate-peut-il-renoncer-son-immunite-diplomatique-une-analyse-de-maxime-didat/>.

Criminal Court are featured in *The Court* from 2013,[17] the genocide in Rwanda and the fate of Canadian General Roméo Dallaire was covered in *Shakehands with the devil*,[18] and the UN was criticised polemically in *U.N. Me.*[19]

Students can be motivated through interdisciplinary teaching methods, by inviting them to watch documentaries and write reviews from an international law perspective. Practical examples include the seminar "Cinema and Human Rights" at the University of Vienna where students receive free tickets for an annual human rights movie festival (*This Human World*) and are asked to write a seminar paper on one of the movies (for example, a discussion on the freedom of assembly on the basis of *Everyday Rebellion*).[20] Another innovative example comes from Andreas von Arnauld's and Arne Reißmann's interdisciplinary seminar "Völkerrecht im Film" ("International law in movies") at the University of Kiel where students watched movies together and subsequently analysed the legal aspects contained therein on the basis of methods used in film studies.[21]

For those preferring a more traditional approach to implementing alternative teaching methods, the large collections of videos from the UN Audiovisual Library of International Law[22] – while probably not as exciting as Hollywood movies – offer a great opportunity to bring the "big names" of international law scholarship and their legal thought into the classroom. In addition to the more general lectures on international law, those on the sources of international law have proven a great resource in class. In addition, one may find lectures on virtually every subtopic of international law.

Moving into actual practice, YouTube is loaded with official speeches by world leaders and outtakes from TV news. These may not only serve as opportunities to discuss current developments (for example, one may show former US Secretary of State Mike Pompeo' interview on how and whether the drone strike on Qasem Soleimani was justified by a direct and immediate threat to the US,[23] or Donald Trump's announcement of his tariffs on steel and aluminium

17 http://www.thecourt-movie.com/.

18 https://www.imdb.com/title/tt0424435/. In addition to the documentary, there is also a movie with the same name.

19 https://www.unmemovie.com/.

20 https://everydayrebellion.net/the-project/.

21 See Arne Reissmann, "Innovative Lehrformate für die Didaktik der Völkerrechtswissenschaft" *Völkerrechtsblog* (21 March 2016) <https://voelkerrechtsblog.org/innovative-lehrformate-fur-die-didaktik-der-volkerrechtswissenschaft/>.

22 http://www.un.org/law/avl/.

23 https://youtu.be/0FETxb3-IUQ.

based on the argument of national security interests)[24] but also the impact of international law in general.

Comparing world leaders' rhetoric or coverage of the same incident from a variety of TV channels from different countries or regions can also serve to show that the domestic understanding of international law varies (for example, I – Ralph – showed both CNN's[25] and Russia Today's[26] coverage of the November 2018 Kerch incident to highlight the similarities and differences and discuss whether reporting was legally biased or not).

As most of us know, many students have the impression that international law is not "real law" (to paraphrase John Austin) and that it does not really play a role in international affairs. Hearing leaders like Vladimir Putin or Barrack Obama talk about the need to uphold international law or the importance of the United Nations and human rights (as they did during their speeches at the UN general assembly, which are all available on YouTube)[27] might change their mind. At the very least, it could make them understand the relevance of international law as the common language in international *fora*.

V Graphs and Charts

Beyond the obvious tools of images and film, graphs and charts may also serve as useful means to reach the "visual learner". These types of visualisations are a particularly effective way to show numbers and concepts, depict processes, and illustrate relationships. At Leiden University (where Melanie teaches), a whole book dedicated to accompanying the regular textbook by illustrating EU law in charts is available to master students.[28]

The simplest and most common charts are those depicting numbers or categories and their relationships. The popular bar graph features several vertical or horizontal columns and is typically used in order to compare various categories or to show quantitative growth over time. Think of illustrating, for instance, the explosion in the number of international organisations over the last decades. The pie chart, a circle cut up into segments that visualises parts

24 https://youtu.be/eEoEicH6Yf4.
25 https://youtu.be/yssaYlkXe1o.
26 https://youtu.be/leoGExvvnso.
27 Barrack Obama's final speech includes references to the "liberal world order", democracy, the United Nations, see https://youtu.be/ji6pl5Vwrvk. For Putin's speech, where he highlighted the origins of the United Nations, can be found at https://youtu.be/q13yzl6k6wo.
28 Christa Tobler and Jacques Beglinger, *Essential EU Law in Charts* (5th ed, HVG-ORAC 2020).

of a whole, is particularly useful to show, for example, how budgets (of international organisations, for example) are constituted or spent.

Flow charts are an excellent tool to illustrate processes. In its most basic form, this chart shows a sequence of steps in a process. Think of illustrating the sequence of sub-analyses required for a particular assessment, the several steps in the assessment of international responsibility for example (equivalent to the "Prüfungsschemata" that students at German-speaking Universities strive to collect). More complex versions of the flow chart allow for the depiction of different choices within a process together with their impact, ideal to visualise multi-layered treaty-making processes, for instance.

Charts also serve to illustrate complex relationships in a more straightforward manner than text or speech can. This is true for instance for the common three-way relationships, such as between a sending sate, a host state, and an international organisation in the area of diplomatic representation of international organisations or between a "perpetrator" state, an aiding state, and an injured party in the application of the rules on responsibility for rendering aid or assistance in the commission of an internationally wrongful act.

Of course, there are no limits to creating more customised graphs, charts, and other diagrams from scratch. The universally recognised depiction of the EU before the entry into force of the Lisbon Treaty as a temple with three pillars under a common roof is testament to that. Spatial regimes, such as the law of the sea or air and space law, are particularly suitable to explore the potential of such illustrations.

But how does the lawyer with limited IT know-how beyond simple word processing software go about including graphs and charts in their teaching toolbox? Word and Powerpoint, software most academics are already familiar with, provide useful and easy to use templates for the most common types of charts. Excel offers tools beyond that, in particular the possibility to draw graphs, but requires a dose more of technical skill. For more extravagant or customised graphs and charts, there is a broad range of specific software, often available online, designed with the non-expert illustrator in mind and simple to use.[29] In any case, the hesitant teacher can rest assured, there is no need for fancy 3D columns or animated pies. In our experience, simple and neat graphs work just as well, if not better, and help to focus on the core message.

For those not wishing to venture into the creation of graphs and charts themselves, there is plenty of material online, provided by various actors of

29 See, for instance, yEd: https://www.yworks.com/products/yed; or Creately: https://creately.com/.

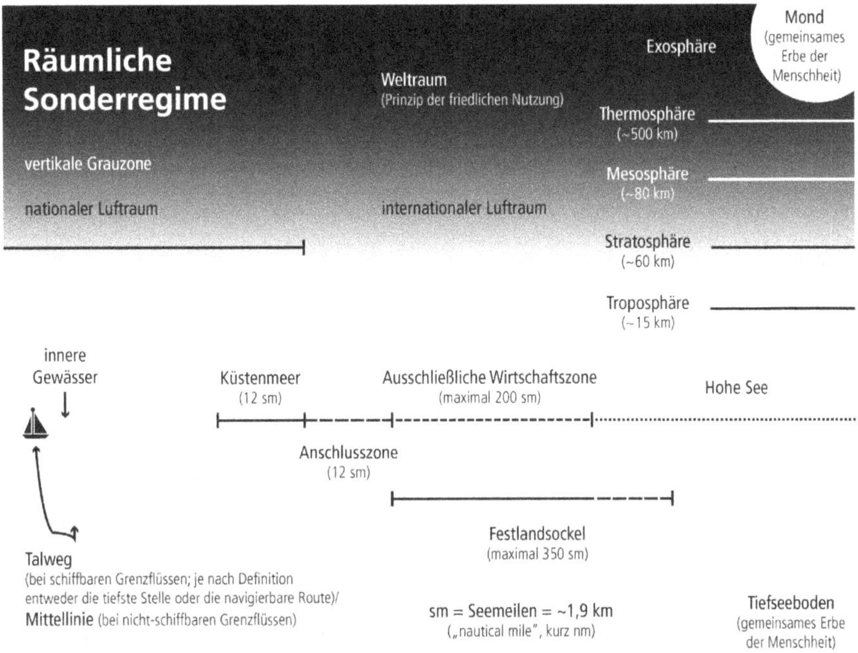

FIGURE 1 An example of how illustrations can be used to illustrate spatial regimes
NOTE: MARKUS BEHAM, MELANIE FINK, RALPH JANIK, *VÖLKERRECHT VERSTEHEN* (3RD EDN., FACULTAS 2021) 310

international relations. The Sustainable Development Goals, for instance, appear as multicoloured, numbered bricks.[30] Another good example are the visualisations through treaty ratification maps provided for human rights treaties by the Office of the United Nations High Commissioner for Human Rights (OHCHR)[31] and for investment agreements by UNCTAD,[32] while the WTO provides a handy overview of regional and preferential trade agreements.[33] Last but not least, the ICRC has a panoply of different visual teaching materials online.[34]

30 https://www.un.org/sustainabledevelopment/sustainable-development-goals/.
31 http://indicators.ohchr.org/.
32 https://investmentpolicyhub.unctad.org/IIA.
33 http://rtais.wto.org/UI/PublicMaintainRTAHome.aspx.
34 https://www.icrc.org/en/document/creating-and-teaching-ihl-course.

Annex: Teaching materials

For convenience, we have included a small collection of movies and specific episodes from TV series which include international law-related topics that we found useful in the past (by showing clips or as references).

Title	Topic	Relevant content
13 Hours: The Secret Soldiers of Benghazi	diplomatic law	Includes a scene depicting the 2012 attack on the US consulate in Benghazi.
Argo	diplomatic law	The introductory scene includes a summary of the historic background from the Iranian revolution to the Tehran hostage crisis itself.
Black Hawk Down	international humanitarian law / use of force	"Targeting" in wars where fighters are hardly distinguishable from civilians, including against guerrilla tactics on the basis of the battle of Mogadishu 1993.
Columbo, Season 5, Episode 2	diplomatic law	Columbo repeatedly violates the basic principles of diplomatic law when going after the "prime secretary" of the delegation of a fictional country whom he suspects of a homicide; the final scene has already been discussed above
Homeland, Season 1, Episode 10	diplomatic law	Blackmailing of a Saudi diplomat (WARNING: explicit dialogue!).
Homeland, Season 2, Episode 5	human rights	Torture scene with a "ticking time bomb" scenario.
Hotel Rwanda	human rights	Movie on the genocide in Rwanda, specifically depicting the dilemmas of a UN peacekeeping unit.
House of Cards, Season 3, Episode 7	United Nations	Discussion of an "emergency session" of the United Nations General Assembly on the basis of the "Uniting for Peace" Resolution.

Title	Topic	Relevant content
Iron Sky	space law	Political satire of a fictional Security Council dealing with the peaceful use of outer space.
Jack Ryan, Season 2, Episode 6	diplomatic law	Declaration of the entire personnel of a US-embassy as *persona non grata*.
Lone Survivor	international humanitarian law	Depiction of "rules of engagement" and consequences of their violations.
Lord of War	international criminal law	Features a warlord modelled on Charles Taylor and his role in the Sierra Leone war. Various issues of arms trade and violations of international law.
New Girl, Season 3, Episode 1	law of the sea	One of the main characters (Nick) flees from Hotel securities after dodging the bill and tries to thwart them off by shouting that he was in international waters.
Quo Vadis, Aida?	genocide	Portrayal of a UN interpreter during the Srebrenica genocide
Room 2806: The Accusation	diplomatic law	Documentary on the "DSK affair" concerning former managing director of the International Monetary Fund (IMF), Dominique Strauss-Kahn.
Simpsons, Season 2, Episode 1	pacific settlement of disputes	Difference between individual and state responsibility and between the International Criminal Court and the International Court of Justice, since there is trial against Krusty the Clown in front of the International Court of Justice (for "crimes against clowndom").
Simpsons, Season 25, Episode 11	human rights	Upon discovering that Mr. Burns has handed out Google Glass goggles to all of his employees so as to spy on them (he can see what they see). Simpson explicitly refers to the right to privacy.

Title	Topic	Relevant content
Simpsons, Season 25, Episode 9	diplomatic law	Charged with violating US copyright laws, the Simpson family hide in the Swedish consulate; Lisa describes the difference between consulates and embassies and the police – just like in the example of Noriega – tries to pressure the Simpsons by playing loud Rock music.
Sometimes in April	human rights	Movie on the genocide in Rwanda.
The Act of Killing	human rights, international criminal law	Documentary on the mass killings in Indonesia during the era of the Suharto regime from 1965 to 1966.
The Hunting Party	international criminal law	Humorous depiction of the hunt for Radovan Karadžić.
The Martian	law of the sea/ space law	The main character muses on the law applicable to Mars, mingling the treaty regulation of the law of the sea with space law.
The Unforgiven	international criminal law	Documentary about the convicted war criminal Esad Landžo who served as camp guard at the Čelebići camp during the Bosnian War.
U.N. me	United Nations	Polemic critique of the United Nations, in particular its anti-Israel bias.
Zero Dark Thirty	human rights	Depiction of the "enhanced interrogation techniques" used by the US after 9/11.

Detailed descriptions of these movies and TV series can be found in the Internet Movie Database (IMDb). In addition, collections of movies[35] and other media dealing with international law may be found online.[36]

35 See, generally, http://iiljfilms.blogspot.co.at/. For a collection including short descriptions see Lyonette Louis-Jacques, "Foreign, Comparative, and International Law and Justice on Film and TV: An A to Z List", <https://uchicago.app.box.com/s/ptoy1v3zbgax8nogutc9ki0vb-2kqaoqv>. For a list on international criminal law and related movies and documentaries see http://www.genocidescholars.org/resources/filmography. For a list on international humanitarian law see http://www.redcross.org/humanityinwar/for-students.

36 http://cdi.ulb.ac.be/culture-pop-et-droit-international/.

Bibliography

Beham, Markus, Melanie Fink, Ralph Janik, "Völkerrecht und Film: Von A wie 'Argo' bis Z wie 'Zero Dark Thirty', in: Georg Nolte and Stephan Hobe (eds.), Lehre des internationalen Rechts – zeitgemäß?! (C.F. Müller 2017) 63.

Beham, Markus, Melanie Fink, Ralph Janik, "Völkerrecht verstehen – Wie gewinnen wir die anderen 99%?", Völkerrechtsblog (9 March 2016) <https://voelkerrechtsblog.org/volkerrecht-verstehen-wie-gewinnen-wir-die-anderen-99/>.

Beham, Markus, Melanie Fink, Ralph Janik, Völkerrecht verstehen (3rd edn., Facultas 2021).

Boon, Kristen, "International Law Movies", Opinio Juris (10.2.2016) <http://opiniojuris.org/2016/02/10/international-law-movies/>.

Dawkins, Richard, The Selfish Gene (Oxford: Oxford University Press, 1976).

Didat, Maxime, "Columbo (Ted Post,1975, saison 5, épisode 2): un diplomate peut-il renoncer à son immunité diplomatique?", Centre de droit international, Université Libre de Bruxelles <http://cdi.ulb.ac.be/columbo-ted-post1975-saison-5-episode-2-un-diplomate-peut-il-renoncer-son-immunite-diplomatique-une-analyse-de-maxime-didat/>.

Heller, Kevin Jon, "The Problem with 'Crossing Lines'", Opinio Iuris (24.6.2013) <http://opiniojuris.org/2013/06/24/the-problem-with-crossing-lines/>.

Louis-Jacques, Lyonette, "Foreign, Comparative, and International Law and Justice on Film and TV: an A to Z List", <https://uchicago.app.box.com/s/ptoy1v3zbgax8>.

Milanovic, Marko, "Eye in the Sky", EJIL: Talk! (9.5.2016) <http://www.ejiltalk.org/eye-in-the-sky>.

Milanovic, Marko, "House of Cards and International Law", EJIL: Talk! (11.3.2015) <http://www.ejiltalk.org/house-of-cards-and-international-law/>.

Reissmann, Arne, "Innovative Lehrformate für die Didaktik der Völkerrechtswissenschaft" Völkerrechtsblog (21 March 2016) <https://voelkerrechtsblog.org/innovative-lehrformate-fur-die-didaktik-der-volkerrechtswissenschaft/>.

Tobler, Christa, and Jacques Beglinger, Essential EU Law in Charts (5th ed, HVG-ORAC 2020).

CHAPTER 15

Writing an International Law Textbook

James Summers

1 Introduction

This chapter is a personal reflection on the process of writing an international law textbook. It looks at the dynamics and limitations inherent in the textbook writing process and considers some of the features of the proverbial 'good' textbook for teaching international law. It draws from my own experience of writing an International Law: Text, Cases and Materials book, first, for Pearson and then for Cambridge University Press. This writing process is nearing completion but not yet complete. Therefore, these reflections are on writing a textbook rather than publishing or revising one. The first part of this chapter will explore the element of originality in a textbook and how this informs its structure. The second part will consider the necessary attributes of 'good' textbook, including authority, reliability, clarity, engagement with the reader and precision, and how these can be approached. In both cases, the chapter will consider how the factors of time, word count and the market influence the textbook writing process.

2 What Is Your USP?

"What is your USP?" This is one of the first questions that people will ask when they hear that you are writing a textbook and it is important to have a clear answer. The 'unique selling point' is the rationale for a textbook project. There is no shortage of high-quality textbooks by distinguished authors, so an initial challenge for any textbook project will be not just to add to the literature but make a distinct and desirable contribution. A particular question is why people would purchase your textbook instead of other established works, which in many cases have been steadily refined over years or even decades.

2.1 *Constraints on Writing a Textbook*

Despite a wide range of titles that might support the perception that "everyone's writing one", producing an international law textbook is a minority pursuit and will always be one. There are good reasons for this. There are benefits

 DOI:10.1163/9789004678880_019

from writing a textbook. Teaching is an obvious one. The process of writing a textbook helps builds a more holistic understanding of international law. Perhaps the only negative from the process for teaching is the temptation to overload your and students with excess information. One textbook chapter could be the source of several hours of teaching. However, there are also benefits, more immediately tangible ones, from not writing a textbook. A textbook requires an enormous commitment and any benefits from a textbook can be weighed against reduced research output.

International law poses a unique challenge for textbook writing. An early pioneer of the form, Henry Wheaton in his *Elements of International Law* reflected in 1836 on "those who know the difficulties of the undertaking."[1] Nevertheless, up to the mid-twentieth century, international law was just another specialism. Since then it has grown into a legal system in many ways as complex and varied as national ones. The central challenge in any general international law textbook is condensing an immense volume of information into an accessible and readable account. The scale of this task should not be underestimated.

Academic institutions may also create disincentives.[2] The time allocated for writing by research-active staff may not extend to a textbook project. If this is the case, textbook writing necessarily becomes a side-project, undertaken alongside or more likely at the expense of research. "Oh, you are working on a textbook", one head of department told me, "we've banned that". Authors may take a strategic decision not to continue with a textbook or pare back its content to complete it.

The single biggest constraint on textbook writing is time. To put this factor in perspective, consider the number of chapters needed in a textbook. This varies but is unlikely to be much below twenty. Some chapters are more demanding than others and time will also be needed to review, consolidate and update the textbook at the end. A good rule of thumb might, therefore, be to take the time needed to write one chapter and multiply it by twenty-five.

How long does it take to write one chapter? Publishers encourage textbook authors to write a chapter in a month or a month-and-a-half. In my experience, this is optimistic. Nonetheless, on the basis of a month-and-a-half per chapter, a textbook would take over three years. This assumes that the author can work continuously on the project for the whole three years. If other commitments

1 H. Wheaton, *Elements of International Law* (2nd edn, Little Brown and Co. 1863) xviii.
2 See C. Warbrick, 'Brownlie's Principles of Public International Law: An Assessment' (2000) 11 EJIL 621, 629.

are factored in and the chapter takes more than a month-and-a-half, then a project can take much, much longer.

What can be covered in the timeframe of a month to a month-and-a-half per chapter? A textbook chapter can be compared in length to a journal article. How long does it take to write an article for publication? It is usually more than a month-and-a-half. It could be argued that these are different things. A research publication needs to show greater originality than a textbook chapter and this takes time to develop and refine. However, if both are to be engaging, insightful and clear, rather than a technical summary, they must show a confident understanding of the issues and a firm grasp of the material. In some ways an article could be less demanding. It must show a clear insight and original research but this will often fall narrowly within an author's specialisation and build on their previous work.

A textbook, by contrast, is a generalist project.[3] However, the fragmented nature of international law means that generalism is really the linking of a series of specialisms. A lecturer who has taught an international law module will, of course, be familiar with the specialisms that make up the different regimes of international law but addressing them in a textbook requires a new level of care and attention. In a system defined by competing interests, the devil in international law has always been in the detail. Getting the detail right is fundamental to the quality of a textbook and the unavoidable reality is that this takes time. In principle, the perfect chapter could take a year to write. Multiple that by twenty-five and a textbook could be the project of a lifetime. You could leave the royalties to your grandchildren, though it is likely that the publishers will have lost patience by then. In reality, textbooks will be completed far sooner but this means that inevitable time pressures impact on their content.

There are ways to reduce the timeframe for the completion of a textbook. One way is for an author to rework and update an established textbook by another author. Recent examples include new editions of Brownlie's, Brierly's, Akehurst's, Cassese's and to an extent Oppenheim's works.[4] This has not been my experience, so I cannot comment on it, though the challenge is to both

3 See, e.g., G. Hernández, *International Law* (OUP 2019) VII.

4 J. Crawford, *Brownlie's Principles of Public International Law* (9th edn, OUP 2019); A. Clapham, *Brierly's Law of Nations: An Introduction to the Role of International Law in International Relations* (7th edn, OUP 2012); A. Orakhelashvili, *Akehurst's Modern Introduction to International Law* (8th edn, Routledge 2019); P. Gaeta, J. E. Viñuales and S. Zappala, *Cassese's International Law* (3rd edn 2020); R. Higgins, P. Webb, D. Akande, S. Sivakumaran and J. Sloan, *Oppenheim's International Law: United Nations* (OUP 2017).

respect the legacy of the previous author while moving the project forward. Another approach that reduces time with the added benefit of drawing from a range of expertise is the multi-authored edited collection. Examples include Malcolm Evan's *International Law*,[5] Mohammed Bedjaoui's *International Law: Achievements and Prospects*[6] or James Crawford and Martti Koskenniemi's *Cambridge Companion to International Law*.[7]

2.2 *The Factors in Uniqueness*

Despite these challenges, there is a rich variety of textbooks by distinguished authors, enough to fill almost every teaching niche. However, not every niche can be permanently filled. Textbooks are a long-term project that take considerable time to produce and maintain. Books become out of date for various reasons and a new niche opens up. Moreover, these gaps cannot be quickly filled. Textbook projects come with a substantial gap between initiation and completion. The USP of any textbook project will be to find a niche, a gap in the market that has not been effectively covered (and is actually worth filling) and then convincingly establish itself within it. It is possible to identify such a gap and approach a publisher, but another scenario is that a publisher will have identified it themselves and then look for a writer to produce this content. Either way, the publisher will make an assessment of the project and on that basis help you through the process of approval.

This centres on independent academic peer review. A textbook proposal, including its proposed contents and sample chapters will be sent to a small number of academics for review. Those reviewers will not only comment on the quality and viability of the proposal, but also its potential marketability. Will it have wide or only niche appeal? These reviewers, of course, are a sample of the audience for the book. They will be the people who may (or may not) ultimately select it for their module reading lists.

There are two ways to demonstrate uniqueness. The first is format. Textbooks can be categorised by length and on this basis fall into three types. First, there are the short 'introductions' to international law. This aim to be concise, readable and easy to digest. They do not go into great detail, sometimes skipping over complex areas, and are lightly referenced.[8] Second, conversely, there are

5 M. Evans (ed.), *International Law* (5th edn, OUP 2018).
6 M. Bedjaoui, *International Law: Achievements and Prospects* (UNESCO 1991).
7 J. Crawford and M. Koskenniemi (eds.) *The Cambridge Companion to International Law* (CUP 2011).
8 "[R]efreshingly free from the ballast of footnotes". C. H. Alexandrowicz, 'Review of J. E. S. Fawcett, The Law of Nations' (1969) 18 ICLQ 521.

the heavy-weight 'practitioner' books. These offer considerable depth and length and are heavily referenced, not only supporting the analysis but also acting as a gateway to cases and literature. As such, they are a crucial for both practitioners and researchers, though they are primarily intended for students[9] and their detail can sometimes be overwhelming for a first-time reader.[10] The length of chapters can also create practical difficulties for assigned reading for lectures and seminars. If a week's teaching covers two or more topics, such as jurisdiction and immunities or the various territorial regimes, then it may be difficult to fit more than one lengthy chapter into a reasonable list of recommended reading. Third, there are medium length 'intermediate' works that include some of the detail missing in short introductions, but do not have the same level of detail and referencing as practitioner books.

Length connects to level, which concerns the intended audience. Again, this divides into three groups. First, there are undergraduate students who will be studying international law for the first time. If they are law students, they will be familiar with the discipline of law, especially if they take international law in their second or third year of study. Second, there are postgraduate masters students. These are a more diverse group. Some will have previously studied international law at an undergraduate level. These students will be already familiar with the discipline and will look for a higher level of engagement. Alongside these students, however, there will be others with a non-legal background, such as politics or history, who will be approaching international law and indeed law itself for the first time. They will need a clear introduction in much the same way as undergraduates. Third, there are researchers and practitioners who do not need an introduction but specific details on an area of law and concise direction to its associated material. These roles are not mutually exclusive. At an undergraduate level, there may be different demands from a textbook depending on its use as background reading for lectures and seminars or for research in assignments and dissertations. Shorter textbooks are tailored for the first role, but they can also be adapted for the latter too with

9 "[T]he essential international law text for students and practitioners." Crawford (n 4) back cover publicity.

10 See, e.g., James Crawford: "To speak of a thousand-page compilation of our subject as 'introductory' raises serious pedagogical issues. How much can students be expected to absorb, and how much to understand?' J. Crawford, 'Review of Gillian Triggs, International Law: Contemporary Principles and Practices' (2007) 56 ICLQ 213, 214. See also O. Sender and M. Wood, 'Review of Brierly's Law of Nations and Brownlie's Principles of Public International Law' (2013) 107 AJIL 959, 962; M. Koskenniemi, 'Review of Brownlie's Principles of Public International Law' (2013) 83 BYIL 137, 137–138.

further reading lists or annotated bibliographies. These can be calibrated to provide basic reading for a standard student essay.

In addition, there is the relationship between textbooks and primary sources. It is expected that students will become familiar with relevant cases and instruments. Some textbooks are associated with a separate volume of materials[11] and almost all are nowadays accompanied by a website with additional material. Alternatively, an international law text could be combined with cases and materials in a single 'TCM' package.[12] This has an advantage in allowing the text and materials to interact with each other, though the effect is to greatly expand the overall length. How much depends on the ratio of text to materials. Conversely, there are cases and materials books that include commentaries, which over successive editions have effectively expanded into an alternative version of a text, cases and materials book – a materials, cases and text book.[13] Nonetheless, almost all the material found in these collections is also available on the internet. This can allow module convenors to bypass these books and create their own materials collections for their module websites.

A second way to assert the unique nature of a book is with a distinct methodological approach. It is argued here that the scope for this is more limited as the primary organisational basis of a textbook but is likely to be more prominent in informing some of its content and structure. It can also be noted that there is a blurring between textbooks and general monographs can be used in teaching, such as Rosalyn Higgins' *Problems and Process*,[14] or edited collections like Martti Koskenniemi's *International Law*[15] or Hilary Charlesworth and Christine Chinkin's *The Boundaries of International Law*.[16]

The process of writing a textbook creates pressures against a radical new methodology as the primary basis for structuring a textbook. The expectation is that an international law textbook, as a teaching tool, will conform to general expectations on how that law is taught. This includes the general structure of lectures. How likely is it that lecturers will restructure their teaching to fit a new textbook? The overwhelming methodology for international law is positivist and if a textbook were to deviate strongly from this, it could be

11 See, e.g., I. Brownlie, *Basic Documents in International Law* (5th edn, OUP 2002); J. Klabbers, *International Law Documents* (CUP 2016).

12 See, e.g., A. Abass, *International Law: Text, Cases and Materials* (2nd edn, OUP 2014).

13 See D. J. Harris and S. Sivakumaran, *Cases and Materials on International Law* (8th edn, Sweet and Maxwell 2015).

14 R. Higgins, *Problems and Process: International Law and How We Use It* (Clarendon 1994).

15 M. Koskenniemi (ed.), *International Law* (Dartmouth 1992).

16 H. Charlesworth and C. Chinkin (eds.), *The Boundaries of International Law: A Feminist Analysis* (Manchester University Press 2000).

questioned how useful it would be as a teaching tool. This is not to say that there no scope for critical engagement or innovation. The advertising for textbooks emphatically rejects the notion that they are simply descriptive of the law, instead emphasising their critical perspective,[17] and their intent to challenge the underlying assumptions of the system,[18] reveal its essential context[19] or adopt a wider, more inclusive perspective.[20] The trends and tensions within international law – state and non-state actors, international institutions, horizontal and vertical structures, new technologies, different cultures and marginalised voices – give considerable scope for such innovation. Nonetheless, these are likely to be perspectives that inform the text of a book rather than define its organisation.

The process of writing a textbook creates other pressures that tend to relegate distinctive methodologies to a more limited role. One of the key questions for a textbook publisher is how it will be used. Will it be adopted as a main/core text or will it be consigned to the more marginal role of additional reading? A textbook that conforms to teaching expectations is more likely to be adopted as a main text, while distinctive approaches to international law might tend towards additional reading. Likewise, the reviewers who are asked to make this distinction may be more likely give positive feedback on chapters that correspond with their own teaching expectations and the existing structure of their modules.

The process of textbook writing proceeds through a series of batches, each batch containing several chapters, which are peer reviewed. This allows the publisher and author to check on the quality of the work as it progresses and how it matches reviewer expectations. For example, with my own book, one batch of chapters contained a particularly lengthy history chapter. A reviewer pointed out, quite rightly, that such a long history chapter did not fit with contemporary account of international law. A key feature of textbooks is that they are up to date and forward-looking. The chapter was correspondingly edited down but this illustrates a process in which authors are shepherded towards a work that conforms with existing expectations. This review process also covers the structure of the textbook and the organisation of chapters. Publishers

17 See back cover publicity for M. Shaw, *International Law* (8th edn, CUP 2017); V. Lowe, *International Law* (OUP 2007); A. Henriksen, *International Law* (2nd edn, OUP 2019); Hernandez (n 3).

18 Evans (n 5) back cover publicity.

19 D. J. Latham Brown, *Public International Law* (Sweet and Maxwell 1970) back cover publicity.

20 Orakhelashvili (n 4) back cover publicity.

will ask reviewers if there are any chapters that are unnecessary or ones that should be added. The responses to this will again push the project towards general perceptions of what a textbook should look like.

This is not to suggest an unduly restrictive process. Authors enjoy considerable freedom in how they write their books. Publishers, in my experience, are not seeking to lever an author into a rigid predetermined mould. On the contrary, I have found them to be flexible when chapters have been divided, merged and reorganised as the textbook has developed. Authors also have a general freedom in deciding the content of their chapters and perhaps to develop signature chapters that reflect their particular interests – provided that they are positively reviewed. There is plenty of scope to innovate and an incentive to do so in order to be contemporary, original and distinctive. Part of the originality of a textbook is that the author is seen to bring their own approach to a subject. The marketing of new textbooks tends to emphasise their "distinctive"[21] "innovative"[22] or "unique"[23] take on the law. This is an expectation that needs to meet. Incorporating new methodologies to a certain degree is a way to do this. The textbook process, therefore, arguably discourages innovative methodologies in a dominant organising role but encourages a more limited but still informative use.

2.3 *National and Internationalist Perspectives*

A final factor shaping the focus of a textbook is the intended market. This can impact on whether a textbook is seen as 'national' or 'internationalist'. International law textbooks are, in principle, freed from the more limited scope of other law textbooks focussed on the national law of a particular state. However, this does not mean that they will necessary be 'internationalist', eschewing a national orientation. Discussion in the Committee on the Teaching of International Law of the International Law Association in 2010 revealed divisions among scholars over whether an internationalist or national approach was most beneficial. The latter was considered particularly valuable for legal practice.[24]

21 Id.

22 J. H. Currie, C. Forcese, J. Harrington and V. Oostervold, *International Law: Doctrine, Practice and Theory* (2nd edn, Irwin 2014) publicity.

23 J. L. Dunoff, M. Hakimi, S. R. Ratner and D. Wippman, *International Law: Norms, Actors, Process: A Problem-Orientated Approach* (5th edn, Wolters Kluwer 2020) publicity.

24 ILA, Hague Conference 2010, Final Report of the Committee on the Teaching of International Law 6.

International law has an inherent relationship with national law, drawing from domestic practice, and being implemented through legislation and in national courts. Indeed, the interaction between national courts in their interpretation of international law has become a factor in its development.[25] The significance of this national-international interaction will vary between chapters. It is obviously central to the 'interaction between national and international law' chapter and is also prominent in jurisdiction, jurisdictional immunities and state recognition. This means that any textbook will have some national orientation and the issue, as Anthea Roberts has noted, is finding an appropriate balance:

> Something is certainly lost if the main way international law is understood is through a state's own domestic case law and materials. But something is also lost when a state's international law textbooks and casebooks supply almost no focus on how that state interacts with the international legal system or how international law is incorporated into and approached within that state's domestic legal system.[26]

In Roberts' own comparative study of international law textbooks, the degree to which a book may focus on the national law of a particular state can be influenced by its legal tradition, size and relationship to the traditional centres of international law scholarship. In states in which international law teaching has relied on textbooks from other counties, nationally-orientated textbooks may be necessary to allow students to understand their own domestic practice.[27]

The range of national practice covered by textbooks may be influenced by time, word count and the market. While the market for an international law textbook is potentially broader than a national one, most international law textbooks are focussed on a specific national or regional market. This applies even among countries, such as common law ones, with a shared language and legal tradition. A British international law textbook will not necessarily sell well in the American market. Thus, publishers will approach a textbook with a primary market in mind and direct authors towards it, though, it should be

25 See E. Benvenisti, 'Judicial Misgivings Regarding the Application of International Law: An Analysis of Attitudes of National Courts' (1993) 4 EJIL 159–183. E. Benvenisti and G. W. Downs, 'National Courts, Domestic Democracy, and the Evolution of International Law' (2009) 20 EJIL 59–72.

26 A. Roberts, *Is International Law International?* (OUP 2017) 152.

27 Id. 152. See, e.g., J. Dugard, M. du Plessis, T. Maluwa and D. Tladi, *Dugard's International Law: A South African Pespective* (5th edn, Juta 2019).

added that in my experience this has not been done in prescriptive fashion. The market will then inform the selection of national material. The law and practice of some states will be essential to the intended market of a textbook, while other national practice might be desirable but not strictly necessary. How this choice of material plays out depends on the length and depth of a textbook. Nonetheless, considering that a textbook project will be pressed for space and time, choices will need to be made on its content and focus.

3 Reads Like a Textbook

"This reads like a textbook". This is a comment that many of us have written on student feedback sheets. It is not intended as a compliment. The negative tone may come, in large part, because an essay reads like *a particular* textbook. Nonetheless, the 'textbook' label is often used to confer the idea that a text is dull, descriptive, unoriginal and not particularly insightful.

What attributes should be attached to the proverbial 'good' textbook?[28] The self-image of textbooks, reflected in their publicity, often centres on a pairing of rigour and clarity, in a mutually reinforcing role. After all, the best way to demonstrate expertise in international law is to explain it clearly. The publicity for Anthony Aust's *Handbook of International Law* describes it as "written by an expert international lawyer" in a "user-friendly format"[29] Jan Klabbers' *International Law* is highlighted as a book that combines "both academic rigour and clarity of expression" and breathes "new life and energy into the subject".[30] Malcolm Shaw's *International Law* is advertised to offer an "unbeatable combination of clarity of expression and academic rigour",[31] while Antonio Cassese's *International Law* is "stimulating and authoritative".[32] The fundamental importance of this pairing is likewise affirmed in reviews.[33]

What elements can be identified in this pairing of rigour and clarity? The first is authority. Textbooks are conceived as authorities to inform students, researchers, practitioners, professionals, organisations, and perhaps most

28 See Warbrick (n 2) 632.

29 A. Aust, *Handbook of International Law* (2nd edn, CUP 2010) back cover publicity.

30 J. Klabbers, *International Law* (2nd edn, CUP 2017) back cover publicity.

31 Shaw (n 17) back Cover Publicity.

32 A. Cassese, *International Law* (2nd edn, OUP 2005) back cover publicity.

33 See M. Fitzmaurice, 'Review of Akehurst's Introduction to International Law' (1999) 48 ICLQ 721; D. Guilfoyle, 'Review of Anthony Aust, Handbook of International Law' (2006) 55 ICLQ 769.

desirable of all, judges. In principle, a textbook should be considered as a writing of a most qualified publicist under Article 38(1)(d) of the ICJ Statute. Authority is, therefore, a basic necessity. Authority relates to the status of the writer but in terms of the text it attaches to a second attribute, reliability. Can the information in a textbook be relied on? Can the analysis by the author be relied on? A reliable text at a minimum needs to be accurate and contemporary. This means that slips in the dates of cases or article numbers in treaties, which can so easily happen in a long writing project, need to be checked and a constant eye kept on new developments. These attributes can be considered basic necessities but other attributes go to the heart of the 'textbook' jibe. A textbook needs to be clear and engaging if it is to perform its role in teaching and conferring knowledge.

Textbook publicity invariably lauds how 'accessible'[34] it is to the reader – in a style that is "refreshingly clear",[35] "clear and elegant",[36] "clear and balanced",[37] "simple et aussi complète",[38] "lucid, untechnical",[39] delivered "in plain terms",[40] "conversational and easy to read",[41] and delivered in a format that is "user-friendly".[42] However, underpinning all these elements in the need for precision. Perhaps the most common word textbooks use to describe themselves, aside from 'accessible', is 'concise'.[43] The essential function in writing a textbook is to distil the enormous volume of information that forms international law into a single accessible work. How this is done will define whether a book is clear, engaging and authoritative. It is hard to be informed and engaging if you are struggling to condense the relevant material.

---

34 See, e.g., E. Tourme Jouannet, *A Short Introduction to International Law* (CUP 2013) back cover publicity.

35 Klabbers (n 30) back cover publicity.

36 G. von Glahn and J. L. Taulbee, *Law among Nations: An Introduction to Public International Law* (8th edn, Pearson 2007) back cover publicity.

37 G. D. Triggs, *International Law: Contemporary Principles and Practices* (2nd edn, LexisNexis 2010) back cover publicity.

38 P. Daillier, M. Forteau, N. Q. Dinh and A. Pellet, *Droit international public* (8th edn, LGDJ 2009) publicity.

39 M. Akehurst, *A Modern Introduction to International Law* (3rd edn, George Allen and Unwin 1977) back cover publicity.

40 Henriksen (n 17) back cover publicity.

41 A. Kaczorowska-Ireland, *Public International Law* (5th edn, Routledge 2015) back cover publicity.

42 Back cover publicity for Aust (n 29).

43 See back cover publicity for R. M. M. Wallace and O. Martin-Ortega, *International Law* (8th edn, Sweet and Maxwell 2016); M. Dixon, *Textbook on International Law* (7th edn, OUP 2013); Henriksen (n 17); Orakhelashvili (n 4); Aust (n 29); Klabbers (n 30).

Whether or not you subscribe to the fragmentation of international law, the international legal system is a huge system that consists of numerous specialist regimes. It is unlikely realistically that as a writer all of these specialisms will be your specialism. The challenge then is to distil this information without sacrificing essential detail, accuracy or insight. As mentioned earlier, any particular textbook chapter might be expected to be about the length of a journal article. (Journal articles vary in length but then so do textbooks). However, the material covered in this space can be found in hefty books spanning hundreds of pages. Many books on treaty law, human rights or international environmental law, to name just three, are longer than the average international law textbook. The question is how this information is distilled into a much shorter format, without losing insight and becoming a dry summary of the law.

Dispassionate legal writing can be described as 'matter of fact' and 'down to business'[44] and that is no bad thing. There is a lot of mileage in a no-nonsense style that gets straight to the point. A 1906 review of the original Oppenheim's *International Law* in *The Spectator*, for example, complemented the text for its "acumen and moderation".[45] Arguably, the most important task of a 'good' textbook writer is to carry their readers with them. The worst attribute of a textbook writer is to be aloof from the reader and the biggest failure to leave them behind. There is, after all, a lot of ground to cover.

To avoid this, it is important to bear in mind the reader you are addressing. Most academic writing is inter-professional. It does not come with explanations for many of the concepts used, as to do so would be excessively disruptive. It should be remembered that the initial interaction between a textbook and its readership will be on this level too. The first people to read a textbook will be academics who teach international law modules and their role will be pivotal in its subsequent selection for students.

However, ultimately the majority of the readers of a textbook and ones with most to gain from an effective introduction to international law will be students. Unless, the book is solidly aimed at practitioners, the most common reader should be presumed to be a late teens/early twenties undergraduate student with no previous knowledge of international law. If they are law students, international law will be different from the national law they have previously studied. If they are not, those students will also need to understand law as a discipline.

44 See, e.g., "It treats the contemporary world situation in a practical manner, with reality and without ideology". G. Schwartzenberger and E. D. Brown, *A Manual of International Law* (6th edn, Professional Books 1976) back cover publicity.

45 *The Spectator* (7 April 1906) 545.

Being clear, direct and concise means avoiding the obscure formulas, convoluted sentences and meandering paragraphs that often appear in legal analysis and academic writing. But, distilling information into a textbook is not about summarising – which leaves it dry and technical – but explaining it succinctly. One of the challenges we set for PhD students is to explain their thesis in one or two sentences. The challenge for a textbook is to take that same approach and apply it to an entire book. The distillation of information in a textbook involve capturing the essential details of a series of principles, procedures, institutions or actors. The discipline is to explain each of those elements it as clearly as possible in a few sentences. Then repeat.

In doing this, I have found it useful to draw inspiration from people whose job involves being able to coin a phrase, such as journalists, novelists and even screenwriters. Some of the best feedback I received from reviewers involved a discussion of the concept of impossibility in the defence of *force majeure*. I explained the concept with a sentence inspired from a line in a film on the nature of impossibility – the Tom Cruise action vehicle Mission Impossible II. Some readers might recoil at this admission, and this is not to suggest that a textbook should read like a Hollywood screenplay. Nonetheless, a writer should positively look for phrases that capture a concept as succinctly as possible. There is, of course, a danger of going too far down a popular route. International law has the material to allow this. There are colourful stories – from embassy sieges to a burning boat falling down a massive waterfall – but a textbook is not a page-turning novel. Eye-catching details might be an easy way to engage the reader but they distract from the real narrative, the development of the law. The need for academic rigour sets limits on the acceptable style, with interesting asides kept on the side. If the style appears to undermine the rigour of the book's analysis then its credibility will be damaged.

Lastly, international law literature has its own high cultural tradition with liberal use of Latin phrases that throw up their own barriers to communication. The days have long passed when most students could be expected to understand what they mean. Indeed, a reasonable assumption, given the diversity of backgrounds of students in any law classroom, is not to presume any particular linguistic skills. At the same time, Latin terms are part of the vocabulary of international law and not engaging with those terms is to fail to equip students with the necessary skills to read an international law text. The clearest approach seems to be to accompany them as much as possible with a translation or explanation aided with a separate glossary of terms.

4 Conclusion

The aim in this chapter has been to lay bare the textbook-writing process and the constraints within it. It identifies two key challenges in an international law textbook – the unique selling point and developing the necessary attributes of a good textbook in terms of accuracy, reliability, clarity, engagement and precision. The textbook writing process can be seen as one in which the writer has considerable freedom but is also constrained by time, word count, peer review and the market. In terms of originality, these factors encourage a certain level of innovation but work against more radical changes to the structure and content of a book. The attributes of the good textbook can be seen as a process of distilling a large amount of information into a relatively concise format. The challenge is not simply to reduce this information to a smaller format but to communicate it in a clear and effective way.

This chapter has been cautionary in tone as it has sought to make a realistic assessment of the challenges and pressures inherent in the textbook writing process. Still, there are clear benefits to writing an international law textbook in terms of better-informed teaching and a more holistic understanding of international law. A textbook also has the potential to introduce you to a much wider range of readers – people who might not otherwise read your more specialist work. In 2011 US special forces stormed the secret compound of Al-Qaeda leader Osama bin Laden in Abbottabad. In his bedroom, they found a stack of books for bedside reading. At the top of the pile was a copy of Anthony Aust's *Handbook of International Law*.[46] Once you write a textbook there is no knowing who it will reach.

Bibliography

Abass, A., *International Law: Text, Cases and Materials* (2nd edn, OUP 2014).

Akehurst, M., *A Modern Introduction to International Law* (3rd edn, George Allen and Unwin 1977).

Alexandrowicz, C. H., 'Review of J. E. S. Fawcett, The Law of Nations' (1969) 18 ICLQ 521.

Aust, A. *Handbook of International Law* (2nd edn, CUP 2010).

Bedjaoui, M., *International Law: Achievements and Prospects* (UNESCO 1991).

Benvenisti, E., 'Judicial Misgivings Regarding the Application of International Law: an Analysis of Attitudes of National Courts' (1993) 4 EJIL 159–183.

46 Anthony Aust Obituary, *The Times* (30 May 2018).

Benvenisti, E., and Downs, G. W., 'National Courts, Domestic Democracy, and the Evolution of International Law' (2009) 20 EJIL 59–72.

Brownlie, I., *Basic Documents in International Law* (5th edn, OUP 2002); J. Klabbers, *International Law Documents* (CUP 2016).

Cassese, A., *International Law* (2nd edn, OUP 2005).

Charlesworth, H., and Chinkin, C., (eds.), *The Boundaries of International Law: a Feminist Analysis* (Manchester University Press 2000).

Clapham, A., *Brierly's Law of Nations: an Introduction to the Role of International Law in International Relations* (7th edn, OUP 2012).

Crawford, J., 'Review of Gillian Triggs, International Law: Contemporary Principles and Practices' (2007) 56 ICLQ 213.

Crawford, J., *Brownlie's Principles of Public International Law* (9th edn, OUP 2019).

Crawford, J., and Koskenniemi, M., (eds.) *The Cambridge Companion to International Law* (CUP 2011).

Currie, J. H., Forcese, C., Harrington, J., and Oostervold, V., *International Law: Doctrine, Practice and Theory* (2nd edn, Irwin 2014).

Daillier, P., Forteau, M., Dinh, N. Q., and Pellet, A., *Droit international public* (8th edn, LGDJ 2009).

Dixon, M., *Textbook on International Law* (7th edn, OUP 2013).

Dugard, J., du Plessis, M., Maluwa, T., and Tladi, D., *Dugard's International Law: a South African Pespective* (5th edn, Juta 2019).

Dunoff, J. L., Hakimi, M., Ratner, S. R., and Wippman, D., *International Law: Norms, Actors, Process: a Problem-Orientated Approach* (5th edn, Wolters Kluwer 2020).

Evans, M., (ed.), *International Law* (5th edn, OUP 2018).

Fitzmaurice, M., 'Review of Akehurst's Introduction to International Law' (1999) 48 ICLQ 721.

Gaeta, P., Viñuales, J. E., and Zappala, S., *Cassese's International Law* (3rd edn 2020).

von Glahn, G., and Taulbee, J. L., *Law among Nations: an Introduction to Public International Law* (8th edn, Pearson 2007).

Guilfoyle, D., 'Review of Anthony Aust, Handbook of International Law' (2006) 55 ICLQ 769.

Harris, D. J., and Sivakumaran, S., *Cases and Materials on International Law* (8th edn, Sweet and Maxwell 2015).

Henriksen, A., *International Law* (2nd edn, OUP 2019).

Hernández, G., *International Law* (OUP 2019).

Higgins, R., *Problems and Process: International Law and How We Use It* (Clarendon 1994).

Higgins, R., Webb, P., Akande, D., Sivakumaran, S., and Sloan, J., *Oppenheim's International Law: United Nations* (OUP 2017).

ILA Final Report of the Committee on the Teaching of International Law (Hague Conference 2010).

Kaczorowska-Ireland, A., *Public International Law* (5th edn, Routledge 2015).

Klabbers, J., *International Law* (2nd edn, CUP 2017).

Koskenniemi, M., (ed.), *International Law* (Dartmouth 1992).

Koskenniemi, M, 'Review of Brownlie's Principles of Public International Law' (2013) 83 BYIL 137.

Latham Brown, D. J., *Public International Law* (Sweet and Maxwell 1970).

Lowe, V., *International Law* (OUP 2007).

Orakhelashvili, A., *Akehurst's Modern Introduction to International Law* (8th edn, Routledge 2019).

Roberts, A., *Is International Law International?* (OUP 2017).

Sender, O., and Wood, M., 'Review of Brierly's Law of Nations and Brownlie's Principles of Public International Law' (2013) 107 AJIL 959.

Shaw, M., *International Law* (8th edn, CUP 2017).

Schwartzenberger, G., and Brown, E. D., *A Manual of International Law* (6th edn, Professional Books 1976).

Tourme Jouannet, E., *A Short Introduction to International Law* (CUP 2013).

Triggs, G. D., *International Law: Contemporary Principles and Practices* (2nd edn, LexisNexis 2010).

Wallace, R. M. M., and Martin-Ortega, O., *International Law* (8th edn, Sweet and Maxwell 2016).

Warbrick, C., 'Brownlie's Principles of Public International Law: an Assessment' (2000) 11 EJIL 621.

Wheaton, H., *Elements of International Law* (2nd edn, Little Brown and Co. 1863).

CHAPTER 16

Teaching International Law Massively

*Pierre d'Argent**

Peter Hilpold invited me to contribute to the second "Teaching International Law" conference he organized in Innsbruck following the publication of a contribution I authored in the proceedings of the Amsterdam's conference of the European Society of International Law.[1] Due to time constraints, Peter graciously agreed that I participated remotely to the Innsbruck conference. While my oral contribution largely drew from my chapter on "Teachers of International Law" written as a follow-up to the Amsterdam conference, it will not be summarized nor repeated here. Rather, the pages below elaborate on the teaching experience I also briefly shared during the Innsbruck conference. As this teaching experience concerns the international law Massive Open Online Course I pioneered on www.edx.org in 2015, it was actually quite fitting to take part in the Innsbruck conference remotely.

Since that conference and the first draft of this contribution submitted for publication, the COVID-19 pandemic struck the world. As a result, universities shut down classrooms and auditoriums. The teaching profession moved online, and we all got more familiar with Zoom, Webex, Teams and other videoconferencing systems. Countless pedagogical experience took place, with more or less success, i.e. more or less boredom on the part of the students and the teachers alike. Most online classes during the pandemic have not taken the form of MOOCs since the pandemic was sudden and MOOCs require months of preparation. Rather, online teaching during the pandemic very often (and even if multiple experiences and formats were tried) resembled teaching in real auditoriums, save for the camera and the screen. However, being able to rely on a pre-existing MOOC during the pandemic certainly facilitated the transition to better distance learning strategies, even for students who would have attended on campus classes in normal times.

---

* Full Professor at the University of Louvain Member of the Institute of International Law Member of the Brussels Bar.

1 P. d'Argent, "Teachers of International Law", *in* J. d'Aspremont, T. Gazzini, A. Nollkaemper, W. Werner (eds.), *International Law as a Profession* (Cambridge: Cambridge University Press, 2017) 412–427.

 | DOI:10.1163/9789004678880_020

This short paper recalls the reasons that incited me to author an International Law MOOC (I), the difficulties and choices in making it (II), the specific challenges of teaching international law to a far-away audience (III) and to on-campus students when a MOOC is assigned, including during the pandemic (IV). The paper briefly concludes (V).

I The Inspiration

During the academic year 2012–2013, Anant Agarwal – a professor of civil engineering at the Massachusetts Institute of Technology, founder and CEO of www.edx.org[2] – visited Louvain university and introduced colleagues of all faculties and research institutes to Massive Open Online Courses (MOOCs), the new pedagogical tool that was trending at the time and since then became part of the higher education landscape.

There are currently two main platforms for university MOOCs: Coursera[3] and edX.[4] EdX was founded by Harvard and MIT; it is an open and non-profit platform that today draws from about 120 of the top-ranked universities in the world, with the ambitions of "transforming traditional education, removing the barriers of cost, location and access".[5] Hosting hundreds of MOOCs in all scientific disciplines, edX has become the learning home of more than 20 million people around the world. Not only are individual online courses accessible through edX, but full-scale Master programmes are now on offer and edX has pioneered MicroMasters programmes also.[6]

I attended Anant Agarwal's conference in my university half a decade ago with a mixed feeling of bewilderment and excitement. It was impossible to remain indifferent to the immense possibilities that MOOCs were offering: the combination of text, images and videos, immediate online assessments and feedbacks, the flexibility of updates and the incorporation of public resources available on the web – all this made the software developed by edX a revolutionary tool compared to traditional teaching in class, including when using reading assignments. Moreover, MOOCs were offering the possibility to open widely the windows of the teaching rooms and, quite literally, to reach out to the world. However, at the time, very few MOOCs had been developed and

2 https://www.edx.org/about-us.
3 https://www.coursera.org/.
4 https://www.edx.org/.
5 https://www.edx.org/about-us.
6 See below.

nobody knew if they were worth the effort. Would they create a bubble of innovation for a few years and disappear as suddenly as they came to existence, or were they there to stay on the long term? Reflecting on what was presented to us during Anant Agarwal's conference, I thought that MOOCs were like a speed train: it was on the move, but from what I was seeing I could not tell its destination. Where was it heading to? Then I thought: either I stay on the side and look at the moving train, like cows look at trains in the countryside, or I jump on board even if I do not know where it will lead me.

And so, I jumped: Louvain joined edX as a Charter Member and I responded to a call for projects issued by the Louvain Learning Lab[7] that serves within the university as focal point for the development of MOOCs and pedagogical improvements.

Beyond the excitement and the curiosity that come with new possibilities, a more substantial reason led me to jump in the MOOCs' train. It is to be found in a very old paper that I had read a few years back and that crossed my mind when discovering the incredible possible outreach offered by MOOCs. The paper was published in 1907 by the *American Journal of International Law*; in fact, it was the very first paper published by *AJIL* in the form of an inaugurating editorial. Authored by Elihu Root, its title sounded like an imperative to any international law scholar living at the age of MOOCs: "*The Need of Popular Understanding of International Law*". In his paper, Root wrote:

> The increase of popular control over national conduct, which marks the political development of our time, makes it constantly more important that the great body of the people in each country should have a just conception of their international rights and duties.
>
> [...]
>
> it is very important that in every country the people whom negotiators represent and to whom arbitrators must return, shall be able to consider the controversy and judge the action of their representatives in [an] instructed and reasonable way. One means to bring about this desirable condition is to increase the general public knowledge of international rights and duties and to promote a popular habit of reading and thinking about international affairs. The more clearly the people of a country understand their own international rights the less likely they are to take extreme and extravagant views of their rights and the less likely they are to be ready to fight for something to which they are not really entitled.

7 https://uclouvain.be/fr/etudier/lll.

> The more clearly and universally the people of a country realize the international obligations and duties of their country, the less likely they will be to resent the just demands of other countries that those obligations and duties be observed. The more familiar the people of a country are with the rules and customs of self-restraint and courtesy between nations which long experience has shown to be indispensable for preserving the peace of the world, the greater will be the tendency to refrain from publicly discussing controversies with other countries in such a way as to hinder peaceful settlement by wounding sensibilities or arousing anger and prejudice on the other side.
>
> [...]
>
> the true basis of the peace and order in which we live is not fear of the policeman; it is the self-restraint of the thousands of people who make up the community and their willingness to obey the law and regard the rights of others. [...] Of course, it cannot be expected that the whole body of any people will study international law; but a sufficient number can readily become sufficiently familiar with it to lead and form public opinion in every community in our country upon all important international questions as they arise.[8]

These wise words of more than 116 years ago could not be more relevant today. They point at the inherent frailty of international law which cannot hold its promises of peace and justice by taming politics without a certain degree of popular support for the rationalization of behaviour and discourse it provides. International law is of course a professional language of justification and you need to be trained in it to use it properly; however, if international law remains the private discourse of a certain class of experts who are just content with themselves and their superb futility – in other words, if only "the style survives"[9] – it cannot but fail. On the contrary, the more a wider public understands and values international law, therefore making the respect for it a domestic political issue, the less rulers are likely to disregard it bluntly and gain political traction from such sombre cynicism.

Suddenly, at the beginning of the 21st Century, MOOCs opened possibilities to bring international law to the attention of a wider audience; an audience that could be interested in international law but would never buy a textbook,

8 *AJIL*, Vol. 1, No. 1 (Jan. – Apr., 1907), pp. 1–3.

9 M. Koskenniemi, "The Politics of International Law", *EJIL*, 1990, p. 4–32 (at 12). Interestingly, Koskenniemi's paper was the first to be published by *EJIL*.

sit and read it. And with such possibilities, maybe a new era was beginning for international law?

With those very naïve thoughts – which, for once, simply acknowledged that teaching always bears some resemblance with preaching – I embarked on the MOOC journey.

II The Making

Thanks to the financial support of a generous benefactor[10] of Louvain University who specifically allocated funds for the development of MOOCs, I was able to hire a half-time assistant[11] to help me in the making of the MOOC. The Louvain Learning Law provided indispensable coaching and support throughout the conception, development and realization of the MOOC, together with the technical realization of videos and animated drawings. While those supports proved indispensable, the structuring and actual writing of each and every video, reading, quiz and discussion forum was a personal endeavour that took me more than 6-month on a full-time basis. Having taught a general course of public international law for about 15 years was of great assistance when it came to adopt its structure and content to the MOOC format.

In designing and making my International Law MOOC, the challenge was to come up with a course that would be accessible both to a wider audience (i.e., a learned public, but not necessarily familiar with the law) and be useful in a course taught to students reading law at the university at the master's level. Indeed, in order to be financed and supported by the university, the MOOC project had to correspond to an on-campus course, part of a university degree, and be used in that course. However, at the same time, the MOOC would be accessible free of charge to learners around the world through the edX platform.

MOOCs are divided into "weeks" of teaching that correspond to parts or chapters in a textbook. Each "week" is divided into several sections, and each section into learning sequences which alternate videos, readings, quizzes and discussion forums or other activities like words clouds or Wikis. My International Law MOOC is divided into eight "weeks", each with a specific heading that uses action verbs.[12] Together, the eight weeks cover what would

10 https://www.treetopam.com/en/.

11 Ms Fanny Declerq, to whom I would like to extend publicly my gratitude. Fanny is now a journalist at *Le Soir*, the main daily French-speaking newspaper in Belgium.

12 1. Introducing International Law ; 2. Setting the international law stage; 3. Making International Law (Part I); 4. Making International Law (Part II); 5. Applying International Law; 6. Claiming Responsibility; 7. Seeking Justice; 8. Upholding Peace.

be found in any general course of public international law: subjects, sources, responsibility, settlement of dispute, use of force. Each week is made of three to six sections,[13] and each section is divided into various learning sequences.

There are 101 videos in the course,[14] of between 3 to 13 minutes each, and about twice as many reading sections that alternate with the videos. Videos convey in a very efficient way more lasting information of an historical, conceptual or structural nature. The transcript of the video runs on its right side and can be read while the video is in progress. Students can navigate the video by clicking on the transcript; control buttons also allow to speed up or slow down the video. Readings allow to go further and illustrate, while at the same time bringing back students to the essential need of learning law by reading it. Because of the way a learning sequence is organized by the MOOC software, students are naturally invited to go through it step by step, reading the texts that appear before their eyes – in contrast to a textbook where they could jump a few pages and just skim through.

All the readings are drawn from primary sources, i.e. treaties, documents of the International Law Commission or, for most of them and by pedagogical choice, cases from the International Court of Justice. The cases are each time introduced and contextualized, with selected excerpts. The full text of cases is always easily accessible for the interested learner through hyperlinks. Maps, pictures or animated drawings are used in the videos or incorporated in the reading sections to illustrate the content. While the videos are more perennial, the reading sections, quizzes, discussion forums etc. can be easily modified and updated. Learners are also invited to contribute to several Wikis, thus elaborating together a glossary page, a list of international organisations and describing the application of international law in their respective domestic legal orders.

All along the way, learners are invited to check their understanding of the videos and readings by taking short quizzes; they receive immediate feedback to their answers with a brief explanation. Except for the first introductory "week", each "week" ends with a "weekly exam" made of multiple-choice questions. At the end of the MOOC, learners who have opted for the "verified certificate"[15] must, in order to gain it, successfully complete an exam made of

13 For more details on the structure of the course, see https://www.edx.org/course/international-law.

14 All videos have also been posted on Youtube and are viewed by many people who do not enrol in the MOOC: https://www.youtube.com/channel/UCGasG4aiJ2_8ar-EXGHI1kQ.

15 The Verified Certificate costs 135 EUR.

two parts: (a) an additional multiple-choice questionnaire that cuts through the various "weeks" of the course and (b) two short essays of 1000 words each.

The MOOC is of the level of a master course at law school. Its eight "weeks" are best taken over a period of about 12 real weeks, the student's weekly workload being of about 6 to 8 hours per week. The full transcript of the videos and readings is available in PDF format for each week, totalizing 570 pages. Learners are also provided with a detailed outline and a "reading material", i.e. a collection of essential documents.

III Teaching International Law to the World

The first edition of my MOOC opened on-line on 30 April 2015. By the middle of 2021, the 9th edition was on offer on the "self-paced" mode which allows learners to enrol at anytime during the entire period when the current edition is running. While previous editions were released twice a year, the current self-paced edition is open for about 11 months, and a new edition will open with the new academic year at Louvain University in the Fall of 2023.

The first edition attracted 16.252 learners from 187 countries – the US representing 18% of the enrolment, followed by India (6%) and Brazil (5%) – the median age being 31. The gender balance was relatively even, with 52,9% of male learners, and 46,6% female. The educational background was significantly high, with 40,4% of learners having a college degree and 32,8% an advanced degree.

As is usual with MOOCs, only a fraction of the enrolled learners take part in the MOOC. Out of the first 16.252 enrolled learners, 3.000 actually started the first section and about 1.600 took part in the first weekly exam. This number dropped regularly throughout the weeks to reach about 850 learners taking part in the final exam. While about 60% of the learners taking part in the weekly exams were successful, 70% succeeded in the final exam. While 252 learners enrolled and paid for the verified certificate during the first edition of the MOOC, 144 received it. Out of the thousands of the "audit-track" learners who enrolled free of charge, 441 received an honour certificate, testifying that they completed the course with an overall score of 60% for their active participation, weekly exams and final exam. In other words, a total of 585 individuals successfully completed the first edition of the MOOC.

Those statistics remained stable with the second edition of the MOOC, but Belgium became the second country of origin of learners as the MOOC was assigned to my 550+ students. As a result, the average age of learners dropped to 27 and the gender balance slightly tilted in favour of women. Each of the next editions attracted an average number of 10,000 leaners worldwide, always with a relatively small percentage finishing the course and gaining the certificate. In 2016, from the third edition onwards, edX changed its policy concerning the delivery of certificates: while enrolment free of charge was still possible, only learners having enrolled for the "verified certificate" track, and paid for it, would be issued a certificate upon successful completion of the course. Between 2016 and 2018, during which five editions of the MOOC were offered, a total of 771 learners enrolled for the new verified certificate track and 244 such certificates were issued.

Although this last number remains modest, the enrolment statistics testify of the interest of the greater public for international law. Most students dropping out of the course do so realizing its difficulty and because they failed to realize how demanding it is when they enrolled. The edition that ended in the Fall of 2021 attracted 12,732 learners, of which 1,378 enrolled for the paid "verified certificate". The specific reasons for such increase are difficult to assess, but the COVID-19 pandemic probably is a factor.

From the 2nd to the 7th edition of the MOOC (2015–2018), I organized live questions & answers sessions by videoconference, using www.zoom.us and tacking hyperlinks to connect into the edX webpage of the MOOC. This allowed me to interact on a monthly basis for about 90 minutes with a dozen verified certificate learners from, literally, around the world. Because students from Manilla to Lima were involved, the only real concern was to find a time-zone accessible to all. The live sessions were recorded and put online for all to see. Aside from this direct interaction with learners, the discussion forums provided a free space of exchange between the students. Because international law touches on very sensitive topics, debates can be lively and frank. Some teaching assistants and graduate students monitored those debates; however, I had to intervene only once to cool down heated exchanges.

In 2018, edX initiated "MicroMasters programs". MicroMasters programs are designed to offer learners a pathway to an advanced degree and can count as credit toward completing a Master's degree program. Learners who successfully earn a MicroMasters program certificate may apply for admission to a Master's program, and if accepted, the MicroMasters program certificate will count towards the degree.

Putting my MOOC together with those authored by my Louvain colleagues Olivier De Schutter (International Human Rights Law),[16] Raphaël van Steenberghe (International Humanitarian Law)[17] and Yannick Radi

16 https://www.edx.org/course/international-human-rights-law.

17 https://www.edx.org/course/international-humanitarian-law.

(International Investment Law),[18] we initiated a MicroMasters program in International Law.[19] So far, 53 students have successfully completed the verified track of each of the four MOOCs, therefore gaining the MicroMasters certificate. Learners who complete the MicroMasters program may apply to be admitted in the (on-campus) Advanced Master (LL.M.) in International Law offered by Louvain University.[20] Each MOOC in the MicroMasters program is worth 5 credits. Therefore, the entire MicroMasters program is valued at 20 credits, or 33% of the full residential master's program. Many MicroMasters learners have expressed the wish that the Advanced Master program be fully offered remotely.

Authoring a MOOC is making your discipline and your knowledge accessible to a much wider and more diverse audience than the students attending on-campus classes. It forces you to think through a course you may have taught for years, to redesign it to make it sharper and more accessible, to balance theory and examples – and it also helps, after a couple of decades in academe, to re-boost enthusiasm for teaching.

Teaching a MOOC is also accepting to expose yourself to the world, therefore receiving praise and criticism – and accepting both with humility.[21] One of the most rewarding comment I received after the first edition of my MOOC was an email from a US pensioner who, after having written many nice things about the content of the course, confessed that next time he would go to the polling station, he would "think twice before casting [his] vote". It is difficult, upon reading such email, not to remember the 1907 editorial of Elihu Root and think, with a certain degree of professional satisfaction: mission accomplished!

IV Using a MOOC On-Campus

From its second edition onwards, my MOOC has been an integral part of the Public International Law course I teach to the students of the 1st year of the Master of Law degree at the Law Faculty of Louvain University. That course is

18 https://www.edx.org/course/international-investment-law.

19 https://www.edx.org/micromasters/louvainx-international-law. From the Fall of 2021 onwards, a fifth MOOC, on Asylum and Refugee Law and authored by my colleagues Jean-Yves Carlier and Sylvie Saroléa, will be added to the MicroMasters program.

20 https://uclouvain.be/en-prog-2019-drin2mc.

21 See the reviews of my MOOC on https://www.coursetalk.com/providers/edx/courses/international-law-2.

compulsory and followed by more than 550 students. It takes place during 14 weeks of the Fall semester, at the pace of two lectures of two hours per week.

The way I have integrated the MOOC in the on-campus course has changed over the years, but my most recent experiment is really to use it as a textbook. On Moodle, students are provided with a detailed calendar of the course; each date of lecture is given a theme and students are invited to prepare at home in anticipation of the lecture by reviewing specific sections and learning sequences of the MOOC that are listed. Students are also invited, at the end of each "week" of the MOOC, to test their understanding and knowledge by taking the online "weekly exam". They can also prepare for the final exam taking place on-campus by taking the MOOC final exam made of multiple choices and essays. I have experimented over the years to value MOOC participation or to organize monthly multiple-choice mini-exams on Moodle but had unfortunately to abandon such continuous evaluation for technical reasons.

Assigning the MOOC to the students and offering them a detailed step-by-step calendar has allowed me not to repeat every year some basic conceptual elements and use the teaching time in class to build from what they were supposed to have learnt at home. Even with a very large group of students, this has allowed me to increase their participation by taking cases to illustrate further what the MOOC taught them and elaborate from there. The MOOC has also dedramatized the symbolic importance of lectures because they know that the essential is conveyed on-line and that they can always returned to it. I would not go as far as pretending that classrooms have been turned into chat rooms. Indeed, regular classroom is still taking place – notably during 7 lectures during which the application of international law by Belgian courts is studied in French – but teaching time has become more conversational even with hundreds of students attending. It is probably possible to attain such result through a well-designed pedagogical use of a textbook, but I gather from my experience and the students' feed-back that the MOOC format is more engaging and more dynamic compared to dry pages of a book.

My only regret concerning the use of my MOOC by my Louvain students is that they appear to be utterly not interested in engaging with the discussion forums to which learners from around the world take part. At the beginning, I tried to lure them into the MOOC by mentioning that they would be able to widen their horizon and deepen their understanding of the diversity of the planet by exchanging with their peers from all continents. However, very much to my regret, I must admit that on-campus students have been astonishingly shy in that regard.

The availability of my MOOC when the pandemic struck and forced us to move teaching online made that transition rather smooth. The on-campus lectures were replaced by online lectures on Teams, but the entire articulation between homework for the students through the MOOC and the lectures was basically unchanged.

V Assessment

As the reader will have gathered from above, with a class of about 550 students, I was already teaching international law massively. This burden has become an opportunity with the technology and the new pedagogical possibilities offered by MOOCs. I have now two categories of students: my Louvain students and learners from around the world that, 10 years ago, I could not have dreamt to address and teach. For scholars with a certain taste for teaching and outreach, MOOCs offer a true existential satisfaction. The train of education and knowledge never stops.

Bibliography

d'Argent, P. International Law, Online MOOC: https://www.edx.org/course/international-law.

Harber, J. *MOOCs* (*The MIT Press Essential Knowledge series*), MIT Press, 2014, pp. 248.

Losh E. (ed.), *MOOCs and Their Afterlives: Experiments in Scale and Access in Higher Education*, University of Chicago Press, 2017, pp. 384.

Root, E. "The Need of Popular Understanding of International Law", *AJIL*, Vol. 1, No. 1 (Jan.–Apr., 1907), pp. 1–3.

Zhang, K. C. J. Bonk, T. C. Reeves, T. H. Reynolds (eds.), *MOOCs and Open Education in the Global South: Challenges, Successes, and Opportunities*, Routledge, 2019, pp. 392.

PART VI

Scholarship on Teaching of International Law

CHAPTER 17

Scholarship on the Teaching of International Law

An Overview of the State of the Art

*Lucas Lixinski**

1. Introduction

There is a growing body of interest in writing about the teaching of international law, as this volume so comprehensively demonstrates. Nonetheless, there is little in the way of analysis of what this growing body of scholarship on teaching does, what its key concerns are, and what the trends are in the teaching of international law as seen through the eyes of those international law teachers who write about teaching itself in addition to their own disciplinary subfields (I refer to them in this chapter as "teacher-authors"). This chapter aims to address that gap, surveying scholarly literature on the teaching of international law.

While I aimed to be as comprehensive as possible, my research was limited by the languages with which I am sufficiently familiar, which are European languages (English, French, Italian,[1] Portuguese, and Spanish). While most of these languages are spoken in multiple continents, they still exclude a full engagement with practices in certain parts of the world, particularly Asia and the Middle East. Therefore, the trends I indicate here should take this caveat into account, a particularly important limitation considering one of the main trends is precisely the localization of international law, as discussed below.

The literature on the teaching of international law is primarily the work of practitioners of teaching. Most of the literature is written by accomplished scholars in their own respective subfields who write in those subfields from theoretically informed, nuanced analytical positions. When they write about teaching, however, they tend to write as practitioners first, with theoretical and analytical engagement giving way to more self-reflexive pieces which may

---

* Professor, Faculty of Law & Justice, UNSW Sydney. PhD in Law, European University Institute. This chapter builds significantly upon work previously made available online. See Lucas Lixinski, 'Teaching International Law: An Annotated Bibliography' (2015), at https://www.academia.edu/23383446/Teaching_International_Law_An_Annotated_Bibliography.

1 Despite my best search efforts, however, I was unable to locate relevant scholarship in Italian.

 | DOI:10.1163/9789004678880_021

sometimes nod at pedagogical literature, but more often than not leverage other literature on international law instead. As a result, when this scholarship dialogues with other bodies of literature, it tends to intervene on substantive issues of international law, rather than on pedagogical theory. This mode of intervention, while useful within the field, and attentive to the primary readership (other international law teachers and researchers), also tends to fall short of engaging with best pedagogical practice.

Consequently, there is relatively little literature that deeply connects with pedagogical scholarship or theory in the context of teaching international law. Most of it is grounded in the experience of those who teach, and then write self-reflexively.

In terms of systematic reviews of teaching beyond the individual experiences of teacher-authors, these modes of intervention have largely fallen by the wayside. The reason is not only a predilection for self-reflection of teacher-authors, but also, markedly, an increasing rejection of certain attempts at comprehensiveness in favor of more granular understandings of what international law is. Specifically, while there were some more systematic attempts up until the 1980s and 1990s to create uniform curricula for teaching international law, those efforts have since been largely abandoned in favor of more region-specific or even country-specific teaching, as a means to embrace local politics and cultural diversity. Part of the reason for this move might be that those international legal scholars more prone to self-reflective scholarship also tend to align with critical movements or New Approaches to International Law, which have led the way in rejecting universalistic claims of international law more broadly as a field, thereby also impacting on pedagogical practice. Practice may be different in (continental) Europe, where one of the prevalent views is still to think of international law as a universalizing project, even if this view is also increasingly subjected to scrutiny in the unpacking of the European legal tradition.[2] Further, there is among its critics a growing realization that perhaps the reason for the persistent hold of the universalist project in Europe is because that universal view is, at its core, Eurocentric.

Another tranche of scholarship focuses on the way international law sits within the curriculum of a single institution, thus comparing the international law teacher to its colleagues not in the field, but within their departments. Namely, much of the literature centres on the place of international law in the

2 For a recent collection of essays, see Hilpold, Peter (ed.). *European International Law Traditions* (Springer, 2021) (surveying European traditions through the lenses of Austria, France, Germany, Italy, the Netherlands, Russia, Scandinavia, and the United Kingdom).

broader curriculum of legal education, and what that means for the position of international legal scholars vis-à-vis their peers in other legal fields.

Related to this concern about the place of international law in the curriculum, or in relation to other legal fields, there is a great concern in the literature about the connection between international law as an intellectual endeavour and something that affects ordinary legal practice. With very few exceptions that embrace international law teaching as a broader intellectual endeavour that does not necessarily need to be connected to everyday practice, a large number of texts in the literature tries to convey the relevance of international law teaching as being of immediate use to law graduates, whether they practice as private lawyers or work for government. All of these concerns seem to echo early 20th-century discussions about whether international law is "real" law, and reflect an urge to validate a field of inquiry that in all likelihood does not need validation.

I argue that, considering these trends, what is needed is more critical reflection on how international law is taught, for what purposes, and based on what premises about the place of international law in the broader legal discipline. Reflections about the doctrinal teaching of international law and literature engaged in the political dimensions of international law teaching would both benefit from being more seriously grounded on pedagogical theory. Some literature to that extent already exists, and has made important contributions to the field, renewing interest in the teaching of international law as an important part of the international lawyer's role, as opposed to an activity that detracts from research. There are even more calls for those modes of engagement, even if the texts themselves only scratch the surface of doing this work. Nevertheless, this literature also highlights the importance of interdisciplinary conversations in the discipline in the classroom, and of grounding international law in everyday reality. International law thus moves away from something that is done at the distant halls of diplomacy, to become an important means of articulating everyday political struggles. International law is thus made relevant to everyone, and the teaching of international law is secured a place in legal curricula.

To support this thesis and the trends indicated in this introduction, what follows further expands on each of these trends, woven around different descriptors to showcase how they are placed pervasively across the field. My aim is not to engage with every single text in depth in its own merits, but rather to connect texts to one another to weave a tapestry of the state of the art in this field in ways seldom attempted in legal scholarship. This chapter is therefore primarily a critical literature review, and is structured as such.

2 General Overviews and Reference Works

Historically, there are a range of significant reference works dedicated to the subject. These texts look more broadly at teaching international law, and are usually the product of larger projects backed by learned societies, particularly the American Society of International Law (ASIL). The first volume, published in 1992, is the product of an extensive survey funded by the Ford Foundation on the status of international law teaching in the United States and Canada. The study was compiled through questionnaires sent to law schools and political science departments, offering important systemic insights which have become rarer in the available literature.[3] A few years later, ASIL sponsored a second volume, this time bringing together theoretically-grounded contributions and case studies on specific materials and techniques for the teaching of international law, building upon the descriptive insights of the first volume.[4]

The United Nations Educational, Scientific, and Cultural Organization (UNESCO) has also backed a significant project in the area.[5] This volume is an early attempt to promote more cooperation in the design of international law curricula in a specific region. It surveys the status of teaching in nine countries (Australia, India, Indonesia, Japan, Republic of Korea, Pakistan, The Philippines, Sri Lanka and Thailand), and includes suggestions for closer cooperation. Despite the call for cooperation being based on an impulse towards universalization in this volume, it is worth noting that calls for regional approaches still persist in the literature, but with different objectives (further regional grounding), as discussed below.

Among those works by individual scholars without specific institutional backing, Bin Cheng edited an important collection in the early 1980s, which examines the relationship between international law teaching and diplomatic practice. This edited volume brings together contributions from authors such as Rosalyn Higgins and Robert Jennings to discuss the relationship between diplomatic practice and the teaching of international law. It is enlightening reading to stress the need to focus on international law teaching as an enterprise grounded on reality, rather than abstract categories and doctrines.[6] The theme of grounding international law in everyday life is a recurring one in the

---

3 Gamble, John, *Teaching International Law in the 1990s* (1992).

4 Gamble, John, and Joyner, Christopher (eds.), *Teaching International Law: Approaches and Perspectives* (1997).

5 UNESCO Regional Office for Education in Asia and the Pacific, *Teaching and Research in International Law in Asia and the Pacific* (1985).

6 Cheng, Bin (ed.), *International Law Teaching and Practice* (1982).

literature henceforth, as discussed further below. This aspiration, while generally concerned with the place of international law in legal training, also extends to other disciplines. Joyner for instance explores the perspective of teaching international law in political science or international relations. He focuses on international law's political utility, and ultimately tries to unify curricula for the teaching of international law, with a focus on collaborative learning.[7]

Authors like Manfred Lachs undertook broader intellectual enterprises about the role of the teacher in shaping students.[8] His book focuses on the role of the teacher in shaping the minds of students, more broadly than simply imparting knowledge. It focuses on the diversity and individuality of ideas that the teacher can transmit, and fights against the idea that the teacher transmits "doctrine", which is simply "an image against which to test and adjust one's perception of reality."[9]

These major survey works showcase a tendency towards universal insights. It is somewhat telling that few similar efforts have been undertaken in the twenty-first century, with the notable exception of Anthea Roberts' book on whether international law is truly international.[10] Before getting to this volume, however, and its call for more specificity in international law teaching, it is worth focusing on some historical texts on the teaching of international law, the focus of the next section.

3 Historical Texts

These texts are for the most part not exercises in history, they are historical themselves. They are included here because they mark specific moments where large events shaped debates about the teaching of international law. Whittuck for instance situates the teaching of international law in its role in the waning British Empire.[11] He centres on the United Kingdom experience, and other parts of the waning British Empire (Ireland, Australia, Canada, New Zealand and South Africa are discussed). Whittuck instrumentalizes the teaching of international law to governmental needs, particularly diplomatic and

---

7 See also Joyner, Christopher, 'Teaching International Law: Views from an International Relations Political Scientist' (1998) 5 *ILSA International & Comparative Law* 377.

8 Lachs, Manfred, *The Teacher in International Law: Teachings and Teaching* (1982).

9 Id., pp. 1–2.

10 Roberts, Anthea, *Is International Law International?* (Oxford University Press, 2017).

11 Whittuck, E A, 'International Law Teaching', (1917) *Problems of the War – Papers Read before the Society in the Year 1917* 43.

military. In this way, international law teaching, and a universality-aspiring curriculum, become a clear instrument of the imperial project, a trend later rebuked by other scholarship.

Other historical texts have less overt global ordering aspirations. Merrills, for instance, is one of the earlier attempts to engage with the possibility of uniform curricula in international law teaching. This historical text focuses on what the author perceives as the five key problems of international law that need to be in any course: (1) the size of the field; (2) the importance of background knowledge; (3) understanding the international system; (4) the relationship to politics; and (5) whether international law is really law (the Austinian handicap).[12] These trends still reoccur in much of the later scholarship, even into the twenty-first century.

Stone explores the connection between the teaching of international law and the general public as an audience of someone who was taught international law. This text, written by a United States State Department and from that vantage point, stresses the need to connect the teaching of international law to diplomacy and the education of the public at large. The teaching of international law becomes a part of United States cultural diplomacy.[13] It foregrounds a need to connect international law to the everyday lives of citizens, while also nodding to the importance of the teaching of international law to pursue foreign policy agendas, imperial or otherwise.

Somewhat similarly, Wilson et al. consider specifically teaching international law to non-lawyers. This text, the proceedings of a panel at an ASIL Conference immediately after the end of the Second World War, focuses on the needs of the post-war world in terms of teaching of international law. It is centred on the teaching of international law in political science and international relations courses, once again highlighting the connection to US diplomacy. In the view of the panellists, the connection to practice is needed to validate the discipline.[14]

These texts remark on specific events that help set up global ordering, underscoring the awareness of international law teachers of the value of pedagogics to promote substantive agendas in the field, and larger political projects. These trends are still reflected in contemporary scholarship, and are also

12 Merrills, J. G., 'On Teaching International Law' (1968) 10 *Journal of Society of Public Teachers of Law* 169.

13 Stone, William, 'The Teaching of International Law in Adult Education of the General Public' (1947) 41 *American Society of International Law Proceedings* 88.

14 Wilson, Robert, 'The Teaching of International Law in Undergraduate and Graduate Courses in Political Science' (1947) 41 *American Society of International Law Proceedings* 77.

noteworthy in a thread of scholarship on the teaching of international law that highlights the importance of teaching to help shore up the then new United Nations organization and the global ordering project it sought to further.

3.1 *Teaching as a Response to the United Nations Era*

These texts document the influence of the Second World War in how international law was imagined and taught. Many leading figures of mid-twentieth-century international law participated in this body of scholarship, such as Philip Jessup, Georg Schwarzenberger, and Arnold McNair.

Jessup documents the effects international law teaching can have on judicial practice. While focused on the United States experience, and an older text, here Jessup highlights a phenomenon that is still felt today: the lack of teaching of international law means that domestic judges, when faced with cases requiring the use of international law, create bad judicial practice. In his view, international law training was needed for the entrenchment of international legal doctrine, which was essential for a world where the UN mattered.[15]

Schwarzenberger considers the role of the new "international society" in shaping the way the discipline was taught. He focuses on the need to include more sociological approaches in the teaching of international law. Schwarzenberger also admonishes that teaching international law based primarily on the division between war and peace is an artificial division that should be reconsidered. It is primarily focused on the United States and United Kingdom experiences, but showcases key concerns about re-establishing a new world order after the Second World War, aligned with the UN project.[16]

McNair goes a step further and argues for the need to train international lawyers to staff United Nations agencies. He speaks in his position as President of the International Court of Justice, focusing on the need to internationalize the curriculum, emphasizing the connection to practice, and the need to supply law graduates to international organizations (most notably the then young United Nations) and diplomatic service.[17]

Connected to the UN project, but more recent, John Gamble explores the potential of the United Nations Decade of International Law as a means to raise the profile of teaching of the discipline. John Gamble is one of the most prolific

15 Jessup, Philip, 'The Teaching of International Law in Law Schools' (1947) 41 *American Society of International Law Proceedings* 66.

16 Schwarzenberger, Georg, 'On Teaching International Law' (1951) 4 *International Law Quarterly* 299.

17 McNair, Arnold, 'The Wider Teaching of International Law' (1952) 2 *Journal of Society of Public Teachers of Law* 10.

authors in the area of teaching of international law. In this piece, published in 1993, he highlights the need for more systemic data on the ways international law is taught in the United States, all the while being celebratory of the United Nations Decade of International Law, which he sees as having the potential to boost teaching in the field.[18] The piece's publication around the end of the Cold War can be read as an attempt to reinvigorate the teaching of international law as a mechanism to shore up international legal ordering.

These pieces do not comprise the entire work in the field at the time, however. Other work is less grounded on the needs of universal enterprises like the UN, and focus instead on the experience of specific countries.

3.2 *Specific National Experiences in Historical Perspective*

These texts include numerous references to the status of international law teaching in specific countries. However, rather than make explicit calls for localization and critical engagement that twenty-first literature does (discussed further below), these texts tend to focus on a stock-taking of practice in specific countries. Their ambitious scope often results in more descriptive insights, which, while useful at the time and still of historical relevance, tell us little about contemporary preoccupations in the field. Nevertheless, they are important in setting the foundations for a concern with local experiences in teaching international law.

W.E. Butler for instance discusses the Soviet Union. He tells the story of how every law school in the Soviet Union adopted the same international law curriculum, imposed centrally by the state. It also contains a translation of said curriculum, as an annex.[19] Elsewhere in the communist space, Wang Tieya explored the Chinese perspective historically, particularly framing the moment of recovery of (international) legal education in the aftermath of the Cultural Revolution.[20]

Many other scholars look at the United States specifically. Gamble and Natalie Shields map out numbers of scholars teaching international law across the US, while also mapping out the number of scholars engaged in research. It is written from the perspective of teaching international law in political science or international relations, but still a useful stock-taking of the field, and what

18 Gamble, John, 'The Decade's Emphasis on Education in International Law' (1993) 87 *American Society of International Law Proceedings* 362.

19 Butler, W. E., 'The Teaching of International Law in the USSR' (1982) 8 *Socialist Law Review* 183.

20 Tieya, Wang, 'Teaching and Research of International Law in Present Day China' (1983) 22 *Columbia Journal of Transnational Law* 77.

it meant to be an international law teacher in the US at the time.[21] Louis Sohn emphasizes the need to connect the teaching of international law to practice and government, in alignment with other scholarship discussed above.[22] Sohn, alongside Louis Henkin, Oscar Schachter, and others, was also the subject of a symposium organized by the Harvard International Law Journal interviewing a number of international law teachers in the United States, reflecting on the strengths and weaknesses of international legal teaching, considered across the spectrum of public and private international law, and its connection to practice.[23] The same theme animates Michael Reisman, who wrote a piece aligned with the mandates of the New Haven School, of which he is one of the founders. He discusses the need to connect international law teaching to its practice, and mainstreaming international law across the legal curriculum.[24]

Just north of the US boarder, Ronald St John McDonald does a "deep dive" into one prominent law school in Canada, and analyses the practice of international law teaching through the prism of the biographies and interests of teachers themselves.[25] He stresses the biography of all teachers, their adopted textbooks and areas of expertise, and institutional reactions to the expansion of international law teaching and its place in the broader curriculum. While fundamentally a descriptive piece, it foreshadows later scholarship on the teaching of international law that is animated by the same concerns, from a more granular or even individualistic perspective.

A similar effort was undertaken by Ivan Shearer in relation to Australia, but this time focused on all looks schools in the country. He undertakes a stocktaking of the field of international law in Australia, not confined only to teaching. He includes biographies of scholars in specific schools in Australia, and discusses the founding of the Australia-New Zealand Society of International Law in 1933. Shearer also discusses the challenges of teaching international law in an "unreceptive community," a concern that animated much scholarship then, and is perhaps still echoed in the preoccupation in more recent

21 Gamble, John, and Shields, Natalie, 'International Legal Scholarship: A Perspective on Teaching and Publishing' (1989) 39 *Journal of Legal Education* 39.

22 Sohn, Louis, 'The Present Importance of Teaching International Law and Organization' (1954) 7 *Journal of Legal Education* 199.

23 'Special Feature: The State of International Legal Education in the United States', (1988) 29 *Harvard International Law Journal* 239.

24 Reisman, Michael, 'The Teaching of International Law in the Eighties', (1986) 20 *International Lawyer* 987.

25 McDonald, Ronald St. John, 'International Law at the University of British Columbia, 1945–2000' (2003) 41 *Canadian Yearbook of International Law* 3.

scholarship with the grounding of international law on the everyday reality of students.[26]

This prevalence of scholarship on the experience of English-speaking countries has effects on scholarship produced about other parts of the world in the period, too. Speaking to the Spanish experience, for instance, Jorge Pueyo Losa draws comparisons with the United States, United Kingdom and France. The piece also contains a relevant summary of initiatives of international learned societies like the International Law Institute on the matter of teaching of international law. He writes in the context of imminent reforms to the Spanish university system, and ultimately advocates for the adoption of the Socratic method for the teaching of international law, which is a staple of teaching in common law jurisdictions (particularly the United States).[27] Therefore, even these more localized experiences, perhaps because of other available scholarship at the time, perhaps in sharing a fundamental aspiration of universality in the discipline, still look for transplantable practices, if anything as reform mechanisms, in a direction that suggests a hegemony of certain (particularly English-speaking) countries. These perspectives come to be challenged in later literature, which I discuss next, as part of a shift to greater theoretical and critical engagement with the practice of teaching of international law.

4 Theoretical and Critical Works

This is the body of literature on the teaching of international law that is growing most quickly at the time of writing. Most authors who have based their writings on international legal education on theory come from a critical perspective. This literature relies centrally on self-reflection, positioning the scholar in the position of practitioner, and often connects to broader theoretical concerns in the substantive field of international law, especially international law's relationship to power and hierarchy. Increasingly, this literature also refers to pedagogical theory, particularly the writings of the Brazilian scholar Paulo Freire, a central figure in critical pedagogical theory.[28]

26 Shearer, Ivan, 'The Teaching of International Law in Australian Law Schools' (1983) 9 *Adelaide Law Review* 61.

27 Pueyo Losa, Jorge, 'Reflexiones sobre la Enseñanza del Derecho Internacional Público', (1987) 5 *Revista de la Facultad de Derecho* 303.

28 For more insights, see the work of the foundation that bears his name, at https://www.freire.org/paulo-freire/.

David Kennedy, for instance, wrote an article based on his own personal reflections as a student and then teacher of international law. He stresses (negatively) the connection between international law teaching and legal practice that has the result of perpetuating, among other things, ethnocentrism in the field. He calls for "alternative points of access to the field", and makes a number of suggestions that have since come to fruition, such as the increase in clinical offerings.[29] Similarly, Anne Orford engages with the ethics of teaching more generally, and the notion of lawyers being located in "global networks of power". Coming from critical, feminist and Marxist perspectives, the author puts forth the idea of understanding international law "as a process that is implicated in the reproduction of inequality."[30] Later work of hers focuses on the discipline of international law more broadly, using teaching practices as a device to assess the discipline. In a section specifically dedicated to teaching, she accuses international law of being a means of reproducing hierarchies, by portraying international law as the lofty ideals and aspirations of white, male, heterosexual and property-owning persons. International law thus is normally framed in an exclusionary way, which has the effect of stripping it of its potentials as a vocabulary of resistance.[31] And Gerry Simpson adds to this thread in a piece that, although ostensibly not engaging with theory, contains a lot of theoretical depth. It is a critical take on the connection between doctrine and theory in the teaching of international law, which discusses the position of international law vis-à-vis other legal fields. Similarly to Kennedy, he concludes with a call for more experiential learning, as long as it is grounded in theory.[32]

Other texts in the critical tradition tackle pedagogical theory more openly. Ignacio Forcada also engages with theory, drawing upon insights from linguistics and cognitive psychology to articulate critical means of perceiving and teaching international law. He launches a thorough critique of the discipline's teaching in Spain, and articulates what he sees as the key ideas of a critical international law course.[33] Dianne Otto builds on the pedagogical theory of

---

29 Kennedy, David, 'International Legal Education', (1985) 26 *Harvard International Law Journal* 361.

30 Orford, Anne, 'Citizenship, Sovereignty and Globalisation: Teaching International Law in the Post' (1995) 6 *Legal Education Review* 251.

31 Orford, Anne, 'Embodying Internationalism: The Making of International Lawyers' (1998) 18 Australian Yearbook of International Law 1.

32 Simpson, Gerry, 'On The Magic Mountain: Teaching Public International Law' (1999) 10 *European Journal of International Law* 70.

33 Forcada, Ignacio, 'La Enseñanza del Derecho Internacional Público en España: Una Perspectiva desde el "Análisis Crítico del Discurso"', (2001) 3 *Revista Electrónica de Estudios Internacionales*.

Paulo Freire as a means to question the role of international law teaching in reproducing and reinforcing hierarchy. The hierarchical practices with which she engages have to do with hetero-normative, sexist, colonialist, racist and nationalist ideologies. Specifically, she argues that "progressive possibilities do not emerge from the argument over which side of the public-private dichotomy can be relied upon to deliver economic and social justice, but rather from the recognition of the complex interactions between the two discourses in their shifting boundaries and multiple ideological purposes", and suggests, "as a strategy for contesting global hierarchies, exploration of the intersections between the public and private domains of international law in legal education."[34]

Christine Schwöbel-Patel makes a forceful call for greater engagement with pedagogical theory, applying the pedagogical theory of Paulo Freire to the teaching of international law. In her view, teaching conveys either conformity or transformation. She emphasizes as a result the relationship between doctrine and theory, and that international law teaching should foreground theory more as a means of disrupting these hierarchies that plague the discipline.[35] Later work of hers pursues this agenda further, bringing in the German concept of *Bildung*. For her, this concept, "as opposed to training, encompasses a sense of activity rather than passivity; it includes the idea of reflexiveness and critique. I suggest that this notion of *Bildung* may be a starting point for a counter-hegemonic approach to teaching law, and in particular international law."[36]

Schwöbel-Patel stands in contrast with Kennedy and Simpson in relation to the importance of connections to practice in the teaching of international law. Higgins contributes to this debate from her own perspective, focusing on need to connect the teaching of international law to practice, particularly judicial and diplomatic practice. She discusses how a growing number of domestic cases before courts have international elements, and how international law is misapplied or rejected by judges with no training on the subject.[37] In doing so,

34 Otto, Dianne, 'Handmaidens, Hierarchies and Crossing the Public-Private Divide in the Teaching of International Law' (2000) 1 *Melbourne Journal of International Law* 35.

35 Schwöbel-Patel, Christine, 'Teaching International Law Critically – Critical Pedagogy and Bildung as Orientations for Learning and Teaching', in Bart van Klink and Ubaldus de Vries (eds.), *Academic Learning in Law: Theoretical Positions, Teaching Experiments and Learning Experiences* (Edward Elgar, 2015).

36 Schwöbel-Patel, Christine, "I'd like to learn what hegemony means' Teaching International Law from a Critical Angle' (2013) 3(2) *Recht en Methode in onderzoek en onderwijs* 67.

37 Higgins, Rosalyn, 'Teaching and Practicing International Law in a Global Environment: Toward a Common Language of International Law' (2010) 104 *American Society of International Law Proceedings* 196.

she invokes threads in earlier historical scholarship, echoing the role of international legal education in shoring up global legal governance projects.

Similar elements occur in a text by Freya Baetens and Wui Ling Cheah, which resurrects earlier practices of massive surveys. Their work is an ambitious mapping across 150 law schools around the world, covering all continents. Looking at coverage of topics in survey courses and electives, whether international law mandatory in curriculum, and other key issues pointed out in earlier literature. It is a useful descriptive exercise, precisely because of its scale, even if it does not offer many insights in terms of pedagogical tools, nor is it not grounded in theory. A chief concern of the authors is the link between scholarship and practice of international law. They make a case for a connection to practice in international legal education, and research-led teaching.[38]

Other authors bring theory not from pedagogy, but from international law itself, to bear on pedagogical analysis. Thio Li-ann for instance offers a critique of the teaching of international law based on its Eurocentrism. The text stresses the need for post-colonial understandings of international law to permeate teaching across Asia, and how at the same time one cannot essentialize "Asia". It concludes by stressing that the teaching of international law inevitably shapes the identity of the field in any one region.[39] Similarly, Karin Mickelson leverages Third World Approaches to International Law (TWAIL) to serve pedagogical purposes. She argues for more engagement with TWAIL scholarship in teaching, particularly in the "developed" world (where the author is based). She suggests that TWAIL works best when it is one of the methods or approaches students are confronted with, and that it helpfully helps critique and undermine students' assumptions about their roles as "saviours" of the third world "victims" or "savages".[40] Juan Amaya-Castro similarly makes the case that place matters for international law teaching. He seems to leverage that insight into a call for taking learners' lived experience into account in teaching international law, which is a key and well-established pedagogical trope, even if the author seems to articulate it as a relative novel insight from his practice,

---

38 Baetens, Freya, and Cheah, Wui Ling, 'Being an International Law Lecturer in the 21st Century: Where Tradition Meets Innovation' (2013) 2(4) *Cambridge Journal of International and Comparative Law* 974.

39 Li-ann, Thio, 'Formalism, Pragmatism and Critical Theory: Reflections on Teaching and Constructing an International Law Curriculum in a New (Post-Colonial) Asia' (2001) 5 *Singaporean Journal of International and Comparative Law* 327.

40 Mickelson, Karin, 'Rethinking Modes of Diffusion and Research and Teaching Methods: A TWAIL Perspective", in Mark Toufayan, Emmanuelle Tourme-Jouannet & Hélène Ruiz-Fabri, eds., *Droit International et Nouvelles Approches sur le Tiers-Monde: Entre Répétition et Renouveau* (Societé de Legislation Comparé, 2013).

with relatively little reference to pedagogical literature.[41] This text showcases, unfortunately, a potential shortcoming of self-reflective pieces that are not sufficiently grounded on pedagogical theory, since a substantive insight about international law is re-packaged as if a novel pedagogical insight, disregarding decades of pedagogical literature.

Luis Eslava instead makes much more extensive use of pedagogical theory. But he still seems to be making a disciplinary substantive intervention in international law. Unlike others who use substantive disciplinary insights to discuss pedagogy, Eslava uses pedagogical insights to articulate a vision for both the teaching of international law and its theoretical underpinnings.[42]

Hengameh Saberi undertakes a similar effort, also reflecting on agency theory to offer "new avenues for a more reflective stance on international law as an intellectual medium through which to relate to the world more responsibly." He seeks to do so "by shifting the focus from ontology to epistemology; by offering an integrative approach without the moralizing baggage of foundations; by accounting for experience without the risk of subjectivity; and by reconciling intellectual demands and dispositional traits to avoid a hegemonic pedagogical blueprint and instead allow for responsible creativity."[43]

With few exceptions, these attempts at theoretically grounded and critical engagement with the teaching of international law so far speak only to the experiences of individual teachers, and do not aim at providing systematic insights. Nonetheless, more comprehensive work also with theoretical ambition has been undertaken in the field, usually under the stewardship of learned societies, particularly the ASIL and the International Law Association (ILA). These deserve separate analysis.

4.1 *Reports of Learned Societies*

Learned societies have often produced their own reports on teaching of international law, often attempting to leverage collective insights from the experiences of their members. Therefore, while these texts are still largely grounded on the individual experiences and reflections of teachers, in the aggregate they

41 Amaya-Castro, Juan M, 'Teaching International Law: Both Everywhere and Somewhere', in Juan Carlos Sainz-Borgo et al. eds., *Liber Amicorum in honour of a Modern Renaissance Man His Excellency Gudmundur Eiriksson* (OP Jindal Global University, 2017).

42 Eslava, Luis, 'The teaching of (another) international law: critical realism and the question of agency and structure' (2020) 54(3) *The Law Teacher* 368.

43 Saberi, Hengameh, 'Virtue Pedagogy and International Law Teaching', in Luis Eslava, Michael Fakhri, and Vasuki Nesiah eds., *Bandung, Global History, and International Law: Critical Pasts and Pending Futures* (Cambridge University Press, 2017).

showcase a significant level of ambition. Some of these expand their views further by recording audience reactions to their insights as well.

One example are the recorded minutes of a panel, alongside the ensuing discussion, focused on topics such as the role of politics in teaching international law, the influence of practical work on the way scholars teach and think about international law, the role of interdisciplinary studies on teaching, and the way teaching is shaped by textbooks (their coverage and organization).[44] Other published work also records panels, such as an ASIL meeting in the 1980s. ASIL devotes to this day significant efforts to the exchange of best practices among teachers. One of the noteworthy records of these discussions focuses on international law as a discipline of crises. It emphasizes the connection to politics in the teaching of international law, and the need to historicize the field. It also highlights the need to educate the general public on international law matters, and the potential role of the United Nations Institute for Training and Research (UNITAR) in this realm. The panel also decries Eurocentrism in the teaching of international law, foreshadowing important discussions later in the field, and that continue to this day.[45] Another panel is built around six main questions, with the aim of coming up with general guidelines for a somewhat uniform international law curriculum, covering everything from themes in a course, teaching materials, assessment, and the place of international law in the curriculum. The panel conveys experiences from both law and political science or international relations, stressing, among other things, the potentials of using hypothetical cases from international law moot court competitions like the Jessup Moot as teaching tools in larger courses.[46]

These efforts by ASIL are important in foregrounding important tensions later attended to by other scholars in the field. Similarly, the ILA had an important Committee devoted entirely to collecting information and best practices on the teaching of international law across the world, leveraging the ILA's extensive (if sometimes still Eurocentric) membership. The first report of the now defunct Teaching of International Law Committee of the International Law Association briefly examines the experiences of members in South Africa, Brazil, the United States, the United Kingdom and Australia. It also highlights the potential of clinical legal education, and the connection between teaching

44 Alvarez et al., 'The Politics of Teaching International Law' (2008) 102 *American Society of International Law Proceedings* 305.

45 Weston et al, 'Promoting Training and Awareness – The Tasks of Education in International Law: Remarks' (1981) 75 *American Society of International Law Proceedings* 159.

46 Osakwe et al., 'Reexamination of the Teaching of International Law' (1984) 78 *American Society of International Law Proceedings* 198.

and diplomatic practice.[47] Subsequent work of the ILA focuses on assessment practices,[48] and the committee concluded its work and dissolved in 2010, turning into an interest group within the Association. In its final report, the ILA Committee highlighted the use of technologies in the teaching of international law, as well as means of increasing student participation.[49]

The work of these learned societies is worth highlighting because it showcases the intuitive nature of the work many scholars produce on the teaching of international law. Many insights are gained from sharing experiences among peers in these fora, which provide supportive networks for international law teachers to discuss their own positioning vis-à-vis one another, but, also importantly, vis-à-vis their colleagues in their home institutions. A significant body of scholarship exists focusing on the position of international law in the broader legal education curriculum, which intersects with debates about the role of international law for legal practice and the grounding of international law in everyday reality, already discussed above. The next section devotes further attention to these issues of internationalization of the legal education curriculum.

5 Internationalization of the Curriculum

These texts are broadly divided in two categories, taking aim at different pedagogical aspirations in relation to international law. Some of the texts advocate for international law to be "mainstreamed" across the legal curriculum, driving home the idea of international law as an essential and pervasive component of everyday life (or at least everyday legal practice). This aspiration, while ambitious and sound, poses difficulties in terms of teacher expertise. In contrast, other work focuses instead on simply ensuring that international law is a mandatory subject in the legal curriculum, a practice that is still not prevalent around the world.

In the first thread, Afshin Akhavari for instance discusses three ways in which legal education is being or can be internationalized in law schools: (1) creating a global law degree to equip students for international legal practice;

47 International Law Association, *'Teaching of International Law Committee: Conference Report New Delhi' (2002)[http://www.ila-hq.org/en/committees/index.cfm/cid/1009]*.

48 International Law Association, *'Teaching of International Law Committee: Discussion Document Berlin' (2004)[http://www.ila-hq.org/en/committees/index.cfm/cid/1009]*.

49 International Law Association, *'Teaching of International Law Committee: Committee Report The Hague' (2010)[http://www.ila-hq.org/en/committees/index.cfm/cid/1009]*.

(2) strengthening the domestic curriculum to include foreign and international materials when teaching domestic law; and (3) catering to the needs of foreign students. The text also decries the fact that it is existing possibilities within law schools that have been driving internationalization, as opposed to alternative views about legal education more generally.[50] Magdalene D'Silva focuses on the ways in which legal ethics instruction should incorporate foreign and international law dimensions. The focus of the article is on the teaching of ethics in England and Wales, but reference is also made to experiences in the United States and Australia.[51] Vai Io Lo focuses on Australia, and stresses the connection between teaching of international law and legal practice, decrying the idea of tokenism in the internationalization of the curriculum. Lo argues that international content should be mainstreamed across domestic offerings, and offers a number of other strategies, that include offering courses abroad, and enhancing exchange programs.[52] And Claudio Grossman discusses the need to make foreign and international law a part of teaching in all law courses, particularly as students need to be prepared for "practice in a global world (where the distinction between domestic and international is becoming increasingly blurred)".[53] Note the Anglophone bias in these pieces, but authors speaking to civil law experiences like Gerard Tanja emphasize the need to connect the teaching and practice of international law, particularly the practice of law firms. His work is primarily focused on transnational business law, with an European focus, and it also explores the connections between the common law and civil law worlds.[54] Somewhat similarly, Catherine Valcke also focuses on the teaching of "transnational" law, as opposed to international law. She focuses on questions such as teaching means, depth of coverage, level of expertise required of instructors, and the connection to domestic law subjects.[55] This scholarship in particular underscores a connection between international law and everyday legal practice as a reason for the mainstreaming of international law.

50 Akhavari, Afshin, 'The Opportunities and Possibilities for Internationalising the Curriculum of Law Schools in Australia' (2006) 16 *Legal Education Review* 75.

51 D'Silva, Magdalene, 'A new legal ethics education paradigm: culture and values in international arbitration' (2013) 23 *Legal Education Review* 83.

52 Lo, Vai Io, 'Before Competition and Beyond Complacency – the Internationalisation of Legal Education in Australia' (2012) 22 *Legal Education Review* 3.

53 Grossman, Claudio, 'Integrating International Law into the First-Year Curriculum' (2005) 24 *Penn State International Law Review* 835.

54 Tanja, Gerard, 'The Teaching of International Law: The Need for Curriculum Change' (2002) 4 *International Law forum du droit international* 199.

55 Valcke, Catherine, 'Global Law Teaching' (2005) 14 *Legal Education Digest* 8.

This connection to practice also animates the second thread of scholarship in relation to the position of international law in the curriculum. Ellen Hey for example discusses the relationship between public and private international law, and how both are necessary themes in the legal curriculum, especially if the curriculum is to be connected to contemporary legal practice.[56] Somewhat against the grain, Hans Corell calls for broader use of philosophy and history in the teaching of international law, and how international law should be a part of the mandatory curriculum of all law schools. He argues for mainstreaming, and adding international and foreign aspects to traditionally domestic law courses.[57]

These pieces that attempt to locate international law in the broader legal education curriculum speak to the connection to practice, and the need to mainstream international law content in domestic legal subjects as well. Doing the latter in particular helps ground international law, answering to calls for more localization of international law that defy classic universality aspirations of the discipline. These calls connect to a growing trend in the scholarship on the teaching of international law, which focuses on country-specific experiences as means of grounding international law on everyday reality in practical and theoretical terms. The next section engages with this literature.

6 Country-Specific Experiences

A significant part of the more recent scholarship on the teaching of international law responds to this trend. This trend aligns with ideas foreshadowed in some older scholarship, but also goes against the majority of that scholarship. Rather than embracing international law as a universalist project, which tries to create global legal ordering that applies equally to everyone, this trend of scholarship focuses instead on the way international law experienced locally, and therefore should be treated differently from one jurisdiction to the next. This move towards localization is important in that it responds to a desire, prevalent in the scholarship, to ground international law in everyday reality. What the original proponents of this grounding probably did not anticipate, however, is that international law would itself be fragmented in this grounding.

56 Hey, Ellen, 'The Teaching of International Law, L'Enseignement du Droit International' (2002) 4 *International Law forum du droit international* 189.

57 Corell, Hans, 'International Law and the Law School Curriculum' (2002) 4 *International Law forum du droit international* 195.

These localized accounts give us a better sense of how international law can be perceived differently in different countries, and also often the connection between the teaching of international law and the needs of that country's government. Scholars in this trend engage in both orthodox and critical theoretical traditions of international law, as we will see below. While these scholars align in the need for grounding the experience of international law, orthodox scholars tend to see this need more as tied to the importance of legal training for practice (therefore, an external mandate), whereas critical scholars tend to tie the grounding of international legal teaching to more substantive projects about the field of international law itself (therefore, an internal mandate).

In relation to the external mandates of localizing international legal education, Robert Beckman discusses national experiences with a focus on problem-based teaching, which the author claims is needed in Singapore, and a better method of teaching international law. He puts significant emphasis on the relationship between teaching and the content of courses on the one hand, and the needs of government and industry on the other.[58] Sam Blay, contextualizing the discussion about the place of international law in the curriculum in Australia, argues that internationalizing the curriculum more broadly should be accomplished by making courses on international and comparative law mandatory. This need is inspired by a close connection to the needs of a changing legal profession, and also the needs of the foreign student cohort, responsible for a significant proportion of revenue in a number of law schools in Australia.[59] James Crawford also focuses on Australia, but broadens the landscape by engaging with the history of the early courses in international law in Australian law schools, as well as details of the curriculum of each law school such as courses offered, and the biographies of the early teachers. He also highlights themes of particular interest for Australian foreign policy. The article finally outlines the status of the field in general (including research), and relationships to the profession.[60] In a similar vein, and elsewhere in the Commonwealth, MacDonald published a monumental work discussing the implementation of international law teaching across all law schools in Canada. The work includes detailed biographies of people who taught in Canadian law

58 Beckman, Robert, 'International Law at the National University of Singapore – Personal Reflections and Prospects' (2001) 5 *Singaporean Journal of International and Comparative Law* 426.

59 Blay, Sam, 'The Function of International and Comparative Law in Australian Legal Education' (1996) *Australian International Law Journal* 80.

60 Crawford, James, 'Teaching and Research in International Law in Australia' (1981) 10 *Australian Year Book of International Law* 176.

schools, as well asreferences to their teaching materials, philosophical leanings, and so on.[61] These comprehensive mappings are insightful in locating international law in a domestic tradition, but go further in underscoring how local needs and traditions are only part of the equation, and much leeway is still left to individual teachers, in the exercise of their academic freedom.

Botha Neville discusses how the new South African Constitution in the aftermath of apartheid created the impetus for more international law teaching, because of its provisions referring to international law. Neville also highlights the influence of the politics of the day in teaching. In the South African case, legal reform directly drives the need for more teaching of international law.[62] Khushal Vibhute also explores the external law reform incentives for teaching international law in his country (India). Specifically, he focuses on the relationship between the teaching of international law and the regulatory environment for the higher education sector in India. He offers three periods for analysis: (1) the separation from British content and the "indianization" of the curriculum; (2) efforts around the regulation of the legal profession; and (3) modernization of legal education to make it more socially relevant.[63]

BS Chimni, also speaking to the Indian experience, takes a different turn. He interrogates the relationship between the teaching of international law and the experiences and needs of third world countries. Chimni argues sensitivity towards these experiences and needs is lacking in education, and as a consequence international law is taught in an apolitical way, whereas it should be political.[64] Similarly, Hikmahanto Juwana highlights the mismatch between the theory and the reality of international law, and the challenges of teaching it in Indonesia. Juwana indicts international law with being taught at an exceedingly abstract level, without taking into account the challenges of a developing country. The text concludes by calling for a challenge to the Eurocentrism of international law teaching.[65] Laura Betancur and Enrique Prieto-Rios make a

61 MacDonald, Ronald St. John, 'An Historical Introduction to the Teaching of International Law in Canada' (1974) 12 *Canadian Yearbook of International Law* 67. Note this is the first in a series of four articles published in the same journal in 1974, 1975, 1976 and 1983.

62 Botha, Neville, 'Teaching International Law in South Africa Ten Years into Democracy' (2004) 29 *South African Yearbook of International Law* 243.

63 Vibhute, Khushal, 'International Law in India – Developing Curricula and Teaching: Some Reflections' (2001) 5 *Singaporean Journal of International and Comparative Law* 388.

64 Chimni, B. S., 'Teaching, Research and Promotion of International Law in India: Past, Present and Future' (2001) 5 *Singaporean Journal of International and Comparative Law* 368.

65 Juwana, Hikmahanto, 'Teaching International Law in Indonesia' (2001) 5 *Singaporean Journal of International and Comparative Law* 412.

similar call in the Colombian context.[66] Forcada also critiques the teaching of international law's focus on practice, and argues for more critical engagement with human emancipation projects, even though, focused on Spain, he is not as interested in the impacts of colonialism. He uses this critique to reposition the student at the centre of the pedagogical experience, as opposed to a spectator.[67]

These critiques of international law's Eurocentrism are not contained to domestic contexts, however. Fabia Carvalho surveys a series of historical congresses of Latin American universities, which sought to introduce curricular reform "towards the Latin American", leveraging this sensibility to modernize the continent, and showcasing the importance of explicit political projects.[68] Adriane Brito and Salem Nasser take up this call more contemporarily, surveying the Brazilian landscape of the teaching of international law to make a call for more Latin American cooperation in this area, so as to build a stronger Latin American tradition to both the teaching and the substance of international law.[69] Mohamed Helal makes a similar argument in relation to Africa and the engagement of the African Union, particularly to promote African interests on the international stage (so, leveraging a mix of internal and external mandates).[70] Rohini Sen also takes aim at Eurocentrism in the teaching of international law in Asia, but writes more self-reflexively about classroom and disciplinary frustrations with the apparent assumption of universality in Eurocentric international law.[71]

These regionalizing efforts are not only undertaken by individual scholars and loose associations of scholars. Besides the Pan-American initiatives discussed by Carvalho, other regional groupings have also focused on their localized needs in relation to the teaching of international law.

66 Betancur Restrepo, Laura; and Prieto-Rios, Enrique, 'Educación del derecho internacional en Bogotá: un primer diagnóstico a partir del análisis de los programas de clase y su relación con las epistemologías de no conocimiento' (2017) 39 *Revista Derecho del Estado* 53.

67 Forcada, cit.

68 Carvalho, Fabia Fernandes, 'História e crítica em direito internacional na América Latina: revisitando discussões pretéritas sobre ensino jurídico na região' (2017) 39 *Revista Derecho del Estado* 91.

69 Brito, Adriane Sanctis de; and Nasser, Salem Hikmat, 'Ensinar direito internacional no Brasil: panorama de uma prática e seus desafios' (2017) 39 *Revista Derecho del Estado* 119.

70 Helal, Mohamed, 'Teaching Public International Law: Reflections on the State of the Art in an Era of Uncertainty' (2017) 416 *Public Law and Legal Theory Working Paper Series*, at http://ssrn.com/abstract=3046633.

71 Sen, Rohini, 'Teaching International Law in Asia: The Predicated Pedagogue', *AfronomicsLaw* (24 September 2020), at https://www.afronomicslaw.org/2020/09/24/teaching-international-law-in-asia-the-predicated-pedagogue.

6.1 *Learned Societies with Specific Geographical Coverage*

A number of learned societies have decided to undertake reflection on the teaching of international law with a specific focus on their region or country. Isabel Castaño for instance reports on the VII Jornadas de la Asociación Española de Profesores de Derecho Internacional y Relaciones Internacionales, and summarizes four lectures and five shorter talks that paint a comprehensive picture of the teaching of international law in law and international relations schools across Spain.[72]

The efforts of ASIL have generally tended towards broader generalizations, as indicated above, but they have also on occasion taken very US-specific questions. The records of an ASIL roundtable in the 1990s for instance focus on the US national experiences. Participants highlight that the connection between teaching and practice is rather small, but that it does not necessarily matter. They also discuss the impact that teaching international law can have on untenured faculty in US law schools, and the need for mainstreaming foreign and international elements across the entire curriculum. An European (French) perspective is also offered by one of the participants.[73] The US branch of the ILA has also analysed the US experience, with a particular focus on the role of internationalizing the curriculum and specific techniques (clinical education). In this report, the US branch of the ILA focused in particular on the experience of New England School of Law in mainstreaming foreign and international content across domestic legal courses, and on the experience of clinical legal education at Suffolk University Law School.[74]

South of the Rio Grande, Paola Acosta et al. are leading a project titled "Rethinking Education in International Law in Latin America" (*Repensando la Educación en Derecho Internacional en América Latina* – REDIAL). This grouping aims to explore the role of international law in social reform and transformation projects, contextualizing and politicizing it, thus responding to a critical internal mandate of reimagining not only education, but also the boundaries of the discipline.[75] The same is the aspiration of learned societies in Asia, as Kevin Tan reports. He summarizes the efforts of two learned

---

72 Castaño Garcia, Isabel, 'Enseñanza e Investigación del Derecho Internacional y las Relaciones Internacionales' (1983) 4(3) *Revista de Estudios Internacionales* 553.

73 'Roundtable on the Teaching of International Law: Remarks' (1991) 85 104 *American Society of International Law Proceedings* 102.

74 Epps, Valerie, and Scharf, Michael, 'Report of the Committee on the Teaching of International Law' (2001) *Proceedings of the American Branch of the International Law Association* 78.

75 Acosta Alvarado, Paola Andrea et al., 'Repensar la educación del derecho internacional en Latinoamérica: reflexiones para un diálogo global' (2019) 1 *TWAILR: Reflections*.

societies in mapping the status of teaching of international law across Asia. He focuses on third-world / post-colonial / North-South relationships and their impact on teaching, decrying the lack of Asian state practice and values in the teaching of international law in the region, while at the same time noting the widespread use of English-language textbooks.[76] I will return to textbooks in the next section, in discussing specific techniques or courses that leverage local, universalistic, diplomatic, and critical ideas about international law.

7 Specific Techniques or Courses

The trend towards self-reflexivity has also led many scholars to focus on their specific courses as a starting point for their analysis of the teaching of international law. Many scholars have also attempted to extrapolate by reflecting on their own production of specific teaching materials, or, more recently, there have been more ambitious projects focused on the ways in which international law is taught through the analysis of teaching materials. Finally, there are also texts on specific experiential learning techniques, or the use of technological tools, which will be discussed further in subsections below. These texts underscore many of the tensions discussed so far, particularly the relationship between international law teaching and the discipline more broadly, the competing aspirations of universality and localization of the discipline, and the impact of specific techniques on bringing students to the centre of the learning experience, reflecting pedagogical insights that these authors seem to grasp intuitively, but generally without much anchoring on pedagogical theory or scholarship.

Fabián Salvioli is a typical example. He engages with his own experience in fully redesigning the international law curriculum for his faculty, in Argentina. The article focuses on the design objectives of the course, more specifically: (a) dynamic and flexible planning; (b) promotion of interactive teaching in the classroom; (c) enhancing academic freedom for teachers in the course; (d) enable internal capacity-building and research; (e) facilitating more interaction with other courses in the law degree; (f) democratic decision-making among the teachers of the course in the process of making changes to content; (g) centralized evaluation across the many groups that are being taught the course simultaneously; and (h) integration of interdisciplinary and contextual

76 Tan, Kevin, 'The SILS-DILA Conference on Teaching and Researching International Law in Asia: Report and Reflections' (2001) 5 *Singaporean Journal of International and Comparative Law* 441.

approaches.[77] Henrique Marcos undertakes similar observations in relation to Brazil, reflecting on the importance of international legal teaching to contextualize the law more broadly, and to broaden students' universes. He also emphasizes the importance of research-led teaching, and even of introducing research projects as central elements of assessment in order to facilitate student ownership of their own learning.[78]

Carlos Espaliú engages with the need to adjust international law teaching not to pedagogical imperatives, but to regulatory requirements. He considers the use of the jurisprudence of international (mostly European) tribunals as a means to conform international law curriculum to the requirements of the Bologna process. He engages with the case method, in the way it is taught particularly in the United States. The article is centred on the possibilities of using this method to meet the requirements of the Bologna process that attempts to harmonize higher education standards across the European Union. The article frames the Bologna process and the case method also in the context of the Spanish regulatory environment for higher education.[79]

Carmelo Cattafi is a notable exception to this lack of engagement with pedagogical theory. He goes to great lengths to decouple pedagogical insights from specific educational contexts, and, unlike the bulk of scholarship that does nod to pedagogical theory, discussed above, Cattafi's primary intervention is on pedagogical theory itself, without a commitment to an intervention on the substantive field of international law. He describes a specific multisdiciplinary project for training higher education teachers, titled "Enseña con Pasión, Aprende con Imaginación" (Teach with Passion, Learn with Imagination), which "aims that the teacher achieves a personal change through self-knowledge and artistic awareness to strengthen their creative thinking and impact on their academic work." Educational improvement is at the centre of this project, and enhancing student engagement with international law as a consequence not of directly

77 Salvioli, Fabián, 'Algunas Consideraciones sobre la Enseñanza Contemporánea del Derecho Internacional Público', (2002) 11(22) *Revista Relaciones Internacionales* 1.

78 Marcos, Henrique Jerônimo Bezerra, 'Didática, Ensino E Pesquisa Jurídico-Dogmática Em Direito Internacional', in Wagner Menezes ed., *Direito Internacional em Expansão – Volume XIX* (Arraes Editores, 2020).

79 Espaliú Berdud, Carlos, *'La Enseñanza del Derecho Internacional Público Basada en las Decisiones de Los Tribunales Internacionales en el Marco de la Implantación del Espacio Europeo de Educación Superior'[https://www.uco.es/docencia_derecho/index.php/reduca/article/view/22]*, (2010) 1 *Docencia y Derecho*.

centring the student, but of empowering the teacher to be more responsive to student needs and better showcase their own passion for the discipline.[80]

Other scholarship focuses on specific courses as pathways to ask broader substantive questions about the field. Fleur Johns and Steven Freeland discuss an experiment offering a course simultaneously and jointly in two universities also as a pathway to unpack basic assumptions about international law's universality, even in the same nominal jurisdiction. Their article focuses on an experiment conducted between the two teachers of bringing together students in their courses at different law schools in Sydney, Australia. One school is highly privileged, whereas the other is in a relatively economically depressed part of the city. The course brought the two cohorts together and highlighted tensions between the two cohorts, catalysing them into teaching that took two forms: a student conference, and a series of negotiations where students role-played different countries.[81] Marjorie Florestal goes further, bringing together US and Guatemalan students, in Guatemala, to confront the mismatches between the promises and reality of international trade and development law.[82]

Turning to specific elements or techniques of teaching international law, Davis et al. highlight the need for teaching of foreign and international law research as a specific subject, discussing issues such as position of such research courses in the curriculum, whether they should be taught jointly with substantive courses on international law or separately, as well as specific teaching techniques. The text is formed of vignettes contributed by each individual author, who are international law librarians in US law schools.[83] Similarly, Terry Hutchinson focuses on the role of legal research in the training of the transnational lawyer. This article also highlights the need to design curricula connected to the needs of both government and industry, and the use of technologies in achieving these goals.[84]

Ku et al. reflect on methods of assessment. They focus on the idea of mainstreaming international legal education in law school curricula, highlighting

80 Cattafi, Carmelo, 'Teaching Methods in International Law' (2018) 14(2) *Journal of International Education Research* 9.

81 Johns, Fleur, and Freeland, Steven, 'Teaching International Law across an Urban Divide: Reflections on an Improvisation' (2007) 57 *Journal of Legal Education* 539.

82 Florestal, Marjorie, 'A Tale of Two *Compadres*: Teaching International Trade and Development Across Cultures' (2013) 26 *Pac. McGeorge Global Bus. & Dev. L.J.* 33.

83 Davis et al., 'Perspectives on Teaching Foreign and International Legal Research' in Hill et al. (eds) *Teaching Legal Research and Providing Access to Electronic Resources* (2001) 55.

84 Hutchinson, Terry, 'Educating the Transnational Lawyer: Globalisation and the Effects on Legal Research Skills Training' (Paper presented at the 61st Annual ALTA Conference, Melbourne, 4 July 2006).

that there are three elements needed for success in mainstreaming: faculty or staff interest, student interest, and administrative support. They also discuss the tension between transnational and international law in teaching, as well as ideas around courses offered abroad, and a few examples of syllabi. In other words, they take up the cause of mainstreaming of international law in the curriculum, but position in specifically in relation to techniques that would allow for the implementation of this goal.[85]

Techniques of implementation of pedagogical goals are also central to scholarship that focuses specifically on the potential of simulations as means of centring the student in the learning process. John Knechtle examines his own attempts to integrate his experiences in diplomatic work in domestic law-and constitution-making contexts, so as to mainstream international law throughout the legal curriculum. He stresses the need to connect the teaching of international law to its practice.[86] Timothy McCormack and Simpson discuss a specific technique for classroom teaching, in which a significant part of the semester is dedicated to a single, multi-layered role-playing exercise of treaty negotiation as a tool to teach the law and politics of international law. Differently from Knechtle, though, they emphasize this technique not just to ground international law in its practice, but also to engage broader theoretical tensions and reimagining the very foundations of the field, instead of assuming its technique.[87]

A similar objective is outlined by Michelle Badin, Arthur Giannattasio, and Douglas Castro, who look at the use of a case method adapted from business schools as a means to unpack the law, and its operation, beyond narrow documents like judgments and other primary sources. This case method is a pathway to contextualize international law, ground it in the everyday reality of the people affected by it, and ultimately empower the student.[88] Other work by the same team further details the technique behind assembling these teaching materials, and how this process simultaneously provides pedagogical value

85 Ku et al., 'International Law and the Legal Curriculum' (2002) 96 *American Society of International Law Proceedings* 54.

86 Knechtle, John, 'Teaching, Decision-Making, and International Law in the Twenty-First Century' (2003) 97 *American Society of International Law Proceedings* 217.

87 McCormack, Timothy, and Simpson, Gerry, 'Simulating Multilateral Treaty Making in the Teaching of International Law' (1999) 10 *Legal Education Review* 61.

88 Badin, Michelle Ratton Sanchez; Giannattasio, Arthur Roberto Capella; and Castro, Douglas, 'O Caso Didático no Ensino do Direito Internacional: Um Instrumento para um Aprendizado Interdisciplinar com Relações Internacionais' (2017) 47(18) *Meridiano*: 1.

and consciousness-raising for teachers.[89] Katia Fach also engages with similar techniques, focusing instead on Problem-Based Learning as a pathway to centre international law teaching on the student, and creating reflective habits on students.[90]

These specific techniques require the production of specific teaching materials. The production of teaching materials is also the focus of an increasing number of forays into the scholarship of the teaching of international law, particularly through textbooks. Some of this scholarship is produced by the authors of textbooks, while others focus on meta-analyses of textbooks.

On the former, Gleider Hernández reflects on his own process of producing a textbook, in what he describes as "a confessional posture, a sharing of certain moments of unease as I ealized the limitations of the medium and perhaps also was confronted with the pragmatism of my own methodological standpoint and training." He struggles with the line between establishing the field and its techniques, and conveying critical theory that goes against this canon.[91] In some ways, his reflection echoes Schwöbel-Patel's above, in which she queries the differences of teaching international law as technique-or theory-centred. Hernández insists that "legal education can equally be a political act, in that it can constitute the exercise or reproduction of existing modes of thinking, and thus existing structures of ideas and even power imbalances", and that textbooks "establish the grammar and structure of thinking about international law; they set the boundaries of relevance, establishing what sources can be validly invoked, what counts as an acceptable legal argument, and what outcomes and remedies may be sought."[92] He laments the inevitability of presenting international law through Eurocentric lenses, and argues that the contestation happens best pedagogically when set against the canon, not in its absence.[93] He shares Florian Hoffmann's view that international law is best taught "as an objective reality, a particular language game, the grammar and syntax of which must be learned more than understood, a particular professional idiom,

89 Badin, Michelle Ratton Sanchez; Giannattasio, Arthur Roberto Capella; and Castro, Douglas, 'As Eleições Implícitas na Pesquisa para a Elaboração e Aplicação de Casos em Cursos de Direito Internacional' (2016) 3(2) *Revista Pedagogía Universitaria y Didáctica del Derecho* 195.

90 Fach Gómez, Katia, 'Ventajas del Problem Based Learning (PBL) como método de aprendizaje del Derecho Internacional' (2012) 64(1) *Bordón. Revista De Pedagogía* 59.

91 Hernández, Gleider, 'Inculcating International Law: The Textbook as Gateway' (2018) 9 *European Society of International Law Conference Paper*.

92 Id.

93 Id.

fluency of which is the distinguishing mark of the lawyer as opposed to the non-lawyer."[94]

On meta-analyses of textbooks and the work they do for the field and teaching, Christina Binder and Jane Hofbauer for instance focus on reviewing international human rights law textbooks. They query the absence of problematization of the "socio-political construction of contemporary society with a clear normative drive. From a practical viewpoint, there emerges the danger of taking human rights for granted and disregarding the political context in which they apply."[95]

Anthea Roberts's comprehensive discussion of whether international law is international also focuses on meta-analyses of textbooks, aiming at the five permanent members of the United Nations Security Council. She does so with the aim of primarily mapping out the field, using pedagogical practice as a pathway to that, offering useful insights in claiming that textbooks "play an important socializing role in shaping understandings of which issues are core and form part of the field, which sources are important, which debates are controversial, which norms are settled, which rules are liable to change, and who and what the leading authorities are." She demonstrates that international law is much more context-specific than the Eurocentric canon might suggest, despite important areas of spillover in the movement of scholars who write textbooks, who train in European nations and have those insights reflected in the textbooks themselves.[96] She asserts that "cross-country differences between the approaches adopted in textbooks and casebooks are not limited to areas involving clashes of ideology or high politics." She further contends that "these divergences often betray deeper differences in the approaches and cultures of different legal systems regarding such issues as whether it is possible to distinguish between public and private law", and that "the books in different states often adopt one approach without describing the competing approaches or attempting to reconcile them. [...] As a result, divergent approaches are often accepted by distinct communities of international lawyers, and passed down to their students, without much reflection or dialogue."

This indictment of the acritical reception and flow of Eurocentric insights to the teaching of international law is further expanded in the Brazilian context

94 Hoffmann, Florian, 'Teaching General Public International Law', in J d'Aspremont and J Kammerhofer eds., *International Legal Positivism in a Post-Modern World* (Cambridge University Press, 2014).

95 Binder, Christina; and Hofbauer, Jane A, 'Teaching International Human Rights Law: A Textbook Review' (2017) 28(4) *EJIL* 1397.

96 Roberts, Anthea, *Is International Law International?* (OUP, 2017).

by a research project led by Fabio Morosini and Luiza Leão that coded all international law textbooks in use in Brazil.[97] Because Brazil responds to the vast majority of the Portuguese-speaking world in terms of population, it has its own extensive production of legal textbooks, including in international law. The participants in this project examined the biographies of textbook writers,[98] their normative commitments,[99] and the sources used by these scholar-teachers.[100] Ultimately, the project showed that, despite the importance of calls for particularization of international law, it is still largely taught as a universalized enterprise, at least as seen through textbooks as the primary teaching materials.[101]

These insights are central to the body of scholarship on the teaching of international law. Despite many calls for the grounding of international law teaching on local realities, and an intellectual rejection of Eurocentric approaches by many orthodox and critical legal scholars-teachers, the fact of the matter is that there is still a strong canon, at least within the legal discipline. Boundary-breaking is needed, with the help of tools drawn from pedagogical theory (as is the current trend in scholarship), or even with the use of other fields.

In relation to the engagement of international law teaching and other fields, there are two bodies of scholarship. The first is the teaching of international law in disciplines other than law, for their benefit. Howard Schiffman for instance focuses on training non-lawyers in international law, echoing calls for the mainstreaming of the discipline for the benefit of world-making at the end of the Second World War and the advent of the UN, discussed above. Many of

---

97 Morosini, Fabio; and Leão, Luiza, 'Research Symposium – Direito Internacional "Na Palma da Mão" – Parte 1', *International Law Agendas* (6 April 2021), at http://ila-brasil.org.br/blog/direito-internacional-na-palma-da-mao-lendo-as-entrelinhas-dos-manuais-brasileiros/.

98 Macedo, Julia et al., 'Research Symposium – Direito Internacional "Na Palma da Mão" – Parte 2. Análise das Biografias dos Principais Autores', *International Law Agendas* (6 April 2021), at http://ila-brasil.org.br/blog/analise-das-biografias-dos-autores/.

99 Ratzkowski, Fernanda; Souza, Jamille Batista e; and Ospina, Julia Britto, 'Research Symposium – Direito Internacional "Na Palma da Mão" – Parte 4. Manuais-Projeto e Manuais-Instrumento: Uma Possível Tipologia dos Manuais de Direito Internacional Público Brasileiros', *International Law Agendas* (6 April 2021), at http://ila-brasil.org.br/blog/manuais-projeto-e-manuais-instrumento/.

100 José, Diego Flávio Fontoura; Brondani, Isadora; and Areosa, João Antonio Coutinho, 'Research Symposium – Direito Internacional "Na Palma da Mão" – Parte 3. Resultados Preliminares sobre os Manuais de Direito Internacional Público no Brasil', *International Law Agendas* (6 April 2021), at http://ila-brasil.org.br/blog/resultados-preliminares/.

101 Leichtweis, Matheus et al., 'Research Symposium – Direito Internacional "Na Palma da Mão" – Parte 5. Sobre o Eixo Universalismo/Particularismo na Pesquisa dos Manuais Brasileiros de Direito Internacional', *International Law Agendas* (6 April 2021), at http://ila-brasil.org.br/blog/sobre-o-eixo-universalismo-particularismo/.

Schiffman's techniques focus on managing the expectations of students, and the underlying message is to focus less on imparting knowledge, and more on conveying passion for the field.[102] Focusing specifically on teaching international law in political science contexts, Dana Zartner highlights the benefits of using cases, mooting and problem questions to teach students in these fields, as opposed to relying only primarily on textbooks and scholarly literature.[103] Zartner therefore calls for less engagement with textbooks as a repository of the (Eurocentric) canon, and with other materials, much like Badin et al. and Fach, discussed above.

The second body of scholarship on how international law engages with other fields focuses not on how international law teaching is exported to other disciplines, but rather how other disciplines can shape the teaching of international law. This body of scholarship, more important for our purposes, deserves separate treatment in the next subsection.

7.1 *Bringing Other Fields into the Teaching of International Law*

Scholars in this thread highlight the potential of bringing in ideas from fields separate from ("classic") public international law to bear on the teaching of the discipline. Egon Schwelb for instance focuses on how to integrate international human rights in mainstream courses on public international law, particularly United Nations Charter-based human rights principles and concerns.[104] In doing so, he echoes calls for using the teaching of international law to shore up the UN's architecture, discussed above. Catherine Magallanes considers insights from business to the teaching of international law. She focuses on specific techniques for teaching, such as substantive skills in public and private international law, communication skills, and adaptation skills. The main focus is in training transnational practicing lawyers.[105] Otto looks at the possibilities of gender, focusing on specific techniques to include gender in classroom discussions of international law. She outlines four specific techniques or strategies: (1) naming what goes unspoken in terms of gender; (2) acknowledging

102 Schiffman, Howard, 'Teaching International Law to Undergraduates and Other Non-Legal Audiences: Practical Suggestions for Pedagogical Approaches' (2002) 9 *ILSA International & Comparative Law* 321.

103 Zartner, Dana, 'An Interdisciplinary Approach to Teaching International Law: Using the Tools of the Law School Classroom in Political Science', (2009) *PS: Political Science and Politics* 189.

104 Schwelb, Egon, 'The Teaching of the International Aspects of Human Rights' (1971) 65 *American Society of International Law Proceedings* 242.

105 Magallanes, Catherine J Iorns, 'Teaching for Transnational Lawyering', (2005) 55 *Journal of Legal Education* 519.

and legitimating the narratives behind the dominant narrative; (3) linking the global with the local; and (4) understanding the law as a socially constructed and contestable discourse, as opposed to static rules.[106] In a similar vein, Ben Saul looks at Indigenous peoples' voices in the teaching of international law. He compares the places of Indigenous law and international law in the legal curriculum, and discusses the possibilities of mainstreaming the two areas, and merging them. He argues that Indigenous content can be better integrated in international law teaching, also as a means of changing attitudes in the profession over time.[107] Francis Snyder, lastly, focuses on what an anthropological perspective can offer: "a new focus combining the 'inside' and 'outside' perspectives on law, which I encourage students to develop, even though often there are difficulties in distinguishing these perspectives and even though ultimately it is impossible fully to enjoy both perspectives."[108]

These perspectives, while useful in adding new voices and perspectives, do not seem to fundamentally challenge the basic assumptions about the teaching of international law elsewhere in the literature, even if their reinforcement of insights gained through other means are welcome. A theme articulated by this thread of literature is the connection to everyday practice and reality of international law, a theme reinforced in specific literature on experiential learning.

7.2 *Experiential Learning in International Law*

Experiential learning is broadly understood as the techniques that allow students to experience international law as a living discipline with tangible and immediate repercussions. This thread of literature reinforces themes that already emerged elsewhere in this review, like the use of clinics and simulations, as well as cross-cultural teaching.

On clinical teaching, Richard Wilson brings together perspectives from the United States, The Netherlands and Canada in terms of clinical education in international law. The participants in this panel address two main questions: (1) the method or philosophy in clinical legal education; and (2) the move towards

106 Otto, Dianne, 'Integrating Questions of Gender into Discussion of the Use of Force in the International Law Curriculum' (1995) 6 *Legal Education Review* 219.

107 Saul, Ben, 'Indigenous Peoples, Laws and Customs in the Teaching of Public and Private International Law' (2012) 4 *Ngiya: Talk the Law* 63.

108 Snyder, Francis, 'The Contribution of Anthropology to Teaching Comparative and International Law', in Marie-Claire Foblets, Gordon Woodman and Antony Bradney eds., *The Trials and Triumphs of Teaching Legal Anthropology in Europe* (Ashgate Publishers, 2015).

international human rights clinics.[109] Deena Hurwitz discusses clinical teaching participants as "transnational norm entrepreneurs", articulating the potentials of clinical legal education for better integrating international law into the principal legal experiences of law students. She discusses in particular two models of clinical legal education in international law: clinics based on international litigation, and clinics based on broader law reform projects.[110]

Another significant experiential tool is the use of simulations, whether full-blown treaty simulations discussed above, or specific moot court competitions. Craig Brown engages with the Jessup moot as a means of outlining the benefits of complex problem-solving in the teaching of international law for participants in the competition and students in general,[111] a theme echoed also by Osakwe et al.[112]

Lastly, an emerging experiential technique is to take international law students to specific sites where international law affects reality. Florestal, discussed above, took students to Guatemala.[113] Mitchell et al. describe two different courses put together by the authors, both of which are offered as experiential learning opportunities. One focuses on the work of international agencies, and the other on the work of the "global lawyer". The authors describe the connection between the courses and international careers, as well as the logistical challenges of taking groups of students abroad.[114] Similarly, Ben Saul and Irene Baghoomians look at the experience of creating an experiential learning course in Nepal on international law and development. They cover many of the logistical challenges associated with creating the course, and the potentials of experiencing international law and development issues on-site. Socio-legal research methods are used as a learning tool, and it is a research-driven substantive curriculum.[115]

109 Wilson, Richard 'Teaching International Law: Lessons From Clinical Education' (2010) 104 *American Society of International Law Proceedings* 87.

110 Hurwitz, Deena, 'Teaching International Law: Lessons From Clinical Education' (2010) 104 *American Society of International Law Proceedings* 95.

111 Brown, Craig, 'The Jessup Mooting Competition as a Vehicle for Teaching Public International Law', 16 Canadian Yearbook of International Law 332 (1978).

112 Cit.

113 Cit.

114 Mitchell et al., 'Education in the Field: A Case Study of Experiential Learning in International Law' (2011) 21 *Legal Education Review* 69.

115 Saul, Ben and Baghoomians, Irene, 'An Experimental International Law Field School in the Sky: Learning Human Rights and Development in the Himalayas' (2012) 22(2) *Legal Education Review* 273.

This thread of literature is important in presenting clear examples, or almost how-to guides, to other teachers of international law as they design new experiences aimed at responding to the major threads in the literature, such as the localization of international law and its effects, and the contextualization of international legal knowledge, theory, and practice in relation to student experiences and the experiences of those most affected by international legal ordering. They also show a concern with how international law is a practical discipline. These techniques are valid guides, as are those that grapple with the use of technology to facilitate international law teaching.

7.3. *Use of Technology*

While many texts discussed above (particularly the reports of learned societies, but also for instance texts focused on legal research) also inquire on the use of technologies for teaching international law, there is scarce literature focused primarily on the use of technology to teach international law, indicating a gap that warrants further exploration, particularly as events like COVID-19 force more engagement with technology-aided learning.

Of particular importance in the response to COVID-19, but predating it by over a decade, Robert Beck examines specific blended learning techniques. He engages with a number of strategies for teaching international law. The blended approach consists of greater use of online resources to make available beforehand parts of the course that would be "taught" or "lectured", so that classroom time can be devoted just to discussion. In this way, classroom time can be decreased. The article focuses on the teaching of international law to students of political science or international relations, but offers many insights for a traditional legal curriculum as well.[116]

Gamble focuses on general technological tools. He calls for more surveys in the area, but also highlights the need for international law teaching to be related to the practice of international law, remarking on the potentials and pitfalls of using new technologies in the classroom.[117]

More recently, pedagogical literature has explored the potential of gamification for learning. Luke Moffett, Dug Cubie, and Andrew Godden explore this possibility in relation to the teaching of international humanitarian law. They argue that video games via a tactical war simulator offer formative scenarios

116 Beck, Robert, 'Teaching International Law as a Partially Online Course: The Hybrid/Blended Approach to Pedagogy' (2010) 11(3) Journal of International Studies Perspectives 273.

117 Gamble, John, 'International Law Teaching: Glass(es) Half Full – Rose Coloured – Red/White and Blue' (2012) 37 *South African Yearbook of International Law* 283.

to ground international legal rules more vividly to decision-making on the ground during conflicts.[118]

The use of technology can be a great aid in the teaching of international law, not only due to external imperatives like COVID-19, but also because it creates other opportunities for students to experience international law as it is translated, and has effects on, a wider range of scenarios and realities. If well-grounded in pedagogical theory and insights, the use of technology can offer promising pathways to addressing many of the dissatisfactions indicated by scholars-teachers writing in this field.

8 Concluding Remarks

This chapter showcased the major trends in the scholarship of international law. Growing theoretical ambition, the international legal scholar's self-reflective take on their own practice, and an increasing emphasis on granularity of experience and the grounding of international law on the everyday, whether from theoretical or practical perspectives. The field is still concerned with the role of international law in the curriculum, but the aspiration to use international legal education to pursue universalist projects or backing specific legal governance projects seems on the wane in many parts of the world, particularly outside of Europe. Many of the chapters in this volume attest to, represent, or challenge these trends. The field is ever-moving, and its growth is welcome. But, for growth to be sustainable and productive of real impact, scholars writing about the teaching of international law need to pay more than lip service to pedagogical theory, and we need to take the time to learn and think about the pedagogy we acquired as a practice. I make this call aware of its irony, as this review itself engages little with pedagogical theory. But I hope this review contributes to the realization of how much important work has already been done, and how to continue this work we need to push past the current plateau in the scholarship, and embrace educational theory insights.

118 Moffett, Luke; Cubie, Dug; and Godden, Andrew, 'Bringing the battlefield into the classroom: using video games to teach and assess international humanitarian law' (2017) 51(4) *The Law Teacher* 499.

References

Alvarado, Acosta Paola Andrea et al., 'Repensar la educación del derecho internacional en Latinoamérica: reflexiones para un diálogo global' (2019) 1 *TWAILR: Reflections.*

Akhavari, Afshin, 'The Opportunities and Possibilities for Internationalising the Curriculum of Law Schools in Australia' (2006) 16 *Legal Education Review* 75.

Alvarez et al., 'The Politics of Teaching International Law' (2008) 102 *American Society of International Law Proceedings* 305.

Amaya-Castro, Juan M, 'Teaching International Law: Both Everywhere and Somewhere', in Juan Carlos Sainz-Borgo et al. eds., *Liber Amicorum in honour of a Modern Renaissance Man His Excellency Gudmundur Eiriksson* (OP Jindal Global University, 2017).

Badin, Michelle Ratton Sanchez; Giannattasio, Arthur Roberto Capella; and Castro, Douglas, 'O Caso Didático no Ensino do Direito Internacional: Um Instrumento para um Aprendizado Interdisciplinar com Relações Internacionais' (2017) 47(18) *Meridiano*: 1.

Badin, Michelle Ratton Sanchez; Giannattasio, Arthur Roberto Capella; and Castro, Douglas, 'As Eleições Implícitas na Pesquisa para a Elaboração e Aplicação de Casos em Cursos de Direito Internacional' (2016) 3(2) *Revista Pedagogía Universitaria y Didáctica del Derecho* 195.

Baetens, Freya, and Cheah, Wui Ling, 'Being an International Law Lecturer in the 21st Century: Where Tradition Meets Innovation' (2013) 2(4) *Cambridge Journal of International and Comparative Law* 974.

Beck, Robert, 'Teaching International Law as a Partially Online Course: the Hybrid/ Blended Approach to Pedagogy' (2010) 11(3) Journal of International Studies Perspectives 273.

Beckman, Robert, 'International Law at the National University of Singapore – Personal Reflections and Prospects' (2001) 5 *Singaporean Journal of International and Comparative Law* 426.

Betancur Restrepo, Laura; and Prieto-Rios, Enrique, 'Educación del derecho internacional en Bogotá: un primer diagnóstico a partir del análisis de los programas de clase y su relación con las epistemologías de no conocimiento' (2017) 39 *Revista Derecho del Estado* 53.

Binder, Christina; and Hofbauer, Jane A, 'Teaching International Human Rights Law: a Textbook Review' (2017) 28(4) *EJIL* 1397.

Blay, Sam, 'The Function of International and Comparative Law in Australian Legal Education' (1996) *Australian International Law Journal* 80.

Botha, Neville, 'Teaching International Law in South Africa Ten Years into Democracy' (2004) 29 *South African Yearbook of International Law* 243.

Brito, Adriane Sanctis de; and Nasser, Salem Hikmat, 'Ensinar direito internacional no Brasil: panorama de uma prática e seus desafios' (2017) 39 *Revista Derecho del Estado* 119.

Brown, Craig, 'The Jessup Mooting Competition as a Vehicle for Teaching Public International Law', 16 Canadian Yearbook of International Law 332 (1978).

Butler, W. E., 'The Teaching of International Law in the USSR' (1982) 8 *Socialist Law Review* 183.

Carvalho, Fabia Fernandes, 'História e crítica em direito internacional na América Latina: revisitando discussões pretéritas sobre ensino jurídico na região' (2017) 39 *Revista Derecho del Estado* 91.

Castaño Garcia, Isabel, 'Enseñanza e Investigación del Derecho Internacional y las Relaciones Internacionales' (1983) 4(3) *Revista de Estudios Internacionales* 553.

Cattafi, Carmelo, 'Teaching Methods in International Law' (2018) 14(2) *Journal of International Education Research* 9.

Cheng, Bin (ed.), *International Law Teaching and Practice* (1982).

Chimni, B. S., 'Teaching, Research and Promotion of International Law in India: Past, Present and Future' (2001) 5 *Singaporean Journal of International and Comparative Law* 368.

Corell, Hans, 'International Law and the Law School Curriculum' (2002) 4 *International Law forum du droit international* 195.

Crawford, James, 'Teaching and Research in International Law in Australia' (1981) 10 *Australian Year Book of International Law* 176.

D'Silva, Magdalene, 'A new legal ethics education paradigm: culture and values in international arbitration' (2013) 23 *Legal Education Review* 83.

Davis et al., 'Perspectives on Teaching Foreign and International Legal Research' in Hill et al. (eds) *Teaching Legal Research and Providing Access to Electronic Resources* (2001) 55.

Epps, Valerie, and Scharf, Michael, 'Report of the Committee on the Teaching of International Law' (2001) *Proceedings of the American Branch of the International Law Association* 78.

Eslava, Luis, 'The teaching of (another) international law: critical realism and the question of agency and structure' (2020) 54(3) *The Law Teacher* 368.

Espaliú Berdud, Carlos, *'La Enseñanza del Derecho Internacional Público Basada en las Decisiones de Los Tribunales Internacionales en el Marco de la Implantación del Espacio Europeo de Educación Superior' [https://www.uco.es/docencia_derecho/index.php/reduca/article/view/22]*, (2010) 1 *Docencia y Derecho*.

Fach Gómez, Katia, 'Ventajas del Problem Based Learning (PBL) como método de aprendizaje del Derecho Internacional' (2012) 64(1) *Bordón. Revista De Pedagogía* 59.

Florestal, Marjorie, 'A Tale of Two *Compadres*: Teaching International Trade and Development Across Cultures' (2013) 26 *Pac. McGeorge Global Bus. & Dev. L.J.* 33.

Forcada, Ignacio, 'La Enseñanza del Derecho Internacional Público en España: Una Perspectiva desde el "Análisis Crítico del Discurso"' (2001) 3 *Revista Electrónica de Estudios Internacionales*, at http://www.reei.org/index.php/revista/num3/agora/ensenanza-derecho-internacional-publico-espana-una-perspectiva-desde-analisis-critico-discurso.

Gamble, John, 'The Decade's Emphasis on Education in International Law' (1993) 87 *American Society of International Law Proceedings* 362.

Gamble, John, and Joyner, Christopher (eds.), *Teaching International Law: Approaches and Perspectives* (1997).

Gamble, John, and Shields, Natalie, 'International Legal Scholarship: a Perspective on Teaching and Publishing' (1989) 39 *Journal of Legal Education* 39.

Gamble, John, *Teaching International Law in the 1990s* (1992).

Gamble, John, 'International Law Teaching: Glass(es) Half Full – Rose Coloured – Red/White and Blue' (2012) 37 *South African Yearbook of International Law* 283.

Grossman, Claudio, 'Integrating International Law into the First-Year Curriculum' (2005) 24 *Penn State International Law Review* 835.

Helal, Mohamed, 'Teaching Public International Law: Reflections on the State of the Art in an Era of Uncertainty' (2017) 416 *Public Law and Legal Theory Working Paper Series*, at http://ssrn.com/abstract=3046633.

Hernández, Gleider, 'Inculcating International Law: the Textbook as Gateway' (2018) 9 *European Society of International Law Conference Paper*.

Hey, Ellen, 'The Teaching of International Law, L'Enseignement du Droit International' (2002) 4 *International Law forum du droit international* 189.

Higgins, Rosalyn, 'Teaching and Practicing International Law in a Global Environment: toward a Common Language of International Law' (2010) 104 *American Society of International Law Proceedings* 196.

Hilpold, Peter (ed.). *European International Law Traditions* (Springer, 2021).

Hoffmann, Florian, 'Teaching General Public International Law', in J d'Aspremont and J Kammerhofer eds., *International Legal Positivism in a Post-Modern World* (Cambridge University Press, 2014).

Hurwitz, Deena, 'Teaching International Law: Lessons From Clinical Education' (2010) 104 *American Society of International Law Proceedings* 95.

Hutchinson, Terry, 'Educating the Transnational Lawyer: Globalisation and the Effects on Legal Research Skills Training' (Paper presented at the 61st Annual ALTA Conference, Melbourne, 4 July 2006).

International Law Association, *'Teaching of International Law Committee: Conference Report New Delhi' (2002)[http://www.ila-hq.org/en/committees/index.cfm/cid/1009]*.

International Law Association, *'Teaching of International Law Committee: Discussion Document Berlin' (2004)[http://www.ila-hq.org/en/committees/index.cfm/cid/1009]*.

International Law Association, *'Teaching of International Law Committee: Committee Report The Hague' (2010)[http://www.ila-hq.org/en/committees/index.cfm/cid/1009]*.

Jessup, Philip, 'The Teaching of International Law in Law Schools' (1947) 41 *American Society of International Law Proceedings* 66.

Johns, Fleur, and Freeland, Steven, 'Teaching International Law across an Urban Divide: Reflections on an Improvisation' (2007) 57 *Journal of Legal Education* 539.

José, Diego Flávio Fontoura; Brondani, Isadora; and Areosa, João Antonio Coutinho, 'Research Symposium – Direito Internacional "Na Palma da Mão" – Parte 3. Resultados Preliminares sobre os Manuais de Direito Internacional Público no Brasil', *International Law Agendas* (6 April 2021), at http://ila-brasil.org.br/blog/resultados-preliminares/.

Joyner, Christopher, 'Teaching International Law: Views from an International Relations Political Scientist' (1998) 5 *ILSA International & Comparative Law* 377.

Juwana, Hikmahanto, 'Teaching International Law in Indonesia' (2001) 5 *Singaporean Journal of International and Comparative Law* 412.

Kennedy, David, 'International Legal Education', (1985) 26 *Harvard International Law Journal* 361.

Knechtle, John, 'Teaching, Decision-Making, and International Law in the Twenty-First Century' (2003) 97 *American Society of International Law Proceedings* 217.

Ku et al., 'International Law and the Legal Curriculum' (2002) 96 *American Society of International Law Proceedings* 54.

Lachs, Manfred, *The Teacher in International Law: Teachings and Teaching* (1982).

Leichtweis, Matheus et al., 'Research Symposium – Direito Internacional "Na Palma da Mão" – Parte 5. Sobre o Eixo Universalismo/Particularismo na Pesquisa dos Manuais Brasileiros de Direito Internacional', *International Law Agendas* (6 April 2021), at http://ila-brasil.org.br/blog/sobre-o-eixo-universalismo-particularismo/.

Li-ann, Thio, 'Formalism, Pragmatism and Critical Theory: Reflections on Teaching and Constructing an International Law Curriculum in a New (Post-Colonial) Asia' (2001) 5 *Singaporean Journal of International and Comparative Law* 327.

Lo, Vai Io, 'Before Competition and Beyond Complacency – the Internationalisation of Legal Education in Australia' (2012) 22 *Legal Education Review* 3.

MacDonald, Ronald St. John, 'An Historical Introduction to the Teaching of International Law in Canada' (1974) 12 *Canadian Yearbook of International Law* 67.

Macedo, Julia et al., 'Research Symposium – Direito Internacional "Na Palma da Mão" – Parte 2. Análise das Biografias dos Principais Autores', *International Law Agendas* (6 April 2021), at http://ila-brasil.org.br/blog/analise-das-biografias-dos-autores/.

Magallanes, Catherine J Iorns, 'Teaching for Transnational Lawyering', (2005) 55 *Journal of Legal Education* 519.

Marcos, Henrique Jerônimo Bezerra, 'Didática, Ensino E Pesquisa Jurídico-Dogmática Em Direito Internacional', in Wagner Menezes ed., *Direito Internacional em Expansão – Volume XIX* (Arraes Editores, 2020).

McCormack, Timothy, and Simpson, Gerry, 'Simulating Multilateral Treaty Making in the Teaching of International Law' (1999) 10 *Legal Education Review* 61.

McDonald, Ronald St. John, 'International Law at the University of British Columbia, 1945–2000' (2003) 41 *Canadian Yearbook of International Law* 3.

McNair, Arnold, 'The Wider Teaching of International Law' (1952) 2 *Journal of Society of Public Teachers of Law* 10.

Merrills, J. G., 'On Teaching International Law' (1968) 10 *Journal of Society of Public Teachers of Law* 169.

Mickelson, Karin, 'Rethinking Modes of Diffusion and Research and Teaching Methods: a TWAIL Perspective", in Mark Toufayan, Emmanuelle Tourme-Jouannet & Hélène Ruiz-Fabri, eds., *Droit International et Nouvelles Approches sur le Tiers-Monde: Entre Répétition et Renouveau* (Societé de Legislation Comparé, 2013).

Mitchell et al., 'Education in the Field: a Case Study of Experiential Learning in International Law' (2011) 21 *Legal Education Review* 69.

Moffett, Luke; Cubie, Dug; and Godden, Andrew, 'Bringing the battlefield into the classroom: using video games to teach and assess international humanitarian law' (2017) 51(4) *The Law Teacher* 499.

Morosini, Fabio; and Leão, Luiza, 'Research Symposium – Direito Internacional "Na Palma da Mão" – Parte 1', *International Law Agendas* (6 April 2021), at http://ila-brasil.org.br/blog/direito-internacional-na-palma-da-mao-lendo-as-entrelinhas-dos-manuais-brasileiros/.

Orford, Anne, 'Citizenship, Sovereignty and Globalisation: Teaching International Law in the Post' (1995) 6 *Legal Education Review* 251.

Orford, Anne, 'Embodying Internationalism: the Making of International Lawyers' (1998) 18 Australian Yearbook of International Law 1.

Osakwe et al., 'Reexamination of the Teaching of International Law' (1984) 78 *American Society of International Law Proceedings* 198.

Otto, Dianne, 'Handmaidens, Hierarchies and Crossing the Public-Private Divide in the Teaching of International Law' (2000) 1 *Melbourne Journal of International Law* 35.

Otto, Dianne, 'Integrating Questions of Gender into Discussion of the Use of Force in the International Law Curriculum' (1995) 6 *Legal Education Review* 219.

Pueyo Losa, Jorge, 'Reflexiones sobre la Enseñanza del Derecho Internacional Público', (1987) 5 *Revista de la Facultad de Derecho* 303.

Ratzkowski, Fernanda; Souza, Jamille Batista e; and Ospina, Julia Britto, 'Research Symposium – Direito Internacional "Na Palma da Mão" – Parte 4. Manuais-Projeto e

Manuais-Instrumento: Uma Possível Tipologia dos Manuais de Direito Internacional Público Brasileiros', *International Law Agendas* (6 April 2021), at http://ila-brasil.org.br/blog/manuais-projeto-e-manuais-instrumento/.

Reisman, Michael, 'The Teaching of International Law in the Eighties', (1986) 20 *International Lawyer* 987.

Roberts, Anthea, *Is International Law International?* (Oxford University Press, 2017).

'Roundtable on the Teaching of International Law: Remarks' (1991) 85 104 *American Society of International Law Proceedings* 102.

Saberi, Hengameh, 'Virtue Pedagogy and International Law Teaching', in Luis Eslava, Michael Fakhri, and Vasuki Nesiah eds., *Bandung, Global History, and International Law: Critical Pasts and Pending Futures* (Cambridge University Press, 2017).

Salvioli, Fabián, 'Algunas Consideraciones sobre la Enseñanza Contemporánea del Derecho Internacional Público', (2002) 11(22) *Revista Relaciones Internacionales* 1.

Saul, Ben and Baghoomians, Irene, 'An Experimental International Law Field School in the Sky: Learning Human Rights and Development in the Himalayas' (2012) 22(2) *Legal Education Review* 273.

Saul, Ben, 'Indigenous Peoples, Laws and Customs in the Teaching of Public and Private International Law' (2012) 4 *Ngiya: Talk the Law* 63.

Schiffman, Howard, 'Teaching International Law to Undergraduates and Other Non-Legal Audiences: Practical Suggestions for Pedagogical Approaches' (2002) 9 *ILSA International & Comparative Law* 321.

Schwarzenberger, Georg, 'On Teaching International Law' (1951) 4 *International Law Quarterly* 299.

Schwelb, Egon, 'The Teaching of the International Aspects of Human Rights' (1971) 65 *American Society of International Law Proceedings* 242.

Schwöbel-Patel, Christine, "I'd like to learn what hegemony means' Teaching International Law from a Critical Angle' (2013) 3(2) *Recht en Methode in onderzoek en onderwijs* 67.

Schwöbel-Patel, Christine, 'Teaching International Law Critically – Critical Pedagogy and Bildung as Orientations for Learning and Teaching', in Bart van Klink and Ubaldus de Vries (eds.), *Academic Learning in Law: Theoretical Positions, Teaching Experiments and Learning Experiences* (Edward Elgar, 2015).

Sen, Rohini, 'Teaching International Law in Asia: the Predicated Pedagogue', *AfronomicsLaw* (24 September 2020), at https://www.afronomicslaw.org/2020/09/24/teaching-international-law-in-asia-the-predicated-pedagogue.

Shearer, Ivan, 'The Teaching of International Law in Australian Law Schools' (1983) 9 *Adelaide Law Review* 61.

Simpson, Gerry, 'On The Magic Mountain: Teaching Public International Law' (1999) 10 *European Journal of International Law* 70.

Snyder, Francis, 'The Contribution of Anthropology to Teaching Comparative and International Law', in Marie-Claire Foblets, Gordon Woodman and Antony Bradney eds., *The Trials and Triumphs of Teaching Legal Anthropology in Europe* (Ashgate Publishers, 2015).

Sohn, Louis, 'The Present Importance of Teaching International Law and Organization' (1954) 7 *Journal of Legal Education* 199.

'Special Feature: the State of International Legal Education in the United States', (1988) 29 *Harvard International Law Journal* 239.

Stone, William, 'The Teaching of International Law in Adult Education of the General Public' (1947) 41 *American Society of International Law Proceedings* 88.

Tan, Kevin, 'The SILS-DILA Conference on Teaching and Researching International Law in Asia: Report and Reflections' (2001) 5 *Singaporean Journal of International and Comparative Law* 441.

Tanja, Gerard, 'The Teaching of International Law: the Need for Curriculum Change' (2002) 4 *International Law forum du droit international* 199.

Tieya, Wang, 'Teaching and Research of International Law in Present Day China' (1983) 22 *Columbia Journal of Transnational Law* 77.

UNESCO Regional Office for Education in Asia and the Pacific, *Teaching and Research in International Law in Asia and the Pacific* (1985).

Valcke, Catherine, 'Global Law Teaching' (2005) 14 *Legal Education Digest* 8.

Vibhute, Khushal, 'International Law in India – Developing Curricula and Teaching: Some Reflections' (2001) 5 *Singaporean Journal of International and Comparative Law* 388.

Weston et al, 'Promoting Training and Awareness--The Tasks of Education in International Law: Remarks' (1981) 75 *American Society of International Law Proceedings* 159.

Whittuck, E A, 'International Law Teaching' (1917) *Problems of the War – Papers Read before the Society in the Year 1917* 43.

Wilson, Richard, 'Teaching International Law: Lessons From Clinical Education' (2010) 104 *American Society of International Law Proceedings* 87.

Wilson, Robert, 'The Teaching of International Law in Undergraduate and Graduate Courses in Political Science' (1947) 41 *American Society of International Law Proceedings* 77.

Zartner, Dana, 'An Interdisciplinary Approach to Teaching International Law: Using the Tools of the Law School Classroom in Political Science', (2009) *PS: Political Science and Politics* 189.

CHAPTER 18

Manfred Lachs and His 'Teacher in International Law'

The Lessons He Gave Us

*Bartłomiej Krzan**

Why to Rely on Manfred Lachs?

The question may seem trivial, yet not only from the Polish perspective Manfred Lachs remains one of the most eminent diplomats, international law scholars, academic teachers, and judges. On different occasions, and in all his different capacities Manfred Lachs considerably affected modern international law in an astonishing variety of fields. These include the law of armed conflict, and international criminal law,[1] the law of treaties,[2] and the law of international organisations. Last but not least, Manfred Lachs was one of the fathers of space law.[3]

Here is not the proper place to discuss in too great a detail his fascinating life.[4] Instead, what is offered here is merely a brief recapitulation of his achievements, which may reveal some additional background crucial for learning his message on teaching international law. Born on 21 April 1914 in Stanisławów (now Ivano-Frankivsk in western Ukraine), Lachs graduated in Law from the Jagiellonian University, Cracow where in 1937 he also was promoted to *doctor iuris* and then continued his studies.[5] During the Second World War he served

* University Professor at the Department of International and European Law, Faculty of Law, Administration and Economics, University of Wrocław; email: bartlomiej.krzan@uwr.edu.pl; ORCID: 0000-0003-3964-114X.

1 His first monograph *War Crimes: an Attempt to Define the Issue* was published with Stevens in 1945.

2 In addition to his first Hague lecture (of 1957), the Polish community of international lawyers remembers and still frequently refers to the splendid monograph on this (Manfred Lachs, *Umowy wielostronne: studium z prawa traktatowego* (PWN 1958), later translated into Russian (1960), Hungarian (1962) and Spanish (1962).

3 Manfred Lachs, *International Law of Outer Space: A Law in the Making* (Sijthoff 1972).

4 See, e.g. Francis Lyall, 'Manfred Lachs (21.4.1914–4.1.1993)' in Stephan Hobe (ed), *Pioneers of Space Law*, (Nijhoff 2013) 193ff.

5 At the Universities of Vienna and Nancy (another doctorate in 1939). After the Second World War broke out, he was at the London School of Economics and the University of Cambridge.

 DOI:10.1163/9789004678880_022

the Polish Government in Exile, both as a legal adviser and as a member of the Polish National Council, and later became a member of the delegation to the UN War Crimes Commission (1944). After returning to Poland, Lachs continued his diplomatic service.[6] In the 1960's he served as Chairman of the Legal Sub-Committee on the Peaceful Uses of Outer Space and was elected to the International Law Commission.[7] Parallel to his diplomatic career, Manfred Lachs continued to be involved in university activities.[8]

Manfred Lachs was also a typical representative of a personal union between judges and teachers/writers.[9] He became a member of the UNESCO Arbitral Tribunal in 1949, and of the Permanent Court of Arbitration in 1956. But the crowning moment for any international lawyer was the election to the ICJ. Indeed, Lachs was on the Bench of the latter Court for the longest time ever. Elected President of the Court exceptionally early in his career (1973–1976), he served with an unusual flair and panache.[10] It is also thanks to him that several important improvements of the ICJ rules have been adopted.[11] He greatly contributed to restoring the Court's reputation and the prestige of the ICJ as a truly international body,[12] by improving its hitherto frayed relations with other

6 As Director of the Legal and Treaties Department of the Polish Ministry of Foreign Affairs (1947–60), and then as a legal advisor (1960–1966), Minister Plenipotentiary (1959–1960), and Ambassador (1960–1966).He was one of the architects of the Rapacki Plan for a nuclear-free zone in Central Europe and then represented Poland during the negotiations of the non-proliferation regime, being involved as a member of the Disarmament Committee (1962–1964).

7 Where he was particularly active in the discussions concerning the Law of Treaties as well as on state succession.

8 First as a professor at the Academy of Political Sciences (1949–1952), and since 1952, Professor of International Law at the Faculty of Law, University of Warsaw. In the 1960s, he served as Director of the Institute of State and Law of the Polish Academy of Sciences.

9 Manfred Lachs, 'Teachings and teaching of international law', (1976-III) 151, Recueil des cours 161, 220.

10 Stephen M. Schwebel, 'On the Bench: Lachs the Judge' (1993) 87 American Journal of International Law 416, 418.

11 E.g. Lachs was instrumental in changing the ICJ rules to make chambers user-friendly (see also Bartłomiej Krzan, 'Izby sądowe Międzynarodowego Trybunału Sprawiedliwości' [= The Chambers of the International Court of Justice] in Zdzisław Galicki, Tomasz Kamiński and Katarzyna Myszona-Kostrzewa (eds), *Manfred Lachs: wybitny prawnik świata* (SAWPiA UW 2011) 267). His attempts to authorize the UN Secretary-General to request advisory opinions were less effective. See also Manfred Lachs, 'The Revised Procedure of the International Court of Justice' in Fritz Kalshoven (ed) *Essays on the Development of the International Legal Order in memory of Haro F. van Panhuys* (Nijhoff 1980) 21, 33.

12 Lord Elwyn-Jones, 'Manfred Lachs', in Jerzy Makarczyk (ed), *Essays in International Law in Honour of Judge Manfred Lachs* (Nijhoff 1984) 108.

UN organs.[13] In the words of Boutros Ghali, "Manfred Lachs was above all a champion of the law, devoted to promoting international legality".[14]

It is a firm suspicion by those who knew him well that despite the many and different roles Manfred Lachs played in his professional life, it would have been that of a teacher which Lachs would like to have been remembered for.[15] In the latter role, Lachs showed young people the development paths of international law, but also its alleys and astray, weaknesses and strengths. "These were not lectures, but a constant dialogue with them: these constant questions from students, seeking explanations as to why the norm and the fact were in conflict, and in particular their interest in contemporary phenomena: why it happened this way and not otherwise".[16] And those led him to admit: "this is what inspired me so often in my practical and scientific work: perhaps one of the greatest stimuli in my work".[17] *Docendo discimus!*

As an academic teacher, Professor Lachs was able to enchant students with substantive competences, beauty, and precision of the language,[18] as well as a

13 Lachs introduced the practice of the ICJ making an annual report to the UN General Assembly, and frequently attended its sessions. See Edward McWhinney, 'The Inaugural Manfred Lachs Memorial Lecture Manfred Lachs and the International Court of Justice as Emerging Constitutional Court of the United Nations' (1995) 8(1) Leiden Journal of International Law 41.

14 The former UN Secretary General further noted: "The law was not for him a disembodied universe, but on the contrary a world that rested on values. He was deeply convinced that international law can find its true justification only in the ends it pursues"-see Boutros Boutros-Ghali 'Foreword: Tribute to Manfred Lachs, Champion of the Law' in Nandasiri Jasentuliyana (ed) *Perspectives on International Law* (Kluwer Law International 1995) x, xiii.

15 Eugeniusz Wyzner 'Preface: A Dedication' in Nandasiri Jasentuliyana (ed), *Perspectives on International Law* (Kluwer Law International 1995) xv, xvi: "Although a master of compromise and a champion of consensus, he was never willing to compromise on such essential values such as honesty, integrity, tolerance and understanding of the views which differed from those he himself professed".

16 Manfred Lachs, 'W podróży, którą nazywamy życiem' [=In the journey called living] *Polityka* (Warsaw, 12 January 1985), 11.

17 And continued: "I admit that often a question asked by a student, an answer that did not satisfy him, incited my further thinking processes, led me to reject old ones and look for other solutions, and thus fostered the birth of new concepts or theories" Lachs (n 16) 11.

18 Cf. Kazimierz Równy, 'Professor Manfred Lachs – inspirujący nauczyciel, pionierski współorganizator badań interdyscyplinarnych, dociekliwy naukowiec i nieugięty obrońca pokoju na świecie (we wspomnieniach wczesnego ucznia)' [=Professor Manfred Lachs – inspiring teacher, pioneering co-organizer of interdisciplinary research, inquisitive scientist, and relentless defender of peace in the world (in the memories of an early student)] in Zdzisław Galicki, Tomasz Kamiński and Katarzyna Myszona-Kostrzewa (eds), *Manfred Lachs: wybitny prawnik świata* (SAWPiA UW 2011) 35, 38–39. His eloquent lectures always

way of being so different from the then prevailing norm.[19] He did more than teach law, he gave his students an outlook on life.[20]

He was a generous and forward-looking educator, very actively engaged in moot courts, frequently presiding over the annual Telders International Moot Court Competition at The Hague. As President of the International Institute of Space Law, Lachs was then instrumental to create, in 1992, the space law moot court now bearing his name.

But one of the most important things was the way how Lachs fostered the careers of many younger Polish international lawyers.[21] He established an annual scholarship for Polish students to study at the Hague Academy. In his last will, Lachs donated a substantial sum of money to establish a foundation in his name to award annual awards for the best books in the field of public international law (in two categories: for an author's début, and then his or her successive book).[22]

Lessons Taught, Learnt and to be Learnt

Lachs' strong interest in teaching was manifested in his *Teacher in International Law.*[23] Based on his 1976 Hague lecture, the book was first released in English in 1982 (with the second edition of 1987), and then subsequently translated into Polish[24] and into French.[25] It received the ASIL award for creative scholarship in 1982. Indeed, it had a remarkable impact. It dazzled all who read it with

discharged themselves into a well-balanced political message, shining through a veil of poetry – see Wil Verwey 'In Memoriam: Manfred Lachs (1914–1993)' (1993) 40 Netherlands International Law Review V, VI.

19 Andrzej Makarewicz, 'Manfred Lachs we wspomnieniach współpracowników' [= Manfred Lachs in the memoirs of associates] in Zdzisław Galicki, Tomasz Kamiński and Katarzyna Myszona-Kostrzewa (eds), *Manfred Lachs: wybitny prawnik świata* (SAWPiA UW 2011) 43, 44.

20 Wyzner (n 15) XVI.

21 Oscar Schachter 'The UN Years: Lachs the Diplomat' (1993) 87 American Journal of International Law 414, 415.

22 The present author did not have the chance to meet Professor Lachs in person but is proud to have been awarded this prestigious distinction for his habilitation thesis ("the Manfred Lachs Prize" for the best monographs in International Law of 2013 and 2014).

23 Manfred Lachs, *The Teacher in International Law* (*Teachings and Teaching*) (Nijhoff 1982).

24 Manfred Lachs, *Rzecz o nauce prawa międzynarodowego* (Zakład Narodowy im. Ossolińskich 1986).

25 Manfred Lachs, *Le monde de la pensée en droit international: theories et pratique* (Economica 1989).

its erudition, historical knowledge, and contemporary insight.[26] For Thomas Franck the reviewed book was 'a graceful compliment to those who live and labor in the world of ideas [...] likely to encourage and strengthen whatever residual intellectual tendencies lie largely dormant in the young law student of the utilitarian 1980's.".[27]

Instead of discussing teaching techniques, curriculum and similar issues, the masterpiece deals with the position and influence of teachers or the doctrine of international law.[28] The relationship between theory and practice in public international law seems to be (or remains) stronger than in many other disciplines.[29] In fact, one could not think of a comparable system of law with such a telling influence of scholars over the substance of principles and rules.[30] Yet, in order to strike a sound balance, one could rely on the succinct assessment by Pearce Higgins, who rejected the idea of international law as "a body of rules which lawyers have evolved out of their own inner consciousness [or] a system carefully thought out by University Professors, Bookworms, or other theorists in the quiet and seclusion of their studies".[31] Everyone should be fully aware of the political importance of international law, which has become, for governments, something too important to be left to lawyers and, especially, to teachers.[32]

An obvious point of reference at present would definitely be Article 38(1)(d) of the ICJ Statute. Some would even claim that the relevance of the provision is limited to the doctrine of international law.[33] Of course, like judicial decisions, "the teachings of publicists are not rules to be applied, but sources to be resorted to for finding applicable rules".[34] Lachs was very clear in showing that

---

26 Rosalyn Higgins, 'Obituary: Judge Manfred Lachs' *The Independent* (London, 16 February 1993).

27 Thomas M. Franck, 'Book Review' (1983) 77 American Journal of International Law 169.

28 In the Author's own words: (n 23) 1: the theme of my reflections is The Teacher in International Law: the subject-matter of his teachings, his role in shaping the minds of others – of his [or her] immediate audience and, beyond, all who receive his message – the impact he can and should have on the law itself.

29 Abdulqawi Ahmed Yusuf, 'The Role of International Lawyers between Theory and Practice' (2017) 15(3) Journal of International Criminal Justice 603, 604.

30 Robert Jennings, 'International Lawyers and the Progressive Development of International Law' in Jerzy Makarczyk (ed), *Theory of International Law at the Threshold of the 21st Century: Essays in Honour of Krzysztof Skubiszewski* (Kluwer Law International 1996) 413.

31 A. Pearce Higgins, *The Binding Force of International Law* (CUP 1910) 3.

32 Michel Virally, 'A propos de la <<lex ferenda>>' in *Mélanges offerts à Paul Reuter: le droit international, unité et diversité* (Pedone 1981) 519, 520.

33 See Albert Bleckmann, *Grundprobleme und Methoden des Völkerrechts* (Alber 1982) 150.

34 Manley O. Hudson, *The Permanent Court of International Justice 1920–1942* (MacMillan 1943) 612.

"It is obviously not a question of "doctors" dictating the law [as suggested by the English Court of Admiralty in the *Renard Case* (1778)[35]], but of their influence on their pupils – first during their actual studentship and then after they have gained responsible positions as teachers or practitioners; of their influence on the better understanding of the law, their impact on its application by government departments, States, groups of States, international organizations or even the international community as a whole".[36]

As obvious as it is, teachers "vary considerably in skill, diligence, intellectual honesty, independence and eminence, but it may be thought invidious to distinguish between them".[37] Sometimes literature may be said to be "unduly theoretical, insufficiently practical, and prone to over-simplification".[38] It has recently been admitted that "subjective factors enter into any assessment of juristic opinion and individual writers will tend to reflect national and other prejudices".[39] In a similar fashion, Sir Hersch Lauterpacht indicated that "the divergence of view among writers on many subjects as well as apparent national bias may often render citations from them unhelpful".[40] The growing quantity of publications led to the diminishing of the authority of the commentators.[41] Against that background, one can only follow Georg Schwarzenberger, who succinctly reduced the value of any exposition of international law to "the degree of accuracy with which it reflects the true state of the law as it stands at a given moment".[42] Such a view resembles what with utmost clarity was stated several decades later when Judges Higgins, Kooijmans and Buergenthal

35 'A pedantic man in his closet dictates the law of nations; and who shall decide, when doctors disagree? Bynkershoek, as it is natural to every writer or speaker who comes after another, is delighted to contradict Grotius'. (165 English Law Reports 51).

36 Lachs (n 23) 168.

37 Maurice Mendelson, 'The ICJ and the Sources of International Law' in Vaughan Lowe and Malgosia Fitzmaurice (eds) *Fifty Years of the International Court of Justice* (CUP 1996) 63, 83–4.

38 Clive Parry, *The Sources and Evidences of International Law* (Manchester University Press 1965) 105.

39 James Crawford, *Brownlie's Principles of Public International Law* (OUP 2012) 43.

40 Hersch Lauterpacht, *The Development of International Law by the International Court* (Stevens 1958) 24.

41 Parry (n 38) 104.

42 Georg Schwarzenberger, *A Manual of International Law* (5th edn, Stevens 1967) 17. The quoted author held further: "In this respect, writers in any age can at the most hope to approximate closely to this goal. Some may be thought to have succeeded better than the others in this endeavor". This goes in line with the assessment by J. Crawford: "some publicists see themselves to be propagating new and better views rather than providing a presentation of the existing law, a tendency the more widespread given increasing specialization" – Crawford (n 39) 43.

appended their Joint Separate Opinion to the Judgment of the ICJ in the Arrest Warrant of 11 April 2000 (Democratic Republic of the Congo v. Belgium) (Merits): "[The writings of eminent jurists], important and stimulating as they may be, cannot of themselves and without reference to the other sources of international law, evidence the existence of a … norm. … the policy arguments advanced in some of the writings can certainly suggest why a practice or a court decision should be regarded as desirable, or indeed lawful; but contrary arguments are advanced too, and in any event these also cannot serve to substantiate an international practice where virtually none exists".[43]

Not as a source of international law, the doctrine indeed has influence on the international law-making process.[44] Thus, legal academics serve as "grammarians of formal law ascertainment who systematize the standards of distinction between law and non-law".[45] Instead of only acting as "crusaders battling for a better world in which international law was to play a larger part", international law teachers may play a very needed role and contribute with "advocacy in favour of change in the law" by "asserting that a proposal *de lege ferenda*, if not already law, is near-law, or law in the process of being made" or by "suggesting that the *le*[*x*] *lata* is corresponding[ly] weakened, or obsolescent".[46]

Thus, the role of academic writers at present consists in the analysis of facts and opinions and in drawing conclusions on binding customary rules and on trends of their evolution. Their conclusions, "like all generalizations of this

---

43 ICJ Reports 2002, 3, Joint Separate Opinion of Judges Higgins, Kooijmans and Buergenthal, 63, at 75, para. 44.

44 GJH Van Hoof, *Rethinking the Sources of International Law* (Kluwer 1983) 178.

45 Jean d'Aspremont, *Formalism and the Sources of International Law: A Theory of the Ascertainment of Legal Rules* (OUP 2011), 209.

46 Robert Y. Jennings, 'Teachings and Teaching in International Law', in Jerzy Makarczyk (ed), *Essays in international law in honour of Judge Manfred Lachs* (Nijhoff 1984) 127. In another contribution, Sir Robert Jennings continued his respective line of argumentation in the following words: "And it is still important to distinguish between lege lata and proposals de lege ferenda; not merely as a technical matter but because of the trap into which the layman so easily falls of supposing all international law to be a proposal. Certainly, it is still the position that international law, or rather civilised humanity, has still to solve the problems of war and violence and inhumanity, which international law has sought to cure from the very beginning. But hope lies perhaps not so much, or only, in new laws directly concerned with the endeavour to control war and violence, as in the gradual but undoubted penetration of international law into new parts of routine, peaceful life, thus building up the habit and expectation of legal ordering of international society" – see Robert Y Jennings, 'An International Lawyer Takes Stock' (1990) 39(3) International and Comparative Law Quarterly 513, 528. Cf. Agata Wnukiewicz-Kozłowska, 'Doctrine as a Source of International Law' in Jan Kolasa (ed), *The Nature of Source in International Legal Order* (E-Wydawnictwo. Prawnicza i Ekonomiczna Biblioteka Cyfrowa 2017) 249, 257.

kind, involve unrestricted supplementation by introducing elements lacking, and hence, a creative factor".[47] One needs to remember, that an international lawyer should never be "a mere slave of the norm, a sort of automaton who squeezes "one-size-fits-all" norms onto reality"[48] but in the process of interpretation should use his/her imagination[49] and, at the same time "to grasp reality to the fullest extent possible".[50] What comes to one's mind is a distinction between a lawyer and an intellectual, or perhaps even a figure of a lawyer not being a mere technician, but rather a person having a broader mind and trying to contribute to changing the law in addition to interpreting the existing law.[51] This is exactly the situation of Schachter's *pénétration pacifique* of ideas from the nongovernmental into official channels.[52] In this fashion one is reminded of the French distinction between the *doctrine académique/doctrine de réflexion* and the *doctrine finalisée/doctrine d'action*.[53]

Manfred Lachs was fully aware that "law" and "teachings" have become so closely interwoven that it is, at times, not easy to distinguish between the object of the study and its creation.[54] He made it clear in the most explicit terms that

47 See Karol Wolfke, *Custom in Present International Law* (2nd edn, Nijhoff 1993) 77, who then added "Further, by attracting attention to international practice and appraising it, the writers indirectly influence its further evolution, that is, the development of custom" (ibidem). Yet, "[w]here juristic commentary provides critical analysis and the exploration of new ideas, writers will make a significant contribution in advisory opinions, law reform and in supporting the work of international organisations, the UN committee system and the ILC" – see Gillian Triggs, 'The Public International Lawyer and the Practice of International Law' (2005) 24 Australian Year Book of International Law 201, 205.

48 Peter Hilpold, 'What Role for Academic Writers in Interpreting International Law?' (2009) 8 Chinese Journal of International Law 291, 297–8.

49 To "re-imagine the game, reconstruct its rules, redistribute the prizes" – see Martti Koskenniemi, *From Apology to Utopia: The Structure of International Legal Argument* (2nd edn, CUP 2005) 561.

50 Hilpold (n 48) 298.

51 See Antonio Cassese, *Five Masters of International Law: Conversations with R-J Dupuy, E Jiménez de Aréchaga, R Jennings, L Henkin and O Schachter* (Hart 2011) 143.

52 Oscar Schachter, 'The Invisible College of International Lawyers' (1977) 72 Northwestern University Law Review 217, 218.

53 André Oraison, 'Reflexions sur la Doctrine des Publicistes les Plus Qualifies des Differentes Nations' (1991) 24(2) Revue Belge de Droit International 507, 509. Yet, as concluded, "One cannot establish in the science of law a too tight partition between basic research and applied research (at 579).

54 Lachs (n 23) 8: "Teachings" have evolved with the "law", almost becoming inherent in it. In analysing law, explaining its birth and development, and seeking its improvement, the Teacher almost "intervenes" in its operation. There is a continuous interaction and feedback operation. Here, inter alia, lies the importance of his work".

"the Teacher, as such, is not a legislator nor a law-maker. To become one, he [or she] must wear a different gown, be vested with special authority".[55]

It is interesting to look at a splendid combination between the utmost modesty of the eminent author and the wealth of his analysis how "the Teacher has been an active element of history: influencing law-making, decision-making, and the application of the law".[56] Striking such a balance, Lachs intended to provide "a brief summary", to project "a panorama in which the state of those "teachings" at a given time is represented by the Teacher then expounding international law according to his lights".[57] Yet, instead of presenting "a complete collection of those who have contributed to our science", his purpose was "to examine their functions, and those of their teachings and to see why this is so".[58] On other occasion Lachs revealed his awareness that "the law is not a favorite of gods or muses, but only a frequent subject of satire, and a lawyer is its hero"[59] but did not refrain from frequently relying on erudite examples from literature.

He warned against considering teaching as "a closed fortress, a phenomenon – within the realm of law – isolated from other branches of knowledge and life".[60] When trying to identify the domains of activity to which the public international lawyer must pay heed, Lachs pointed, as obvious as it is, to economics, as well as to philosophy and other branches of the humanities, but then extended the scope to all the social sciences (while invoking a common effort towards unity of all of them), and even further, to all science.[61] Each of them, therefore, – including teachings of international law,-must participate in the common effort towards unity of all the social sciences. In the latter regard,

55 Lachs (n 23) 8.

56 Lachs (n 23) 8.

57 Lachs (n 23) 9.

58 As declared by Lachs: "it would be fascinating to play the Cicerone in this international gallery, where the great diversity of colours would complement, set off or clash one with another, reflecting the varieties of vision and temperament. I will pause at certain of the portraits, to expound the significance of the sitter in his historical frame. Nevertheless, of none, not even of my heroes, could I say: "this man-made law", though he may have contributed to its making; he may be one of "the most highly qualified publicists of various nations." [footnote omitted] This in itself is no mean status, for without them the law would certainly not be what it is".

59 Lachs (n 16) 11. And pointed further to '[h]ow significant it is that Cervantes made a judge of Sancho Panza; Guy de Maupassant, Chekhov, Čapek and Shakespeare wrote about them' to arrive at a rather bitter conclusion that 'law in literature is a system of regulations that do not meet the needs of life or of people and nations'.

60 Lachs (n 23) 131–2.

61 Lachs (n 23) 132–134.

attention was paid to "continuous great achievements of modern science and technology",[62] stressing that "The relationship to the environment, the use of and control over natural resources, in brief, man's and society's place in nature, have come to be recognized as major factors in the development and collective survival of humanity".[63] Not only against the background of the present challenge of climate change may his words of caution remain very telling.[64]

Lachs drew attention to the need to consider the development and achievements of exact and natural sciences, as well as the impact of technological progress in the process of teaching international law. One can once again but subscribe to his position on challenges facing the teachers and his appeal to continuing "the great dialogue of 'teachers' and 'teachings'".[65]

With regard to transmission of knowledge, Lachs played with the claim by a historian that textbooks "are cemeteries in which knowledge is buried"[66] and then continued: "This in many ways justified remark would suggest that they are more likely to create a distaste for the subject and hold the students at arm's length from the mysteries of his vocation, rather than provide him with the key he needs. This may be true, especially where they are not supplemented by personal contact with the author or some stimulating exponent. The sheer bulk, moreover, of the textbooks available is daunting to the student who lacks criteria of selection. Here as elsewhere the "information explosion" has produced its effects".[67] The accuracy of this assessment does not lose anything of its topicality despite the passage of several decades, and the increased availability, now also comprising electronic sources.

---

62 Lachs (n 23) 134. In a later article, Lachs wrote: "All I wished to do was to confirm that science and technology have become essential parts of history and the present; that law neither of yesterday nor of today could be studied and understood without taking due account of their vital contribution to the lives of nations and states; that the future will to an even greater degree be dependent on the various methods and tools used to make products of human genius serve the needs and interest of mankind and the international community" – see Manfred Lachs, 'Thoughts on Science, Technology and World Law', (1992) 86 American Journal of International Law 673, 699.

63 Lachs (n 23) 135. On other occasion Lachs' was even more explicit: "with each passing day it becomes obvious that man must cooperate with nature as a constituent part of it, protect it from degradation and destruction: nature conservation is related to the tomorrow of life on this planet" – Lachs (n 16) 11.

64 Lachs (n 23) 136: Modern science has immensely increased man's understanding of his physical environment and his ability to manipulate it. Yet its miracles have, of course, not produced a panacea for the world's ills. In the very act of solving problems, science has created many new ones in its own domain and in its relations to man.

65 Lachs (n 23) 136.

66 Lachs (n 23) 137.

67 Lachs (n 23) 137.

One feels like again subscribing to the ironic conclusion that "the spate of publications has grown to such proportions that the severest problem may lie in selecting the book or article most apposite to the enquiry at hand".[68] Still, Lachs was fully aware that such an optimistic situation is not always the rule.[69] This notwithstanding, one may ponder on the value added by the numerous 'novel' textbooks which are offered 'anew' each year.

For Lachs, as probably for most, "teaching", in a more precise sense, means university education (even if international law was rather a latecomer to the universities of Europe).[70] One of the lesser-known facts, which was described in the Lachs' seminal exposition, is that Polish scholars, most notably Professor Stanisław Hubert and his disciples (Jan Kolasa, Kazimierz Kocot) examined the teaching of international law in XVIth and subsequent centuries.[71] Interestingly, the learned judge noted also that there will "remain discrepancies between teaching in various countries in view of national or cultural differences, and different schools of thought are bound to come to the foreground, but this should not constitute an obstacle in the increase and expansion of the teaching of international law".[72] Yet, he strongly warned against viewing the inculcation of international law as a closed field ("hermetically sealed off from other subjects of study").[73] Therefore, it would not be advisable to separate international law from other branches of law: "[t]o be well versed in international law, a solid background of general knowledge of law, i.e., municipal law,

68 Lachs (n 23) 138.

69 "Nevertheless, there remain, regrettably, vast regions of the world where important works of international law are still not easily available, where there is a serious shortage of knowledge in this field. The remedying of this situation calls for special attention and can be envisaged to some extent within the United Nations Programme for the wider appreciation of international law", Lachs (n 23) 138.

70 Lachs (n 23) 138–139.

71 Lachs (n 23) 140ff. (referring to the Hague lecture by Ludwik Ehrlich and the work by Franciszek Kasparek) See also Anna Przyborowska-Klimczak, 'Poglądy Profesora Manfreda Lachsa na temat nauczania prawa międzynarodowego' [=Professor Manfred Lachs' views on the teaching of law] in Zdzisław Galicki, Tomasz Kamiński and Katarzyna Myszona-Kostrzewa (eds), *Manfred Lachs: wybitny prawnik świata* (SAWPiA UW 2011) 65, 66f.

72 Lachs (n 23) 148.

73 "It is true we live in an age of specialization, an age when learning is becoming equated with knowing more and more about less and less. Yet, while specialization has become in many ways unavoidable, since each of us has only one lifetime and the rate at which the human mind can assimilate knowledge is limited, it does not make sense to embark on a concentrated study of what is avowedly only a part of a whole without first having acquired a working knowledge of the whole. The result can be but distortion" – see Lachs (n 23) 150.

is indispensable".[74] One could consider the precedingly quoted words as a very eloquent invitation to discuss the fragmentation of international law, which would definitely go beyond the remit of the present study. But the scope of teaching also reaches into other dimensions – the whole vast and rich field of international relations,[75] which opens the floor for discussing the interdisciplinary character of teaching.

In advocating the indispensability of the interdisciplinary approach,[76] Lachs in very strong words[77] criticized the claim that enlarging the study of international law to include related branches of knowledge must result in the distortion of the *legal* character of the teaching. According to him, this has proved to be a false problem.[78] For Lachs, the wider background of "international relations" was required but "[t]his should not [...] amount to identifying the two subjects [...], for this may lead to submergence of law, its depreciation or even negation. The Teacher must therefore thread a narrow path and maintain distinction between diplomatic practice as such (with whatever aspects of law it may be intertwined) and the legal basis of international behavior. The identity and distinct role of international law must remain unaffected – and it is essential only to see it in the context of other spheres of knowledge and international activities, hence the need for the complex approach [..] both within the world of social sciences and beyond it".[79]

It is again interesting to see how implications of all those manifestations were addressed by the learned judge: the teacher should again help to bridge three gaps – the interdisciplinary communication gap, the gap between men of science and the public and the generation gap-while restoring confidence in the teaching of law.[80] Outside the judicial context one could also sense the

74 However, the same applies to students who seek a career in other fields of law: without an adequate knowledge of international law, their education is bound to be incomplete (ibidem).

75 Lachs (n 23) 150–151.

76 Lachs (n 23) "In the "teaching", as in the "teachings", of international law a much wider view must be taken. We have to go beyond law into other areas of social phenomena and of the relevant sciences, all of which are no less interdependent than the events which shape the course of society of nations".

77 In an even stronger manner, this proves to be visible in a Polish version of the book (Lachs (n 24) 187) where he used the term *mętniactwo* (turbidity).

78 Then he continues: "The study of international relations, of which international law is a part – should be seen in a different perspective. In no circumstances can it, as an encyclopedic subject, replace international in its true function and perspective. But international law subsists in an element, environment, ignorance of which must be harmful".

79 Lachs (n 23) 156.

80 Lachs (n 23) 159.

idea of bridging the gaps. For Vladen Vereshchetin, "Professor, Diplomat, Judge Manfred Lachs personified an important link, a kind of "bridge" over the gap which existed between Soviet and Western doctrines and practices of international law" for his "authority, expertise, and skill [...], equally recognized by both sides, immensely facilitated affirming common values of international law notwithstanding the existing gap between social and economic systems".[81] Admittedly, Lachs' inclination for compromise and impact greatly affected his approach to international law and the respective roles for international lawyers.

During a ceremony at the Polish Academy of Sciences celebrating his 70th birthday anniversary, Lachs further revealed his approach: "Acquiring the art of persuasion, peace, and patience even in the face of serious crises – this is what determines the importance and role of a diplomat and international lawyer: he should not draw narrow boundaries, and this will enable the end of the war before it begins. this is what life has taught me: it has taught me the art of listening. This does not mean giving up or abandoning the fight to defend certain principles and for a better tomorrow, on the contrary, it only makes them more real and allows for a proper understanding of the facts, the course of events, protects against illusions that inevitably facilitate an escape from reality, to an isthmus leading to the world of metaphysics, and in fact leading nowhere. The only way until tomorrow is an agreement, unimposed decisions, unforced contracts".[82] *Concordia parvae res crescunt!*

But a natural talent for conciliation in the search of a common denominator was skillfully blended with the coolly logical approach of a perfect lawyer.[83] This feature should not be hidden behind a very erudite way of formulating the views. Far beyond it, Lachs was able to identify 'real-life human problems behind virtually every, seemingly purely legal issue'.[84]

To learn his vision of international law even better, it is worth mentioning one of the concluding thoughts Lachs included in the fourth lecture delivered at the Hague Academy: "In truth, international law of today is a product of historical development and of a causation chain which has embraced both

---

81 Vladen Vereshchetin, 'Authors recollect Judge Lachs' in Nandasiri Jasentuliyana (ed), *Perspectives on International Law* (Kluwer Law International 1995) 529, 535.

82 Lachs (n 16) 1, 11.

83 Wyzner (n 15) xvii.

84 As recalled by Wyzner, 'He approached every case with an uncannily balanced mixture of icy legalistic perfection and deep human compassion and understanding. He could be reserved, but was never aloof. He recognized that it was human to err, and was always willing to acknowledge that he himself was no exception to the rule' (Wyzner (n 15) xvii).

subjective and objective elements, represents a consolidation of what has come to be regarded as proper conduct, and is designed to provide a framework in which each State, without jostling its neighbours, can do "what it is eager to do", and what is not incompatible with the common interest of all".[85]

The message was quite explicit and of general application for the role of a(n) (international) lawyer. At the end of his last Hague lecture, Lachs suggested that "in order to perform his task the jurist cannot be parochial or myopic; he must be imaginative and critical, fight against myth and falsehood, have a vision of a coherent law which must rhyme with history and do his utmost to influence events for the betterment of inter-State relations".[86]

Not only against this background, it is important to note that a historical approach to understanding international law was always one of the dominant themes of the lectures by Lachs.[87] According to him, law is prone to ossification and therefore "it is a matter for the legislator, teacher and judge to constantly develop it through new norms and interpretations in the dimensions of time and events".[88]

As obvious as it is, Lachs criticized the practice of the pushing international law "into a small corner of the curriculum" and advocated that "while exaggerated hopes should not be encouraged, intellectual exploration, deeply rooted in reality, is the essence of the adventure of learning"[89] – this is the position all students (potentially being co-responsible for interpreting international law) and teachers are to subscribe without any reservation!

As the main objective of education, Lachs referred to "build[ing] in the minds of men the defences of peace", but then immediately added a warning that "the road to peace, if by peace is meant more than a state of armed truce, must pass through the creation of a more just humane world, and this requires

85 Manfred Lachs, 'The Development and General Trends of International Law in Our Time' (1980) 169 Recueil des cours 9, 258.

86 Lachs (n 85) 260. See also Hilpold (n 48) 297–8.

87 Sudhir K. Chopra, 'The Teacher: Lachs at the Hague Academy', (1993) 87 American Journal of International Law 420, 421.

88 Lachs (n 16) 11: "Today, with the increasing rhythm of life, it requires more oxygen than ever in the past, so that its pulse adapts to the realities of today and that it reaches its perspective into the future". In a similar fashion, during the Convocation Address at Simon Fraser University in Vancouver, in 1976 he stressed that: "It is the international jurist's task to make international law work, to fight against the dethronement of reason, to act with passion and imagination for the attainment of order and concord. He must not only know the law, but he must have a vision to create new rules for which the new phenomena of human activity cry-out" – see Eugeniusz Piontek, 'Professor Manfred Lachs: Wise Man of International Law' (2011) 13 International Community Law Review 81, 85.

89 Lachs (n 23) 157.

an understanding of the realities of life. While knowledge does not in itself solve the problems it identifies, it sows the seeds of wisdom and paves the way to their solution".[90] Also, outside the remit of his outstanding book, Lachs was very keen to quote Albert Einstein's words: "knowledge pervades all aspects of life".[91]

But when analysing the goals of education Lachs may be considered a forerunner of the Life-long Learning Program, not simply by claiming, as he did, that "the idea of acquiring, at an early age, a set of intellectual or technical equipment valid for a lifetime [was] out of date"" and that "the fundamental axioms of traditional education [were] crumbling".[92] This reflects again a very open approach to innovative education.

While relying on the report *Learning to be: the world of education today and tomorrow* by the International Commission on the Development of Education,[93] Lachs identifies the goal of international law education: as "an indispensable intellectual tool for the proper understanding of relations between the States of the world today: in economics and communication, politics, culture and technology, science and exploitation of natural resources".[94] Tools for dissemination of knowledge are of course textbooks, and other books used beyond the scholastic. In a more present fashion one would be tempted to also include more modern types of teachings, including e.g., blog posts.[95] Writing several decades ago, Lachs in a similar fashion, warned against overlooking the leading educational role of radio and television, strongly advocating for the inclusion of the new techniques.[96] Now, his message could be extrapolated to the broader use of Internet for research and distant learning, an even more pressing need, given the pandemic.

---

90 Lachs (n 23) 163.

91 Manfred Lachs, 'Conclusion' (1988) 21(1) Revue Belge de Droit International 361.

92 Lachs (n 23) 164.

93 Edgar Faure et al., *Learning to be: The world of education today and tomorrow* (Unesco 1972) XXXIII, https://unesdoc.unesco.org/ark:/48223/pf0000001801: If all that has to be learned must be continually reinvented and renewed, then teaching becomes education and, more and more, learning.

94 Lachs (n 23) 164.

95 See e.g., Sandesh Sivakumaran, 'The Influence of Teachings of Publicists on the Development of International Law' (2017) 66 International and Comparative Law Quarterly 1, 23.

96 Lachs (n 23) 165: "it is up to those who know to impart their knowledge to those whose task it is to present the current events of international life and to lend their willing participation to the educative work of news and documentary features. It is moreover high time that courses in international law became an accepted feature of educational radio and courses broadcasting".

For Lachs, "the process of education in international law has to be continuously improved in all dimensions, adapted, and perfected – its study made to respond to the paramount needs of humanism in our age". From his perspective, "the Teacher is called on to commit himself to the cause of international law, to understand and help it fulfil its proper place in the international relations of our age. Only by taking a broad scientific and life-oriented approach can he fulfil his true, his sacred mission".[97] The words just bring to mind the assessment by Thomas Franck, according to whom, "Lachs became a missionary for the law and, specifically, for adjudication so that law was the civilized religion and courts were its churches: he did not think it inappropriate to propagate his faith".[98] In a similar fashion, another commentator considered that Lachs 'until the very end [...] remained preoccupied with his profession, international law was his life'.[99]

It comes as no surprise that academic lawyers' influence consists in teaching future practitioners.[100] The impact of the teachers, and their teachings radiates well beyond the sphere of pedagogical activity.[101] The uses and application of teachings and teachers were discussed in separate sections on courts, diplomatic correspondence, Advisers to Governments, Counsel in Disputes, Umpires and Judges, as well as The Development of International Law, and its Codification.

Many writers work as counsel or judges at some point in their career. Their professional engagement may consist in being an academic, activist, advocate, judge, government official, or any combination thereof.[102] It may be claimed that the vocation of a lawyer is to become a justice.[103] For any roles, also those

---

97 Lachs (n 23) 166. At this point he would rely on the words of Hans Wehberg, who pronounced in 1929 that belief in the future of international law and the ability to inspire the student with devotion for progress in international law are both indispensable in order to teach international law – as referred to in fn 76, p. 166.

98 Thomas M. Franck, 'The Private Lachs: Life As Art' (1993) 87 American Journal of International Law 419.

99 Verwey (n 18) VII.

100 William Twining, 'The Role of Academics in the Legal System' in Mark Tushnet and Peter Cane (eds), *Oxford Handbook of Legal Studies* (OUP 2005) 927.

101 Lachs (n 23) 167.

102 Gleider Hernández, 'The Responsibility of the International Legal Academic: Situating the Grammarian within the 'Invisible College'' in Jean d'Aspremont et al. (eds.), *International Law as a Profession* (CUP 2017) 160.

103 Fritz Münch, 'Zur Aufgabe der Lehre im Völkerrecht' in *Recueil d'études de droit international en hommage à Paul Guggenheim* (Imprimerie de La Tribune Genève 1968) 490. Cf. Ian Brownlie, 'The Calling of the International Lawyer: Sir Humphrey Waldock and His Work' (1983) 54 British Yearbook of International Law 68 (the ICJ at the centre of the world of the professional international lawyer).

of legal advisers of international organizations, or NGO lawyers, competence or craftsmanship in interpreting international law is necessary.[104] In this respect one has to refer to the late C.W. Jenks, who advocated for good craftsmanship in international law to "rest upon a solid foundation of sound scholarship",[105] no matter what (practical) role he or she is to play alongside the scholarly career.

Naturally enough, a reader is tempted to return to the Schachter's concept of an invisible college. One is of course to concentrate on the mingling of the scholarly and the official as well as the accompanying tension for individuals moving from one role to another or perceiving themselves as acting in the dual capacity of objective scientist and government advocate.[106] This is not merely, as Schachter put it, international lawyers, jurists being part of the active professional community and 'who maintain intellectual contact with the scholarly side of the profession',[107] but more the lack of a sharp dividing line in professional lives between theory and practice.[108] Lachs also recalled that for decades, he had worn two caps: one of a practician, the other of a theoretician, and has changed them many times a day.[109]

His remarks offer many interesting insights on the impact of teachings. It would be hard to disagree with Lachs' assessment that "for long time writers played an important role in influencing judges on matters of international law".[110] It should come as no surprise that "teachings" have frequently been referred to in separate and dissenting opinions.[111]

Subsequently, when dealing with diplomatic correspondence, Lachs admits that "the name of the teachers and their views have rung out in many halls of the world's capitals" and continues that "their authority has been appealed to, as representatives of the science of law, and has for several centuries played an important role [...], even though they have had no formal standing".[112] He concludes that "by donning other robes or taking up the professional life [the

104 Andraž Zidar, 'Interpretation and the International Legal Profession: Between Duty and Aspiration' in Andrea Bianchi, Daniel Peat, and Matthew Windsor (eds), *Interpretation in International Law* (OUP 2015) 133, 135.

105 C. Wilfred Jenks, *The Common Law of Mankind* (Stevens 1958) 409.

106 Schachter (n 52) 218.

107 Schachter (n 52) 217.

108 Yusuf (n 29) 610.

109 Lachs (n 16) 11.

110 Lachs (n 23) 170. With regard to the World Court he held that both PCIJ and the ICJ "far from ignoring "teachings" [...] [had] considered them as what they really were intended to be: subsidiary means – to be resorted to only when the main sources were not adequate, or were lacking in clarity", p. 172.

111 Lachs (n 23) 172.

112 Lachs (n 23) 176–177.

Teacher] does not leave the world of science but links in various capacities theory and practice, a phenomenon common to all branches of law".[113]

When discussing the necessary synergy of the respective roles of teachers and those of advisers to governments, Lachs first identified the need for legal advice: "in general, to prevent a government from running into conflict with law in the quest for its objectives, but also, in regard to those objectives which are lawful, to promote the choice of only those means of achieving them which strengthen the rule of international law" to rhetorically ask: "who could be more competent to do this than the Teacher?".[114] After discussing numerous examples of combining the two roles, Lachs refrained from offering a definite answer on whether the distinguished jurists had in fact been successful in exercising influence on the practice of states. Such a question is of course difficult to answer, therefore one needs to be satisfied with a balanced reply by the learned Scholar when he firmly stated that "governments tend to heed their advice [as] attested by ample evidence", yet adding that "there is no certainty that on many occasions, those which were pregnant with serious conflict or strife, the legal adviser's views were accepted or even sought".[115]

The involvement as counsel in disputes by international lawyers is frequent and thus obvious.[116] In fact, the more distinguished the international legal academic, the more likely it is that he or she gets engaged in multiple professional capacities with international law, beyond their research and teaching.[117]

Interestingly, Lachs paid attention not only to the influence of a teacher-adviser on his/her government but also a remaining question of their

113 Lachs (n 23) 177.

114 Lachs (n 23) 177–178. Cf. Jennings (n 46) but note also Fitzmaurice observed that "the parties, their advocates and the tribunal itself, view in quite a different light such (material) sources of law, as, for instance, the opinions of jurists (however eminent) and a decision, even if the tribunal given is composed of less eminent persons" Gerald Fitzmaurice, 'Some Problems Regarding the Formal Sources of International Law' in FM van Asbeck et al (eds), *Symbolae Verzijl: présentées au professeur J.H.W. Verzijl à l'occasion de son LXX-ième anniversaire* (Nijhoff 1958) 153, 171–172.

115 It was further held that "Sometimes the "political element" so very much overshadows the case that heads of ministries or departments fail to see that there is a "legal aspect" too, and one seriously to be considered. On other occasions the legal advisers are sought too late – he is intended to act as a "fireman". If one is to judge events, with due consideration given to one of the actors, i.e., the legal adviser, one must conclude that not infrequently the Teacher has been overridden, or that the situation had gone beyond the point where his advice could be implemented. Yet, as in so many walks of life, it is the successes which go unnoticed, for when all goes smoothly there is nothing to observe" – Lachs (n 23) 180–181.

116 Lachs (n 23) 183.

117 Hernández (n 102) 167.

independence. Against that particular background, he referred to occasions where teachers had held and expressed views not necessarily coinciding with the policy of their countries, even if he was still aware that "bearing in mind the great hold the bond of nationality has upon men, some may nurture a lurking suspicion of the supposed impartiality of the Teacher".[118] Despite this, as a concluding remark, Lachs wrote: "the thinking cap of the Teacher cannot in general be viewed as sewn in the colours of his country's flag".[119] He warns against questioning his integrity or suggesting that he acts against his own convictions or teachings. To substantiate his view, Lachs mentioned cases "of some great jurists refusing to plead in particular disputes or situations or resigning their posts when in disagreement with the government on important of law, or in regard to general policies".[120]

But of course, greater attention was paid to elevation to the bench of most highly qualified publicists, to become umpires and judges. Also in that regard, Lachs strongly defended the integrity of judges, unfortunately having to rely on his own experience. It was with the US reaction on Nicaragua[121] that Lachs expressed in a very clear fashion his vision of serving at the ICJ and underlined the overriding requirements for judges: integrity and independence.[122] Indeed, Lachs belonged to the most eminent and renowned members of the ICJ.

118 See Lachs (n 23) 182, mentioning the allegations about Grotius' change of position between *De mare liberum* and *De jure praedae*, with the latter work allegedly having been written in the interest of the Dutch West India Company, contrary to the views expressed in the former. See the telling anecdote provided by Anne Peters, 'Rollen von Rechtsdenkern und Praktikern – aus völkerrechtlicher Sicht', in *Paradigmen im internationalen Recht: Implikationen der Weltfinanzkrise für das internationale Recht* [= (2011) 45 Berichte der Deutschen Vereinigung für internationales Recht] (Müller 2012) 105 107.

119 Lachs (n 23) 182. since "Teachers of international law constitute the greatest majority of what one may call the international bar; it is from among them that in most cases counsel are chosen. For the (further) development see James Crawford, 'The International Law Bar: Essence Before Existence?' in Jean d'Aspremont et al. (eds.), *International Law as a Profession* (CUP 2017) 338.

120 See also Peters (n 118) 128.

121 See Marian Nash Leich, 'Contemporary Practice of the United States Relating to International Law' (1985) 79 American Journal of International Law 431, 440.

122 See Military and Paramilitary Activities in and against Nicaragua (Nicaragua v. United States of America), Separate opinion of Judge Lachs, ICJ Rep.1986, p. 158. He further held: "A judge – as needs no emphasis – is bound to be impartial, objective, detached, disinterested and unbiased" (ibid.). See also his letter to the Editors of American Journal of International Law (1990) 84 American Journal of International Law 231 and Manfred Lachs, 'Some Reflections on the Nationality of Judges of the International Court of Justice'(1992) 4 Pace Yearbook of International Law 49. Cf. Schwebel (n 10) 418. The critical remarks by another Judge, Sir Robert Jennings, should be also noted (Military and Paramilitary Activities in and against Nicaragua (Nicaragua v United States), Merits,

As admitted by the author himself, he could not resist the temptation of dealing with how becoming a judge affects the "thinking cap" of a great teacher or publicist. According to Lachs, such a person undoubtedly "remains a representative of a school of thought [...] and this is bound to have a bearing on his thinking [even though] one cannot escape the feeling that, having become a judge, he has from now on to act somehow differently on the legal question he faces, not only think and persuade but take part in decision-making, sometimes lead others along the road".[123] Lachs also illustrated this with a quotation from McNair giving his own testimony both as a teacher of law and as a practitioner and "struck by the different appearance that the rule of law may assume when it is being examined for the purpose of its application in practice to a set of ascertained facts".[124]

But Lachs was also eager to note a converse phenomenon as a confirmation of the role of the teacher or a writer: that "an increasing number of judicial decisions, handed down by courts with many former "teachers" on the bench, which are quoted and in time relied other "teachers", e.g., in textbooks.[125] In discussing the commitment of the Teachers to the growth of law and its progress by contributing as judges. Lachs was well aware, and also critical, of the difficulties of some teachers, when turning judge, "in refraining from traversing larger tracts of their theories than the issues may warrant – yet the moderate use of the right of comment may most usefully supplement the judgment or draw attention to alternative approaches which remain available for future application".[126]

Again, within the monograph, he maintained that "it should not be forgotten that a judgment attracting the adherence of a majority of fifteen judges cannot but represent a nucleus of all the reasoning which may plausibly lead

Judgment, ICJ Reports 1986, p. 14, at 528 (Judge Jennings, Dissenting Opinion): "I also wish to express my regret that, in a Court which by its Statute is elected in such a way as to assure 'the representation of the main forms of civilisation and of the principal legal systems of the world', the United States in its statement accompanying the announcement of the non-participation in the present phase of the case should have chosen not refer to the national origins of two of the Judges who took part in the earlier phases of the case").

123 Lachs (n 23) 184.

124 Lord McNair, *Selected Papers and Bibliography* (Sijthoff 1974) 257–8, as quoted by Lachs (n 23) 184 fn 58, further holding "As stated in a textbook it may sound the quintessence of wisdom, but when you come to apply it many necessary qualifications or modifications are apt to arise in your mind ... it is probable that the legal element in the resulting solution will be a more useful and more practical rule of law than a rule elaborated by a teacher or writer in his study working alone and in the abstract".

125 Lachs (n 23) 185.

126 Lachs (n 23) 186–187.

to its *dispositif*, a common denominator of all the legal values upheld by the decision. Given the small number of judgments handed down, and the tiny number of those on any specific point or aspect of the law, it is a necessary enrichment of jurisprudential science that the individual judge should share his apposite thoughts with the legal community".[127]

In that sense, Lachs revealed his approach to adjudication. "Master of compromise and a champion of consensus",[128] Manfred Lachs always tried to build the majority, as in his opinion, the consensus was always the best way to solve problems".[129] This feature may be first of all (but not only!) drawn from his activities when on the Bench of the ICJ, where throughout over a quarter of century he only dissented twice. As recalled by Dame Rosalyn Higgins, his influence in the formulation of majority views was remarkable, both when he was President and otherwise.[130]

To capture Judge Lachs' approach to judging and formulating the eventual decision by the Court, it may be helpful to recall his declaration appended to Fisheries Jurisdiction Cases (UK/Iceland and FRG/Iceland, respectively), in which he laid down his approach: "I am in agreement with the reasoning and conclusions of the Court, and since the Judgment speaks for and stands by itself, I would not feel it appropriate to make any gloss upon it".[131] As rightly noted by a commentator, the declaration implicitly suggested that the reasons for separate statements by a judge must be substantial, if not compelling. Thus, it may be inferred that, where Lachs voted with the majority, he was able to get included in the Courts opinion any views which he had regarded as significant, which may mean that he had played a major role in the drafting of the decision/opinion.[132]

Both the international judicial decision and the exposition of particular points in individual opinions may remove doubts on several issues, even only loosely related to the case.[133] While the decisions rely on judicial reasoning, law is developed. From Lachs' perspective, judgments are also indispensable

127 Lachs (n 23) 186.

128 Wyzner (n 15) xvi.

129 Karolina Wierczyńska, 'Judge Manfted Lachs and His Role in International Adjudication' (2007) 7 Baltic Yearbook of International Law 113, 118.

130 Rosalyn Higgins, 'Fundamentals of International Law' in: Nandasiri Jasentuliyana (ed), *Perspectives on International Law* (Kluwer Law International 1995) 3.

131 ICJ Rep. 1974, p. 35 and 206 respectively.

132 Lyndel V. Prott, 'The Judicial Philosophy of Manfred Lachs' in Jerzy Makarczyk (ed), *Essays in International Law in Honour of Judge Manfred Lachs* (Nijhoff 1984) 423, 425.

133 Lachs (n 23) 186.

instruments in the education of the international community – and not only of the parties to the dispute.[134]

Finally, it is worth recalling the brilliant remarks on the impact of teachers on the development of international law and its codification. The latter's aim is, as Lachs succinctly put it, "to consolidate, certainly, but not to immobilize".[135] A reader may sense the experience of the writer dealing with "the risk of sanctifying the rules of yesterday and thereby halting progress in the name of progress".[136] In the "Teacher", Lachs concentrated also on who the codifiers were and are.

When discussing the age of imperial expansion and the collaboration by Paul Fauchille with other eminent scholars, Lachs noted the passing of "the era of the isolated scholar and innovator in international law" and that "that of co-operation had begun to be transformed into the age of collective research".[137] His own comment is both ironic and positive,[138] underlining the paradox that "the first codifiers of international law would not have embarked upon their work if consolidation, as mere inventorizing and tidying-up, had been their sole motive".[139]

In discussing the impact of teachers, and noticing the difference between their teachings, he once again provided his inclination to compromise: "Frequently when facing a concrete dispute or the need of formulating or re-formulating a rule-agreement between ostensibly warring scholars has proved possible. All meet on the bench, or at a conference, in the International Law Commission, or in other forums – and find themselves able to iron out

134 Lachs (n 23) 187.

135 Lachs (n 23) 187 explaining in a telling way "for to what purpose does a climber secure his foothold but to mount higher still?".

136 Ibidem.

137 Lachs (n 23) 78.

138 Lachs (n 23) 189: "Why do we nowadays need committees for what used to be accomplished by heroic individuals? Might we not expect that all the Pegasuses they design will turn out to be flightless camels? A word in favour of committees and commissions is in order here, for the answer lies in the very nature of the subject: hence the specific character of the law-making process. However perhaps lacking in brilliance and fancy, therefore a committee-made code will always be nearer the mark than an individual compilation. But there is another reason, also, why a code must result from the collaboration of several minds. It is because no one mind can be expected to be equally adept in the different facets of codification, namely: consolidation, harmonization and discipline. It is obvious that different kinds of mind will be better equipped to tackle each".

139 Lachs (n 23) 190. Given that "the codifier in the early days was something of a pioneer and no mere chronicler in spirit" one may extrapolate this onto present times to find that "the proposed codification is no mere compilation or orderly restatement of the explicitly accepted"-see ibidem.

their disagreements in concrete cases".[140] One could conceive of no better formulation of the approach by the learned scholar.

Concluding Remarks

The present analysis has aimed at paying tribute to an outstanding scholar, diplomat, and judge, as well as to his lasting legacy. Naturally, attention has been paid to "The Teacher in International Law" by his pen. With this seminal examination, a reader was presented with a journey in time stressing the importance of the international law teacher and the (sometimes even *decisive*)[141] roles he or she is to play.

"The Teacher" embodies a combination of in-depth and broad reading, a thorough knowledge of history, a sharp scientific mind, and an alert sense for the innovative,[142] and could thus be recommended as obligatory reading for all (future and already established) teachers. Some lessons have been taught; some need still to be learnt. One may but hope that the growing number of scholars dealing with what seemed to be Lachs' favourite topic are going to pay attention to, and remember, his great contribution (which is unfortunately not always the case).

One could conceive of no better concluding remarks than those final ones included in Lachs' seminal book: "It is within the reach of the Teacher of international law – armed with imagination and reason – while relying on true social humanism, to move across new frontiers, to help and inspire, to make the study of international law more humane, and law itself a meaningful part of our culture, an effective instrument of a lawful world, and important agency for the betterment of mankind".[143] *Aurea dicta!*

References

Bleckmann A, *Grundprobleme und Methoden des Völkerrechts* (Alber 1982).

Boutros-Ghali B, 'Foreword: Tribute to Manfred Lachs, Champion of the Law' in Nandasiri Jasentuliyana (ed) *Perspectives on International Law* (Kluwer Law International 1995) x.

---

140 Lachs (n 23) 199.
141 Lachs (n 23) 209.
142 Verwey (n 18) VI.
143 Lachs (n 23) 209.

Brownlie I, 'The Calling of the International Lawyer: Sir Humphrey Waldock and His Work' (1983) 54 British Yearbook of International law 68.

Cassese A, *Five Masters of International Law: Conversations with R-J Dupuy, E Jiménez de Aréchaga, R Jennings, L Henkin and O Schachter* (Hart 2011).

Chopra SK, 'The Teacher: Lachs at the Hague Academy' (1993) 87 American Journal of International Law 420.

Crawford J, *Brownlie's Principles of Public International Law* (OUP 2012).

Crawford J, 'The International Law Bar: Essence Before Existence?' in Jean d'Aspremont et al. (eds.), *International Law as a Profession* (CUP 2017) 338.

d'Aspremont J, *Formalism and the Sources of International Law: a Theory of the Ascertainment of Legal Rules* (OUP 2011).

Elwyn-Jones F, 'Manfred Lachs', in Jerzy Makarczyk (ed), *Essays in International Law in Honour of Judge Manfred Lachs* (Nijhoff 1984).

Faure E et al., *Learning to be: the world of education today and tomorrow* (Unesco 1972).

Fitzmaurice G, 'Some Problems Regarding the Formal Sources of International Law' in FM van Asbeck et al (eds), *Symbolae Verzijl: présentées au professeur J.H.W. Verzijl à l'occasion de son LXX-ième anniversaire* (Nijhoff 1958) 153.

Franck TM, 'Book Review' (1983) 77 American Journal of International Law 169.

Franck TM, 'The Private Lachs: Life As Art' (1993) 87 American Journal of International Law 419.

Hernández G, 'The Responsibility of the International Legal Academic: Situating the Grammarian within the 'Invisible College'' in Jean d'Aspremont et al. (eds.), *International Law as a Profession* (CUP 2017) 160.

Higgins AP, *The Binding Force of International Law* (CUP 1910).

Higgins R, 'Fundamentals of International Law' in: Nandasiri Jasentuliyana (ed), *Perspectives on International Law* (Kluwer Law International 1995) 3.

Higgins R, 'Obituary: Judge Manfred Lachs' *The Independent* (London, 16 February 1993).

Hilpold P, 'What Role for Academic Writers in Interpreting International Law?' (2009) 8 Chinese Journal of International Law 291.

Hudson MO, *The Permanent Court of International Justice 1920–1942* (MacMillan 1943).

Jenks CW, *The Common Law of Mankind* (Stevens 1958).

Jennings RY, 'International Lawyers and the Progressive Development of International Law' in Jerzy Makarczyk (ed), *Theory of International Law at the Threshold of the 21st Century: Essays in Honour of Krzysztof Skubiszewski* (Kluwer Law International 1996) 413.

Jennings RY, 'Teachings and Teaching in International Law', in Jerzy Makarczyk (ed), *Essays in international law in honour of Judge Manfred Lachs* (Nijhoff 1984) 127.

Jennings RY, 'An International Lawyer Takes Stock' (1990) 39(3) International and Comparative Law Quarterly 513.

Koskenniemi M, *From Apology to Utopia: the Structure of International Legal Argument* (2nd edn, CUP 2005).

Krzan B, 'Izby sądowe Międzynarodowego Trybunału Sprawiedliwości' in Zdzisław Galicki, Tomasz Kamiński and Katarzyna Myszona-Kostrzewa (eds), *Manfred Lachs: wybitny prawnik świata* (SAWPiA UW 2011) 267.

Lachs M, 'Conclusion' (1988) 21(1) Revue Belge de Droit International 361.

Lachs M, *International Law of Outer Space: a Law in the Making* (Sijthoff 1972).

Lachs M, *Le monde de la pensée en droit international: theories et pratique* (Economica 1989).

Lachs M, *Rzecz o nauce prawa międzynarodowego* (Zakład Narodowy im. Ossolińskich 1986).

Lachs M, 'Some Reflections on the Nationality of Judges of the International Court of Justice' (1992) 4 Pace Yearbook of International Law 49.

Lachs M, 'Teachings and teaching of international law', (1976–III) 151 Recueil des cours 161.

Lachs M, 'The Development and General Trends of International Law in Our Time' (1980) 169 Recueil des cours 9.

Lachs M, 'The Revised Procedure of the International Court of Justice' in Fritz Kalshoven (ed) *Essays on the Development of the International Legal Order in memory of Haro F. van Panhuys* (Nijhoff 1980) 21.

Lachs M, *The Teacher in International Law (Teachings and Teaching)* (Nijhoff 1982).

Lachs M, 'Thoughts on Science, Technology and World Law' (1992) 86 American Journal of International Law 673.

Lachs M, *Umowy wielostronne: studium z prawa traktatowego* (PWN 1958).

Lachs M, 'W podróży, którą nazywamy życiem' *Polityka* (Warsaw, 12 January 1985) 1.

Lachs M, *War Crimes: an Attempt to Define the Issue* (Stevens 1945).

Lauterpacht H, *The Development of International Law by the International Court* (Stevens 1958).

Leich NM, 'Contemporary Practice of the United States Relating to International Law' (1985) 79 American Journal of International Law 431.

Lyall F, 'Manfred Lachs (21.4.1914 – 4.1.1993)', in Stephan Hobe (ed), *Pioneers of Space Law*, (Nijhoff 2013) 193.

Makarewicz A, 'Manfred Lachs we wspomnieniach in Zdzisław Galicki, Tomasz Kamiński and Katarzyna Myszona-Kostrzewa (eds), *Manfred Lachs: wybitny prawnik świata* (SAWPiA UW 2011) 43.

McNair A, *Selected Papers and Bibliography* (Sijthoff 1974).

McWhinney E, 'The Inaugural Manfred Lachs Memorial Lecture Manfred Lachs and the International Court of Justice as Emerging Constitutional Court of the United Nations' (1995) 8(1) Leiden Journal of International Law 41.

Mendelson M, 'The ICJ and the Sources of International Law' in Vaughan Lowe and Malgosia Fitzmaurice (eds) *Fifty Years of the International Court of Justice* (CUP 1996) 63.

Münch F, 'Zur Aufgabe der Lehre im Völkerrecht' in *Recueil d'études de droit international en hommage à Paul Guggenheim* (Imprimerie de La Tribune Genève 1968) 490.

Oraison A, 'Reflexions sur la Doctrine des Publicistes les Plus Qualifies des Differentes Nations' (1991) 24(2) Revue Belge de Droit International 507.

Parry C, *The Sources and Evidences of International Law* (Manchester University Press 1965).

Peters A, 'Rollen von Rechtsdenkern und Praktikern – aus völkerrechtlicher Sicht', in *Paradigmen im internationalen Recht: Implikationen der Weltfinanzkrise für das internationale Recht* [= (2011) 45 Berichte der Deutschen Vereinigung für internationales Recht] (Müller 2012) 105.

Piontek E, 'Professor Manfred Lachs: Wise Man of International Law' (2011) 13 International Community Law Review 81.

Prott LV, 'The Judicial Philosophy of Manfred Lachs' in Jerzy Makarczyk (ed), *Essays in International Law in Honour of Judge Manfred Lachs* (Nijhoff 1984) 423.

Przyborowska-Klimczak A, 'Poglądy Profesora Manfreda Lachsa na temat nauczania prawa międzynarodowego' in Zdzisław Galicki, Tomasz Kamiński and Katarzyna Myszona-Kostrzewa (eds), *Manfred Lachs: wybitny prawnik świata* (SAWPiA UW 2011) 65.

Równy K, 'Professor Manfred Lachs – inspirujący nauczyciel, pionierski współorganizator badań interdyscyplinarnych, dociekliwy naukowiec i nieugięty obrońca pokoju na świecie (we wspomnieniach wczesnego ucznia)' in Zdzisław Galicki, Tomasz Kamiński and Katarzyna Myszona-Kostrzewa (eds), *Manfred Lachs: wybitny prawnik świata* (SAWPiA UW 2011) 35.

Schachter O, 'The Invisible College of International Lawyers' (1977) 72 Northwestern University Law Review 217.

Schachter O, 'The UN Years: Lachs the Diplomat' (1993) 87 American Journal of International Law 414.

Schwarzenberger G, *A Manual of International Law* (5th edn, Stevens 1967).

Schwebel SM, 'On the Bench: Lachs the Judge' (1993) 87 American Journal of International Law 416.

Sivakumaran S, 'The Influence of Teachings of Publicists on the Development of International Law' (2017) 66 International and Comparative Law Quarterly 1.

Triggs G, 'The Public International Lawyer and the Practice of International Law' (2005) 24 Australian Year Book of International Law 201.

Twining W, 'The Role of Academics in the Legal System' in Mark Tushnet and Peter Cane (eds), *Oxford Handbook of Legal Studies* (OUP 2005) 927.

Van Hoof GJH, *Rethinking the Sources of International Law* (Kluwer 1983).

Vereshchetin V, 'Authors recollect Judge Lachs' in Nandasiri Jasentuliyana (ed), *Perspectives on International Law* (Kluwer Law International 1995) 535.
Verwey W, 'In Memoriam: Manfred Lachs (1914–1993)' (1993) 40 Netherlands International Law Review v.
Virally M, 'A propos de la <<lex ferenda>>', in *Mélanges offerts à Paul Reuter: le droit international, unité et diversité* (Pedone 1981) 519.
Wierczyńska K, 'Judge Manfted Lachs and His Role in International Adjudication' (2007) 7 Baltic Yearbook of International Law 113.
Wnukiewicz-Kozłowska A, 'Doctrine as a Source of International Law' in Jan Kolasa (ed), *The Nature of Source in International Legal Order* (E-Wydawnictwo. Prawnicza i Ekonomiczna Biblioteka Cyfrowa 2017) 249.
Wolfke K, *Custom in Present International Law* (2nd edn, Nijhoff 1993).
Wyzner E, 'Preface: a Dedication' in Nandasiri Jasentuliyana (ed), *Perspectives on International Law* (Kluwer Law International 1995) xv.
Yusuf AA, 'The Role of International Lawyers between Theory and Practice' (2017) 15(3) Journal of International Criminal Justice 603.
Zidar A, 'Interpretation and the International Legal Profession: Between Duty and Aspiration' in Andrea Bianchi, Daniel Peat, and Matthew Windsor (eds), *Interpretation in International Law* (OUP 2015) 133.

PART VII

Final Remarks

Conclusions

Peter Hilpold and Giuseppe Nesi

The readers of this book will have noticed the enormous wealth of information already available on the issue of TIL. In the last decades there has been an intense discussion in this field, often, however, starting from disparate positions and with limited reciprocal interaction. Many of these efforts were therefore like ships passing in the night. Learned societies showed sporadic, and for some periods also intense interest but there was no real continuity. Much work was carried on by experts in their individual capacity, as an expression of individual interest. The results mirror these particularities.

Nonetheless, over the years the insights, the knowledge in this field has become ever more detailed.

The perception by the editors of this book was that time has come for a stocktaking, to attempt to bring the various strands of the discussion together. Of course, there is still no "general theory" of TIL but nonetheless some traits in this discussion can be discerned that evidence a perception for the existence of some common ground and for main research interests for the future. As Charlotte Ku wrote, "there are a variety of approaches that are equally valid", but nonetheless or maybe exactly because of this variety of alternatives it appears to be so important to gain a broader overlook of the situation in TIL.

Much research is still individualistic and expression of self-reflection and these elements are also present in the contributions to this book. And necessarily so as academics dealing with TIL are regularly teachers of ("substantive") IL. They are often at an advanced stage of their career and turning to theoretical issues of TIL either because they have noticed deficits in the teaching system, or because they are intended to share what they perceive to be important insights in this field or they are motivated by both intents.

A further step, once clarity has been achieved about what common grounds exists in legal theory about TIL, would consist in reaching out to pedagogics.[1]

More and more international lawyers are paying at least lip service to this need (see Lucas Lixinski). This might, perhaps constitute a prelude to an effective engagement with interdisciplinary inquiries (often presented as a necessity for IL studies in general, see the contribution by Sergio Dellavalle).

1 The editors are, however, convinced, that in advance clarity has to be gained on aim and function of TIL on the legal ground. This book is purported to contribute to this specific function.

 | DOI:10.1163/9789004678880_023

Unfortunately, from the vantage point of pedagogics the barriers to address IL issues seem to be even higher. For true interdisciplinarity it would be useful to try a rapprochement starting from both sides in a somewhat egalitarian manner. In view of the diversity of approaches towards TIL, having in mind that particularism also affects visions of and perspectives on teaching one might gain the impression that fragmentation and specialization is a general trend in IL affecting also the subject of teaching. International lawyers have become prudent when it comes to pronounce overarching principles, to issue statements that should claim general validity. For the matter of teaching, things are, however, somewhat different. Notwithstanding the broad awareness as to the misleading and patronizing character of "great designs" with regard to TIL many authors recognize the potential for making a difference, for bringing about important improvements.[2] In teaching lies an important key for change. The great inspirational ideas of peace, human rights protection and self-determination that have undergirded UN law since its inception have still an enormous motivational force for teaching.

It was attempted to show that it is surely not up to the teacher of IL to design the way autonomously, governments should head, but nonetheless teachers can provide important insights and acting from prominent, influential positions, they are also called to stand up in case democratic achievements appear to be imperiled. To be able to do so, both morally and materially, teachers have to enjoy a sufficient degree of freedom. Academic freedom has to be defended permanently. "New Managerialism" has proven to be a particularly insidious threat to academic freedom in those country in which it has been implemented. Token arguments such as the quest for more efficiency or more productivity are easy at hand, when the real intent it to weaken the status of Universities or of teachers with the further aim to introduce authoritarian systems and to limit the freedom of expression. This freedom, as well as the freedom of teaching, are, however, essential achievements in the fight for fundamental rights. As a subject very close to politics, IL is especially exposed to political pressure. On the other hand, international lawyers are in the best position to connect internationally and already for professional reasons they should be best prepared to avail themselves of the relevant international instruments suited to defend their academic freedoms.

Authoritarianism and new sovereignism often go hand in hand with restrictions and protectionism or, presented the other way round, opening up borders,

2 Again, however, we have to consider that also in this respect perspectives in various region differ. See the contribution by Lucas Lixinski.

enhancing the mobility of academics, creating a truly international labor market for teachers of IL can be ideal antidotes to these modern challenges for democracy. In this book, the image of the "Invisible College of international lawyers", so happily crafted by Professor Oscar Schachter is often cited as a vision of a community that interacts across borders, which exchanges ideas and participates in debates without being restricted by time, space and separate legal orders. Of course, this vision is an ideal, but perhaps also a "realistic utopia" (Cassese) in the sense that it can at least partly become true in the foreseeable future. The evolving technology provides continuously new instruments to approach this aim more easily on the technical level. At the same time, however, also mental and legal barriers have to be torn down to make this interaction possible and happen in practice. The situation within the European Union is a good example in kind to show how an area of relatively small geographic proportions has become highly segmented on the practical level notwithstanding the fact that, at least in theory, the freedom of circulation of workers (and therefore also of academic teachers) would apply. As a consequence, competition not only of teachers but also of ideas has become restricted in a field that for its very subject should provide a forum for keenest contest.

Teachers of IL keep therefore struggling for ideals, in various fields also for ideas that, for the time being, might seem utopian but over time might become reality. At the same time their work is very much down to earth when they have to convince a broader audience that dealing with IL issue is no longer (in reality it has never been) a pastime for an elitist academic circle but a task that should involve larger groups of society and in particular lawyers in general. As IL is now closely connected to and interwoven with subjects and law disciplines that once were considered to be of a typical internal nature nearly all teachers of law have now become also teachers of IL. The same holds true at the practical level: Practitioners of law mostly are (or should be) also practitioners of IL (see also the contribution to this book by Charlotte Ku). This finding is further confirmed if we adopt, as it should be, a broad understanding of "teaching" (see for this also the contribution by Carlo Focarelli).

The editors are therefore rather optimistic that the subject of TIL will come out of its niche, that it will continuing to gain importance and that to deal with it will become a natural part of the professional understanding of any law teacher and, of course, of IL teachers in a qualified form. The editors hope to have provided with this book a further impetus to make this happen.

Index

www.ingramcontent.com/pod-product-compliance
Lightning Source LLC
LaVergne TN
LVHW012051011026
849162LV00017B/34